The Sociology of Education in Canada

Critical Perspectives

Fourth Edition

Terry Wotherspoon

OXFORD
UNIVERSITY PRESS

OXFORD

UNIVERSITY PRESS

Oxford University Press is a department of the University of Oxford.
It furthers the University's objective of excellence in research, scholarship,
and education by publishing worldwide. Oxford is a registered trade mark of
Oxford University Press in the UK and in certain other countries.

Published in Canada by Oxford University Press
8 Sampson Mews, Suite 204,
Don Mills, Ontario M3C 0H5 Canada

www.oupcanada.com

First Edition published in 1998
Second Edition published in 2004
Third Edition published in 2009

Library and Archives Canada Cataloguing in Publication

Wotherspoon, Terry
The sociology of education in Canada : critical perspectives / Terry Wotherspoon. — 4th ed.

Includes bibliographical references and index.
ISBN 978-0-19-544548-0

1. Educational sociology—Canada—Textbooks. I. Title.

LC191.8.C2W67 2013   306.430971   C2013-901117-X

Cover image: P Wei/Stockphoto

Oxford University Press is committed to our environment.
This book is printed on Forest Stewardship Council® certified paper
and comes from responsible sources.

Printed and bound in Canada

1 2 3 4 — 17 16 15 14

Contents

Figures, Tables, and Boxes

Figures

Tables

Boxes

International Case Studies

Preface

Education and learning, and the world within which learning activities take place, have undergone remarkable transformations even in the relatively short time since the first edition of this book was being developed. Children are entering schools with a significant range of experiences, capacities, and expectations that their parents and teachers did not encounter at a similar life stage. In the process, many people are questioning what schools and other educational institutions are doing, and must do, to keep pace with rapid social, economic, and technological changes. Lots of people have ideas about what's wrong with schooling, or what needs to be fixed or changed, but others can point equally to dimensions of schooling that are working well or improving. This book addresses many of these debates, highlighting the need to understand them in the context of the social environments in which they have emerged and the relationships of which they are part. Education, because of its importance for individuals, communities, and societies, is a complex and often contradictory undertaking in Canada and around the globe.

Regardless of how schools have changed over time, many of our formative experiences continue to occur within the context of schooling. Throughout the courses of our lives, we are far less likely than previous generations to stray too far from formal learning situations even as we engage in a far-reaching array of informal learning situations. In social contexts heavily shaped by knowledge and information exchange, increasingly more of us are augmenting our initial schooling by taking post-secondary, adult, and continuing education programs and by pursuing a wide range of alternative learning opportunities. Lifelong learning, marked by innovation, adaptability, and the capacity to manage vast amounts of information, is widely touted as the key to success in a globally competitive environment. At the same time, we need to pose questions about which sorts of knowledge and learning systems are most appropriate for the worlds we encounter and seek to shape. Public scrutiny over education has produced varying answers to questions about what kinds of education we should promote, who should pay for it and who should control it, who should have access to it, and how it should be recognized.

Education is regarded more seriously as the stakes associated with it rise, and consequently is criticized heavily on some fronts and praised on others. Educational options have expanded dramatically even as some alternatives have been cut back. The benefits from forms of learning that are inclusive, flexible, fun, and engaging are being rediscovered at the same time that learners are being subjected to more testing, scrutiny, procedures, and expectations that often generate frustration and stress. Patricia Clifford (2008: 76), writing in *Education Canada*, observes how the contemporary world requires us to seek innovative solutions to problems that may not have definitive answers, yet our learning is mostly shaped and evaluated with reference to answers that somebody already knows. There is some hope, nonetheless, that much educational debate is moving from entrenched positions based on uncritical acceptance of presumed truths to serious efforts to understand the strengths and limitations associated with various options and their consequences. There is an emerging impetus to engage in decision-making based on empirical findings from educational research, signified especially in the form of several major collaborative initiatives among researchers, policy bodies, and diverse educational communities. There is also growing emphasis that knowledge and learning are multi-faceted, with mutual benefit derived from sharing and exploring diverse alternatives.

Much of my life has revolved around formal education, first as a student at various levels of study, later as a high school and junior high school teacher, and then as a university faculty member. My own observations, insights, and predispositions have been shaped directly and indirectly by many of the educators, students, colleagues, and communities with whom I have worked and interacted over the years. I acknowledge, in particular, the contributions of several people whose efforts and support have been especially important in the writing and production of this book. My nascent efforts to understand and appreciate the nuances associated with educational matters have been broadened considerably by members of numerous research consortia and educational bodies I have been fortunate to be associated with in Saskatchewan, across Canada, in China, and elsewhere. My colleagues and students in the Department of Sociology at the University of Saskatchewan have provided a supportive environment to encourage ongoing debate, discussion, and scholarship. Several former and current graduate students, including Joanne Butler, Jason Doherty, Trina Evitts, Darlene Lanceley, Beverly LaPointe, Artin Lahiji, Andy Livingstone, Kevin Shearer, Qianru She, and Yixuan Wang, have contributed directly or indirectly in various ways, including assisting in the preparation of the manuscript and supporting materials, offering useful commentary on the manuscript, and providing fresh insights into educational issues. I am indebted to the anonymous readers of the manuscript whose suggestions have enriched the work in many ways. I am especially grateful to Oxford University Press and its personnel for providing a consistently high quality of support, direction, and professional expertise throughout the development and publication process. Some key people, notably Euan White, Phyllis Wilson, and Richard Tallman, have played central roles from the beginning, nurturing the work from its initial stages through all four editions. I want to acknowledge, as well, the excellent guidance, support, and professional competence of Meagan Carlsson, Patti Sayle, and Caroline Starr, along with others who have made possible and contributed to the publication of the current edition.

I am especially indebted to Barb for her support in all ways. This book is dedicated to Rachel and Nicole, and all the teachers who have made schooling for them a wondrous and exciting experience.

The author and the publisher would like to thank the following reviewers and those who chose to remain anonymous for offering outstanding feedback and guidance:

John Marshall Mangan, Western University
Amir Mirfakhraie, Kwantlen Polytechnic University
Kathleen Moss, Carleton University
Lisa Trimble, McGill University

Chapter 1

The Sociological Analysis of Education

Learning Objectives

In this chapter, you will:

- be introduced to the discipline of sociology, its defining characteristics, and its core concerns;
- understand how sociological analysis has been applied to an understanding of education systems and educational issues.

Introduction

Education is a vital part of our social existence. Whether it occurs in formal settings or in less formal ways, **education** helps to shape our personalities as well as our life choices and chances. In many respects, all human experiences are educative. We continually engage in processes of self-development, modifying and recreating the world through our everyday activities. Both structured and unstructured forms of education are taking on greater significance in Canada and throughout the world within what is commonly called the information society or knowledge economy in which knowledge and learning occupy centre stage in social relationships and economic activities. The central role of education challenges us to investigate the implications of educational transformation, including how and why education systems have taken their present shape.

This chapter introduces several of the main themes pertinent to a critical examination of education. Its aim is to guide the development of a distinctly sociological understanding, but this is also augmented with insights derived from a variety of academic disciplines and interdisciplinary perspectives. Following a brief introduction to the discipline of sociology and the core questions and frameworks associated with sociological understandings, the chapter identifies four critical approaches to the analysis of education—critical pedagogy, feminist pedagogy, anti-racism education, and political economy—that inform the analysis employed throughout the book.

The Sociological Understanding of Educational Problems

Usually when we think of education, we identify it with formal institutions—schools, colleges, universities, and other structured institutional or learning processes. Viewed in these concrete terms, education tends to be associated with teachers, texts, and tests; knowledge, skills, and values; credentials, opportunities, and rewards; and policy, budget, and public representation. Consider the following questions:

- How and why has formal schooling come to be associated with education?
- Why do some people fail or drop out of school while others achieve success through post-secondary education?
- Why do most school classrooms have a readily identifiable character that distinguishes them from other social settings?
- Which social groups are served by educational institutions, and with what outcomes?
- How does teaching compare with other types of work?
- Why is Canadian education financed mostly by governments, and primarily by local, provincial, and territorial governments?
- What do people really learn at school, and how important is it for jobs and life outside of school?
- What impact do social, economic, and technological changes have on educational processes and achievement levels?
- What is the relationship between formal education and other learning activities?
- Who decides what is in the curriculum and how is the curriculum translated into educational practice?

Each of these questions can be answered in many different ways. Canadians hold diverse opinions about many of them. Most of us tend to take education for granted, but there are disparate views about what education systems should focus on and how they should be organized, resulting in extensive controversy surrounding many contemporary educational issues. Some answers involve historical facts or information that can be gathered through simple observation. Responses to other questions require more detailed data collected statistically, through interviews, or by other methodologies. Nearly all questions are subject to competing interpretations.

Sociology is a discipline or field of inquiry that provides particular frameworks through which we can make sense of questions like those outlined above as well as of the diverse responses they generate. Sociologists are interested in education because it is so central to human social experience, to our direct and indirect relations with other people. Education, in its various guises, conveys important insights about particular kinds of societies and the people within them. The analysis of educational structures, practices, and outcomes can help us to understand, for example, what kinds of values, beliefs, and ideologies prevail in a given society, how people learn about and become organized within particular social structures, and how open and democratic that society is.

The purpose of this book is to analyze Canadian educational practices, structures, and problems from a critical sociological framework. In many cases, international examples are employed to highlight the broader context within which Canadian education is situated. Emphasis is on formal education or **schooling**, as opposed to other types of education, since it is in its institutional forms that education has become most highly integrated into wider social, economic, and political organization. We also explore the changing boundaries between educational institutions and other learning sites. Reference is made to a variety of sociological studies and perspectives developed within and beyond Canada to provide the reader with a sense of how distinct research traditions have been employed to understand schooling. The book adopts a critical orientation, which reveals how education in Canada has been from the outset a complex, contested, and contradictory endeavour. The book is not intended as a manual or an exhaustive history that details all aspects of our education systems. Instead, it employs analytical tools derived from sociology and related disciplines in an effort to answer questions about why education has developed as it has and how educational issues are interconnected with fundamental characteristics of social organization and

Box 1.1 Sociological Interest in the Growth and Social Significance of Education

The growing significance of education for Canadians is illustrated in Figure 1.1, below, which demonstrates how, over the past half-century, the share of the population with university degrees has overtaken that portion of the population with less than a Grade 9 education. Sociologists have offered numerous interpretations of this educational growth, and have also examined its significance for society as a whole and for different subgroups within the population.

Figure 1.1 Proportions of Canadian Population, 15 Years and Over, with University Degrees and Less Than Grade 9 Education

Sources: Data from Guppy and Davies (1998:19); Statistics Canada, Census of Canada, various years; and CANSIM Table 2820004. This is an updated version based on a figure in Clarke (2000:7).

social life. The remainder of this chapter examines the issues and approaches central to sociological analysis. The chapter concludes with a brief discussion of how these insights can be applied to educational questions in such a way as to provide a framework for the chapters to follow.

Sociology and Its Relation to Other Disciplines

Sociology is the investigation of the relationships between individuals and society. It examines how social structures (relatively enduring patterns of social organization) and social practices (ongoing social activity) both shape and are shaped by human beings. It is a scientific discipline in the sense that it is based on research and theories that attempt, in a systematic and organized manner, to describe and explain important features of social reality. Sociologists analyze such institutions as schools, families, economic and political organizations, religion, the mass media, and the criminal justice system, as well as interpersonal relations, small groups, informal social practices, and much broader and sometimes less visible social forces, such as power and control.

In its scope and methods, sociology overlaps with and draws on several other disciplines and fields of inquiry. Sociology—or particular subfields of the discipline—can share much in common with such other social sciences as economics, political science, psychology, and anthropology, as well as with studies in the humanities, such as history and philosophy, and with interdisciplinary approaches in such areas as Native studies, women's studies, environmental studies, cultural studies, and regional studies. Some sociological work is influenced by and influences other fields of inquiry, including human geography, biology, medicine, demography, policy studies, and administrative studies.

Despite its complementarity with various academic disciplines, sociology developed from the vision of eighteenth- and nineteenth-century intellectuals who wanted to construct a distinct science of society modelled after physics, biology, and other natural sciences. In common with closely related social sciences like psychology and economics, many of the tools that sociologists employ to examine the social world involve principles of research methodology and theory construction shared with scientists who study the natural world. However, the studies of the social and natural worlds differ in crucial ways. Social reality, complex and dynamic in nature, is not governed strictly by law-like regularities and it is not readily amenable to definitive statements about cause and effect that are the objective of much scientific inquiry. Social structures and practices are constantly being reshaped and reinterpreted by human activity. Moreover, the sociological investigator, as part of the social world being studied, may have an impact on social actions and how they are understood. Social research involves an ethical dimension that raises questions about what kinds of research activities are socially acceptable and what their consequences are for social life. These problems are shared by other sciences, since all scientific activity involves to some extent human interpretation, phenomena that are subject to change, and ethical questions, but they are much more evident within or central to sociology and other human sciences than in the scientific investigation of non-social phenomena.

With this wide array of influences, it might seem unusual that a discipline like sociology should exist, since most questions like the ones listed earlier can be investigated through one or more of the other disciplines. Two somewhat opposing points can be made in response to this concern. First, it is true that boundaries between disciplines are somewhat flexible, so that it may seem that the only clear distinction between areas is evident in the field by which people identify themselves (e.g., psychologists, educational administrators, and sociologists may all use similar methods to conduct research into the question of why some students drop out of school). The second point, however, involves the recognition that each discipline is constituted around core questions and approaches that can clearly be distinguished from one another. In the example noted above, the psychologist may be most interested in identifying the personality characteristics of school dropouts in comparison with students who stay in school; the researcher in educational administration may be most concerned with identifying ways to keep students in school longer; and the sociologist may be most interested in determining how characteristics of school organization contribute to the dropout phenomenon. The distinguishing characteristics of sociology are discussed below.

The Nature of Sociological Inquiry

Sociology, like most social sciences, emerged relatively recently compared to the humanities and physical sciences. A prolonged period of social, economic, and political upheaval in Europe, particularly during and after the mid-eighteenth century, fostered an interest in sustained inquiry into the nature of society and its relationship to the individual. The rapid advancement of the Industrial Revolution, combined with new social and political arrangements, led to serious questioning about the nature and consequences of social change. People's life experiences were altered amid challenges to existing social conventions and institutions. Among the transformations was a growing emphasis on democracy and individual rights as opposed to more traditional, hierarchical bases of social order. Out of these circumstances emerged both intellectual and pragmatic concerns to understand the conditions that produced social change, to assess the impact of the changes taking place, and to consider the possibilities and prospects for future social transformation. "Sociology," a term first used by the French writer Auguste Comte in the nineteenth century to signify the need for a scientific study of society, was developed to study these issues by examining the relative impact of social stability and social change on people's lives.

Although the thematic focus and methodological substance of sociology have taken on different forms since Comte's time, many of the issues that concerned early sociologists remain at the core of the discipline. Sociology is both a scientific discipline and a moral or human undertaking in which theoretical analysis and empirical research are applied to an understanding of important social problems and issues in order to enhance the world in which we live. The contemporary significance of this historical vision for the discipline has been articulated in the work of recent sociologists. Patricia Hill Collins (2007: 112), for instance, stresses the continuing inspiration offered through the works of such classical social theorists as Karl Marx, Max Weber, Georg Simmel, Émile Durkheim, W.E.B. Dubois, and others whom she characterizes as public sociologists offering a "commitment to bring the tools of sociology to bear on the important issues of their time. . . . So much of what they did was on behalf of bettering the public." Similarly, Steve Fuller (2006: 1) contends that, "The central aspiration of sociology—and the social sciences more generally—has been to make good on the eighteenth-century Enlightenment promise of creating a 'heaven on earth' [with an aim] to create a world in which humans exercise dominion over nature without exercising dominion over each other."

As a discipline concerned with understanding and building upon relations between individuals and society, sociology has been guided by several fundamental questions and debates, including the following:

1. At which level—individual or social—should analysis begin?
2. To what extent are individuals the products or the producers of social structures?
3. Is social life characterized more by social stability and consensus or by social conflict?
4. How do we study the social world, and to what ends? Should the study of society be guided by a search for observable facts and laws (positivism) or by human interpretations of the world?

Individual versus Society

All sociological analysis is concerned at some level with relations among individuals and societies. Sociologists do not study individuals in isolation from one another, but focus instead on how people interact with each other either directly (at a face-to-face level) or indirectly (through internalized rules and expectations, the products of human activity, consciousness of others, and institutionalized patterns of behaviour). Different forms of sociological analysis emerge around questions about which factor or set of factors is regarded as most important.

The debate concerning the relations between individuals and society can be illustrated with reference to two key sociological theorists, Émile Durkheim and Max Weber, whose works were instrumental in establishing sociology as a viable academic discipline in the late nineteenth and early twentieth centuries. Durkheim defined sociology as the study of "social facts," referring to features of society (such as rates of marriage or death, religion, law, and economic systems) that existed in their own right and had an influence on individuals' thoughts and actions. Society, in these terms, can be studied as if it is a real thing because it is present before we are born and after we die, and it affects the life and character of each human being. Weber, by contrast, defined sociology as the "interpretive understanding of social action," by which he meant that the discipline should emphasize how people's social decisions and behaviours are guided by interpretation or meaning. Unlike Durkheim, Weber argued that society has no independent existence outside of people's thoughts, motives, and actions (although human actions and creations have a powerful impact on our choices and actions). Posed in simpler terms, Durkheim represents a version of sociology in which the study of relations between individuals and society begins with society, while Weber's analysis begins with individuals and proceeds from there to study social relations. Contemporary sociologists continue to look to these starting points, or some intermediate position, as the basis for analyses.

Human Agency versus Structural Determination

An important question that accompanies the investigation of how individuals are interrelated with society concerns the role that free choice plays in our lives. Although we tend to think of ourselves as unique individuals, we must also recognize that our thoughts, personalities, and actions are heavily influenced by our social background and surroundings. Sociologists do not always agree about the extent to which individuals are shaped by social factors, and vice versa. One view, that of human **agency**, asserts that human beings are active "agents" whose behaviour and thoughts make society possible. People are seen to be relatively free to make sense of the world in such a way as to make decisions that guide their lives and conduct. The world, according to this approach, is socially constructed—our language, cultures, and institutions are created, maintained, and changed through human activity.

A contrasting, structuralist view emphasizes that people are social products. **Social structures**, or relatively enduring patterns within society and social life, give rise to our personalities and thoughts, to the choices we face, and to the courses we take in our lives. When we are born, existing social structures determine limitations and opportunities dependent on such factors as gender, race, the wealth and status of our parents, and so on. Our freedom, in other words, tends to be highly constrained by social rules and expectations.

Most sociologists and other social thinkers take a position somewhere between the two extremes of individual agency and structural determination. As Karl Marx (1963: 15) observed, people "make their own history, but they do not make it just as they please; they do not make it under circumstances chosen by themselves, but under circumstances directly encountered, given and transmitted from the past." A more contemporary sociologist, Anthony Giddens (1987: 11), has expressed the same point through what he calls "the 'double involvement' of individuals and institutions," in which "we create society at the same time as we are created by it." In other words, whatever their starting points, most sociologists agree that society is something more than a collection of individuals such that it must be studied with sensitivity to the reciprocal impact of human beings and social structures on each other.

Stability versus Conflict

As noted earlier, sociology emerged through systematic efforts to understand significant social changes occurring in conjunction with the Industrial Revolution and social upheaval. Some early social commentators feared that the changes were destructive of a social order that could never be retrieved while others welcomed the changes as a mark of progress and hope for the future. These dual concerns, of a search for social stability and a desire for social change and improvement, remain central to the discipline.

Sociologists continue to address these issues from different stances. Some sociologists, following the tradition of Auguste Comte, have attempted to uncover laws governing social order and conditions for social change. Their assumption is that stable social order, supported by consensus about fundamental values, is the normal state of a society. The development of sociology as a science, in these terms, is to identify factors that foster social harmony as opposed to those that are socially harmful or destructive. Excessive conflict and social change that proceeds too rapidly are deemed to threaten the long-term survival of a society. A contrasting approach to social analysis depicts conflict and struggle as normal features of societies. Societies, particularly if they are relatively complex in nature, are likely to contain a diversity of different collectivities and subgroups, each with specific needs and interests. Although overt conflict is not always present or apparent, social change is driven by the demands and actions of social groups to have their interests represented and their needs met. The task of sociology, in this view, is to identify and analyze the social circumstances that give rise to each set of interests.

Positivism versus Interpretative Analysis

There are different ways of looking at the world as well as of determining what should be looked at. The task of social science, for some sociologists, is to replicate, as much

International Case Study

The Sociology of Education as a Tool to Address Educational Problems

Unlike many branches of sociology that are sometimes concerned with highly technical or abstract theoretical and methodological issues of greatest interest within the discipline, many strong linkages exist between the sociological analysis of education and educational policy and practice. This is partly a result of the early interest in sociology among educators and educational administrators who saw that sociology could serve as a tool to generate information about and answers to pressing educational problems. These relationships have helped foster widespread interest in sociology of education research, but they have also attracted important criticisms—research driven by the interests of governments and educational administrators often leaves few channels to address more significant educational problems and limits opportunities to explore fundamental causes of the problems being investigated (Banks, 1976: 1-3; Ball, 2008).

After World War II, researchers and policy-makers began to focus on questions about the extent to which, and how best, education could contribute to improved social and economic opportunities, especially for those coming from lower- or working-class positions. This work was initially developed in the United Kingdom in the 1950s when interest in exploring how education could advance the goals of the welfare state emerged out of an earlier "political arithmetic" tradition concerned with research for effective population management (Ball, 2008: 654–5). In the United States, educational research dedicated to understanding differences in educational performance and improving socio-economic outcomes through schooling has factored centrally in major policy initiatives like the War on Poverty in the mid-1960s and the "No Child Left Behind" legislation introduced in 2001 (Lauen and Tyson, 2009: 73). In many nations, including the UK, attention turned after the late 1980s to issues of school effectiveness and organizational studies focusing on which characteristics produced different outcomes from one school to another. Ball (2008: 662–5) sees in much of this research focus a lack of attention to critical sociological and contextual factors, thereby reducing the work to a tool employed by policy-makers. Paradoxically, researchers in the US and other nations express concern that educational policy development often proceeds with limited or selective attention to evidence produced through research by sociologists and other educational researchers (Stevenson, 2006: 559–60).

Some policy-relevant educational research is open to analysis from a variety of perspectives. One of the predominant issues in the sociology of education in a wide range of national contexts is race and ethnic relations, with the focus shifting depending on the composition of minority groups within particular settings. Saha (2008: 305), observes that:

> In the United States, sociologists are particularly interested in the educational attainments of African American and the Hispanic populations.

But in general, similar attention has been given to all minority groups, especially since movements of populations across national boundaries have increased, both voluntarily and nonvoluntarily. The study of racial and ethnic minorities has included indigenous, migrant, and refugee populations. Sociologists of education in the United States, Britain, Canada, and Australia have been particularly active in this research.

In developing countries, much of the early work in the sociology of education either drew from structural functionalism and other models that had been abandoned in the West, or produced unique work not widely known outside of specific national or regional contexts. As in Western nations, educational research in the developing world has tended to address questions defined by governments and educational officials, but it has also been driven by the interests of development agencies and financial bodies seeking to advance particular agendas to foster modernization or economic liberalization. Ball (1981: 311) points to striking gaps in earlier analysis that fail to take account of important day-to-day realities in schools in much of the developing world: "The vital differences between elite and mass schooling, urban and rural schooling, Christian and Muslim schooling, day and boarding schooling, etc., have been glossed over. The education of women is virtually ignored and so too is the vast amount of non-formal education taking place in the cities, towns and countryside of Africa, Asia and Latin America." Many of these issues, as well as other problems identified in developing nations, have been taken up in more recent research, but in some contexts the range of questions that may be explored through sociology of education research remains restricted as a result of various political, financial, or logistical factors.

The overall field of research in the sociology of education is diffuse and dynamic. Unique national, regional, and linguistic factors influence the kinds of problems and orientations adopted in particular settings, but the prevalence of a few dominant research traditions and interest in several common thematic areas (such as relationships among education and social change, inequalities in educational access and outcomes, and the impact of globalization on education), as well as often top-down policy agendas, mean there is considerable convergence in the focus of research. Access to data and research facilitated by digital technologies, translation of key works across various languages, and interest in comparative and international dimensions of education hasten some of this convergence, but these processes also open new possibilities for alternative research perspectives such as those emerging through subaltern voices within both developing and highly industrialized nations.

Discussion Question

1. To what extent should educational research pursue questions of interest to educational policy-makers and administrators, as opposed to the academic interests of educational researchers? Justify your answer, and provide examples to illustrate your response.

as possible, the rigorous approaches associated with physics, chemistry, and other scientific disciplines. The goal of science, understood this way, is to formulate laws and statements about regular patterns of cause and effect in the social world, and to specify the conditions under which these causal relations will occur. This approach, known as **positivism**, emphasizes that science must concern itself with phenomena that can be readily identified and measured. Like many scientists who study the natural world, these sociologists assume that the social world has a definite structure of reality that can be observed, classified, and controlled as we gain objective knowledge about each of its parts.

Other sociologists, by contrast, contend that positivism's claims to uncover objective knowledge about laws that regulate society are false. They argue that all human knowledge, including scientific observation, is based on particular interpretations of reality. Social reality, moreover, is continually being shaped and reshaped because it is based on human actions. For interpretative sociologists, therefore, the proper task of science is to identify the social bases and meanings attached to particular phenomena, and to explore how those meanings are related to people's social actions. This assessment, expressed in its most radical form within some postmodernist orientations, suggests that any scientific quest for universal truths or general laws is necessarily misguided because it does not take into account the diverse meanings and viewpoints characteristic of human life. Other interpretative sociology does not reject the possibility of science, but cautions that we must be aware of the limitations associated with science and the claims or authority that it carries with it.

Sociological Perspectives

Sociologists, like anyone else who investigates nature or society, must make decisions about what they study and how they study it. They require guidelines to help them focus their observations and make sense of what they see. In their most general form, these guidelines are provided in the form of what are called sociological perspectives, or ways of looking at the social world. Perspectives point to what is important, based on particular assumptions about social reality and how to study it.

Sociology, it should be emphasized, is not unique in offering perspectives to its practitioners. All sciences rely on specific assumptions that lead to different ways of conducting scientific investigation. In medical research, for example, some researchers emphasize the factors that cause a certain disorder so that appropriate cures or remedies can be prescribed, while others adopt a more holistic orientation that examines health in the context of a wide range of environmental conditions, which themselves must be modified before effective healing can take place. In physics, the study of quantifiable characteristics of matter is contrasted with the analysis of unobservable, changing forces. In all disciplines, perspectives identify ways to address these kinds of issues in a systematic manner.

It should be emphasized that sociologists share some common goals regardless of the perspectives they adopt. All theory is an attempt to enhance our ability to understand aspects of the social and natural worlds, and all research is conducted as part of an effort to provide us with information that tells us something about what those worlds are like. Scientific inquiry is unified by a search for knowledge and understanding, even though there are differences over how that search should be conducted, what the ultimate aim of that search should be, and what should be done with the information generated.

Sociological perspectives are aligned around questions governed by debates outlined in the preceding sections. Although there are different ways of labelling and organizing them, it is generally agreed that the discipline has been shaped by several sociological perspectives, in particular three identified here as structural functionalism, interpretative sociology, and critical analysis.

Structural Functionalism

Structural functionalist analysis examines social institutions and other elements of society in relation to the social system as a whole. It is sometimes known as the order perspective because it is concerned with factors that ensure the maintenance of social stability. As the name suggests, structural functionalism examines phenomena by asking questions about what functions they serve and how they contribute to the orderly operation of the social system. Formal education, for example, serves the social order by transmitting vital knowledge and social aptitudes to successive generations and by sorting and selecting people for entry into roles or positions required by the social system.

Structural functionalist analysis commonly employs an organic analogy in which societies are compared to living organisms. Each part of the social system, like each feature of the organism, has specific roles to play to keep the organism alive and functioning properly. Some functions are more crucial than others to the unit's overall health and existence, but with increasing specialization, as the unit becomes more complex in nature, the system's survival requires each element to be integrated with the others in a unified way. Sociological analysis, as with the analysis of organic structures, proceeds to describe these interrelationships and to identify the conditions required for social stability. The long-term survival of society, according to this analysis, requires that elements (whether individuals or institutional processes) that do not fit with the whole, or are not functioning properly, must be eliminated or modified, analogous to the Western medical treatment of a diseased body.

Although the perspective is highly abstract through its concern with general features of social systems, research conducted by structural functionalists tends to be positivistic in nature. It seeks to outline regular relationships among phenomena through measurement of specific social dimensions, such as degrees of socio-economic inequality, pupil dropout rates, or racial categorizations. In their assumptions that the social world has a definite, observable structure that can be made known through scientific investigation, structural functionalists often attempt to give sociology the status of a more established natural science like physics or biology.

Structural functionalism was highly influential in the development of North American sociological theory and research throughout much of the twentieth century. Its major contributions have been to demonstrate the impact of social structures on social groups and individuals and to point out how various components of societies are interrelated. Nonetheless, the limitations of structural functionalism are evident in a critical examination of many of its central assumptions and procedures.

A first major criticism is most apparent to sociologists who adopt an interpretative orientation to social analysis. Structural functionalism, in its concern to "map out" the social system and its constituent structures, ignores much of the richness of everyday life. It is frequently open to the charge that it portrays society in such a mechanistic way that it has no place for the activities and realities of living human beings, who in fact are the producers (or agents) of society and social change.

Critical sociologists have pointed to a second main limitation of structural functionalism: its emphasis on social order and consensus tends to undermine or draw attention away from struggles or tensions that operate within society. Many conflicts are more than merely transitional in nature; indeed, significant social divisions may be built into the structure of a given society. Therefore, inequalities and power struggles may be a normal rather than an abnormal occurrence. Social order, when it is evident, may itself be the consequence of political force rather than an indicator of widespread agreement about social goals. The use of coercion to achieve social stability is most obvious in societies ruled by totalitarian regimes, but it is a regular feature of life even in democratic societies. Taken together, these major criticisms sometimes portray structural functionalism as an approach limited by its attempts to impose order and control arbitrarily onto social circumstances rather than to subject them to sustained analytical inquiry.

Interpretative Analysis

Sociologists who work within interpretative traditions portray the social world as produced and interpreted by human activity. As the name of one important branch of interpretative sociology—symbolic interactionism—denotes, the main focal points for social analysis are social interactions and social symbols. People develop and share meanings with one another as they engage in social activity and attempt to make sense of their activity within a social context.

Interpretative sociology, in contrast with structural functionalism, is concerned with the analysis of social processes rather than social structures. Structures serve as guidelines for interaction that comes into being, and can be changed or modified through social activities. Individuals act, comprehend, and have motives; social structures do not. The world, viewed this way, is seen to be "socially constructed" because the nature and meaning of social reality have no existence independent of our relations with other people, either at a face-to-face level or through the language, beliefs, knowledge, and modes of communication created and shared by people.

Because sociology and other scientific investigations are forms of social activity, scientific data and observations, like other social products, must be understood in terms of how they are processed by the human mind. Science, therefore, is subject to varying interpretations, as are other forms of social interaction. These insights do not mean that it is impossible to conduct scientific inquiry into the social world. Rather, our understanding of science (whether we are studying society or the natural world) must take into account the importance of human values and interpretations in shaping the world and how we see it.

Interpretative analysis is sometimes called microsociology because it is concerned with patterns of interaction at an everyday, interpersonal level, as opposed to the broader, macrosociological orientation of structural functionalism and much critical sociology. While it may seem that the individualistic starting point is not sociological because it does not focus on social structures, it is important to recognize that interpretative analysis studies individuals as participants in social interaction and shared meaning rather than as isolated units. The task of sociology, presented this way, is to help people develop a clear awareness of their own identities and subjectivity, their relations with others, and their place within society.

Interpretative sociology makes a valuable contribution to sociological analysis by showing the importance of our interactions with other people. It highlights the significance of everyday encounters and situations, and emphasizes how meanings are created and shared through social interaction. As opposed to structural forms of analysis that emphasize society at more abstract levels, it places active human beings at the core of sociological inquiry.

Despite its insights, interpretative sociology often fails to provide a comprehensive analysis of social life. The tendency within this approach to focus on immediate social settings is more oriented to description than to explanation. This ahistorical emphasis makes it relatively unable to explain problems such as how it is possible for enduring social inequalities to persist or how broad social positions and expectations may change. In the analysis of education, for example, an emphasis on interactions within the classroom is often unconnected with social structures and practices that shape the organization of the classroom, the curriculum, and the forces that condition the opportunities and experiences of the educational participants. Similarly, an acknowledgement that particular social circumstances and definitions are socially constructed does not necessarily indicate whose definitions are employed or what barriers stand in the way of attempts to introduce new definitions and social constructions.

Critical Sociologies

Various forms of critical analysis have been posed as alternatives to the traditional variants of sociology represented by structural functionalism and interpretative analysis. Critical analysis, as the term suggests, engages in a critique of social structures and practices by probing beyond descriptions of the status quo. The social world, as opposed to something neutral or mutually beneficial to all its members, is characterized by fundamental structural inequalities constituted in part by oppression by dominant groups over subordinate social groups. Critical sociology, in this regard, is committed to social change as well as to social analysis. This does not mean that the approach is unscientific. Instead, in common with interpretative approaches, it argues that science is a necessary human activity uncovering aspects of social reality that tend to be hidden from us in our everyday lives.

These characteristics can be illustrated with reference to two main branches of critical analysis, Marxism and feminism. Marxist analysis emphasizes that class, defined according to ownership and control of productive resources, is the fundamental basis of social inequality and oppression. Feminist analysis sees patriarchy, or male domination of personal and institutional life, as the primary basis of social differentiation. From different starting points, both Marxist and feminist approaches share the view that extensive analysis is required to uncover the dynamics and roots of social oppression and structured inequalities. Both theoretical stances also share a common commitment to changing repressive social conditions, although each contains varying assessments of the nature of, and strategies to advance, social change.

Despite this common ground, there are important differences among particular forms of critical analysis. Even general orientations to analysis such as Marxism and feminism contain sharply divergent approaches. Whereas radical feminism and orthodox Marxism, for example, disagree fundamentally about the origins of social oppression and how best to conduct social research, Marxist feminism and socialist feminism argue that the two approaches can be highly compatible.

Critical educational theories have been subject to recent challenges both internally and externally. Within critical analysis, proponents of various positions have

Box 1.2 Research Orientations in the Sociology of Education

Research, particularly through the systematic collection and analysis of data, is a fundamental part of any scientific discipline. Just as there are differences in how sociologists understand and explain educational problems, researchers in the sociology of education employ a wide range of research approaches and methodologies in their work. This work has produced important new knowledge and provided support or countervailing evidence related to existing theoretical insights. Sociological research on education has also introduced or popularized many significant methodological innovations. Émile Durkheim, whose work provided an explicit empirical and methodological foundation for early social scientific research, explored educational issues throughout his career.

Major studies on the impact that schooling had on social inequality across generations have introduced advanced statistical techniques into social science research in North America, Europe, and other regions since the mid-1950s, while research based at the University of Chicago and other places has provided a long tradition of innovative qualitative analysis of education. Detailed records, reports, and massive statistical databases—collected and maintained by national and provincial governments, international bodies such as UNESCO, and other central agencies involved in education—often serve as rich data sources for educational researchers. Growing sophistication and co-ordination characteristic of many large data sets are enabling researchers to gain a better understanding of complex educational issues, but there continue to be gaps in some of this information. Canada lags behind many nations in its ability to collect comprehensive national data necessary to make many international comparisons of education spending and outcomes (Cappon, 2007). Also, many researchers fear that the

often dismissed or ignored possibilities for shared insights such as an exploration of how factors like class, gender, and race interact with one another or an assessment of strategies for effective educational and social change. Shifting economic, cultural, and political alignments, along with increasing attention to challenges associated with globalization, new technologies, and environmental issues, have also been accompanied by new ways of thinking about the social world and relations between people and nature.

Several researchers, drawing on interpretative analysis, postmodernist critiques, and insights developed within other disciplines, have argued that no single approach is sufficient to provide an adequate understanding either of education or, more broadly, of human life in general (Davies, 1995; Kanpol, 1992). Postmodern thought, in particular, has emerged as a theoretical alternative suggesting that contemporary social life and personal experiences are so multi-dimensional and fragmented that no unified theory or set of ideas can adequately explain social reality. Despite these challenges, however, critical educational perspectives are able to demonstrate their resiliency when they identify issues and present analytical tools that not only advance our understanding of social problems but also seek to find effective solutions to them.

Canadian government's decision in 2010 to replace the mandatory long-form census with a voluntary household survey will distort census findings related to key variables regarding education.

However, these statistical resources can have limited utility for researchers who may not be able to gain access to them and who may require information collected for different purposes and categorized in different ways from those determined by the sponsoring agencies. Recent emphasis in fields like education and health care on the use of empirical research evidence for policy and professional decision-making has provided an impetus for large-scale initiatives to co-ordinate more systematically research initiatives, databases, and findings. In the United States, the implementation of federal legislation, designated the No Child Left Behind Act of 2001, represents one of the most visible examples of evidence-based decision-making in education. On a more modest and less controversial scale, initiatives in Canada, such as the creation in 2004 of the now disbanded Canadian Council on Learning, have provided new opportunities for researchers, policy-makers, and other partners to co-ordinate research-related activities focused on key dimensions of education and lifelong learning.

Educational researchers typically rely on data collected from a variety of sources. While some specialize in quantitative methodologies and techniques, drawing upon data collected through secondary sources as well as surveys and instruments they have developed through their own research, others employ qualitative methods such as interviews, focus groups, observation, documentary analysis, and narrative accounts. Researchers are increasingly combining research methods or developing detailed case studies to gain a richer understanding of educational structures, practices, and meanings. Throughout the book, references are made to findings derived from studies and approaches that represent an extensive range of these diverse orientations.

Emerging Directions in the Critical Analysis of Education

This book adopts a critical stance towards the analysis of education, in particular drawing on four interrelated forms of critical analysis that have influenced recent thinking about educational matters: critical pedagogy, feminist pedagogy, anti-racism education, and political economy. They will be outlined briefly here, discussed more fully in Chapter 2, and integrated into the analysis employed in subsequent chapters.

Critical Pedagogy

Critical pedagogy is influenced by several critical traditions and motivated by the desire to integrate educational theory and educational practice. Like Marxism and feminism, its advocates emphasize the deeply rooted power imbalances and social inequalities that infuse schooling structures and processes. In common with interpretative and postmodern analysis, critical pedagogy also stresses the symbolic importance of knowledge, language, and social action within educational practices. Education has both cultural and economic significance as a mechanism that gives shape and meaning to people's life experiences, thereby reinforcing the privileges of advantaged groups relative to powerless segments of society. Educational practices, according to critical pedagogy, must be restructured to represent the voices and experiences of all social groups, not just those who have sufficient resources and power to advance their own interests.

Feminist Pedagogy

Feminist pedagogy, like critical pedagogy, challenges the common view that education is neutral, and commits itself to transform the education system as a consequence of the critique it offers. **Feminist pedagogy** argues that educational theory and practice must take into account the differential experiences, life chances, and ways of knowing that prevail for men and women in society. As teachers, mothers, and students, women tend to be excluded from key roles in educational decision-making and research, which thereby serves both to reflect and to perpetuate their socio-economic subordination relative to men. As a basis for achieving the true function of education, which is the empowerment of human beings, feminist pedagogy seeks to sensitize educators, students, and researchers to the ways in which gender structures men's and women's lives.

Anti-Racism Education

Educational approaches informed by anti-racism emphasize the powerful social impact of inequalities and ideologies based on race. **Anti-racism education** aligns itself with critical and feminist pedagogies in its quest to empower marginalized persons, while it shares with political economy a critique of material circumstances that produce fundamental social inequalities. The critical race theory in which anti-racism education practices are grounded emphasizes the intersections among relations of power and inequality embedded within social and legal structures. Critical race analysis and anti-racism education orientations are concerned not only with the analysis of minority and subordinated groups, but draw attention as well to the social construction of "whiteness" and the social relationships in which it is embedded. Educational institutions and the knowledge and practices associated with them are implicated in the production and legitimation of racial categories and how these are expressed in notions of difference and various forms of discrimination and racism. However, schooling and post-secondary education can play a crucial role in working to address these problems.

Political Economy

Political economy stresses the interrelationships that prevail among the various segments of society, including the economic, political, and social realms. Like other approaches, there are various strands within political economy, ranging from traditional and liberal thought to orthodox Marxist perspectives. This book is informed by recent developments in critical political economy that examine the interplay among class, race, gender, and other central factors that shape and are shaped by people's life experiences. This approach argues that to make sense of social reality, we must examine how people collectively produce and reproduce both the material and symbolic conditions of their social existence. Education, viewed this way, has importance as a site in which people's personalities and life options take shape through interaction among the characteristics and experiences they bring with them into educational settings, the structures and practices that constitute education on an ongoing basis, and the linkages between education and the socio-economic context within which it operates. More recent political economic analysis, informed by practices associated with globalization, has shifted its focus from education in specific national or regional settings in order to understand linkages with comparative and international dimensions of education.

Conclusion

The sociology of education, parallel to the educational realities it seeks to investigate and explain, is a multi-faceted and changing endeavour. Sufficient scope and diversity in the analysis of education are needed to capture the richness of education in its various forms. At the same time, because educational research and theory can be used to guide policy and practice, we must ensure that our understanding of educational matters develops in a comprehensive way, based as much as possible on complete and accurate information sensitive to its potential impact on people's lives.

The task of developing a socially meaningful understanding of education is especially daunting at a time when education faces serious challenges often considered to be of crisis proportions. Canada's growing integration into new global economic and political alignments is forcing a reassessment of how education should best be employed for competitive advantage. Significant changes occurring across institutional spheres of contemporary life are accompanied by transformations in how we engage with and make sense of our identities and our relations with social and natural environments. Educational reform and reorganization are further promoted through changing government priorities and operations, important demographic and economic transformations, and strategies developed in response to issues related to regional diversity, national unity, and shifting global relations. Media attention and public outcries periodically focused on real or imagined concerns, such as declining educational standards, intolerable illiteracy and school dropout rates, lack of discipline and respect for authority, increasing crime rates among young offenders, and lack of moral guidance and focus among youth, have drawn attention to the limitations of existing educational bureaucracies and to desires for accountability and choice in schooling. Changing gender relations, new patterns of immigration, and prospects for self-determination among First Nations have forced educational institutions to be increasingly responsive to issues of representation, cultural diversity, and equity. Shifting arrangements and tensions related to work, income, and family life, and transitions throughout the life course have carried over into schooling, creating pressures for increased flexibility and demands for new educational supports and services at the same time that budgetary needs for public education and social services must be justified in such a way as to ensure they do not fall behind other priorities.

In the chapters that follow, historical and contemporary dimensions of Canadian education, its structure and participants, and the challenges facing it are examined through critical sociological inquiry. Each chapter highlights a theme of particular importance within the sociology of education. Chapter 2 provides an overview of major theoretical approaches and issues, contrasting traditional perspectives with more recent critical analysis. Chapter 3 is concerned with the historical development of formal education in Canada, showing how divergent objectives and contestation have shaped educational policies and practices. Chapter 4 examines the organization and dimensions of contemporary education systems in Canada and other nations. Chapter 5 examines classroom interaction and educational practices, revealing how day-to-day educational activities reflect the tension between the need to produce distinct educational outcomes and less clearly delineated elements of human social development. Chapter 6 explores the nature and development of teaching, analyzing how teachers' work is subject to many of the same forces, such as control by external managers and demands for increased productivity, as other occupations—at the same time as its orientations to educational and social processes lend it a unique professional character. Chapter 7 addresses the relationship between education and work, highlighting in particular the notion that, contrary to persistent demands that schooling and work training should be more closely linked, the nature and purposes of formal education also are determined by other competing priorities. Chapter 8 highlights the ways in which education contributes to both socio-economic opportunity and the reproduction of structured inequalities among various segments of the population. Chapter 9 draws together key themes covered in the previous chapters, focusing in particular on alternative visions of educational reform framed through diverse social and economic vantage points in a context in which the composition of educational participants and expectations about education's social and economic roles are changing rapidly. The discussion links contemporary debates over such issues as educational finance, accountability and choice, technological change, and social inclusion to accommodate diverse educational communities. These related debates reveal the importance of education to fundamental social and political choices and directions.

Annotated Further Readings

Apple, Michael W., Wayne Au, and Luis Armando Gandin, eds. 2009. *The Routledge International Handbook of Critical Education*. New York: Routledge. Several influential educational researchers present analysis and research from a wide range of national contexts to explore relations among power and knowledge in education.

Ballantine, Jeanne H., and Joan Z. Spade, eds. 2012. *Schools and Society: A Sociological Approach to Education*, 4th edn. Thousand Oaks, Calif.: Sage. This collection draws together excerpts from several classic contributions to the sociology of education as well as more recent research contributions, particularly from the US. Core topics include school organization and relationships, social and political contexts of schooling, equity and inequality, higher education, educational reform, research methods, and globalization.

Davies, Scott, and Neil Guppy. 2014. *The Schooled Society: An Introduction to the Sociology of Education*, 3rd edn. Toronto: Oxford University Press. The authors introduce core themes and concepts in the sociological analysis of education that enable us to understand how schools are organized, and how they select and socialize students to fulfill social requirements associated with the emergence of contemporary knowledge-based economies.

Dei, George J. Sefa, Irma Marcia James, Leeno Luke Karumanchery, Sonia James-Wilson, and Jasmin Zine. 2000. *Removing the Margins: The Challenges and Possibilities of Inclusive Schooling*. Toronto: Canadian Scholars' Press. Drawing on varied accounts and experiences with Canadian schooling, the authors outline a framework for the creation of inclusive educational practices that focus on how educational success must be oriented to the needs of students from diverse social and cultural backgrounds.

Jenks, Chris, ed. 1998. *Core Sociological Dichotomies.* London: Sage. The contributors to this edited collection provide an overview of the central debates and themes the discipline is concerned with, including structure/agency, fact/value, local/global, race/ethnicity, and numerous others.

Lauder, Hugh, Phillip Brown, Jo-Anne Dillabough, and A.H. Halsey, eds. 2006. *Education, Globalization, and Social Change.* Oxford: Oxford University Press. This is one of the most comprehensive collections to analyze contemporary education systems from a variety of perspectives, with contributions highlighting theoretical developments, substantive issues, and research findings from leading researchers representing diverse disciplinary and national contexts.

Key Terms

Agency Recognition that human beings act on the basis of various degrees of choice and free will.

Anti-racism education An approach to educational theory and practice oriented to identifying and changing attitudes, policies, and practices that discriminate on the basis of race.

Critical pedagogy An approach oriented to progressive educational change by linking educational practices and experiences with social critique and a vision of educational alternatives.

Education The process by which human beings learn and develop capacities through understanding of their social and natural environments, which takes place in both formal and informal settings.

Feminist pedagogy An approach to educational analysis grounded in a critique of gender inequalities in education and the factors that give rise to them, and committed to practices to change those inequalities.

Interpretative analysis An approach to understanding social life that emphasizes the role played by meanings and intersubjective relationships in social activity.

Political economy An approach that emphasizes the interrelationships among social, economic, and political factors in social life; critical political economy examines the causes and consequences of deep-rooted forms of social and economic inequality.

Positivism A philosophic approach that emphasizes sensory experience as the basis for all knowledge, applied as a scientific framework that seeks to derive and test laws based on empirical evidence from systematic observation and measurement.

Schooling Education systems and processes organized through formal educational institutions.

Social structure Elements of social life that are relatively patterned, interconnected, and enduring, often understood with reference to the rules and boundaries associated with different forms of social action.

Sociology An academic discipline concerned with the nature and organization of societies and the relationships that exist among individuals and societies.

Study Questions

1. What is education? How does education differ from schooling and training?
2. Why is it important to examine education from different disciplines and perspectives?
3. Discuss the relationship between sociology and other disciplines with respect to the analysis of educational issues. What distinct contributions can a sociological analysis make to an understanding of education?
4. Select an issue related to education from discussions in mass media or popular websites. Specify the different positions or arguments being made, and identify major characteristics of the individuals and groups advancing each position. Indicate what strategies you might employ to conduct further research to offer a sociological understanding of the issue and what it tells us about relationships between education and society.
5. What major social and economic forces need to be taken into account for an adequate understanding of education? With reference either to your own educational experiences or to issues such as one selected to address question 4, above, provide some examples of how these forces operate in contemporary societies.

Chapter 2

Sociological Theories of Education

Learning Objectives

In this chapter, you will:

- gain an understanding of what theory is and why it is important to sociological understandings of education;
- compare and contrast the major theoretical approaches employed in classical and contemporary sociological analyses of education;
- apply theoretical understandings to specific educational problems and examples;
- identify core factors needed to gain a comprehensive understanding of education systems and issues.

Introduction

Theories exist to help people explain how and why particular phenomena occur as they do. They are employed as tools that enable us to make sense of the world, and are systematically developed from existing knowledge and tested against empirical evidence.

Sociological theories of education have arisen to explain everything from why some people fail and others succeed to problems of educational finance and everyday classroom interaction. It is sometimes difficult to categorize and assess the importance of sociological theories of education. Because particular groups, including educational administrators, governments, educational participants, and researchers in several academic disciplines, conduct educational research for different reasons, theories of education often are either absent from research or else are highly diverse. Parelius and Parelius (1987: 15) warn about educational research findings that lack any theoretical perspectives: "A glut of discrete findings, with no organizing framework, can be as useless as the untested speculations of the 'armchair' theorist." At the same time, it can be an imposing task to make sense of the sometimes bewildering array of theoretical alternatives in a field like the sociology of education, which is commonly characterized as being in a "constant state of flux" represented in the "3Ds" of divergence, disagreement, and difference (Levinson and Sadovnik, 2002: 3).

Building on the central sociological questions discussed in Chapter 1, this chapter examines representative theories of education. The discussion starts by focusing on distinctive assumptions and representative theorists associated with each of the three main theoretical perspectives, identified as structural functionalism, interpretative sociology, and critical analysis. From these foundations, the chapter also reveals theory to be a challenging, dynamic, and complex enterprise, drawing attention to debates among proponents of these approaches and showing as well how several hybrid or integrative theories have emerged out of these core theoretical approaches or critical alternatives to them. Because of this complexity, the material covered in the chapter illustrates significant developments and theoretical issues related to the sociological analysis of education, and is not intended to be exhaustive and comprehensive in nature. The chapter closes with an outline of several key factors we must remember as we work towards an adequate sociological understanding of educational problems.

Structural Functionalism and Liberal Theory
Émile Durkheim

The earliest influential sociological theories of education emerged within structural functionalist analysis. In the late nineteenth and early twentieth centuries, French sociologist Émile Durkheim, one of the first writers to develop an explicitly sociological framework, made the examination of education systems a central part of his analysis of society. The crucial problem guiding Durkheim's sociological inquiry is at the heart of **structural functionalism**—"Why does the individual, while becoming more autonomous, depend more upon society?" (Durkheim, 1933: 37). Durkheim's concern, which remains highly significant today, arose from the observation that it was necessary to discover the bases of cohesion or solidarity that keep societies from disintegrating amid an increase in individualism, individual rights, and self-interest. He was especially concerned, through critical engagement with earlier work by Auguste Comte, Herbert Spencer, and others who advocated a scientific analysis of social organization and orderly change, to understand relationships among "social facts," or the uniquely social phenomena that transcend and influence individuals. Durkheim stressed education's importance as an integrative and regulative mechanism that would bind people together and help them develop consciousness of their responsibilities and relationships within the wider society. He emphasized that societies, like individuals, have unique characteristics that set them apart from others. The purpose of formal education is to provide each individual with the knowledge and capabilities that are essential for meaningful participation in particular societal contexts. Education, understood in this way:

> is the influence exercised by adult generations on those that are not yet ready for social life. Its object is to arouse and to develop in the child a certain number of physical, intellectual, and moral states which are demanded of [him or her] by both the political society as a whole and the special milieu for which [he or she] is specifically destined. (Durkheim, 1956: 71)

For Durkheim, the task of sociology with respect to education and other social facts is, therefore, to uncover and specify the "normal" characteristics for any given society in order to ensure closer integration between the individual and society and among all members of that society. Durkheim's writings on education have received less attention among sociologists than other aspects of his work. Nonetheless, recurrent themes in his work, such as a concern to preserve social solidarity, have gained recent prominence as social policy-makers turn to educational solutions to problems associated with social diversity and cohesion.

Assumptions of Structural Functionalism

Durkheim's assumption—that a core set of social factors is general and shared widely within a society—is a defining feature of structural functionalist and liberal analysis. The work of Talcott Parsons, extending many of Durkheim's insights to the analysis of American social systems, represents the functionalist view that central social institutions like the education system play a key role in maintaining social order. Parsons, like Durkheim, views the task of schools to be more complex than simply to transmit knowledge and values to students. Rather, such knowledge and values are to be internalized by individuals as part of their personalities. The properly "schooled" person is one who knows intuitively and can act productively on the expectations, rules, and behaviours that accompany and give shape to social life.

Parsons (1959) conveys the most central assumptions and propositions of structural functionalist analysis in his article "The School Class as a Social System: Some of Its Functions in American Society." As the title suggests, Parsons portrays schools as social systems that reflect and serve the interests of the wider society. Within industrial democracies, schools redirect individuals from the emotional, person-centred demands of home and family life to the more formalized, competitive, and achievement-oriented world of work and public life. In the primary grades, for instance, school subjects are not rigidly divided like they are in high school. Rather, emphasis is on learning fundamental social and intellectual skills without comprehensive testing, and pupils are taught by one teacher (usually a woman, to provide continuity from the mother figure in the home environment). In progressively higher grades, however, there is greater emphasis on competitiveness, merit-based performance, and instruction by several teachers, primarily men, akin to the structure and division of labour that prevail in the workplace (Parsons, 1959: 314–15). Schools, in these regards, have two primary functions—allocation and socialization—that contribute to the maintenance of the social system. First, through the mechanisms of grading, granting credentials, and more informal selection processes, schooling sorts individuals to fill distinct positions in the social hierarchy. Second, schooling contributes to individual personality formation by inculcating the dispositions necessary for successful participation in general social life as well as the values and behaviours suited for the specific social roles and experiences that accompany each person's expected social position.

Structural functionalist analysis, as illustrated clearly in the work of both Durkheim and Parsons, offers a particular perspective on the question of schools' role in social reproduction. Structural functionalists view social reproduction, the process by which social order and continuity are maintained from generation to generation, as consensual and harmonious in nature. Much like in a natural ecosystem or physical organism, the normal state of society is portrayed as one in which each element (including individuals and institutions) plays a specific part that combines and is interdependent with others in such a way that the vitality of the whole system is maintained. Because all members of an organization or society have a stake in the system, mutual respect and common goals are emphasized. While tensions and conflict may emerge, a successful social organization, in this view, is able to develop mechanisms to manage conflict and change and reduce the possibility that they may cause damage to the social or institutional system.

Some structural functionalist writers carry these notions further by highlighting what they call the "hidden curriculum." Whereas the formal curriculum conveys the social expectations attached to learning and educational outcomes, the hidden

Box 2.1 A Functionalist Perspective on the Sociology of Education

Talcott Parsons (1959: 277–8) has presented one of the most influential structural functionalist accounts of education in his discussion of the socialization and allocative functions of schooling:

> Our main interest, then, is in a dual problem: first of how the school class functions to internalize in its pupils both the commitments and capacities for successful performance of their future adult roles, and second of how it functions to allocate these human resources within the role-structure of the adult society. The primary ways in which these two problems are interrelated will provide our main points of reference.
>
> First, from the functional point of view the school class can be treated as an agency of socialization. That is to say, it is an agency through which individual personalities are trained to be motivationally and technically adequate to the performance of adult roles. It is not the sole such agency; the family, informal "peer groups," churches, and sundry voluntary organizations all play a part, as does actual on-the-job training. But, in the period extending from entry into first grade until entry into the labor force or marriage, the school class may be regarded as the focal socializing agency.
>
> The socialization function may be summed up as the development in individuals of the commitments and capacities which are essential prerequisites of their future role-performance. Commitments may be broken down in turn into two components: commitment to the implementation of the broad values of society, and commitment to the performance of a specific type of role within the structure of society. Thus a person in a relatively humble occupation

curriculum refers to the more informal or less explicitly defined characteristics that, nonetheless, are regular features of the schooling process. School-based learning consists of much more than simply the content of lessons, textbooks, and rules that students are presented with. Important knowledge and skills are also conveyed by daily participation, extended over several years, within the social context of schooling. Students learn values of conformity, competitiveness, deferred gratification, obedience to authority, and adjustment to success and failure through their experiences in classrooms and other school settings (see, especially, Dreeben, 1968; Jackson, 1968).

It is useful to consider here a central assumption of structural functionalist analysis: the presupposition that social stratification and inequality are necessary structural features of advanced societies. The reproduction of society involves an assumed hierarchy of positions that must be filled with suitably qualified and motivated people. This requirement gives rise to the specified functions of schooling, including the tasks of sorting and socializing individuals and contributing to common values. As long as the social system appears to be operating smoothly, with no threats to the system's breakdown, few questions are raised about the kinds of values and inequalities being fostered or about which groups, if any, are their main beneficiaries.

may be a "solid citizen" in the sense of commitment to honest work in that occupation, without an intensive and sophisticated concern with the implementation of society's higher-level values. Or conversely, someone else might object to the anchorage of the feminine role in marriage and the family on the grounds that such anchorage keeps society's total talent resources from being distributed equitably to business, government, and so on. Capacities can also be broken down into two components, the first being competence or the skill to perform the tasks involved in the individual's roles, and the second being "role-responsibility" or the capacity to live up to other people's expectations of the interpersonal behavior appropriate to these roles. Thus a mechanic as well as a doctor needs to have not only the basic "skills of his trade," but also the ability to behave responsibly toward those people with whom he is brought into contact in his work.

While on the one hand, the school class may be regarded as a primary agency by which these different components of commitments and capacities are generated, on the other hand, it is, from the point of view of the society, an agency of "manpower" allocation. It is well known that in American society there is a very high, and probably increasing, correlation between one's status level in the society and one's level of educational attainment. Both social status and educational level are obviously related to the occupational status which is attained. Now, as a result of the general process of both educational and occupational upgrading, completion of high school is increasingly coming to be the norm for minimum satisfactory educational attainment, and the most significant line for future occupational status has come to be drawn between members of an age-cohort who do and do not go to college.

Source: Reprinted by permission of *Harvard Educational Review*.

The assumptions about consensus and stratification in structural functionalist theory focus attention on the identification of mechanisms that will assure that the social reproduction process operates effectively and efficiently. In the late 1950s and 1960s, theoretical consideration of the link between schooling and socio-economic needs was enhanced by policy concerns to produce a scientifically and technically sophisticated workforce. Rapid expansion of industrial production and mass-marketed goods and services were stimulated by a combination of factors, including military production in World War II and the subsequent Cold War, the creation of new household consumer products, and relatively high wages and stable labour markets. In North America, the "space race" between the Soviet Union and the United States served as a symbolic rallying point around which new workforce requirements, driven by science and technological knowledge, were to be implemented. At the same time, the promise of social and economic security fostered growing emphasis on the domestic sphere and the cultivation of closer ties between schools and family life. Schools figured prominently in these transitions, as enrolments were boosted by rising birth rates associated with the post-war "baby boom" and new educational activities that accompanied expectations about domestic life and leisure-time activities.

Educational expansion was further fuelled by demands for a more highly educated labour force and a scientifically grounded curriculum to train experts and service workers required by the new economy. Subsequently, social scientists interested in the prospects education held for wider social and individual advancement extended functionalist orientations through a number of interrelated strands of structural and liberal analysis, including technological functionalism and **human capital theory**, which view education as an investment to stimulate productivity and economic growth.

Variations of Structural Functionalism

One variant, status attainment research, emerged as a means to provide empirical evidence that would test the strength of linkages among background characteristics (like gender, race, and socio-economic status), formal education, and other life chances. The research findings, typically drawn from large-scale quantitative data, consistently demonstrate the pervasive nature of social inequality, but are surrounded by conflicting interpretations. Blau and Duncan (1967), for example, suggest that their data offer support for the Parsonian thesis that education has come to replace family background as the primary determinant of occupational placement in the United States. However, other high-profile empirical analyses, notably the Coleman Report (Coleman et al., 1966) and the work of Jencks et al. (1972) in the United States and of Floud, Halsey, and Martin (1956) in the UK, attribute the origins of social inequality more to the home and other non-school sites than to schooling. Coleman (1968) emphasizes, as well, that it is crucial to distinguish between equality of results and equality of opportunity. Schools cannot compensate for social disparities on their own, but they can make an impact by providing enriched learning conditions that give all students the chance to compete for access to desired social positions. With respect to Canadian data, Porter (1965) provides a functionalist analysis of education's contribution to social mobility, but adds the important proviso that domination by elites, selected through social factors such as class, ethnicity, and religious affiliation, places limits on the opportunity structure.

It is noteworthy that the studies cited above, conducted primarily between the mid-1950s and the late 1960s, reflect an optimistic faith in education's ability to promote social progress and democratic opportunities. While the optimism is sometimes tempered with warnings that social reforms may be required to fulfill the promise of schooling, very little in these studies challenges the prevailing liberal and functionalist assumptions that inequality is socially necessary. What becomes crucially important is that social stratification must be seen to be based on open and fair selection mechanisms. The major point of debate concerns the degree to which schools could or could not contribute to the equalization of opportunities. It is perhaps not surprising, therefore, that status attainment research, like human capital theory, frequently has been cited to justify social policies and reforms that affect practices both within and outside of education systems, as illustrated in the case study in this chapter.

Another influential strand of liberal analysis, *educational progressivism*, offers a critique of existing social arrangements, but retains faith in the ability of schools to improve those conditions. Originating within the nineteenth-century progressive movement that promoted a humanistic vision of social change guided by the state, educational progressivism contributed strongly to restructuring educational thought and practice in the early part of the twentieth century. Sociologist Jane Addams (1910) promoted social improvement through co-operation and democratic social ethics,

International Case Study

Theory, Policy, and Practice

Theories, while often thought of as abstract and separate from the real world, are always linked to real social practices and issues. Sociological theory has had widespread influence on how policy-makers, media, and publics understand and approach important issues in education and other areas. In both highly industrialized and developing nations, public debates and policies in education and other spheres have been informed by sociological analysis and concepts associated with many of the discipline's core themes, such as power relations; public opinion; cultural capital; social movements; and class, gender, race, and other dimensions of social inequality. In European contexts, policy discussions for several decades have been infused with important sociological reference points from classic themes such as Durkheim's focus on social cohesion and solidarity and Weber's analysis of bureaucracy and credentials to more recent work related to such themes as social inclusion and social capital.

Various theories associated with human capital have been especially prominent in ongoing educational policy considerations. Both the Coleman Report in the United States and the Plowden Report (Central Advisory Council for Education, 1967) in England, for instance, were commissioned by the respective governments as tools to address issues of poverty and provide initiatives to stimulate the social and economic advancement of disadvantaged groups. They drew from structural functionalism the relatively optimistic and unquestioning assumption about the role of education in the service of individual, social, and economic development, although this view was often tempered by research findings and philosophical orientations that gave rise to skepticism about how much difference schooling, at least in its present forms, could make to social change.

Sociological analysis of education focusing on institutional structures and institutional change has also influenced approaches to policy and administration in many fields, especially in the United States. A relatively recent orientation known as "new institutionalism" draws attention to the importance of predominant beliefs, expectations, or "myths" in shaping institutional frameworks. Schools, universities, and other institutions take on distinct characteristics not because of functional or technical requirements so much as because in their efforts to maintain legitimacy, decision-makers and social actors orient their activities to what they think is necessary to maintain the trust and faith of public audiences (Meyer and Rowan, 2006).

Educational policy and actions have also been influenced by more critical analysis of formal educational and policy structures, sometimes giving rise to substantial reforms or posing alternatives to these systems. The goal of theory within perspectives informed by feminism, critical pedagogy, anti-racism, Marxism, and other critical stances is not to stand apart from but to be part of social practice and to foster social change. Critical theories have been at

continued

the heart of several important educational initiatives and transformations. Singer and Pezone (2003) observe that, "In the United States, there has frequently been a close connection between advocacy for mass public education and demands for expanding democracy, social equity, and political reform." They cite as examples Horace Mann's role in promoting public education as a foundation for strong citizenship in the nineteenth century, John Dewey's early twentieth-century vision of schooling as a tool for human liberation, and Paulo Freire's advocacy for literacy and self-directed learning as a tool for social change extending from his native Brazil to many other national contexts.

While the impact of sociological analysis of education on educational policy and practice has been limited by many factors as well as highly intertwined with or subordinated to other influences, at times sociologists and social theory have been accused of being too influential. Dorn (2003), for instance, criticizes sociological analysis for creating a distorted understanding of artistic activity that has influenced the decisions about arts funding and education made by policy-makers and other influential groups. He points to sociologists working within diverse theoretical orientations—notably Marxism, critical theory, symbolic interactionism (Howard Becker's labelling theory), and Pierre Bourdieu's analysis of art and social preferences—who have undermined appreciation for artistic creation and aesthetic values by posing the arts as a "cultural industry" determined by class and other social forces. The challenge, he asserts, is one of "reclaiming art and arts education policy from the sociological agenda" so that the focus returns to "the individual encounter with all aspects of art-man [sic] as individual thinker, not as part of a herd. Any productive new theory of the art world must take this point of view" (Dorn, 2003: 11).

Regardless of one's perspective on these issues, it is clear that theoretical issues involve much more than abstract scientific concerns.

Discussion Questions

1. Based on your understanding of educational matters, what impact do you think sociological theories have had on educational policy and practice? How does this compare with the influence of theories from other disciplines such as economics, psychology, political science, or educational administration?

2. Discuss the relationship between theory and practice in education. Should theory be combined with practice or undertaken separately as a scientific pursuit?

integrating education, social theory, and community-based practice in order to encourage the collective realization of social benefits for all members of society. Interest in this work has been revitalized through recent initiatives to promote lifelong learning, community–school collaboration, and stronger integration of formal education with other social experiences.

John Dewey, probably the best-known advocate of educational progressivism, was influenced by Marx as well as by liberal theory, and also was an associate of Addams, as well as G.H. Mead and other interpretative sociologists at the University of Chicago. Like Marx, Dewey (1966) was critical of a growing uniformity of life within industrial capitalism and advocated the creation of more meaningful connections between school and practical experience. However, reflecting his liberal orientations, Dewey promoted schooling as a mechanism that would ameliorate such pressing social problems as poverty, crime, ethnic antagonism, and social dislocation caused by rapid urbanization, industrialization, and economic change. Dewey sought to replace the adherence to routine and orientation to future rewards in traditional education with child-centred educational practices. He contended that schools should act autonomously from the industrial system and its inherent dangers in order to foster individual growth and social responsibility.

Dewey's progressive, humanistic philosophy seemingly was at odds with some of the major educational reforms derived from industry early in the twentieth century. Influential administrative reformers like Ellwood Cubberly, J.F. Bobbitt, and R.W. Tyler advanced the implementation of rational models of educational management and curriculum construction based on the application of scientific principles to school organization and practice. These approaches, in stark contrast to the liberal emphasis on human development, portrayed education as an endeavour that should be planned and operated as an efficient business enterprise. There was, however, an affinity between the scientific management of schooling and the progressive vision of a better society produced through the intervention of state authorities and scientific expertise. The convergence of these orientations contributed to growing emphasis in the 1920s and 1930s on such innovations as psychological testing of student intelligence and aptitudes, systematic curriculum planning, increased demarcation of school subjects and grade levels, especially at the high school level, bureaucratic school administrative structures, and streaming of pupils by programs and ability.

Progressivism re-emerged as an influential force in educational practice and theory in the 1960s and 1970s. Educational reforms such as "open" classrooms, curricula and teaching styles that emphasized pupil choice and participation, sensitivity to learners' backgrounds and values, and awareness of the relevance of schooling to everyday life signified a supposed shift from traditional to progressive educational philosophies in an era characterized by widespread challenges to authority and prevailing social structures. Some critics, labelled by Carnoy and Levin (1985: 16–17) as critical progressives, condemned the schools for perpetuating rather than eradicating the problems of mass society, "arguing that far from being an instrument of social progress, education was actually deadening—much more oriented to producing failure than to developing creative, critical minds that could be the basis for a more humanistic, democratic society."

The titles of significant studies from this period—*How Children Fail* (Holt, 1964), *Death at an Early Age: The Destruction of the Hearts and Minds of Negro Children in the Boston Public Schools* (Kozol, 1967), and *De-Schooling Society* (Illich, 1970)— convey the message that schools foster, at best, boredom and restricted opportunities for success or, worse, dehumanization and habituation into destructive routines. Unlike the more optimistic assessment of the possibilities that schooling contains for a democratic society, as advanced by educational progressivism, the critical progressive stance contends that schools are not organized and equipped to fulfill their promise and overcome the damaging aspects of the hidden curriculum. These arguments have influenced many proponents of home schooling and other recent movements to adopt alternative forms of educational delivery. Nonetheless, in common with other liberal approaches, these orientations tend to give less prominence to analysis of the root causes of educational problems than to a preoccupation with individual bases of success, failure, and opportunities.

Limitations of Structural Functionalism

The theories that have been examined in this section have pointed to the real and potential contributions made by formal education to social and economic development. With a few exceptions, they portray education as a progressive force that can expand opportunities for individuals as well as for whole societies. The key to a successful education system is the establishment of mechanisms that will ensure a proper "fit" between individuals' social background, on the one hand, and the demands of the social system, on the other.

Structural functionalism is rarely employed as an explicit theoretical orientation in current educational research, in part because of some of the problems outlined below, as well as because of the impact that newer theoretical frameworks have had on the field. However, structural functionalism is highly significant for its formative impact on the development of the sociology of education. It has drawn attention to crucial questions about the relationship between education and other spheres of social life as well as to the role that persistent social inequalities play in advanced societies. Liberal analyses of education, by contrast, have remained popular among both academic researchers and policy-makers due to their generally optimistic assessment about prospects for expanding individual opportunity and social productivity. Several writers have suggested, as well, that Durkheim's educational analysis warrants rehabilitation as societies look for solutions to challenges posed by social diversity, moral uncertainty, changing relations between individualism and community, and issues of citizenship in a global context (Walford and Pickering, 1998). In a similar vein, other researchers have begun to reconsider structural functionalism and Parsonian systems theory because of the tools they provide for making sense of the complex interactions between education and other fields in contemporary societies. While acknowledging limitations in earlier functional and systems theories, several writers point to the importance of understanding how education functions as a distinct social system while interacting more intensively with other major components of social and economic systems in knowledge-based societies (Luhmann and Schorr, 2000; Vanderstraeten, 2003; Baker, 2011).

Despite their influence, structural functionalist and liberal theories of education are unable to account adequately for important dimensions of the social phenomena with which they are concerned. In particular, the theoretical models tend to offer a description of an ideal state of affairs rather than an explanation of social reality. As will be documented later, much substantial evidence runs contrary to, or at least makes questionable, the assumption of a meritocratic social structure in which educational achievement and individual effort, and not one's social origins, account for social success or failure. Even when there is a clear relationship between educational achievement and social status or occupational attainment, it is necessary to consider whether schooling reinforces or eradicates social inequalities already in existence. The impact of such factors as wealth, control, and restructuring of jobs, and of intrinsic rewards such as personal satisfaction with particular jobs or life situations, is often not considered in the measuring of social and educational inequality. While inequality is a complex, changing phenomenon, it is also reproduced in both overt and subtle ways. Opportunities for social advancement may be restricted even if we assume an open, fair, and meritorious process by which individuals are allocated to social positions. Functionalist and liberal analyses tend to overestimate the extent to which social reforms can contribute to social change, in the process ignoring or minimizing the significance of more deeply embedded power relations associated with class, gender, race, and related factors. By the late 1960s, the contradiction between promised socio-economic opportunities and people's life experiences resulted in a rethinking of liberal assumptions among many educational participants and analysts. Growing consciousness of the subordination of women and racial minorities, the emergence of the student protest movement, and the persistence of poverty produced a fertile environment in which alternative perspectives in academic research could flourish.

Interpretative Analysis of Schooling

Interpretative analysis has tended to focus on two features of schooling: (1) the meaning and nature of school practices for educational participants; and (2) the importance of language, knowledge, curricula, and other symbolic aspects of schooling. Learning and interaction with others are viewed as social processes, not simply as aspects of social positions and structures as they are portrayed within structural functionalist analysis. Consistent with a broad social constructivist orientation, interpretative sociologists argue that society and social outcomes are not fixed; rather, they are created, recreated, and modified continuously by human activity. Schooling, in this view, is a site of perpetual adjustment as participants attempt to decipher and share meanings with one another and, in the process, shape their personalities and lives. As expressed by Karl Mannheim (1936: 156),

> Modern education from its inception is a living struggle, a replica, on a small scale of the conflicting purposes and tendencies which rage in society at large. Accordingly, the educated [person is] . . . determined in a variety of ways.

In common with other approaches examined in this book, there are diverse roots and strands to the interpretative analysis of schooling.

Max Weber

Max Weber, whose work is at least as influential as that of his contemporary, Émile Durkheim, stressed the importance of education and educational credentials to the rationalization of society. Rationalization, for Weber, is a process that involves science, technical knowledge, and other elements related to systematic planning for the achievement of predetermined objectives. Rationality is perhaps most strongly apparent in bureaucratic organizations governed, at least in a formal sense, by written rules and procedures, a hierarchy of authority, impartial treatment of clients, and hiring and career advancement of officials based on formal credentials. In this context, formal education has special significance as a bureaucratic site in which training is systematically organized to provide individuals with necessary social attributes and legitimate credentials. While this analysis parallels that of functionalism in important respects, Weber is especially concerned with the ways in which credentials are used by officials and other interest groups to advance their own positions (see, e.g., Gerth and Mills, 1946: 240–4, 416ff.). Despite the overwhelming tendency towards control and

Box 2.2 An Interpretative Perspective on the Sociology of Education

Interpretative analysis emphasizes the meanings and interactions within schools and other social settings, highlighting their implications for social actors themselves. Ogle and Eckman (2002: 169–70, 184–5), analyzing media coverage of the tragic circumstances surrounding the shooting deaths of 15 persons at Columbine High School (CHS) in Colorado in 1999, illustrate the powerful role that socially constructed images—in this case focusing on dress codes—can play in our orientations to youth, violence, and identity:

> Even in articles published the day of the shootings, media writers invoked appearance as a potential explanation for this act of youth violence. Through this coverage, certain types of appearances were constructed as part of the Columbine problem. These appearances were linked to three different CHS social groups—the Trench Coat Mafia, the Goths, and the jocks—and consequently were imbued with meanings reflective of the values and lifestyles purportedly embraced by members of these groups. The identification of certain appearances as part of the Columbine problem—and thus, as in need of regulation—can be traced to numerous newspaper articles that included descriptions of the gunmen's appearances. . . .

predictability in modern life, in other words, Weber maintains that the processes by which these outcomes are sought or resisted are of utmost importance. Weber's work has given rise to later studies in both critical analysis and interpretative sociology.

One such approach, known as neo-Weberian analysis, employs Max Weber's theories of bureaucracy and power to analyze contemporary schooling. C. Wright Mills (1951, 1956), who adopts elements of both Marxian and Weberian analysis in his scathing social critique, argues that the process of rationalization has contributed to the rise of a mass society dominated by a power elite of business, political, and military leaders. Formal education, particularly within private schools and colleges, is an important mechanism through which access to elite positions can be controlled and elite solidarity fostered. Schooling and training practices facilitate rational processes of planning and management so as to produce a cadre of technical experts.

Neo-Weberian analysis of power relations is often linked with conflict theories as well as with interpretative orientations. These connections are emphasized in the critique of the role of education in advanced industrial society offered by Randall Collins (1971), who disputes liberal functionalist arguments that increased technical requirements for skilled labour are responsible for the expansion of the public education system. Collins argues that the link between schooling and jobs is often marginal, and, in fact, that the skill requirements for many jobs have not increased. Rather, the increase in the levels of formal education required for entry into particular occupations is a consequence of competition among status groups. The major purpose of schooling, therefore, is to provide credentials and offer legitimacy to particular status cultures within the social and occupational structures. Murphy (1994), employing international and Canadian examples, extends Collins's analysis by showing

For example, the argument that control of the school environment can be achieved by control of student appearances echoes the premise that by regulating the dress of students, school officials can control the symbolic messages communicated by students' appearances and thereby direct their behaviors, interpersonal interactions, and thus the academic climate. A specific example of such logic can be found in the claim that by prohibiting dress symbols used to express group affiliation, and thereby disallowing the use of dress cues to identify another as a member of a certain peer group, schools could effectively reduce negative feedback exchanged (e.g., taunting) and hostile interactions among rival student groups such as the Trench Coat Mafia and the jocks. Similarly, banning appearances (e.g., black trench coats) that could communicate a message of affiliation with the gunmen or an inclination for violence so as to prevent altercations among individuals who might mistakenly define the situation (i.e., assume another is violent based on his or her dress and behavior, accordingly) also reflects the notion that humans use appearance symbols to assign identities, to formulate behavioral expectations, and to guide their interpersonal interactions.

Source: Jennifer Paff Ogle and Molly Eckman, "Dress-Related Responses to the Columbine Shootings: Other-Imposed and Self-Designed," *Family and Consumer Sciences Research Journal.* © 2002 American Association of Family and Consumer Sciences. Reprinted by permission of SAGE publications.

that Weber's theory enables us to assess how credentials are used in different ways by both dominant and subordinate groups in various struggles over status and **cultural capital** (cultural resources). Teachers' associations, for instance, may rely on the credentials of their members as a way of distinguishing teachers from laypersons wanting to become involved in educational matters, but they may also seek support or alliances with political parties and other organized groups to protect their own interests against more powerful forces.

Weber's analysis of processes of rationalization and legitimation and his comparative study of organizations have also been major influences on the development of **new institutional theory**, which has been employed widely in management and policy studies as well as the sociology of education (Davies and Zarifa, 2009). Institutional analysis emerged out of challenges to the predominant emphasis on individual outcomes of schooling, highlighting the substantial effects education has come to have on societies and populations as a whole (Meyer, 1977). Although educational organizations are bureaucratically organized, the institutional connections and levels of control within educational structures are not as strictly imposed as commonly believed. This approach attributes the remarkable similarity in educational models and institutional practices across contexts to shared beliefs or myths that foster conformity to institutionalized norms and organizational patterns (Meyer and Rowan, 2006: 5–6).

The Chicago School

The interpretative analysis of schooling and other social institutions rose to prominence through a branch of investigation that came to be called the Chicago School of sociology. This approach, which continues to have a strong influence within the discipline, was most active in the 1920s through the work of sociologists and other scholars at the University of Chicago, who used their dynamic city, with its changing mix of industry, urban development, and social composition, as a living laboratory. The Chicago School stressed the interdependent nature of the personality, or self, and social interaction. Two writers previously discussed in the context of educational progressivism played a formative role in and were mutually influenced by the emergence of Chicago School sociology. Jane Addams sought not only to understand how individual selves and collectivities intersected with one another but also to demonstrate how research and theory can be integrated with social practice. Philosopher John Dewey, who emphasized the interrelationships between consciousness and human behaviour, also had close ties with Addams, with George Herbert Mead, who taught at Chicago, and with other sociologists and educational theorists. W.I. Thomas's notion of the **"definition of the situation,"** which highlights the powerful role that perceptions and shared meanings play in guiding social action, and C.H. Cooley's concept of "the looking-glass self," which alerts us to the process by which our behaviour and identity are shaped by our awareness of the reactions of others, illustrate the interpretative aspects of this approach. Mead's analysis of the dynamic, interactive nature of personality formation contributed to the development of **symbolic interactionism** in sociology and social psychology. For Mead, as recognized by later developmental psychologists, education is part of an ongoing process of human development in which the individual learns and shares social meanings with other people (Ritzer, 2011: 436–7).

One of the earliest, most complete analyses of schooling within the Chicago School tradition is Willard Waller's *The Sociology of Teaching*, originally published in 1932. Waller (1965: 6) examines the school as a "social organism" constituted through "a unity of interacting personalities." His analysis moves directly into the classroom and other school sites, providing rich examples of the complex social relations that link pupils, teachers, administrators, parents, and other educational participants within a distinct school culture. School and social structures are viewed as maps to guide these interactions, but Waller emphasizes that schooling remains a fluid process marked by changing, sometimes conflicting, definitions of the situation. Several writers, informed by Arlie Hochschild's (1983) influential analysis of emotional labour, have extended this analysis to explore how gender relations and caring and emotional dimensions intersect in classrooms and other core sites of human interaction (Bellas, 1999).

Howard Becker (1952, 1953; Becker et al., 1961), who employed detailed interviews to explore such issues as how medical students develop identities as doctors and how teachers define and act on their roles and circumstances, extended the interpretative tradition of classroom research. Becker's analysis points to the process by which identities and educational outcomes are shaped through social expectations, school cultures, and social interactions framed within particular labels or socially constructed categories. A substantial body of later research elaborates how particular definitions of the situation held by educators result in **self-fulfilling prophecies**. Teachers create and apply particular labels to children and their parents (as well as to other individuals, and vice versa), based on common-sense assumptions, background information, and observations from encounters. This labelling influences subsequent educational and social career paths. Rosenthal and Jacobson (1968), in a frequently cited study of children in a San Francisco elementary school, demonstrate that teachers' presuppositions about pupils' learning potentials, even if false, tended to have more impact on student performance than did actual ability. Studies by Cicourel and Kitsuse (1963) and Rist (1970) in the United States, Hargreaves (1967) and Lacey (1970) in the United Kingdom, and Stebbins (1975) in Canada, among many others, support the finding that self-fulfilling prophecies operate as powerful influences on educational outcomes, but this research emphasizes much more fully than do Rosenthal and Jacobson the complex interactions that take place within schools.

Many research findings within the interpretative tradition ultimately support functionalist and critical analyses of social reproduction that show social outcomes of schooling as highly predictable in nature. However, interpretative analysis emphasizes that schooling cannot properly be viewed as a "black box" that produces preselected results; instead, the most compelling interest lies with what happens inside the school (Karabel and Halsey, 1977: 60). Other classroom studies, including Canadian research by Martin (1976) and Stebbins (1971, 1975), portray schooling as a site within which complex processes of negotiation and decision-making are undertaken by all participants. Albas and Albas (1993), for instance, through observation of students' behaviour in examinations in a western Canadian university, demonstrate that students employ a wide range of actions to avoid being labelled as cheaters. Interpretative analysis, by probing into the sometimes devious ways that people engage with one another and their social surroundings, often conveys a strong sense of cynicism, expressed clearly in a chapter entitled "School is a Lousy Place to Learn Anything In" in which Howard Becker (1996) reflects upon many of his earlier influential studies.

The "New" Sociology of Education

A conscious effort to question both school practices and the structure of knowledge and curricula emerged within what came to be known in the early 1970s as *the "new" sociology of education*. Critical of previous conventional sociological and educational analysis that took for granted what happens in schools, the new sociology of education sought explicitly to expose the power relations embedded within educational practices (Gorbutt, 1972; Young, 1971). While this approach drew inspiration from emergent critical sociological analyses, its orientation to research problems and methodologies was primarily interpretative. Karabel and Halsey (1977: 47–8) observe that the new sociology of education was predominantly a British phenomenon that paid little heed to previous, mostly North American, classroom research, such as the studies referred to above. However, the attention given by contemporary policy-makers and educators to priorities associated with the emergence of knowledge-based societies has rekindled interest in the kinds of questions posed within new sociology of education explorations concerning what is meant by knowledge and whose knowledge counts the most (Moore and Young, 2011).

The strength of the new sociology of education is its ability not only to bring the schooling process to the centre of educational research, but also to challenge many of the prevailing assumptions about the content of schooling. Knowledge is produced, defined, and given meaning and importance through the social contexts in which it appears. Consequently, much of the research in the new sociology of education, like other forms of interpretative analysis, is devoted to providing detailed descriptions and outlines of the significance of everyday occurrences, such as patterns of joking and teasing in the classroom or the hidden meanings contained within school textbooks. Whereas other forms of analysis tend to overlook or trivialize day-to-day activities, interpretative sociology brings these to the forefront as crucial components of social life.

Limitations of Interpretative Sociology

While offering detailed insight into such crucial features of schooling as classroom processes, interpersonal interactions, and the curriculum, interpretative sociology is often limited by its failure to link what happens in schools with the world beyond schooling. Attention to the intricacies of everyday processes tends to leave unanswered historical questions about change and how things got that way in the first place. Moreover, there is a tendency to ignore the impact of broader social structures, opportunities, and decision-making processes on educational practices and outcomes. Negotiation between teachers and pupils for grades or teachers' contributions to students' self-esteem may influence students' career choices, for instance, but these choices cannot be understood without reference to such factors as labour markets, families, and other socio-economic determinants. Ultimately, like much structural functionalist analysis, interpretative sociology makes its strongest contribution in the description of social life but falls short in its explanatory powers.

Critical Analysis

The various strands in the critical analysis of schooling are unified by their concern to find the underlying causes of educational inequalities and change. Critical analysis, like the other approaches to the sociology of education, has a long history, but in North America, at least, it has really only achieved a position of some prominence since the mid-1970s. Critical analysis stresses that the education system has largely failed in its promise to promote a more egalitarian society. Moreover, this failure is not an accidental by-product that can be corrected by simple reforms. Instead, schooling, in content and process, contributes to the subordination of substantial segments of the population. The meritocratic and democratic visions promoted by liberal and functionalist analysis are criticized as ideologies that serve the interests of dominant social groups. Three distinct orientations to critical analysis of schooling—political economy, influenced by Marxism; feminism; and critical **pedagogy**—are discussed below, with reference to their unique emphases as well as to recent integrative approaches informed by insights derived from diverse critical and traditional perspectives.

Marxism

Marxist educational theory shares with neo-Weberian analysis the assessment that education systems within capitalist societies are unable to fulfill their democratic potential because of the profound influence of dominant social forces. Marxism, however, attributes the root causes of social inequality to structures of class and economic production rather than to competition between status groups.

While Karl Marx wrote very little on formal education, his theories and his method for analyzing capitalist society offer a foundation for critical analysis, known as historical materialism, that is absent in other approaches. Marx's analysis begins with the premise that all societies emerge around the ways in which people meet their basic survival needs. As human beings we develop socially, distinct from other species, by virtue of our ability to labour. Labour, for Marx, refers in a broad sense to conscious activity devoted to the fulfillment of specific human needs. Marx's social critique emphasizes how our labour comes to be alienated through processes by which others gain control over our labouring activity and the products that we generate through it. Alienation is most extreme in capitalist society, which is distinguished from other types of societies and modes of production by the ways that capitalists are able to control and organize work to maximize profit.

Although most of Marx's analysis focuses on the structural mechanisms that drive the capitalist system and produce social class antagonisms, Marx also comments on the contradictory nature of schooling. Like other institutions within capitalism, the education system constrains human potential that is otherwise necessary for social progress. Schooling, when it is integrated with work and other crucial social activities, provides opportunities through which people can develop both critical consciousness and meaningful skills in such areas as literacy and vocational practice. Organized to serve capitalist priorities of profit and labour market discipline, however, schools fall far short of their potential, becoming more like "sausage factories" than places for human fulfillment. Schooling, under capitalism, is a vehicle for the production of a compliant workforce, providing just enough knowledge to ensure a supply of workers ready for monotonous jobs while advancing ideologies that serve capitalist interests (see, e.g., Marx, 1977: 613–15; Wotherspoon, 1984: 211). Despite the deadening effects of work and other social practices within capitalism, however, Marx's theory emphasizes possibilities for the revolutionary transformation of society. Public schooling, Marx contends, would remain an essential part of communist society, although, by linking work and education, its aim would be to foster personal and social development rather than to serve the bourgeois order (Marx and Engels, 1965: 55, 60).

Neo-Marxism

Marx's work, by virtue of its political orientation, has had a major impact on educational practice. Literacy campaigns and revolutionary movements, inspired at least in part by Marx and incorporating interpretations of his work adapted to fit particular circumstances, have contributed to various kinds of educational reform in many parts of the world. The student protest movement that emerged in Western Europe and North America in the late 1960s also created a receptive atmosphere for Marxist analysis in the social sciences. Schooling began to be portrayed as an "ideological state apparatus" (Althusser, 1971) or a form of cultural imperialism (Carnoy, 1974) that contributes ideologically and materially to the perpetuation of fundamentally unequal class relations.

Insights offered by Harry Braverman (1974) exemplify the emergent Marxist critique of work and other social conditions under advanced capitalist society. In common with neo-Weberian analysis advanced by writers like Collins, Braverman challenges the popular liberal assessment that technological change has created enhanced skill requirements and more meaningful white-collar work opportunities. However, Braverman (whose analysis will be elaborated in more detail in subsequent chapters) contends that capitalist control over work involves managerial strategies that produce increasing degradation and deskilling within virtually all occupations. Education, despite its apparent contribution to individual and social development, serves primarily to prepare students for adjustment to the routines of a world dominated by monopoly capital.

Probably the most influential neo-Marxist study of schooling to appear in the wake of the 1960s challenges to political orthodoxy has been *Schooling in Capitalist America* by Samuel Bowles and Herbert Gintis, published in 1976. Bowles and Gintis make explicit the connections between the capitalist economy and schooling only noted in passing by Braverman, beginning with a critique of the failure of liberal educational reform to deliver on its promise of a more egalitarian and democratic society. They contest, as well, conservative arguments that attribute educational inequality to inherent differences in intelligence and ability. Bowles and Gintis argue, rather, that educational reform can do little in itself to alleviate social inequality insofar as inequality is rooted in the class structure of capitalist society. They identify a **correspondence principle** that operates between educational reform and economic change. They argue that capitalism, in common with totalitarian political systems, restricts democratic participation in order to maintain material and ideological conditions to generate profit and ensure a productive labour force.

According to Bowles and Gintis, formal education in the United States has undergone three major historical changes that correspond to changes in the capitalist economy. Initially, the rise of mass public schooling accompanied the need in the mid- to late nineteenth century for a disciplined wage labour force. During the second transition, between 1890 and 1930, progressive educational reforms converged with the growing concentration of corporate capital and a diversified workforce to produce a bureaucratic education system based on standardization, testing, and systematic control. The third phase involved correspondence between the rapid expansion of post-secondary education and the post–World War II growth of professional and white-collar occupations needed to coordinate labour and capital under intensified control by state and corporate agencies. Educational change frequently is marked by struggle because, as Bowles and Gintis (1976: 235) argue, "Conflicts in the educational sphere often reflect muted or open conflicts in the economic sphere." However, formal education serves primarily to facilitate the transformation of capitalist development in such a way as to maintain social order.

Bowles and Gintis's analysis has advanced the understanding of educational structures and practices by demonstrating that schooling, at least indirectly, is a central part of the logic that drives capitalist development and reproduces systematic social inequalities. Their work also provides a historical account, lacking in most previous studies, of forces that have contributed to the formation and growth of contemporary educational institutions.

Despite the acuity of their critique of both traditional educational theories and schooling processes in capitalist societies, the insights offered by Bowles and Gintis have sufficiently strong parallels with structural functionalist analysis that some writers (e.g., Carnoy and Levin, 1985: 21–2) consider their work to be "critical functionalist" in nature. Among both traditional and critical analyses, in other words, there is general agreement that schools contribute to social, ideological, and labour force reproduction. Yet, there is considerable debate over what kinds of reproduction occur, how fair the system is, and who benefits from it. On either side of the debate, there is a tendency to understate the complexities characteristic of educational realities.

Livingstone (1994: 65–7) summarizes three major problems with the correspondence principle advanced by Bowles and Gintis: (1) a failure to recognize that different forms of knowledge, and not exclusively capitalist knowledge, exist and are produced within educational settings; (2) the accumulation of historical evidence suggesting that the correspondence between schools and economic change is, at best, incomplete and not necessarily determined by capitalist production relations; and (3) a failure to develop a complete explanation of education that goes beyond relatively simple statements about its functions. Bowles and Gintis, in response to criticisms of their work, have commented that more attention needs to be paid to the contradictions that characterize education and other social relations in advanced capitalism (see, e.g., Gintis and Bowles, 1980). Their work, despite its limitations, has remained a significant reference point for critical analysis of schooling because of the crucial questions it raises about how education contributes to social reproduction.

Within much subsequent educational analysis informed by Marxism, there has been a tendency either to take for granted the existence of a correspondence principle or else to elaborate the mechanisms through which schools are linked to state and economic structures. These trends are apparent in critical analysis from a Canadian political economy tradition oriented to explaining the development of Canada's resource-based economy, the Canadian class structure, the social and economic impact of Canada's dependence on European and American capital, and subsequent attempts to delineate the emergence of one or more distinct Canadian nations. A preoccupation with historical preconditions and patterns of economic development has often left schooling as an unproblematic or absent force in such literature. In Wallace Clement's (1974) influential analysis of *The Canadian Corporate Elite*, for instance, education is mentioned only in passing as a device for conveying class-based privilege from one generation to the next, while more thorough subsequent reviews of the "new" political economy literature in Canada (Clement and Williams, 1989; Clement and Vosko, 2003) offer only incidental, if any, allusions to schooling and education despite covering such themes as immigration, gender, labour markets, welfare state policy, media, and youth.

There is, however, a substantial body of political economic analysis of Canadian education. Two important books published in the 1970s focused on a growing literature of critical analysis that emphasized how schooling was integrated with the corporate order under capitalism. *The Politics of the Canadian Public School*, edited by George Martell (1974), documents in a manner that continues to be highly relevant several issues of importance to Canadian education, including the reinforcement of class inequalities, the infusion of corporate values and profit-making strategies into the curriculum, and the political mobilization of teachers' movements. *Reading, Writing, and Riches: Education and the Socio-Economic Order in North America*, edited by Randle Nelsen and David Nock (1978), extends this analysis, detailing such additional issues as corporate control over post-secondary education and the subordination of Native peoples.

These books, along with analyses presented by Lockhart (1979), Schecter (1977), Livingstone (1983, 1985), Wotherspoon (1987), and others, have revealed the extent to which the Canadian education system has been infused with class-based ideologies and practices. Growing concern about the role that corporate interests are playing in aligning education more closely with business and market priorities has stimulated a revival of critical analysis of education (Harrison and Kachur, 1999; Robertson et al., 2003; Taylor, 2001). However, preoccupation with economic reproduction within Marxist and political economy frameworks has often tended to overgeneralize the powers that capitalism, capitalists, and dominant economic forces have in shaping social life, and thereby to undermine education's capacity to change and be changed through interaction among educators, students, community members, and other social forces. Gaskell (1992: 22) observes that "Critical theory and Marxist theory, despite their impact on scholarship, made few inroads with educational practitioners, who were frequently the targets of the critique, or with policy-makers, who were told

Box 2.3 A Neo-Marxist Perspective on the Sociology of Education

Herbert Gintis and Samuel Bowles (1980: 52–3) outline the correspondence principle that links schooling with the economy:

A main proposition in *Schooling in Capitalist America* held that a major objective of capital, in its interventions into the formation and evolution of the educational system, was precisely the preparation of students to be future workers on the various levels in the hierarchy of capitalist production. Given the quite significant success of capital directly and indirectly structuring schools and in the face of the undemocratic nature of economic life, schools could not fulfill their egalitarian and developmental objectives. We concluded that the only means towards the achievement of progressive educational reform is the democratisation of economic life, allowing for a democratic and emancipatory school system which does not conflict with the formation of adults capable of effective participation in the system of production.

We also argued specifically that the current relationship between education and economy is ensured not through the content of education but its form: the social relations of the educational encounter. Education prepares students to be workers through a correspondence between the social relations of production and the social relations of education. Like the division of labour in the capitalist enterprise, the educational system is a finely graded hierarchy of authority and control in which competition rather than co-operation governs the relations among participants, and an external reward system—wages in the case of the economy and grades in the case of schools—holds sway. This correspondence principle explains why the schools cannot at the same time promote full personal development and social equality, while integrating students into society. The hierarchical order of the school system, admirably geared towards preparing students for their future positions in the hierarchy of production, limits the development of those personal capacities involving the exercise of reciprocal and mutual democratic participation and reinforces social inequality by legitimating the assignment of students to inherently unequal "slots" in the social hierarchy.

there was not much to be done anyway within the framework of a capitalist economy." Ironically, some Marxist analysis can also be criticized for its commitment to social change, in which the impression is created that, with proper revolutionary consciousness and effective political agents, radical social transformation appears to be inevitable (Davies, 1995: 1465–6).

Growing recognition of the dual nature of education, as a force that can foster critical sensitivity and empower people to take control over aspects of their lives as well as one that contributes to subordination and disempowerment, forced educators and educational researchers to develop more sophisticated educational critiques. Analysis came to focus not only on what is wrong with schooling, which has commonly been the main theme of orthodox Marxism and political economy, but also how education might facilitate individual and social transformation. Political economic analysis is

The correspondence principle, we believe, makes four positive contributions to progressive educational strategy. First, its explanatory value is great. Despite the considerable scepticism which greeted publication of our book, critics have made little headway in overturning our major empirical conclusions. Indeed the one major subsequent statistical investigation of sources of educational and economic success—Christopher Jencks et al.'s *Who Gets Ahead?*—dramatically confirms our own findings. Second, in an era where the failures of liberal school reform have become increasingly evident to policy-makers and the public, the correspondence principle shows a positive alternative. Egalitarian and humanistic education are not unattainable due to some inherent defect in human nature or advanced industrial society, but to the undemocratic nature of participation in economic life. Educational reform requires at the same time economic transformation towards democratic socialism. Third, our formulation rectifies an earlier pre-occupation of both liberal and Marxian analysis with the overt content of schooling. By focussing upon the experience of schooling, the correspondence principle provides a consistent analytical framework for understanding the school as an arena of structured social interaction. Fourth, our formulation of the correspondence principle contributes to a more positive understanding of the goals of socialist transition. In older critiques of capitalist society, almost unique stress was laid on the private ownership of means of production. At least as far as educational reform is concerned, we have been able to show that not ownership, but control is central to social inequities. Merely passing from private to social ownership without challenging in any substantial way the social relations of economic life, can have no impact on the egalitarian and humanistic goals of progressive educational reform. The correspondence principle then represents a powerful antidote to the authoritarian tendencies all too often found in an otherwise progressive social movement.

Source: Gintis, Herbert, and Samuel Bowles, 1980. "Contradiction and Reproduction in Educational Theory," in Barton et al., eds, *Schooling, Ideology and the Curriculum*. Reprinted by permission of Falmer Press.

often integrated with insights derived from other critical theories, including feminism and anti-racism, as well as statistical, historical, and comparative research, to produce richer critiques of contemporary educational issues and to suggest alternative visions (Livingstone, 2004; Sears, 2003; Taylor, 2001; Torres and Mitchell, 1998).

Theories of **cultural reproduction** offer possibilities to link detailed examination of specific educational practices, akin to interpretative studies, with processes that contribute to the maintenance of social structures. This approach is heavily influenced by the work of Pierre Bourdieu (1977, 1984) in France, Paul Willis (1977) and Basil Bernstein (1977) in Britain, and Michael Apple (1995, 2004) in the United States.

Bourdieu agrees with the Marxist position that education contributes to the perpetuation of class inequalities and other dimensions of unequal social structures. However, he is more concerned with social practices that affect how these inequalities can be variously reproduced or altered. Capital exists in the form of social, cultural, and symbolic assets as well as being an economic factor. Power and prestige convey definite advantages to members of privileged social groups, which in turn can be transmitted across generations, but these are only effective to the extent that they can be converted from potential to real benefits. For Bourdieu, a person's family background and social circumstances contribute to "habitus" (dispositions) or deeply ingrained experiential leanings that influence their options and actions in relation to specific types of social situations (which he terms "fields" of interaction). Schools and other educational institutions are infused with class-based assumptions and expectations related to such things as rules of conduct, manners of expression, and background knowledge, giving some people a competitive advantage over others in their understanding and application. However, education, as it gains significance as a mechanism to grant credentials and provide legitimate access to social and economic opportunities, also becomes a site through which various social groups struggle for position and advantage. Bourdieu and Passeron (1979: 77), echoing neo-Weberian analysis of credential inflation, observe that, "When class fractions who previously made little use of the school system enter the race for academic qualifications, the effect is to force the groups whose reproduction was mainly or exclusively achieved through education to step up their investments so as to maintain the relative scarcity of their qualifications and, consequently, their position in the class structure."

The framework introduced by Bourdieu has gained increasing prominence as researchers pay greater attention to the intricate interconnections among schooling, human agency, and structural inequalities (Lareau and Horvat, 1999; Lareau and Weininger, 2003; Sullivan, 2002). In Canada, this approach has been especially useful for offering insights that take us beyond statistical regularities to highlight the ways in which social background and personal circumstances influence choices that have longer-term significance. The analysis of strategies that draw on different forms of capital has been applied, for example, to the exploration of how British Columbia students' social backgrounds and schooling experiences affect the educational and occupational pathways that they subsequently follow (Andres Bellamy, 1993); the economic, cultural, and institutional factors that limit post-secondary educational horizons and access for students from rural areas (Andres and Looker, 2001); the selective mechanisms that contribute to and reinforce gender segmentation in information technology fields (Taylor, 2005); and the intersecting class, social, and cultural factors that have a decisive impact on whether a student continues with or drops out of higher education (Lehmann, 2007).

Willis, through extensive observations and interviews, traced a group of boys in a working-class town in the United Kingdom from their secondary schooling into their early post-school working lives. Willis demonstrates that, while economic reproduction occurs in predictable fashion in the sense that the boys are destined for occupational futures consistent with their class backgrounds, there is a complex interplay among the social and cultural factors that produce those outcomes. Jobs and social positions are not mechanically predetermined but develop through specific choices and experiences that arise, in part, through life in schools. The working-class "lads" Willis observes engage in forms of resistance and rebellion to schooling that range from mocking school authority to verbal abuse, theft, and vandalism because they see in the middle-class standards of schools little that is of interest or relevance to their lives. By withdrawing from the mainstream of school life, the lads select a path leading to short-term work that at first offers excitement and independence but eventually results in low-paying jobs with few prospects for meaningful working lives. Willis argues that these choices reveal what he calls "partial penetrations." In other words, students are able to see through or penetrate weaknesses in the dominant meritocratic ideology because their experience contradicts the official argument that school success and hard work lead to social success. However, their insights are only partial in the sense that the options they choose lead them to a life of deadening routine that reinforces rather than transforms social inequalities.

Michael Apple's analysis of schooling proceeds from the recognition that schools contribute actively to the production, as well as the reproduction, of cultural practices and social structures. Apple, like Willis, accepts the Marxist argument that schools contribute to social control and the maintenance of structured inequalities, but he argues—consistent with the new sociology of education—that schools also create and process knowledge. This work has given rise to a rich tradition of work demonstrating how schools do more than simply transmit knowledge and ascribe places for individuals in society. Within schooling, ideas and understandings about the world and our place in the world are shaped by the actions of educational participants, which in turn are circumscribed by power relations and political economic structures (see especially Weis et al., 2006).

The work of Apple and Willis has helped to advance what has come to be known as **resistance theory**. Resistance theory, unlike the more one-dimensional accounts of social reproduction that tend to be conveyed by structural functionalist and orthodox Marxist analyses, portrays schooling as a venue continually subjected to contestation. Students do not blindly and automatically move from schooling into preordained social positions. Rather, their active participation in schooling involves diverse responses that range from enthusiastic acceptance to blatant rejection of the curriculum, of the manner in which it is transmitted, and of other aspects of the schooling process. Moreover, there are significant variations in how curricula and educational practices are presented to and experienced by various categories of students as distinguished by such factors as gender, race, ethnicity, and age. Boys and girls, for instance, are often taught differently and bring with them distinct frames of reference through which they subsequently interpret the curriculum.

Resistance theory, in more general terms, brings to the forefront the dynamic elements of educational practices and cultures without losing sight of the social, economic, and political contexts within which schooling operates. This work is being extended in many important ways to explore the complex ways in which people are coping with uncertainties associated with existence and identity in a world being transformed by global challenges (Dolby and Dimitriadis, 2004). Nayak (2003), for instance, returning attention to the northeast of England where Willis conducted his ethnographic research, explores how diverse youth subcultures are created both within and across boundaries of race, class, and gender as young people attempt to negotiate meaningful places and identities in a world full of risk (a theme also discussed by Nolan and Anyon, 2004). Apple (2006: 681), reviewing notable recent American contributions to the critical analysis of education in the United States, reiterates the vital role this analysis serves "to illuminate the ways in which educational policy and practice are connected to the relations of exploitation and domination in the larger society" at the same time as such policy and practice point to the visions and possibilities for radical change.

Feminism

Feminist theory has also advanced considerably our ability to understand education, in particular its divergent forms and interests. Feminist analysis has an extensive history that has been reformulated into systematic academic and political discourse over the past four decades. Critiques of schooling that we would now characterize as feminist were prevalent, for instance, in eighteenth-century arguments that access to education was a fundamental right for women as well as for men; in nineteenth-century debates over whether boys and girls should take or be in the same classes as one another, and whether women should be admitted into universities; in nineteenth- and early twentieth-century struggles by women teachers to gain recognition for their work and to improve their working conditions; and in later efforts to incorporate subjects and knowledge pertinent to girls' and women's lives into the curriculum. British social analyst Harriet Martineau (1837) was one of the first writers to link explicitly principles for the scientific analysis of society with an understanding of the condition of women's lives in relation to marriage, education, and other social spheres. Jessie Bernard (1964) explored the experiences of women who engaged in academic work in conjunction with her extensive and sophisticated analysis of a broad range of social issues, including the impact of sexism on women's lives in marriage, education, and economic activities. The emergence of a distinct feminist analysis of schooling drawing from these sources and other historical roots can be traced to the rising consciousness in the late 1960s and early 1970s of gender inequalities in education as well as in other spheres of social, economic, and domestic activity (Gaskell et al., 1989).

The several forms of feminist analysis are unified by recognition of women's disadvantage and lack of privilege relative to men and of the need for social action to redress women's oppression. Most early feminist analyses of schooling focused on questions about sexism in the classroom and curricula and unequal distributions of men and women in different positions within the education system (Kenway and Modra, 1992: 140–8). These concerns are most characteristic of liberal feminism, which proposes reforms to alleviate sex bias and create more equitable gender representation in socially important positions. In schools, for example, employment equity measures are commonly identified as a response needed to compensate for the fact that, while women teachers outnumber men at nearly all levels of schooling up to the senior grades, most educational administrators are male. Liberal feminists advocate change, but argue that gender equity can be attained through modifications within existing social, educational, and economic arrangements.

Other feminists contend that effective change requires a more fundamental restructuring of social practices and structures. It is not sufficient simply to ensure equitable numbers of women and men in socially important positions, or that textbooks contain language and examples that apply to girls' and women's as well as to boys' and men's lives. Radical feminism has pointed out that patriarchy, or the systematic devaluation and oppression of women, is embedded within all forms of social organization. Language, science, politics, the economy, and other spheres of activity are organized around ways of knowing and doing that take male experience as the norm. Women's experience, by contrast, is undermined and relegated to the margins of what is considered to be socially important. Women—and spheres of life such as the domestic and sexual realms that give particular shape and meaning to their lives—are frequently absent as subjects and objects of study. In the sociology of education, for instance, feminist analysts have criticized classroom studies, such as Willis's, for ignoring the central role that gender plays in the construction of student school experience and school outcomes (Weiler, 1988: 41–2). More radical versions of feminism, in the process, have also inspired researchers and educators to take seriously questions about sexuality, body practices, social identity, and related issues that have typically been excluded from education and related discourses.

Socialist feminism, like radical feminism, views liberal reforms as insufficient to overcome gender inequalities, but emphasizes social differences among, as well as between, men and women. Women's subordination must be understood in terms not only of gender but also of class (as well as race and other important aspects of social experience). How gender influences people varies insofar as our lives are shaped by the distinct positions we occupy within society, including the opportunities we have for access to power and other crucial resources.

Feminist pedagogy has emerged as a way to unify women's common concerns, moving beyond specific labels towards clearer articulation of strategies to address practical problems (Luke and Gore, 1992). Feminists argue that the incorporation of women and their experiences into research is an important part of the wider process within which women are to make sense of and reclaim their lives. This involves the recognition of issues that are meaningful in an everyday context but commonly absent from curricula and public discussion, such as domestic violence, public safety concerns, competing family and career demands, and personal encounters with sexism. Women's voices, often emerging through accounts of their own experiences, become an important device to identify, clarify, and seek positive solutions to social problems (Brookes, 1992). In this way, possibilities are created to realize the potential education holds to be truly liberating and progressive. Dorothy Smith (1987) demonstrates how daily routines enacted in the course of mothering, which are often mirrored in teaching-related practices, both reveal and reinforce unequal gender-based divisions of labour. bell hooks (2000: xiii), emphasizing the need for a critical feminism grounded in an understanding of how gender, race, and class intersect, emphasizes that, "Just as our lives are not fixed or static but always changing, our theory must remain fluid, open, responsive to new information."

These insights have encouraged recent feminist scholarship, often in conjunction with critical pedagogy, new political economy, and post-structuralist and post-modernist critiques, to develop a vision of social justice that proceeds from an understanding of the multiple causes of oppression (Arnot and Weiler, 1993; Kenway and Willis, 1998). Increasing recognition is also given to analysis that links personal or biographical experiences with wider structures of power and inequality. Gaskell (1992), for example, details how changes in schooling, labour markets, and socialization processes are intertwined with life choices and chances to produce different educational and vocational career patterns for girls and boys and for women and men. Diverse frameworks such as those elaborated by Bourdieu, as well as other critical studies of power, hold considerable potential for advancing feminist engagement with issues associated with hierarchy, domination, and alternative possibilities (Dillabough, 2004).

As with many other theoretical perspectives, feminist analysis has increasingly sought to incorporate a more complex understanding of how personal identities and social opportunities are being reshaped by the complex interplay among shifting political, social, cultural, and economic relationships. The impact of changes associated with globalization and more localized processes tends to be highly uneven. Arnot and Dillabough (1999: 184–5) emphasize a need for struggles for democracy in education to be recast to take into account these changing and contested circumstances, thereby requiring feminist analysis

> to go beyond a feminist engagement with questions of voice, subjectivity, and difference. It also must remain committed to the idea that women, as agents of knowledge (not foundationalist knowledge!), need to make claims about their identity in order to effect broad social and political change. These agents are not uniform in character; they take multiple, dynamic positions that often are in tension. However, they must be viewed as members of a heterogeneous community who are concerned with how new social and political formations (e.g., neo-liberalism) structure the relationship between gender and democratic education.

There are important gender-based differences in how contemporary social and economic transitions are experienced and understood. These transformations have also forced us to reconsider the meaning of gender and how it intersects with other important social characteristics, including class and race. The expansion of educational opportunities, both in general and in new opportunities in several non-traditional fields, has advanced women's social, economic, and political prospects in numerous ways. At the same time, many women have not had equitable access to or returns from education as a consequence of domestic, occupational, social, and cultural circumstances, as well as institutional and structural factors. Feminist analysis has highlighted, for instance, the disproportionate impact of economic restructuring and state cutbacks that affect employment in government services and non-unionized sectors in which high proportions of women are employed. In the process, women often face further pressures to care for dependants and take on added responsibilities to manage the impact of economic uncertainty in the household and community. Later chapters (particularly Chapters 4, 6, and 7) discuss significant barriers that restrict educational advancement, especially for women in non-privileged segments of North American populations and for girls and women in many less-developed nations. Feminism places questions about gender and strategies to foster democratic social change at the heart of our understanding of the social world.

Feminist scholarship has stimulated important questions and insights regarding sexuality and gender roles and identities more generally. Masculinity studies have addressed questions of gender identities and stereotypes both in relation to traditional roles associated with boys and men and with respect to changing patterns associated with feminist empowerment and broader social transformations. Much of this work, taking its cue from feminist orientations, has explored the meaning and nature of gender-based expectations and experiences in the lives of men and boys, but some media and educational literature have also raised questions of "male disadvantage" as rates of educational participation and achievement by females have overtaken those of males in Canada and other highly developed nations (Connell, 2000; Weaver-Hightower, 2003). This analysis has enhanced appreciation of the challenges in ensuring policy and practice are based on solid understanding of the nuances of gender roles and relationships, but care also has to be taken to avoid alarmist thinking that frames gender relations in narrow, competitive terms (Frank et al., 2003; Kenway and Willis, 1998). Writers who focus on gay and lesbian studies as well as bisexuality and transgendered behaviours and identities that do not correspond with male-female dualisms and heterosexual norms have further questioned prevailing assumptions about gender and the stability of gender-based identities. As with feminism, these studies are concerned with developing a stronger sense of how sexual identities and related social practices intersect with one another while advancing conditions to overcome bias and discrimination against those who do not conform to heterosexual norms. Queer theory, influenced by postmodernist critiques of language and practices seen to categorize and regulate people arbitrarily, adopts a more radical stance by contending that no sexual or gender identity is normal. Judith Butler (1990), in particular, argues that specific categories such as male, female, lesbian, gay, or transsexual act as labels that fix expectations about behaviour and identity and thereby constrain and channel our actions in specific ways. Gender, for Butler, is performed as we express various dimensions conveyed through these categories in our dress, speech, and other actions. Butler's theory of performativity has been influential well beyond research on gender and sexuality in the sociology of education, informing studies in such areas as race, ethnicity, class, disability, youth cultures, and teachers' work (Ball, 2004; Youdell, 2010).

Critical Pedagogy

Critical pedagogy is a related form of analysis that has emerged in an attempt to link educational theory with practice. This is not unique insofar as all critical theory, including Marxism, feminism, and other critical approaches, is unified by the researcher's commitment to try to change the world, rather than to act as an external observer who is studying it in an apparently detached and objective manner. A frequent limitation of the critical theories of education discussed to this point, though, has been their tendency to have little application to real educational settings. Educational participants who have been informed by critical analysis may develop a heightened awareness of their place within schooling as they attempt to rectify problems associated with social and educational disadvantage. However, a tendency in much critical analysis to focus on powerful oppressive forces often produces a sense of futility that things cannot be changed. Critical pedagogy aims to overcome the gap between understanding educational reproduction and taking action to provide social and educational transformation.

Education, as presented within critical pedagogy, contributes to the perpetuation of knowledge and power structures that foster the oppression of subordinate groups by dominant groups, but it also contains possibilities to empower persons in subordinated positions to change their lives and the social contexts within which they live. In this sense, while critical pedagogy, as a label, is relatively new, it builds on recognition of numerous historical examples of struggles in which oppressed groups have sought to use education as a means to gain control over their lives—from colonized peoples in Asia, Africa, and Latin America to marginalized inner-city residents and First Nations peoples in North America.

Some variants of critical pedagogy are heavily informed by **postmodern** theory and poststructuralist analysis. Postmodernism and poststructuralism challenge theories and practices that emerged with the development of Western modern societies, especially those rooted in assumptions that human activity is guided by rational thought, which supposedly enables us to establish truth and certainty about the world in such a way as to advance towards progressively higher levels of social development. Poststructuralism shares with interpretative analysis an emphasis on the socially constructed nature of knowledge, focusing more explicitly on how language and textual symbols impose boundaries and meanings that come to be taken as indicators of reality. Poststructuralists advance what is often called a linguistic turn that exposes the

Box 2.4 A Feminist Perspective on the Sociology of Education

Feminist analysis has become increasingly concerned not only with questions related to gender-based differences in social positions and identities, but also with a social world that has been transformed, in part, through previous feminist struggles for equity and voice. Johanna Wyn, Sandra Acker, and Elizabeth Richards (2000: 444–6) explore the experiences of women who have moved into managerial positions in universities in Canada and Australia in contexts in which universities themselves are under pressure to adhere to logics based on market forces and new managerial imperatives:

> [W]e can conclude that the women in this study have consciously striven to "make" themselves senior academics and managers, "differently" from their perceptions of the traditional male academic. As the research reveals, even as relatively powerful players, they are also conscious of the impossibility of being assimilated fully into the taken-for-granted university processes.
>
> Hence, to be a woman manager in a university is indeed to be reminded of an identity one is not, and constantly to have to define the identity one is.
>
> Our study depends on qualitative, narrative techniques to focus on the fine details of everyday experience in the lives of senior women in faculties of education. Their tales of inclusion and exclusion, centrality and marginalisation, innovation and tradition are documented, with attention to the contradictions apparent in the stories of women who find themselves in senior positions in situations where they have few predecessors. Their perspectives support the view that, while we have much to gain from studying women's participation in the management of universities, their contribution cannot be simply characterised as a "women's way" of leading (Blackmore, 1999: 56). The study has provided a perspective on a cohort of women that has engaged in similar struggles in universities across two countries during the 1970s, 1980s and 1990s. Their overwhelming concerns reflect the ideals of this period: those of the improvement of educational opportunity for disadvantaged groups, and the creation of more diverse and inclusive practices within the institution.

arbitrary nature of these signifiers by exploring their social impact and reading alternative meanings into them.

Michel Foucault (1980), in particular, emphasizes how relations of knowledge and power are embedded in social practices as well as discourses, or truth claims, about the world and its phenomena. Schools and other social institutions, along with state agencies and scientific disciplines, including sociology, contribute to the diffusion of power relations throughout society as they categorize, discipline, and regulate populations (Foucault, 1977). Postmodernist theory extends this analysis through various spheres of life, rejecting notions that knowledge can be objective and offer any absolute truth and dismissing as myths notions that history has an inner logic or is driven by overarching forces like class or gender. Individuals and societies have multiple bases of identity, through which they may be able to construct various narratives

In both countries, these senior women saw themselves as being forces for change, with greater or lesser success. Many had feminist commitments (although they might deny feminism in individual ways) and wanted to make the academy a better place for both women and men. Many believed they had something unique to offer as women in leadership roles. Some had instituted specific practices towards that end, for example, making special efforts to mentor and support junior faculty. Both optimism and disappointment framed their accounts. Paradoxically, they were simultaneously central and marginal within their institutions. They might be well placed to innovate and improve aspects of academic work or university practice, but at the same time, they were frequently themselves isolated and acutely conscious of their "difference" from men senior colleagues and sometimes from other women colleagues as well. . . .

Feminist knowledge production and political work would seem to be at odds with the direction of these changes. Yet, the informal demands on women's emotional labour are likely to increase as women "struggle to undertake feminist work in conditions which are both increasingly hostile to it and increase the need for it" (Kenway and Langmead, 1998: 30). Not all the women interviewed considered themselves feminists, but as we have shown, all were committed to "making a difference," often along feminist lines. Is the university to which women are making a difference more in tune with the university of the past than that of the future? To the extent that the answer is "yes," there is a need to develop a new understanding of the role of women in leadership. The women whose perspectives are described in this article have used a range of strategies in "fortifying the difference," and their views provide a key to understanding what it means to be leaders and managers in these times. We would suggest that the insights gained from their experiences over the last quarter of a century are an important element in the process of developing a new feminist politics of leadership for the twenty-first century.

Source: Wyn, Johanna, et al. "Making a Difference: Women in Australian and Canadian Faculties of Education," *Gender and Education*. Reprinted by permission of the publisher (Taylor & Francis Ltd., www.tandf.co.uk/journals).

and adopt shifting personas. Social science theories, and scientific analysis overall, represent elements of more general "regimes of truth" that seek to legitimize particular orientations to the world as power and truth reinforce one another (Gore, 1993).

Drawing from poststructuralism and postmodernism, critical pedagogy adopts a skeptical stance towards discourses and the power relations embedded in linguistic and institutional practices. At the same time, it focuses on the capacity to work across boundaries that divide academic disciplines and impose identities. However, most critical pedagogy also remains committed to a vision of social transformation that is dismissed by postmodernist analysis.

Critical pedagogy begins with a dialectical and dynamic understanding of the relationship between theory and action that locates research, like all human activity, within changing relations of domination, subordination, and resistance (see, e.g., Freire,

Box 2.5 A Critical Pedagogy Perspective on the Sociology of Education

Joe L. Kincheloe (2007: 16–17) addresses the role that critical pedagogy must play in a complex world by linking people's lived experiences with an analysis of social structures and power relations in order to work towards social transformation through the empowerment of both teachers and students:

In order to develop a critical pedagogy as a form of cultural politics, it is imperative that proponents of a complex critical pedagogy appreciate the fact that all educational spaces are unique and politically contested. Constructed by history and challenged by a wide variety of interest groups, educational practice is an ambiguous phenomenon as it takes place in numerous settings, is molded by numerous and often invisible forces and structures, and can operate under the flag of democracy and justice in oppressive and totalitarian ways. Practitioners of critical pedagogy report that some teacher education students, educational leaders, parents, and members of the general public often have difficulty appreciating the fact that schooling can be hurtful to particular students from specific backgrounds in unique social, cultural, and economic settings—for example, indigenous and aboriginal students. Many individuals often have trouble empathizing with students harmed by such negative educational dynamics because schooling in their experience has played such a positive role in their own lives.

Thus, a complex critical pedagogy is a domain of research and practice that asks much from those who embrace it. Critical pedagogical teacher education and leadership, for example, involve more than learning pedagogical techniques and the knowledge required by the mandated curriculum. In addition to acquiring teaching methods, teachers and leaders steeped in critical pedagogy also understand the social, economic, psychological, and political dimensions of the schools, districts, and systems in which they operate. They also possess a wide range of knowledge about information systems in the larger culture that serve as pedagogical forces in the lives of students and other members of society: television, radio, popular music, movies, the Internet, podcasts, and youth subcultures; alternative bodies of knowledge produced by indigenous, marginalized, or low-status groups; the ways different forms of power operate to construct identities and empower and oppress particular groups; and the modus operandi of the ways sociocultural regulation operates.

Democracy is a fragile entity, advocates of critical pedagogy maintain, and embedded in educational policy and practice are the very issues that make or break it. Understanding these diverse dimensions and structures that shape schooling and the knowledge it conveys is necessary, critical pedagogues believe, to the very survival of democratic schooling—not to mention the continued existence of democracy itself. The analysis of the ways these complex forces evolve in a globalized, technological, electronic communications-based era marked by grand human migrations is central to the complex critical pedagogy proposed here.

Source: Reprinted by permission of *Harvard Educational Review*.

1985; Giroux, 1983, 1988; Livingstone, 1987: 7–9; McLaren, 2007: 196ff.; Darder et al., 2009). Giroux and McLaren (1989: xxi) emphasize that critical pedagogy involves a "language of protest" and a "critical theory of education" directed towards the task of "constructing a new vision of the future." The analysis offsets its portrayals of the despair of everyday life and the social structures that contribute to poverty, de-humanization, and hopelessness with the promise of hope and prospects for meaningful change.

More than most other approaches within the sociology of education, critical pedagogy is grounded in the actions of classroom practitioners. Theory is oriented to address their concerns directly by enabling them to comprehend their own educational realities in relation to wider struggles for liberation. This has sometimes proven to be problematic, in part because the language and philosophical discourse of critical pedagogy have little meaning for all but a few students and educators. While writers like Paulo Freire and Peter McLaren are careful to integrate their analysis with everyday educational experience, there is a tendency in much critical pedagogy to become overly abstract and removed from socio-cultural realities. This is especially true of critical pedagogy that, in its heavy reliance on postmodernist critiques of conventional theory and practice, often appears to favour the quest for clever turns of phrase while neglecting significant social reference points.

To educators who have become cynical about recurrent waves of fashionable educational ideologies and prescriptions for change, the idealistic and Utopian visions of radical educational reform can be readily dismissed as irrelevant to immediate classroom problems. Nonetheless, critical pedagogy has forced educators and analysts to clarify the nature and significance of educational practices while they maintain awareness of the social contexts that shape educational possibilities and limitations.

Critical Race Theory and Anti-Racism Education

One of the persistent though often unspoken concerns within the analysis of education has been the ways in which race, racism, and racialized identities are constructed and reinforced within education and other social structures and practices. Although researchers have long debated with one another over various explanations as to why there have been often profound differences in the educational outcomes associated with students of diverse racial origins, questions related to how and why racial groups are categorized as they are, and what implications those categorizations hold for particular social groups, have often been ignored. These concerns are the focus of social analysis within frameworks of critical race theory, post-colonial theories, and anti-racism education. Like other theories, these orientations have extensive roots, influenced by the formative work of writers like sociologist W.E.B. Du Bois, who explored the relationship between race and socio-economic inequality at the beginning of the twentieth century. The roots of these theories extend, as well, to the civil rights movement in the United States and to lessons derived through struggles for independence by people in regions colonized by Western societies in many parts of the world.

Critical race theory and *anti-racism education* share many of the concerns central to feminism and critical pedagogy, including a commitment to social change guided by social analysis, with a more explicit focus on differential and unequal treatment based on race. Race, understood in this way, does not exist as a static social category or identity, but is implicated in processes of power associated with **racialization** through which individuals and groups are defined and treated on the basis of ascribed racial characteristics, often ignoring other bases of identity or differences within groups. Racial inequality, understood within post-colonial and critical race theories, involves much more than socio-economic differences or unequal opportunities for particular racialized populations in relation to the dominant groups; it is important, as well, to analyze how experiences associated with relations of domination and subordination are expressed through and shape language, identities, and social encounters (Ladson-Billings and Tate, 1995). Post-colonial theories, in particular, share with postmodernist analysis and critical pedagogical orientations a concern to explore the centrality of cultural practices and discourses to these relations (Rizvi et al., 2006: 255–6).

Anti-racism education is intertwined with critical orientations to the analysis of race and other social inequalities, integrating theoretical understanding with the development of strategies and social practices dedicated to social change. It is not the same as multicultural education, with which it is sometimes confused. Multicultural education shares with liberalism and human capital approaches a focus on rights and cultural differences but gives relatively limited attention to the underlying causes of racial inequalities (Kailin, 2002: 52–4). Racism is perpetuated through social practices and structures that subordinate racial minorities, including the language used to categorize and describe people from various racial and cultural backgrounds. Anti-racism analysis extends beyond the simple categorization of people on the basis of racial characteristics to highlight the diverse ways in which people's lives are affected by intersecting forms of oppression based on class, gender, race, and other social characteristics. Racism has played a powerful role in limiting the life chances for specific groups, such as African-American students (Ogbu, 1994) and Aboriginal people in Canada (Monture-Angus, 1995).

Anti-racism education has three main concerns—to expose how racism, in itself and in conjunction with other types of oppression, contributes to the suppression of opportunities for specific racialized groups; to examine the impact of racism; and to develop strategies to counter racially based subordination. Schooling is a primary focal point in anti-racism theory. Educators and their educational contexts have a significant impact on issues and practices associated with racial difference and inequality. Education contains the potential, alternatively, to critique and modify, or to ignore and reinforce, unequal racial identities and associated practices (Dei, 1996; Dei and Calliste, 2000). Anti-racism education has sensitized educators to the continuing significance of race-related oppression in and beyond schools. It has also posed important questions about how racialized forms of inequality can best be countered. While much anti-racist analysis has focused on "talk" and awareness related to individual encounters with racism, there is a critical need to embed anti-racism within more systematic practices aimed at fostering effective institutional and organizational change (Srivastava, 2007: 308–9). Part of this analysis has expanded our consideration not only of school practices, but also of the nature of knowledge. Schools historically have severed the links that many minority communities have with traditional forms of knowledge and ways of knowing. However, many racialized populations, including First Nations and some African-Canadian groups, have sought to reclaim and gain recognition for their particular cultural or indigenous knowledge systems as part of wider strategies for social and economic empowerment. These challenges have forced educators and educational researchers to reconsider deeply embedded assumptions about what we mean by knowledge, and what the application of these assumptions within schooling practices means for different student bodies. They have also expanded the focus on anti-racism from preoccupation with the racialization of "visible minority" categories to critical "whiteness" studies that take into consideration the practices and discourses around which "whiteness" has been constructed as an invisible but powerful social entity (Dei et al., 2004).

Guidelines for Research and Analysis in the Sociology of Education

This chapter has presented an overview of several influential and representative theories within the sociological analysis of education. These diverse approaches offer distinct ways of defining research problems, collecting and analyzing data, and explaining educational phenomena, as summarized in Table 2.1. Each provides important insights into educational practices and structures. As we have noted, several factors must be taken into consideration to assess the adequacy of any particular theory or approach. What assumptions do we make about the world and how we study it? Does our interest lie, for example, with an explanation of what happens inside classrooms or are we more concerned with social, economic, and political structures (such as questions about educational finance, policy-making, and social inequality) that operate beyond the classroom? Is our focus on

- current issues or historical developments?
- educational practices or the outcomes of schooling?
- formal or informal aspects of the curriculum?
- factors that give rise to educational stability, or educational change and conflict?
- understanding and explaining education systems and practices in abstract terms, or influencing changes in those structures and practices?

No single theory can address all of these questions adequately. Increasingly, educational analysis has emphasized the paradox that, while certain problems are more amenable than others to particular theoretical questions and research methods, sometimes more common ground exists between differing perspectives than is often supposed. These considerations do not mean, however, that all theories are equally valid or that we can simply "pick and choose" an approach in an attempt to investigate social or educational phenomena. Rather, we must be aware of guidelines to ensure that our analysis is systematic and provides an accurate account of the realities we are trying to understand.

It is useful, in this regard, to identify several aspects of educational realities that must be accounted for if we are to develop an adequate sociological understanding of education. These include the following:

- We must recognize education as a broad set of practices that is not restricted to specific institutional forms like schools, colleges, and universities. Education takes place both formally and informally in all aspects of our lives. Educational practices have both intended and unintended consequences.
- Formal education is riddled with contradictions. It can contribute to enhanced social and economic opportunities, individual self-awareness, and greater understanding of our place in the world, but it can also lead to oppression, subordination, and restricted socio-economic opportunities.

Table 2.1 Summary of Major Theoretical Perspectives in Sociology and the Sociological Analysis of Education

	Structural Functionalism and Liberal Analysis	Interpretive Sociology	Conflict Sociology	Integrative Theories
Main purpose of theory	• to provide an objective model of reality in order to organize, understand, and explain social phenonema	• to help illuminate and explain the social world especially as a guide to nform practical activity	• to transform social practices and structures through understanding social phenomena and their root causes	• may be used to understand social phenomena and foster change, or to represent competing "regimes of truth"
Major assumptions	• highlight parallels in how societies and living organisms can be understood; • social order and stability maintained by individual roles and institutional functions; • problems arise if social change is too rapid or uneven; • individual factors or the social importance of positions people occupy as major sources of social inequalities	• meanings and symbols are central to human activity; • how people make sense of the world can count more than objective reality; • societies, social institutions, and knowledge produced through human activity; • everyday life is an important focus for sociological analysis; • social structures do not exist independently from the social interactions and encounters that give rise to social organization	• focus on structures and relations rather than individuals; • deep inequalities based on class, gender, race, and other significant social factors; • relations of power enforced by coercion, ideology, and structural factors; • effective social change involves fundamental transformations rather than minor reforms to policy and practice	• social analysis involves insights from diverse perspectives; • causality may be multiple (or, for postmodernists, not possible to establish); • important to acknowledge social position or standpoint of researcher; • emphasis on complex interactions rather than single or dual dimensions of phenomena; • focus on mutual interactions among human agency and social structures
Foundational influences	A. Comte H. Spencer E. Durkheim T. Parsons	M. Weber K. Mannheim J. Addams H. Becker J. Dewey G.H. Mead	H. Martineau K. Marx J. Bernard C. Wright Mills	P. Freire P. Bourdieu B. Bernstein A. Giddens D. Smith M. Foucault

Key concepts for sociology of education	• functions and social order; • social integration; • norms and morality; • socialization, allocation and stratification, merit; • equality of opportunity	• definition of the situation; • social construction; • social interaction and negotiation; • rationalization; • labelling, self-fulfilling prophecy	• power, domination, and subordination; • structural inequality; • exploitation, patriarchy, racism; • commodification	• multiple forms of capital (social, economic cultural, symbolic); • identity, difference, and intersectionality
Main elements in sociological analysis of education	• educational institutions understood in relation to their functions or how they meet societal needs; • the growth of education systems is integral to modernization; • credentials serve as legitimate bases to validate knowledge and determine access to social positions	• school as negotiated site or "unity of interacting personalities" (W. Waller); • social structures and routines involve adaptation within general frameworks or scripts; • labels and expectations held by parents, teachers, and others influence educational outcomes; • credentials are established in the process of competion among social groups	• schools shaped through unequal power relations and dominant ideologies; • school knowledge and practice reinforce class inequalities and patriarchal relations; • significance of state regulation and control; • educational change is limited without changes to structures beyond education	• school practices are shaped and influenced by intersections of class, race, gender, and other bases of identity; • important to understand relations between formal and informal curricula; • power relations are not simply imposed externally but take shape within everyday practices and discourses
Major variants and contemporary contributions to sociology of education	• human capital theory; • status attainment and technological functionalism; • relations between education and social opportunity structure explored through empirical research (J. Coleman, J. Porter) • neo-functionalism (J. Alexander) and systems theory (N. Luhmann)	• credentialism (R. Collins); • "new" sociology of education and critique of school knowledge; • emotions and emotional labour (A. Hochschild); • new institutionalism (J. Meyers)	• neo-Marxism (H. Braverman (H. Braverman; S. Bowles, H. Gintis), • analysis of globalization and world systems; • critiques of marketization and corporate influences on education	• theories of social and economic reproduction, culture, and resistance (M. Apple, P. Willis; A. Lareau); • postmodernist and poststructural analysis; • critical and feminist pedagogies (P. McLaren, H. Giroux, b hooks); • queer theory (J. Butler); • risk society and reflexive modernity (Z. Baumann, U. Beck); • postcolonial theories

■ We must be able to understand, and link together, what happens inside schools and the organization and operation of the education system as a whole. The analysis of education, in turn, must be integrated with an understanding of wider social processes and structures and strategies for transformation.

■ We must be aware of the historical factors that have given rise to educational systems and processes of educational change.

■ Formal education involves the production and dissemination of knowledge and skills of various forms. We must be aware of how these processes are contested and often selective in nature, so that we can understand the extent to which they do or do not include and represent diverse social interests.

■ We must be sensitive to how the needs and actions of educational practitioners, including students, teachers, administrators, and policy-makers, can both inform and be informed by educational analysis and research. It is important, in this regard, to recognize that none of these groups is homogeneous; rather, they reflect varied experiences characterized by gender, race, ethnicity, class, and other important social characteristics.

Conclusion

This chapter has emphasized the importance of theory as a tool to guide our understanding of education and its connections with other social phenomena. Illustrative theories have been presented from three main sociological frameworks—structural functionalism, interpretative analysis, and critical approaches—to highlight the diversity of questions and explanations drawn on by sociologists. The chapter has concluded with a series of issues that need to be taken into account in order to arrive at a comprehensive understanding of education, with the recognition that any single study or theory cannot encompass all of these concerns.

The chapters that follow—informed especially by the insights of critical theories of education—address these issues. Critical analysis enables us to move beyond the surface of educational activities to examine the underlying causes and consequences of educational practice. Through this analysis, ultimately, our aim is not only to understand the contradictory nature of education but to work towards a plan of action that allows us to make progressive changes in educational practices and outcomes.

Annotated Further Readings

Apple, Michael W., Stephen J. Ball, and Luis Armando Gandin, eds. 2010. *The Routledge International Handbook of the Sociology of Education*. Abingdon, UK: Routledge. Articles cover recent theoretical developments in the sociology of education, as well as applications of theory and research on a broad range of themes highlighting educational issues in several national contexts.

Arnot, Madeleine, and Mairtin Mac An Ghaill, eds. 2006. *The RoutledgeFalmer Reader in Gender and Education*. London: Routledge. This comprehensive reader integrates classic articles on feminist theory with research that explores significant questions concerning relationships between gender and education. Themes include knowledge and pedagogy, gender variations in educational achievement, debates concerning boys' and girls' schooling, curriculum and classroom relationships, and gender, power, and identity.

Bowles, Samuel, and Herbert Gintis. 1976. *Schooling in Capitalist America: Educational Reform and the Contradictions of Economic Life.* New York: Basic Books. This highly influential book emphasizes that, in contrast to prevailing assumptions about education's contributions to social opportunity and equality, educational reform has maintained social inequality by contributing to ideologies and labour market requirements driven by the dynamics of a capitalist economy.

Darder, Antonia, Marta P. Baltodano, and Rodolfo D. Torres, eds. 2009. *The Critical Pedagogy Reader,* 2nd edn. New York: Routledge. This collection integrates core foundational work and more recent theoretical and empirical investigations employing critical pedagogy. Contributions from several authors cited in this chapter, as well as many others, employ various critical perspectives including anti-racism education, feminist pedagogy, and critical pedagogy to investigate classroom practices, globalization and education, teaching, and other important educational issues.

Dolby, Nadine, and Greg Dimitriadis, eds. 2004. *Learning to Labor in New Times.* New York: Routledge. Focusing on Paul Willis's influential study on youth culture and schooling and work relationships, several contributors draw from perspectives that include feminism, critical pedagogy, race relations, and cultural studies to illuminate social experiences and life transition processes encountered by contemporary youth.

Durkheim, Émile. 1956. *Education and Sociology.* New York: Free Press. This book, bringing together English translations of several of Durkheim's papers, is a classic work that makes the case for, and outlines the foundational elements of, the sociological analysis of education.

Torres, Carlos Alberto, and Theodore R. Mitchell, eds. 1998. *Sociology of Education: Emerging Perspectives.* Albany: State University of New York Press. Contributions to this book examine theoretical developments in the sociology of education and the significance of different types of educational reform and inequality in comparative perspective.

Key Terms

Correspondence principle The view that presents educational reforms and outcomes as consequences of economic requirements, labour market needs, and inequalities within a capitalist economy.

Cultural capital The resources that people possess for economic and social success, which include not only wealth and economic assets but also knowledge and understandings about social expectations, dominant values, and other pertinent information that institutions use in their ongoing operations.

Cultural reproduction Recognition that, while education contributes to ongoing social inequalities, it does so through cultural and social practices as well as economic requirements.

Definition of the situation The acknowledgement that our perceptions can influence social actions. Interpretative analysis draws attention to how socially constructed and shared meanings play a crucial role in shaping, reinforcing, or altering social frameworks.

Human capital theory A theoretical approach, with frequent policy applications, that emphasizes education, skill development, and other learning processes as investments that enhance capacities and opportunities among individuals, thereby contributing to general economic growth.

New institutional theory A theoretical orientation drawn from research in several disciplines including sociology, economics, and organizational studies that focuses on the distinctive characteristics of institutions and institutionalized arrangements and explores their impact on broader social and economic processes.

Pedagogy Processes associated with the organization and practice of teaching. The term refers more generally to various kinds of interactions (and how these are understood and organized) in teaching–learning situations.

Racialization Categorizing and treating people based on observed physical group characteristics and the stereotypes of group differences that are products of historical and social processes.

Resistance theory Analysis that highlights children, youth, and other students as active participants who can oppose and shape their education and social futures rather than as passive institutional clients.

Self-fulfilling prophecies The notion that the assumptions and expectations that teachers and other service workers hold about students can influence students' lives and futures.

Structural functionalism A theoretical perspective that explains social phenomena with reference to their mutual influence on one another, especially through the social needs they fulfill and the contributions they make to social order.

Symbolic interactionism A theoretical perspective that emphasizes the importance of language, meaning, and use of symbols in our development of self-awareness and, through our relations with others, as the basis of societies.

Study Questions

1. Why, rather than a single approach, are there several distinct theoretical frameworks within the sociological analysis of education?

2. Which approach to sociological analysis offers the most comprehensive explanation of educational practices and developments in Canada? Justify your answer.

3. Looking at your own educational experiences, identify the major factors that have contributed to your educational aspirations and attainment to date. Which of these factors are the result of individual characteristics and which ones have a social basis? Which, if any, of the theories outlined in this chapter might best explain these experiences? What factors cannot be accounted for by the theories?

4. Discuss the relationship between theory and practice in education. To what extent, and with what consequences, can theory and practice exist without informing one another?

5. Discuss which set of factors—those related to what happens inside educational institutions, or those brought in from outside educational institutions—has the strongest impact on educational outcomes. How well are these factors accounted for in the main sociological theories of education?

6. In what ways do educational institutions mirror other major institutions in contemporary societies? How, by contrast, can educational institutions be considered as distinct from other institutions? Discuss the impact of these similarities and differences on the development of a theoretical understanding of education.

Chapter 3

Historical Dimensions of Canadian Education

Learning Objectives

In this chapter, you will:

- identify the main phases and factors associated with the historical development of Canadian education systems;
- gain an understanding of important social, economic, and political factors that have influenced these processes of educational development;
- be introduced to public controversies related to education that have emerged over the years.

Introduction

The Canadian education system, as a whole, is one of the largest enterprises in Canadian society. In Canada, over $100 billion annually are spent directly on education, constituting just over 6 per cent of the gross domestic product (the total value of goods and services produced in the nation), while increasing amounts are spent on indirect support for schooling, educational services, and other learning activities. Over six million Canadians are enrolled full-time in elementary, secondary, and post-secondary education programs, and close to 800,000 more are enrolled in part-time programs (AUCC, 2011: 5; Brockington, 2011; CAUT, 2012: 39). Education also employs substantial numbers of people in teaching, administrative, and support positions. In 2010, more than 700,000 people in Canada worked either full-time or part-time as teachers and professors, with more than 1.1 million persons employed in educational services fields overall, representing 7.9 per cent of the total labour force (Statistics Canada, 2011b, 2012).

Canadians, like people in other developed nations, accept formal education as a normal part of the experience of children and youth. It has become, for many people, a central feature of ongoing development throughout the life course. In many ways, current educational realities stand in marked contrast to the situation at the beginning of the twentieth century, when most people had very little, if any, formal schooling. Those few individuals who graduated from high school often became teachers or, on rare occasions, continued into post-secondary studies to gain entry into select professional fields or round out their intellectual development for social and political reasons. The dramatic expansion of **public education** in just over a century, from a localized and voluntary pursuit to a highly formalized bureaucracy accompanied by an increasingly large selection of alternatives, is largely taken for granted, as is the fact that almost entire populations participate in schooling and rely on formal educational credentials for career and social advancement. Nonetheless, in common with contemporary public policy discussions about how schooling should be organized and financed, and what kinds of reforms are required to maintain relevant and competitive educational programming, the expansion of public education and efforts to modify or standardize the educational base were topics of heated public debate in the late nineteenth and early twentieth centuries.

This chapter provides an overview of historical factors that have shaped educational growth and transformation in Canada, setting the stage for the next chapter, which outlines the structure, size, and scope of contemporary Canadian education systems. The nation has a rich and highly convoluted educational history that, while unique, is also interwoven with influences, traditions, and developments imported from or occurring in conjunction with events and practices in other nations. The discussion here highlights major dimensions of this development to illuminate issues discussed in other chapters—detailed accounts that offer a more complete understanding of Canada's educational history are widely dispersed in academic and popular written work as well as in diverse oral traditions. Throughout this chapter, particular emphasis is placed on the contested nature of educational reform and on the changing role of state involvement in the organization, financing, and delivery of educational services.

The Historical Development of Education in Canada

The story of education in Canada, like other institutional histories, involves much more than a straightforward description of key events. Some of the key markers in the development of the education system are associated with significant events and milestones, such as the establishment of schools and universities and the passage of legislation concerning education, as well as with influential individuals. Conventional educational histories have emphasized the prominent role played by influential white men such as Bishop Laval in New France, Egerton Ryerson in Upper Canada, and John Jessop in British Columbia, whose visions and leadership contributed to the advancement of a stable education system in Canada (see, e.g., Johnson, 1968; Wilson et al., 1970; Titley and Miller, 1982). Women's education and the role of women and other minority groups in educational development and reform have been relatively absent in much of the historical analysis of education, reflecting in part a preoccupation with formal political, administrative, and academic matters, which historically excluded from formal education many segments of the population (Fahmy-Eid, 2003: 32–3). Subsequent educational researchers have come to appreciate more fully the significant contributions that women and men representing diverse communities have made to educational development, often in the face of hostile or recalcitrant authorities and complex regulations (see Box 3.1). Education systems are also the product of more mundane events and activities involving countless interactions among students, teachers, parents, and other educational participants (see, e.g., Axelrod, 1997; Houston and Prentice, 1988).

Historical, legal, and practical factors have combined to produce a unique and complex array of education systems in Canada. Under the initial terms of the British North America Act (now known as the Constitution Act, 1867), existing denominational rights to schooling were to be maintained, and provisions were also outlined for the operation of separate schools. Through these historical and legal foundations, along with subsequent developments and constitutional amendments, Quebec has maintained an education system (based initially on "confessional" or religious

Box 3.1 Obstacles and Progress: Two Notable Contributions to Educational Reform

We commonly take for granted the existence of educational programs and services that are, in fact, the result of sustained efforts of many committed educators and community leaders, often in the face of sustained resistance or difficult procedural barriers. Helen Raptis (2005: 302–3, 308) details the experiences and strategies of two women, Edith Lucas and Mary Ashworth, whose work with minority students in the mid-twentieth century awakened their awareness of the need for change. Lucas's experience reveals their dedication to new programs, policies, and approaches to language instruction and school–community interactions even when there was no apparent route to advance such change:

Although Lucas, a seasoned teacher and principal, had never before prepared lessons for adult immigrants, she was cognizant that their needs differed from those of children and adolescents. Finding there was "no book on the market suitable for teaching English to intelligent adults," Lucas devised her own strategy.[1] On her own time after work Lucas organized a class of newcomers to meet in the evenings in her Victoria office, a stone's throw from the YWCA's quarters. Once she had prepared and "field tested" a lesson with her own students, she had it "mimeographed and sent to the YWCA classes for their guidance."[2]

Lucas eventually compiled her lessons into two books, entitled *English I* and *English II*, each totalling over 300 pages. Upon completing *English II*, students could sit [for] an examination that entitled them to a "certificate in English and citizenship," a document they could present as evidence of readiness

distinctions and later on linguistic factors) that in curriculum, structure, and various other respects is markedly different from systems in other provinces. Schooling was also organized and funded on a religious basis in Manitoba until 1890 and in Newfoundland and Labrador until the late 1990s, while Alberta, Ontario, and Saskatchewan have separate school systems with provision for public schooling based on the dominant religious group in a region as well as minority separate schools. British Columbia, Prince Edward Island, New Brunswick, and Nova Scotia officially adopted a single non-denominational public school system, but the three Maritime provinces (along with Manitoba) made some compromises and introduced arrangements to provide support for separate schools (Manzer, 2003: 40ff.; Wilson et al., 1970; Young et al, 2007). Governments in the northern territories, until recently, have maintained single public school systems, eventually adopting provisions for schooling in indigenous languages and French. Over time, several provinces, beginning with Alberta in 1967 and now including also Quebec, Manitoba, Saskatchewan, and British Columbia, have also introduced measures to provide some public funding for independent or private schools. These developments, along with numerous other circumstances, reveal an educational reality that cannot be made sense of through simply defined narratives.

From a critical sociological standpoint, it is important, in acknowledging different ways in which the story can be told, to focus not strictly on what happened but, when applying for Canadian citizenship. By 1954, there were over 115 night schools in BC using Lucas's textbooks, which she described as "instruction in the rights and responsibilities of Canadian citizenship, teaching at the same time practical English and our customs."[3] . . .

As a member of the Canadian Citizenship Council and an immigrant to Canada herself, Lucas considered the development of *English I* and *II* to be a "labour of love," produced mostly during her own, unpaid time. Lucas preferred to produce her own materials from scratch since she disapproved of many of the available language texts, whose pages were rife with stilted, formulaic phrases such as "the pen of my aunt is under the lilac bush." Lucas took pride in her works, which were well illustrated with phrases built around the daily needs of the adult immigrants "in the sort of sequence in which they are naturally spoken."[4] . . .

Notes

1. "Book Enables 'New Canucks' To Outshine 'Old Canadians'," *Vancouver Sun*, 7 Jan. 1956, 11.
2. Ibid. Each lesson consisted of formal grammar, vocabulary drill, and pages of reading material about a fictitious immigrant family experiencing various aspects of Canadian life, such as government, banking, property insurance, taxation, home decoration, and workmen's compensation.
3. "Personality of the Week: Dr. Edith E. Lucas," *Colonist*, 3 Feb. 1952, 16.
4. Ibid.

more crucially, on why things happened as they did, how they are significant for the analysis of social life, and how they can be understood in relation to the social context in which they emerged. Educational practices and changes take shape through the intentions and actions of particular historical actors who, in turn, influence and are influenced by other actors, organizations, and structures. The following brief historical overview outlines some of the most significant features of the education system.

Colonization and Settlement: Education in Canada Prior to the Mid-1800s

The school system as we know it is a relatively recent development, not a natural or inevitable feature of social life. It has been produced and modified within particular social circumstances, often subject to serious contestation over its direction or resistance to its presence and forms. Schooling, by nature, is oriented to change. Implicit within the aims of formal education are the objectives to produce new knowledge, transform individual personalities, and modify or improve social conditions. While there may be little disagreement, at least at a general level, that these are worthy objectives, the demands for educational changes frequently originate within groups or forces that have distinct social agendas or interests, however much these may be challenged and modified by other factors.

Indigenous Beginnings

Education was a central part of life in what came to be Canada long before there were any formal schools. Early education was distinguished by its incorporation into the daily life practices of First Nations people. Education was crucial for the fulfillment of material needs and cultural survival. According to Kirkness and Bowman (1992: 5), "It was an education in which the community and the natural environment were the classroom, and the land was seen as the mother of the people. Members of the community were the teachers, and each adult was responsible for ensuring that each child learned how to live a good life." The integration of education with everyday life suggests a highly informal system of socialization. There is evidence, however, that many First Nations had sophisticated forms of social organization more than 15 centuries ago (Sewid-Smith, 1991: 19–20). While oral traditions such as storytelling were central to learning, complex systems of knowledge were systematically transmitted among generations, sometimes with the aid of visual symbols. First Nations each had their own distinctive bodies of traditional or **indigenous knowledge**, supported by social practices to preserve and transmit core beliefs, values, and competencies. Many of these were endangered through subsequent efforts by European colonizers to undermine or deny such knowledge (Battiste, 2000; Royal Commission on Aboriginal Peoples, 1996a: 526–7).

The First Nations pattern of "organic" educational practices suited to the practical needs of family, clan, or community has characterized education among many other groups in Canadian society. This has been the case most commonly for children living in regions with no established educational facilities, such as families of early European settlers, Hudson's Bay Company officials, and homesteaders on the Prairies. On some occasions, family or community members attempt to resist, or even assert control over, public education despite the ready accessibility of formal educational services. Situations of this kind are most likely to arise when members of minority groups, such as those based on ethnicity or religion, dispute central features of the dominant school system, when parents assert their right to educate the children themselves, or when parents see schooling as interfering with competing demands on their children's time for work, care of family members, or other responsibilities.

European Education and Colonization

The earliest formal schooling in Canada was established by missionaries and religious orders. It was oriented primarily to the replacement of indigenous lifestyles and knowledge with European concepts of morality and consciousness. However benevolent the intentions of religious authorities may have been, denominational education was promoted zealously in the belief that Europeans were morally and intellectually superior to the original inhabitants of North America. Later, myths of the illiterate or noble savage served both to undermine and romanticize Aboriginal life. The representation of Aboriginal peoples as uncivilized or less than full persons enabled colonizing forces to attack traditions they characterized as naive or backward.

These early educational efforts had varying degrees of success. In some cases they were rejected, while in others they were embraced by Aboriginal people. Jaenen (1986), for instance, identifies four distinct phases in the education of Aboriginal people in New France, ranging from missionary education of children and families in the mission field beginning in the seventeenth century to nineteenth-century boarding schools. Changing educational practices reflected colonial desires to devise new strategies to accomplish educational objectives, particularly those oriented to the assimilation of First Nations peoples into European-based life conditions.

Education figured prominently in the fragmentation of First Nations societies. The impact of education was destructive both in content and in form. Not only were Native children taught that their traditional ways were inferior and unacceptable, but the routines and spatial organization of schools often contributed even more strongly to the separation of children from their families and communities. Assimilation was to be accomplished at the cost of breaking down existing social relationships. Schooling was particularly destructive when it attempted to transplant European cultural and educational forms to replace stable indigenous patterns attuned to the demands of life in North America. At the same time, Native people were not given opportunities to participate fully and equally in the new social order (Jaenen, 1986: 60). Boarding and residential schools, introduced as official policy by the federal government in the 1870s, acted as "total institutions" in which children were taken from their parents so as to be removed from "regressive" influences. Children were subject to harsh disciplinary measures for such offences as speaking in their Native language, and often they were unable to associate with other family members except for brief periods each year.

Missionaries and other individuals who were privately contracted also provided early schooling for children of British and French origin in Canada. These schools were intended primarily to keep alive connections with established European traditions or to train individuals for specific purposes. Examples of the latter include the provision of training for religious orders, political elites, and teachers. Among the general population, education tended to be sporadic, oriented to the cultivation of loyalty to religious or political orders rather than to anything more than the most basic formal lessons (see, e.g., Titley, 1982).

It is essential to have a sense of the context of the general social structure to understand fully the origins of schooling. The initial development of Canada by European and, subsequently, North American interests was motivated primarily by territorial or commercial concerns. Resource-based industries such as the fur trade, gold extraction, logging, and fishing were highly volatile, and priority was given to measures that would ensure that adequate supplies of labour and access to resources were available. Moreover, with a few exceptions, such as colonial officials, merchants, and service suppliers who were in a position to settle and raise families, most of the labour force consisted of men who were single or geographically mobile. Because many regions had no children other than those who performed domestic chores or engaged in paid labour, and the relatively privileged groups could arrange to have their children tutored privately or sent to schools elsewhere, there were few demands for a general system of public schooling until the late eighteenth and early nineteenth centuries.

The Development of a Public School System (mid-1800s to the early 1900s)

Increased immigration and settlement of families, the influx of United Empire Loyalists from the United States, and political and economic threats to Canadian lands and resources gave rise to new demands for a system of free public schooling. Whereas schooling under denominational and colonial control fostered loyalties to traditional sources (Church, class, and old-country ties), the most ardent proponents of a common public school system sought the development of distinctly Canadian identities.

Box 3.2 Truth, Reconciliation, and Residential Schooling

Most Canadians do not know the full story of residential schooling for First Nations, Métis, and Inuit and its devastating consequences that continue to haunt indigenous people and communities well after the last schools closed. The appointment of a national Truth and Reconciliation Commission in 2008 in conjunction with a public apology issued by the federal government has provided a forum for greater awareness about the damaging practices and legacy associated with forcible removal of Aboriginal children from their homes and confinement in residential schools. An account by one residential school survivor (Guss, 1993: 91–2) contrasts the freedom of traditional First Nations education with the regimentation that prevailed in residential schools:

Normally, in a Native family, a child is allowed to learn by trial and error, with love and support being freely given. My experiences in residential school were a sharp contrast to this. There, our natural curiosity was impeded by the outlook of nuns, who had no experience in life and no experience as a parent. Even the natural curiosity of the opposite sex was discouraged and one was made to feel ashamed for even having such curiosities.

There were very few times you could enjoy life as it was so regimented. There was no freedom of thought or expression allowed. Everyone had to conform to a rigid set of standard rules: pray, learn, pray, obey, pray, eat, pray. Up at 6:30 a.m., Mass at 7:00 a.m., breakfast at 8:00 a.m., class at 9:00 a.m., lunch at 12:00 noon, class at 1:00 p.m., sewing and mending at 4:00 p.m., supper at 6:00 p.m., bed at 9:00 p.m. The next day it started again.

Even our bodily functions were regimented; there were certain times to go to the washroom, and castor oil was administered once a year. We had a bath once a week, and laundry duty every Saturday. We attended church once a day and twice on Sunday. On Sundays we had a few hours of free time but we were unaccustomed to such freedom, so we usually looked to an older student to organize our activities.

Schooling for the general population was to be secular—to overcome the particular intentions of denominational authorities; open to all pupils—to ensure that the entire population had a common education; and suited to the cultivation of social and political bonds within Canada. Education was a significant factor in struggles to break ties with the colonial powers of Britain and France and to preserve Canadian autonomy against American influence. In some instances, such as among Loyalist emigrants from the United States, parents agitated for schooling in order to extend opportunities they had previously experienced. In many other cases, however, the strongest advocates for public schooling were politicians, business people, educated professionals, and educators themselves who sought the establishment of stable communities (Curtis, 1988; Prentice, 1977). The presence of a school in a community signified a commitment to future planning and growth. The **curriculum**, while facilitating basic literacy among the population, could also be used to cultivate new attitudes and allegiances, along with prospects for democratic participation, necessary for the growth of a stable social order.

Beyond strict discipline and regimentation, children in residential schools often had to perform physical labour and other chores to sustain and raise funds for the schools. More seriously, physical beatings, whipping, and extreme forms of punishment frequently occurred well in excess of standards tolerated in public school systems even during an era in which corporal punishment was commonly practised. Sexual abuse, disease, malnutrition, deficient facilities, and other serious issues fostered deliberately and through negligence contributed to health problems, starvation, high death rates, and physical and emotional trauma. In its interim report, the Truth and Reconciliation Commission observes that, "Overall, the residential schools system often amounted to a system of institutionalized child neglect, compounded by the behaviour of specific individuals who used their authority and the isolation of the schools to physically and sexually abuse those in their care. Within this context, students could be prey not only to abuse from staff, but also from older or better organized students." The legacy of the residential school experience has affected not only those who attended the schools, but subsequent generations who have continued to come to terms with the encounters and the scars they have implanted deep within indigenous communities. Chrisjohn and Wasace (2009: 226–7; italics in original) are blunt in their assessment of the institutionalized cultural destruction represented in the residential school system:

> Let us be clear: *the crimes of the Indian residential school system are not reduced to the individual injuries experienced by those compelled to suffer them. . . . The schools were not created to destroy the lives of Bill, Dave, Ann, and Elizabeth but to destroy forms of life that were surviving and growing within them. Making individuals whole does not thereby reconstitute the Indigenous forms of life residential schooling was mandated to destroy.*

Tragically, the residential school experience was not isolated to Canada, as attested to by the widespread adoption and damaging legacies of residential and boarding schools for indigenous populations in the United States, Australia, and many other nations (Smith, 2009).

The factors that contributed to the development of public school systems in Canada reveal the dual objectives of formal education. First, schooling provides formal learning opportunities through the curriculum. Fundamental skills and knowledge are made available to all learners, and people are given a chance to encounter new ideas and challenges. At the same time, however, formal education also contributes to **moral regulation** and the reshaping of people's identities. In both structure and content, schooling is centrally involved in the process of disciplining the individual through emphasis on rules and habits rather than on lessons alone (Corrigan et al., 1987; Curtis, 1988). Political reformers recognized that schooling could be an important contributing factor to the process of Canadian nation-building. This process involved, in part, the shaping of individual subjects committed to the Canadian state and its institutions and values. School facilities were among the first and most prominent structures in many communities in recognition of education's importance in state formation and community-building.

Educational promoters faced three main obstacles in their quest to construct a solid educational system as part of the **state apparatus**, or within the framework of the government services and regulations. First, it was necessary to raise money to build schools, hire qualified teachers, and operate school programs. Funds for education had to be raised against competing priorities such as economic development and the construction of roads and other services. Current debates over the extent to which governments should be responsible for educational finance need to be understood in the context of a history of a long, contested, public discourse concerning the proper role of the state in the provision of public services. Second, educational promoters had to mobilize support for public schooling in the face of considerable opposition or indifference from various sources, including religious denominations, supporters of private schools, and community members who saw schooling as an intrusion into private life. Records reveal that just over half of the children in Canada attended schools regularly by the early part of the twentieth century. As late as 1910–11, when over 1.3 million students were enrolled in schools in Canada—which was a substantial proportion of the 1.5 million children in the 5- to 15-year-old age group—the average daily attendance rates remained below two-thirds of those children registered (Dominion Bureau of Statistics, 1924: 157; Leacy, 1983: W67–8). Attendance patterns tended to reflect regional differences in socio-economic circumstances as well as families' material conditions and class backgrounds. There were wide variations in children's school attendance, depending on family means, periodic illness, and local economic conditions such as irregular wages among labourers and shifting labour and employment patterns for children at home, on farms, and in industry (Davey, 1978; Gaffield, 1982). A third problem that plagued early school development was the shortage of a steady supply of trained teachers. Teachers had to have adequate preparation to teach the curriculum, but, more crucially, they had an important role to play in the promotion of schooling. As school employees, they also needed to be loyal to the cause of educational goals as capable representatives in the service of the state (Wotherspoon, 1993).

Difficulties in Maintaining Schools in All Communities

These problems left many schools in jeopardy, particularly in the poorer and less established regions of the country. Lack of public support and revenue for schooling led to substandard school facilities and low wages for teachers, which in turn made it difficult for some municipalities to attract pupils and suitable teachers. An illustrative case occurred in Victoria when teachers left their jobs for two years, beginning in 1870, after they had not been paid their full wages. The strike action was precipitated by a lack of funds following the refusal of the school board to enforce collection of an educational tax of $2 per resident (Wotherspoon, 1993: 88–9). Until well into the twentieth century, the option of closing down or being left to operate with little or no funding plagued schools across the country.

In the struggle of schooling to survive, educational ideals continually gave way to the demands of harsher realities. While nineteenth-century educational promoters initially sought to advance schooling's status by attracting a corps of male teachers of high moral character and strong educational background, school boards most often had limited resources and hired the cheapest, most readily available teachers, most of whom were young women whose formal qualifications fell far short of desired standards (Prentice, 1977: 108–9; Wotherspoon, 1993: 93). While critics were tempted to blame the worst educational problems on the young women who entered the classroom, it was in fact often the zeal and resourcefulness of these teachers and supportive community members, rather than any higher educational motives, that enabled schooling to flourish (Shack, 1973). Ironically, when schooling became successful in attracting large numbers of students, there was an even greater reliance on hastily prepared teachers to ensure that all schools could be staffed.

In part to compensate, education came to be governed by a growing array of formal regulations. Most jurisdictions, by the late nineteenth century, introduced rules governing everything from textbooks to school behaviour, often in the form of legislation to ensure compulsory attendance, regular taxation, and other matters, as part of an effort to regularize schooling. Strict adherence to daily attendance records and specific classroom routines enabled school authorities to monitor teachers and pupils carefully, while provisions for school finance helped to secure educational stability. Classroom life could be a deadening process of enforced order with rituals of repetition to memorize information (Axelrod, 1997: 57–8). In combination, these measures were important because they represented standards and practices that distinguished schooling from everyday life. Formal education became a central element in the expansion of state rule.

Social reformers promoted schools as critical tools in the state's crusade against the social disorganization that accompanied significant social transformations in the late nineteenth and early twentieth centuries. North American social and institutional life was altered by new industries and technologies, urban growth, the promotion of settlement in the West, and massive immigration. Public optimism about the future was mixed with uncertainty about new challenges. Unemployment, displacement from work, crime, poverty, unwelcome intrusions by "foreigners," family breakdown, and generally declining moral standards loomed as supposed threats to the social order.

Many diverse reform movements that advocated education and other social intervention into private life grew around and played upon these fears. Government officials, churches and religious orders, employers, workers' associations, community leaders, and numerous other groups (often with different motivations and degrees of success) influenced the shape and direction that formal schooling eventually would take at the centre of public life (Charland, 2000). Some of these interests were driven by concern that rapid changes were undermining the social order and leading to declining standards of living, while others acted out of concern for the welfare of families and individuals disadvantaged by social changes (Moscovitch and Drover, 1987). The state or authorities acting on behalf of the state, representing public as opposed to more particular or parochial interests, gained new powers to act as legal guardians for individuals who were deemed socially unfit or problematic in some way. The Juvenile Delinquents Act, enacted in 1908, enabled the state to provide "assistance" to young offenders who were portrayed as "misdirected and misguided." Similarly, during the 1890s, provincial governments authorized teachers to act in loco parentis, effectively granting them parental responsibilities for the time that children were at school. Other reforms, demanded by such groups as charitable and welfare organizations and mental and public health movements, were based on the designation of particular groups as problematic or incapable of supporting themselves, thereby warranting the personal and professional services of official agents.

The arguments employed by social reformers emphasized the need for state intervention in the absence of proper guidance by parents (Sutherland, 1976). A plea written in the late 1860s by school officials in Prince Edward Island for compulsory

Box 3.3 Teachers' Duties, 1875

This excerpt from the 1875 rules and regulations for public schools in British Columbia (1875: 47) not only spells out teachers' duties, but, more importantly, it indicates the significance of discipline, habit, morality, cleanliness, and order in the operation of schools:

It shall be the duty of every teacher of a Public School—

1. To teach diligently and faithfully all the branches required to be taught in the school, according to the terms of his engagement with the Trustees, and according to the rules and regulations adopted by the Board of Education:

2. To keep daily, weekly, and monthly registers of the school:

3. To maintain proper order and discipline in his school, according to the authorized forms and regulations:

4. To keep a visitors' book (which the Trustees shall provide) and enter therein the visits made to his school, and to present such book to such visitor, and to request him to make therein any remarks suggested by his visit:

5. At all times when desired by them, to give to Trustees and visitors access to the registers and visitors' book appertaining to the school, and upon his leaving the school to deliver up the same to the order of the Trustees:

6. To have at the end of each half-year public examinations of his school, of which he shall give due notice to the Trustees of the school, and, through his pupils, to their parents and guardians:

7. To furnish to the Superintendent of Education, when desired, any information which it may be in his power to give respecting anything connected with the operation of his school, or in anywise affecting its interests or character:

8. To classify the pupils according to their respective abilities:

9. To observe and impress upon the minds of the pupils, the great rule of regularity and order,—a time and place for everything, and everything in its proper time and place:

attendance legislation to counteract the "evils of irregular attendance" is typical of the justifications of the need for public education and other mechanisms to ensure compliance with state rule: "If then, from the poverty, the cupidity, or the apathy of parents, the education of their children be neglected, it is surely the duty of the State to interpose its authority in their behalf, by means of a compulsory law" (cited in Prentice and Houston, 1975: 165). This kind of appeal blamed individual children and their parents for ignorance or neglect, leading to social problems that demanded a social solution by the state, which was posed as the protector of the public or common interest. In this case, compulsory schooling was a mechanism to keep children off the streets, teaching them in the process rules of discipline, proper conduct, and perhaps even useful skills and knowledge.

10. To promote, both by precept and example, cleanliness, neatness, and decency. To personally inspect the children every morning, to see that they have their hands and faces washed, their hair combed, and clothes clean. The school apartments, too, should be swept and dusted every evening:

11. To pay the strictest attention to the morals and general conduct of the pupils; to omit no opportunity of inculcating the principles of truth and honesty; the duties of respect to superiors, and obedience to all persons placed in authority over them:

12. To evince a regard for the improvement and general welfare of the pupils; to treat them with kindness, combined with firmness; and to aim at governing them by their affections and reason rather than harshness and severity:

13. To cultivate kindly and affectionate feelings among the pupils; to discountenance quarrelling, cruelty to animals, and every approach to vice:

14. To practice such discipline in school as would be exercised by a judicious parent in the family, avoiding corporal punishment, except when it shall appear to him to be imperatively necessary; and then a record of the offence and the punishment shall be made in the school register for the inspection of trustees and visitors:

15. No teacher shall compel the services of pupils for his own private benefit or convenience:

16. For gross misconduct, or a violent or wilful opposition to authority, the teacher may suspend a pupil from attending school, forthwith informing the parent or guardian of the fact, and the reason of it; but no pupil shall be expelled without the authority of the trustees:

17. When the example of any pupil is very hurtful, and reformation appears hopeless, it shall be the duty of the teacher, with the approbation of the trustees, to expel such pupil from the school; but any pupil under public censure, who shall express to the teacher his regret for such a course of conduct, as openly and explicitly as the case may require, shall, with the approbation of the trustees and teacher, be re-admitted to the school.

Industry, Science, and the Bureaucratic Organization of Schooling (1910s–1940s)

While the historical evidence indicates that schools were not established simply to meet employers' demands to produce a compliant industrial workforce, industry doubtless affected the rise of public schooling in significant ways. Educational administrators sought to ensure the success of schooling by making the education system relevant—and perceived as useful—to life in industrial societies. They emphasized that students had to be trained to adapt to a changing world and to come out of schools with skills and knowledge that would contribute to their gainful employment. While business and industry officials often had little to do directly with schooling, educational authorities sought to cultivate the support of business leaders, parents, and other public interests in order to stabilize the education system.

Education officials also looked to industry for models to govern curriculum and school organization. The physical arrangement of the classroom, with its rows of desks under the watchful gaze of the teacher, the division of the school day into distinct periods or blocks of time, an early emphasis on memory work and rote exercises, and concern for punctuality, proper manners, and good habits were derived from military and religious training, but they were also highly amenable to a factory system of industrial production. Modern industry, moreover, provided models of organizational and classroom management oriented to educational efficiency. Many educational administrators promoted scientific management, a strategy by which employers could assert control over industrial production processes by dividing tasks into their simplest, cheapest operations, as a most effective method of lesson planning. Curricula were to be organized and planned systematically, not left to guesswork and reliance on teaching methods that were used simply because they seemed to work in the classroom (Wotherspoon, 1995a).

Educational reform has also been highly influenced by non-economic factors beyond an industrial logic and work preparation. In the early twentieth century, many educators advocated a philosophy of **educational progressivism**. Educational progressives, combining faith in the twin virtues of science and humanism, viewed schools as institutions that contributed to the realization of social progress by allowing students to develop their full human potentials. They wanted to replace earlier models of child development, which emphasized routine tradition and factory-like regulation, with approaches that provided opportunities to foster interest, creativity, and positive personal growth. Progressivism advocated the incorporation within schooling of subjects that allowed for artistic and interpersonal development rather than strict academic courses. Teachers, in turn, required specialized training, in part to learn the scientific principles on which pedagogy and human development were grounded. In the process, a series of educational reforms emerged. These reforms were driven simultaneously by objectives for a more democratic and humanistic learning environment and by a desire for the creation of "an educational system that was highly centralized, bureaucratic, autocratic, geared to the development of a meritocracy of intelligence, and designed to lead and direct an adequately socialized majority" (Mann, 1980: 115).

As the school system became governed increasingly by principles of rational organization derived from business and industry, there was a contradictory significance for the development both of schooling and of teaching as a professional occupation. Increasingly specialized training, grounded in science, gave teaching a degree of expertise that could advance its status as a professional occupation. By World War II, schools in most regions of Canada had become centrally organized as bureaucratic structures within larger school units. The average school size in Canada increased from 66 pupils per school in the mid-1920s to 156 in 1960 and 350 in 1970 (Manzer, 1994: 131). Amalgamation of smaller schools and school districts into larger units was attractive for several reasons. Many smaller schools were not financially viable, and although each school was required to provide a range of basic programs and services, it was often not possible for many schools to offer complete programs or attend to diverse educational needs. Larger schools offered better prospects for stable educational services accompanied by more extensive facilities, more complete educational programs, and a variety of curricular and extracurricular choices. It became possible for school districts to offer teachers better pay and job security and, particularly in the senior grades, to provide conditions in which teachers would be better able to teach in their areas of specialization.

Both community input and teacher professionalism, however, faced direct and indirect constraints that limited their influence on educational practice. Teachers were subordinated within an educational bureaucracy, subject to the supervision of educational administrators and guided by regulations set by officials outside the occupation. Indirect control over teaching was extended by the development of scientific curricula and central planning, which tended to move educational decision-making on many crucial issues, such as selection of textbooks and the organization of curricula, from the classroom to sources outside the school (Popkewitz, 1991). In the process, the treatment of educational matters as technical problems also minimized opportunities for meaningful community involvement in the education system. Experts, claiming legitimacy through training and knowledge related to principles of educational management, child development, curriculum planning, and pedagogy, assumed authority over a growing domain of issues beyond the reach of most public participants.

Canada's education systems have also been shaped in highly significant and often unique ways through struggles over language and minority rights. Both nationwide and in specific provincial circumstances, Canada's educational history is marked by periods of fierce contestation over such issues as language of instruction, alignment of curricula with particular religious or cultural values and beliefs, adherence to religious practices, and public funding to support denominational or minority education programs and systems. In many instances, accommodation has been accomplished by measures to enable more specialized forms of instruction to coexist with public education systems through education programs offered by minority groups on evenings, weekends, or other periods outside of regular public school hours. In other cases, tensions over minority rights have had significant impacts on the administration, curriculum, and financing of entire education systems. At the time of Confederation, the constitutional division of powers outlined in section 93 of the British North America Act granted provinces jurisdiction over education but also included provisions to ensure protection for existing denominational rights. Manzer (1994: 40) observes that, within this context, "Both before and after Confederation, the 'school question' was consistently one of the most explosive and deeply divisive issues of Canadian politics, resulting in four distinct regimes of public instruction" representing diverse mixes of public and separate school systems. Education systems, governments, and courts have also been required to address minority rights and learning needs associated with increasing cultural and linguistic diversity produced through immigration. In the early twentieth century, provincial authorities in many cases took action to prevent or restrict the operation of schools in languages other than English or French (McLeod, 1993). Later waves of immigration, beginning with changes to liberalize immigration policy in the late 1960s, have produced new challenges as well as opportunities within education systems, such as pressures to accommodate diverse cultural practices or meet demands to provide adequate education in English or French as a second language. In many cases, contention over linguistic and minority rights has been at the core of and further facilitated by subsequent legislation, failed and successful attempts to amend the Constitution, and numerous court challenges and legal rulings in conjunction with implementation of the Canadian Charter of Rights and Freedoms in 1982. The legislation and events summarized in Box 3.4 illustrate the

Box 3.4 Language, Minority Rights, and Education in Canada: Selected Key Developments

Canada (Federal Government)

1867: Section 93 of the British North America Act allocates education as an area of provincial jurisdiction while education for Indians is designated a federal responsibility.

1876: The Indian Act outlines federal responsibilities for providing education to Indians, including terms to enable the establishment of residential schools.

1951: Amendments to the Indian Act outline provisions for transfer of responsibilities for education of status Indians to provinces and territories.

1969–70: Official Languages in Education program is established to promote second-language training in provinces and provide funds to support French-language education for francophones outside Quebec and English-language education for anglophones in Quebec; support introduced for French immersion programs.

1971: Policy of "multiculturalism within a bilingual framework" is adopted to provide support for cultural minorities and assistance to foster integration of diverse populations within Canadian society (augmented by later initiatives such as the 1977 Cultural Enrichment Program to support teaching of non-official languages).

1982: Charter of Rights and Freedoms is incorporated as part of new Constitution Act, 1982, and includes section 23, which specifies conditions to provide for second- and minority-language instruction in the provinces. More generally, and often amid extensive public controversy, the Charter increases opportunities for challenges to education and related legislation concerning religious instruction, cultural observances, and several other matters.

1988: Canadian Multiculturalism Act reaffirms and expands support for visible minorities and heritage cultures while introducing provisions to promote social equality and eliminate barriers to participation in Canadian society.

1996: The last Indian residential school (in Saskatchewan) is closed, and the *Report of the Royal Commission on Aboriginal Peoples* calls for a fundamental transformation in relations between governments, Aboriginal peoples, and non-Aboriginal peoples.

2008: Truth and Reconciliation Commission of Canada is established as part of a settlement in conjunction with a court challenge by residential school survivors against the federal government and church organizations.

Newfoundland and Labrador

Pre-Confederation: Both denominational and non-denominational schools are supported with public funding beginning in 1836, with the latter also shifted to denominational control starting in 1843.

1949: Upon union with Canada, existing rights to operate publicly funded schools are maintained by six denominations existing alongside the government-funded public education system.

1967: Controversial Royal Commission report recommending replacing denominational school boards by non-denominational boards is not implemented.

1996: Francophone school board is approved.

1998: Establishment and election of non-denominational school boards proceeds following referenda in 1995 supporting the placement of both denominational and non-denominational schools under regional boards, and stronger support in 1997 to create a single publicly funded and administered school system.

Prince Edward Island

Pre-Confederation: Non-denominational common schooling is organized but some schools operate as Roman Catholic institutions; legislation in 1852 creates a single public board of education, followed by extensive conflict over denominational rights and use of the Bible in classrooms.

1877: Public School Act outlines provisions for a non-sectarian public school system.

1972: Recognition of first francophone school district.

New Brunswick

Pre-Confederation: Non-denominational common (locally operated) schools begin in 1802 but some schools operate as Roman Catholic institutions, with legislation in 1858 authorizing grants to some of the latter.

1871: Common Schools Act is implemented, with public schools to be non-sectarian; protests, at times violent, result in limited provisions to enable support to Catholic schools.

1969: Official Languages Act permits instruction in French or English, depending on mother tongue within community, in conjunction with official designation as a bilingual province.

Nova Scotia

Pre-Confederation: Non-denominational common schooling begins in 1808 but some schools operate as Roman Catholic institutions.

1864–5: Education legislation provides framework for provincial (post-1867) public non-denominational school system; public funding for francophone schools is abolished.

1950: French is reintroduced in public schools.

1983: The last segregated black school in Canada is closed.

1998: The Mi'kmaq Education Act is the first agreement to transfer jurisdiction over education from the federal government to First Nations self-government.

Quebec

Pre-Confederation: Legislation authorizes separate Roman Catholic and Protestant school bodies in Montreal and Quebec City (1846); legal provisions establish non-denominational common schools in rest of Canada East; in addition to common schools, minority groups can elect school boards and maintain separate schools in Canada West beginning in 1841.

1869: Legislation establishes a dual (Roman Catholic/French and Protestant/English) education system.

1965: The first French immersion program is established in St-Lambert (followed over the next decade by French immersion programs throughout Canada).

continued

1966: Parent Royal Commission recommendation to replace denominational school boards with secular French and English ones is not implemented due to opposition from several sources; subsequent measures to implement secularization and challenges to these measures continue for over 30 years.

1968: Legislation enables parents to choose language of instruction for their children; public grant is introduced to eligible private or independent schools.

1977: Bill 101, requiring French as the language of instruction for kindergarten to secondary school and placing tight restrictions on entry into English-language schools, results in legal challenges from other linguistic minorities and provokes controversy across Canada.

1998: School boards based on language replace denominational boards in conjunction with federal and provincial government actions the previous year; a policy and action plan is introduced to foster intercultural education and newcomer integration.

Ontario

Pre-Confederation: Local non-denominational common schools are established in Upper Canada (1816).

1867: Rights to establish separate Protestant and Roman Catholic denominational schools are recognized under terms of BNA Act.

1913: Provincial government passes regulation to limit French-language instruction in schools.

1965: Last segregated black school in the province is closed.

1966: Canada's first community school opens in North York, focusing on school as a resource for the community even after school hours.

1968: Legislation is amended to authorize French instruction in schools with sufficient numbers of students, followed by wider legislation in 1974.

1993: Guidelines are introduced by NDP government (abandoned by a new Conservative government two years later) to develop policies on anti-racism and promote ethnocultural equity.

2001: Tax credits are brought in (repealed in 2003) for tuition paid to private schools; the issue of support for private and religious schools remains a periodic source of political debate and controversy.

Manitoba

Pre-Confederation: Both French and English school boards and schools operate (a majority of Manitoba residents were French-speaking at the time of entry into Confederation in 1870).

1871: School Act authorizes publicly supported Catholic and Protestant schools and districts.

1890: Legislation abolishes separate denominational schools in favour of a unified publicly funded non-denominational school system, resulting in protests and court challenges from francophone Catholic groups.

1896: School Act is amended to ensure hiring of Roman Catholic teachers and permit instruction in French in public schools that meet designated criteria.

1916: Rights to French-language instruction are abolished.

1967: School Act is amended to enable schools to offer instruction in French language for up to half the school day.

1970: Further amendment to School Act recognizes both French and English as languages of public school instruction, determined by student numbers.

1979: Amendment to school legislation permits instruction in bilingual programs that include languages other than English or French.

1981: Provincial grants to private schools are established.

Saskatchewan

Pre-Confederation: Denominational (Roman Catholic and Protestant) school districts are authorized within a single board of education for North-West Territories; provisions in 1901 allow some instruction in languages other than English.

1905: Legislation retains right of instruction in languages other than English but no public funds for francophone schools; the first school in a district must be a public (majority) school, but separate (minority) schools are then permitted.

1918: English is designated as the single language of instruction (although instruction in French is permitted until 1931 for students' first year at school).

1968: Along with BC, the province becomes the first outside Quebec to offer a publicly supported French immersion program.

1978: The province follows the lead of Alberta with amendment to school legislation to permit bilingual instruction in languages other than English or French.

1995: Education Act amendment enables registration of independent (private) schools.

2011: Partial provincial funding is announced for designated categories of independent schools, beginning in 2012.

Alberta

Pre-Confederation: A single board of education for North-West Territories authorizes denominational (Roman Catholic and Protestant) school districts.

1905: The first school in a district is established as a public (majority) school, but separate (minority) schools are then permitted.

1967: Alberta is the first province to establish provincial grants to private schools.

1968: School boards can authorize instruction in French for up to half of the school day.

1971: Amendment to school legislation makes Alberta the first province to permit bilingual instruction that includes languages other than English or French (initially Ukrainian and later bilingual programs in several other languages).

1988: Language Education Policy establishes guidelines for instruction in English, French, and other languages.

1990: Supreme Court ruling extends right to separate schooling and school boards for minority-language education where numbers permit, which serves as a precedent for rulings and action in other provinces.

1994–5: Legislation authorizes francophone population to manage French-language schools.

2000: Project to enhance training in French as a second language, heritage and international languages, and Aboriginal languages is initiated.

continued

British Columbia

Pre-Confederation: All public schooling is declared to be non-denominational (1865).

1872: Education Act reinforces provision of public schooling on a non-denominational basis.

1968: Along with Saskatchewan, BC becomes the first province outside Quebec to offer publicly supported French immersion program.

1977: Provincial grants to private schools are established.

1995: Language education policy guidelines reinforce English-language proficiency as the core competency, but outline provisions for instruction in French, Aboriginal languages, English as a second language, and other languages; French school board is established.

Yukon

1906: English is designated as official language.

1990: Education Act outlines provisions for French-language instruction and school boards and for instruction in Aboriginal languages.

Northwest Territories

Pre-Confederation: Denominational (Roman Catholic and Protestant) school districts are authorized within a single board of education for North-West Territories.

1906: English is designated as official language.

1969: Education authority is transferred from federal government.

Nunavut

1999: Nunavut Act includes provisions for public and separate schools, as well as instruction in Inuktitut languages.

Sources: Information compiled from federal, provincial, and territorial government websites, and from Cummins and Danesi (1990); Tetley (1982); Manzer (2003: 40–55ff.); Wilson et al. (1970); Young et al. (2007).

prominent role language, religion, and minority rights issues have played at specific junctures in the development of education systems within Canada.

Educational Expansion in the Post–World War II Period (1940s–1970s)

The role of schooling in society increased in complexity throughout the twentieth century. The dynamic growth of education systems was accompanied by extensive reconsideration and debate concerning the purposes of education in a changing society. Educational practices expanded in two general ways. First, an increasing array of educational institutions, programs, and curricula emerged, incorporating a broad range of courses and subject areas not previously taught. Second, growing numbers of people enrolled in educational programs and remained in them for longer periods of time. The result has been massive increases in enrolments and educational attainments since the end of World War II. At the same time, significant changes occurred in the nature and quality of schooling. For the most part, classrooms were better equipped, teachers were better qualified, and curricular offerings were more diverse than ever before.

Formal education also gained an increasingly central place in social and economic life beyond the schools. Three interrelated developments—the Cold War, scientific and technical advancement, and the growth of the **welfare state**—had a profound impact on schooling after World War II. Canada, to a certain extent echoing concerns expressed in the United States about the growing influence of the Soviet Union and the possible spread of communism, turned to the education system as a mechanism to ensure citizenship, loyalty, and a knowledge base that would protect the supremacy of North American interests. The war effort had also contributed to highly co-ordinated, productive economic output in many industries, making it possible to invest in new technologies, advanced skills formation, and various forms of state services to stabilize social order and foster social security. By the mid-twentieth century, formal education gained increasing recognition as a credentialling mechanism. The attainment of educational certification became a mark of entry into specific occupations and jobs, in some cases involving requirements for advanced education and training beyond minimal levels previously associated with initial entry into the labour force.

New employment opportunities were created in a context of rising industrial productivity, mass distribution of consumer goods and services, and the expansion of employment in human services through the growth of the state sector. At the same time, educational achievement and the attainment of stable jobs with good wages and working conditions were closely related. Social reformers also looked to schools as sites where people could be taught to develop interests that would enable them to use their leisure time and meet the diverse demands of advanced liberal democracies more fruitfully.

By the 1960s, formal education appeared to be well positioned to fulfill its promise to contribute to a more equitable social order. Educational expansion, combined with favourable social and economic circumstances, suggested that all persons, regardless of social background, had potential opportunities for social and economic advancement.

Although there was considerable reason to be optimistic, heightened emphasis on the value of schooling prompted a reassessment of educational realities that claimed education could not always deliver what it promised. Beginning in the late 1950s, as observed in the previous chapter, several studies framed within what came to be known as status attainment research highlighted the continuing association of schooling with substantial socio-economic inequalities. Moreover, people's life experiences did not always accord with emergent expectations. As schooling and the ideologies surrounding its social benefits gained in prominence, it became easy to blame individuals for their failure to take advantage of opportunities for socio-economic advancement.

However, schooling itself also proved to be vulnerable to criticism. On one side critics like Hilda Neatby (1953), in her controversial *So Little for the Mind*, attacked schools for straying from their intellectual roots by catering to an overly broad range of interests. The problem, viewed from this perspective, was that schooling was becoming too diverse, weakening its ability to provide a common core of essential knowledge and values. Other critics, by contrast, maintained that schools were not keeping pace with changing socio-economic realities. They saw it as essential for schools to offer socially relevant knowledge, vocational training, and courses related to new employment requirements. These demands intensified after 1957, when the Soviet Union's launch of the Sputnik satellite prompted fears that North America was losing its technological advantage. Educational institutions came under fire for their failure to produce technically sophisticated and innovative graduates.

Elementary and secondary schools responded by revamping their curricula to emphasize programs in mathematics and the natural sciences. Enhancement of scientific and technical training, prompted by federal funding initiatives, also fuelled postsecondary educational expansion. Nationally, the number of bachelor's degrees awarded in mathematics and the physical sciences increased substantially, from 1,617 in 1960–1 to 7,730 a decade later (Dominion Bureau of Statistics, 1963; Statistics Canada, 1973). Enrolment was encouraged by the addition of programs and research facilities to existing institutions as well as by the creation of several new technical institutes and community colleges throughout the nation. Between 1960 and 1970, education spending increased from 14 per cent of all government expenditures in Canada to 21.6 per cent (Lockhart, 1979: 229), and by 1975 there were 170 public community colleges in Canada compared to just one a decade earlier (Dennison, 1981: 213).

The expansion of the welfare state and focus on scientific training helped fuel the growth of **post-secondary education** in the 1960s and 1970s as demands increased for educated professionals and for workers in the social and human services and in skilled scientific occupations. In Canada, the number of bachelor's degrees awarded in education increased 5.8 times between 1960–1 and 1970–1, while those in law increased by a factor of 5.2 times, those in nursing 4 times, and those in the physical sciences 4.9 times; over the next decade, the number of social work degrees awarded increased by nearly 5 times. Educational and occupational growth in these areas was especially important for providing opportunities for women. The proportion of bachelor's and first professional degrees awarded to women doubled from one-quarter to one-half between 1960–1 and 1980–1. By 1980–1, women received 73.5 per cent of Bachelor of Education degrees (compared to 37.2 per cent in 1960–1), 77.3 per cent of Bachelor of Social Work degrees (44.3 per cent in 1960–1), and nearly all of the degrees awarded in nursing. While only 5 per cent of recipients of Bachelor of Law degrees in 1960–1 were women, that proportion had climbed to over 33 per cent two decades later. By contrast, however, women received only 8.4 per cent of bachelor's degrees awarded in engineering and applied sciences, and 29.6 per cent of first degrees in mathematics and physical sciences in 1980–1 (calculated from Dominion Bureau of Statistics, 1963: 22, 44–9; Statistics Canada, 1973: 456–8; Statistics Canada, 1984: 69–74).

These trends illustrate the strong paradox that characterizes formal education. Expansion of post-secondary education after World War II offered legitimacy to the belief that formal education could provide individuals with meaningful social and economic opportunities. The attainment of higher education credentials not only enabled individuals to gain access to secure and well-paying jobs, but it also opened up possibilities previously unavailable to women and members of other minority groups. At the same time, the issues of who could achieve educational success and what kinds

International Case Study

Alternative Educational Practices for Social Justice

Many of the strongest demands for supporting alternatives to mass public schooling have been associated with conservative groups and libertarian advocates of private, religious, or home-based schooling. The long and rich history of various educational models, ranging from early childhood education to adult learning and literacy movements in the United States and Canada, reveals that this is not always the case. The progressive movement in education, beginning in the late nineteenth century, rejected traditional schooling that emphasized reading, writing, and discipline in favour of curiosity-driven classrooms that fostered social engagement. The participatory community-based work of sociologist Jane Addams was particularly important for inspiring John Dewey and other scholars at the University of Chicago to link education with skills and reforms that addressed pressing social matters related to poverty, services for immigrants, women's and children's rights, and other critical issues rather than technical concerns. Progressive educational ideologies, though stripped of many of the initial core principles and modified in other ways, motivated liberal curricular reforms (as well as extensive critical backlash) in North American schools in the mid-twentieth century, and continue to inform the aims of alternative schools in many communities (see, e.g., Cremin, 1988: 174ff.; Spring, 2011: 207ff.).

Schools guided by principles derived from British and European educational models or philosophies emphasizing self-discovery and self-directed learning or creative expression, such as Summerhill, Montessori, Waldorf, and Reggio Emilia, operate in many provinces and states. Many communities across North America have also given rise to more radical educational movements that pursue commitment to social justice, socialism, and other progressive values in part through instruction to promote literacy, basic skill development, and critical engagement with other community members. While these schools encompass a disparate and often bewildering range of influences, histories, and experiences, they have often overlapped or shared some common influences or key personnel. Some of the best-known or most representative cases include the following:

- Arbeter Ring (Workmen's Circle), I.L. Peretz, and other radical Jewish schools were introduced in many North American cities at the beginning of the twentieth century, combining teaching of Yiddish language and Jewish cultural heritage with activities to promote socialism and social justice. The Jewish progressive school movement is often associated most strongly with New York and other American cities that had large Jewish populations, but many active and successful programs, ranging from kindergarten to high school and evening programs, were established in Montreal, Winnipeg, Toronto, and

continued

other Canadian cities. Many of the schools and related programs closed or fragmented due to external pressures or internal disagreements over the schools' mandates, resulting especially in the abandonment or softening of their radical roots. Nonetheless, the legacy of these roots is evident in schools, learning activities, and organizations that remain active in many communities (Gonick, 2010; Tulchinsky, 2008: 124ff.).

- Highlander Folk School was established in Tennessee in the early 1930s, influenced by folk schools introduced in Denmark in the nineteenth century to foster rural development. At Highlander, adult learners gained basic literacy skills while establishing social connections and competencies that would enable them to mobilize to take action to promote workers' rights and address poverty and other fundamental social problems. Although each had unique and sometimes conflicting orientations, schools that shared the goal of expanding higher education and democratic engagement among industrial workers were also introduced into many other regions of the United States in the early twentieth century (Cobb, 2000; Horton and Freire, 1990; Longo, 2007).

- In Canada, a long history of co-operative and adult education combining collective community organization and critical pedagogies includes several notable examples. The Antigonish Movement, begun at St Francis Xavier University under the leadership of two priests, Fathers Moses Coady and James Tompkins, was a response to social and economic problems in the Maritimes during the Great Depression. Frontier College, originally the Reading Camp Association, was founded at the beginning of the twentieth century by a Presbyterian minister to introduce literacy and basic learning skills to labourers in northern Ontario lumber camps and other remote areas, and in more recent years it has reached into Aboriginal communities. In addition, several Folk Schools in Ontario and the Prairies have been informed by a spirit of co-operation and local engagement to meet local educational, economic, and social needs (Parsey and Friesen, 1953; Selman et al., 1997). In many communities, participatory action, informal learning practices, and activities organized in conjunction with local and indigenous knowledge systems continue to mobilize participants for social change while offering connections with knowledge, skills, and competencies beyond those within narrowly defined formal or technical criteria.

- Freedom Schools were introduced in Mississippi and other southern states in the 1960s to advance the goals of the civil rights movement. These schools promoted literacy skills, civic participation, and mobilization for social change within black communities, informed by principles and practices drawn from other radical adult education and leadership training programs including Highlander, where Rosa Parks, Martin Luther King, and other prominent civil rights leaders had visited or participated in workshops. More recently, the Freedom

School model has been revived in conjunction with the Children's Defence Fund in order to provide educational opportunities, youth leadership skills, and social justice engagement in communities with limited educational and economic resources (Cobb, 2000; Hale, 2007; Payne, 2003).

These examples represent only a small sample of diverse learning initiatives and schooling models undertaken within the North American context. Some have disappeared or been nearly forgotten, while others have thrived, continued in modified form, or inspired new initiatives. Education debates and discussion stand to gain considerable insights by exploring the full spectrum of educational developments and experiences.

Discussion Questions

1. What are the common elements of the schools and educational practices described in this case study? Discuss the extent to which these common features are or are not compatible with the aims and practices of mass public schooling.

2. Look for historical records and materials related to any one of these initiatives, or describe a similar initiative in your own community. Discuss the core aims and objectives of the initiative you are exploring, and identify factors related to its success as well as impediments to its success. How can understandings derived from this example be used to inform discussions about contemporary educational reform?

of educational programs were available to different groups remained problematic. As formal education was relied on more frequently as a screening mechanism for entry into jobs and other social venues, disadvantaged groups were in danger of being left even further behind. Social advancement became that much more difficult for people who, for various reasons, were denied educational success. Moreover, as revealed in the distribution of university degrees to men and women, education itself remained highly stratified, producing different opportunities and career prospects for different social groups. While increasing numbers of people were attaining higher levels of formal education, considerable discrepancies existed in the kinds of benefits that people received from their educational credentials.

Educational Crisis and Reassessment since the mid-1970s

Debate and controversy over educational priorities were not restricted to labour markets and credentials. The increasing centrality of education to social life drew attention also to the educational process and to people's experiences within educational institutions. By the end of the 1960s, popular demands for educational reform intensified in an atmosphere characterized by sensitivity to drastic social changes and critical questioning of fundamental social institutions. Technological developments altered

Box 3.5 Education Problems in Canada, 1958

After World War II, educators, policy-makers, and media reports highlighted the need to link education with technological advancement. Following the development of nuclear weapons and the launch of the Sputnik satellite by Russia, educational reformers advocated the adoption of education systems like those in the Soviet Union and other nations, and increased investment in human capital, to encourage the expansion of scientific and technical expertise. In 1958, the Canadian Teachers' Federation, the Canadian Manufacturers' Association, the Canadian Labour Congress, and other organizations sponsored a national Conference on Education, described here by the then-president of the British Columbia Teachers' Federation (Cottingham, 1958: 398–9, 407), to reassess educational practices and establish new educational priorities:

> For years people closely connected with education have been increasingly alarmed about the magnitude of the task which we have set ourselves in Canada—to provide the maximum formal education at public expense for every man's child. Perhaps those with most reason to be alarmed at the growing crisis have been the teachers and professors who face their classes every day and know to what extent the time and talents of students and instructors are being wasted or used to best advantage, despite the rising costs of education. Never in the history of our country have so many boys and girls been kept in school and university so long at such great expense as now. Never have teachers and professors been in such short supply. Never have their tasks been so heavy. Never has the supply of well prepared professional, industrial, and technological workers been so far short of the needs of our society.
>
> No matter how critical the problem, in a democratic nation the solution must await the awakening of public opinion and only through the time-consuming democratic process can action be effected. . . .
>
> This conference was planned long before USSR launched its Sputniks into outer space, but these evidences of scientific achievement on the part of our

how people lived and worked. Media coverage of international events, particularly US involvement in the Vietnam War, made startlingly evident the significance of global events for everyday life. University campuses and other educational sites were crucial nurturing grounds for the emergence of anti-war protests, radical student movements, and feminism. Many of the concerns were motivated by increasing awareness of the reality that graduates were not getting the kinds of jobs and social opportunities they felt they had been promised through education.

Schooling, in this context, came under attack from nearly all sides. Left-wing and radical movements, while often mobilized and empowered by educational experiences, dismissed schooling as a bastion of bureaucratic traditionalism that stifled, rather than enhanced, creativity and genuine opportunity. The ideas of such writers as Ivan Illich (1970), who advocated alternatives to schooling that required the dismantling of the present education system, gained popularity as well as notoriety both within and beyond educational circles. From the right, critics argued that social radicalism both northern neighbor increased the significance of this national discussion on the problems of education in Canada, where our strange scale of values causes us to spend twice as much on liquor and tobacco as we do on formal education and almost four times as much on defense.

Dr Wilder Penfield, distinguished brain specialist and Director of the Conference, gave the keynote address. "Dissatisfaction with the support of education and the performance of educationists has led to this meeting," he said, "and the educationists have it in their power to mould our future." Dr Penfield had visited USSR two years ago. There he found the prestige and the level of pay for teachers and professors considerably higher comparatively than they are in Canada. Russia had a better system of scholarships for its able students and its training of prospective teachers and university professors was far more rigid and exacting. However, he suspected that in Russia students specialize too early without being grounded in the humanities.

"The specialist who has a broader educational basis leads a better life." At the same time Dr Penfield felt that more emphasis should be put on trade schools and technical colleges in Canada.

He set the whole problem squarely before the delegates when he said:

"Looking to the future we face two possibilities: the ending of this civilization such as it is, or its final flowering and fulfillment in greater progress. Education is our only hope, our challenge in the peaceful competition of the future. But, if war should come, our wits might well save us. We would be well advised to spend on the cultivation of those wits a sum comparable with what we are spending on explosive defense." Especially in the field of higher education, Dr Penfield felt that financial support must be doubled, but that support must leave these institutions complete freedom of development. Responsibility for support of teaching at all educational levels rests with the provinces, but industry, labor and the federal government could provide scholarships. . . .

Source: Reprinted with permission from the BC Teachers' Federation.

produced and was a product of educational failure. Formal education had strayed from its disciplinary and instrumental purposes, according to this viewpoint, and needed to return to fundamental values, knowledge, and respect for authority in order to prevent social breakdown.

Officially, though, the most successful educational ideology was embodied in liberal and human capital positions. Educators as well as policy-makers revealed renewed interest in issues of equality of opportunity and educational progressivism, modified to meet contemporary demands. Several influential reports presented in the late 1960s and early 1970s, such as those known popularly as the Hall-Dennis Report in Ontario (1968) and the Worth Report in Alberta (1972), stressed that child-centred learning opportunities and educational flexibility were crucial elements in people's ability to adapt to a changing society.

The spirit of change embodied in recommendations contained within the various reports was translated into a flurry of initiatives to restructure schooling and educational practices across Canada. Where resources were sufficient, students were presented with many new options beyond the traditional core curricula in areas such as law, family life, sex education, band and music appreciation, psychology, creative arts, and social studies. The goal was to broaden their development and to better prepare them for the diverse demands of a post-industrial society. Experimental and innovative practices were encouraged in educational circles to overcome what came to be regarded as overly rigid and outmoded pedagogical models based on military and industrial principles. Schools were designed or modified to incorporate open classrooms and learning resource centres to counteract the rigid, box-like structure of existing school spatial organization; boundaries between disciplinary subjects and grade levels were broken down; student evaluation and reporting emphasized a wide range of skills, competencies, and subjective observations rather than strictly letter or numerical grades; and teachers were encouraged to draw out the child through critical thinking and social interaction rather than focus strictly on cognitive knowledge and prescribed curricular content.

Some of the changes had immediate impacts on educational practices and outcomes. Curricular revisions and modification of programs and practices to meet local needs or to improve responsiveness to disadvantaged groups, for instance, were long overdue. However, there was considerable resistance to the process of change, and in many cases little evidence could be found to support widespread perceptions that schooling was being transformed in fundamental ways. Many teachers felt that educational reforms had been imposed on them with little consultation and inadequate training and resources to implement them properly. Traditionalists pointed to the chaos, wasted time, and lack of tangible results as evidence that educational liberalization was a drastic failure, which provoked demands for centralized curricula with a "back to the basics" emphasis. Still other critics pointed out that the changes, as dramatic as they appeared to be, were mostly cosmetic and did not reach the real sources of social and educational problems, thereby perpetuating socio-economic inequalities and failing to acknowledge that school-age individuals and their needs were undergoing transitions (Tomkins, 1981: 147–9). "In short," as one commentator observed in the early 1970s, "having failed to satisfy the exaggerated expectations created by its promoters, education is now enjoying an excess of abuse for its considerable shortcomings" (Myers, 1973: 11).

A recurrent problem with educational reform has been that too much attention was focused inside the education system without consideration of crucial social, economic, and political factors that limited what formal schooling could do. Initiatives like the ones outlined above, which were intended to broaden the scope of education, were introduced during a period of fiscal restraint and reorganization of public services. Debate over educational goals and relevance exposed education as a vulnerable target for state measures to control public expenditures (Lockhart, 1979). From the late 1960s into the early 1970s, governments took several steps to contain education, including legislated reductions to wages and costs in the education sector and more centralized control over educational decision-making. Teachers' organizations in several provinces, notably British Columbia, Ontario, and Quebec, became increasingly militant in response to the deterioration of teaching and working conditions (LeBlanc, 1974; Repo, 1974). Symptomatic of the position of education generally, teachers felt that they were being made scapegoats for much deeper social and economic problems.

The nature and form of public education remained a core focus of political struggle throughout the 1980s and 1990s. Governments had to contend with significant economic and social transformations, including desires by firms and investors for easy access to the most profitable markets, aging population structures, and competitive pressures from rapidly developing regions of the world. In this context, neo-liberal policy agendas gained ascendancy in many parts of Canada and other nations, frequently targeting education in a series of measures to reduce public expenditures, limit the size of state activity and employment, and expand market-based forms of competition. By the mid-1990s, the volatile atmosphere was captured in a proliferation of media accounts under headlines like "What's Wrong with Our Schools?" as well as in popular literature that carried such titles as *Class Warfare: The Assault on Canada's Schools* (Barlow and Robertson, 1994), *School's Out: The Catastrophe in Public Education and What We Can Do About It* (Nikiforuk, 1993), and *Busting Bureaucracy to Reclaim Our Schools* (Lawton, 1995). Teachers' fears that their profession and schools were under assault were not assuaged by declining birth rates and public concerns that schools based on models designed several generations previously had become redundant for life in a global age. The next chapter explores how these issues have influenced the reshaping of education into the twenty-first century.

Conclusion

This chapter has traced educational development in Canada from an array of practices organized around specific familial, cultural, and local circumstances and requirements to the massive, complex, and often highly contested mélange of public and private enterprises that schooling represented at the end of the twentieth century. The core framework for formal education in Canada, taking shape over several decades, was cemented by the early 1970s when an expanding array of post-secondary institutions and early childhood educational programs augmented the consolidated school systems that delivered compulsory elementary and secondary programs. In the process, formal education systems have grown to encompass a diverse range of participants, curricular programs, and social learning experiences far beyond those that appeared in the earliest schools.

Ongoing economic, labour market, and policy transformations continue to have profound impacts on people's working and private lives (Li, 1996: 136–45; Clement and Vosko, 2003). During the periods highlighted in the last sections of this chapter, demands for both low-skill and highly qualified labour have increased in conjunction with growth in service industries relative to manufacturing and primary industries. Economic and social changes have contributed to shifting social relations and divisions of labour in both the workplace and households. Women's labour force participation rates, now close to two-thirds of all women ages 15 and over, increased steadily, from 20 per cent in 1941 to 40 per cent in 1971 and 60 per cent by 1991. Canada has also imported substantial numbers of workers and family members from other nations, turning since the late 1960s from a focus on Western European and American immigrant sources to Asia, Africa, the Middle East, and the Caribbean to meet demands for highly skilled and professional labour. In the early 1970s, multiculturalism emerged as a new policy emphasis that, along with political demands for recognition of unique rights for francophones and Aboriginal peoples, has been associated with periodic political tensions around race and ethnic relations as well as questions about national unity and relations between individual and collective rights.

Other demographic shifts have affected schooling through changes in the size, concentration, and composition of student populations. The high enrolments that accompanied baby boomers and their children through the education system have given way to declining enrolments in many elementary and secondary school systems and concerns about longer-term prospects for post-secondary enrolments. The increasing urban concentration of the Canadian population, as well as other demographic changes, has had an uneven impact on the ability of school districts to provide adequate and equitable services for all students. The growing concentration of immigrant populations in larger cities, for instance, poses a demand both for increased institutional space and for programming and services that address the needs of diverse student bodies.

The educational changes described in this chapter represent part of a broad reshaping of social, economic, and political landscapes that have affected the character of the nation and the experiences of individuals. These domains and the world they are part of have become simultaneously more specialized and more highly interconnected. Today, public and policy focus on a knowledge society has offered prospects for formal educational institutions and educators to regain much of the respectability and fiscal stability that appeared to be lost at the end of the twentieth century. Nonetheless, this promise is accompanied by significant challenges as educational stakes increase and educational participants and relationships become more diverse.

Annotated Further Readings

Axelrod, Paul. 1997. *The Promise of Schooling: Education in Canada, 1800–1914.* Toronto: University of Toronto Press. Axelrod provides a concise overview of the early history of education in Canada, emphasizing how education has been shaped by and has affected complex class, gender, racial, ethnic, cultural, and political factors.

Curtis, Bruce. 1988. *Building the Educational State: Canada West, 1836–1871.* London, ON: Althouse Press. Focusing on a crucial period of educational history in Canada, the author offers a sociological analysis of the dynamics associated with the establishment of public education within the broader process of state formation.

Gidney, R.D., and W.P.J. Millar. 2012. *How Schools Worked: Public Education in English Canada, 1900–1940.* Montreal and Kingston: McGill-Queen's University Press. The authors approach a significant period in the development of modern education systems in Canada by focusing on school environments and the characteristics of those who participated in them.

Lawr, Douglas A., and Robert D. Gidney. 1973. *Educating Canadians: A Documentary History of Public Education.* Toronto: Van Nostrand Reinhold. This rich resource contains policy statements, legislation, administrative documents, and submissions from parents and other community representatives pertinent to key issues and phases in the development of formal education systems in Canada.

Manzer, Ronald A. 1994. *Public Schools and Political Ideas: Canadian Educational Policy in Historical Perspective.* Toronto: University of Toronto Press. The author examines the development of Canadian education through the interaction of political, economic, and ideological forces.

Truth and Reconciliation Commission of Canada. 2012. *They Came for the Children: Canada, Aboriginal Peoples and Residential Schools.* Winnipeg: Truth and Reconciliation Commission of Canada. The interim report of Canada's Truth and

Reconciliation Commission is essential reading for all Canadians. Introduced by a history of residential school policy and practice, the report details residential school experiences, providing a solid context in which to understand the consequences for Aboriginal individuals, families, and communities.

Key Terms

Curriculum Programs, courses, and materials arranged and presented formally to meet the objectives of educational institutions.

Educational progressivism An educational movement based on the progressive philosophy that the development of humans, as individuals and societies, advances through the broad cultivation of intellectual, physical, and emotional growth. Popularized in the "child-centred" orientation of John Dewey early in the twentieth century, the approach has influenced many school reforms since the late 1960s.

Indigenous knowledge Systems of knowledge and ways of knowing, premised on the interrelationships among humans with one another and the environments of which they are part, transmitted among generations through integrated cultural traditions and social systems.

Moral regulation Processes by which notions of right and wrong, and the sense of how to act in ways deemed to be socially appropriate, are internalized as part of individual personalities.

Post-secondary education Formal education leading to degrees, certificates, or diplomas beyond high school graduation levels, normally through universities, community colleges, or other accredited institutions.

Public education Educational institutions and programs organized, administered, and funded by governments or state agencies.

State apparatus Institutions, agencies, and regulations established, organized, and administered by governments.

Welfare state A policy framework in which governments, rather than individuals, families, or other agencies, are responsible for ensuring the economic security and physical and social well-being of all citizens, including a network of government institutions organized to carry out major social welfare and development functions.

Study Questions

1. How and why did elementary and secondary schooling in Canada and comparable nations become organized through the state rather than privately?

2. Which social and economic factors have had the greatest impact on the massive expansion of education systems and educational attainment levels over the past five decades?

3. What factors contributed to increasing stabilization of education systems in Canada over time? What difficulties did these systems and their advocates encounter in the process?

4. What are some of the main visions of schooling advanced by different groups or interests in the development of Canada's education system?

Which of these have been most influential in the shape that education has taken, and why?

5. How is schooling portrayed in mass media newspapers, influential blog sites, and television reports? Select a prominent education-related issue, and indicate what it reveals about the state of contemporary education compared to that of a century ago.

6. Critically discuss the relationship between public education and minority groups in the development of education in Canada. What have been some of the major issues in these relations, and how, if at all, have they been resolved?

Chapter 4

The Structure of Canadian Education Systems

Learning Objectives

In this chapter, you will:

- be introduced to the main characteristics of Canadian educational institutions and systems;
- gain an understanding of the major debates over educational organization and the alternatives presented by different groups;
- learn to identify, understand, and explain some of the major similarities and differences between Canadian education systems and those in other nations.

Introduction

This chapter examines the nature and organization of contemporary educational activities in Canada, focusing primarily on the structure and core dimensions associated with formal education. In Canada, formal education is a collection of diverse systems rather than a single system. The previous chapter emphasized how most formal education has been regulated and operated through the state, although there is increasing pressure to deregulate and privatize educational services. Here, we consider the arrangements by which education in Canada is regulated and delivered, and summarize key trends associated with educational enrolments, expenditures, and organizational patterns. While much of the focus is descriptive, the discussion points to emerging themes and controversies, many of which are addressed in more detail in subsequent chapters. The chapter closes with a brief discussion of comparative educational trends, pointing to debates and issues surrounding educational reform in the context of major social and economic transformations.

An Overview of Educational Activities in Canada

Canadians engage in a broad and expanding range of educational activities. The discussion in this chapter and throughout the book emphasizes *formal education*, that is, organized study through state-certified institutions aimed towards the achievement of a degree, diploma, or certificate. Nonetheless, it is important to acknowledge that growing emphasis on lifelong learning, educational choice, and knowledge societies has been accompanied by increased participation in and interaction among diverse forms of educational practices for nearly all members of industrially developed societies. These include *non-formal and adult education*, which refers to courses, educational activities, and training programs organized through clubs, associations, and workplaces to augment formal credentials or to meet selected personal or employment-related needs and interests. Another significant type of educational activity, **informal learning**, generally encompasses all learning activities that occur outside of formally organized educational sites. Informal learning normally focuses on the acquisition of specific knowledge or skills in ways that are more structured than the everyday or incidental learning that occurs through socialization processes (Livingstone, 2004: 14).

In Canada, formal education is a provincial jurisdiction under the terms of the Constitution Act, 1867, and the subsequent Constitution Act, 1982. However, in practice, several agencies and levels of government are involved in the organization and delivery of education. Much of the responsibility for the actual delivery of educational services rests at the local level. School boards, along with recently recognized First Nations educational authorities, generally are accorded the most active role in the day-to-day operations of elementary and secondary schools. Both public and private interests operate post-secondary educational institutions, which are supported by a combination of grants from federal and provincial governments, tuition fees, and funds from corporate and private sources. Increases at all levels in the number of private schools, training institutes, and programs, and the expansion of educational programs outside formal educational institutions, have added to the diversity of educational service providers in Canada.

Because so many different levels of government and non-government agencies are involved in education, Canada does not have a single unified education system. Diverse institutions and jurisdictions share with one another several major educational characteristics, with a long-term tendency towards greater convergence, but as observed in the previous chapter, each one also possesses unique features.

Figure 4.1 provides a broad overview of the structure of formal education in Canada. The diagram indicates the general transition process followed by individuals through major levels of the education system. The pathways depicted in the figure provide a simple, formal description of the general organization of education in relation to labour markets; the boundaries and flows that describe the actual patterns of transitions across different sites of learning, work, and social experience are becoming increasingly more fluid and complex, as will be discussed in Chapter 7.

Elementary and secondary schooling constitutes the largest component of the education system. Most students are introduced to formal education systems through kindergarten, which normally begins at ages 5 to 6, but increasing numbers of children are engaged in preschool programs offered by provincial systems or privately as kindergarten is expanded from half days to full days in a growing number of jurisdictions. Elementary schooling typically continues from kindergarten to Grades 6, 7, or 8 in most provinces and territories. Curricula at this level tend to focus on a limited number of subjects, where all pupils are exposed to core areas, including language, mathematics, science, social studies, creative arts, physical education, and a few other options. In the early grades, students often receive instruction from only one or two teachers. More distinct boundaries between subjects and exposure to greater numbers of teachers generally prevail by the middle grades. Most provinces and territories classify Grades 7 to 9 as the middle or junior high school level, which provides students with a transition period into high school, though this is not universally the case. The junior or middle grades are classified as Grades 6 to 8 in the New Brunswick English school system, 6 to 9 in Saskatchewan, and 5 to 8 in Manitoba, while the transition

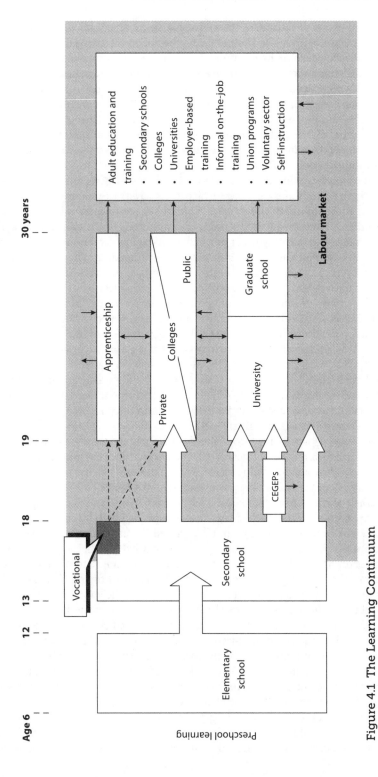

Figure 4.1 The Learning Continuum

Source: Reprinted from Industry Canada (1992: 17). Reproduced with permission from the Minister of Public Works and Government Services Canada 1997.

from elementary to secondary school occurs after Grade 6 for most Quebec schools and after Grade 9 in British Columbia and the Yukon (Statistics Canada, 2011a: 90).

Secondary or senior high school, which normally continues to Grade 12, is organized around more distinct subject areas, providing core courses and electives associated with specific streams tailored to requirements and interests for academic, vocational, career, and other paths. High school graduation is generally required for admission into post-secondary educational programs. In Quebec, however, students proceed from Grade 11 to programs in a CEGEP (Collège d'enseignement général et professionnel) that are preparatory for entry to either university education or particular vocations.

Post-secondary education includes universities, which are institutions that grant degrees, and community colleges, which offer diverse programs that may lead to transfer to a university program or to diploma certification. Once they are accredited through provincial legislation, post-secondary institutions usually are granted considerable autonomy to set programs and course requirements, hire faculty or instructors, and establish and enforce academic standards. The traditional distinctions between universities and colleges are blurring as increasing numbers of colleges expand their academic offerings. Several provinces and territories also are transforming colleges into universities or accrediting them with degree granting status as "university colleges" to promote agendas for enhanced university graduation rates. Trades or vocational training incorporates specific programs, usually of short-term duration, as well as longer apprenticeship programs combining work experience with classroom training, that are oriented to qualification for specific trades or occupations. High school graduation has not always been required as a prerequisite for many of these programs, but this is changing as trades/vocational training encompasses more specialized knowledge and skills and is integrated into the post-secondary level (for details, see Statistics Canada, 2011a: 87–8).

The trends depicted in Figures 4.2 and 4.3 offer a sense of perspective on changing patterns in educational enrolments and expenditures since the mid-twentieth century. The figures illustrate the significant increases in the size and cost, as well as the shifting composition, of the education system since the early 1950s.

Demographic changes have had a profound impact on educational enrolments and expenditures. Student numbers rose sharply as children born in the post-war baby boom reached school age and progressed through different stages of schooling from the mid-1950s to the early 1970s. Somewhat less markedly, the subsequent progression of baby boomers' children through schooling into the 1980s and 1990s maintained elementary and secondary school enrolment figures close to the historical high point reached in 1970–1. By the early 1970s—the point at which educational expenditures reached their highest levels as a proportion of the gross national product—individuals from the baby-boom cohort were graduating from high school and entering universities, community colleges, and trade programs. Declining birth rates since the mid-1960s have been partly offset by the tendency for more people to stay in school for longer periods of time and by high immigration levels, but total student numbers in elementary and secondary levels have been declining since the late 1990s.

Another striking characteristic of the trends depicted in Figures 4.2 and 4.3 is the growing significance of post-secondary education. Universities and community colleges began to establish a strong presence by the late 1960s, with significant growth since that time, especially at the university level, as enrolments have roughly doubled

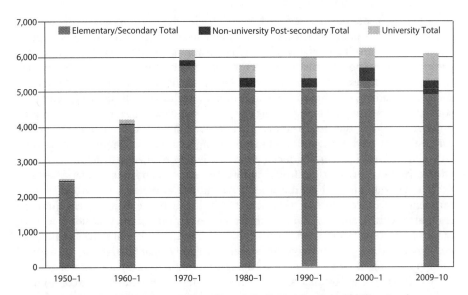

Figure 4.2 Full-Time Enrolment in Canada (000s) by Level of Study

Sources: 1950–1 to 1970–1: compiled from Statistics Canada, *Historical Compendium of Education Statistics* (Ottawa: Minister of Industry, Trade and Commerce, 1978), Catalogue no. 81–568; 1975–6 to 2000–1: compiled from Statistics Canada, *Education Quarterly Review* (Ottawa: Minister of Industry, Science and Technology, various issues), Catalogue no. 81–003; 2009–10: compiled from Statistics Canada (2011b, 2013) and CAUT (2012: 39).

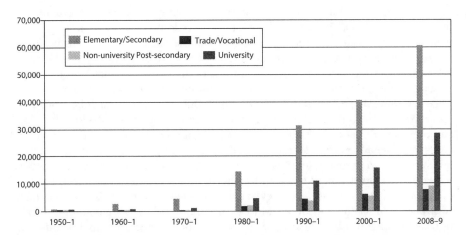

Figure 4.3 Education Expenditures by Level, Canada, Selected Years, 1950–1 to 2008–9

Note: Figures for 2008–9 are estimates and include 2009–10 data for non-university post-secondary. Sources: 1950–1 to 1970–1: compiled from Statistics Canada, *Historical Compendium of Education Statistics* (Ottawa: Minister of Industry, Trade and Commerce, 1978), Catalogue no. 81–568; 1980–1: compiled from Statistics Canada, *Education in Canada* (Ottawa: Minister of Supply and Services Canada, various years), Catalogue no. 81–229; 1990–1 to 2000–1: compiled from Statistics Canada (2011a: Table B1); 2008–9: compiled and estimated from data in Statistics Canada and CMEC (2012b: Tables B1.1.1 and B2.1) and CAUT (2012: 2, 5).

in each 20-year period since the mid-1960s. While Chapter 7 discusses the implications of post-secondary expansion for different social groups, for now it is important to observe how increasing emphasis on educational priorities is reflected in these patterns of educational growth. One way to understand this is to look at Figure 4.3, which demonstrates, in comparison with Figure 4.2, first, that the amount of money spent by Canadians on education has risen even more dramatically than the number of students and, second, that the funding for post-secondary education has grown even more rapidly over the period under consideration. The disproportionate expenditures reflect, in part, the fact that education at higher levels costs more because post-secondary education typically includes more highly qualified instructors as well as additional costs for infrastructural support, laboratories and research facilities, and other operating costs. These increased expenditures also reveal the growing commitment, especially since the 1960s and 1970s, to investment in higher education associated with an emphasis on human capital development and expansion of a post-industrial or knowledge-based economy in which individuals and governments have been more inclined to promote investment in highly qualified labour. Substantial funding, enhanced by new expenditure programs supported by the federal government, facilitated the introduction of new institutions and programs at the community college and university levels to promote the development of knowledge and workers, particularly in scientific and technical fields. Since the early 1990s, the federal government, in common with most other highly developed nations, has elevated education and learning-related activities to a major priority as part of its innovation strategy to undertake investment for a knowledge-based economy (Wolfe, 2002).

Funding

The data in Table 4.1 and Figure 4.4 indicate the changing basis of educational finance in Canada since 1950. The most striking feature is predominance of public, or government, funding of education relative to private sources. Consistent with constitutional responsibility for jurisdiction over education, over half of all spending on education is by provincial and territorial governments. Until the 1980s, provincial governments assumed growing fiscal responsibility for education, although patterns have varied since that time. While several recent government initiatives and fiscal policies seem to indicate the likelihood of a continuing pattern of downloading of costs for education and other social spending programs to both local and private sources, there is also a counter-tendency towards centralization of educational planning and programming both federally and provincially. It is likely that further variations in these patterns will occur as governments move to streamline expenditures and consolidate their spheres of operations. Since the late 1990s, several provinces have adopted measures to tighten control over educational spending. Most of these reforms have sought to limit discretionary funding by school boards, to cut back on the number of school boards (see Table 4.2), and to ensure that public bodies are more accountable to those who pay for government services (Council of Ministers of Education Canada, 2001: 18–19). They have also sought to place limits on teachers' salaries and other personnel costs associated with education while relying more heavily on private sources to fund education and education-related activities.

Patterns of educational spending, organization, and reform vary considerably from one jurisdiction to another. The data in Table 4.2 illustrate some of the unique characteristics that emerge through specific demographic, historical, and social compositions

Table 4.1 Total and Relative Expenditures ($ millions) on Education in Canada, 1950–1 to 2008–9

Year	Total Expenditures on Education	Total Education Expenditures as % of GDP*
1950–1	439	2.4
1960–1	1,706	4.4
1970–1	7,675	8.5
1980–1	22,202	7.1
1990–1	48,586	7.1
2000–1	67,666	6.3
2008–9	95,009	6.0

*Figures from 1950–1 to 1960–1 are for gross national product, which results in slightly higher percentages than for gross domestic product.
Sources: 1950–1 to 1960–1: Statistics Canada, *Historical Compendium of Education Statistics: From Confederation to 1975* (Ottawa: Minister of Industry, Trade and Commerce, 1978); 1970–1 to 1980–1: Statistics Canada, CANSIM Tables 3800015 and 4780001; 1990–1 to 2000–1: compiled from data in Statistics Canada (2011b, Tables B1.1 and B1.5); 2008–09: compiled from data in OECD (2011).

within each province and territory. Provincial and territorial legislation determines the definition, number, size, responsibilities, and powers of school boards and related bodies. As part of this equation, the educational climate can swing in various directions depending on the policy leanings of the government in power, the influence of the major educational organizations, and public sentiment and mobilization, tempered by the many layers that have become part of educational decision-making in Canada (Levin, 2005).

Shifting patterns in educational spending also point to the changing nature of federal government participation in education. Under the Canadian constitutional framework, the federal government's role in education is limited to matters that relate to minority languages, denominational schooling, and the education of designated groups under federal jurisdiction, such as registered Indians, the armed forces, and penitentiary inmates. In some of these areas, federal involvement has diminished through program reductions and jurisdictional transfers, particularly as First Nations and Yukon, the Northwest Territories, and Nunavut have gained responsibilities broadly comparable to provincial powers with respect to education and related areas. In other respects, the federal presence has expanded in education. Arising out of attempts to stimulate the development of various training initiatives and to coordinate labour market development strategies, the federal government has initiated several types of funding arrangements and programs, particularly in relation to postsecondary education, vocational training, and research and development initiatives. The federal government has also taken a leading role in promoting educational activities in areas such as multiculturalism, investment in innovation and knowledge-based initiatives, adoption of protocols to ensure comparable standards and transferability

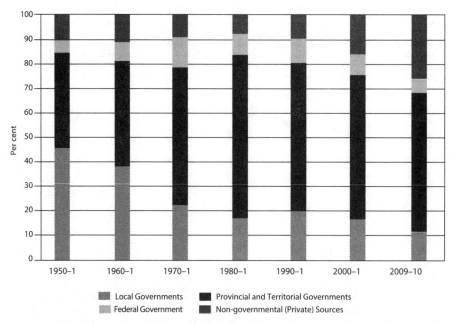

Figure 4.4 **Share of Expenditures on Education in Canada, by Direct Source of Funds, 1950–1 to 2009–10**

Note: Figures for 2009–10 are estimates.
Sources: 1950–1 to 1970–1: Statistics Canada, *Historical Compendium of Education Statistics: From Confederation to 1975* (Ottawa: Minister of Industry, Trade and Commerce, 1978); 1975–6 to 1990–1: Statistics Canada, *Advance Statistics of Education* (Ottawa: Minister of Industry, Science and Technology, various years); 1995–6: Statistics Canada, *Education Quarterly Review* 5, 3 (Mar. 1999); 2000–1: Statistics Canada, *Education Quarterly Review* 8, 3 (June 2002); 2009–10: compiled from Statistics Canada CANSIM tables 385-0007, 478-0001, and 478-0004, and OECD (2012b: 232, 248).

of credentials across jurisdictions, and mechanisms to integrate educational planning and policy-making.

The federal government asserted its presence in promoting educational expansion beginning in the 1960s and 1970s. The federal share of educational funding more than doubled, from just under 5 per cent of total educational expenditures in 1950–1 to over 12 per cent two decades later. The relative share of federal spending on education has now fallen below 10 per cent of all spending on education in Canada, reflecting a wider pattern of diminishing federal involvement in education and social program spending areas despite growing concerns about Canada's capacity to provide equitable opportunities for all citizens while remaining economically competitive. Organizations such as the Council of Ministers of Education Canada and the recently disbanded Canadian Council on Learning have advocated a more highly coordinated national strategy for education. Global competition and related social and economic transformations have contributed to pressures to reorganize and streamline educational finance and service delivery amid demands to co-ordinate educational programming and standards on a national level and shifting conceptions of federal, provincial, and First Nations constitutional jurisdictions.

Table 4.2 Number of School Boards, by Province and Territory

Provnce/Territory	Number of School Boards		
	Mid-1990s	2011–12	Type of Organization
British Columbia	75	60	59 public, 1 francophone education authority
Alberta	181	66	42 public, 19 Catholic, 5 francophone + 13 charter schools
Saskatchewan	121	29	19 public, 9 Catholic separate, 1 francophone
Manitoba	57	38	37 public, 1 francophone
Ontario	172	72	public: 31 anglophone, 4 francophone; Catholic: 29 anglophone, 8 francophone
Quebec	158	72	60 French, 9 English, 3 special status First Nations
New Brunswick	18	14	9 anglophone, 5 francophone
(reduced			to 4 anglophone, 3 francophone as of 1 July 2012)
Nova Scotia	22	8	7 regional, 1 provincial francophone
Prince Edward Island	5	4	2 anglophone, 1 provincial
francophone,			1 Mi'kmaq elementary school
Newfoundland and	27	5	4 anglophone, 1 provincial
francophone			
Labrador			
Yukon	1	1	1 francophone (+ 27 school councils)
Northwest Territories	10	2	2 public school (+ 8 Divisional
Education			Councils + 1 non-official French DEC)
Nunavut	n.a.	1	1 francophone (+ 27 District Education Authorities)

*School boards were abolished in 1996 and reinstated in 2001.
Sources: Canadian School Boards Association, *Cross-Canada Chart, Education Governance in Canada* (1999), and information from provincial and territorial education departments and school board associations.

Structure

Efforts to reappraise and restructure education systems have drawn increased attention to privately funded and operated educational institutions and programs. Traditionally, in Canada, education by or within the private sector has been heavily overshadowed by public education. Governments have been reluctant to extend support and endorsement for private education beyond nominal levels on the grounds that schooling is a public enterprise that provides common learning experiences and

Box 4.1 Educational Reorganization, School Size, and Student Performance

The ongoing process of administrative reorganization of schooling gives rise to significant questions about what impact changes are likely to have on student performance and other educational activities. Issues of school and class size are of particular concern among educators and educational researchers, and they often become a focus of controversy during periods of educational reform. Like many dimensions of education, questions about what should be the optimum school and class sizes meet with mixed responses. Larger schools and classes can be cost-effective, providing students with a wider range of programming, services, and activities that may not be available in smaller ones, but they may also alienate students and limit the capacity to attend to particular student needs. The issue is complicated because class size has served frequently as a rallying point in efforts by political parties, teachers' organizations, and other groups to draw attention to the impact of particular educational reforms or budgetary measures. Governments in several provinces have legislated limits to class sizes, while in other cases the question of the right to negotiate class size remains highly contentious. Quebec teachers in 2005 threatened strike action to advance their demands for smaller classes, while British Columbia teachers more recently have engaged in a series of job actions and legal challenges to maintain their right to negotiate class size in collective bargaining with school boards.

In this context, many Canadian school districts or governments have sponsored studies to provide a better understanding of the key factors associated with class or school sizes. The findings, collectively, reveal that there are some advantages to maintaining smaller schools and classes, but these are tempered by broader factors that are part of school climates. Jones and Ezeife (2011) observe that in Ontario, in common with previous studies conducted in Alberta and New Brunswick, no statistical significance is found between school size and student achievement overall,

opportunities for all segments of the population. The creation of local school boards and implementation of property-based taxation to support schools were designed to ensure that residents could gain input into and have a stake in educational matters. Without these measures, early school reformers feared that private and sectarian interests would dominate and fragment schooling, keeping it out of reach of much of the population.

The development of Canadian education has been heavily influenced by periodic demands by organized religious minorities for instruction appropriate to their beliefs. One type of compromise was the establishment in several provinces of provisions to allow for publicly funded and regulated separate or denominational schooling to operate parallel with public school systems (Wilson, 1981). Historically, Roman Catholic and occasionally Protestant minorities were the predominant advocates for separate schooling, but this has changed as Canada has become increasingly more multicultural and multi-faith. Initially, parents or groups who sought alternative forms of education were forced to finance these themselves with no assurance that programs and credentials would be officially certified or recognized. However, recent although some variations are found in specific curricular areas. It is especially important to focus on ways to achieve an appropriate balance between school size and capacity to provide equitable, high-quality educational services. Leithwood and Jantzi (2009: 484–5), surveying studies published after 1990 on school size, observe that smaller schools typically offer advantages with respect to student and organizational outcomes, but that "one size may not fit all purposes." Citing the importance of social context and composition of the student body, they suggest that an optimum school size for schools with a heterogeneous or relatively advantaged student body is about 500 students at the elementary level and 1,000 at the high school level, while for schools serving a disadvantaged student population, optimum numbers are about 300 elementary students and 600 secondary students. Presenting the findings to members of the Regina public school board, one of the authors (Leithwood) highlighted the significance of socio-economic status, especially for disadvantaged students who are often less well equipped than relatively advantaged ones for larger school settings, noting that, "It's hard to get too small a school for students who really struggle" (Pacholik, 2007: A1–2).

Similar patterns are observed with respect to research on class size. Research in Edmonton reveals that reductions in class size can improve student achievement if these are implemented in conjunction with appropriate forms of professional support for teachers (Edmonton Public Schools and University of Alberta Faculty of Education, 2001). Bascia (2011: 19), in a study for the Ontario Ministry of Education produced through the Canadian Education Association, concludes that smaller class sizes offer instructional benefits and are well received by teachers, students, and parents, but reduction in class sizes in primary schools must not be viewed as a "magic bullet" and cannot be implemented effectively without parallel strategies that focus attention on the overall social and educational context.

All of these findings reveal that no single dimension of educational practice or reform can be understood in isolation from the institutional and community environments in which schools operate.

trends have seen a blurring of traditional boundaries that once separated public (secular), separate (denominational), and private schooling, sometimes accompanied by an escalation of tensions between advocates of different kinds of schooling. Sustained pressure from religious organizations and other groups resulted in legislative changes in many jurisdictions, beginning with the western provinces and Quebec since the late 1960s, to provide public funding for private schools that meet provincial criteria in prescribed areas like curriculum and teacher certification. Because these issues cut across several deeply embedded and often opposing values and interests, they resurface periodically in the form of intense controversy over different kinds of educational alternatives. The next two sections explore significant aspects of those challenges in relation to issues of market choice and accountability.

School Choice and the Educational Marketplace

Disparate views of education have been accompanied by various measures in the direction of making individuals and family members, as opposed to governments, more responsible for their own welfare. Volatile social, economic, and political conditions have accompanied globally competitive economic markets, rapid acceleration of new technologies, and significant demographic changes, and these conditions have implicated education in what has been called a "new politics of the welfare state." Consequently, social and economic arrangements in advanced industrial democracies have been drastically modified in recent years (Pierson, 2001).

In the realm of education, governments in every major jurisdiction in Canada and other Western nations have adopted numerous measures, including initiatives to modify arrangements for educational finance and governance, regulate teaching and teachers' organizations, reorganize curricula and service delivery, and implement mechanisms to assess performance outcomes and contribute to public accountability in education. The kinds of educational reforms vary considerably within each national, provincial, and territorial setting, and the impacts these reforms have had on public schooling and other educational delivery systems also differ. Nonetheless, a remarkable degree of uniformity is evident in the overall direction of change towards stronger emphasis on individual responsibility and a closer match between education and economic imperatives (Portelli and Solomon, 2001; Taylor, 2001; Lauder et al., 2006: 47ff.). The notion of education as a public responsibility, organized and delivered through the state, is being fragmented—by design and by specific events and practices—into multiple educational systems and forms. While numerous competing and contradictory dynamics are at work, educational thinking and decision-making have been influenced in important respects by neo-liberal orientations that characterize schooling and other services as a marketplace subject to the choices of individual consumers.

Private Education

Expansion of private education and other alternatives to mainstream school systems have been driven by several factors, hastened by government funding constraints and interrelated concerns about educational quality, curricular options, and standards, and by gaps in the programming options available through public educational institutions (Sweet and Gallagher, 1999). Individuals and parents are also increasingly looking to position children and youth more competitively by pursuing educational options that best suit their interests and aspirations.

The data in Figure 4.4 illustrate the escalation of trends towards growing reliance on private spending in education. For much of the duration represented in Figure 4.4, private sources constituted 10 per cent or less of educational spending, even declining briefly in the 1960s and 1970s when government spending was increased to stimulate massive educational expansion. However, the proportion of funding from non-government sources, such as tuition fees and private donors, has more than doubled since the early 1990s, approaching one-quarter of all reported expenditures on education in Canada by 2010. This figure would be even higher if all educational expenses, such as private tutoring or assistance services and family spending on educational materials and learning tools, were included.

Steady increases also have occurred in the number and proportion of children attending private elementary and high schools in Canada, hastened in part by legislation to allow or provide public funding for alternatives to the public school system. Private schooling now represents about 6 per cent of total school enrolments across Canada, rising from 4.6 per cent two decades ago. These rates are even higher in some regions, notably British Columbia and Quebec, revealing in part a drift of children from public school systems as well as a more general demographic shift that has left many school jurisdictions with fewer school-age children (Canadian Council on Learning, 2006b; Davies et al., 2006; OECD, 2011). There are several types of **private schools**, including elite or "preparatory" schools, alternative or "free" schools, and schools oriented to distinct groups based on racial, ethnic, or cultural traditions, as well as schools operated by religious organizations. A growing array of private institutions provides or sponsors educational services in post-secondary programs, vocational and career training, and adult education. In addition to formal school-based programs, private agencies are increasingly involved in the delivery of educational services such as tutoring, special education programs, preschool and after-school programs, adult education, corporate training, and educational franchises (Davies et al., 2006; Aurini and Davies, 2005).

Parental Choice and Alternative Education

Parallel growth has occurred in other forms of educational alternatives, including the number of children educated at home. Home-based schooling has expanded

International Case Study

Comparative Perspectives on Public and Private Schooling

Private schools represent a small but growing part of the education sector in Canada. Private schooling and debates over public involvement in education feature much more prominently in many other nations.

Education continues to be a prime target for critics of government spending in the United States despite years of falling budgets that, in some cases, have produced substandard learning conditions. In the United States, which like Canada has a federal structure of government, states typically provide close to half of all schooling expenditures. Over half of all states reduced their funding for schools between 2008 and 2011, and three-quarters reduced funding between 2010 and 2011 (Oliff and Leachman, 2011). The funding reductions, most of which have occurred in both absolute and per student terms, have resulted in layoffs or wage cuts for teachers and support staff, increased class sizes, reductions in programming and music, athletic, and other co-curricular activities, and loss of support services. Many districts and states have introduced fees or tax increases to avoid further declines in education-related programs, increasing pre-existing gaps between wealthier communities and those in which low- and medium-income families predominate. The situation is even more severe at the post-secondary level, as government funding declined in nearly all states over the past three decades, with every state except North Dakota and Wyoming reducing funding for universities and colleges between 14.8 per cent and 69.4 per cent

continued

from 1980 to 2011 (Mortensen, 2012). While critics highlight the contradictions entailed by the loss of state support for education at a time when education is becoming globally more significant, greater attention is being paid to the consequences of the shift towards privatization of education in other contexts.

The share of private expenditures on total elementary, secondary, and vocational education costs is about 10 per cent in Canada and the United States, well above levels for many OECD nations such as Sweden, Finland, Austria, Italy, and France, but also below those for Germany, Australia, New Zealand, Mexico, Chile, and the United Kingdom (UNESCO 2011a: 288–91). Rates of private expenditure, especially in the form of tuition fees, are typically much higher for post-secondary education levels, but significant variations reveal the different capacities and priorities that governments have to invest in education. Households in many of the poorest regions of the world, especially in sub-Saharan Africa as well as nations in Latin America and the Caribbean and parts of Asia, typically contribute between four to six times as much to education as do those in North America and Europe (UNESCO, 2011a: 75–6). These patterns reinforce serious inequalities based on socio-economic status, gender, and other important social characteristics.

Discussion Questions

1. Compare education in your region with a corresponding region or state in the United States. What are the similarities and differences in how education is financed and organized, as well as in curriculum areas and practices?

2. Why is the share of education expenditures paid from private expenditures rising in many nations? What impact do these trends have for different social groups?

3. What factors account for the phenomenon by which individuals or families in many of the poorest nations pay a higher share of education costs than do those in many of the most developed nations? What policies and practices would have to be adopted to change this situation?

significantly as many parents opt to keep children out of public schools. There are different types of home-schooling practices, ranging from philosophies of "unschooling" to arrangements with school boards for children unable to attend regular classes for particular reasons. Much home schooling is based on religious considerations, but several other factors motivate home-based schooling, such as concerns about academic quality and learning styles, flexibility, or school-based victimization. Most estimates place the number of children of elementary and secondary school age regularly schooled at home in Canada at between 60,000 to 95,000 (about 1.5 per cent of the school-age population)—concentrated most heavily in Alberta, British Columbia, and Ontario—although advocates suggest that at least 100,000 families are engaged in home schooling (Canadian Council on Learning, 2006b; Priesnitz, 2008; Ray, 2001: 28).

The proliferation of private alternatives has been accompanied by an expansion of public educational delivery and program options. Public school systems and post-secondary institutions have modified and diversified their offerings to attract and maintain enrolment in competition with other agencies and in response to broader educational challenges and needs. School districts have relaxed or removed policies that previously required most students to attend their neighbourhood schools. Many school districts have introduced specialized schools targeted to particular groups, such as immigrant populations, Aboriginal inner-city youth, academically talented students or those with special learning needs, students with specific cultural and arts-oriented interests, adult learners, and students with disabilities. Publicly funded post-secondary institutions have expanded programming and developed alternative modes of course or program delivery, sometimes through contractual arrangements with private agencies. Governments and public school boards have also made arrange-ments to co-operate in various ways with home-based educators and other agencies, while educational institutions have altered admission policies to acknowledge or give credit for a variety of educational alternatives.

Despite these trends, market-based educational reforms, both as a focus for public debate and in their implementation, appear to be less pervasive in Canada than in many other jurisdictions, including several American states. Advocates of a market or consumer choice model of education claim that educational choice is required to en-sure that schools will be more flexible and responsive to community concerns (Easton, 1988: 71–6; Wilkinson, 1994). Chubb and Moe (1990), in their influential argument for school choice, contend that school improvement follows as a logical outcome from the removal of constraints on parents, teachers, and schools, whereby schools (posed as distinct enterprises) would have the autonomy to make changes necessary to attract and retain students and their parents (posed as consumers).

One of the most actively promoted models of educational choice is the establish-ment of charter schools. Charter schools operate on the basis of a "charter" or agree-ment between particular schools and governments that identify specific mandates and features of governance by which each school will operate in conformity with general principles of public education. They are premised on the notion that parents are edu-cational consumers who should be provided with effective input and choices in order to make rational decisions about their children's schooling.

Advocates of charter schools argue that viable alternatives are needed because pub-lic schools have become too firmly entrenched in the hands of educational elites and have experienced declining educational standards by attempting to be all things to all people. Some options, such as home schooling and private or independent schooling, are beyond the reach of parents without sufficient time or resources to invest in these alternatives or who do not share the values embodied in these special forms of educa-tion. Charter schools, by contrast, are promoted on the basis that they offer the best elements of both public and private schooling. Charter schools, like public schools, are funded by government grants, are ideally open to all pupils, and are subject to provincial curriculum and teacher certification guidelines. Like private schools, how-ever, they have greater autonomy to define their own particular mandates, to make decisions about staffing, resource allocation, and instructional matters, and to ensure that parents' voices are incorporated into educational planning (Lawton, 1995: 68–9; Nikiforuk, 1993: 100–2; Raham, 1996). Others argue that governments should issue educational vouchers that enable parents or students to select their schools (public or private), in lieu of current funding arrangements whereby grants are provided directly to school boards.

Joe Freedman (1995: 40), one of the strongest early promoters of charter schooling in Canada, argues that they offer a "middle ground between choosing schools by voucher and allowing the system to fix itself." Their success, Freedman claims, is driven by "the challenge of removing the exclusive franchise from school boards, creating choice for parent clients, providing a focus on outcomes, establishing real autonomy through school status as a legal entity, and creating genuine accountability through the threat of school closure or loss of teaching position."

One of the most broadly based initiatives to introduce charter-like schooling is in New Zealand, which in 1989 required all school jurisdictions to develop charters as part of a series of initiatives to deregulate and privatize government services. Considerable pressure from interest groups in the United States has led to various forms of charter arrangements in several states, beginning with Minnesota in 1991, which was joined within the next two years by four other states (Lawton, 1995: 70–81). Within the next decade, the number of charter schools had increased to over 1,600, serving close to half a million students in 34 states (Fuller, 2000: 7). There have been several vocal advocates of charter schooling in Canada, notably in Alberta, which has remained the only province to authorize charter schools since the passage of facilitating legislation in 1994 (Bruce and Schwartz, 1997: 408). Three charter schools opened in 1995, with the number rising to 11 by 1997 and reaching 22, operated by 13 different charter school authorities, by 2009; the schools are oriented primarily to particular groups or a specific focus such as traditional "back-to-basics" instruction, foreign language instruction, English as a second language, street youth, academically talented learners, arts immersion, and science and technology (Richie, 2010).

Despite the inroads and popular support it has gained in some jurisdictions, charter schooling also faces considerable opposition from educators and educational organizations, as well as from broader community and policy groups. Some opposition arises from concerns that charter schooling is an affront to public education that may undermine established educational structures and bodies. However, serious concerns also arise from prospects that charter schools can be divisive, inequitable, undemocratic, and ineffective in addressing major educational problems (Canadian Teachers' Federation, 1997). Critics argue that educational choice is already provided, or possible, within existing structures of public and private schooling and that charter schooling diverts control and resources from schools that serve the wider community (Crawley, 1995: 168–9; Friesen and Friesen, 2001).

Although charter schools may have some general appeal, advocacy for charter schools and other market models of education is being pursued most actively by individuals supported by or representing groups that have the most economic, political, and cultural capital (Robertson, 1998: 263–6). Critics contend that these advocates stand to gain the most from a bifurcated education system in terms of both individual competitive advantage and the benefits that accrue from the redirection of public funds into private hands. They add, moreover, that while public schools are intended to serve and be responsive to diverse social groups, charter schooling is likely to contribute to the diversion of resources and opportunities away from disadvantaged groups that have the greatest educational needs. There are strong contradictions in both the logic and practice of market-based initiatives in education. Initiatives to regard education as a market governed by consumer choice have simultaneously fostered arrangements in which private firms enter into exclusive contracts with educational institutions to supply particular services or products such as beverages, electronic equipment, or food and cleaning services (Berthelot, 2006: 90–1). Finally, charter schooling and related shifts in the direction of educational accountability and measurement may contribute to the deskilling of teachers' work by setting and controlling performance standards and conduct in such a way as to restrict professional autonomy and increase workloads.

The early evidence from charter schooling and other private alternatives supports many of these contentions, though some evidence is mixed (Davies and Aurini, 2008; Richie, 2010). Charter schools have drawn students who have been disengaged or dissatisfied with the mainstream education system as well as those from more privileged groups. Similarly, whereas public schools are most likely to enrol students from a diverse mix of backgrounds, children who attend private schools are drawn predominantly from households situated at the top and bottom ends of family income groups (Statistics Canada, 2001b). Discourses of school choice are especially appealing to more privileged parents who are able to mould the educational futures they consider most advantageous to their children's future pathways (Davies and Aurini, 2008). Private school advocates point to data from comparative student assessment programs that indicate students in private schools achieve higher scores than those in public schools (though this trend is less pronounced in Canada than in many other nations). However, this trend tends to disappear when social class, school diversity, and other background factors are taken into account (Bussière et al., 2001: 38).

Regardless of the impact of particular types of school reform, debates over school choice will continue to be ineffectual as long as they ignore more fundamental issues, including the structural causes of poverty and social and income polarization (Fuller, 2000: 10). Without these factors as a priority, such debates may be more about competitive positioning for corporate resources and family advantage than about meaningful educational reform and improvement. The analysis of alternative forms of educational delivery suggests that no single form of educational governance is likely to address complex questions about educational quality, and that models transferred from other realms, such as business management, are not automatically applicable in an educational context (Fiske and Ladd, 2000: 312–13).

In summary, the various options promoted for educational reform and alternatives to public schooling represent divergent social and ideological interests. It is important not to discount the genuine concerns that all people have for changes that will make education more meaningful and rewarding in its varied economic, cultural, social, and moral purposes. The kinds of reform strategies being pursued, however, follow distinctly different courses, leading, in one direction, to a market-driven orientation to the education "industry," and, in another, to a more person-centred focus on human development, opportunity, and social justice. Labaree (2010: 6) stresses the contradictory significance of market-based discourses employed by more advantaged groups drawing upon notions of equality and inclusivity while pursuing strategies to preserve their own privilege through exclusivity: "Consumers have wanted schools to allow them to accomplish goals that are less noble socially but more resonant personally: to get ahead and stay ahead. . . . In short, the vision of education as a private good (formed by the self-interested actions of individual consumers) has consistently worn out over education as a public good (formed by the social aims of reform movements)."

The growth of private and home-based schooling and the increased involvement of non-government organizations in education have tremendous significance for educational organizations and practices. As a result, these issues are often fiercely debated. Advocates promote private schooling on the basis that choice is necessary to provide a range of educational options that cannot be accommodated or afforded in a single, public educational system. Private schooling, viewed this way, promotes both human rights and free-market principles by enabling parents and learners to select the kind of learning environment most suited to their beliefs and interests. Critics argue, to the contrary, that the **privatization** of education contributes to fractionalization and reduced opportunities for much of the population. Education is not a commodity meant to be governed by price and market forces but a complex undertaking that contributes to human development and social responsibility as well as to the acquisition of knowledge and skills. Agencies that fund and operate private educational services are often more interested in their own profitability or are governed by specialized interests that run contrary to broader public concerns. As private operations, they are not subject to the same scrutiny and regulations that prevail in state-operated educational institutions to ensure that standards are met and public input is maintained.

The Governance and Financing of Canadian Education

Recent policy and institutional changes and program initiatives make it difficult to provide a comprehensive overview of contemporary educational patterns in Canada. However, several distinctive and competing tendencies are evident. On the one hand, educational restructuring, driven by fiscal rationales and market-based principles or neo-liberal ideologies, has contributed to a number of significant trends. These include

- institutional downsizing and reorganization;
- **amalgamation** and centralization of educational administration and program delivery;
- the transfer of educational funding and programming from the public to the private sector;
- renewed emphasis on "basic" or "core" curriculum areas;
- the definition and measurement of specified learning standards used to determine achievement and placement in and beyond education programs; and
- intensified measures to scrutinize and control the activities of educators and learners (Simon, 2001; Wotherspoon, 1991: 17; Taylor, 2001; Lessard and Brassard, 2009).

On the other hand, various public, community-based, and private educational initiatives have emerged to serve diverse educational requirements. Programs and services tailored for socially and educationally disadvantaged groups, such as children living in poverty, learners designated "at risk" or vulnerable to school failure or early school leaving, and cultural minorities, coexist with expensive training programs oriented to narrow, specialized markets. Public educational institutions continue to be governed by principles of effective community participation, relevance to heterogeneous constituencies of learners, and responsiveness to changing social and occupational demands.

It is important to acknowledge that education in Canada continues to be funded predominantly by provincial and territorial governments (supplemented with transfers from the federal government), even with the gradual shift towards heavier reliance on private and local sources of funding. Although its massive size and cost (representing in total between 6 and 8 per cent of Canada's gross domestic product, second only to health as a priority for total government spending) have exposed the education system as a visible target within strategies to reduce government spending or compensate for tax cuts and spending priorities in other areas, public education has also been defended under the guise of human capital approaches as a vital investment in the nation's future.

This double significance is reflected in mixed orientations to education spending held by particular social groups. Hart (2012: 9–10), for instance, reports that a majority of Ontario residents surveyed in 2012 favour increased spending for schools and would be willing to pay higher taxes to support education; however, while levels of support for increased educational spending are significantly higher than they have been in previous decades, they have moderated or declined since peaking in 2007. Yet, even if public opinion is softening in some respects, the analysis offered by Hart (2012: 9–10) suggests continuing uneasiness about the future of education, with concerns for fiscal responsibility offset in part by fears that potential spending cuts could undermine the quality of education. While the evidence does not point to a "crisis of confidence" or tax revolt such as that advanced in some neo-liberal discourse promoting market-based reforms, most jarringly in anti-government "tea party" rhetoric prominent across parts of the United States, it does not fully match the expectations of enhanced commitment to a strong public school system advocated by organized labour, teachers' and parents' organizations, and other community groups (Lewington and Orpwood, 1993: 16–17; Hart, 2012).

Debates over educational funding and organization are often more about priorities than about absolute spending levels. This helps to explain how funding or program cutbacks may be experienced by some educational participants or sectors even as educational expenditures rise or remain relatively constant. While there is general consensus that education is crucial for personal, social, and economic development, there is considerable disagreement about the kinds of education and educational organizations there should be.

It is often difficult to pinpoint the social bases of educational debates because views about education appear in complex and sometimes contradictory ways, expressed by persons who represent diverse social perspectives. People with a broad range of educational experiences and social backgrounds may come together, for instance, to either support or oppose a "back-to-basics" orientation to curricula, culturally sensitive educational practices, or demands for greater discipline and safety in schools.

The New Right

Apple (2000: 20ff.) analyzes the impact on education of the rise of the New Right in the United States and Britain, and some of his insights apply, to a certain extent, to the

Box 4.2 Funding Cuts, Commercialization, and Educational Inequality

Schools and other educational institutions have become more dependent on funding and sponsorships from private sources, including individuals, families, and corporations, as governments have cut or restricted funding. About one-third of Canadian households reported spending on education tuitions, supplies, and textbooks in 2009, with average expenditures on these items nearly doubling since 2000 (Statistics Canada, 2011a: Table B.2.7). Statistics Canada (2007e) estimates that individuals and households in Canada spend close to $14.5 billion simply to outfit children for the school year, including clothing and accessories ($249.9 million for girls, $229.2 million for boys, and $106.9 million on unisex clothing); computer hardware and software ($1.1 billion); books, newspapers, and other periodicals ($749.6 million); and stationery, office supplies, and other material ($921.7 million). School fundraising initiatives are also increasingly reliant on families and private sponsors. These trends can have an adverse impact on educational equity and the quality of education, as made clear in the results of a national survey conducted by the Canadian Teachers' Federation, the Canadian Centre for Policy Alternatives, and the Fédération des syndicats de l'enseignement (Canadian Teachers' Federation, 2006):

Beyond the bake sale: Exposing the many faces of commercialism in public schools

How many chocolate almonds does it take to buy an education?

The underfunding of public education has forced schools and school communities to compensate in a variety of ways: door-to-door fundraising campaigns, advertising revenue, exclusive marketing contracts, and seeking donations or handouts from the private sector. Awareness of these activities has been largely anecdotal, up to now.

. . . Among the study's findings (contained in the report *Commercialism in Canadian Schools: Who's Calling the Shots?*) are the following:

- About a third of schools reported the presence of advertising in or on the school, with higher rates in secondary schools than in elementary schools.
- 27 per cent of schools had an exclusive marketing arrangement with Coke or Pepsi.
- The majority of schools reported charging user fees for a variety of services and programs.
- 15 per cent of elementary schools and 21 per cent of secondary schools reported selling services to generate revenue.

Fundraising activities are common in schools, with money being raised for school trips, library books, athletic programs and technology; 60 per cent of elementary schools reported fundraising for library books.

Schools reported raising—through fundraising and other activities including user fees, advertising revenue and partnerships/sponsorships—amounts of money ranging from a few hundred dollars to, in some cases, several hundred thousand dollars.

The study raises some fundamental questions about the implications of commercialism and privatization for students, teachers, schools and public education as a whole.

When schools and communities have varying degrees of capacity to fundraise and attract outside funding, what is the impact on equity? Which students in which communities have access to programs enhanced by private funding, and which do not? As schools compete with each other for external funding (from corporations and individuals), how does education suffer? Do the time and other resources spent on fundraising detract from the quality of education schools can provide? To what extent does an over-reliance on private funding erode the decision-making authority of elected school boards? Are there strings attached to private funding—and with what effects? Who ensures that curriculum and classroom materials provided by private sources are unbiased, complete and accurate? As schools are increasingly dependent on private funding sources, what happens in times of economic instability or dwindling corporate largesse, or when parents are unable to fundraise to the same extent? . . .

The classroom is an environment like no other, a fact not lost on corporate marketers. They openly describe it as an ideal environment in which to reach this increasingly influential consumer group—students—required by law to be in school, five days a week, six hours a day, 10 months of the year, until they reach the age of 16. The school also offers an implicit endorsement of products, organizations and messages associated with it. . . . One has to wonder if comments from governments about our commitment to the "knowledge economy" are predominantly rhetorical, particularly in light of how dependent schools are becoming—in the absence of adequate public dollars—on private funding sources.

While fundraising is hardly a new activity (ask yourself how many chocolate almonds you've bought to support your community school), the results of this first national survey indicate that school commercialism has clearly moved beyond bake sales and raffles, assuming many forms. They also demonstrate that the goals of these new fundraising campaigns are no longer just for band trips but for books, or desks, or yes, even bathroom facilities. These are hardly "frills" or "extras," but rather what most of us would consider part of a basic education.

Source: Material reprinted with the permission of the Canadian Teachers' Federation, The Canadian Centre for Policy Alternatives, and the Fédération des syndicats de l'enseignement.

politics of education in Canada. The New Right is characterized as a broad movement supporting principles of market-driven free enterprise; opposing state regulation; cynical of state bureaucracy; and fearful about loss of authority, tradition, and standards in personal and public life. Rather than operating as a unified group or force, however, the New Right is better understood as an amalgam of disparate forces such as the pro-family movement, business lobbyists, opponents of the welfare state, neoliberal groups, right-wing organizations, and other populist forces that seek a return to "traditional" values. Education, because it touches family life, economic futures, and other concerns vital to people's lives, hopes, and aspirations, has been a prime target for reform by the New Right. Apple (2000: 22) argues that

> The sphere of education has been one of the most successful areas in which the Right has been ascendant. The social democratic goal of expanding equality of opportunity (itself a rather limited reform) has lost much of its political potency and its ability to mobilize people. The "panic" over falling standards and illiteracy, the fears of violence in schools, the concern with the destruction of family values and religiosity, all have had an effect. These fears are exacerbated, and used, by dominant groups within politics and the economy who have been able to move the debate on education (and all things social) onto their own terrain, the terrain of "tradition," standardization, productivity, and industrial needs.

One of the major features that such critics of the education system point to is the size and power of the educational bureaucracy, which is often depicted as a monopoly resistant to change. These images are widely promoted throughout North America in media accounts as well as popular books with titles such as *Fallacies in Education: Why Schools are Mired in Mediocrity* (Trani and Irvine, 2010). Fears about unchecked growth of the education system are enhanced with depictions of educational administrators, teachers, and other entrenched interest groups who are distant from the real concerns of students, parents, and community members. Canadian journalist Andrew Nikiforuk (1993: 57), for instance, argues this in his book *School's Out*:

> Just as the Canadian oil industry did during the boom of the 1970s, educators have spent, built, and added on programs and services without any coherent plan or realistic sense of limits. Unlike the oil patch today, however, educational institutions cannot be effectively regulated or reformed by market forces. As essentially social monopolies, they appear to have become unmanageable because of their autonomous nature.

Similarly, Lawton (1995: 14–15) criticizes the "bureaucratic bondage" that has removed control over education from parents and other segments of the public into the hands of bureaucrats, professional educators, and administrators. Hepburn (1999: 1), in a report published by the right-wing Fraser Institute to make the case for school choice in Canada, states the apparent problem more bluntly: "Canadian education is not just inefficient but seriously inadequate. Statistical evidence of poor student performance coupled with the deterioration of public confidence suggests that, if it is not to become obsolete, public education must be redesigned."

These criticisms have a common-sense appeal because they pose a unifying framework for a series of problems that most people can identify with or have experienced in one form or another. Taken as a whole, the kinds of issues we see or hear about in our educational institutions—rising costs, declining standards, uncaring teachers, lack of accountability to taxpayers and communities, student violence and vandalism, irrelevant curricula, meaningless reporting practices, wasted instructional time—may convey an image of an education system in serious crisis.

There is a danger, however, in adopting an uncritical approach to such a critique. Despite numerous concerns, no consensus necessarily exists over the idea that the education system is failing or in crisis. In fact, as is noted throughout this book, public opinion on most educational issues is divided and highly complex. In a social context within which public and private institutions are regarded with skepticism and declining confidence overall, public schools are rated relatively well, maintaining higher levels of confidence than many other major institutions (Guppy and Davies, 1999; Roberts, 2007).

Education Reform

Wickstrom (1994: 6–7) identifies seven distinct models to characterize the diverse demands that exist for educational reform:

1. the factory, emphasizing productivity, uniformity, and quality control;
2. the department store or large convention, stressing variety and consumer choice;
3. the family, with a focus on love, compassion, and co-operation;
4. the garden or "untended meadow," in which growth, interest, and beauty and diversity are crucial;
5. the Olympics, highlighting excellence and competition;
6. the freedom march, oriented according to passion and indoctrination to a specific cause;
7. the clinic, regulated by diagnosis, prescription, precision, and successive stages of sophistication.

While each of these models can be applied to specific groups or philosophies of educational change, most educational practices and opinions encompass a mixture of elements from various models.

One way to gauge the extent to which educational practices and reforms have or have not been able to match the level of expectations surrounding education systems is to examine public attitudes. Major public opinion surveys reveal mixed sentiments about the direction and impact of education change, though levels of confidence in public education systems have remained relatively high throughout the past several decades.

Historical comparisons reveal that public expressions of general concern or dissatisfaction with education have tended to be highest during periods in which education systems have been confronted with expansionary pressures or diminished resources. In response to a Gallup Poll question asking "Do you think children today are being better educated or worse than you were?" the proportion of those who indicated that they felt children were worse educated rose from 12 per cent in 1948 to 33 per cent in 1976, while the proportion who felt children were better educated declined from 74 per cent to 49 per cent over the same period (Canadian Institute of Public Opinion, 1976: 2). Public concerns over the quality of education also rose during the 1990s, especially in provinces affected most heavily by funding restraints and program disruptions, but these have subsequently abated as funding and service delivery arrangements for schools and other educational institutions have recovered over the past decade.

Box 4.3 Growing Emphasis on Parent Involvement in Schools

As schools seek to become more accountable and relevant to the interests of the communities they work with, they have placed increased emphasis on issues of community engagement and parent involvement. Extensive evidence shows the benefits of parent involvement of various types. This involvement ranges from volunteer support for classroom and in-school activities, meetings with teachers and school staff, and parent–child co-operation on homework, reading, and other activities outside of the school to participation on school councils and in other forms of educational governance. In its most positive forms, parental engagement provides opportunities for parents or guardians, children, teaching staff, and administrators to work together to enhance educational experiences and outcomes. Most Canadian educational jurisdictions have created formal mechanisms to institutionalize these relationships, taking various forms, such as parent advisory councils, district education councils, parent–school support committees, and parent involvement committees. These arrangements, unlike more traditional home and school or parent–teacher associations, provide regular opportunities for community members to play a part in decision-making on school policies and other major education-related activities.

Despite the strong advantages these kinds of arrangements can offer through strengthening relationships among homes, communities, and schools, there are several reasons to be cautious. The focus on parental involvement has divergent and sometimes contradictory roots, signifying from various standpoints the expansion of democratic possibilities or the subordination of education to narrow political and economic influences in a context in which public investment in education is falling behind. It represents the growing recognition of education as both an investment and a form of social development for individuals and communities. Educators seek to enhance their legitimacy by drawing community members into schools, but they can also feel threatened by what they see as potential challenges to their expertise and sphere of decision-making. Schools frequently struggle to find truly inclusive and effective forms of involvement. Parental involvement is often defined in unclear terms, is understood in different ways by different participants, and requires adequate bases of agreement and support for it to succeed (Stelmack, 2004). Social, economic, and cultural resources also have a strong impact on the extent to which parents are able to participate and feel confident in engaging with educators, especially in a sustained manner. Several factors, including social class, race, and family status, influence the extent to which parents have the cultural and economic resources to meet school expectations or have the time and confidence to participate in a meaningful way (Lareau and Horvat, 1999; Sweet and Mandel, 2005). Like many educational reforms, the expansion of initiatives to promote parental involvement includes several dimensions that must be understood in relation both to their specific components and to the wider context in which they have emerged.

The Canadian Education Association (CEA), for example, has periodically tracked Canadian attitudes since 1979, asking opinion on a variety of matters, including requests to assess school performance on the basis of a letter grade. The proportion of those assigning an A grade to schools in their community declined from 19 per cent in 1979 to 6 per cent in both 1990 and 2007, but rose to 14 per cent in 2012; the proportion assigning failing grades has remained relatively constant at levels of 3–4 per cent throughout this time period, and about half (rising to 61 per cent in 2012) assign grades of B or higher (CEA, 2007: 9–10; CEA, 2012: 5). Guppy et al. (2005: 15–16) report similar trends in a national survey in which rising proportions—72 per cent of parents and 76 per cent of teachers in 2005—assigned grades of A or B to public schools in their communities.

However, the most recent CEA survey also suggests that respondents tend to rate schools in their provinces overall lower than those in their communities (CEA, 2012: 4–5). The results of a survey conducted in 2012 by Ipsos Reid for Global News suggest further concerns that schools are having difficulty in meeting public expectations. About three-quarters of respondents assigned public schools a grade of B (35 per cent) or C (39 per cent) while only 5 per cent awarded an A grade; nonetheless, ratings tended to be higher than average in provinces like Manitoba and Saskatchewan, which had relatively healthy economies, and lower in British Columbia and Ontario, where measures to regulate teachers' salaries or working conditions were producing public tensions between governments and teachers (Young, 2012). Respondents to the CEA surveys also hold mixed views about how well schools are responding to demands for change, observing some improvements in the quality of education over time but expressing desires for schools to embrace new ways of doing things with regard to issues like managing differences in student abilities and developing linkages with learning outside schools (CEA, 2007: 15; CEA, 2012: 4, 7).

These findings suggest that the notion that the public is clamouring with one voice for particular kinds of educational reforms is ideologically and socially constructed. Educational reports, policy documents, and anecdotal evidence highlighting problems are merged into an apparent consensus dominated by business and corporate interests rather than by values and practices emerging from people's real experiences (Delhi, 1993: 116–17). Barlow and Robertson (1994) argue that, akin to the New Right in the United States and Britain, a conservative alliance driven principally by business and religious fundamentalist interests has mobilized public opinion to promote school reforms across Canada that exacerbate class divisions and weaken the schools' ability to respond to the needs of less privileged social groups. Dominant class interests have pressured education further, both directly and indirectly, for neo-liberal reforms and market-based orientations through international and multinational trade agreements (Grieshaber-Otto and Sanger, 2002: 129–30; Robertson, 1998). Within these ideologies and associated reforms, property rights gain ascendancy over personal rights by regarding individuals, variously, as consumers, clients, and products of education. Molnar (2005: 10, 21–6) suggests that the increasing alignment of North American schools with corporate interests is evident across eight categories of commercialization:

- corporate sponsorship of programs and activities;
- exclusive product agreements;
- incentive programs;
- appropriation of space (for advertising, logos, or naming rights);

- sponsored educational materials;
- electronic marketing;
- privatization of educational services;
- fundraising.

He warns that such commercialization is detrimental to academic responsibilities and works against what schools are supposed to be about. Despite the emphasis on personal choice and freedom, real people and their diverse needs and struggles are regarded as abstractions, like inputs and outputs in an industrial system governed by considerations of cost-effectiveness and competitive advantage.

Comparative Educational Growth

Canada's education systems have their own distinct characteristics, but they are highly influenced by education systems and advancements in other nations. In its earliest stages Canadian schooling drew heavily from European forms of school organization and curricula, particularly from France and the British Isles. The historical development of education more generally is highly diverse and uneven. Collins (2006: 214) observes that education today has not emerged through a linear evolution; rather, the history of education reveals varied fluctuations and interactions among different forms. He outlines at least four main educational models, including age cohort (such as adolescent initiation rites), private apprenticeship, professional licensing and university degrees, and bureaucratic schools derived from imperial and religious practices in China and Japan. Globally based patterns of economic development, colonial systems of rule, and expansion of market forces have created some convergence among education systems, but substantial variations and inequalities in education remain both within and across nations.

Education, in developing countries and in highly industrialized countries, is guided by core concerns about how to meet basic skill and citizenship needs particular to local, regional, or national priorities and how to ensure training and skill enhancement for competitive economic growth. Historically, the development and growth of education systems have tended to be marked by a shift in emphasis from the first to the second of these priorities. Many governments, for instance, have adopted policies to ensure that education enhances particular kinds of skill development or channels people directly into the labour market. However, recent educational planning efforts by major international bodies and their participants have tended to pose these objectives as complementary to each other. While the expansion of higher-end skill development and advanced education remain vital priorities within most nations, parallel concern has emerged for the large segments of populations who have limited levels of education, literacy, and other basic skills.

Nations with highly advanced economies, including members of the Organisation for Economic Co-operation and Development (OECD), have identified enhanced educational development beyond compulsory schooling, through post-secondary education and **adult education and training**, as a major priority to drive further economic growth and social development (OECD, 2001: 151). Governments and economic agencies across the globe have intensified their demands for educational reforms, motivated by global competition and desires to link growth in knowledge-based industries with strategies to create strong public- and private-sector connections among education, training, and economic growth (Ashton and Sung, 1997). National and international attention also has shifted to the need for educational improvement at the lower end, both to ensure that all persons have basic education and, especially among the marginalized, to foster continuing education (Bowers et al., 1999).

Many nations and regions have modified their educational policies and practices to position their economies for global competitiveness and to demonstrate that the education they offer meets high-quality standards appropriate for an information society. These changes have contributed to growing convergence as education systems adopt similar objectives, organizational patterns, and practices, especially when motivated by targets or structural adjustment policies established by international bodies like the OECD, World Bank, or International Monetary Fund. Nonetheless, because education remains closely tied with questions of national character, cultural significance, and specific economic and political objectives, extensive variation still exists across different models and patterns of education and school–work linkages (Brown et al., 2001; Stromquist and Monkman, 2000).

Repositioning education within a changing global order is highly challenging. As with the historical development of education in Canada and other highly developed nations, the expansion of education in less developed regions tends to be accompanied by the promises of enhanced democratic participation and greater social mobility. The dramatic expansion of a highly educated subclass, accompanied by new types of employment in non-traditional fields and high consumption lifestyles in India, China, and many other nations, seems to suggest that some of these prospects are being fulfilled.

It is crucial, in a context in which lifelong learning and higher education are stressed, to recognize nonetheless that significant proportions of the world's population have limited education and face continuing barriers to educational participation. The benefits of educational advancement are not shared equally, and much of the world's population—especially females in the most socio-economically vulnerable groups—is losing ground rather than advancing in educational status. The World Educational Forum, organized in conjunction with the United Nations, in 2000 identified broad goals for all nations to achieve by 2015, including universal primary education; the elimination of gender disparity, first (by 2005) in primary and secondary education and later in other education levels; and a 50 per cent improvement in adult literacy levels. UNESCO (2011b: 24) reports that, by 2011, despite some advances, "The bottom line is that progress towards the key goals has been too slow and too uneven. ... Ultimately, at this critical juncture there is evidence that progress is slowing—and that the Education for All targets will be missed by a wider margin than previously assumed." Significant numbers of children do not attend school (more than 67 million in 2008), dropout rates are high, educational quality is poor in many regions, and adult literacy is declining in many nations, especially in sub-Saharan Africa and South and West Asia (UNESCO, 2011b: 24–5). While progress has been made in narrowing gender disparities, a significant "global gender divide" continues to restrict educational opportunities for girls in many parts of the world (see Box 4.4).

Education, throughout the world as in Canada, has emerged over the past several decades as a vital tool for social and economic participation, and as a core priority area for public policy. This reality carries mixed significance because the benefits derived from education, for societies as well as for individuals, simultaneously expose education as a focus of ongoing political and economic contestation. Nowhere has this been more starkly and ruthlessly demonstrated than in Pakistan's Swat Valley,

Box 4.4 Global Inequalities in Basic Education

Although considerable attention is given to the importance of advanced education and skills in the global economy, prospects to fulfill even fundamental educational objectives remain distant in many regions. UNESCO has observed progress by many nations towards achieving the six basic goals of "education for all" targeted to be achieved in 2015, but numerous barriers remain to full and equitable educational participation in some parts of the world. The excerpt below, from a report on progress in the first 10 years of monitoring these targets (UNESCO, 2011b: 73–82), highlights concerns about continuing educational inequity, including acknowledgement that initial targets to achieve gender parity in basic education have been missed. The three figures that follow are based on data from the report, summarizing regional disparities in progress towards achieving three of these goals:

Goal 5: Eliminating gender disparities in primary and secondary education by 2005, and achieving gender equality in education by 2015, with a focus on ensuring girls' full and equal access to and achievement in basic education of good quality.

- Eliminating gender disparity in enrolment at both primary and secondary level by 2005—the original goal—was overambitious and was accordingly missed by a wide margin. Achieving gender equality in access and achievement by 2015 is a more credible ambition. However, many poor countries will not achieve the target without radical shifts of policy and priorities in education planning. . . .
- In fifty-two countries, the ratio of girls to boys—that is, the gender parity index (GPI)—in gross enrolment ratios is 0.95 or less at the primary school level, and twenty-six countries have a primary GPI of 0.90 or less. Of the forty-seven countries not yet at parity with enough data for a projection to 2015, most are moving in the right direction, but thirty-eight will fall short of the target. . . .
- The picture in secondary education is more mixed, and prospects for gender parity by 2015 are less promising. Only about a third of all countries with data have achieved gender parity in secondary school and in many countries significantly fewer girls than boys are enrolled. In 2008, twenty-four countries in sub-Saharan Africa and three in South and West Asia had GPIs in secondary school enrolment of 0.90 or less—and ten had GPIs of less than 0.70. Of the seventy-four countries that had not achieved gender parity and had the data needed for a projection, only fourteen are on track to eliminate their gender disparities by 2015. . . .
- Taken separately, gender inequalities in education and employment have profoundly damaging consequences for the life chances of individuals and for national economies. Those consequences are mutually reinforcing with education disparities reinforcing labour market inequalities, which in turn reduce the incentives for girls to complete secondary school. Governments that tolerate large gender gaps in their school systems are not just depriving young girls of a basic right, but also undermining the national economic interest.

Source: © UNESCO (2011b: 73–4; 82).

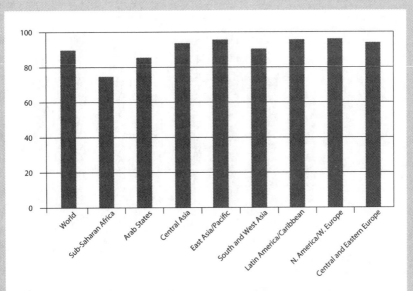

Figure 4.5 Net Enrolment Ratio in Primary Education,
by Region, 2008

Note: Percentage of children of official primary school age who are actually enrolled in
primary school.
Source: Based on data in UNESCO (2011b: 40).

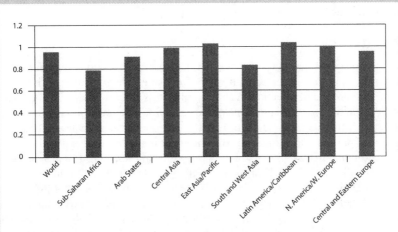

Figure 4.6 Ratio of Females to Males Enrolled in Secondary
Education, by Region, 2008

Source: Based on data in UNESCO (2011b: 73).

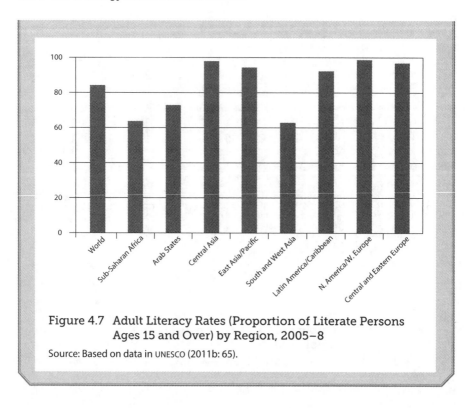

Figure 4.7   Adult Literacy Rates (Proportion of Literate Persons
Ages 15 and Over) by Region, 2005–8

Source: Based on data in UNESCO (2011b: 65).

where, in October 2012, a Taliban assassin sought to murder a 15-year-old schoolgirl for becoming an activist for the right of girls to obtain an education. The girl, Malala Yousafzai, was shot in the head on her school bus but survived, barely, and soon was transported from Pakistan to London for treatment and rehabilitation.

Conclusion

As education systems gain prominence in a world where credentials and learning take on central importance, they remain sites of considerable controversy and struggle over their mandate and direction. As more Canadians than ever before are engaged in educational activities, proclamations about the value of education are accompanied by debates concerning the extent to which this value is being realized. Thus, rising educational participation and **educational attainment** levels coexist with concern over phenomena such as illiteracy, school dropouts, uneven educational achievement, and underutilization of vital forms of learning, as depicted vividly in Livingstone's (2004: 13) imagery of "pyramids" of formal learning and "icebergs" of informal and voluntary learning. The contradictory character of educational reform is in large part an expression of the intersection of dynamics of global competition and cultural and social change with a contemporary education system that, as the previous chapter has emphasized, derives much of its prevailing structure and orientation from a period of early capitalist development and industrialization. Education is directed towards the transformative potentials in human beings and their societies, but it is organized and structured in such a way that routine, standardization, and restrictions of opportunity often prevail over creativity, flexibility, and innovation. Ultimately, the varied educational systems and practices that have arisen in the midst of recent socio-economic transformations and challenges are not a consequence of any single evolutionary historical process; rather, they represent what education fundamentally is: a somewhat paradoxical and contentious network of social relations and institutional structures.

Issues related to educational reform, relevance, and public confidence in a changing society are revisited in the last chapter, which offers a more thorough examination of the reasons for mixed sentiments expressed in recent debates over educational reform. Formal education is not neutral insofar as it is subject to competing priorities, objectives, and visions about social possibilities. Whether viewed as preparation for work, preparation for life in general, or an essential activity in its own right, education both reflects and influences the social world of which it is a central component. The next chapter explores these complex dynamics further by taking us inside educational processes.

Annotated Further Readings

Council of Ministers of Education Canada. 2008. *The Development of Education: Reports for Canada*. Toronto: Council of Ministers of Education Canada. Following a concise summary of the major features of Canadian education systems, the reports provide a multi-level government focus on emerging issues in education, with special emphasis on inclusive education as populations and learning needs diversify.

Friesen, John W., and Virginia Lyons Friesen. 2001. *In Defense of Public Schools in North America*. Calgary: Detselig. The authors make the case for the benefits of public schooling, presenting a concise summary of the history, purposes, and outcomes of public schooling in Canada, an overview of contemporary educational issues and problems, and a critique of alternatives advocated by critics of public schooling.

Levin, Benjamin. 2005. *Governing Education*. Toronto: University of Toronto Press. The author, drawing on his extensive experience as an educator, school board member, university administrator, and deputy minister of education, provides knowledgeable "insider" perspectives on the education system and policy-making process.

Robertson, Heather-jane. 2007. *Great Expectations: Essays on Schools and Society*. Ottawa: Canadian Centre for Policy Alternatives. This volume collects the author's insightful and powerful commentary on important educational matters.

Sears, Alan. 2003. *Retooling the Mind Factory: Education in a Lean State*. Aurora, ON: Garamond. The nature and impact of various dimensions of educational reform are examined critically in the context of political and economic transformations driven by neo-liberal policies and the expansion of market forces.

Young, Jon, Benjamin Levin, and Dawn Wallin. 2007. *Understanding Canadian Schools: An Introduction to Educational Administration*, 4th edn. Scarborough, ON: Nelson. This book provides a comprehensive overview of school organization and administration in Canada, addressing issues such as school policy, educational structures, the nature and role of various educational participants, and school reform.

Key Terms

Adult education and training Educational and training activities engaged in by persons, normally aged 17 and over, who have completed their basic or initial schooling.

Amalgamation The consolidation of smaller school boards or administrative units into larger units.

Educational attainment The highest level of education that a person has completed, usually expressed in terms of numbers of years of formal schooling or the highest credential achieved by those who are not currently enrolled in an educational program.

Informal learning Learning activities undertaken as part of a conscious or organized effort to gain new knowledge, skills, or competencies outside of programs organized by an institution or agency for specific credit or credentials.

Private schools Educational institutions, which may or may not receive government funding, administered or operated by individuals, associations, or agencies outside the public school system.

Privatization A process in which services or programs operated by the state sector or governments are shifted to private or for-profit firms or agencies.

Study Questions

1. What challenges have education systems been confronted with by periodic growth in the school-age population and the increasing lengths of time that people stay in school?

2. Who makes the major decisions about educational resources, curricula, and program requirements? What are the implications of these decision-making arrangements and power structures for different social groups?

3. Select two nations—one industrially advanced and the other in a less developed part of the world—and compare their education systems. How is the system organized and funded? What are the levels of participation and attainment (by the overall population as well as by gender)? What factors account for the patterns you observe? What do these patterns reveal about opportunities and priorities in each of these nations?

4. What are the major public expectations for Canada's education systems in the knowledge or information society? What varied and often conflicting reforms are being proposed by different participants in order to produce a more effective education system? Critically discuss these issues, exploring the positions advanced in websites such as the Canadian Education Association blog (www.cea-ace.ca/blog) where educational debates are articulated.

5. How are educational institutions being influenced by recent emphasis on lifelong learning and global competitiveness? What educational alternatives are viable to meet these challenges?

6. Discuss the impact that social diversity among student populations has had on educational practices and outcomes.

Chapter 5

The Process of Schooling

Learning Objectives

In this chapter, you will:

- be introduced to the predominant sociological characteristics that constitute schooling processes;
- gain an understanding of how educational practices both directly and in less obvious ways help to shape individual life experiences and opportunities;
- explore how educational practices influence and are shaped by interactions related to major social characteristics, including class, race, gender, sexual orientation, and age.

Introduction

One of the remarkable features of schooling is its consistency over time. Despite the many changes that have occurred in educational philosophies and practices over several generations, educational institutions and classrooms have retained a distinctive quality that makes it difficult for them to be mistaken for any other setting. Children who are driven to spacious, well-equipped urban composite schools replete with innovative technological devices may not immediately identify with the experiences of ancestors who walked or rode horseback to attend one-room schoolhouses with few books and blackboards made of tarpaper, but people's reminiscences of their school days tend to evoke common themes regardless of when and how they were educated. This commonality is, in part, a consequence of the integral role that schooling has come to play in developmental processes associated with childhood and adolescence and its importance in the transmission of basic knowledge and beliefs from one generation to the next. It is also a product of the massive scale of educational bureaucracies and institutional enterprises. Despite periodic modifications, fundamental patterns of classroom interaction, school organization, and curricula in Canada have remained relatively faithful to nineteenth-century roots. The school system's resistance to particular kinds of change is the focus of extensive discussion and controversy as educators, policymakers, and various social groups struggle with the issue of what schooling should be like to ensure it remains relevant to the needs of contemporary societies that place a substantial premium on knowledge and its application.

This chapter explores the main patterns of activity that occur within educational processes, examining their significance both for individuals and for more general social relations. Although schools are likely to reveal features that are peculiar to the demographic and social characteristics of the communities they are located in, the school system as a whole is one of the most socially inclusive agencies in contemporary societies. The face of the student body has changed significantly, through patterns of immigration, lengthened periods of education from early childhood to adult education, integration of students with disabilities and others who often were excluded from regular schooling, and shifting cultural practices and expectations. This chapter looks at how educational institutions variously include and exclude particular individuals and groups throughout the schooling process. It begins with a general discussion of how sociologists analyze the dynamics between human interactions and educational institutions, then examines significant dimensions associated with what might be considered the three Rs of reproduction, regulation, and resistance.

The Multi-faceted Nature of Educational Practices

A common characteristic in traditional sociological research on education, as observed in Chapter 2, has been a tendency to concentrate either on the details of life within schools or on the expectations placed on schooling through external social pressures and organizations. This dualism of focus is in part an expression of debates over whether human agency or social structures play the greatest role in influencing social life and human behaviour. In practice, internal and external forces, agency, and structure all are important determinants of educational realities. Some aspects of these dynamics, and in particular how they contribute to making educational practice such a varied and often contradictory undertaking, are discussed below and expanded on in subsequent sections of this chapter.

Structural analysis stresses how labelling and hierarchy, as employed both formally and informally within educational settings, contribute to the reproduction of the social order. The standard imagery, from this vantage point, portrays classrooms structured by rows of desks occupied by students facing a teacher or professor at the front of the room. Education is viewed as little else than a form of preparation for work or **socialization** for adult life. Whatever the variations on this theme, the image conveys certain salient features of much educational life—schooling is organized around expectations of conformity, compliance, and standardization, whereby the instructor's position and authority are privileged in comparison with those of the learners. Despite their analytical differences, both structural functionalist and Marxist theorists of education share the position that student classification and streaming are central functions of schooling driven by the requirements of advanced industrial or capitalist social structures. Educational practices are examined not for their intrinsic or unique characteristics, but for their ability to produce individuals who are ready and able to occupy the social positions that await them after they leave the education system.

Interpretive analysis, by contrast, focusing on human agency, portrays labelling, categorization, and social identities within schooling as more fluid and changing processes, often expressed in terms used by educational participants themselves. High school pupils in Newfoundland and Labrador surveyed by Martin (1982), for instance, viewed classroom culture as a series of practices constructed around two main categories of pupils—"teachers' pets" and "class victims." Students also categorize themselves and others through various designations, based on factors like academic performance, cultural identification (signifying recreational pursuits, musical or sports-related interests, racial or ethnic identities, drug or alcohol preferences, or gender and sexual identities), or physical characteristics. Teachers also apply labels to pupils as they differentiate among "good kids," "troublemakers," "bullies," "mean girls," "yahoos," "overachievers," "underachievers," and so on. Many of these labels, and the social interactions they are associated with, reflect or contribute to more enduring patterns of success and failure, but they are also important signifiers of the ways educational settings are constituted as rich and varied sites of social activity.

Many studies of schooling fail to integrate analysis of activities inside the classroom—and other sites where educational interactions occur—with life beyond the classroom, and to comprehend the relationship between official and unofficial school activities. Similarly, more general boundaries and distinctions characterize common perceptions about schooling. People tend to accept formal education as an inevitable part of their lives. When individuals do talk about schooling, it is usually with reference to people they hung around with, interesting or embarrassing moments, successes and failures, and overall impressions rather than about curricula and content that was learned. People are sometimes uneasy because these informal considerations seem to be at odds with the identification of school as the official world of lessons, homework, tests, rules, school-sponsored organizations, and other scheduled activities.

When asked to describe the purpose of schools, for instance, students often revert to language that could almost be quoted from official school documents, even though students rarely pay attention to such statements. A typical conception of schooling, in this case from a Grade 12 female student interviewed in the course of my own research, is that "School is a place of learning, a place where we learn to interact with people and learn skill[s] that will help us deal with the problems in life with basic reason and understanding." Whether or not they agree with particular features of schooling, people rarely question the legitimacy of formal education as a mechanism to structure learning, regulate lives, and confer **credentials**. This acceptance is based on distinctions we make that place boundaries between school and other aspects of our lives. As another student, this one a Grade 9 male who generally had a positive orientation to school, observed, "I dislike the hard work and homework because I like to go home and watch TV and go hang around with my friends." In other words, for students the official part of schooling is important, but it is not the same as, and sometimes interferes with, "real life."

Schooling overlaps substantially with people's social lives to the extent that much school time is occupied by "joking around," finding ways to pass the time, and discussing parents, relationships, parties, popular culture, or personal issues, yet these events are typically discounted as irrelevant or incidental to education (McLaren, 2007; Contenta, 1993). Students often internalize educational success or failure as a personal responsibility, regardless of personal circumstances, as observed in this account from a First Nations student in Grade 12:

> I think if I experienced difficulty [in school] that would be [because of] a low expectation of myself. I have two children, I have a son and a daughter and I have a babysitter, and it takes more responsibility to get them to daycare, to get myself to school and if I can't do that then that's my fault.... I can't make excuses, I can't use them as an excuse because it's something I did and it's my responsibility to get my education regardless.

It is crucial to recognize that schooling, in all of its routines as well as its more unique or exciting moments, is an important social activity in its own right even as it serves as a conduit into other spheres of social activity. Life in educational institutions carries its own rhythms and meanings, but it also reveals the pervasive influence of the world beyond the classroom door. The sometimes chaotic experiences of organized schooling leave indelible impressions about what is possible and expected in people's social lives.

Much recent sociological analysis of classroom processes has explored the linkages between social interaction in educational settings and more general historical and structural arrangements. Given the strong correlation between social privilege and success in education and life beyond school, what is it about schooling that preserves this relationship in spite of the supposed role that education plays to provide equal opportunities for all? What are the features of schooling that produce relatively enduring patterns of success and failure? To what extent, and in what ways, does education impose control over people, and how much does it provide opportunities to empower them? Critical inquiry has attempted to address these issues by moving beyond individual determinants of educational attainment and school success to highlight the connections between human agency and social structure and between formal and informal aspects of educational practices.

The Contribution of Schooling to the Development of Human Subjects

The observations made in the previous section suggest that the analysis of schooling must recognize formal education as having, in several significant ways, a dual character. Schooling contributes to formal learning and the attainment of knowledge and credentials that can be concretely defined and measured, but it is also characterized by more indefinite tasks associated with its human interactive and social dimensions. As was pointed out in Chapter 2, many important school lessons are derived from a **hidden curriculum** with little apparent connection to formal or overt educational objectives. We learn about such things as competition, success, failure, gender roles, racial identities, cultural understandings, and our place in society through our participation in the daily rituals of schooling. In other words, in addition to its roles of transmitting knowledge and bestowing status, schooling contributes to personality formation. Expressed another way, schooling is involved in the process of **individuation**, which refers to how our identity is constructed through notions of ourselves as distinct subjects.

The idea that our personalities are not fully formed from birth but are shaped as we interact with other people in particular circumstances is a central insight of sociology. Most sociological perspectives, regardless of their specific differences, emphasize the importance of formal education in the process of making us *social* beings. We are expected, through schooling, to develop patterns of co-operation with others and to gain sufficient understanding that we will comply with certain social expectations. Ironically, a fundamental part of our social identities in advanced capitalist societies is oriented towards individualism as a core value. We tend to view successful educational and social outcomes, essentially, as the product of initiative, aptitude, intelligence, and other attributes associated with qualities of the individual, while factors that contribute to failure commonly are given psychological explanations and persistent problems are regarded as ailments in need of treatment. The sociological critique of individualist positions emphasizes that individuals are shaped by society not merely because our social lives are conducted in relation to one another, but also in the sense that individualism itself is constructed through social processes.

It is important, in developing a sociological understanding of individual identities and orientations, that we not dismiss entirely the social role played by individual actors. Fundamental to notions of human agency is the acknowledgement that each

Box 5.1 Aboriginal Students' Perceptions of a Positive School Climate

Several initiatives have been implemented by school systems to address persistent concerns about the lack of educational success among Aboriginal students in Canada. The experiences described by Aboriginal youth in a Saskatchewan high school, which has modified its programming, organizational structure, and social relations to account for difficulties students often face both in and out of school, demonstrate how students can benefit from a proactive, positive school climate:

A. When teachers are teaching they always refer to something to do with Aboriginal people, all the time. If it's Psychology, if it's something, because there are always Aboriginal students that go here ... they use examples or bring up First Nations because everybody gets a little taste of it.

B. [In this school] everybody gets by, everybody has a story, the teacher has a story, they know more about the students than a regular teacher would. ... The classes are smaller, you get to know everybody real quick.... [There is] more of a holistic way of teaching, not just straight out of the textbook, more Native teachers to explain the difference between the traditional and the contemporary.

C. Lots of times [in other schools] the teachers don't understand the situations or they don't understand certain people, they are used to seeing their middle-class kids attending and being good students. I guess if one of those teachers came into this school, their head would spin off their shoulders because there are so many different people with different problems and mostly everybody has some problem because most of the students are young parents. Eighty per cent of the student population here ... is considered at risk.

D. ... most of the teachers here will help you out if you have the time to go early ... it's not just, "do your work," they take the time to help you.

E. [I can] almost identify the school as a community.... The people are really friendly, and I know [it] kinda has a bad reputation ... but that's always not true, there's a lot of people that have come here and they say it's so mellow and there's like no fighting, you're not really in little groups. Everybody is friends with everybody. There's no prejudice ... it's small and caring.

person must accept some responsibility for his/her decisions and actions as well as for the consequences that follow from them. At the same time, however, we must be attentive to how schooling and other social circumstances set parameters around which those decisions, actions, and consequences can be meaningful and effective.

The Role of Schooling in Shaping Identities

Educational practices play a major role in the process by which people's lives and identities are constructed as individual subjects. Most school learning revolves around individual competencies. The individual pupil is monitored, expected to complete assignments, graded, promoted from one grade to the next, and disciplined. Educational credentials are acquired on a competitive basis, separating and distinguishing the identity and performance of each person from all others. We therefore come to identify success and failure, and learn to deal with their consequences, as products of our own efforts. A continual focus within schooling on individual characteristics, efforts, and achievements reinforces similar orientations prevalent within the mass media, workplaces, families, and other social sites, creating an impression that the individual is the natural, inevitable basis of social existence. School knowledge involves the development of an identity based on a modified sense of place or position in society. Education sorts students through continuous assessment and evaluation of pupils within schooling and in the presentation of grades and credentials for the outside world. The operation of the hidden curriculum and the informal interactions among educational participants also serve to construct and reinforce identities both within and beyond schooling.

The processes by which formal education contributes to personality and character formation can be illustrated with reference to the historical example of boarding and residential schools for children of Aboriginal ancestry. Boarding schools, operated by religious denominations, and residential schools, operated by the churches under federal government standards and with government funds after the mid-nineteenth century, were oriented to the assimilation of First Nations children into the dominant social order. Children were separated—sometimes forcibly—from their families for at least 10 months a year. The schools were organized in accordance with the principles of what Goffman (1961) terms **total institutions**, which are isolated from external social settings and governed by strict regimes of administrative scrutiny and control. Authorities in residential and boarding schools had complete control over children's lives for the duration of schooling. In addition to class work, their social lives and labour time (justified as necessary to provide essential job skills) were highly regimented and regulated. They were treated as inmates, subject to extreme scrutiny and strict disciplinary measures for transgressions such as speaking their indigenous language. The schools were organized to alter the children's identities away from their original cultures to one that was regarded by authorities as appropriate for life in the dominant society. The intended transformation was a radical one, as described by the Royal Commission on Aboriginal Peoples (1996a: 365):

> At the heart of the vision of residential education—a vision of the school as home and sanctuary of motherly care—there was a dark contradiction, an inherent element of savagery in the mechanics of civilizing the children. The very language in which the vision was couched revealed what would have to be the essentially violent nature of the school system in its assault on child and culture. The basic premise of resocialization, of the great transformation from "savage" to "civilized," was violent. "To kill the Indian in the child," the department [of Indian Affairs] aimed at severing the artery of culture that ran between generations and was the profound connection between parent and child sustaining family and community.

"The result," according to Kirkness and Bowman (1992: 12), "was a tragic interruption of culture" that produced a legacy "of cultural conflict, alienation, poor self-concept and lack of preparation for independence, for jobs and for life in general." The residential schooling experience not only affected students directly, but, as observed in

Chapter 3, it contributed to a legacy of destruction and "cycle of abuse" whose powerful impact remains deeply embedded in many Aboriginal communities (Truth and Reconciliation Commission of Canada, 2012; Schissel and Wotherspoon, 2003: 60–3).

Boarding and residential schools are not necessarily representative of schooling in general, given the extreme circumstances in which they functioned as total institutions oriented to the modification of individual personalities, in this case from their grounding in Aboriginal knowledge systems based on relationships with the land to identities viewed by officials as being more suited for life in a society dominated by Euro-Canadian people and Christian values. Nonetheless, parallels are found among all types of schooling. Formal education, by its nature, shares the general objective to transform individual character and consciousness. Gracey (1977), in an influential article entitled "Learning the Student Role: Kindergarten as Academic Boot Camp," shows how formal education is oriented from the outset to establish military-like classroom order and discipline. Various humanistic and progressive reforms, along with recent emphasis on the importance of creativity and innovation to a knowledge-based economy, have softened or concealed much of the disciplinary structure of the classroom. Nonetheless, the rise of a security state that has accompanied the post 9/11 American "war on terror," in which Canada has been a complicit participant, mass shootings in schools and other public places, and fears about external threats and youth violence have renewed a "law and order" ethos for many schools (Chomsky, 2011).

The structure of many classrooms continues to resemble late nineteenth-century factory organization, but school regimentation comes from roots that precede mechanized industrial production just as it is transformed by new production and social processes. Nineteenth-century school reformers, in particular, were blunt in their assessment that mass public schooling should involve discipline and habit at least as much as it should be concerned with the acquisition of knowledge and work skills. Schools were consciously constructed to mould the individual and foster new loyalties and allegiances. Educational authorities devised measures, such as the timetabling of the school day, the physical organization of the classroom, and monitoring and assessment of pupils and teachers, in such a way to ensure that schooling produced disciplined individual subjects (see, e.g., Corrigan et al., 1987; Curtis, 1988; Wotherspoon, 1993). Today's schools may be less overtly concerned with discipline and personal virtues, but issues of character, order, and hierarchy remain fundamental to schooling processes.

Thus, it is important to recognize how educational practices shape and are shaped by what happens outside schooling. The activities we engage in and the identities we develop tend to be mutually reinforcing. Both individually and socially, educational outcomes tend to be affected more deeply by "things that happened" than by "what we learned in school." The extent to which these events may become meaningful depends, in turn, on such factors as our relations with parents and family members, out-of-school interests and obligations, racial and gender characteristics, and the social and economic resources available to us.

Regulation and Resistance in Schooling

One way in which sociologists have attempted to make sense of educational dynamics is to conceptualize schools as sites in which regulation and resistance occur. Schools regulate individuals and social activities as they fulfill tasks associated with their varied expectations, including the dissemination of knowledge, the development of student skills and aptitudes, the production of recognized credentials, and the shaping and provision of direction to individuals' lives. In its most extreme and visible forms, as in the case of residential and boarding schools, regulation is evident through rules, disciplinary procedures, the organization of time and space, and scrutiny by school officials over pupils' activities. Regulation also occurs in subtler forms, such as the recognition of some forms of knowledge and viewpoints as valid and the denial of alternative frameworks and experiences. In schooling, as in any regulative institution, however, official objectives and practices are not always passively accepted by participants. Educators and learners alike use varied strategies and coping mechanisms as they attempt to make their lives alternatively meaningful or simply bearable. Students may mock teachers they dislike, for instance, overtly flout school rules, or vandalize school property, just as teachers may introduce materials not on the curriculum, refuse to carry out official regulations, or employ a wide repertoire of other actions in expressing their responses to either specific or general features of schooling. Notions of resistance, whether they reside in disillusionment, optimism, rebellion, or even ridicule and humour, point to the ways in which educational practices can be indeterminate and contested, regardless of the limitations imposed by dominant educational structures and the agents who act on their behalf.

The discussion thus far has portrayed life in educational institutions as a volatile combination of formal and informal, official and unofficial, and determinate and indeterminate features. These educational realities create opportunities for individual and social transformation at the same time as they contribute to the reproduction of existing social circumstances and structures. People carry with them into schooling various background characteristics and predispositions—such as race, gender, income, employment status, parental support, family responsibilities, and emotional states—that affect and are shaped by their educational experiences in complex ways. One of the most difficult tasks in the analysis of education is to isolate the relative impact of these various influences on people's life conditions, choices, and chances. As noted in Chapter 2 (and elaborated on in Chapters 7 and 8), there are strong correlations between educational experiences and outcomes and social characteristics such as class, gender, and race. Social forces interact with unique aspects of our lives to produce distinctly different opportunity structures. As a consequence, regardless of our individual predispositions, our experiences are also strongly affected by whether we are male or female, Aboriginal or non-Aboriginal, poor or wealthy, of urban or rural origin, and so on. Similar interrelationships operate within the education system. Within Canadian education, for example, most senior-level teachers and administrators are men, while women are concentrated in lower-level teaching positions. To understand this reality, it is not sufficient to consider the specific elements that influence day-to-day decision-making within the scope of the classroom or other aspects of individual teachers' lives. We must also know something about how such factors as gender discrimination and differential labour market opportunities for men and women have contributed to the historical development of teaching. While particular career paths are the result of unique experiences, those experiences are preconditioned by strikingly regular patterns defined by social boundaries and expectations.

By recognizing these boundaries and the interactions that take place within them, we can begin to understand how relations of regulation and resistance may produce distinct social and educational outcomes. In subsequent sections of this chapter, these dynamics are explored through discussion of four significant types of practice that structure educational experience: (1) *streaming*, whereby students are channelled into distinct learning groups and programs; (2) an emphasis on *official knowledge*, which designates the kinds of topics, information, and content considered to be legitimate or worth knowing within schooling; (3) *hegemony*, through which domination is experienced in people's everyday life experiences; and (4) *silencing*, which refers to processes through which particular kinds of social experience and alternative voices are devalued, marginalized, or denied a place within educational practice.

Streaming

Streaming refers to the placement of students into different programs based on their aptitude, ability, or special interests and needs. Streaming is most visible in situations where learners are differentiated into broad program areas such as vocational or academic streams. Streaming occurs between schools both when the choice of a school is related to the programs it offers and when it is recognized (by teachers, students, and parents) that the nature and quality of education vary from one school to the next. It also takes place within schools and classrooms in the form of various measures such as ability grouping in which pupils are divided into regular, remedial, or advanced streams in basic subject areas.

Streaming tends to be more voluntaristic and less systematically co-ordinated in Canadian schools in comparison with nations such as the United Kingdom, Japan, and Germany, where highly structured educational streams are prevalent, and even the United States, where tracking (grouping within classrooms) and stratified institutional arrangements are widely practised. Pedagogical justifications for streaming are based on arguments that students of similar backgrounds, interests, and abilities can be taught more efficiently and effectively than is possible in mixed classes. According to this justification, pupils receive instruction and assignments appropriate to their levels of interest and understanding, thereby facilitating success and making the educational process more rewarding for the individual. Streaming is also promoted for its potential to make education more relevant to the learner and better oriented to student futures. It is sometimes argued that educational and individual resources are wasted when all students are expected to be taught from the same curriculum at the same pace. This position asserts that people should receive training directly related to the kinds of jobs and futures they can expect.

Critics of streaming contend that these arguments confuse important issues while they hide the damaging realities of streaming. Much of the problem, at least on a day-to-day basis, is associated with the labels and identities that accompany student categorization. Students are highly aware of their status in relation to others and look for cues such as the classroom or work group they are placed in to identify where the system has slotted them. Responses like "How come I'm with the dummies?" or "I'm here because I want to go to university" signify pupils' attentiveness to groupings that may not even be officially acknowledged to the students by teachers or administrators. While the occasional placement of students in particular groups may not be highly significant, students' educational careers are given shape by recurrent labels and groupings that affect their self-concepts and educational performance. As noted in Chapter 2, the complex workings of the self-fulfilling prophecy, in which students eventually adopt behaviours consistent with the perceptions and expectations of their ability and roles held by teachers and other officials, have been demonstrated repeatedly through classroom research (Rosenthal and Jacobson, 1968; Stebbins, 1975; Contenta, 1993; Martel et al., 1999).

A regular consequence of streaming is that it does not affect students randomly but, instead, produces results that tend to correspond to existing patterns of social inequality, particularly in terms of race, class, and gender. This operates in several ways.

Schooling and Gender Differentiation

Gender relations illustrate both how streaming can affect students on a differential basis and how processes related to streaming can change over time. Nearly all school programs are open to males and females alike, but often there are pronounced differences in the kinds of schooling that boys and girls, and men and women, experience. Consequently, as Jane Gaskell (1992: 37) emphasizes, "Gender itself matters" in the education system:

> At the university level, the small number of women enrolled in engineering and science has frequently been noted. Women are much more likely than men to be enrolled in nursing, education, the fine arts, and most humanities disciplines. At the college level, women are under-represented in trades training and in technologies, but are over-represented in community services and in secretarial and accounting courses. In high schools, the differences occur not so much between academic and non-academic courses, where racial and class differences are found, but within each. Young women are more often in senior French and history courses than in senior physics and computer science courses. They are more often in domestic science and business education than in industrial education.

Gender differentiation is produced by a combination of individual choices and organizational features of the school and wider society. Directions and comments from parents, teachers, guidance counsellors, peers, and others reinforce differential expectations about what kinds of behaviours and choices are appropriate for boys and girls. Many researchers have observed that teachers interact differently with boys and girls. Eyre (1991), observing students in a Grade 8 home economics program, notes that boys tend to dominate discussions, are more likely to be acknowledged by teachers, and are permitted higher levels of boisterousness than girls. In contrast to this situation, in which teachers have modified the curriculum to attract the attention of boys, McLaren and Gaskell (1995: 152) observe in a senior physics class little effort by teachers or students (male and female alike) to empower girls, challenge male authority, or even confront harassment of female students by some of the male students.

Competing Claims about Boys, Girls, and Schooling

Recent research findings and media attention have posed significant challenges to feminist critiques of gender-based differentiation in education. Feminist analysis initially highlighted mechanisms within education and career pathways that undermined girls' educational achievements or diverted women in directions that did not match their aspirations or capabilities. However, a powerful discourse has emerged since the mid-1990s in Canada and many other nations to suggest that boys, not girls, have become educationally disadvantaged. These claims are based on several types of evidence, including standardized test results that repeatedly show girls outperform boys overall on reading and literacy measures, higher school **dropout** rates for boys relative to girls, post-secondary enrolment and graduation trends in which females outnumber males in most programs, and the preponderance of female students as recipients of major academic awards. Schools have come under pressure from media voices, policy-makers, educators, and parent advocacy groups to tailor programs, teaching styles, and curricular activities to boys' interests and needs, reminiscent of efforts in previous decades to make schools more "girl friendly." The prominence given to standardized test results led to broader scrutiny about issues such as boys' loss of interest in school matters, lack of reading interest, and stages of developmental progress. In 2001, the Durham District School Board in Ontario gained extensive national exposure after it implemented guidelines requiring schools to develop action plans to address systematically the problem of boys' educational difficulties. The board identified several objectives, such as the need for "longer, more complex written assignments from boys; increased use of libraries by boys for recreational reading; more boys in academic after-school programs; [and] more boys being celebrated for reading achievements." These objectives were translated into specific strategies, such as the use of role models to encourage boys, scrutiny of reading materials for gender bias, public acknowledgement of boys' reading achievements, and establishment of after-school programs to attract boys (Fine, 2001: A7; Bauer, 2001).

The introduction of a discourse that has posed boys as educationally disadvantaged has been accompanied by considerable controversy. Many educators are reluctant to embrace strategies to improve boys' educational performance for fear that efforts to target any specific group will reinforce stereotypes about gender and other discriminatory groupings, and undermine efforts to promote education inclusive of all students. Some critics link the focus on male disadvantage to a backlash against feminism that blames previous efforts to make schooling more accessible and rewarding to girls for going too far. There are also concerns that the reframing of the positions of boys and girls in schools reinforces a traditional gender duality that identifies the masculine as the rational and the feminine as the irrational.

Walkerdine (1998: 168) observes that

[t]he ideal child it seems is still a boy, a boy indeed with potential, whose success is being thwarted by women and girls, indeed by the very notion of female success. It is instructive therefore to examine the discourses through which this situation is understood and the way in which what at first appears as a problem with and for boys is too easily translated into a female problem: such a translation certainly accords with educational discourses which target mothers, female teachers, and of course, latterly, feminism.

In practice, the purported reversal of the gender gap can be understood fully only after several key questions are asked about such factors as the basis of comparisons, the processes that contribute to students' selection of particular subject and academic programs, the relative status attached to specific subjects, and the employment and life prospects that follow from specific educational outcomes. Kenway and Willis (1998: 57) illustrate, in part, how these mechanisms may operate:

Although not wanting to draw attention to themselves as high achievers, many students try to avoid being labeled as low achievers by enrolling in higher status subjects. Thus many—predominantly boys—enroll themselves in physics and chemistry with little chance of success. In contrast, a lack of confidence or ambition—or both—are perceived by many teachers to prevent girls from enrolling in physics and chemistry when they *are* able to cope with them. Gender policies and programmes which define able students' choices as acceptable when they are based on physical science and high-level mathematics, and less acceptable when they are not, serve to privilege success in male and academic terms and to devalue success in other areas. Overwhelmingly, this works against girls, who recognise that their futures are not likely to be the same as those of boys. Less obviously, it also works against "less able" boys, who inappropriately choose subjects which are not likely to match the kinds of post-school options which will be available to them.

While boys and girls alike may be encouraged to aspire to careers in math, science, business, or health care, individual aspirations are modified by specific experiences of success or failure in the classroom, cues received from others about the appropriateness of particular goals, and growing sensitivity to categories produced by gender stereotyping. Despite increasing sensitivity to gender variations, it is still true, for example, that men are much more likely to be engineers and computer programmers while women are more likely to be secretaries and nurses. It is also important to recognize that gender and gender relations are experienced in complex and often contradictory ways. Contentions that a new post-feminist era has heralded the advancement of "girl power" to the detriment of boys are dangerous for obscuring complex social structural factors while falsely suggesting that achievement and success are simply matters of individual initiative (McRobbie, 2009; Ringrose, 2007). While discourses of female empowerment, self-confidence, and enhanced social and educational opportunities for girls and women have reinforced one another, these are often intermingled with encounters with discrimination and less fulfilling scenarios. Pomerantz and Raby (2011), reporting on research in two Ontario high schools, emphasize the mixed signals that girls often encounter: "They spoke of themselves as empowered girls who have the world at their fingertips. But this feeling of optimism is contradicted by experiences of sexism both in and out of the school, and the belief that they will have to do better than boys throughout their lives just to be seen as equal."

These trends have reopened many long-standing debates, including questions about the extent to which biological factors influence educational and career pathways. Recent developments in genetic science and brain research have added a degree of sophistication lacking in previous nature–nurture controversies insofar as empirical evidence appears to support claims that boys and girls are fundamentally different with respect to aptitudes, learning styles, and other attributes. While such analysis can be compelling and powerful, it can also lead to conclusions that nothing can be done to change human "nature," in the process potentially overstating the veracity of specific findings and the extent to which they can be generalized to apply to wider phenomena. At the same time, this analysis can undermine the complex mechanisms through which social practices intertwine with biological factors to produce any given social outcome. The new politics of genetics and renewed nature–nurture controversies, as with previous iterations of debates over whether social or biological factors contribute more to social outcomes, tend to be highly charged and often misguided due to deep political convictions and ideological positions adopted by proponents of differing views. On one side, neo-liberal and socially conservative forces frequently see in genetic research a powerful "scientific" antidote to feminism and social welfare orientations, often without exploring fully the limitations inherent in this "science" and the claims associated with it; from an opposing perspective, social constructionists and advocates of state intervention frequently dismiss research findings that in some instances do have to be taken seriously.

Debates about gender and other nature–nurture controversies often obscure serious examination of how social structures and educational processes interact among themselves and with varying biological dimensions to restrict or foster educational and social opportunities. The polarization of gender identities and dualist gender-based understandings of success draw on and reinforce assumptions that do not represent the full scope of children's experiences. Blaise and Taylor (2012: 92) point out that, while children "draw upon dominant heteronormative discourses to 'perform' or 'act out' stereotypical gender performances, it is also possible for children to 'perform' being a girl or a boy in other ways. By drawing upon alternative gender discourses, children can choose a range of gender performances." Kehler (2010) observes the contradiction emerging as schools adopt policies designed to eradicate discrimination based on sexual orientation at the same time that youth who do not conform to the heterosexual norm "are further marginalized through a dominating and oppressive power differential underlining literacy strategies that aim at allowing 'boys to be boys' in the face of a perceived 'masculinity crisis.'"

It is important to understand the interrelationships among gender-based educational streaming and other significant processes of social differentiation. While much attention has been paid to the differences between boys' and girls' test results in mathematics and literacy, for instance, more substantial variations are produced by social class and inequalities in parental backgrounds (Kenway and Willis, 1998; Bussière et al., 2007: 41–2). Krahn and Taylor (2007), analyzing data on courses selected by 15-year-olds in four Canadian provinces, observe that, "Young people from more advantaged families were more likely than those from families where neither parent had a postsecondary education and where family incomes tended to be lower to be taking the type of math, science, and English courses that would keep all their postsecondary options open." Without a clear understanding of how race, gender, and class operate within schooling, the characteristic focus on differences in educational performance can advance a neo-liberal emphasis on the individual at the expense of an awareness of the fundamental social bases of inequality (Burman, 2005).

Race, Class, and Streaming

Class and racial and ethnic relations are reproduced in similar ways, as discussed in more detail in Chapter 8. Working-class children predominate in lower streams while children of professionals and those from more privileged families tend to be placed in academic streams and schools that are better equipped to produce success (Curtis et al., 1992). Educational experiences and attainments are also highly segmented through similar processes that operate along racial and ethnic lines (Li, 1988; Young, 1987). Henry and Tator (2009: 206–7), in a summary of Canadian research findings, observe that streaming repeatedly works to the detriment of immigrant and visible minority students, often as a consequence of assessment and decision-making processes related to the placement of students in particular streams. They cite as prominent cases the disproportional placement of black students in low-level academic programs and vocational programs, and the concentration of Southeast Asian students in mathematics, science, and computer post-secondary programs. The impact of streaming also extends beyond the allocation of students among distinctive programs or courses. Often, when programs and services such as English/French as a second language or anti-racism programs are created in response to the needs of specific student groups, they remain vulnerable to cutbacks through resource constraints and educational restructuring decisions (Canadian Race Relations Foundation, 2000: 9).

The contradictory dynamics that operate within formal education are evident within streaming. Practices overtly concerned with grouping learners and providing instruction appropriate to their aptitudes and competencies can also operate insidiously to reinforce or produce systematic patterns of inequality. To the educator and educational administrator, grouping and categorization are likely to signify viable practical and

---

Box 5.2 Racism and Anti-Racism in Canadian Education

Canada is widely recognized for its formal recognition of multiculturalism, tolerance for racial and cultural diversity, and receptive immigration policies. In contrast with many European nations and parts of the United States, where some organized group or political parties openly campaign against immigration or selected racial minority populations, racialized discourse and practice tends to be somewhat muted in Canada. Nonetheless, racism is experienced both overtly and in covert forms across Canada. A comparative survey on racism conducted for the Canadian Race Relations Foundation and Association for Canadian Studies (2011) reveals that about one-third (31 per cent) of Canadians reported witnessing a racist incident in the previous year, the same proportion as in Spain, compared to 34 per cent of American respondents and only 10 per cent of German respondents, although when asked whether whites and visible minorities were treated equally at their place of work, respondents in Canada were only slightly less likely than those in Germany to indicate agreement (62 per cent and 66 per cent, respectively), compared to 57 per cent in the United States and Spain. Among Canadians who reported witnessing a racist incident in 2010, rates were highest in the Prairie region (45 per cent in Alberta and 40 per cent in Manitoba and Saskatchewan) and lowest in the Maritimes (33 per cent), and also highest in the younger cohorts (58 per cent among those 18 to 24 years) than in older cohorts. However, while close to half of Canadian respondents (46 per cent) considered racism to be on the rise, those in the younger age cohorts were less likely than older respondents to agree with this sentiment (CRRF/ACS, 2011). These findings point to the continuing presence of racism within Canadian society as well as increasing awareness of racism and its impact. Henry and Tator (2009: 10–17) contend that as blatant racial discrimination becomes less acceptable in liberal democratic societies, the persistence of racism is maintained through institutionalized practices and covert forms that produce "democratic racism," conveyed especially through discourses that justify racism even as they deny or seek to trivialize its occurrence.

Educational institutions are not immune to racism and discrimination against minority groups. Research findings and personal accounts from across Canada reveal some of the numerous forms and consequences of race-based discrimination in educational contexts:

- Several schools and universities across Canada have experienced incidences of verbal abuse, physical attacks, graffiti, and destruction of property pedagogical responses to differences among students that do not necessarily imply any inherent advantage or disadvantage for one category relative to another. At the same time, the direct and indirect messages sent to students, in conjunction with disparate resources and opportunities associated with each stream, have important consequences that contribute to inequalities in educational experiences and outcomes. These dynamics are explored further with respect to the importance of official knowledge and hegemony in schooling and the silencing of particular voices in the educational process.

directed against Muslim, Jewish, and other targeted minority groups in recent years.

- Anishinabe youth in Ontario schools often feel unwelcome, confronted by name-calling and stereotypes from peers that teachers do not respond to (Hare and Pidgeon, 2011).
- A Quebec commission on racial profiling observes that targeted scrutiny of blacks, Latinos, and other racialized minority youth, based on assumptions about gang violence and anti-social activities, contributes to excessive disciplinary measures and other responses that are related, in turn, to leaving or failing school (Eid et al., 2011: 58–60).
- The impact of encounters with racism and discrimination is often indirect and prolonged, as evident in the educational underperformance across generations of black Canadian youth in Halifax and youth of West Indian and Caribbean ancestry in Toronto, despite their high educational aspirations and optimism about prospects for educational success (Smith et al., 2005).
- Aboriginal teachers across Canada report encounters with various forms of racism, including discounting of the professional education and teaching qualifications; exclusion, marginalization, and silencing by colleagues; resistance to inclusion of indigenous content in the curriculum; lowered expectations by many teachers for Aboriginal students; and discounting of the history and impact of colonization of Canada's indigenous people (St Denis, 2010: 40–1).
- "Democractic racism" against international students occurs as post-secondary institutions impose differential tuition fees or institutional practices for students from selected regions, respond to student language and cultural characteristics in accordance with stereotypes based on country of origin, maintain practices that marginalize and exclude international students from campus life, and treat cultural characteristics as obstacles to integration (Crosby, 2010).

Provincial and territorial governments, school boards, and educational institutions in Canada have implemented various policies and initiatives to promote anti-racism, multiculturalism, and respect for diversity. Nonetheless, even in those few cases where compliance is enforced, much more comprehensive strategies are required to ensure widespread awareness of and action to address racism in Canadian society.

Official Knowledge

Education is centrally concerned with issues related to knowledge. We commonly view educational institutions as sites in which knowledge is transmitted or disseminated to the learner from teachers, textbooks, and course materials. In fact, knowledge relations in education are much more complex than they appear to be. Knowledge is not simply conveyed in a strict top-down, one-way flow and accumulated through what Freire (1970) calls a "banking" approach to learning. Instead, knowledge is dialogical and interactive in the sense that all educational participants, whether they acknowledge it or not, share in the ongoing transfer and interpretation of knowledge.

The revitalization of debates over school curricula and standards has opened up important questions about what kinds of knowledge, and whose knowledge, are part of the educational process. Periodic calls for "back-to-basics" teaching to a standardized curriculum or reliance on a selected list of core reading materials are opposed by competing claims that the curriculum is too narrowly framed and unrepresentative of student, community, and cultural diversity.

We must recognize that knowledge is not only disseminated but produced in educational settings. This is most evident in universities and other post-secondary institutes that encompass within their mandates an ongoing involvement in research and scholarly work. However, all participants at every level of the education system contribute to knowledge production in a variety of ways through discussions, problem-solving, and engagement in everyday activities. Knowledge is shaped not only as it is continuously interpreted, processed, and reinterpreted in the interactions among instructors and learners in educational settings, but also through the experiences and understandings brought in from outside of schooling.

The top-down view of knowledge dissemination that dominates conceptions of formal education originates in our relatively unchallenged acceptance of official knowledge. As opposed to recognition of knowledge as something that arises from social interactions in everyday life in and out of school, emphasis on official knowledge gives legitimacy only to those ideas and beliefs that are in some way authorized by designated officials or agencies. What this means is that not all knowledge counts as "true" or "real" knowledge. Relations of power and authority act to differentiate between official knowledge, which is regarded as a valued commodity, and knowledge that we use in our everyday experiences, which tends to be devalued or treated as common sense (Apple, 2000: 42–4). The learned or knowledgeable individual, viewed in these terms, is someone who has book learning or formal educational credentials, whereas a person who has considerable expertise in practical matters or know-how is not recognized in the same way if these skills have not been formally acquired or certified (Jackson, 1993: 170–1).

Educational institutions are centrally implicated in the process whereby official knowledge is distinguished from and given privileged status over other forms of knowledge. This occurs in part because of the imperative for formal educational institutions to maintain their own legitimacy so that they are not undermined by other social sites that might wish to disseminate knowledge and bestow educational credentials.

Curricula as Socially Constructed

The state plays a central role in granting legitimacy to educational agencies by establishing, coordinating, and regulating standards for the recognition of curricula, programs, and instructors. In Canada, provincial education departments are normally responsible for the formal approval of elementary and secondary school curricula and textbooks and, either directly or through bodies they authorize, for the certification of teachers and the establishment of procedures and standards for evaluation, promotion, and graduation. Provincial governments also grant accreditation to universities, colleges, public schools, and some private educational institutions, enabling them to structure their programs, hire qualified instructors, and grant certificates and degrees.

Because the state is expected to act as an arbiter among competing groups and interests, educational practices and forms of knowledge incorporated within these formal structures have a legitimacy that is absent in less official social settings. Schools operate within an ideology of value neutrality in the sense that the curriculum is supposed to convey beliefs and knowledge representative of the society as a whole. Education's apparent objectivity is reinforced by the dismissal of ideas seen to represent overtly the views of "special interest groups." Many school boards have policies that forbid explicit product advertising or the display of corporate logos, for instance, while curriculum materials that depict gay lifestyles or readings produced by groups such as pro-life or pro-choice advocates are commonly protested if not banned from classrooms.

In practice, what comes into the schools is filtered through a selection process influenced by power relations and idea systems that prevail in the wider society. Schooling, like other social sites, conveys particular representations of reality that are not neutral in their origins and impact. This is not always readily apparent, nor is it a simple matter of one group imposing its ideas and values on all others. Several steps within educational and curricular processes allow for input and participation by diverse social agents, contributing to prospects for control by dominant groups as well as to resistance and unanticipated consequences. Apple (2000: 50–9) shows how textbooks can contain ideas that support dominant interests (by presenting one-sided, uncontested views of controversial or complex issues) at the same time as they depict the events and experiences that are meaningful to subordinate groups. Curricula that allow for discussion of issues like working-class history, gay rights, and racial and gender equity can be used exploitatively as well as progressively. Not all library books, texts, or curricular materials have an equal chance of making it into schools. Because textbook publishing and production of curricular materials can be a highly lucrative market, some major companies are able to allocate significant resources to promote products to teachers, administrators, and other decision-making bodies. Intensive lobbying efforts by religious organizations and other groups can also affect curricular options both directly, such as by exerting pressures on schools to keep specific resources out of school libraries, and indirectly, by constraining publishers from producing materials that some groups might deem to be offensive. The curriculum is constructed through selection from a range of material eligible for inclusion into school systems, in conjunction with what is adopted and how that material is used and integrated into other personal and educational experiences.

Considerable flexibility and variation exist in the framing and delivery of school curricula. In Canada, most decisions about curricula and textbooks are made in the first instance by committees in various subject areas composed of administrators, teachers, specialists, government officials, and often representatives from universities, parent groups, and other community organizations. Curriculum-established limits to what is officially considered to be "school knowledge" will vary from setting to setting, depending on such factors as the range of choices that teachers are given in lesson planning, frameworks established through specific core curriculum requirements, and the presence or absence of standardized or provincial examinations based on prescribed content or learning objectives. Teachers, working within curriculum guidelines, generally have high degrees of discretion to determine what, when, and how particular material will be taught. Curricula and teaching effectiveness are shaped further by informal and unstructured classroom interactions. Classroom practices are marked by a meandering, often indeterminate path that wanders between what is represented as official knowledge and the lessons and understandings that students exhibit after they leave their schools and classrooms.

Regardless of how curriculum-related decisions are made, distinctions between what is and is not considered valid educational content have important implications for different educational participants. Many students, particularly those from white middle-class families, arrive in school with a strong familiarity with the language and operations of the classroom. The greater the correspondence between what schools expect and students' background experiences, the less likely the pupils will be to have difficulties with understanding school rules and course materials. Conversely,

International Case Study

Politicizing the Curriculum

In Canada, decisions about what constitutes the curriculum and the materials and teaching strategies required to support curriculum delivery are highly complex. Provincial and territorial legislation establishes broad parameters that are then fleshed out by variously constituted curriculum committees. The end result, it is anticipated, is that curricula will represent general knowledge, values, and priorities in accordance with public expectations in each jurisdiction. Some provinces have maintained historically separate school systems for Catholic or Protestant minorities, while other groups often look to private schools or evening and weekend classes based on religious, cultural, or other salient characteristics. While this division of labour generally accommodates diverse interests within specific jurisdictions, a few high-profile cases reveal the potentially volatile nature of curriculum matters when parents organize to protest the introduction or exclusion of books, topics, or other items they find sensitive.

In other nations, the politics of education can often be more overt or extreme. Political revolutions and regime change are frequently followed by revision of major historical accounts or reorientation of educational values, such as the introduction of Marxist philosophy in schools after the Communist revolutions in Russia and China in the first half of the twentieth century and religious conservatism and initial prohibitions on girls' schooling through the influence of the Taliban in Afghanistan.

In the United States, contestation over the curriculum has intensified with the rise of well-organized religious fundamentalist groups and other challenges to scientific authority. A nationwide public opinion poll in 2011 revealed that, while over half of respondents did not think that any books should be banned completely from school libraries, 16 per cent agreed that children should not be able to get books that discuss evolution, over 40 per cent felt that books with references to sex, violence, drugs or alcohol, and witchcraft or sorcery should not be available, and proportions who responded that the Koran, Torah or Talmud, and Bible should not be in school libraries were 28, 24, and 11 per cent, respectively (Braverman, 2011). These perspectives are being translated into action in many communities and states, most prominently in periodic court challenges against mandated teaching of evolutionary theory and pressure to introduce alternative, religious-based perspectives of creationism and "intelligent design." Supporters of the religious right, combined with mobilization by segments of the population expressing dissatisfaction with government bureaucracies and paying taxes, have elected numerous school board members and state and federal representatives who have targeted schools for budget cuts and curriculum reform, especially since 2010. Growing numbers of states are introducing legislation that makes it easier for parents to withdraw their children from classes they find objectionable, to restrict availability of selected books and curricular material, or to introduce alternative curricular content. Some states allow parents to exempt their children from specified subjects over which they have objections. The range of designated areas, initially focusing on topics like sex education, has grown to encompass evolution, climate change, and other subject matter. The decision by a California school board to modify an environmental science curriculum—to require teachers to "balance" the teaching of scientific facts about climate change with other perspectives—drew reactions from science teachers across the country who indicated they received threats and pressure from parents and groups opposed to their own scientific teaching (Reardon, 2011). The New Hampshire House of Representatives passed legislation in early 2012 that would enable parents to request alternatives to any course material they find objectionable in any subject (Robelen, 2012). Legislation was introduced the same year in other states, including Oklahoma and Tennessee, to encourage science teachers to introduce non-scientific arguments in areas like evolution, origins of life, global warming, and human cloning (National Center for Science Education, 2012).

Discussion Question

1. Should parents have greater control over books and curricular material available in schools? Compare the Canadian experience with recent efforts in the United States to make the curriculum more responsive to religious and other special interest groups.

Box 5.3 A Holistic Framework for Redefining Success for First Nations, Métis, and Inuit Learning

Considerable attention has been given to problems and deficiencies associated with conventional indicators of educational participation, progress, and attainment experienced by Aboriginal students. Recent initiatives to create meaningful options for the kinds of education system that will engage Aboriginal communities and their members more fully have pointed to the need to integrate Western educational values with models of education that provide cultural affirmation of indigenous knowledge, values, and cultural traditions. The Aboriginal Learning Knowledge Centre of the Canadian Council on Learning (2007b: 5–7) worked with a diverse cross-section of Aboriginal communities and educators to develop a framework that redefines educational success to address these issues. The framework builds on several key dimensions in which learning is

- holistic and nurturing, and develops the individual (emotionally, physically, spiritually, and intellectually) and the collective;
- a lifelong process, illustrated in the four quadrants of the medicine wheel, highlighting continuity through individual and generational life cycles;
- experiential in nature, in which observation and participation occur beyond the classroom, in communities and natural environments;
- rooted in Aboriginal languages and cultures;
- spiritually oriented;
- a communal activity, involving family, community, and Elders;
- an integration of Aboriginal and Western knowledge.

Three models are presented to guide this process (ibid., 18, 20, 22):

First Nations Holistic Lifelong Learning Model

For First Nations people, the purpose of learning is to develop the skills, knowledge, values, and wisdom needed to honour and protect the natural world and ensure the long-term sustainability of life. Learning is portrayed as a holistic, lifelong developmental process that contributes to individual and community well-being. This process is both organic and self-regenerative in nature, and integrates various types of relationships and knowledge within the community.

The First Nations Holistic Lifelong Learning Model uses a stylized graphic of a living tree to depict learning as a cyclical process that occurs throughout the individual's lifespan. This learning tree identifies the conditions that foster cultural continuity and provide the foundation for individual learning and collective well-being.

students who lack the "cultural capital" underlying educational practices are likely to be at a relative disadvantage.

Basil Bernstein, a British sociologist of education, offers useful insights into how cultural capital is related to power and control in educational processes. His work,

The model contains four main components. They depict the dynamics that enable First Nations people to experience holistic lifelong learning as a purposeful developmental process. The components include: the sources and domains of knowledge (the roots), the individual's learning cycle (the rings), the individual's personal development (the branches), and the community's well-being (the leaves).

Inuit Holistic Lifelong Learning Model

The Inuit Holistic Lifelong Learning Model presents a stylistic graphic of an Inuit blanket toss (a game often played at Inuit celebrations) and a circular path (the "Journey of Lifelong Learning") to portray the Inuk's learning journey and its connection to community well-being.

The model contains four main visual components that convey the Inuit approach to holistic lifelong learning. The components include: the determinants of community well-being, Inuit values and beliefs (the 38 community members [each core value and belief is associated with a representative ancestor or family and community member]), sources and domains of knowledge (the learning blanket), and the journey of lifelong learning (the pathway).

Métis Holistic Lifelong Learning Model

For the Métis people, learning is understood as a process of discovering the skills, knowledge, and wisdom needed to live in harmony with the Creator and creation, a way of being that is expressed as the "Sacred Act of Living a Good Life." Although learning occurs through concrete experiences that occur in the physical world, this *learning by doing* is grounded in a distinct form of knowledge that comes from the Creator.

This sacred knowledge reveals the laws that govern relationships within the community and the world at large and provides the foundation for all learning. To illustrate the relationships between knowledge and the dynamic processes that comprise the "sacred act of living a good life," the Métis Holistic Lifelong Learning Model uses a stylized graphic of a living tree.

The tree depicts Métis learning as a holistic, lifelong process, an integral part of a regenerative, living system, as represented by the life cycle of the tree. Like the tree, Métis learning is governed by the Natural Order, an all-encompassing entity that regulates the passage of seasons and the cycles of birth, death, and rebirth. . . . The model contains four main components that represent various aspects of Métis learning. The components are: determinants of community well-being (the roots), the stages of lifelong learning (the learning rings), the sources of knowledge and knowing (the branches), and the domains of knowledge (the leaves).

in part, proceeds from a distinction between "visible" and "invisible" pedagogies (Bernstein, 1977). Visible pedagogies are educational processes with obvious hierarchies of authority and knowledge: teachers have explicit control over pupils; the curriculum is organized, directed, and transmitted by teachers; and pupils are monitored and evaluated by teachers in accordance with relatively explicit standards. Invisible pedagogies, by contrast, are characteristic of more open teaching/learning situations in which teacher control over pupils is more implicit; children have greater apparent opportunities to select, arrange, and pace their activities and social interactions; and greater emphasis in teaching and assessment of students is placed on process than on specific measurable outcomes.

Bernstein's analysis focuses on the development of what at the time were newer forms of open preschool classes based more on activity and play than on work, but it does have relevance for schooling at other levels as well. The open classroom seems progressive because it allows greater flexibility and concern for the learner than is possible under more authoritarian models of schooling. However, Bernstein argues that, under visible pedagogies, students (and parents) recognize explicitly what is expected of them, even if their ability to succeed depends on culturally biased materials and expectations that favour the middle classes. Under invisible pedagogies, by contrast, the standards are much less clear and, moreover, more of the child's activity becomes exposed to the scrutiny of the teacher. Successful performance now requires that students have the know-how or skills to uncover hidden rules and expectations. This educational structure gives a tremendous advantage to children (particularly those whose parents are of professional backgrounds) who have insight and experience to point them in the direction of activities and behaviours that are rewarded rather than penalized.

Hegemony

Critical sociology often makes reference to the concept of hegemony to illustrate how social structures give shape to our daily activity. **Hegemony,** as elaborated in the work of Antonio Gramsci, refers to a process of domination by consent, in which the general population adopts a world view that reflects the interests of the dominant classes (see, e.g., Gramsci, 1971: 12ff.). This analysis allows us to see how our common-sense way of looking at things, which we derive from our traditions and experiences, is constructed so that ruling practices are maintained without usually being evident to us.

Two examples illustrate how educational practices are hegemonic. The first is the way that knowledge is organized and presented in the classroom. The curriculum is usually understood, arranged, and transmitted to pupils, and often even to teachers, in the form of prearranged units of information. Facts, ideas, and subjects are divided and separated from one another in such a way that they sometimes seem to bear no relationship to each other, with little reference to the context within which they emerged and came to be seen as important. Assignments and tests are often based on recall and reference to discrete bits of information. The learning process is narrowly defined around material that can be readily presented and retrieved (Apple, 2004). Schools are hegemonic insofar as they contribute to a taken-for-granted sense of the world by failing to encourage critical thinking and a sense of how various practices and ideas are interconnected.

A second example of how hegemony is produced in the schooling process is the ethic of individualism referred to earlier in this chapter. As we have already observed, we are taught—through schools, the media, and other venues—that our social position and worth are based on individual effort and initiative. This view, for many of us, is beyond question; we accept it because it seems natural to us. In doing so, however, we fail to consider seriously any alternative viewpoints there might be. Individualism is an ideology that draws attention away from the social origin of practices and ideas. In fact, many elements of our realities are socially constructed—they are produced through the interplay among human actors, social forces, and already existing social structures. Viewed in this way, individual ability and initiative count, but they can only be made sense of against a backdrop that places strict limitations on what is possible for any given individual. To ignore these aspects of reality leads to sets of beliefs and circumstances that favour the dominant social interests at any given point in time.

Schools are hegemonic institutions to the extent that they do not address or encourage the posing of fundamental questions about the nature of our social reality. They are not necessarily organized to favour explicitly the interests of the wealthy and powerful over the poor and disenfranchised, but when social inequality is not discussed as a central part of curricula and when the world is seen as a collection of individuals rather than as a system based on distinct social positions, one consequence is that prevailing patterns of domination and subordination are understood and experienced as natural and inevitable rather than as something to be questioned. As we have noted repeatedly, formal education also affords the possibility for alternative ways of seeing the world and for resistance to official knowledge and hegemony. These will be discussed later in this chapter, following the consideration of another process—silencing—that limits the scope of learning and understanding in educational practices.

Silencing in Educational Processes

Silencing operates in two interrelated ways. First, it exists when particular issues are excluded from or discouraged in the classroom. Second, silencing also occurs when the lives, interests, and experiences of particular educational participants are made irrelevant to the schooling process. By dealing with "the curriculum" or "the business at hand," schools and other institutions send clear messages about what is and is not important. In the process, some topics and experiences, however central they may be to students' lives, are placed outside the boundaries of what are defined or understood as legitimate areas of classroom discussion.

As we observed with respect to the official knowledge that is central to educational processes, some forms of knowledge and behaviours are rewarded while others are marginalized. Considerable attention has been given in recent years to the cultural bias inherent in standardized curricular material and instruments like aptitude and intelligence tests. Test items, like many classroom activities, often rely on knowledge or experiences that may seem to the teacher or tester to be universal but that in fact reflect a particular orientation to reality not shared by all groups. What occurs is that some world views are given voice, or legitimized, while others are silenced. Many common-sense approaches to problems are dismissed as irrelevant or inappropriate for the classroom. An Aboriginal child from a northern reserve and a black pupil in an inner-city school, for instance, may possess considerable knowledge about complex social activities that they encounter daily outside the school setting, whereas in school their worlds are rarely acknowledged. This is not necessarily a deliberate or calculated attempt to privilege one group over another, yet it has the effect, especially when reinforced over time, of compounding the disadvantage faced by subordinate groups.

Analysis conducted through various critical perspectives demonstrates that silencing operates in numerous ways to control classroom interaction and regulate individual identities. Talking in the classroom is commonly discouraged, unless it is directed by teachers and authorities who are lecturing or giving instructions, or where students are allowed to conduct discussions related to a specific pedagogical task (Shor, 1980: 72). Silencing may operate more symbolically than literally in the sense that students, when they do respond to teachers or professors, may subordinate language or dialect they employ informally in favour of patterns of discourse that are rewarded in educational settings. Remaining silent also functions as a way students may protect themselves from scrutiny by educators or from embarrassment at exposing too much of themselves and their lives (Ellsworth, 1992: 104–5). Bourdieu and Passeron (1977) examine how "self-silencing" occurs as a result of "symbolic violence" in the education system. Students who are unfamiliar with or unable to meet the demands that arise from educational standards and expectations are likely to undermine their own capabilities and personalities if they cannot change to achieve conformity. Rather than question how and why such standards reflect social privilege associated with dominant social groups, the individual internalizes educational failure while reinforcing existing power relations. Educational processes can operate in these ways to silence teachers as well as students, depoliticizing participants by undermining their "authentic voices," thereby reinforcing hierarchies of gender, race, and class (Nugent and Bell, 2006).

Box 5.4 Africentric Schooling

The establishment of an Africentric alternative school within the Toronto District School Board has been surrounded by extensive controversy and sometimes highly emotional responses by critics and defenders of the initiative. The first school was approved in 2008 and opened a year later, guided by principles to integrate the heritage and knowledge of peoples of African descent throughout the entire curriculum and school experience. Its aim is to address serious deficiencies in educational retention, performance, and attainment among many black students, especially those of Caribbean descent, in the city's schools. Critics attack the initiative as a form of ghettoization, segregation, and regressive policy that could lead to the eventual fragmentation of the entire education system; proponents point to evidence that the present system is not working. Often missed in the most extreme debates are the historical roots of the problem and the precedents that exist in other contexts, including a prior trial in Toronto and a Nova Scotia school that has operated on Africentric principles since the mid-1990s (White, 2008; Dei, 2006). While issues associated with the relationship between racial segregation and schooling are well known, especially in the southern United States, many black communities in Canada have similar experiences of marginalization and social isolation. Black communities established their own schools due to prejudice and barriers that blocked participation in public schools as early as the 1830s in Canada West (Ontario) and the 1840s in Nova Scotia. Subsequent school and human rights legislation formally ended race-based discrimination in the latter parts of the twentieth century, but the exclusion of racial minorities through various socio-economic, geographical, and cultural factors has contributed to the perpetuation of clustering of school populations along racial lines (Kelly, 1998: 30–4). An influential Nova Scotia document, widely known as the BLAC report (Black

The Impact of Silencing on Minority and Marginalized Learners

Proponents of inclusive education and anti-racism in schooling and other institutional settings point out the deep impact that silencing can have on people's lives. For some persons, challenges to or devaluation of their lived experiences can have damaging psychological consequences. Invisible messages transmitted in the classroom that are based on white, male, middle-class standards, for instance, can lead minority students to see their own identities as undesirable or unacceptable (Ng, 1991). Silencing produces invisibility, which through normal school practices results in negations of self and identity that "erase the social, cultural, historical, and political realities of marginalized groups in society through the exclusive practices of Eurocentrism" (Dei et al., 2000: 172). Pupils, in response to these processes, may become marginalized and withdraw from participation in school activities, especially if there are conflicting messages between home and school about what is culturally and socially important. Such withdrawal, in turn, can lead to social isolation or to incorporation into alternative groups such as youth gangs or "counter-school cultures" that define themselves through their defiance against authority (Willis, 1977).

The lack of connection between schooling and student background is a major contributing factor to educational problems experienced by Aboriginal and visible

Learners Advisory Committee, 1994: 35), highlights the numerous systemic barriers encountered by black learners and community members in that province:

> During the BLAC research, we encountered widespread condemnation of the education system as *biased, insensitive* and *racist*. Systemic racism was seen as manifested in student assessment and placement; in labelling of large numbers of Black students as slow learners or having behaviour problems; in streaming; in low teacher expectations; in denigration by and exclusion of Blacks from the curriculum; and in the total lack of responsiveness to the needs of Black learners and concerns of the Black community.

Proponents of Africentric or black-focused schooling see the schools as complementing principles of public schooling but offering effective alternatives within systems that continue to fail to deliver on promises to ensure effective educational options for a substantial segment of the population. Sociologist George J. Sefa Dei (2006: 28) contends that

> [i]f we are to define "educational success" broadly, then we must recognize that alternative/counter visions of schooling may enhance learning for these young people. While my enthusiasm for Black-focused/African-centred schooling is primarily based on its potential to address issues of Black and other minority youth disengagement and "push out" from the Canadian school system, the same fundamental principles may help to transform conventional schooling in Euro-Canadian/American contexts, as well.

While the Toronto school continues to be the subject of various concerns, its initial success, reflected in rising enrolments, improved test scores, and high parental engagement, has contributed to expansion of the school in 2012 and approval for a new Africentric high school (Hammer, 2012).

minority children and youth. Schools and other educational sites that fail to do so, or are not able to make a connection between what they do and the lives of the students and communities they work with, increase the likelihood that students will become disengaged from, or disaffected with, their education. Highlighting the gap that Aboriginal youth frequently identify between life in and out of school, the Royal Commission on Aboriginal Peoples (1996b: 482) observes that, "Education as they experience it is something removed and separate from their everyday world, their hopes and dreams." Sometimes, even content specific to students' cultural backgrounds can pose confusion or mystification when school representations conflict with what students are told in community contexts. The comments of one Grade 12 First Nations student in a prairie inner-city school are typical of this concern: "There is quite a contrast [between what I am told in school and what my people tell me], like the Crazyhorse [the Lakota leader whose legacy is represented in distinctly different ways in Western and indigenous knowledge traditions], the old people know, like my grandpa used to talk about them a lot, and then when you learn about them in school ... it's a lot different, and I was saying, ok, somebody is lying to me." Dei et al. (2000: 20–1) contrast educational practices that exclude and marginalize minority students with inclusive schooling; the latter is characterized by an acknowledgement by educational personnel and practices of students' cultural backgrounds in a manner that integrates the community into the school context.

Like other hidden aspects of schooling, therefore, silencing can deeply affect both the schooling experiences and the social futures of students. Beyond the content and skills directly transmitted through the curriculum, the knowledge, attitudes, and emotions absent from or subordinated within educational practices convey to educational participants critical signals about how the world is organized and should be encountered. Both overt and silent understandings in the classroom contribute to a complex process of manoeuvring and differentiation in which the successful or "good" students are distinguished from those characterized by alternative or deviant labels and identities.

Student Response and Resistance

Students must become accomplished actors in a number of ways in the course of their schooling experiences. Their actions contribute to the continuously changing nature of classroom activity. The school day is rarely the smooth-flowing progression of tightly integrated lessons and transitions between classes that appears in official accounts of schooling. Instead, it involves uneven pacing, constant interruptions, and shifting back and forth among planned and unplanned occurrences. Within even just a few moments, students are likely to alternate their behaviour to reflect varying degrees of attentiveness, boredom, overt and covert gestures, dialogue with teachers, and exchanges with other pupils. In contrast with common conceptions of pupils as passive consumers of curricular knowledge, students are continuously engaged in shaping and making sense of the educational process. As Michael Apple (2000: 57) observes, "students are active constructors of the meanings of the education they encounter."

Researchers who analyze educational settings frequently employ the concept of "resistance" to understand how students engage in and respond to their schooling experiences. Most of this research is focused on adolescents at the stage where resistance tends to be most overt. The notion of resistance conveys most immediately a sense of rebellion or rejection of schooling as demonstrated through such acts as vandalism and destruction of school property, overt disregard for school rules, defiance of teachers' authority, refusal to complete assignments, absenteeism, or dropping out. However, students often exercise resistance in subtler ways. Lack of attentiveness to lessons and instructions, whispered comments and notes passed to other pupils, informal mocking of teachers, repeated errands and trips to the washroom, and pressure to discuss issues not on the formal curriculum all can signify reactions against school activities that students consider boring, meaningless, or oppressive.

The concept of resistance adds to our understanding of school processes a sensitivity to the unofficial and interpersonal elements of schooling. Educational dynamics are characterized by continual dialogue and interchange, both verbal and non-verbal. Students, far from being passive recipients of schools' efforts to shape and control the individual, are highly implicated in the directions that their schooling takes and the outcomes to which it contributes.

The presence and significance of resistance should not be exaggerated. Deviant forms of behaviour, such as bullying or resentment against authority, are often confused with resistance to schooling (Giroux, 1983; Lynch, 1989: 15; McLaren, 2007: 216). Resistance is more appropriately understood as student responses to the dehumanizing and restrictive aspects of schooling that diminish creativity, enlightenment, and self-worth or that devalue meaningful social experiences. Such resistance is usually individual in nature, but it may also be collective. Sometimes, collective resistance is spontaneous, such as when students support a pupil they feel is being picked on unfairly by a teacher, or when students persuade their teacher that playing ball would be more beneficial than doing a math quiz on a sunny day. Woods (1983: 56–8) emphasizes how both students and teachers employ laughter and other apparent deviations from the formal curriculum as means to negotiate daily classroom interactions. School resistance can also be more organized, as when students engineer a walkout from class or circulate a petition to complain about such issues as overly harsh school regulations or the transfer of a popular teacher to another school. In these kinds of situations, it is noteworthy that student actions generally tend to be accommodative to schooling, with resistance limited to specific instances or features of educational practices.

Understanding the Significance of Resistance

There is considerable debate about the meaning of different forms of resistance. Kanpol (1992: 57), for instance, distinguishes between institutional political resistance, which is directed against specific features of particular schools or educational environments, and cultural political resistance, which involves movement from a critique of education towards the formulation of alternative ideas and practices. Many educators, politicians, and media analysts point to school violence, vandalism, and lack of student respect for authority as alarming indicators of the extent to which educational and social standards have declined in recent years. Other commentators, particularly those who adopt a critical pedagogy orientation, portray student resistance as an outcry against oppression or a noble struggle to preserve their humanity in a dehumanizing world. Schools and school rules, in this view, signify externally imposed authority structures that are threatening to students, particularly those for whom access to meaningful, secure jobs and influential social positions seems unattainable. Several researchers have commented on the frequent tensions arising between teachers and students around issues of physical appearance. Even schools that do not have strict dress codes have unspoken or informal standards regarding appropriate kinds of clothing, hairstyles, and student demeanour. Students, however, often adopt non-traditional styles of dress and attitudes that enable them to express their sexuality and assert a rebellious stance against school authority. A rich tradition of research in Canada and many other nations explores the diverse ways in which students from working-class and minority backgrounds express themselves through particular actions and symbolic representations in order to set themselves apart from dominant values or groups (e.g., McRobbie, 1978; Connell et al., 1982; McLaren, 2007).

This literature has broadened to encompass resistance against the regulation of sexuality, ability status, and other characteristics in which schools and youth cultures can work variously to reinforce or undermine dominant normative and behavioural standards. Schools and post-secondary institutions have focused increasingly on strategies seeking to foster student engagement. In an overview of the research, Dunleavy and Milton (2008: 6) find an emphasis on two dimensions of engagement—social engagement ("participation in the life of the school") and academic engagement ("participation in the requirements for school success")—and introduce a third form, intellectual engagement ("participation in learning with serious psychological and cognitive investment in learning"). As educators explore diverse ways to draw students into meaningful learning experiences, they are also confronted with new challenges. The significance of new technologies in student life has proven especially troublesome in many educational contexts. Teachers and instructors often adopt innovative ways to incorporate handheld devices, laptops, and new applications in order to enhance learning opportunities for students who might not otherwise be engaged in conventional classroom activities. However, technological innovations also introduce new issues into school relations, including distractions from other tasks, different skill levels and device categories among students and teachers and between school and home, sharing of sensitive information, and cyberbullying.

Youth Cultures and Moral Panics

Schools represent a focal point around which considerable attention has been directed to the contemporary status of children and youth. As gathering places that often crystallize distinct youth cultures built around such designations as punks, metalheads, freaks, skids, skaters, ravers, gangsta' rappers, hackers, and many others commonly drawn from popular entertainment and sports, schools have also been targeted by many critics for their role in fostering some of the more questionable aspects of youth experience. Various youth identities and expressions are typically part of the attachments and insecurities that arise through the developmental process, especially in a context in which roles and expectations for young people are undergoing significant transformations. These identities sometimes encourage a degree of peer acceptance and "acting out" of tensions and resentment against a social environment that students otherwise perceive as meaningless or actually hostile to them. In the process, many aspects of youth culture have become the focus of intense public scrutiny, often accompanied by outrage within mass media and other prominent commentary.

Sociologist Stanley Cohen (1972) introduced the concept of **moral panic** to describe situations in which powerful groups mobilize public opinion against what they portray as threats to dominant values. Socially constructed "moral panics" framed through discourses that depict contemporary youth as out of control and excessively engaged in deviant and criminal activity have served in particular to stigmatize disadvantaged groups (Schissel, 2006). The extensive media coverage given to incidences of gang-related activities, school shootings, swarmings, physical bullying, violence by girls and boys alike, drug and alcohol abuse, and the use of public websites and electronic technologies to intimidate and embarrass individuals is reinforced by public outcries and pledges by politicians for disciplinary measures. The resulting hysteria often creates a highly skewed image of youth culture, creating a sense that problems exist far in excess of their true scope while neglecting both positive dimensions of youth life and more direct problems that do concern youth.

Prompted by these fears, schools in many parts of North America have asserted their role as disciplining institutions. Some urban high schools now resemble prisons, with the installation of metal detectors, security cameras, lockdown procedures, locker inspections, and strict monitoring procedures. Governments and schools have also adopted more general measures to address concerns related to public safety and security. Ontario's Safe Schools Act, for instance, implemented in 2000–1, empowers teachers as well as principals to suspend or expel students who are deemed to be engaging in disruptive or violent behaviour. Sometimes called "zero tolerance" policy by critics and supporters alike, the legislation has been challenged for being applied inappropriately, especially for targeting black students as well as other visible minority students and students with learning disabilities (Ontario Human Rights Commission, 2003). The experience related to this legislation, which was amended in early 2008 in response to parental concerns and an investigation by the Ontario Human Rights Commission, exemplifies some of the highly selective and dangerous outcomes that can be produced by moral panics related to children and youth.

Many of the groups most negatively affected by security-based measures—including Aboriginal youth, students from low-income families, those living in domestically fragile situations, inner-city black students, and learning-disabled students—are those who most require support from schools and other agencies to enable them to benefit from education. According to one Toronto high school teacher, disciplinary measures to enforce codes regarding dress and hair covering in her school, along with "the implementation of other security measures in the name of school safety, [were] really a 'crackdown' on the identities of visible minority students, particularly Black students, primarily Black male students." At the same time, others, especially sexual minority students—i.e., those who identify as lesbian, gay, bisexual, or transsexual (LGBT)—feel their safety is at risk in the school environment (Short, 2011: 6). Ironically, many of these students otherwise look to schools to provide inclusive, safe environments, in contrast to higher degrees of vulnerability or insecurity that confront them in other domestic, community, or agency environments.

Youth in a Volatile World

Attention to the most shocking or provocative aspects of youth cultures obscures the more complex and subtle dynamics that characterize the lives and experiences of most young people. Children and youth face a bewildering array of opportunities, challenges, demands, and stimuli. Whereas terms like the "generation gap" were applied to the social and cultural distance that marked differences in lifestyles, attitudes, and identities between previous cohorts of children and youth and their parents and elders, many social, material, and spatial reference points were shared across these cohorts. Contemporary youth, by contrast, have access to an unprecedented and rapidly changing range of technologies and experiences—both "real" and "virtual"—but face incredible pressures and uncertainty regarding future life plans. Rapid developments and widespread accessibility related to information and communications technologies have expanded exposure to information, forms of social interaction, and stimuli that alter youth's expectations and perceptions of the world, often in ways that parents, teachers, and other non-peers cannot fathom or keep pace with. In the process, their lives are shaped by shifting family and economic dynamics and growing sensitivities to new risks and presumed standards of various kinds, ranging from concern for environmental and climate change, to body image and threats to security and even species survival. Half a century ago the Cuban Missile Crisis created fears of a nuclear Armageddon—for a few weeks. Today, with a 24-hour news cycle and many troubling issues that political and economic leaders seem unwilling (or unable) to confront, the level of angst and unknowing about the future is multiplied manyfold, especially for young people.

The pervasiveness of market economies and consumer culture, reinforced by and through various communications devices and media, has hastened the extension of what Steinberg and Kincheloe (1997) have designated as "kinderculture"—a new form of childhood and youth characterized by consumerism, gratification, and identification with disposable objects rather than enduring social and cultural reference points. Leisure time carries many of its own diversions, often leading to the neglect of or opposition to school and what schooling stands for (Nelsen, 2007). In addition, fuelled by a desire for cash (either out of necessity or to support individual consumption) and the recognition that schooling in itself is not enough, many young people are increasingly engaged in paid and volunteer work, which further complicates student life.

Schooling, in the course of these transformations, faces significant challenges. Educators often see themselves competing against media, technology, and consumer culture to capture student interest. Many parents and school critics press for stricter disciplinary measures and educational standards. Others seek educational reforms to ensure greater relevance, incorporating technologies and new methods such as teamwork and problem-solving orientations into the schools.

In the course of these shifts, and despite attention given to the more extreme forms of resistance and deviance, research that has explored in a systematic way what students think of their schooling experiences has shown that they respond to formal education—and other facets of their lives—in mixed and often contradictory ways. A useful categorization of student responses is presented by Connell et al. (1982), who suggest on the basis of their interviews with Australian high school students about 14 years of age that, in addition to resistance, there are at least two other main types of student–teacher relations. The first is compliance, in which students accept school rules and express enthusiasm for their schooling as a way of gaining rewards. The second response is pragmatism, in which students engage in required activities only to the extent that they are seen to be required for achieving objectives, such as passing grades and receiving credentials.

Many other researchers have observed similar processes. McNeil (1986) and Weis (1990), studying American high schools, stress how the ritualistic nature of classroom practices emerges as part of an unspoken agreement between students and teachers. By the time they reach high school, students typically tend to be passive and docile. While the occasional outburst of energetic protest may erupt over particular issues, especially when pupils feel they are being unfairly dealt with by teachers who exercise excessively harsh discipline, double standards, or poor teaching methods (Connell et al., 1982: 84), students rarely challenge either teachers or the school authority structure. Instead, students agree to carry out at least minimal requirements to complete work assignments and keep an orderly classroom—in other words, to do what they think is expected to help the teacher do his or her job properly. In exchange, they expect to get through school with respectable treatment and acceptable grades.

This accord channels potential student dissatisfaction and resistance in such a way that the legitimacy of the education system, and the social system as a whole, is not called into question (see, e.g., Aronowitz and Giroux, 1993; Willis, 1977). Students to a large extent "buy into" the education system, viewing educational success as desirable for social success and blaming themselves for many of the occasions that they experience failure. Even where more severe problems begin to appear, taking the shape, for instance, of frequent skipping of classes, overt resistance, conflict with teachers, or resignation, students are hesitant to express doubt about the school system except when they are probed or encouraged to speak out. Interviews with early school-leavers, such as those conducted by Crysdale and MacKay (1994) in Toronto, Samuelson (1991) and Tanner et al. (1995) in Edmonton, Randhawa (1991) in Saskatchewan, and Crysdale et al. (1999) in Alberta and Ontario, reveal that those who drop out blame the school for producing boredom, alienation, rejection, or lack of preparation for work, but they also express self-doubt and regret over personal factors that contributed to their decision to quit school.

By contrast, as Levin (2009: 17) emphasizes, interpersonal relationships and professional orientations remain critical to school outcomes, as evident in consistent research evidence showing that "the single biggest factor in whether students try or give up, leave or stay, is their sense that somebody in the school knows who they are and cares about what happens to them." Moreover, perspectives portraying children and youth as bureaucratic subjects or victims of global forces run the risk of increasing disaffection with established ideas and orders. Youth are far more insightful, resourceful, and resilient than they are often given credit for. Porfilio and Carr (2011: 8) stress that youth not only are aware of many of the social forces that shape their lives at school and in the world beyond schooling, but they "are channeling their critical insights into outlets and initiatives that can subvert the structures, policies and practices fueling oppression, hate, and inequity" through such platforms as social media. The mixture of hope and despair, of self-blame and bitterness against the school system expressed by students who fail or drop out, is not markedly different from more general student commentaries on their educational experiences.

The Concern for Safe, Inclusive Educational Environments

Students hold sophisticated and often contradictory attitudes with regard to their schooling experiences. These paradoxical stances reflect students' central but subordinate place within educational structures, their changing roles and expressions as children and adolescents, and their uncertain place in broader social and economic structures. Despite the significant challenges and uncertainties they encounter, children and youth tend to be more optimistic than pessimistic about their futures, hold high educational aspirations, and are generally positive and accepting of their

Box 5.5 Bullying and Victimization in Students' Lives

As the stakes associated with learning increase, greater concern is directed to the conditions that foster or inhibit learning for various groups of students. These conditions go well beyond classroom relationships and relate to such factors as homework loads, extracurricular activities, work and other commitments outside school hours, and student safety concerns. Among the most prominent of these factors are problems associated with bullying. A survey conducted on behalf of the Canadian Council on Learning (CCL) (2007e: 33) reveals that four out of five adult Canadian respondents agree or strongly agree that bullying is one of the most serious issues affecting students. While 38 per cent of male respondents and 30 per cent of female respondents indicate that they had been bullied in school, many are concerned that bullying has become more serious in nature (ibid., 35). The problem is compounded, in part, by the pervasive impact of new technologies and the broader ways in which we have come to understand bullying and abusive relationships, as illustrated in the summary of four main types of bullying identified by the CCL (ibid., 32):

Types of bullying

1. Physical bullying

- punching
- kicking
- pushing
- tripping
- pinching
- pulling hair
- forced confinement

2. Relational bullying

- social exclusion
- spreading rumours
- gossip
- sending nasty notes

3. Verbal bullying

- name-calling
- verbal intimidation
- mocking
- insulting

4. Electronic or "cyber" bullying

- similar to relational and verbal bullying but occurs online
- sending false emails using the victim's name
- forwarding private emails, pictures, or information

Behaviour related to bullying is a focus of concern in many nations. Incidents of bullying and victimization occur widely among both boys and girls, although boys are typically more likely to bully others and much more likely to engage in physical fighting in school and other settings in which children and youth are concentrated. Several international and comparative studies reveal reported incidences of bullying in Canada to be higher than average, although not as high as in several other nations. The table below, constructed from data in a World Health Organization survey of youth in different age cohorts in 35 nations, illustrates variations in patterns across several nations, placing Canada relatively high in overall incidences of bullying though somewhat below average in instances of physical fighting.

Table 5.1 Young People (13-year-olds) Who Were Bullied or Who Bullied Others at School at Least Twice in the Previous Two Months, and Those Who Have Been Involved in a Physical Fight at Least Three Times in the Previous 12 Months (%), Selected Nations

Nation	Were Bullied		Bullied Others		Were Involved in Physical Fighting	
	Girls	Boys	Girls	Boys	Girls	Boys
Greece	27	29	13	28	10	27
Turkey	26	29	13	19	16	34
Ukraine	22	20	18	23	4	26
Austria	16	20	11	26	6	25
Russian Federation	17	18	15	22	10	28
Portugal	13	19	9	15	4	18
Canada	13	18	8	13	11	21
Germany	13	16	7	17	4	12
France	14	15	11	15	6	20
Switzerland	11	16	10	19	3	15
Scotland	12	10	4	7	9	22
USA	10	11	9	14	7	16
Poland	8	13	6	14	5	23
England	9	12	5	8	8	20
Finland	9	10	4	6	4	12
Netherlands	8	10	4	12	4	15
Italy	8	10	6	12	8	22
Ireland	7	10	3	7	6	21
Denmark	8	8	6	11	8	27
Hungary	8	7	4	7	13	26
Norway	6	9	1	5	3	15
Czech Republic	5	7	3	6	9	31
Spain	4	6	6	8	4	15
Sweden	4	5	1	4	4	14
Average (40 nations)	13	15	9	15	7	21

Source: Compiled with data from Craig and Harel (2008: 156-64).

continued

The extent of concern over bullying is evident in the wide range of anti-bullying programs and strategies that educators, parents, and school administrations in Canada and other OECD nations have introduced to address these problems. Recent attention has turned as well to homophobic bullying, as lesbian, gay, bisexual, and transsexual (LGBT) youth report consistently higher rates of verbal and physical harassment than heterosexual peers, ranging from denigrating comments to exclusion and violent physical assault. UNESCO (2012: 14–17) reports that about one in five LGBT students in Canada and the United States reports physical harassment or assault, while two-thirds of LGBT students in some nations, including Peru, Chile, Japan, and the United Kingdom, indicate they have experienced bullying. Worldwide attention to the severity of the problem has resulted in the rapid expansion of initiatives like Pink Shirt Day in schools across Canada from its Nova Scotia beginnings in 2007, and the adoption of an annual International Day Against Homophobia and Transphobia following the National Day Against Homophobia first introduced in Quebec in 2003.

school experiences, even if they are not hesitant to point out numerous issues that concern their lives in and out of schools (Bibby, 2001: 133–56; King et al., 1999: 11–25; Schissel and Wotherspoon, 2003: 82–92). They often identify grievances against outdated pedagogies and curricula, unfair treatment or expectations on the part of teachers, lax standards, or lack of opportunities to pursue information and activities that they prefer, but they tend not to challenge the structures of authority and rewards either within or as represented by schooling. There is a general sense that "that's just how things are," even when students retain an uneasiness about their lives and futures that transcends anything they can do to make them better.

Student populations are more diverse, sophisticated, and concerned about social, economic, environmental, and political issues than they are commonly portrayed as being. They are highly aware of and engaged with many of the high-profile issues in both popular and alternative media, including bullying and youth violence, substance abuse, matters related to sex and sexuality, labour market options, consumerism, poverty, social disadvantage, and social justice. Their schooling is a crucial but not isolated part of their lives. It is valued for its contributions to knowledge, skills, social connections, and life prospects, but it is also most effective when it is connected with realities outside the classroom. The educational environment, particularly in situations in which schooling is compulsory and there are few alternatives, can be intense, competitive, alienating, and even terrifying for students who are rejected, picked on, or abused by other students and teachers. Alternatively, schools and the students within them are most likely to succeed when schooling becomes a place in which participants find security, acceptance, validation, and encouragement.

Conclusion

This chapter has considered how the profusion of incidents and the shifting pace of structured and unstructured activities that constitute the school day are channelled into diverse but relatively predictable social outcomes. Since its inception over a century ago, public schooling has changed substantially in several highly visible ways, including subjects taught, school facilities, classroom resources, background and qualifications of teachers, and dress and demeanour of students. However, basic classroom structures and the aims and orientations of schooling have remained remarkably resistant to change. Schools continue to be regarded as factories for producing products—the schooled individual, credentials, and other end results—just as they are sites for human social development. The varied purposes and practices of schooling are not accidental by-products but direct reflections of the contradictory nature of public education.

Annotated Further Readings

Contenta, Sandro. 1993. *Rituals of Failure: What Schools Really Teach.* Toronto: Between the Lines. In a highly readable and engaging book, the author discusses how schools' hidden curricula both restrict future prospects for many students and limit the extent to which true education is accomplished through schooling.

Côté, James E., and Anton Allahar. 2006. *Critical Youth Studies: A Canadian Focus.* Toronto: Pearson Prentice-Hall. The authors examine the changes and difficulties youth are experiencing as the transition period between childhood dependency and adult independence is prolonged. Prospects for those aged 15 to 30 are considered with respect to a broad range of social and economic relationships.

McLaren, Peter. 2007. *Life in Schools: An Introduction to Critical Pedagogy in the Foundations of Education*, 5th edn. Boston: Pearson Allyn and Bacon. Drawing on his experiences teaching elementary students in a Toronto inner-city school, McLaren explores the foundations of a critical pedagogy approach by framing an account of daily school practices within a broader social, economic, and political context, maintaining radical pedagogical reform as a basis for keeping alive prospects for a better future.

Porfilio, Brad J., and Paul R. Carr, eds. 2010. *Youth Culture, Education and Resistance: Subverting the Commercial Ordering of Life.* Rotterdam: Sense Publishers. Several contributors draw from critical pedagogy to examine the impact of social changes in the context of neo-liberalism on the lives and experiences of youth, as well as various forms of resistance and critical engagement by youth in various communities in Canada, the United States, and other nations.

Schissel, Bernard, and Terry Wotherspoon. 2003. *The Legacy of School for Aboriginal People: Education, Oppression, and Emancipation.* Toronto: Oxford University Press. The book combines an analysis of how residential schools and other educational developments have contributed to the subjugation of Aboriginal people in Canada with an overview of recent initiatives and commentary from Aboriginal students that highlight how educational promise may be fulfilled in the future.

Taylor, Catherine, and Tracey Peter. 2011. *Every Class in Every School: Final Report on the First National Climate Survey on Homophobia, Biphobia, and Transphobia in Canadian Schools.* Toronto: Egale Canada Human Rights Trust. Reporting on the accounts of sexual and gender minority youth across Canada, this study presents data and experiences demonstrating the high degree to which these youth encounter verbal, physical, and sexual harassment. The impact of safe schools policies and gay–straight alliances is also discussed.

Key Terms

Credentials Qualifications achieved through formal education or training programs and recognized in the form of degrees, diplomas, certificates, or other legitimate awards.

Dropout A student who leaves school without completing requirements for secondary matriculation or high school graduation. This term is often replaced with "school-leaver" to take into account the many students who interrupt their schooling and return at one or more later stages to complete further education.

Hegemony Domination by consent, or ideologies that foster belief in the legitimacy of existing power relations.

Hidden curriculum The understandings that students develop as a result of the institutional requirements and day-to-day realities they encounter in their schooling. This term typically refers to norms, such as competition, individualism, and obedience, as well as a sense of one's place in school and social hierarchies.

Individuation The process by which people come to see themselves, and are seen by others, as autonomous individuals rather than with reference to the social relations of which they are part.

Moral panic The creation of widespread fears built around images of threats to public safety or order, often related to violence, deviant activity, or health concerns, generated especially by exaggerated or erroneous media and political accounts.

Silencing Mechanisms that restrict student voices or prohibit from the schooling process the inclusion of topics and material that are important to students' lives.

Socialization The ongoing process of learning and discovery through which people internalize the norms and expectations about cultures and their place within their societies.

Streaming Formal and informal educational mechanisms that sort students based on ability, social background, or other characteristics into groups, programs, or institutions that have differential status.

Total institutions Self-contained institutional settings, such as prisons, mental institutions, military sites, and residential schools, separated from the outside world and regulated by formal routines, procedures, and scrutiny with the intent to reshape those who reside, work, or are housed or detained in them.

Study Questions

1. What are the predominant social features of elementary and secondary school classrooms? What explanations can be provided for how these features came about?

2. Critically discuss the nature and impact of residential schooling for Canada's First Nations.

3. Watch the trailer for the video "Imagine a School" produced for the Canadian Education Association (at www.youtube.com/watch?v=tNLAGHdlC6M) or find a library copy of the full video. Discuss the student stories from the video. Consider, from the student perspective and then that of a teacher, how you would respond to incidences in which you observe discriminatory treatment and those in which a student reports such treatment to you.

4. Discuss the importance of the hidden curriculum, relative to the formal curriculum, for what students with various social characteristics learn and retain from their schooling.

5. Which elements of schooling inhibit student participation and engagement? Which ones contribute to greater participation and engagement? Discuss the significance these factors have for students from different social and cultural backgrounds.

6. To what extent are schools self-contained institutions as opposed to sites that are highly influenced by their external environments? Discuss the significance of these circumstances for what students learn in schools.

Chapter 6

Teachers and Teaching

Learning Objectives

In this chapter, you will:

- gain an understanding of the nature of teaching as an occupation;
- be introduced to the major factors that constitute teaching as a particular form of work;
- explore the changing dynamics of teaching with a focus on relationships between professionalization and attempts to control and regulate teachers and their work.

Introduction

Teachers, like students, are central agents in educational processes. Their prominent role in the delivery of educational services makes them nearly synonymous with schooling in the eyes of students, parents, and community members. However, teachers also occupy a somewhat paradoxical position in and out of the classroom. They represent the school and its authority structure to pupils and parents, but they are subordinate to principals and senior administrators in educational hierarchies. They must be highly skilled and competent to gain public confidence to educate and discipline learners behind classroom doors, but they are also subject to public scrutiny with regard to what and how they teach as well as to their overall moral character. They have specialized training and other attributes associated with professionalism, but they do not have the autonomy, authority, or status held by doctors or lawyers. They are advocates for educational causes and learning issues, but they are also waged employees of public or private educational bodies. They are well placed to be seen as leaders in a knowledge-based economy, but their working lives are replete with tensions and constraints. In short, consistent with the complex nature of the education systems teachers work within, teaching is a highly contradictory occupation.

The paradoxical nature of teachers' roles has long been a predominant theme within the sociological analysis of teaching. Willard Waller (1965: 49), in his classic analysis of schooling, *The Sociology of Teaching*, concisely summarizes the special nature of teaching through his conception of the teacher as "stranger" in the community:

> The teacher stereotype is a thin but impenetrable veil that comes between the teacher and all other human beings. The teacher can never know what others are really like because they are not like that when the teacher is watching them. The community can never know what the teacher is really like

because the community does not offer the teacher opportunities for normal social intercourse.

Waller was writing mostly about teachers in small communities at a time (the book
was first published in the early 1930s) when there were likely to be few other relatively
highly trained professional workers active in the human services. His observations
continue to hold relevance by pointing to the combination of respect and devaluation that today accompanies teachers' work and lives, constituting what Lortie (1975:
10) calls a "special but shadowed social standing." Mass media and popular culture,
such as movies and television programs, typically portray teachers and the work they
do through both positive and negative stereotypes that influence how people think
of teaching (Weber and Mitchell, 1999). More crucially, teachers and the work they
do are continually shaped and reshaped through their interactions within schooling and broader social and economic transformations (Robertson, 2000; Tardif and
Lessard, 1999).

This chapter highlights the diverse and often contested nature of teaching.
Following a profile and history of teaching in Canada, consideration will be given to
the changing nature of teaching as a particular form of work. While there are some
common elements to all forms of teaching, this chapter is most concerned with teachers in public elementary and secondary schools. The vast majority of educators in
Canada are public school teachers who, unlike most teachers at other levels, require
specialized teacher training and certification. Moreover, public school teachers are
primarily concerned with teaching and pedagogy, in contrast with university professors or vocational educators, whose work is defined more in terms of such other responsibilities as research or applied skills.

Teachers and Teaching in Canada

About 700,000 persons work as teachers and professors in Canada, with 550,600
reporting full-time employment and another 149,900 working part-time in 2011
(Statistics Canada, 2012). The full-time teaching ranks include about 340,000 full-
time equivalent elementary and secondary school teachers, 44,400 full-time university
faculty, and an estimated 30,000 instructors employed full-time in community colleges and vocational or trade instructional institutions (Statistics Canada, 2011a:
Tables C.2.2, D.3.1). Growth in the total teaching workforce has been most pronounced at the university level, reflecting the rising importance of post-secondary education, in comparison with the number of elementary and secondary school teachers,
which began to increase in 2004 after declining since the 1990s. Educational institutions have met changing enrolment patterns in part by increasing reliance on part-time
teachers. Since 2005, part-time teachers have represented between one-fifth and one-
quarter of teachers at all levels compared to about one in seven in the mid-1980s (calculated from Statistics Canada, 2007b, 2012). Some of the growth in part-time teaching
can be accounted for by the desire by some to combine teaching with family responsibilities, employment in other fields, or educational upgrading. More significantly, as
discussed later in this chapter, the growth in the part-time teaching workforce represents changes in educational funding, organization, and management orientations that
leave a greater share of the workforce in contingent and temporary circumstances.

Teachers are a diverse group, with varying backgrounds, positions, and work experiences. While all teachers may share many common concerns about workloads, student

Box 6.1 The Attractions and Stresses of Teaching

Many aspects of teaching are readily apparent to non-teachers, while others are frequently misunderstood. This paradox is partly a consequence of the nature of teaching as an occupation in which many aspects of the job are performed under public scrutiny while others occur behind classroom doors or outside of regular school hours. Many teachers' organizations have introduced campaigns to ensure that teachers' voices, which are often absent in discussions of educational policy and reform, gain recognition in debates about public education. The results of a national survey conducted by the Canadian Teachers' Federation in 2011 provide several insights into the highs and lows of teachers' work as well as teachers' perspectives on important educational issues. "There aren't many professions where workers pay for their own office supplies," reports Tremblay (2012) in relation to the survey findings, "but for Canadian teachers, it has become a trend. A 2010 online survey by the Canadian Teachers' Federation showed each teacher spent $453 on average that year on classroom materials or class-related activities. It's a sign the education system is underfunded. It's also a sign of the dedication of the professionals tasked to educate Canada's youth."

Additional key findings from the study (summarized from Froese-Germain, 2011) include the following:

- Teachers enjoy their work, and especially working with children. When asked to consider various factors "very important" to their decision to remain in teaching, respondents indicated especially that they "Enjoy teaching/job satisfaction" (cited by 80 per cent) and "Enjoy working with children" (86 per cent), and that they value their role in "Making a difference in children's lives" (82 per cent).

- Respondents cite several factors for why teachers leave the profession; ranked highest among those considered "very important" to the decision to leave are "Heavy workload" (84 per cent), "Work-related stress" (82 per cent), and "High expectations/increasing demands on teachers" (80 per cent).

- Teachers consider themselves capable of addressing diverse student needs, but they seek greater support to ensure they are able to respond adequately to increasing complexity in education driven by issues of "inclusion, workload and work-related stress, class size, access to professional development, inadequate resources, rapidly changing technology, and assessment and accountability strategies combined with other external pressures" (Froese-Germain, 2011).

Whereas outside observers frequently denigrate teaching based on the length of holidays in the school year and the limited number of instructional hours, teachers frequently point to the opposing dilemma that their workloads have increased to such extent that they do not have sufficient time during the year to keep pace with the demands for planning, curricular changes, technological developments, and capacity to engage fully with students, parents, and other educational participants.

demands, pedagogical techniques, and other aspects of their work, there are significant differences in qualifications and conditions associated with teaching at different levels and institutions and in different subject areas. Teachers at each level and jurisdiction are represented by specific organizations. These are usually called federations or associations, avoiding identification—with the exception of Nova Scotia teachers—as a "union." Elementary and secondary teachers are represented by a single organization in most provinces and territories, but there are also distinct organizations for specific groups of teachers in some provinces. Ontario and New Brunswick have separate associations for francophone teachers, while Quebec and Ontario have, in addition to their provincial associations, distinct associations for Protestant and Catholic teachers (as well as an Ontario association for English Catholic teachers). Nationally, the Canadian Teachers' Federation and the Canadian Association of University Teachers bring together affiliates from provincial and territorial organizations and institutional members. Many subject and specialist groups also exist apart from, or in conjunction with, the major educators' organizations. In addition, teachers are often active in initiating or running diverse organizations oriented to educational reform and other matters relevant to education. Post-secondary faculty and instructors are also represented through a variety of occupational and professional organizations. Most Canadian university faculty members are unionized through organizations that, as with teachers, are more typically labelled associations rather than unions. Unionized non-permanent university instructors and college instructors are typically organized through government or public-sector unions or faculty associations.

Teaching is guided by a variety of educational goals and objectives. Three key themes that emerge in the sociological analysis of teaching will be explored in the remainder of this chapter: (1) the development of teaching as a profession; (2) the importance of gender relations in teaching; and (3) the changing nature of teachers' work. Emphasis is given to how teaching exists as a contradictory form of work organized around competing demands. In some ways these demands are similar to changing patterns of work in general, yet they are uniquely shaped by educational priorities.

Teaching as a Profession

The Analysis of Teaching as a Profession

A prevalent theme in the sociological analysis of teaching is an attempt to understand teaching as a profession. The three most common ways of depicting teaching as a profession lie in approaches characterized as *professional trait*, *historical*, and *pressure group theory* (Ozga and Lawn, 1981). As will be shown below, each of these approaches offers useful insights into the development of teaching as an occupation, but each leaves important questions unanswered.

Teacher professionalism is commonly understood through trait approaches that begin with an assessment of how professional occupations differ from other types of work. Major traits that characterize professions usually include such features as formal credentials based on a body of advanced knowledge, social recognition as high-status work, high degrees of decision-making authority in the workplace, and an altruistic commitment to careers and clients (Carr-Saunders, 1966). Authors who employ this approach tend to use recognized professions like medicine and law as a standard of comparison against which to assess the extent to which teaching is a profession. On this basis, it is commonly concluded that teaching falls short of full professional status because it lacks autonomy and prestige, or that teaching is at best a semi- or quasi-profession that remains constrained by external forces such as other professions and bureaucratic school authority structures (Anderson, 1968; Henchey, 1977; Johnson, 2005).

Teaching is often understood through historical accounts, which are related to trait approaches to professionalism. Studies of this type emphasize the evolutionary strides teachers have made towards professional status. Paton (1962), for instance, outlines four historical phases within which Canadian teachers have organized and sought to achieve professional standing:

1. *1850–1914:* Teachers were brought together principally through meetings conducted by school inspectors and senior educational authorities to inform them of new developments in education and reinforce their loyalties to the school system.
2. *1914–35:* Teachers organized to promote teaching and improve their welfare and working conditions.
3. *1935–55:* Teachers' organizations struggled for official recognition and greater participation in educational policy-making processes.
4. *1955 and beyond:* Teachers sought professional status through improved occupational powers and responsibilities.

Many other studies, such as accounts by Chafe (1969) and Chalmers (1968), respectively, of the development of the Manitoba Teachers' Society and the Alberta Teachers' Association, Skolrood's (1967) study of the British Columbia Teachers' Federation, and Phillips's (1957) overview of the role of teachers in Canadian education, concur with the overall assessment that teachers have progressively gained professional status through better training, improvements in teaching and learning conditions, and greater input into sophisticated educational matters, despite barriers to the fulfillment of some of their aspirations.

A third group of studies related to teacher professionalism concentrates on the dynamics of teachers as organized lobby or interest groups. This approach, like the historical studies, emphasizes how teachers have struggled collectively to better their professional status and occupational welfare (Downie, 1978; Martin and Macdonnell, 1982; Muir, 1968). However, the analysis of teachers' organizations as interest groups highlights two aspects of teaching that indicate there is more to the occupation than simply the desire to be recognized as professionals. First, teachers have often found they can pursue their occupational interests more successfully through **collective bargaining,** labour militancy, or political mobilization than through any kind of acknowledgement that they have achieved professional status (see, e.g., Ungerleider, 1994; CEQ, 1974). Second, because teaching is highly constrained by state regulation, such as provincial legislation that outlines the duties and responsibilities of teachers, the degree to which the occupation can influence educational policy and practice is limited (Bascia, 2009; Lawson and Woock, 1987).

Considerable evidence supports the claims made in the literature that Canadian teachers have made significant progress over the past century towards the achievement of professional status. Whereas most teachers received little formal training at the beginning of the twentieth century, today teachers in nearly all provinces require at least four years of university education to qualify for a teaching certificate, with recent pressures to extend and intensify pre-service training. Teachers' pay scales, which were once set at the discretion of trustees who were often unwilling or unable to secure funds to pay teachers adequately, are now bargained collectively and reflect differences in levels of professional training and experience. Teachers are represented on curriculum committees and other educational bodies that set or influence policies relating to schooling. Their work is informed by critical reflection, collaboration, reliance on specified performance indicators, and extensive in-service and continuing learning. They are recognized, through their professional training and school legislation, as professionals who make decisions regarding such matters as curricular planning, pedagogy, discipline, and evaluation of students. **Teachers' associations** have developed codes of ethics regarding professional conduct and have been actively involved in professional development activities for their members. Teachers have also participated in a wide range of educational decision-making activities once left to the discretion of legislators, school trustees, and educational administrators.

Constraints on Teacher Professionalism

Despite marked improvements in the professional status of teachers, factors other than professionalism operate to shape teaching. Legislative and bureaucratic frameworks pose serious limitations to teachers' abilities to act as autonomous professionals. Teachers are the focus of intense scrutiny by parents, politicians, and media commentators who can be quick to dismiss teachers' efforts in the absence of appreciation for the full range of teaching-related activities. However, much of what teachers do is invisible to the casual observer. Ungerleider (2003: 152) highlights how teachers are charged from the outset with managerial responsibilities that few employees in the corporate world are likely to encounter, so that "Those people who have observed teachers at work are often overwhelmed by the sheer volume of teacher–student interaction, the quantity of paper and material to be managed, the movement of students, and the pacing and sequencing of activity."

The mixed signals that teachers tend to receive about their work contribute to considerable confusion over the nature and direction of teaching as an occupation. Teachers have not always been successful in developing collective strategies that would enable them to balance professional objectives and concern for students' welfare with campaigns to improve wages and working conditions. They have gained widespread notoriety as powerful lobby groups through their periodic regional or provincial support for selected political parties, their involvement in a number of important social justice initiatives, such as anti-poverty organizations, and their role in Quebec nationalist movements (Lockhart, 1991: 17; Ungerleider, 2003: 161–2). As a result, Canadian teachers' organizations have frequently found themselves in conflict with provincial governments or at the centre of intense media criticism.

By the 1990s, recurrent media reports on the theme of "what's wrong with the schools" had reinforced notions that teachers are not doing an adequate job of maintaining order, teaching students proper skills for life in the technological age, or keeping students interested in schooling. Nikiforuk (1993: 112) encapsulates many of these sentiments, observing that "Self-absorbed, poorly led, and often lacking in self-criticism (criticism now equals self-esteem bashing in some quarters) the profession or trade tends to prize its contributions too smugly."

Teachers have been able to maintain some public sympathy through acknowledgement that they cannot be held responsible for setting many of the conditions of their work. Attitudinal surveys suggest significant levels of public support for both teachers and for schools overall (Hart, 2012: 6–7), with about 70 per cent of

Canadians (and over three-quarters of respondents in the Prairie and Atlantic regions) indicating that they are very or somewhat satisfied with the jobs that teachers are doing (Canadian Education Association, 2007: 7). Nonetheless, teachers and their unions continue to be the focus of periodic attacks by media and government representatives seeking action to reduce state spending and reform the organization of education (Bascia, 2009: 481–2). Public critiques that fail to take into account

---

Box 6.2 The Impact of Education Reforms on Teaching and Learning Conditions

Successive measures to implement education reforms in Canada and many other nations have created a sometimes overwhelming array of demands that teachers must attend to in their daily work lives. These contribute to new teaching and learning opportunities, but they are also accompanied by extensive tension, stress, and uncertainty. The following summaries, drawn from research conducted with teachers in Newfoundland and Labrador (Younghusband, 2006: 9) and the Prairies (Wotherspoon, 2006: 690–1), highlight these disparate concerns:

Teacher stress and working environments in Newfoundland and Labrador

Teachers talked about being tired, worn out physically and emotionally. As they reflected on a life in the classroom, in a job they loved but found overwhelming, it was clear that the effort to remain effective was taking a toll not only on them, but on their colleagues and, they feared, on their students. "No time to stop, too many changes . . . some not workable, some have negative effects on students" they said. They described themselves as "bombarded, overwhelmed, on overload, always on the run." The word "impossible" was used over and over to describe their job. Increased demands for accountability from so many levels, each requiring a daunting amount of documentation and paperwork, all added to the hours worked. Recently, a teacher told my education students that he now spends more time on documentation than on lesson preparation. We must ask how that benefits students and how it makes the teacher feel.

Teachers discussed dealing with children who are profoundly needy, not only academically, but also socially and emotionally. They talked about teaching courses for which they had no background or training and how challenging that was, the time it took to prepare, and what it was like to feel that they weren't doing a first rate job.

Then there were the multiple roles expected: guidance counsellor, social worker, caregiver, parent, recess and lunchtime supervisor, fund raiser, extracurricular organizer.

"Just let us teach!" they said.

One participant described it this way: "Teaching doesn't end at 5 p.m. Calling parents, tracking things down, preparing for the next day—you're trying to juggle and balance the demands. I don't like being set up as a failure. I don't think there is a physical way of accomplishing it" (Younghusband, 2006: 9).

the realities of teaching and learning conditions often have a demoralizing impact on a teaching workforce concerned that it is not receiving the resources and support essential for fulfilling complex educational mandates. The Canadian Teachers' Federation was sufficiently concerned in 2001 to place a full-page advertisement in *The Hill Times*, which reports on the activities of the federal Parliament in Ottawa, to stress the difficulties schools had in recruiting and retaining teachers because of

Teachers' work in Aboriginal communities in Manitoba and Saskatchewan

Teachers' circumstances frequently lead to questions about the cumulative impact that various demands associated with teaching have for both teachers and students. A teacher of Aboriginal ancestry working in an elementary school in a medium-sized city articulates the contradictions associated with her work: "The school/education systems have been given more and more 'parental' responsibilities which take away from teaching time for basic and other skills children need to have to become competitive in or active participants of society. Schools feed, clothe, and try to impress respect upon children—children who go home at 3:30 to not safe surroundings where even the most basic of their needs are not or cannot be met." . . .

The comments of a teacher working in a remote rural area reveal how the joys of working with the high proportions of Aboriginal students in her district can sometimes be offset by the onus on teachers to take on unrealistic fiscal and professional burdens:

The classroom has become a safe secure environment for many students. Issues of abuse, incest, depression, and alcoholism come up on a regular basis in my class. I do not feel I am equipped to deal with such issues. There are two school counsellors—who are not trained professionals and are often absent—for 445 students. Therefore, they are extremely busy and overwhelmed. I feel I should receive some training to allow me to better deal with these situations. I have been to one professional development workshop, however, [my school district] would not fund it, nor would the school. Therefore, a one-day workshop cost me half my monthly salary. I am also overworked. I teach [six courses]. I receive one hour for preparation time for every six days of teaching. The school also mandates I coach a sport team, run an after-school club, and supervise detention hall after school for one-half hour. I do not think it is possible for many people to work that many hours under duress.

This combined sense of empathy for colleagues and students, accompanied by a litany of duties and expectations, conveys a near-crisis situation for both the individual teacher (who is "overworked" and "overwhelmed") and the education system itself (with a staff "under duress" unable to attend to students who see schooling as a mechanism to address serious problems in their daily lives) (Wotherspoon, 2006: 690–1).

Box 6.3 Two Views on Teachers' Right to Strike

Teaching and teachers' work are given shape through many divergent responsibilities, orientations, and expectations. These elements become especially apparent in periodic debates and controversies over questions of whether, or under what conditions, teachers should have the right to strike. Sharply divergent positions are being expressed in jurisdictions seeking to regulate public costs and rights of public-sector employees. In 2012, teachers' challenges to government actions both in the United States (notably in the city of Chicago) and Canada (Ontario and British Columbia) drew attention to these issues and what they mean for public-sector work. Competing views of teachers' rights to strike are illustrated in the following statements presented in the context of a 2011 court decision in British Columbia that reaffirmed teachers' right to strike in that province. These opposing views are expressed by (1) a representative from the Fraser Institute (Grubel, 2012) and by (2) the president at the time of the British Columbia Teachers' Federation (Lambert, 2011).

1. Stopping Teachers' Strikes Permanently

Like most striking workers, BC teachers tend to believe they are underpaid and overworked. And like most employers today, the BC government is facing tough economic times and can't afford to be generous with its workers. . . .

Fights between the BC teachers union and the government have a long history and transcend party lines. They will always be there. Give people the power to decide what they should be paid, they will always try to use this power to get what they want.

The only permanent solution to this problem therefore is to deprive teachers of the right to strike. The government that granted that right can also withdraw it. Such a policy is consistent with the widely held view that anyone who does not want to work for an organization that is prohibited from striking is free to work for one where the right exists.

The policy will restore the role of market forces. The government as the employer will rationally set wages so that there are neither unfilled vacancies nor teachers looking for work. School curricula and working conditions for teachers will be set in response to demands from parents and the political pressures they generate with input from teachers.

To prevent [not] only strikes but also increase the effectiveness of the educational system, the government should change the current system further by giving all parents vouchers that they spend on schools, which through competition are induced to provide the type and quality of education parents believe their children need.

Under this system, governments continue to meet their commitment to provide universal access to education. The big difference is that parents indirectly hire teachers that meet their standards, replacing the current system which sees teachers hired directly by government agencies that are much less sensitive to their children's needs than are parents. . . .

There is no time like now for at least a debate, if not action, on the possible prohibition of strikes by teachers union and the universal use of vouchers.

The public is tired of strikes, the deficits and debt caused by excessively generous wage package[s] in the past and never-ending demands for better and costly working conditions. The public is looking for political leadership to deal with these problems, not just the band-aid solutions offered by the type of legislation now used (Grubel, 2012).

2. Collective bargaining and the right to strike

As summer winds down, teachers are getting ready for the opening day of school. . . . Once students arrive, teachers will participate in finalizing class groupings and the school year will begin. After the beginning of September however, if there is no progress in bargaining, there are some tasks that teachers won't be doing. Teachers will be teaching, but they won't be doing administrative tasks such as filling out forms, supervision, attending meetings called by administrators and, if there has still been no agreement reached when the time comes, writing report cards. A partial withdrawal of services is designed to convince the employer to address the proposals that teachers have put on the bargaining table. . . . We have set as our priorities improvements to teacher working conditions which are student learning conditions; salaries and benefits on par with teachers across Canada and the right to seek local solutions to local issues.

Collective agreements were stripped of class size and student support provisions in 2002. Since then conditions for B.C. students, and especially students with special needs, have deteriorated to a point that teachers are not prepared to see continue. Teachers are determined to improve services so that each student in the public school has the support she or he needs. Restoring provisions for class size, provisions for teachers who support students with special needs, and for other learning specialists such as English-as-a-second-language teachers and teacher-librarians is a priority for teachers in this round of bargaining.

Parents and the public count on teachers to advocate for good learning conditions for students. Living with the knowledge that a child could do so much better if there were someone who could take time each day to support them in their learning is a pressure that adds to the work stress of teachers. Provisions for class size and special needs services in teacher collective agreements help to protect funding in the school system and ensure that these services are available to students.

Salaries for B.C. teachers rank eighth in Canada, while cost of living in this province is among the highest in the country. Teaching requires five years of university training and new teachers on average spend three to five years working as teachers on call at an average annual salary of less than $15,000. Teachers are not paid commensurate with work in the private sector requiring the same level of certification. When a teacher in Dawson Creek earns $16,000 per year less than a teacher 133 kilometres to the southeast in Grande Prairie, it's clear that there is an imbalance that needs to be addressed.

It is impossible to negotiate a "one size fits all" provision for many issues on the provincial bargaining table. Teachers are looking for opportunities for

continued

> local teacher unions and school districts to negotiate local solutions to local issues.
>
> Teachers, frustrated that these issues are not being addressed in a substantive manner, have responded with a 90-per-cent strike vote to begin actions designed to push for progress at the negotiating table (Lambert, 2011).

government measures to undermine teaching and public educational quality, educational cutbacks, new societal demands, poor employment conditions, and uncompetitive salaries (Willard, 2001). As large cohorts of experienced teachers approach retirement age, concerns about severe teacher shortages in many parts of Canada are exacerbated by high rates of attrition, especially among beginning teachers, and difficulties in attracting new recruits—especially males (Press et al., 2002; Bradley, 2011). The second decade of the twenty-first century has been marked by signs of increasing teacher militancy in several jurisdictions in Canada, the United States, and many other nations as teachers see their working conditions and occupational rights erode while educational expenditures are constrained, despite rising expectations about what education should contribute to knowledge-based societies.

The challenges that teachers face in their work and in establishing an occupational image suggest that trying to determine whether teaching is a profession is misdirected. What does it mean to acknowledge that any occupation is a profession? Professionalism is not static or absolute. Recent measures to restructure health care, for instance, mean that even established professions like medicine are in danger of losing much of the autonomy and respect they once held. In the continually changing world of education, teachers are subject to similar challenges, with the consequence that they are deprofessionalized in some aspects of their work at the same time as they may gain professional powers in others. Moreover, the nature and organization of teaching are governed by factors that both transcend and shape the nature of professionalism. Two of these are considered below—the importance in teaching of gender relations, and pressures in the direction of what has been conceptualized as the **proletarianization** of teaching.

Gender, Diversity, and Teaching

Gender Stratification within Teaching

Much of the discussion so far has presented teachers and teaching at a general or collective level. However, teachers and the conditions in which they work are highly diverse and multi-dimensional. One of the most striking features of the teaching workforce is its highly segmented gender composition. Women are concentrated in elementary school classrooms while men are concentrated at the post-secondary level and in senior administrative positions. In Canada, overall, over eight out of ten primary and preschool teachers, compared with just over two out of ten full university professors, are women. Two out of three full-time teachers in elementary and secondary schools are women while the number and proportion of male teachers, which has declined over the past two decades, is likely to drop further based on demographic trends and enrolment patterns in teacher training programs (Ferrao, 2010: 21; CAUT, 2012: 42; Turcotte, 2011b: 25). The concentrations of women teachers in post-secondary institutions are also increasing, but remain well below those of men, especially in full-time positions and at the highest academic ranks (CAUT, 2012: 29–33). Even more substantial differences are found within each educational level. A 2004–5 national survey revealed that in the kindergarten and elementary grades, women constitute 80 per cent of all teachers but just over half of principals and vice-principals in those schools; at the secondary level, 52 per cent of teachers and about one-third of principals and vice-principals are women (Blouin, 2006; O'Haire, 2005: 16). The number and proportion of female senior administrators at school and district levels have been increasing but remain disproportionately low relative to those of men and in comparison with the proportion of female teachers in jurisdictions across Canada (Rees, 1990; Reynolds et al., 2008).

There is an even more sharply defined pyramidal structure in the gender distribution of positions at the post-secondary level (see Figure 6.1). At the university level,

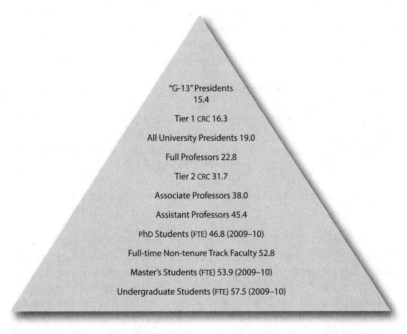

Figure 6.1 Post-Secondary Pyramid: Gender Distribution of Personnel in Key Roles and Positions, Canada (% female)

Data are for 2010–11 unless otherwise indicated.

"G–13" refers to the group of 13 leading research-intensive universities in Canada.

CRC = Canada Research Chairs.

Sources: Adapted from Canadian Federation of Humanities and Social Sciences (2012). Data for presidents compiled by Wendy Robbins and Bill Schipper, PAR-L, with assistance from the Canadian Association of University Teachers and the Canadian Federation for the Humanities and Social Sciences; data for students, faculty, and CRCs compiled from CAUT (2011, 2012).

about two-thirds (67 per cent) of tenured faculty, 55 per cent of faculty in positions leading to tenure, and over three-quarters (77 per cent) of faculty at the highest academic rank of full professor are men (CAUT, 2012: 29–31). Among full-time university faculty, women are much more likely than men to be concentrated at the lowest academic ranks, although this gap has declined in recent decades (Ornstein et al., 1998: 18; CAUT, 2012: 29–31). Male and female teachers throughout the education system are also concentrated in particular subject areas in accordance with traditional divisions of labour—for instance, most teachers in mathematics, sciences, and engineering are men while most teachers in general classrooms, health care (other than medicine), business education, and household sciences are women.

Differences in the kinds of teaching positions that men and women occupy have been reflected historically in teachers' salaries. Although the wage gap is diminishing, men continue to earn more, on average, than women at all levels and ranks of teaching. Among full-time university faculty, the average salary for women in 2010–11 was $12,137 (or about 10 per cent) below comparable levels for men, while at the full professor rank, the relative salary gap was about half that, at $6,849 (about 4.9 per cent) (CAUT, 2012: 9). Much of the disparity can be accounted for by differences in rank, qualifications, age, and experience. Personal factors, such as family commitments, specialized interests, and background in particular subject areas, and age–grade preferences also often contribute to distinct career choices and teaching priorities among men and women. Taken together, however, these elements are indicative of how individual and structural forces combine to produce unequal opportunities for men and women in teaching, as in many other occupations and spheres of life.

An overview of the historical development of public school teaching in Canada offers some insight into how gender inequities have become incorporated into the occupation. Table 6.1 shows the gender composition of the national school-teaching workforce since Confederation. In contrast with recent experience, in which women have constituted between one-half and two-thirds of the teachers, most teachers until the late 1860s were men. During the first quarter of the twentieth century, fewer than one in five teachers was male, although the relative proportion of male teachers gradually increased from a low of 16.6 per cent in 1920 to nearly 45 per cent in the early 1980s, before dropping to current levels of just over one-third.

The Feminization of Teaching

The national trends illustrated in Table 6.1 do not show provincial and regional variations in the **feminization** of teaching. By the time of Confederation, the numbers of male and female teachers were roughly equal in most jurisdictions. In Quebec and many regions of Ontario, however, women teachers outnumbered men by large margins much earlier; in much of western Canada, men predominated until at least the 1880s; and there were more men than women teaching in Prince Edward Island schools until after the turn of the century (see, e.g., Danylewycz et al., 1991; Leacy, 1983: W150–91). Among rural school districts in many provinces, particularly those that employed teachers working in one-room schools, men tended to outnumber women until late in the nineteenth century. In such districts, gender parity often continued for several years after that, although there were variations in the trends from one region or school district to another (Danylewycz et al., 1991).

Danylewycz and Prentice (1986: 60–1) emphasize that many commentators hold mistaken views associated with historical processes through which teaching became feminized. One such myth is that the preponderance of young female teachers at the turn of the century devalued teaching and made it susceptible to extensive regulation by educational authorities, thereby delaying or preventing the occupation from becoming a full profession. While it is true that teachers were frequently subjected to paternalistic control by educational administrators, it is also important to emphasize

Table 6.1 Full-Time Teachers in Elementary and Secondary Schools, by Gender, Canada, Selected Years, 1867–2009*

Year**	Male (%)	Female (%)	Total
1867	3,312 (53.8)	2,840 (46.2)	6,152
1870	5,143 (38.6)	8,180 (61.4)	13,323
1875	5,338 (34.1)	10,329 (65.9)	15,667
1880	6,181 (35.1)	11,411 (64.9)	17,592
1885	5,772 (28.2)	14,719 (71.8)	20,491
1890	5,797 (25.7)	16,753 (74.3)	22,550
1895	6,069 (24.5)	18,652 (75.5)	24,721
1900	6,205 (22.7)	21,164 (77.3)	27,369
1905	6,392 (19.8)	25,818 (80.2)	32,210
1910	7,849 (19.4)	32,627 (80.6)	40,476
1915	8,789 (17.5)	41,453 (82.5)	50,242
1920	9,600 (16.6)	48,178 (83.4)	57,778
1925	12,069 (18.9)	51,771 (81.1)	63,840
1930	14,255 (20.3)	55,990 (79.7)	70,245
1935	18,492 (25.3)	54,593 (74.7)	73,085
1940	19,417 (25.8)	55,970 (74.2)	75,387
1945	17,415 (22.5)	60,064 (77.5)	77,479
1950	24,064 (26.8)	65,618 (73.2)	89,682
1955	31,058 (26.8)	84,777 (73.2)	115,835
1960	44,593 (29.1)	108,447 (70.9)	153,040
1965	67,832 (34.4)	129,261 (65.6)	197,093
1970	100,820 (38.4)	161,637 (61.5)	262,457
1975	110,429 (41.8)	153,833 (58.2)	262,262
1980	121,537 (44.4)	152,170 (55.6)	273,707
1985	119,400 (43.9)	152,659 (56.1)	272,059
1990	119,143 (40.1)	177,963 (59.9)	297,106
1995	113,198 (37.9)	185,478 (62.1)	298,676
2000***	108,277 (35.0)	201,085 (65.0)	309,362
2005***	97,954 (31.6)	212,027 (68.4)	309,981
2009***	86,348 (29.0)	211,127 (71.0)	297,475

*Data not available for Nova Scotia and Quebec in 1867; Prince Edward Island, in 1875 and 1895; Manitoba and British Columbia, until 1885. Data for Alberta and Saskatchewan not included until 1905; Newfoundland, until 1950; and Yukon and Northwest Territories, until 1960.
**School year beginning in the year shown.
***Figures are estimates.
Sources: For 1867–1975: F.H. Leacy, ed., *Historical Statistics of Canada,* 2nd edn (Ottawa: Statistics Canada, 1983), W150-2; for 1980–90: Statistics Canada, *Education in Canada* (Ottawa: Minister of Supply and Services Canada, various years); for 1995–2009: Statistics Canada and CMEC (2011b) and OECD databases.

the strong professional commitment demonstrated by many early women teachers in their efforts to provide effective education despite personal and occupational difficulties (Poelzer, 1990; Prentice and Theobald, 1991; Wilson, 1991). Sometimes, young women entered teaching on a temporary basis until they were married, but many teachers saw the occupation as a lifelong vocation. A spirit of adventure and the ability to innovate were often essential ingredients for the success of those who assumed teaching positions in remote rural areas. Although such teachers initially may have lacked formal training and experience, they played a crucial role in promoting public education and maintaining the school as a vital part of social development in many communities across Canada.

A second misconception related to the feminization of teaching concerns the devaluation or invisibility of teaching as a form of work (Danylewycz and Prentice, 1986: 61). Teaching traditionally has been discounted as something less than a "real job" or else has been analyzed separately from other work by virtue of its nature as non-manual labour performed primarily by women. Instead, it is often considered as an extension of unpaid social roles associated with mothering and domestic work (Gaskell and McLaren, 1991). In addition to undermining teaching as work, these views have been used to justify discriminatory practices in teaching, including the maintenance of pay schedules in which female teachers were paid less than men until the mid-twentieth century, as well as the periodic requirement of provincial governments and school boards for women to resign from teaching positions upon marriage. Despite persistent realities to the contrary, female teachers have been depicted by many administrators and policy-making bodies as less dedicated and well trained than males, and less in need of income and careers to support themselves or their families (Arbus, 1990; Reynolds, 1990).

An analysis of the historical development of teaching in Canada yields important insights about changing gender relations within the occupation. Both men and women have played central, although often distinctive, roles in all phases of Canadian schooling. Gendered divisions of labour were established early. In New France, distinct schools for boys and girls tended to be run, respectively, by parish priests and female teaching orders in the seventeenth century (Johnson, 1968: 8–9). Beyond elementary schooling, at least until the nineteenth century, teaching tended to be conducted by men for men, usually by clergy in colleges or seminaries that offered professional training, or by highly educated men who provided elite training to other men of privileged classes.

In general, two kinds of schooling, associated with distinct classes of teachers, prevailed prior to the late nineteenth century. Grammar schools or those established by particular organizations sought teachers who were somewhat qualified and loyal to the goals of the sponsoring authorities. Common schools open to all children in the community were initially established by anyone who claimed to be a teacher or who could hire others to teach. The former tended to be somewhat better paid and more highly regarded than the latter, although there were frequent reports of public disdain for, if not hostility against, teachers in general (Phillips, 1957: 546–7).

One of the main objectives sought by advocates for a system of free public schools in the nineteenth century was the establishment of a stable, highly respected teaching workforce. This desired form of school organization had contradictory implications for teachers, whose role came to be that of "subordinate partners" in the education system (Wotherspoon, 1993). Teachers gained some degree of job security and occupational legitimacy through the introduction of measures to ensure that communities had schools operated with public funds and other forms of state support. Teachers also experienced increasing status through the expectation that they would promote public education and be entrusted to supervise and teach children. At the same time, though, teachers were more fully monitored by school inspectors and regulated by state educational administrators. Thus, although they had considerable autonomy and authority in the classroom, teachers became public servants in the sense that their primary obligations and loyalties were to the "public good" rather than to any specific social interest.

School promoters and educational administrators were interested in developing a workforce of classroom teachers that met their ideals of public education. Repeatedly, in the speeches, reports, and writings of such educational leaders, the ideal teacher was presented as a relatively well-educated and self-disciplined man of high moral quality (Corrigan et al., 1987; Love, 1978). While educational authorities were not opposed to female teachers, they sought males, who they felt would be more committed to public education as a project of state formation. From its beginnings, then, a paternalistic model of authority was incorporated into the public education system so that senior administrators and state officials were almost exclusively men, as were secondary school teachers and senior teachers in larger schools, while women taught in the elementary grades or in ungraded rural schools.

The development of the Canadian teaching workforce, like many other aspects of education, involved a constant tension between educational ideals and practical considerations. One of the persistent limitations to the fulfillment of educators' visions of the education system was the lack of an adequate supply of suitable, fully qualified teachers. This problem was itself often the consequence of other difficulties within the education system, including negative public images of teachers and low teacher salaries. These factors often reinforced one another. Public schools, by the late nineteenth century, were supported by provincial government grants intended to be supplemented by locally raised funds. The latter, however, were frequently scarce, contributing to inequalities between rural and urban schools and among school districts. Collection of school funds could not always be enforced, especially in poorer regions or districts where the public had little interest in or support for the school system. Therefore, teachers were often paid less than amounts they had been promised, however inadequate those salaries were to begin with (Wotherspoon, 1993). Teachers' salaries, on average, were lower than the wages of unskilled labourers at the start of the twentieth century (Phillips, 1957: 551–2) and they remained well below average occupational salaries until after World War II, when factors such as the consolidation of school districts, increased allocation of central government funding for education, and aggressive collective bargaining by teachers began to stabilize teacher incomes.

This situation exacerbated gender-based differential pay rates for teachers. Table 6.2 reveals that women have been paid about two-thirds to three-quarters of what men received until relatively recently. However, while teachers experience greater gender parity than other Canadian workers, as a whole, the average income for female teachers remains just over four-fifths of that for male teachers. As the data for 2006 reveal, even for full-time full-year workers in mid-career, female teachers' earnings remain at about 90 per cent of those for male teachers. Altenbaugh (1995: 83–4) indicates that differences in pay among men and women throughout North America stemmed in part from the likelihood that male teachers had more formal training and teaching experience and

Table 6.2 Average Elementary and Secondary School Teachers' Incomes
in Comparison with Average Income in Canada, by Gender,
Selected Census Years, 1921–2006

	Teachers			All Occupations		
	Male	Female	Total	Male	Female	Total
1921	$1,395	$818	$914	$1,057	$573	$954
1931	1,575	917	1,066	927	559	848
1941	1,416	793	962	993	490	755
1951*	2,673	1,915	2,050	3,468	1,788	2,898
1961	4,712	3,176	3,734	3,679	1,995	3,191
1971	8,420	5,532	6,424	6,574	3,199	5,391
1981	24,039	15,142	18,111	16,988	8,863	13,635
1991	41,266	27,938	31,864	29,847	17,751	24,329
2001	46,356	38,449	40,751	38,347	24,390	31,757
2006**	61,052	55,026	56,920	50,238	38,111	44,435

*For 1951, figures are for median income; for teachers, data for Quebec are not available.
**Data for 2006 refer to median income for full-time full-year workers ages 25–54 and are not directly comparable to earlier years.
Sources: Compiled and calculated from census data; for 1951, data on teachers are from Dominion Bureau of Statistics, *Survey of Elementary and Secondary Education, 1950–54* (Ottawa: Queen's Printer, 1959).

were concentrated in high schools, where salaries tended to reflect higher qualification levels and where teachers were better able to organize to protect their occupational interests. Altenbaugh emphasizes, further, that gender discrimination played a more fundamental role in teaching, as evident in the fact that women were paid less even when they were teaching high school or had more education and experience than men. It has been noted previously, for instance, that gender differences were institutionalized through separate and unequal pay scales for men and women that were systematically maintained by provinces and school districts until the 1960s.

Gender factors also entered into the regulation of teaching by educational administrators and government officials. Public or common schooling, of which teachers were the most visible representatives in local communities, signified the presence of state rule in everyday life. This placed teachers in a position in which their lives and characters were under surveillance away from school as well as at work. The lack of teachers with adequate training and of presumed character to meet the ideal desired by educational authorities posed a dilemma that resulted in new ways of monitoring and managing the teaching workforce.

In the late nineteenth and early twentieth centuries, legislators and educational administrators introduced several measures to regulate teaching. Many of these initiatives were directed in particular towards the preponderance of young women who entered teaching to meet the demands of a growing school system. A system of school inspection was implemented so that state authority would be represented in schools on a periodic basis to compensate for the difficulties involved in monitoring classroom activity on an everyday basis. The school inspector was instructed to assess the character as well as the competency of teachers. The traumatic nature of school inspectors' visits—and the mysterious authority they represented—has become a recurrent theme in Canadian fiction as well as in biographical accounts of students and teachers (see, e.g., Braithwaite, 1979). The system of classroom inspection had the additional effect of reinforcing paternalism and gender-based divisions of labour within educational hierarchies by creating a career path in which it was possible for loyal male teachers to be promoted to the rank of inspector (Fleming, 1986). In the larger urban schools, supervision of teachers was often more directly accomplished through the presence of principals, head teachers, and subject specialists (Danylewycz and Prentice, 1986: 70).

The inspection function was complemented by a second form of control under the guise of legislation and regulations to govern the character and work of teachers. Teachers' duties were specified in law and other directives passed down from both the provinces and school boards. Thus, as exemplified in the regulations of British Columbia in 1875 (see Box 3.3), the teacher not only had to teach "diligently and faithfully" the curriculum set by boards of education, but was also required to promote "both by precept and example, cleanliness, neatness, and decency" and to inculcate "trust and honesty" (British Columbia, 1875: 47). Teachers' duties and the demands on their time expanded in conjunction with increases in school size and enrolment, the duration of school attendance, and the scope of the curriculum. In addition to growing class sizes and the requirements to teach new subjects, teachers were faced with paperwork, documenting everything from student attendance and progress to homework and classroom activities (Danylewycz and Prentice, 1986: 66–8).

However, as the quotation above reveals, teachers' personal attributes and lives, more than just their school-related work, were subject to external scrutiny by educational authorities. This applied to both men and women. School officials frequently criticized male teachers for their apparent lack of commitment to teaching or carelessness in their work and personal habits. The lives and habits of female teachers were subjected to even closer scrutiny. Akin to forms of patriarchal regulation of women's sexuality and social activities that prevailed in the family, school board regulations and teachers' contracts stipulated how female teachers should dress, prohibited them from keeping company with men, proscribed the hours they were to be at home, and made them subject to dismissal if they drank, smoked, or married (see, e.g., Apple, 1986: 72–4; British Columbia School Trustees' Association, 1980). The teacher—especially the female teacher—became a public figure who was governed by specified notions of morality as determined by state authorities.

A third form of regulation, oriented to the governance of women teachers, was the regularization and expansion of teacher training programs. Until the early part of the twentieth century, the qualifications and training required to become a teacher were highly irregular. While many private and secondary schools were able to attract and pay adequate salaries to persons who had undertaken university studies, common schools often hired whomever they could to ensure an adequate supply of teachers. Initially, a person might be considered eligible to teach simply by virtue of having more schooling than the students being taught (or even claiming to have more). State officials, concerned about the quality as well as public perceptions of the school system, promoted the establishment of formal teacher training programs. Teacher training institutions called **normal schools**, which provided prospective teachers with knowledge about curricular subjects and the "art" and practice of teaching, were introduced as early as 1836 in Montreal and 1847 in Upper Canada and New Brunswick (Johnson, 1968:

156). Over the next several decades, provincial governments and school boards made periods of training in normal schools, usually in conjunction with some high school attainment, a requirement for teacher certification. Nonetheless, as Phillips (1957: 579) observes, "actually, in all provinces before 1900 a large proportion of elementary school teachers had no more than two years' secondary school education, and either no professional training at all or no such training at the normal school level."

Normal schools had as their objective the production of a corps of teachers who could at least approximate the ideal advanced by educational authorities. However, these schools also reoriented their focus to the reality that most persons who were entering teaching were "raw, untrained" young women, as they were characterized by at least one school official (British Columbia, 1904: A65). Consequently, normal school training emphasized the cultivation of feminine dedication and loyalty to the public educational enterprise as much as practical classroom knowledge. These paternalistic aims were directed by male administrators in both the school system and the normal schools (Wotherspoon, 1989: 151).

Reconceptualizing Teaching and Teachers' Work

It is necessary to recognize several fallacies in the portrayal by education officials of teachers, and women teachers in particular, as compliant and incompetent novices. First, while there were many "green" teachers who did enter the classroom with little formal training, most school districts had several examples of teachers who, over the course of extended careers, made significant contributions both to the education of several generations of youth and to the increasing public respect that came to be accorded the school system overall. High teacher attrition rates were at least as likely to be the result of inadequate pay or working conditions, or regulations such as the one to force women to resign their positions upon marriage, as the consequence of individual failings.

Second, teachers were, as they generally continue to be, much more resourceful than they have been given credit for. Teaching, in common with other occupations considered to be "women's work," such as clerical work, involves highly complex attributes that tend to be discounted as skills (see, e.g., Jackson, 1994). Considerable skill is involved, for instance, in the day-to-day ability to organize and manage classrooms. Most notably in poorly equipped schools or those located at a distance from major towns and cities with libraries and adequate technological support, teachers have had to develop their own materials and techniques to convey the curriculum and maintain student interest.

Teachers also possess expertise in their ability to facilitate interpersonal relations in and out of the classroom. A fundamental part of teaching is the emotional labour related to teachers' caring and nurturing roles, managing the emotions and feelings of students and other social relationships (Hochschild, 1983; Isenbarger and Zembylos, 2006). As this book has emphasized, the often indeterminate nature of life and social dynamics within schooling is a vital part of educational processes. The teaching relationship includes such things as sensitivity to students' emotional states, informal counselling and advising, mediation between competitive or antagonistic students, and other nurturing activities. These aspects of teaching are often devalued and discredited as real skills because of their parallels with mothering and domestic labour, forms of unpaid labour considered natural. Nonetheless, the "caring" dimensions of teachers' work remain central to capacities regarded as essential for good teaching.

International Contrast Case Study

Teaching in Crisis?

Teachers in Canada and other highly developed nations have made extensive gains in occupational status and improved working conditions, although their efforts to gain full professional recognition for their work and qualifications are sometimes undermined by educational reforms, funding crises, and other serious issues. Processes of intensification, work overload, deprofessionalization, and work-related stress are among many factors contributing to projections of serious teacher shortages around the world within the next decade (MacBeath, 2012: 9–11).

In many parts of the world, teachers' professional status and **work conditions** have been even more seriously eroded, often to the extent that their livelihoods, schools, and lives can be in jeopardy. Teachers' organizations, educational agencies, and major international bodies, including UNESCO and the International Labour Organization, have drawn attention to these issues in the declaration of 5 October each year as World Teachers' Day. The theme of the 2011 World Teachers' Day was "Teachers for Gender Equality," motivated by concerns that

> as the profession has become increasingly feminized, conditions of service, pay and status have deteriorated. . . . It is also important to identify the causes for the shortage of women teachers where they exist. Adequate provisions for maternity protection and parental leave, as well as effective protection from sexual violence and abuse, are essential. If qualified female teachers avoid postings in disadvantaged and rural areas, how can we convince reluctant parents to send their children to school? (International Labour Organization, 2011)

Teachers also encounter severe difficulties of many other kinds, such as the following (Education International, 2009):

- The achievement of universal primary education by 2015 would require 18 million additional teachers. The problem of teacher shortages and unqualified teaching personnel is particularly acute in sub-Saharan and North Africa, the Middle East, and South and West Asia.
- Teachers in many nations, especially in sub-Saharan Africa and South Asia, are experiencing increasing class sizes while their wages, already close to or below poverty-line levels, are being reduced.
- Restrictions on academic freedom and political pressure on university teachers and researchers are reported widely in many parts of the world.
- High incidences of HIV and AIDS, and lack of attention to the problem, are contributing to teacher shortages, discrimination, teacher absenteeism, and decreased performance, particularly (but not exclusively) in sub-Saharan Africa.

continued

- Teachers in several nations, including Colombia, Jamaica, Germany, Norway, Portugal, Nepal, Ghana, and Malaysia, have been the victims of physical and verbal aggression by parents and students.
- Violent attacks including "targeted assassinations of teachers or education unionists, death or injury during destruction of buildings by remotely detonated explosions or acts of burning or ransacking, illegal detention, torture by forces of, or supported by, the state or by rebel groups, abduction of teachers by armed forces for extortion or to spread terror and rape of teachers by military forces" are increasing in many parts of the world such as Afghanistan, Colombia, Nepal, Thailand, Zimbabwe, Palestine, Iran, Mexico, and Brazil (Education International, 2009: 22–3), while school massacres in the United States and parts of Europe are raising more widespread concerns about school safety.

Discussion Questions

1. Why are teachers vulnerable to threats, abuse, and difficult working conditions in many parts of the world? Explore the factors that contribute to these difficulties in particular contexts as well as for teaching as a profession overall.
2. How can teachers, collectively, address most effectively the threats to their work and working conditions?

Acker's (1999: 195) observations with respect to one school are applicable to many teaching situations:

> The fact that most of the teachers were women was also one of its strengths. Many of the women had in the past, or were having concurrently, experience in managing homes and families and balancing competing commitments. They seemed well adapted to the flexibility and tolerance for change required for a successful teacher at the school.

A third problem is the image of docility associated with a highly feminized teaching workforce. The fact that educational administrators and teacher-training officials introduced a broad and frequently changing range of regulations to govern teaching signifies that teachers were not readily subordinated. Many teachers demonstrated courage and determination simply to maintain their positions in the face of parents, trustees, and other officials hostile to them or the school. Teachers adopted both formal and informal means to resist measures they felt were extreme or unfair. Women teachers not only advanced struggles for pay equity, improvement of teaching conditions, and curricular change within the school system, but they were also engaged, often in leadership roles, in the suffragist and later feminist movements as well as in other organized groups in pursuit of social justice. Moreover, women did have some formal opportunities to influence the profession more directly. Although women with university degrees and other superior qualifications were more likely to be bypassed for promotion in favour of men, they were not always completely excluded from administrative and senior teaching positions.

These observations are important in helping us to reconceptualize the notion of professionalism. In contrast to approaches concerned with the question of whether teaching is a profession, historical evidence suggests that professionalism can more appropriately be understood as a strategy or ideology employed by various forces and agencies, both within and external to teaching, in order to shape the occupation in particular ways (Warburton, 1986). In the same way that school officials continually had to revise how they regulated teaching because it was not possible to construct a workforce of idealized teachers, diverse images and consequences of professionalism have contributed to the development of teaching in Canada.

Some school officials, for instance, were opposed to female teachers because they saw the influx of young women as a deterrent to the achievement of professional status by teachers. Viewed in this context, the introduction of normal schools was a way to upgrade teacher professionalism by providing specialized training and improving teacher qualifications, but it was intended to scrutinize teachers and inculcate in them an appropriate orientation to the school system before they entered the classroom. Similarly, teachers working in different educational settings had unique professional needs. For relatively well-paid, highly qualified secondary school teachers, professionalism was a way to increase their status and power in the education system, while teachers in poorly equipped remote rural schools were more likely to see professionalism as a tool for attaining fundamental improvements in teaching and working conditions. Professionalism, as an ideology, has had a moderating impact by restricting the extent to which teachers have adopted overtly political and militant actions, but it has also been influential in raising teachers' occupational profile, sometimes by their aggressive pursuit of policies and practices that go beyond school-specific issues.

The tendency for many teachers, as well as legislators, administrators, trustees, parents, and the media, to establish boundaries that define legitimate spheres of activity for teachers, and to distinguish these from areas that teachers should not be engaged in, continues to have important consequences for gender relations in teaching. Teachers who have advanced equitable treatment for women in teaching, for instance, have sometimes also been leaders in wider feminist movements. Some have encountered criticism from within and outside teaching for dealing with issues characterized by critics as political rather than educational in nature. Frequently, educational administrators and leaders of teachers' organizations have dismissed demands by teachers to address issues such as pay inequity, racism, and sexism in the classroom, and to express concern about poverty in the community, as "unprofessional." These tendencies have made it difficult for teachers' organizations to take decisive action on such problems as sexual harassment, maternity leave, inequitable assignment of duties, competing demands between home and school, and other concerns that emerge through women's experiences in teaching.

The continuing **division of labour** along gender lines in teaching is clearly illustrated by the data in Tables 6.1 and 6.2 on the positions occupied by men and women in the education system. In general, it remains the case that most teachers in the lower grades and subordinate positions are women, while most teachers in high school and administrative positions are men. Although women today have a much greater impact on educational decision-making than in the past, partly reflected in increased participation rates in senior positions, substantial gender inequality remains within teaching and educational administration with respect to numbers, voice, differential expectations about responsibilities, and role performance (Collard and Reynolds, 2005; Young et al., 2007: 193–5). Employment equity programs, increased recognition of the need for women to take more central roles in educational planning and management as well as delivery, and the leadership that some women have provided to change educational realities and serve as successful role models have had an impact on creating more favourable conditions for gender equity. Various factors, including personal choice, positive and negative attitudes of teachers and administrators, and the ways in which teaching-related activities are differentially recognized in career and promotion decisions within teaching, have contributed to the mixed success in achieving equity objectives (Rees, 1990; Reynolds, 2002).

Social Diversity and Teaching

The teaching profession in Canada faces additional scrutiny and challenges in relation to the increasing racial and cultural diversity within schools. Teachers are expected to reflect many of the major characteristics of the communities they work in and to play a leadership role by fostering learning environments that are sensitive to the students and communities they work with. With few exceptions (notably visible minorities teaching at the university level), the proportion of teachers and educators at all levels who are visible minorities or Aboriginal has not kept pace with comparable growth in the student body and the general population (see Figure 6.2). By 2006, visible minorities constituted 16.2 percent of Canada's population but only 6.9 percent of all elementary and secondary school teachers and school counsellors, representing an increasing gap since 2001; the trend was most evident in major immigrant-receiving cities like Vancouver and Toronto, but there is also increasing diversity in smaller centres where there are few minority-group teachers (Ryan et al., 2009: 597–8).

Figure 6.3 reveals that only about one in six Aboriginal persons nationally had attended a school that had any Aboriginal teachers or teachers' aides. Proportional representation was lower than average in the eastern provinces but substantially higher in Manitoba, Saskatchewan, and the northern territories. Among Aboriginal respondents surveyed in 2009 in major urban centres across Canada, 69 per cent indicated that they had no Aboriginal teachers in elementary school and 67 per cent had no Aboriginal teachers in high school (Environics Institute, 2010: 119). This is beginning to change, as more Aboriginal people move into the teaching workforce and governments and school boards adopt more proactive Aboriginal equity programs. However, considerable under-representation across Canada of Aboriginal teachers and educational workers still exists, both overall and relative to the proportions of Aboriginal persons in age cohorts most typically enrolled in formal education programs. When we recognize that the Aboriginal population is much younger than the total population—currently one-third of the Aboriginal population is 15 years old and younger and fully half of Aboriginal persons are under the age of 29—and that these demographic disparities are projected to continue, the relative lack of Aboriginal teachers is seen as an even greater problem (Frideres, 2011: 208–10).

Comprehensive current data are not available, but the proportions of school-age children of Aboriginal ancestry tend to outnumber the proportion of Aboriginal teachers in elementary and secondary schools by factors of at least 2.5 to 3 times in jurisdictions in which data are reported. In Manitoba, for example, persons with

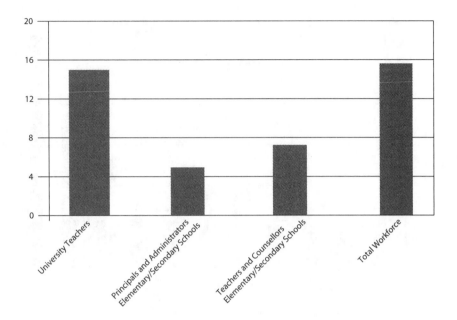

Figure 6.2 Visible Minorities as Proportion of Selected Teaching
Occupations and Total Workforce, Canada, 2006

Sources: Data compiled from CAUT (2012: 36), and 2006 *Census of Canada*, Statistics Canada
catalogues 97-564-XCB2006005F0011XCB2001040 and 97F0011XCB2002053.

Aboriginal identity represented nearly one-quarter of the school-age population (23.8
per cent of those ages 5 to 19) compared to 8.5 per cent of the province's elementary
and secondary school teachers (calculated from Statistics Canada, Census of Canada,
97-558-XCB2006006; Manitoba Education, 2011: 1–2). A similar pattern is evident
in Saskatchewan, where in 2008–9 those who indicated Aboriginal ancestry represented 16.5 per cent of all students in the province's school system compared to 6.4
per cent of the province's teachers (Saskatchewan Ministry of Education, 2009: 71).
Similarly, amid rising numbers and rates of participation in post-secondary education by Aboriginal students, Aboriginal educators represent only about 1 per cent of
all university teachers in Canada (CAUT, 2012: 36). Racial minority groups, especially
within black and Aboriginal communities, frequently cite the lack of representation
within the teaching and educational administrative workforce as a serious deficiency
in the creation of a racially tolerant and culturally supportive atmosphere (Canadian
Race Relations Foundation, 2000: 8–9). Many visible minority and Aboriginal teachers express concern about their work placements, job expectations, lack of acceptance
by other school and community personnel, and encounters with racism (St Denis,
2010: 35–46). Broader concerns are also evident as teachers are mandated to implement anti-racist or culturally inclusive program guidelines despite having limited
background knowledge, administrative support, resources, and time for preparation. These problems coexist with several promising initiatives in which teachers

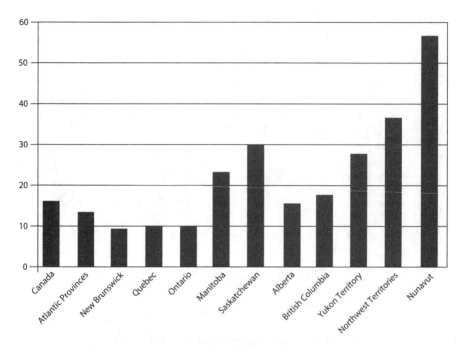

Figure 6.3 Proportion of Aboriginal Population Ages 15 and Over Indicating They Had Attended a School That Had Aboriginal Teachers or Teacher's Aides

Source: Data compiled from Statistics Canada, *2006 Profile of Aboriginal Children, Youth and Adults, Key Indicators from the 2006 Aboriginal Children's Survey and the 2006 Aboriginal People's Survey*, 2009, at: www12.statcan.gc.ca/census-recensement/2006/dp-pd/89-635/index.cfm?Lang=eng.

are strongly supported and committed to develop strong connections and relationships with the communities in which they work (Dei et al., 2000: 141ff.; Schissel and Wotherspoon, 2003: 116–19).

Proletarianization and Intensification of Teaching

Regulating Teachers' Work

In contrast to the view that teaching can be characterized by its strong progress towards professionalism and gender equity, some commentators argue that the dominant tendency is one of proletarianization. Proletarianization refers to the processes whereby teachers, like workers in many industries, are subject to increasing, externally driven forms of control and pressures to intensify their work.

One of the primary claims for recognition of teaching as a profession has been the continual increase in educational qualifications required for teacher certification. At the beginning the twentieth century it was not uncommon for teachers to have less than high school completion, and secondary education and a period of specialized teacher training were required by the early part of the century. By the mid-1970s teacher training in most provinces was established in university degree programs, and today most Canadian jurisdictions require a minimum of four to five years of university education, including one or more years of professional studies, prior to certification. Most administrative positions and some secondary teaching positions are restricted to persons with a master's degree or higher in combination with other forms of professional development (Canadian Teachers' Federation, 2012). By the early 1990s, two-thirds of all teachers who taught at the kindergarten to Grade 3 levels and over 70 per cent of teachers in the higher grades (increasing by level) held university degrees (King and Peart, 1992: 22). Despite these improvements in formal educational qualifications, a common complaint of teachers is that there is a disjuncture between their training and the expectations placed on them in the classroom and in other aspects of the job. Those who argue that teaching is becoming proletarianized rather than professionalized emphasize the necessity for examining how teaching is organized and regulated as work, rather than what the formal entry requirements are, in order to assess how "professional" teaching has become. Moreover, when teaching is analyzed as work, the reasons for teachers' involvement with organized labour and their adoption of trade unionist strategies become more readily apparent.

With respect to teaching, proletarianization can be understood in several different ways. In the most general sense, the concept refers to the attributes that teaching shares with other forms of work that are regulated and controlled by employers or managers outside the shop floor or the classroom. Braverman (1974), in one of the most influential analyses of contemporary labour processes, argues that no occupation is immune from proletarianization and the related process of deskilling, in which workers lose their ability to plan, make decisions, and use a wide range of skills to carry out their work tasks. As was observed in Chapter 2 and will be expanded upon in the next chapter, increases in formal educational credentials and training requirements in many occupations do not necessarily mean that workers use the acquired skills and training on the job. This phenomenon is significant for teachers in two ways: (1) in terms of how teaching is organized as work, and (2) in terms of their responsibilities to educate students whose own work futures are uncertain.

All jobs are organized around the completion of particular tasks. In the case of teaching, the main activities tend to be considered as mental rather than manual labour. Teachers are able to make claims to professionalism in part because many aspects of their work are difficult to codify. This stands in contrast to many other jobs, such as those involved in the making or selling of commercial products, in which employees are expected to follow explicit instructions in accordance with their job descriptions. Teaching, though, is also organized around several technical functions, such as designing lesson plans, grading students, keeping records of student attendance and progress, and following rules and procedures regarding student discipline. For each of these activities, there is likely to be considerable variation from one teaching situation to another with respect to how closely teachers are monitored and expected to perform specified duties or how much leeway teachers have to alter their practices.

Proletarianization occurs as teachers are subject to increasing levels of external control by supervisors or administrators, or when their work is reorganized to minimize the discretion they have over their activities. When standardized curricula or exams are introduced into schooling, for instance, teachers' performance presumably can be assessed as readily as that of students. Educators' reliance on curricula and lesson plans based on rigidly defined behavioural objectives, or on student workbooks that follow a specified progression of lessons and exercises, requires little input from the teacher in the curricular planning and delivery process. While most teachers are likely to use these materials in conjunction with other resources and to innovate in their lesson planning, the likelihood that they will depend largely or entirely on prescribed materials (if, indeed, they are not overtly directed to adopt these materials) increases as class sizes and demands on their time grow. Runté (1998) observes in one Canadian jurisdiction that even when teachers have some discretion over what is taught and how it is taught, the imposition of centralized examinations and standardized tests removes effective education planning and the setting of goals from the school level to more centralized authorities.

The Intensification of Teachers' Work

Apple refers to the process of **intensification** to demonstrate how important aspects of the work of teachers and other professionals can be proletarianized or deskilled. Intensification occurs when the demands associated with a job are increased. Apple (1986: 41) observes that intensification

> has many symptoms, from the trivial to the more complex—ranging from being allowed no time at all even to go to the bathroom, have a cup of coffee or relax, to having a total absence of time to keep up with one's field. We can see intensi- fication most visibly in mental labour in the chronic sense of work overload that has escalated over time.

As school districts reduce teaching and support staff and increase class sizes, for instance, teachers are required not only to teach more pupils but also to perform more duties that were once done by other workers. Changes to school budgets and pro- grams mean that many have to teach in areas for which they have little or no training, especially if subjects outside of the core areas or a full range of extracurricular activi- ties are to be retained. New curricula and modified learning objectives require the in- troduction of new subjects and materials with which teachers have to keep up to date. However, these changes place increased demands on teachers' time in and out of the classroom, especially when there is limited funding and time for in-service training.

These trends are not just hypothetical. Educational researchers and teachers' organ- izations in many nations have pointed to growing concerns about teacher workload, stress, and other problems associated with new demands imposed on teachers through educational reform and changing school contexts (Hargreaves, 2003; Robertson, 2000; Smyth, 2001; Whitty, 1997). Hall (2004), summarizing research on teachers' work in developed nations, identifies four major transformations that teachers are experiencing:

1. teachers' diminishing power to determine the curriculum they teach and how they teach it;
2. a new emphasis on teachers' managerial and administrative role with pupils and with other adults working in school;
3. changing pay structures, and a dismantling of union-won agreements;
4. changing conditions of service and new regulatory controls over competence and behaviour.

Similarly, Macdonald (1999: 839–41) observes that teachers in both highly devel- oped and less developed nations are experiencing increased levels of stress, anxiety, and attrition, a result of factors including deteriorating conditions within schools, inadequate resources to keep pace with emerging student numbers and needs, low pay structures especially in relation to other employment options, declines in teachers' status and collective bargaining powers, student misbehaviour, and work overload.

Research tends to contradict common perceptions of teaching as a job conducted in the classroom within the confines of the school day and school year. For Canadian teachers, like people in many other occupations, one of the biggest issues is time—time in the classroom to meet the demands of the curriculum and attend to the diverse needs of students, administration, and other school-related responsibilities; and time outside the classroom to plan lessons, meet with parents, engage in organizational activities, manage extracurricular activities, and upgrade their professional skills and knowledge related to their jobs. Teachers experience intensification of their work both by working longer and by doing more within their working day. Canadian research in many jurisdictions echoes studies from other nations revealing that teachers over the past two decades are typically working longer hours while experiencing tremendous pressures associated with rising workloads (Smyth et al., 2000: 171–2). In a survey of Canadian teachers commissioned by the Canadian Teachers' Federation (2005), 83 per cent of respondents indicated that their workloads had increased over the previous four years, over half indicated that they were teaching larger classes, and teachers worked an average of 55.6 hours a week. These results correspond with national labour force data showing that full-time educators at elementary, secondary, and university levels worked an average of more than 50 hours of paid and unpaid labour per week in 2005, about 10 hours more than a decade earlier and about 10 hours per week more than the averages for all combined occupations (Lin, 2006).

Increasing workload pressures have caused additional strains for teachers. A study of Saskatchewan teachers, for instance, emphasizes that "Teachers describe a relentless pressure to take care of school work even when they are in poor health or experiencing personal difficulties" (Gallen et al., 1995: 56). Similarly, British Columbia teachers report rising stress and health problems related to a number of factors:

- a large volume of work;
- a wide range of workload duties that have changed over time;
- changing class composition;
- seasonal pressures, with intense periods of work in addition to regular loads;
- extensive curriculum changes;
- a wide range of expectations from government, employers, school administrators, and parents (Naylor and Schaefer, 2002: 35).

Although teachers are expected to become more inclusive in their educational orientations to accommodate greater diversity in teaching and learning circumstances, work overload can sometimes limit effective relationships that schools have with students and communities who most need stronger educational outreach (Tardif and Lessard, 2004; Wotherspoon, 2006: 692–3). Changing educational realities and new knowledge requirements have also meant that teachers are spending additional hours engaged in their own formal and informal learning activities (Smaller et al., 2000).

Teachers' experiences of stress and other pressures, as well as their working patterns within teaching and competing commitments outside of their work, are highly influenced by such factors as gender, marital status, teaching level, and career stage (King and Peart, 1992; Canadian Teachers' Federation, 1993). Because of this diversity

Box 6.4 Trends Associated with the Restructuring of Teachers' Work

Teachers in Canada and other nations are experiencing significant changes in their work amid global economic restructuring. Smyth (2001: 38–9), writing from an Australian perspective, summarizes many of the prevalent forces and trends:

- [Education] is being constrained by the intrusion of external agencies who require that schools operate in the "national interest," a claim that is invariably couched in the economic imperative of increased international competitiveness.
- The fiscal crisis of the state is reducing funding to schools, in contexts in which schools are exhorted to "do more with less."
- The breakdown of other social institutions is occurring at the same time schools are expected to take on a wider and more complex range of functions.
- Control is being re-centralized, having the effect of conveying the message to teachers that they cannot be trusted and that their work is devalued—this happens in contexts in which it is made to look as if teachers are being given more autonomy, self-control, and decision-making power at school level.
- Schools are expected to operate more like private enterprises, to market themselves, to compete against one another for students and resources—functions that take them increasingly away from the reasons for which they exist, namely, teaching and learning.

All of these matters are ripe with implications for teachers' work and have resulted in a number of policy initiatives that:

- require teachers to work within more rigidly defined policy frameworks and guidelines, of one kind or another;

within the teaching workforce, research findings on teachers' work are varied and sometimes contradictory. Female teachers, particularly those who teach kindergarten and early elementary grades, for instance, are less likely to report that they have adequate preparation time during the day, but these teachers are also the least likely to report themselves as being in the high-stress group (Canadian Teachers' Federation, 1993: 62, 68–9). However, female teachers tend to be disproportionately affected by the combined impact of shifting forms of workplace control, emerging educational demands, responsibilities associated with caring for children and other dependants, domestic work, and community activity (Naylor, 2002: 140–1). Overall, though, teachers remain highly committed to their work and the students they work with. Despite increased concern about intensification, growing fears about physical safety in schools, legal action for child abuse, and attacks on the teaching profession by politicians and in media reports, Canadian literature reveals consistently high levels of overall job satisfaction and pride with respect to teaching.

The Multi-Dimensional Nature of Teaching

To understand the apparently paradoxical ways in which teachers describe their work, it is instructive to consider the observations made at the beginning of this chapter.

- place greater emphasis on determining the worth of teaching in terms of measurable outcomes;
- supposedly make teachers more accountable by linking outcomes to the actions and activities of individual teachers, classrooms, and schools;
- move teachers and schools in the direction of processes that are more appropriate to those of the corporate and industrial sector—performance appraisal, curriculum audits, quality assurance, and the like;
- preach the virtues of education and schooling as being no different from any other commodity—to be measured and calibrated according to quality standards; packaged and delivered to targeted audiences; and haggled over in the artificially constructed "user-pays" marketplace of education.

On the other hand, another set of tendencies and trends suggests, erroneously, that the opposite is happening in education. These all have the sound of participation and democracy about them: devolution; competition; choice; autonomy; collaboration; self-management; liberation management; teamwork and partnerships; networking and collegiality; flexibility; responsiveness. While these tendencies might look and sound as if they are about giving teachers more control over their work, and in some cases it is true that they do, it is more a matter of appearances in most instances. The work of teaching is increasingly brought under the influence of politicians, policy-makers, and the captains of industry at the same time as claims are made that teachers and schools should take greater control of their own destiny: deciding on local priorities; exercising greater self-management; breaking away from expensive and inefficient bureaucratic forms of organization; and making schools into leaner organizations able to be more responsive.

Teaching is shaped by divergent and often contradictory expectations and activities framed through various sites, including the classroom, the school authority structure, the community, and the occupation itself. Consequently, intensification, proletarianization, and **professionalization** are not necessarily mutually exclusive processes. This is why it becomes possible for teachers to view additional demands on their time, involving such tasks as learning techniques to manage larger classes or developing lesson plans around new curricula, as an extension of their professional competencies at the same time as their work is being intensified and deskilled. If teachers feel that their expertise and professional judgment are being used in the process of educational change, they may be more willing to endure increased workloads even when it means they are working harder or putting in longer hours. Apple (1986: 45), describing the situation in a school in which much of teachers' work was reorganized around standardized packages of skill-based worksheets, observes

> Professionalism and increased responsibility tend to go hand in hand here. The situation is more than a little paradoxical. There is so much responsibility placed on teachers for technical decisions that they actually work harder. They feel that since they constantly make decisions based on the outcomes of these multiple

pre- and post-tests, the longer hours are evidence of their enlarged professional status.

These factors become even more significant when we come back to the point that teaching tends to be characterized more by social relationships than by strictly technical operations. The human or interpersonal dimensions of relationships between teachers and students (who most often are children or young adults) are defining features of interaction in classrooms and other educational settings. These social aspects of teachers' work are so obvious that they are easy to take for granted in the analysis of teaching. However, by drawing attention to their importance, we can begin to understand how proletarianization and professionalization interact in teaching.

One of the characteristics that makes it possible for teachers to claim professional status, and thereby to seek improvements in their terms and conditions of work, is the fact that they are working with human beings. From an early point in the establishment of a system of mass public education, teachers had to gain public confidence that they were sufficiently competent, trustworthy, and reliable to manage a classroom of children. Gradually, standards of certification and training, backed by legislation and regulations, ensured that teachers were authorized to conduct classes, evaluate pupils, and perform a wide range of other educational functions.

This legitimacy to work with and assess individuals has had a dual significance for teachers. On the one hand, it has given teachers a privileged status that distinguishes them from laypersons and other workers in the community because it allows them to claim expertise over professional matters such as child development, discipline, pedagogy, and curricular content. As certified representatives of the school system, they have a public responsibility, in contrast to parents and other community members whose interests appear to be more fragmented and private. On the other hand, this responsibility, combined with the fact that they are employees, has meant that teachers are also subject to **moral regulation** and intense administrative and public scrutiny even when they are not directly observed performing classroom duties. Teachers are as likely to be monitored informally, through rumours and conversational accounts of their activities in and out of school, as through more formal kinds of assessment. Thus, while school board regulations concerning teachers' dress and public conduct may not be as stringent as they once were, their moral character, as much as their teaching ability, remains the focus of considerable public interest.

Inside the classroom, fears of the school inspectors' visits have been replaced by worries over allegations of sexual abuse, while teachers' social lives continue to be constrained by the dangers of being seen doing the wrong things in the wrong places by students, former students, parents, school officials, and the media. While most jurisdictions now operate within human rights and legal frameworks that prohibit discrimination against teachers based on sexual orientation, gay and lesbian teachers in many communities continue to feel uncomfortable with disclosing their sexuality amid fears of harassment and bullying by other persons, including students (Mombourquette, 2011). Widespread access to smart phones and social networking sites has made it possible for classroom scenarios not otherwise open to outsiders to be transferred instantly or preserved in electronic media.

Several recent high-profile cases involving educators and coaches, in concert with growing awareness of the legacy of residential schools for Aboriginal people, have drawn public attention to instances in which adults have violated their close working relationships with children and youth. Educational contexts are not immune to sexual misconduct by educators, along with other forms of physical and emotional abuse, often resulting in serious consequences for those who have been victimized. Because of the sensitive nature of these issues and the power relations involved, limited information exists about the full scope of sexual misconduct and offences by educators and other adults in educational relationships. In some cases, teachers themselves have been victims of cyberbullying and false allegations of sexual or physical abuse. Regardless of the lack of systematic data, many educational jurisdictions are responding to the gravity of these circumstances by developing more explicit guidelines and protocols concerning legal and ethical conduct. In the process, legislators, courts, and other stakeholders are struggling to balance the rights and interests of students, parents, and educators while ensuring that conditions remain conducive to safe, effective learning environments (Broster and Brien, 2010; Shakeshaft, 2004).

Recognition of the dual nature of teaching also allows us to understand how technical regulation and intensification occur. Because it is difficult for educational managers and administrators to monitor and assess many of the interpersonal aspects of a teacher's work, demands for increased educational quality and output tend to be met by looking at measurable factors, such as standardized test scores and class sizes. Increases in workloads, however, make it less possible for teachers to attend to the varied needs of all students as well as to other responsibilities. As class sizes go up, for instance, it is tempting, for the sake of both classroom control and pedagogical efficiency, for teachers to rely more heavily on lectures, pre-packaged textbooks and assignments, and standardized group activities than on interaction with small groups or individual pupils.

The examples cited above reflect a tendency in which educational productivity is measured in quantitative terms, to favour technical over subjective or interpersonal dimensions of teaching. Chapter 9 considers in more detail how contemporary demands for measurement and accountability in education tend to be framed within limited conceptions of what goes on in schools over approaches that view schooling as a process that contributes to meaningful social participation and opportunities.

Conclusion

This chapter has examined teaching as a highly complex occupation characterized by several paradoxes. Teachers are professionals, but they are also workers whose professionalism is highly constrained. Their special status and responsibilities leave them subject to extensive public scrutiny and criticism. They are expected to perform their work with specialized skills and knowledge, but they work under conditions in which they may not be able to put their capabilities and training to use. They are potentially curriculum planners and innovators who at the same time face or succumb to pressures to routinize their activities to the point of monotony and dehumanization. They are in positions in which they are expected to be community leaders and role models for children and other learners, but they also experience restraints and receive criticisms from people who do not fully understand what schooling and teaching are all about.

These contradictions can be understood as inherent characteristics of the teaching occupation rather than as unfortunate or accidental by-products of the school system. Like other workers, teachers are paid employees who are subject to extensive administrative or managerial control governed by demands for efficiency, accountability, and order. Unlike many other workers, though, teachers are entrusted to work intensively in a formative way with other human beings. It is the uncertain nature of these social characteristics that makes teaching both a potentially rewarding and satisfying occupation and one that can often be frustrating and over-regulated.

Annotated Further Readings

Acker, Sandra. 1999. *The Realities of Teachers' Work: Never a Dull Moment*. London: Cassell. The author provides an in-depth study of the working relationships and lives of teachers at an elementary school, highlighting the complex interactions in and out of the classroom that are vital parts of teaching.

Apple, Michael W. 1986. *Teachers and Texts: A Political Economy of Class and Gender Relations in Education*. New York: Routledge & Kegan Paul. This analysis of economic and cultural pressures to transform education includes a detailed discussion of the changing nature of teaching as a particular, highly feminized, form of work.

Hargreaves, Andy. 2003. *Teaching in the Knowledge Society: Education in the Age of Insecurity*. New York: Teachers' College Press. Building from a critique of the limitations inherent in existing models of schooling and teaching, the author provides a case for remaking schooling to advance teachers' role as knowledge workers dedicated to enhancing human skills and capacities within knowledge societies.

Robertson, Susan. 2000. *A Class Act: Changing Teachers' Work, the State, and Globalisation*. London: Falmer Press. The author explores how teachers' work and educational relationships more generally are being transformed amid social, political, and economic restructuring occurring in a globally competitive environment. Detailed analyses of the politics of teaching in England and the United States highlight the many interwoven currents that frame and play out through teachers' professional and class relations.

——— and Harry Smaller, eds. 1996. *Teacher Activisim in the 1990s*. Toronto: James Lorimer. Several contributors demonstrate the impact of educational reform, driven by global economic restructuring, on teachers, teachers' organizations, and schools in Canada and other nations.

Lawrence, J. Saha, and A. Gary Dworkin, eds. 2009. *International Handbook of Research on Teachers and Teaching*. New York: Springer. This comprehensive collection of articles looks at key dimensions of teaching and teaching-related issues, emphasizing international comparisons as well as general trends. Topics include teacher roles, aspects of specific teaching circumstances, and developments in teacher professionalism and teaching conditions.

Smyth, John, Alastair Dow, Robert Hattam, Alan Reid, and Geoffrey Shacklock. 2000. *Teachers' Work in a Globalizing Economy*. London: Falmer Press. The book addresses the powerful impact of global economic change on teachers' work. Drawing on the analysis of teachers' work and experiences in several developed nations, the authors outline a model for understanding the diverse forces reshaping teaching and teachers' work.

Key Terms

Collective bargaining A process by which members of an occupational group, normally represented by a union, enter into agreements with employers on such matters as wages, benefits, and terms and conditions of employment.

Division of labour The differentiation and distribution of jobs and tasks at different levels, which can occur globally or across a society, within a particular form of work or activity, or among social groups.

Feminization The concentration of women within particular occupations or groups, often discussed in conjunction with gender-based forms of discrimination.

Intensification A process whereby workers lose privileges and autonomy through rules and procedures intended to increase productivity and tighten control over work outcomes.

Moral regulation Scrutiny of teachers and other workers based on expectations related to their personal characteristics, habits, beliefs, and behaviour.

Normal schools Teacher training institutions that operated from the mid-nineteenth to mid-twentieth centuries to provide beginning teachers who had limited educational qualifications with information, guidance, and practical experience related to the varied dimensions of teaching.

Professionalization A trend in which a particular occupation gains status and recognition through specific credentials, specialized knowledge, or access to specified rights and privileges.

Proletarianization A process in which workers lose control over core aspects of their work, or one in which self-sufficient workers are replaced by employees in subordinate positions.

Teachers' associations Organizations that represent teachers in collective bargaining over salaries and conditions of work and provide teachers with opportunities and resources for professional development, advocacy for public education, and services to support teaching and teachers' well-being.

Work conditions The varied dimensions of schooling and educational organization that affect teachers' work, such as overall workload, class size, preparation time, teaching assignments, supervision of students during the school day, participation in extracurricular activities, and resources to support teaching in particular school contexts.

Study Questions

1. Discuss the extent to which school teaching is or is not a unique occupation in comparison with other forms of work.
2. Critically discuss the question of whether teachers should have the same right as other workers to engage in strikes and other job actions in cases of contract disputes over wages and working conditions.

3. How representative is the teaching workforce in relation to the social composition of Canada's population? What is the significance of this relationship for the education of diverse groups of learners?

4. What factors account for the fact that most Canadian schoolteachers are women? What implications does the gender composition of the teaching workforce have for teaching as an occupation?

5. Explore public sentiments about the teaching profession in your community. What is said publicly or in media and web accounts about their work and working conditions? Look at the websites of regional or national teachers' unions or associations to examine teachers' perspectives on these issues. What do these various accounts contribute to an understanding of teachers and their work?

6. Critically discuss the extent to which the promotion of a knowledge economy will benefit educators or detract from their professional interests.

Chapter 7

Learning Objectives

In this chapter, you will:

- explore changing connections between education and work;
- understand the concept of skills and identify its importance to the relationship between education and jobs;
- recognize employment-focused aspects of schooling in relation to several other important goals of education.

Introduction

It is widely accepted that a major purpose of schooling is to prepare people for work. This task is carried out both directly, in the provision of skills and knowledge necessary for work, and indirectly, through the development of aptitudes and credentials whose importance is recognized for employment. The rapid pace of technological change, combined with economic and social transformations of global significance, has given newfound prominence to issues concerning the relationship between schooling and work. In the process, intense debates have raged over the extent to which schooling is relevant, or should become more relevant, to a world that has become so fundamentally transformed. Frequent criticism has been levelled by employers, government agencies, and labour organizations, as well as by parents and students, over the presumed failure of schools and other educational institutions to offer the kinds of preparation that workers require for employment and success in today's globally competitive society. Consequently, the reference points are changing insofar as what happens educationally affects internal as well as global labour markets, economic production, and social relationships.

Education critics contend that schooling contributes to a mismatch between workers and jobs, and also is remiss in its efforts to prepare people to adjust to the social realities of a globalizing economy. Chapter 3 examined the expansion of conventional education systems in Canada and other highly industrialized nations in conjunction with the growing complexity of industrial production, scientific advancement, and bureaucratization. Over the past three decades, the subsequent focus of criticism has been the emergence of what is frequently referred to as a **post-industrial society**, in which service-sector work and knowledge-related activities are superseding industrial work and manufactured goods as the core foundations of economic development (Bell, 1973; Giddens, 1990). The concepts of "brain drain" and "brain circulation" have drawn attention to processes by which people with desirable qualifications and skills are widely sought by governments and industries in several nations. They bring into focus, as well, issues related to investment in specific forms of education, and the degree to which nations may either look to import or risk losing highly qualified workers. These changes have prompted numerous questions concerning how well suited today's schools are for the contemporary world and, more generally, what these transformations signify for life in that world.

This chapter provides a critical analysis of the relationship between schooling and work. It assesses competing perspectives on these relations, broadly framed around approaches that see in post-industrial or knowledge-based economies unprecedented social and economic horizons and those that take a more cautious stance in observing that capitalist economies are limited in the extent to which rewards can be allocated to those with increased qualifications. The chapter begins with an overview of contemporary demands for educational reform targeted to prepare students for work in a globally competitive environment. Major economic changes are making it imperative that students have access to educational services that provide them with both skills and orientations to learning that will enable them to make successful life decisions under highly uncertain circumstances. At the same time, some of the claims made about the apparent inability of formal educational institutions to adjust to economically driven forces are called into question through an understanding of the complex historical factors that have shaped the relationship between schooling and work. Contemporary critiques of the education system's ability to deliver the kinds of work training sought by many segments of society echo those raised on several occasions for more than a century. Educational planning and practices encompass conflicting priorities that cannot be reduced to a simple economic rationale. It is important, ultimately, to understand that because of competing visions and contradictory influences, relationships among schooling, labour markets, and jobs tend to be highly complex in nature.

Contemporary Demands for Educational Reform: The "Mismatch" between Schooling and Jobs

The promotion of educational reform has become an increasingly central component of labour market development strategies in Canada and other advanced industrial nations. The emergence of new forms of work and investment strategy marked by rapid developments in information technology, technological innovation leading to increased productivity, and intense global competition has fostered renewed interest in human capital. Education figures prominently in the equation because of its significance in ensuring basic knowledge and social skills for potential workers and consumers, its contributions to advanced levels of training, its integration into a broad array of lifelong learning choices, its value as a commodity within business and other enterprises, and its contributions to innovation. In a report released in 2012, the Organisation for Economic Co-operation and Development highlights investment in skills, posed as a "global currency" in contemporary economies, through better integration between initial education, lifelong learning, and employment settings:

> Much is expected from initial education and training systems in the 21st century. . . . Education is increasingly expected to develop new ways of thinking, involving creativity, critical thinking, problem-solving and decision-making; new ways of working, including communication and collaboration; new tools for working, including the capacity to recognise and exploit the potential of new

technologies; and, the capacity to live in a complex world as active and responsible citizens. . . .

Preparing young people for their entry into the labour market with up-front education and training is only one facet of skills development; working-age adults also need to develop their skills so that they can progress in their careers and meet the changing demands of the labour market. . . .

Governments need to raise the quality of education and training at all levels so that investment in skills development is effective and people leave education not only with a qualification/diploma, but also with the corresponding skills. (OECD, 2012a: 26, 33, 38)

The central place that education holds in discourses and strategies associated with knowledge-based societies carries mixed significance for education, educators, and learners. The high value placed on learning-related priorities increases prospects that educational institutions will be the beneficiaries of enhanced awareness, resources, and revitalization, thereby mitigating some of the more severe attacks and cutbacks they have endured in previous years. Teachers and other educators may gain some influence and status in the process, while educational programs may benefit from new partnerships with business, governments, and communities. Many proposed educational reforms and calls for enhanced early childhood education and improved support services, including those for disadvantaged groups, echo concerns long held by educators. However, the knowledge or learning agenda also signifies major shifts in existing educational priorities and directions. It increases public expectations about education, posing intense pressure on educators and the institutions they work in to fulfill promises that are not always clearly understood or adequately supported with essential resources, including many issues that lie beyond the realm of education. The **new economy** discourse contains both explicit and implicit indictments of educators and the systems in which they work: its implementation involves measures to contain costs, ensure accountability, outline explicit performance indicators, and pose education as a competition aligned more closely with market-based economic activities. Schools are attributed full or partial blame for alienating youth before graduation or for producing graduates with low literacy levels, inability to integrate into labour markets, and limited capacity or aptitude for innovation and entrepreneurship.

Educational Reform and Life Course Transitions

A steady flow of reports and position papers distributed by Canadian governments, corporate bodies, think tanks, and lobby groups since the mid-1980s outlines the expectations that the new economy holds for education and training in a context driven by globally competitive economic development. Typically, such reports begin with an overview of the nature and size of the "education industry," acknowledging that levels of educational expenditure, involvement, attainment, and outcomes in Canada rank at or near the top, relative to other OECD nations. Education is then posed in terms of productivity, quality, and returns on investment, with emphasis on the need to raise the bar in order to retain a competitive advantage. "Why," it was asked in an influential report by the Economic Council of Canada (1991: 168), "does Canada, as a nation, not appear to be getting a greater economic return on its substantial investment" in formal education?

More recent policy statements have shifted emphasis from indictments of education's failure to meet its fundamental objectives (which were used in part to justify

Box 7.1 The Skills Challenge

Canadians are engaged in unprecedented levels of formal educational activities, but they are also admonished that even more is required due to the accelerated pace and flexibility in learning required to meet challenges posed by global competition and the rapid advancement of a knowledge-based economy. Governments, along with employers' groups and other agencies, insist that "[w]e can and must do more, together," especially in an environment in which "[c]ountries that succeed in the 21st century will be those with citizens who are creative, adaptable and skilled" (Government of Canada, 2002: 5–6). Many of these organizations, such as the Canadian Chamber of Commerce (2012: 2, 4), warn of a growing "skills challenge" that requires an increase in the long-term supply of highly skilled workers for the knowledge-based society:

> Powerful forces are transforming the global economic landscape and challenging Canada's prospects in the world. In the last 20 years, the weight of global economic activity has shifted dramatically from developed to developing countries. . . . Canada's growth and prosperity will depend on our ability to be more innovative and globally competitive. Better trained workers are essential to improving Canada's productivity. A more highly skilled workforce will produce value-added goods and services and the . . . new technologies that can maximize productivity and improve the quality of life for all Canadians. . . . Canada is a middle performer in providing access to undergraduate education and also trails many other nations in the number of graduate degrees

funding cuts to education or reallocation of resources) to its role as a partner in the pursuit of higher levels of training and excellence. Formal education is understood increasingly as part of a continuum of lifelong learning that runs from early childhood, through schooling, into workplace training, and on to adult education and numerous alternative learning opportunities. In the process, in a manner that echoes and embellishes earlier versions of human capital, governments and many other organizations stress repeatedly that increased engagement in learning-related activities is a core precondition for successful participation by both individuals and nations in a globally competitive economy.

These claims have a simple appeal. Widespread acceptance of the view that education is positively associated with socio-economic success is borne out by statistical evidence that, in general, the more education one has the greater the likelihood of labour force participation, the lower the rates of unemployment, and the higher the average incomes. In mid-2012, for instance, the overall unemployment rate for labour market participants aged 15 and over in Canada was just over 7 per cent, ranging from about 5.5 per cent for graduates from post-secondary programs to just below 15 per cent for persons who did not have a high school diploma (Statistics Canada, CANSIM Table 282-0105). Moreover, there is a general sense that the importance of education and technical training for jobs and work is growing. In a report pointing to evidence that Canada's post-secondary educational expansion is not keeping pace awarded. The country falls short in addressing the current and future skills needs of the workplace.

These warnings echo earlier observations in a report by the Canadian Council on Learning (2007d: 5), which cautions against a complacent stance with regard to the state of education in Canada:

Canadians are becoming increasingly aware of the economic benefits of more education, for individual citizens, and for the competitiveness of our country. We are also coming to appreciate the contributions that learning makes to our health and well-being, and to the strength and cohesion of our communities. Nonetheless, there are serious signs of trouble. We ignore them at our peril.

An astounding number of Canadian adults cannot read, write or do arithmetic at the level required to participate fully in today's globally competitive economy. And literacy and numeracy skills decline with age, indicating that many Canadians are not using these skills.

In addition, the amount of workplace training available in Canada is low compared to many other developed countries. And the workers with the lowest levels of literacy—arguably those who would benefit most from further training—are the least likely to have access to employer-supported training.

Our large and growing immigrant population is also trapped in a paradox: while Canada needs to count on our current citizens and those who will join us from abroad, we must provide immigrants with the language, literacy and skills training they need to flourish within our society and help sustain our economic growth.

with growth occurring in many other nations, the Canadian Council on Learning (2007c: 31) stresses that "[t]he majority of the occupations that are forecast to experience excess demand are those requiring post-secondary education. As a consequence, the linkages between the educational institutions and the labour market will be even more critical than in the past." There is increasing consensus around the assessment that job-relevant education and training are critical components of both personal and national success in a global economy.

The evidence so far presents a powerful rationale that job futures are enhanced by higher education. Nonetheless, it is sometimes difficult to gain a clear sense of shifting relations between schooling and work because assertions that schools are failing to provide the kinds of training necessary for today's job market are often embedded within broader ideologies that call for fundamental transformation of the education system. These results suggest that, while there may be some general public uneasiness about the quality and job-specific relevance of education, there is nowhere near consensus on the relationship between education and jobs, including the view that schools are failing in their central missions that is assumed in the rhetoric to promote economically driven educational reform.

The vigorous emphasis on the significance of education for economic development strategies highlights an exchange among educators, business leaders, and government officials that has often been uneasy and uncertain. There are numerous visions of the

International Contrast Case Study

The Growth of the Global Talent Pool

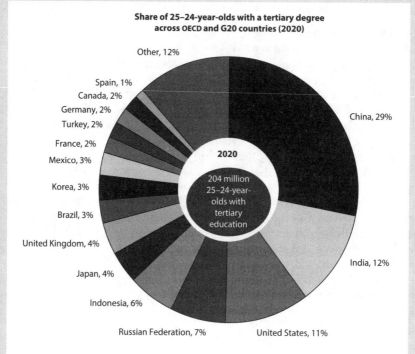

Share of 25–24-year-olds with a tertiary degree across OECD and G20 countries (2020)

Other, 12%
Spain, 1%
Canada, 2%
Germany, 2%
Turkey, 2%
France, 2%
Mexico, 3%
Korea, 3%
Brazil, 3%
United Kingdom, 4%
Japan, 4%
Indonesia, 6%
Russian Federation, 7%
United States, 11%
India, 12%
China, 29%

2020
204 million 25–24-year-olds with tertiary education

Figure 7.1 The Global Talent Pool Projected for 2020
Source: de León et al. (2012).

The introduction of new technologies, movement towards a knowledge-based economy, and shifts in the nature and scale of production and consumption have contributed to substantial changes in recent and projected future employment prospects. These transformations have increased the demand for highly skilled labour to the point that many commentators are suggesting that post-secondary (tertiary) credentials may soon be required for success in the labour market. While previous chapters have demonstrated the steady growth of post-secondary education in Canada, these trends are being eclipsed by the explosion of growth of a **global talent pool** fostered especially by dramatic increases in the numbers of persons with post-secondary credentials in highly populated, rapidly developing nations. In an analysis for the OECD, de León, Heckmann, and González (2012) suggest these trends are likely to accelerate in the near future:

In the last decade alone, the number of younger adults with higher education degrees has grown at a remarkably fast clip. This is particularly true for non-OECD G20 countries like Argentina, Brazil, China, India, Indonesia, the Russian Federation, Saudi Arabia and South Africa, where the number of 25–34 year-olds with a higher education degree increased from 39 million in 2000 to an estimated 64 million in 2010. By contrast, the number of younger adults with higher education degrees in OECD countries increased from 51 million to an estimated 66 million during the same period.

In addition, the rapid expansion of higher education in non-OECD G20 countries has significantly altered the distribution of the talent pool among countries. A decade ago, one in six 25–34 year-olds with a higher education degree was from the United States, and a similar proportion was from China. Twelve per cent came from the Russian Federation, and about 10 per cent each were from Japan and India. But by 2010, China was at the head of the pack, according to OECD estimates, accounting for 18 per cent of 25–34 year-olds with a tertiary education. The United States followed with 14 per cent, the Russian Federation and India each had 11 per cent, and Japan had 7 per cent.

These trends are likely to intensify further in the years ahead. According to OECD projections, there will be more than 200 million 25–34 year-olds with higher education degrees across all OECD and G20 countries by the year 2020—and 40 per cent of them will be from China and India alone. By contrast, the United States and the European Union countries are expected to account for just over a quarter of young people with tertiary degrees in OECD and G20 countries.

In fact, these figures may underestimate the future growth of the global talent pool, because a number of countries—notably China, the European Union countries, and the U.S.—are pursuing initiatives to increase higher education attainment rates even further.

The explosive growth of the talent pool raises a key question: With all of these highly-educated people emerging around the world, will the global labour market be able to absorb the increased supply?

Evidence from science and technology occupations—key "knowledge economy" jobs—suggests that it can. Between 1998 and 2008, employment in science and technology occupations increased at a faster rate than total employment in all OECD and G20 countries with available data. The average annual growth rate was uniformly positive, ranging from 0.3 per cent in China to 5.9 per cent in Iceland.

This consistently upward trend signals that the demand for employees in this knowledge economy sector hasn't reached its ceiling. Applied to the overall labour market, the implication is that individuals from increasingly better-educated populations will continue to have good employment outcomes, as long as national economies continue to become more knowledge-based.

As such, countries may be well-advised to pursue efforts to build their knowledge economies, in order to avoid skills mismatches and lower

continued

> returns on education among their higher-educated populations in the future.
>
> ### Discussion Questions
>
> 1. Is the characterization of the global talent pool presented in the OECD report useful, or is it too broad or limited? Discuss your response.
>
> 2. The report poses and answers the question of whether the global labour market will be able to absorb the growing global talent pool. Indicate whether you agree or disagree with the conclusion provided in the report, outlining reasons for your assessment.

appropriate linkages between schooling and work, just as there are different models in which those relationships are applied. In North America, unlike nations such as Germany or Japan, little direct relationship exists between schooling and employment. Employers and educators often regard one another with skepticism or distrust, with the former assailing schools for their inability to produce the kinds of workers and skills they demand while the latter condemns business for its skewed sense of education and its failure to see that schooling is concerned with much more than simply training for employment and profit. The absence of dialogue and engagement among employers and educators is often posed as an obstacle to effective educational reform. However, this has begun to change through several new partnerships and growing integration of schooling and work innovations such as co-operative learning and internship. The consequences for education and students are mixed, as will be observed later in this and subsequent chapters.

The Relationship between Schooling and Work

The expectation that schools should be evaluated in terms of how well they are preparing youth for work appeals to the logic that schools exist primarily to channel people into the world of work. This assessment, though, ignores the reality that formal education is about much more than job training, and is oriented also to education in a broad sense. Schooling is emphasized throughout this book as a complex, often contradictory set of arrangements that encompass personal development and moral and aesthetic capacities that are not necessarily governed by labour markets and workplaces. It is important, in these respects, to consider as problematic the extent to which, as well as how, schools contribute to work preparation, and how these forms of preparation are related to competing educational objectives.

It is important to acknowledge as well that significant social and economic transformations are changing how we understand, talk about, and experience these relationships. Three interrelated discourses that appear prominently in contemporary accounts of school–work interconnections—as represented in the concepts of lifelong learning, life transitions, and employability—draw attention to the magnitude of these changes. **Lifelong learning** highlights the extension of education and

Box 7.2 Comparative School-to-Work Transitions

Education systems and their role in the transition to work differ across nations. Kerckhoff (2006: 472) examined the educational systems of Germany, France, the United States, and Great Britain and concluded that "the transition process varies greatly among those four societies." Here he summarizes the two different models he found:

> From the review presented, it is possible to construct two ideal types of educational systems. Type One systems are highly standardized and stratified, and their educational credentials recognize vocational specialization. Type Two systems are relatively unstandardized and unstratified and their credentials have little vocational relevance. It appears that Type One societies have a stronger education–occupation association, lower rates of return to full-time school, fewer increases in educational credentials, fewer job changes, and lower rates of early occupational mobility. In effect, the transition from school to work is more orderly and stable in Type One societies.
>
> Germany comes closest to having a Type One educational system, and the United States comes closest to having a Type Two educational system. France and Great Britain have mixtures of the characteristics used in this typology.
>
> Difficult problems in studying the transition from school to work still remain. One is finding a definition of the first job that is wholly adequate for comparisons across societies. A related problem is the societal variation in the opportunities for increasing one's level of educational credentials while in the labour force rather than only while outside the labour force.

learning activities beyond the basic or conventional school years to encompass formal, informal, and continuing learning activities in various sites from early childhood throughout the life course. The related concept of **transitions** points to the increased likelihood for people to combine work and learning or to move across different education, training, and work situations over the course of their lives, as opposed to making a linear shift from initial education to a long-term career. **Employability** also signifies the dynamic conditions produced by the rapid pace of change in jobs, technologies, and knowledge production and application. In contrast with an understanding of the contributions of schooling to "employment" (with regard to linkages between specific educational requirements and specific jobs or careers), the notion of "employability" (understood as the capacity to maintain attachment to the labour market) highlights the mix of core and specialized skills and aptitudes that people will require in order to adapt to rapidly changing social and economic environments.

The following discussion addresses these issues by examining, initially, the kinds of contributions schools do make to work preparation, including (1) the granting of credentials; (2) curricular knowledge relevant to participation in the labour force; (3) the relationship between work and organizational features of schooling that are part of the hidden curriculum; (4) social features of the hidden curriculum related to individual characteristics and interpersonal relationships; and (5) general contributions that schools make to the economy as mass markets and workplaces. It will be seen that a substantial degree of correspondence exists between educational structures and processes, on the one hand, and economic productivity and work training, on the other.

However, there are at least three important limitations to the view that schools should be more responsive to requirements for work preparation. (1) Historical evidence demonstrates that mass public schooling, from its inception, was not intended to be oriented narrowly to jobs or economic considerations. (2) Continuing debate and alternative views identify schooling as an undertaking that must be responsive to diverse educational objectives beyond training for work. (3) There are barriers to the extent to which schooling can and should be the most effective institution for labour market preparation. The next two sections discuss each of these dimensions in turn, before attention is directed to more detailed consideration of how relationships between schooling and work are changing in Canada and in other countries.

The Contributions of Schooling to Work and the Economy

Formal educational institutions make several direct and indirect contributions to labour markets and wider economic processes. Among these are credentialling; explicit employment preparation through the teaching of knowledge and skills; implicit employment preparation through the establishment of the structure and discipline of work; the channelling of students into social and work roles; and the role of education itself as both workplace and market.

Credentials

One of the central functions of schooling is to bestow diplomas, certificates, degrees, and other credentials upon successful completion of particular educational programs and levels of study. Many hiring and promotion decisions, as well as eligibility requirements for certain jobs, are based on specified types of educational achievement or credentials earned through education and training programs. Educational credentials become relevant to employment decisions in different ways. In some instances, possession of a credential implies that the individual has acquired particular kinds of knowledge or met standards of rigour deemed to be essential for a job. In many other cases, educational achievement is used as a screening mechanism to limit the number of qualified applicants seeking particular jobs, regardless of whether the education or training is directly relevant to the work positions. These issues are discussed below, briefly, and developed more fully later in this chapter in the context of debates about work skills.

Workplace Skills and Knowledge

Another important function of education and training programs is to transmit knowledge and skills related to employment situations and the workplace. This knowledge includes information that may be necessary for specific occupations, as well as general know-how considered valuable by employers and that therefore makes a person employable. The role and outcomes of educational institutions have gained increasing prominence in conjunction with the attention given to the rise of post-industrial society or knowledge-based economies for their contributions both to the production of new knowledge and to the cultivation of knowledge workers.

The most direct and apparent relationship between formal schooling and jobs tends to be in vocational training, certification, and professional degree programs required for entry into specific occupations such as welding, hospitality management, animation, law, and medicine. These kinds of programs are organized in accordance with technical specifications and requirements for licensing or certification deemed critical for practice in the specified field. Outside of these areas, various courses, subjects, and programs are usually seen to have a looser connection with jobs, providing either a general background in an area or offering fundamental knowledge desired by employers, beginning with basic competencies like the ability to read, write, and compute through to more advanced, abstract, or specialized types of knowledge and skills. However, contemporary education systems are also faced with expectations that are not always compatible with one another. The rapidly changing nature of many jobs and skill requirements makes it difficult for many education institutions to align themselves too strongly with vocational training at the same time that individuals faced with high tuition costs and uncertainty about job and career prospects look to education to provide them with knowledge and skills that will position them well for meaningful employment.

The connections among technological development, societal advancement, and educational expansion have been articulated most powerfully through *human capital theory* and related strands of sociological and economic analysis focused on understanding the rise of post-industrial societies. Human capital theory regards education as an investment in human resources that offers potentially valuable returns for individuals and society as a whole. Economic development in advanced industrial and post-industrial societies requires not only highly developed material resources, but also sufficiently skilled and motivated individuals. A society's ability to compete successfully in a highly advanced economic environment depends on the extent to which it is able to produce trained, innovative personnel who can contribute to scientific and technological development.

Within sociology, **technological functionalism** influenced the logic of human capital orientations by emphasizing the impact of changing technologies on educational requirements. Social progress, defined in terms of the advancement of technical and scientific expertise, demands an increasingly qualified and specialized population. Consistent with liberal and functionalist theories of stratification outlined in Chapter 2, technological functionalism views formal educational requirements, first, as a means to disseminate socially important knowledge and skills and, second, as a mechanism to ensure the social placement of individuals on the basis of merit. The theory attributes the massive expansion of public education in the twentieth century primarily to technological change, so that increasing numbers of people are achieving higher levels of education while curricula are becoming increasingly more sophisticated and demanding (Clark, 1962). Educational advancement, from this perspective, is necessary to keep pace with and advance technological change as a stimulus for further economic development (Bell, 1973).

Human capital theory and its variants have drawn attention to the expansion of formal opportunities for social advancement, especially those determined by credentials accomplished through schooling, as opposed to more informal mechanisms of sponsorship and restricted mobility that supposedly prevail in non-industrialized nations. A stratified but meritocratic social order, in which individuals achieve jobs and rewards on the basis of merit or competence, is deemed essential for a society whose welfare and progress depend on the skills, technical expertise, and commitment of its members. While these theories were fashioned primarily in North America to highlight the emerging economic competition from highly developed nations in Europe, they have gained subsequent impetus in conjunction with the advancement of technologies in Japan and other Asian nations. They have been applied more recently to the analysis of economic expansion, high-skilled labour, and the growth of a middle class in less developed parts of the world, in part to justify investment in these regions and in part to highlight new competitors seen as potential threats to North American domination.

As these observations suggest, there is much more than theoretical significance to human capital theory. Governments and employers in Canada and other advanced industrial nations and rapidly developing nations have drawn upon concepts and research influenced by human capital approaches as part of the rhetoric and as an active component in labour market development strategies, including massive programs to develop scientific innovation and knowledge transfer. In the latter part of the twentieth century, curricula were reorganized to emphasize mathematics and sciences in elementary and secondary schools, new community colleges and technical institutes were built across Canada and the United States, and government expenditures on post-secondary education increased substantially. The influence of human capital theory remains very much alive through contemporary reforms and ideologies that emphasize competitiveness, human resource development, and the need to match skills with jobs. Business and government leaders draw on such arguments to promote programs to retrain workers, for example, or initiatives to increase productivity in the workplace.

Questioning the True Value of Credentials

Human capital and technological functionalist arguments underlie many discussions of the emergence of a "new economy" based on learning and knowledge related to rapid developments in information and communications technology (Drucker, 1993). These discussions emphasize the imperative for all people to further their education in order to adjust to and work in post-industrial societies. However, they are most focused on high-level knowledge, sometimes termed the "Triple Helix" of university–industry–government synthesis to signify the revolutionary nature of such developments (Leydesdorff and Etkowitz, 1997). While such collaborations are not new, their scale and scope have accelerated dramatically as government agencies and industries, along with participants in various other community groups, engage in strategic partnerships with educational workers and institutions. Education institutions at all levels are involved in these kinds of initiatives, but such activity is concentrated most intensively at the post-secondary level, particularly as university-based researchers are teamed with partners from other sectors in various ways, including major collaborative research projects, centres of excellence, high-tech parks, and innovation clusters (such as California's Silicon Valley or Canada's Ottawa Valley) devoted to develop new technologies, applications, products, patents, and ideas.

These arrangements have produced several exciting innovations and prospects, but they are not without their difficulties. Many analysts dispute the relatively optimistic assessments of relations between schooling and work advanced by proponents of human capital theory and post-industrial society, while other criticism is directed to several dangers inherent in trends that subordinate education to economic priorities.

The first issue—challenges to the assertion that increasing education necessarily contributes to improved job prospects—is discussed briefly here and explored in more detail later in this chapter; the second point, which addresses the limitations of reducing educational practices to economic factors, is the focus of the next section and is revisited in Chapter 8.

Among the more problematic aspects of human capital theories are claims about the levels of education actually required for work and the specific connections between attributes and skills developed through education and those performed on the job. Several factors other than required skill levels or technical requirements can account for levels of education or training associated with particular jobs. Education often serves as a screening mechanism to narrow large pools of potential job prospects or to "signal" to employers those candidates who are likely to have particular attributes and characteristics regardless of forms of training actually needed for the job.

Collins (1971, 2006) offers one of the most pointed critiques of technical and human capital explanations of educational expansion, positing an alternative account that highlights the persistence of *credential inflation*. The dramatic rise in educational attainment throughout the population of highly developed nations can be understood in terms of competition for desired positions as people seek ever greater levels of formal education for entry into job markets in which there is no clear logic between what they learn and the knowledge they need to perform on the job. Despite progressive increases in both the overall levels of education throughout the population and those required for entry into many occupations or jobs, there is often a relatively loose connection between technical requirements associated with particular credentials and skills or tasks performed in the workplace. Consequently, while much recent attention has been focused on the need for workers to gain higher levels of skills and education for work in a knowledge-based economy, many labour force participants reveal that they possess more knowledge and skills than they need for the jobs available to them (Livingstone, 2004).

Before examining empirical evidence pertinent to these contending visions of the relationships among education, skill, and work requirements, and considering the implications these trends have for different groups of learners and workers, it is instructive to acknowledge that the rhetoric to reform education and training in Canada to meet employers' demands for certain kinds of labour is not new. The following passage calling for the introduction of technical and industrial training in the schools was issued 120 years ago in the *Report of the Royal Commission on the Relations of Capital and Labour in Canada* (1889: 119), but it bears a striking similarity to contemporary demands for educational reform in the face of global competitiveness:

> To be successful competitors with foreign manufacturers we must have workmen as highly skilled in their respective callings as those with whom they have to compete. To do so, the same facilities must be provided to give the cultivation and training necessary to acquire skill and knowledge as the workmen of other countries have.

Similar statements have been made repeatedly over the years, perhaps an indication that schools have not responded well to demands that they become more relevant to employers' needs. Despite this impression, though, periodic curricular reforms have been justified by their contributions to changing job markets.

Box 7.3 Credential Inflation and Credential "Creep"

The rising number of students pursuing post-secondary credentials and the uncertain job market are contributing to desires and pressures for many students to extend their education even further. However, media reports and blog sites in Canada, the United States, and other nations reveal increasing frustration with the diminishing payoff that results from experiences in which ever-more costly credentials and program requirements have little bearing on the capacity to secure employment or perform a specific job, as revealed in the three examples, below.

Enrolment in master's and graduate programs is increasing across [Canada], leaving many to wonder if their meagre undergraduate degree will be enough to land them the perfect job. . . .

There was a time when earning your undergrad put you ahead of those with just a high school diploma.

With the rise of those who graduate with an undergrad, many students see the master's as a way of making themselves more employable upon graduation.

"Credential creep . . ."

Credential creep is the phenomenon that puts the MA in the same position the undergrad was in [during] the 1980s. It also means that one day the PhD might turn into the undergrad degree and MA of today. . . .

Getting a job after graduation is easier said than done. Many employers need to weed out the good applicants from the dozens of students that all apply for the same job. Distinguishing by degree is a quick and simple way of doing that. (Bourgon, 2008: A4)

If nurses want to go into research, education, management or some other specialized field, they should be able to continue their education. But the extra courses that are now required simply to graduate are mostly a waste of time and money and are rarely used by the average bedside nurse. I trained at a community college and had more bedside hours than my counterpart who trained in a university. When I started my professional career, I adapted more

Sutherland (1976: 155ff.) documents how schools introduced subjects such as agriculture, industrial arts, domestic science, bookkeeping, and other forms of **vocational and technical education** following vigorous pressure for change from various lobby groups in the nineteenth and early twentieth centuries. More recently, courses in computers and natural sciences have been introduced or modified to keep pace with technological developments and demands for highly skilled scientific workers. Table 7.1, which outlines some of the most important subjects introduced into school curricula over the past two centuries, demonstrates the periodic introduction of vocational subjects into programs initially dominated by academic subjects.

Despite periodic curricular modifications and innovations designed to reflect vocational and employment concerns, educators have tended to oppose the idea of turning schools into training factories. In some cases, vocational and career-oriented quickly and effectively than she did. . . . Sadly, centres of higher education have become big business, and the practice of valuing only those qualifications that are "on paper" is a societal illness. Meanwhile, many talented and gifted people are eliminated from sharing their wisdom and skills, and our society suffers. (Johnson, 2011)

Last summer I attended a free course offered to the unemployed by our local community college. During one session there was a discussion of resume types—how to find the most effective format to list your work experience and match your skills to a job description.

A woman in the back of the class raised her hand. She was in her early fifties and had previously worked at a call center. When she was laid off she went back to school—to the very community college where she now sat— and earned a degree in medical coding. She then spent over a year applying for jobs and going to interviews in that field, with no success. Then, at her most recent interview, she had been told that her not-yet-used skills were now out of date and she should persue [sic] a new certification.

"I haven't finished paying for the first degree yet!" she wailed. "Should I just forget it? Should I go back to school and get a degree in something else?" . . .

Americans' reverence for education and their belief in social and financial mobility are virtues, but an over-reliance on college degrees as the foundation of the American Dream is distorting our economy and may even lengthen the current downturn. . . .

This is not to say that a college education has no value, or that bright young people from financially modest backgrounds shouldn't aspire to college. (In the interest of full disclosure, I was among the first in my family to earn a university degree.) But this mania for requiring all workers to pay thousands for a new certification in order to advance in the workplace has more in common with Scientology than actual education.

On the other hand, it is a great place to stash large numbers of the unemployed. (Deafening Silence, 2010)

courses were introduced more for the pragmatic consideration of gaining employers' support for the school system than for enthusiasm over the academic or curricular merits of the subjects. Vocational and technical subjects continue to remain distinct from core areas of the curriculum in schools with academic programs. Moreover, considerable discrepancies often exist between the formal listing or presentation of a subject in a curriculum description and the actual teaching of that subject in the classroom. These issues, as will be discussed later in the chapter, make the relationship between schooling and work preparation more problematic than it might otherwise appear to be.

The Discipline and Structure of Work

Beyond the teaching of vocational and career-oriented knowledge or subjects, formal education contributes to labour force participation in many indirect ways. Previous

Table 7.1 Summary of Major Changes and Additions to Curricula in Canadian Elementary Schools

1825–50	reading, writing, arithmetic, religion (Bible reading), needlework, cooking
1850–75	grammar, geography
1875–1900	kindergarten classes, literature, history, music, drawing
1900–25	nature study, art, manual training, physical training, hygiene, household science
1925–50	social studies, science, industrial arts, home economics, health, physical education, enterprise, languages, phonics
1950–75	French and French immersion, business and commercial education
1975–2000	whole language instruction, language arts, computer studies, technological education, Native studies, technical vocational education, hospitality and tourism, life transitions
2000–current	wellness, co-op learning and work experience, literacy and new technology education, media literacy, civics and career studies, skills for success in high school, environment and resource management

Sources: Phillips (1957: 433); Katz (1969: 67); various provincial curriculum guides.

chapters have shown that student school experience is shaped at least as much by everyday practices, unwritten rules, and informal expectations as by the overt transmission of knowledge and skills. This hidden curriculum is defined by Apple (2004: 13) as "the tacit teaching to students of norms, values, and dispositions that goes on simply by their living and coping with the institutional expectations and routines of schools day in and day out for a number of years."

The "expectations and routines" that constitute the hidden curriculum—in terms of both the organizational and social characteristics of schooling—are heavily influenced by work. The spatial and temporal structure within most educational institutions has a great deal in common with nineteenth-century factory organization. Physically, schools tend to be arranged as a series of box-like classrooms or special-function areas (gyms, libraries, art rooms, resource centres) oriented to regimentation and control. There are also strong parallels between schooling and industrial work organization in terms of models of supervision and assessment, the division of classes by grade and subject, streaming within grades or subject areas, and the hierarchy of authority that prevails both administratively and in the conduct of classes.

Workplace discipline also is reflected in the regulation of school time. The day is broken into distinct periods, usually signified by the ringing of bells. Students' bodily functions, including eating, are directed by timetables and school rules, and pupils frequently are required to seek permission to use the washroom or get a drink of water. These arrangements are structured in such a way that students internalize routines associated with the day-to-day patterns of life in many workplaces.

Channelling Students into Social and Work Roles

The hidden curriculum is oriented to individual as well as organizational character-istics. Writers working within both traditional (e.g., Jackson, 1968; Dreeben, 1968) and critical (e.g., Bowles and Gintis, 1976; Willis, 1977; Smith and McLaren, 2010) perspectives agree that much of the social reproduction accomplished within school-ing occurs through the cultivation of dispositions and attributes necessary to function in contemporary society (Lynch, 1989). This analysis stresses that what is important is not so much the specific knowledge required for any particular job or social posi-tion as the general preparedness and ability to meet expectations that are attached to out-of-school roles. Through schooling, students encounter circumstances such as competition, success and failure, deference to authority, deferral of gratification, and other situations that prepare them for later social experiences. They must also develop an awareness of how the world is structured and how it operates in order to ease their transition into work and other social settings.

Researchers have become increasingly concerned to adopt approaches that can help to make sense of these complex relationships. As observed in Chapter 2, the framework developed by Pierre Bourdieu (1977, 1984) to integrate interactions among individuals, social backgrounds, and social structures through the analysis of concepts like "habitus," "cultural capital," and other forms of inequality has been especially influential. Lesley Andres Bellamy (1993, 1994) adopts Bourdieu's framework to analyze how Canadian students make choices about their post–high school futures. *Cultural capital*, understood in conjunction with economic capital and other social resources, refers to the attitudes, behaviours, preferences, and general sense of how things operate that individuals must possess to be socially successful. Constituted in this way, cultural capital is neither neutral nor equally accessible to all social groups. Andres Bellamy (1994: 122) observes that, for Bourdieu, "the culture that is transmitted and rewarded by the educational system reflects the culture of the dominant class." This places students who possess the prior knowledge or sensitivity to the qualities that enable them to meet educational expectations in an advantaged position in comparison with students who lack cultural capital. The related concept of **habitus** refers to a "system of dispositions" produced by our past experiences, which are embedded in our perceptions and interact with new social circumstances. It operates as a kind of internal code that affects how we approach and understand everyday practices.

Using data from interviews and surveys involving educational participants in di-verse Canadian contexts, several researchers (e.g., Andres Bellamy, 1993; Andres and Looker, 2001; Taylor, 2005; Lehmann, 2007) demonstrate how educational institu-tions are implicated in complex processes of decision-making, actions, and organi-zational characteristics in such a way that students view their choices about work and post-secondary studies as an unproblematic part of their normal progression from family life. Schools, in this way, contribute to labour force reproduction by fostering dispositions regarding success, failure, and future plans even if they are not directly involved in job training and employment selection. This insight comple-ments the findings of other influential studies, such as those of Willis (1977), Anisef et al. (2000), and Lareau and Horvat (1999), which demonstrate that school organi-zation, social background, and students' daily circumstances affect one another in such a way that students often "choose" predictable futures without being directly pushed into those positions.

Education as Workplace and Market

Schools and other educational settings serve a purpose beyond preparing students for work in that substantial economic activity takes place within them and through them—educational institutions themselves are workplaces as well as markets in which billions of dollars are spent annually on goods and services.

Large numbers of teachers, administrators, maintenance and support staff, purchasing agents, and other personnel are employed in the education sector. As the previous chapter on teachers has emphasized, education workers are subject to many of the same dynamics that operate within wage employment in general, even though educational work also contains unique characteristics related to educational processes. Besides their work with students or educational clients, educational workers engage in economic production insofar as they develop products, knowledge, and skills that may be of benefit to particular employers, corporations, or social interests. While this activity is most evident at the post-secondary level, where faculty members and other researchers are expected to cultivate and disseminate knowledge, classrooms and education systems at all levels are open to experimentation and innovation, the benefits of which may extend beyond the education system.

Education also has economic significance in recognition of the massive quantities of goods and services purchased by educational institutions or in relation to educational activities. Given its size and, in some instances, centralized decision-making, which leads to the adoption and purchase of textbooks, course materials, technologies, and supplies for entire school districts, post-secondary institutions, or even provinces, the educational market is a highly lucrative one. Educational institutions also stimulate economic activities in other ways, beyond their importance for the consumption of instructional resources. The construction of educational facilities, especially during peak growth periods such as the 1960s and 1970s, has had a significant economic impact on communities. Even when few new schools or universities are being built, employment is created through the maintenance and repair of educational facilities, as well as in their day-to-day operation. The food and beverage industry is supported directly by school cafeterias, while there tends to be a concentration of restaurants, bars, bookstores, and entertainment and service operations around universities and community colleges. Large corporations have found schools and universities such lucrative markets that they have entered into sometimes controversial agreements to provide funding for scholarships, sports, and other programs in exchange for exclusive agreements to sell their products. The economic spinoff from education is also important in other respects. The computer industry, for instance, has pursued the educational market aggressively in part because it recognized that many students and parents will purchase hardware or software packages compatible with new technologies employed in the classroom.

The role of business and industry in the classroom has long been debated by educators. As education systems are confronted with declining levels of government funding, prospects for reliance on materials and services that are donated, purchased in bulk, or provided at low cost from corporations and other external agencies are likely to increase. Many corporations introduce curricular materials or sponsor school teams and events, such as essay-writing competitions, that may produce a favourable climate or corporate image at the same time as potential recruits or ideas are being harnessed for corporate objectives (Apple, 2004: 143–4; Klein, 2009; Regnier and MacLean, 1987). While corporate partnerships have promoted some areas of innovation and access to resources that would not otherwise be available to support students, programs, and research in public educational institutions, many educators and observers point to the growing danger that reliance on corporate bodies and fiscally driven planning are skewing educational priorities. Thus, some have argued, basic educational services directed towards a wide range of learning needs and community interests will be sacrificed to more glamorous initiatives based on narrow and unrepresentative agendas (Axelrod, 2002; Currie and Newson, 1998; Robertson, 1998).

Clearly, in a growing number of dimensions, education is highly integrated with economic activity. Through direct labour force preparation and participation, as well as through more general involvement in the production and consumption of particular commodities, education can be considered an industry essential for economic advancement of both individuals and societies. Nonetheless, considerable tension exists between the view that schooling should become guided more fully by economic considerations and the position that education must remain oriented to principles other than commercial ones.

Discontinuities in Relationships among Schooling, Work, and Economic Activity

While the evidence presented so far suggests that there is considerable merit to the idea that schooling has a central role to play in the reproduction of the labour force and in the stimulation of economic activity in general, it is necessary to address some of the limitations to this relationship. In particular, schooling has been responsive to competing priorities that place emphasis on personal and social development as well as economic factors.

Education and Morality

Mass public schooling, from its inception, was not strictly concerned with labour force preparation. Early education officials cautioned against the dangers of reducing schooling to its economic functions. Writing in the early 1880s, for instance, New Brunswick's chief superintendent of education contended that "The primary function of the public school should not be subverted to provide technical instruction"; rather, "the public school is primarily an agency for the general education of all classes of youth," where such basic training consists of the elements of physical health, intelligence, and character (cited in Lawr and Gidney, 1973: 93–4). As Table 7.1 indicates, the core areas of the curriculum have been concentrated in academic areas (such as reading, writing, mathematics, languages, sciences, history, and geography) or subjects oriented to personal development (health, physical education, drawing, and music) rather than workforce training. Certainly, each of these areas contributes in a general way to labour force development, particularly through the provision of basic skills, discipline, and orientations to work required for the performance of wage labour. However, social and political objectives, at least as much as economic ones, figured prominently in the origins and rise of mass public schooling.

In many ways, the Church rather than the factory provided the inspiration for a formal system of public education, although not in a direct way. Order, discipline, and habit may have been amenable to industrial work, but they were more explicitly promoted as essential attributes for individuals attuned to life in a new social and political order. Corrigan, Curtis, and Lanning (1987: 21, 24) argue, for instance, that early school reformers were concerned with "the creation of particular kinds of political selves" in the form of individuals who would engage in social relations through "will-ing" or "cheerful obedience." The school's mission, like that of the Church in this re-gard, was to produce morally regulated individuals. Such morality, however, was to be produced in the public realm, with adherence to the bourgeois state rather than to any particular religious denomination. Across Canada, legislation concerning the estab-lishment and maintenance of public schools addressed this objective by the creation of highly centralized provincial educational administrations, although room was al-lowed for diverse community input through delegation of many responsibilities to local and district school boards (Tomkins, 1977: 11–14).

The location of educational authority within the state was intended to counter the overt influence of groups considered to have narrowly defined interests, including religious denominations as well as business and industry. Industrial leaders were often indifferent to or had little regard for public schooling. During the rise of the factory system, especially into the late 1860s in the more industrialized areas of central and Atlantic Canada, schools were perceived as intrusive to employers who relied on chil-dren as a low-cost labour force. The main value of schooling, from this point of view, was as a vehicle for social control to keep idle children from engaging in crime or other mischief on the streets when they were not working. Ironically, much of this "idleness" was a consequence of children's decision to leave schools that did not provide them with sufficient job-specific skills (Houston, 1982: 139–40). Education authorities were sensitive to these trends, sometimes seeking reforms intended to win the support of employers for educational causes, but they continued to ensure that schooling could not be reduced to any kind of crude vocational training. While education systems have tended to be driven increasingly by economic and instrumental factors, attention to subjects like civic participation, global citizenship, multiculturalism, and environ-mental stewardship illustrate the multiple commitments entailed within schooling.

The Right to Learn

Public education, from the beginning, has been driven by competing forces that are not restricted to training for work or other economic purposes. Carnoy and Levin (1985: 14) point out that schools are driven by the contradictory dynamics of what they call a **capitalist imperative** and a **democratic imperative**. They contend that, "On the one hand, schools have traditionally reproduced the unequal, hierarchical relations of the nuclear family and capitalist workplace; on the other, they have repre-sented the expansion of economic opportunity for subordinate groups and the exten-sion of basic human rights."

These dynamics themselves are subject to debate and contestation. Included within the capitalist imperative, for instance, are employers' demands for appropriately dis-ciplined and skilled workers and working-class demands for education and training that will result in meaningful, well-paid employment (Livingstone, 1987: 62–3). The issue of who benefits from education extends beyond class lines, encompassing de-mands for opportunity and representation from various groups, including women, racial and ethnic minorities, residents of rural areas and remote communities, and many others. Competing interests are reflected in debates over major issues, including what is taught in schools and how extensive the provision of public education should be, as well as more specific concerns such as the length and timing of the school year or what kinds of reading materials are included in school libraries.

A brief look at the major objectives of schools and education systems reveals how diverse educational aims are. The *Report of the Royal Commission on Education* for

British Columbia (1988: 68) observes that, for more than a century, extending their central mandates as "agencies of learning."

> schools have been viewed as multi-purpose institutions whose endeavours go far beyond educational functions—various public elements at various times have seen schools as agencies for civic development, as laboratories for democratic practice, as institutions to sustain a common culture and common values, as places to remediate the behaviour of wayward youngsters, and as centres for community life. Within the public imagination, the potential of schools has sometimes seemed boundless; we have turned to schools to reduce crime, improve public health, inspire patriotism, minimize civil strife, eradicate prejudice, promote social justice, set children on the "right road," and, in the long run, even contribute to international understanding.

The degree to which these varied objectives are given priority varies over time and place as well as among social groups. Coulter (1993: 71, 81) reports that Canadian youth in the 1930s expressed serious concern about unemployment and skill development, but by the mid-1940s a national survey of youth revealed that job preparation was ranked below both "helping to think clearly on the problems of life" and "helping to understand modern society and the responsibilities of a citizen" as key purposes of schooling. Nearly three decades later, a national survey conducted by the Canadian Education Association indicated that the top two reasons for schooling were the attainment of self-satisfaction and the goal "to get along better with people at all levels of society," while only 18 per cent of respondents suggested that the primary reason for schooling was "to get better jobs" (Lauwerys, 1973: 14). By the end of the 1990s, over half of respondents to a national survey indicated that schools needed to devote greater attention to "the basics" such as reading and writing skills rather than areas such as computer skills (Angus Reid Group, 1999: 5, 17). However, public opinion in the twenty-first century reveals increased concern for economic and work-related issues. In its last national survey, the Canadian Council on Learning (2009a: 20–1) reports that fewer than half of respondents agree that schools are meeting or exceeding their expectations in helping prepare students for work; there is strong support by Canadians for high schools to do more to help prepare students for work, including programs that include work experience. Similarly, other surveys (e.g., Strategic Council, 2007: 5) reveal public concerns that universities are not fully equipped to meet labour market needs in particular industries or regions despite the general contributions made by post-secondary education to employability.

Public opinion surveys over time reveal that job preparation and training gain force as priorities in periods of high unemployment and uncertainty or transitions in labour markets. This helps to explain why these issues have once again moved to the forefront in recent debates over educational reform. Employers' interest in having a supply of adequately qualified labour converges with individuals' expectations that education will lead them to a stable employment future at a time when most people have been exposed to harsh realities associated with occupational restructuring and the threat or experience of joblessness.

Job Training in the Schools

Despite the force of recent arguments that schooling should be doing more to help prepare individuals for the labour market, the question remains as to how effective schools could be even if job training were to become their primary orientation.

Formal education, in its current configurations, faces several impediments to directing and placing students into jobs. Considerable changes occur in personal aptitudes, labour markets, employment needs, and technologies over the normal period of 12 to 13 years that it takes an individual to proceed from kindergarten to high school graduation. Even if it could be assumed that schools were vocational in nature (thereby ignoring the varied purposes of public education), it is doubtful whether they would have the resources and ability to meet labour market requirements, particularly in a context in which jobs, technologies, and skills are continually being redefined and reorganized. Several critical questions would need to be addressed:

- Should people be educated for self-employment or wage labour and, if the latter, would major corporations or small businesses prevail?
- Which skills would be common to all pupils and which would be developed within particular educational streams and at what levels?
- Would individual or community interests be outweighed by employers' interests?
- What kinds of credentials and expectations would mesh with prospects for employment after the completion of formal education?

Many of these issues are currently at the centre of both public policy discussions and academic analysis of work–school linkages. The notion of "transitions" has replaced a long-standing sense of a linear transition process as people move through their life courses from family to school to work to retirement (Ashton and Lowe, 1991: 1–2). The rethinking of school–work linkages is given focus by emphasis on lifelong learning, innovations in areas such as adult and continuing education, and the rapid expansion of alternative forms and sites of educational delivery. European research draws attention to a "new life course" dynamic in which individuals are required to become increasingly more self-reflexive and strategically adaptive as conventional social roles and expectations are destabilized by constant social, cultural, and economic changes (Vinken, 2007). The OECD (2012a: 26) acknowledges that

> For any education and training programme, decisions need to be taken about the right mix of knowledge, skills and even behaviour, attitudes and values that it should impart to serve desired economic and social outcomes. Since skills requirements change and people need to adapt and learn new skills over their working lives to ensure occupational mobility, compulsory education is where people should master foundation skills and where they should develop the general desire and capacity to engage in learning over an entire lifetime.

There is also growing awareness that employers and other non-educational agencies have obligations to ensure that labour market entrants are equipped with skills and capacities to complement those developed through schooling. Students as well as employers are paying increasing attention to work experience programs and other mechanisms that provide individuals with options to develop these wider repertoires of knowledge and practice. Given these concerns, discussion turns in the next section to contemporary changes in work as they pertain to education.

Education and Work in Canada

The Canadian labour force and the kinds of jobs that workers have been engaged in have changed significantly over the past few decades. As shown in Table 7.2, shortly

Table 7.2 Employment by Industry, Selected Years, Canada, 1946–2011 (% of total)

Industry, by Sector	1946	1951	1961	1971	1981	1991	2001	2006	2011
Primary									
Agriculture	25.4	18.4	11.2	6.2	4.4	3.5	2.2	2.1	1.8
Forestry	1.8	2.3	1.4	0.9	0.7	0.5	0.5	0.4	0.3
Fishing, trapping	0.6	0.6	0.3	0.3	0.3	0.4	0.2	0.2	0.1
Mining, oil/gas extraction	1.6	1.5	1.3	1.6	1.9	1.4	1.2	1.5	1.6
Primary total	29.4	22.8	14.2	9.0	7.3	5.8	4.1	4.1	3.7
Secondary									
Manufacturing	26.0	26.5	24.0	22.2	19.3	15.1	14.9	12.8	10.2
Construction	4.8	6.8	6.2	6.1	5.9	5.7	5.5	6.5	7.3
Secondary total	30.8	33.3	30.2	28.3	25.3	20.8	20.4	19.3	17.5
Tertiary									
Transportation	7.4	7.8	8.1	7.7	7.1	6.3	5.2	4.9	4.9
Utilities	0.7	1.0	1.2	1.1	1.2	1.1	0.8	0.7	0.8
Trade	12.3	14.1	16.9	16.5	17.1	17.6	15.8	16.0	15.4
Finance, real estate	2.7	3.0	3.9	4.8	5.5	6.1	5.9	6.3	6.3
Services*	16.8	18.0	19.5	26.2	29.6	35.4	42.6	43.6	45.8
Public administration	—	—	5.9	6.5	7.0	6.8	5.3	5.1	5.6
Tertiary total	39.8	43.9	55.5	62.7	67.5	73.3	75.5	76.6	78.8
Total (%)	100	100	99.9	100	100.1	99.9	99.9	100	100
Total number (000s)	4,666	5,097	6,055	7,958	11,398	12,916	14,946	16,484	17,306

* Includes public administration until 1961.
Sources: For 1946–91: Bernier (1996); data for 2001: Labour Force Historical Review (2006), Statistics Canada CS71–0004/2006–MRC; for 2006–11, Statistics Canada, CANSIM table 282–0008.

Box 7.4 Employment Prospects in the Knowledge Economy

Increased competitive pressures and rapid development of new technologies have created a volatile economic climate for many sectors. As new job categories and businesses are created or expand, others have disappeared, fuelling demands for higher education while creating considerable uncertainty with respect to employment prospects. These trends are illustrated in the analysis, by Kanagarajah (2006: 7–9), of employment by firms in high-, medium-, and low-knowledge sectors (defined with reference to ratios that take into account proportions of research and development personnel, workers with post-secondary education, and positions in natural sciences, engineering and mathematics, and professional and technology-related fields):

Of all firms that were created during the 1990s, roughly one-quarter ceased to operate within the first two years. . . . Just over one-third survived 5 years or more and only one-fifth were still in operation after 10 years. The survival rates of firms improved tremendously after the mid-1990s. Those that were created during the second half of the decade were more likely to keep operating than their counterparts born in the early 1990s. This was due partly to the economic recovery that followed the 1990–1992 recession.

On average, the number of businesses grew by about 9,300 each year during the 1990s. This was the difference between the average of 138,100 firms that began operations each year and the average of about 128,800 a year that went out of business. Businesses employing 100 to 499 workers experienced the strongest growth.

In 2003, just over one million businesses were operating in Canada, up 12 per cent from a decade earlier. . . . In 2003, only 0.2 per cent of firms employed 500 or more employees, but they represented 43 per cent of total employment. The vast majority (92 per cent) of companies employed fewer than 20 workers, and they accounted for 21 per cent of total employment.

Strongest Growth in High-Knowledge Sector

Most of the growth in firms between 1991 and 2003 occurred in the services-producing sector. During this time, the number of businesses in this sector increased 15 per cent, while it stagnated in the goods-producing sector, increasing by only 1 per cent. Within the services-producing sector, the number of firms in high-knowledge industries nearly doubled (+96 per cent) from 32,000 to 62,000 firms, while the number in medium-knowledge industries rose 18 per cent from 283,000 to 334,000 firms. The number of firms did not change in low-knowledge industries within the services-producing sector. Examples of industries in the high-knowledge category include high technology and biotechnology industries.

In the goods-producing sector, the number of firms in high-knowledge industries also grew at a much faster pace than in other industries. As a result, high-knowledge industries experienced by far the fastest growth between 1991 and 2003. Overall, their number rose a solid 78 per cent, more than five times the rate of 14 per cent among medium-knowledge industries.

Table 7.3 Percentage Change in the Number of Businesses,
by Knowledge Industry, Canada, 1991 to 2003

Knowledge-based Industries	Goods	Services	All
Low knowledge	−10	0	−3
Medium knowledge	6	18	14
High knowledge	25	96	78
All	1	15	12

Source: Statistics Canada, "Business Dynamics in Canada," 2003, Catalogue no. 61-534,
released 10 March 2006, p. 7. Available at: www.statcan.gc.ca/pub/61-534-x/61-534-
x2006001-eng.pdf.

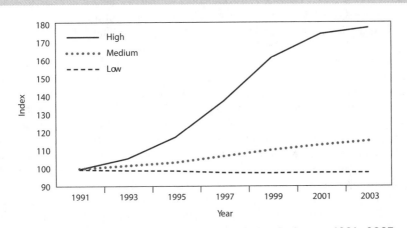

Figure 7.2 Employment Growth by Knowledge Industry, 1991–2003

Source: Kanagarajah, Sri. Report for Statistics Canada, "Business Dynamics in Canada," 2003,
Catalogue no. 61-534, released 10 March 2006, p. 8. Available at: www.statcan.gc.ca/pub/
61-534-x/61-534-x2006001-eng.pdf.

Overall, low-knowledge firms fared even worse, as their number fell 3 per cent
during the 12-year period. Even though business growth was very strong in the
high-knowledge industry, this sector actually accounted for only 30 per cent of the
net increase of 112,000 firms between 1991 and 2003. The reason is that relatively
few firms were operating in this sector at the beginning of the 1990s. In fact, almost
half (53 per cent) of the net increase in the number of businesses originated in the
medium-knowledge industry. This occurred mainly among small firms . . . .

continued

> **Just under one-half of firms in the high-knowledge industries survived five years or more.**
>
> Chances of survival for firms varied by industry; it was the highest for those that started operating in the high-knowledge industries. Between 1992 and 1997, 46 per cent of these companies survived five years or more. In contrast, 39 per cent of medium-knowledge firms lasted for five years or more, as did 33 per cent of low-knowledge industries.
>
> Source: Statistics Canada, "Business Dynamics in Canada," 2003, Catalogue no. 61-534, released 10 March 2006. Available at: www.statcan.gc.ca/pub/61-534-x/61-534-x2006001-eng.pdf.

after the end of World War II, one-quarter of all workers were involved in agricultural work and nearly one-third were blue-collar workers (secondary sector), while fewer than two out of five were classified as white-collar workers (what is now called the tertiary or service sector). By 2011, however, fewer than 2 per cent of workers remained as part of the agricultural labour force and the proportion of blue-collar workers was only about one in six, while nearly four out of every five workers were employed in the service sector. The single largest industry category, identified as "service," encompasses seven major subcategories—education, health care, social services, information, culture and recreation, accommodation, and food services—each of which is larger than the total number of workers in primary-sector industries. This has meant, at least in a general way, that types of work that typically require formal educational credentials have become increasingly central to the labour force as a whole.

In the same way that the occupational classifications of workers have changed, the nature of work and the composition of the labour force have become much more diverse. New technologies, services, product lines, and forms of work organization have altered the jobs we do and the way we work. The transformation of working arrangements, in turn, affects and is shaped by shifting patterns of employment and demands for distinct kinds of workers. Canada's paid labour force, which at the time of Confederation consisted predominantly of men of British and French origin, has become increasingly feminized as well as more racially and ethnically heterogeneous. Today, most men and women, regardless of age, marital status, and social origin, are labour force participants. At the same time, the changing occupational structure has meant that the prospects for and future of work are highly uncertain for substantial proportions of the population. This is particularly true for youth who are about to enter the workforce as well as for persons with disabilities or of minority group status who have historically experienced marginalized labour force participation.

Important social and economic transformations have been mirrored in the changing relationship between schooling and work. In the nineteenth century, schooling had little importance for the majority of the population except as a brief point of contact to gain basic reading, writing, and social skills. Other than for the select few persons who entered professions, such as medicine, law, teaching, and the clergy, education bore little formal relation to the kinds of jobs most people worked at, such as farming, fishing, mining, manufacturing, and commercial work. The primary importance of schooling was in its service as a socially stabilizing force, keeping young people occupied, off the streets, and under public surveillance. As we have seen, however, the importance of formal education increased through the twentieth century to become a major conduit for entry into the labour market.

Job Markets in Uncertain Times

In recent years, the social and economic purposes of schooling have been reassessed. What had been regarded as a relatively fixed pattern of progression through the major individual life roles has been redefined as a process of multiple transitions in the context of global economic changes (see, e.g., Anisef and Axelrod, 1993; Hango, 2010; OECD, 2010a). There is not so much a single point of entry into labour markets as a persistent shifting across educational and work settings. Figure 7.3 illustrates the complex pathways followed by Canadian youth, revealing the proportion of students who leave school or continue to higher levels of education at various stages in relation to various points of entry into labour markets. Just as increasing numbers of students seek part-time employment to gain experience and support themselves during the time they are engaged in formal studies, they are also more likely, after they have started work, to return to educational programs to upgrade their credentials or retrain for new lines of work. Movement between part-time work and studies, periodic unemployment, changes in the nature of work, and changing educational requirements have altered traditional relations between schooling and work. We are being told more frequently that "lifelong learning" has become the norm that will govern our educational futures and that adaptability is the key to success (Livingstone, 2004: 14–15). Some forecasts suggest that, despite the massive numbers of people pursuing post-secondary education across the globe, the supply of highly qualified labour will be insufficient to keep pace with accelerated growth of high-skill, high-pay technical jobs over the next decade (Gordon, 2009).

In general, evidence points to the likelihood that people with higher levels of education and diverse educational backgrounds will be more successful in job markets than those who have more limited educational credentials. Education is positively associated, for instance, with the chances of finding a job, having more meaningful work, and securing better incomes. Table 7.4 and Figure 7.4 provide indications of the relative return from education in relation to labour force participation and income. The data illustrate, as well, the continuing presence of substantial gender inequities within labour markets. Similar trends also hold true for minority groups, including immigrants and Aboriginal peoples (Reitz, 2007; Schissel and Wotherspoon, 2003: 111–14).

The importance of education for job prospects takes on greater significance in light of recent evidence that it has become increasingly difficult for young adults to achieve a secure position in the labour market. Recent labour market entrants, in sharp contrast to their predecessors in the late twentieth century, have an abundance of job options in many regions of Canada, especially as much of the "baby boom" generation approaches retirement age. Nonetheless, many of these jobs are insecure, contingent on the shaky fortunes of resource industries, or, with the exception of positions requiring highly specialized skills or extensive experience, concentrated in low-paying services and related areas. Analysis for the OECD (2010a: 21) reveals strong concern in many nations about the capacity of labour markets to integrate young workers successfully, especially after 2008, as "[t]he recent global economic crisis has hit school-leavers and young workers particularly hard because they are extremely vulnerable to

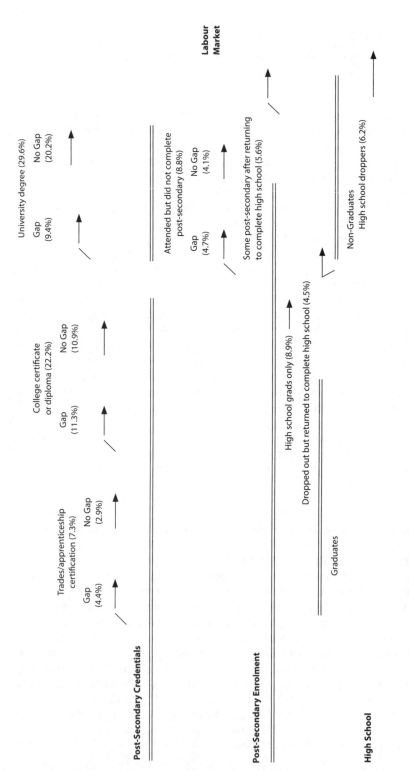

Figure 7.3 Diverse Pathways for Youth in School-to-Labour-Market Transitions

Note: Gap refers to a break of four months or more between high school and post-secondary studies.

Source: Adapted from Figure 1.2 in Hango and de Broucker (2007: 19) and data in Hango (2010: 13).

Table 7.4 Educational Attainment and Labour Force Participation, Canada, 2011

Highest Level of Educational Attainment	Labour Force Participation Rate (%)			Unemployment Rate (%)		
	Total	Males	Females	Total	Males	Females
0–8 years	23.2	32.1	15.2	15.5	14.6	17.1
Some secondary	47.5	54.7	39.8	15.4	15.3	15.6
High school graduate	67.0	75.0	59.4	7.9	8.2	7.4
Some post-secondary	66.8	69.5	64.1	9.7	10.6	8.7
Post-secondary certificate or diploma	75.5	79.0	72.0	5.9	6.2	5.7
University degree	78.7	80.2	77.2	4.9	4.9	4.9
Total	66.8	71.5	62.3	7.4	7.8	7.0

Source: Data compiled from Statistics Canada CANSIM Table 2820004.

joblessness in economic downturns. Over the past two years, youth unemployment rates have doubled in a number of OECD countries and increased significantly across the board." Beaujot and Kerr (2007: 15) summarize data from Canada revealing that "[t]he relative economic position of youth, particularly young men, declined throughout the 1980s and 1990s, despite the fact that they had higher credentials in terms of education." Governments and other agencies in Canada have recently turned to other countries, with stronger linkages between initial education and workforce entry that provide some protection both for young workers and for employers, for examples in beginning a systematic search to develop strategies that would more closely integrate schooling and employment (Taylor, 2007).

As labour markets become more volatile and competitive, there is additional pressure to achieve greater levels of education and training. Just as workers who enter job markets with strong educational credentials have greater employment and career opportunities than those with less education, a growing body of evidence points to the importance of both formal and informal job-related education and training in maintaining employment success. While individuals with a broad range of educational backgrounds are engaging in such training, the benefits are not equally shared among all labour market participants. Livingstone (2004: 26, 27, 30) reports significant increases in adult and continuing education among virtually all social groups, particularly among young adults or those who had previously dropped out of school, but cautions that "[t]hose who have higher levels of formal schooling are more likely to participate in most forms of further education." Findings from research on adult learning in Canada and other OECD nations echo this theme, revealing that those most likely to participate in further adult learning tend to be individuals who are already highly educated and those from households in which higher levels of education and income are more likely, whereas factors associated with low levels of initial education

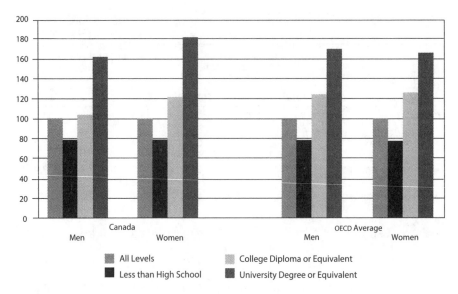

Figure 7.4 Ratio of Earnings ($) to Average for Population, Ages 25–64,
            with Income from Employment by Level of Education Completed,
            Canada and OECD Average, 2009

Source: Data for Canada from OECD (2012: 150) and for OECD average, from OECD (2011: 147–8).

tend to compound themselves over time, contributing to relatively low rates of participation in adult learning activities (Statistics Canada and OECD, 2011).

This evidence seems to reinforce the general argument that individuals, even if they
are already highly educated, require extensive educational credentials and continual
upgrading to remain competitive in today's job market. By implication, those who
fail to achieve high levels of education and up-to-date training are relegated to the
growing pool of marginal or long-term unemployed workers. These factors point to
two common claims regarding educational restructuring: (1) that efforts to improve
credentials are an individual responsibility, and (2) that governments, education systems, and employers must work more actively to overcome the mismatch between
workers and jobs.

Unfortunately, the description of the trends outlined above offers no indication of
the extent to which education and training are actually required on the job. We need
to consider, in other words, whether the increase in educational credentials is a function of the growth of more sophisticated jobs or whether it is, instead, a consequence
of credential inflation and other factors beyond work-related skills and training.

Proponents of the first thesis point to the impact of information technology on
the creation of jobs that require a more highly educated and trained labour force.
The expansion of jobs that require high qualifications occurs in three ways—through
demands created by the emergence of new industries or enterprises in creative, scientific, and technical fields; through the creation of new jobs in high-level professional, technical, and service work; and through upgrading and new skill demands in
already existing jobs. Advanced education is required as work-related tasks become
more specialized and sophisticated. Since the mid-1980s, job growth in Canada, the

United States, and other highly developed nations has been clustered in industries that possess high concentrations of **knowledge workers**, i.e., professionals, engineers, scientific and technical workers, computer specialists, senior managers, and the self-employed who possess high levels of training, specialized skill, and/or decision-making authority. Many of the trends described throughout this chapter are reinforced in the observation concerning data from the 2006 census reported by Statistics Canada (2008b: 15): "The Canadian economy . . . still places a premium on workers with higher levels of education."

The growth of highly skilled jobs and knowledge work is necessary, advocates claim, to drive productivity for both large and small firms in a highly competitive economy. Education and training can increase the degree of complementarity between the interests of workers and employers because they not only assist individuals in their ability to secure employment but also influence the wages, personal benefits, and working conditions of employees. Bowlby (1996: 35) indicates that, in addition to receiving higher wages, "Graduates with a direct education–job relationship are the most likely to be satisfied or very satisfied at work, much more than graduates in unrelated jobs."

A less optimistic view, however, is taken by those who emphasize that the categorization of jobs or industries by job titles and education levels is highly misleading if we do not examine how work is actually changing. Recent economic restructuring has been characterized by the disappearance of stable, better-paying work and the proliferation of low-end jobs as businesses pursue strategies to reduce labour costs. In traditional industries and businesses, existing jobs often are phased out or deskilled while newer jobs, particularly in the service sector, are concentrated in low-skill, low-paying occupations. Education serves as a screening device independent from competencies required on the job. As general education levels rise and job descriptions change, employers are able to keep wages low through competition generated by labour surpluses, claims that available workers do not have suitable skills to match the available work, new labour-saving technologies, and the transfer of production from regions or nations with high-cost labour to those with lower labour costs and living standards. Much recent employment growth has been in service industries characterized by part-time, temporary, or insecure work, low wages, few benefits, and often poor working conditions. Bracey (2006: 94), observing the proliferation of growth in service-sector jobs with low pay, stresses that employers are less concerned with technical knowledge and test scores than with the fundamental social and personal attributes conveyed by job seekers. Those most attractive to employers were

> people who seemed serious about work and eager to get the job, who seemed bright and alert, who seemed courteous and personable, who seemed to have the ability to learn quickly, who had a neat appearance and dressed appropriately, who had good reading ability and ability with numbers, and [noted last] those who had a record of achievement in school.

Increasingly, the absence of secure, high-status jobs drives workers into jobs and fields where they are unable to use their capacities and skills. The problem of lack of credential recognition has gained widespread attention due to publicity surrounding experiences by highly qualified immigrants who are often frustrated by their inability to gain appropriate jobs or official credit for their foreign training and skills. While significant, this issue is related to a more general job deficit. Analysis of the Canadian workforce reveals that about one-third of Canadian workers aged 35 and under with post-secondary educational credentials indicated that they were over-qualified for their jobs, with as many as one in five workers with university degrees holding jobs that required no more than high school (Crompton, 2002: 23; Lowe, 2002; Li et al., 2006: 3; Statistics Canada and OECD, 2011: 280–1). These trends are not confined to Canada. Brown (2003) highlights what he calls an "opportunity trap" in which ever-larger pools of highly educated and skilled persons encounter contemporary global labour markets that are unable to accommodate their career expectations.

Recent evidence on the changing nature of employment has pointed to a much more complex picture than that revealed in the two arguments outlined above. Much attention has been focused on the tendency towards polarization of job growth distributed among high-end and low-end jobs, with a corresponding decline in the share of employment and protections for workers in mid-level jobs over the past two to three decades (Economic Council of Canada, 1991; Heisz, 2007; Osberg, 2006). This analysis highlights the decline of employment in goods-producing industries relative to substantial increases in service-sector employment. Both sectors, in turn, are characterized by diverse clusters of internal characteristics. Demand for highly educated, skilled, well-paid employees in many industries has increased as a consequence of new production and information technologies. However, increased productivity, workplace restructuring, and corporate and public-sector downsizing have also contributed to large-scale layoffs, intensification of work, and **deskilling**. The economic recession that began at the end of the first decade of the twenty-first century affected most deeply the employment prospects for people in the lowest education categories, but the employment growth that did occur for those with more education between 2008 and 2011 was not sufficient to ensure jobs for all university graduates (Statistics Canada and CMEC, 2012b: 7). At the same time, changing workplace demands also require workers to develop new skills beyond those acquired in the course of education, training, and initial workplace experience. A 2012 survey of over 1,000 Canadian workers revealed that nearly two-thirds (63 per cent) indicated that to perform their jobs they had to learn new skills in the previous five years; more than half (54 per cent) of workers indicated that they learned new skills on the job, whereas about one-quarter (27 per cent) had formal training through their company, 22 per cent attended training outside the organization, and others learned new skills through informal means or by job shadowing in which people learn about a specific career by spending part of a day or longer with someone at work in that field (Smith et al., 2012: 8, 30). In general, several prevalent trends emerge, most notably the expansion of service-sector work (in managerial, administrative, professional, clerical, sales, and service occupations), increases in the proportion of non-unionized workers relative to the unionized labour force, the growth of part-time work and self-employment relative to full-time paid employment, and deepening problems for the most vulnerable segments of the labour force (Heisz et al., 2002; Sawchuk and Taylor, 2010).

Education and Labour Market Inequalities

It is often tempting, in the analysis of labour force trends, to look at these patterns in an abstract way as if they affected all workers equally. In fact, however, labour market changes have very different implications for distinct categories of workers. Employment-related polarization encompasses several dimensions, as highly divergent work environments affect different sectors of the workforce in a highly un-even manner—as the workweek has declined for some workers, others are working well beyond standard working hours while increased earnings at the top are offset by lower overall wage and benefit packages across much of the workforce (Lowe, 2007). Since the mid-1980s, the degree of labour market polarization, or the gap between the highest- and lowest-paying jobs, generally has dropped for women, grown for men, increased substantially for workers less than 35 years of age, and remained high for visible minority groups and Aboriginal people (Human Resources Development Canada, 1996: 6; Canadian Council on Social Development, 2003; Usalcas, 2011). Hughes and Lowe (2000) conclude that such factors as the gender and age of workers and occupational conditions are more likely than computer technology to contribute to polarization within the labour market. Occupations associated with high job va-cancies also tend to be polarized among those with relatively high skill requirements and those that are not unionized and have low wages. Galarneau et al. (2001: 33) observe that, "Even in periods of strong economic growth, a substantial share of job vacancies are outside the high technology sectors. In 1999, more than 40 per cent of job vacancies and 50 per cent of long-term job vacancies of profit-oriented establish-ments were in the retail trade and consumer services industries."

The high profile given to the growth of knowledge work also obscures the fact that more than three-quarters of Canadian workers occupy jobs classified as non-knowledge occupations (Baldwin and Beckstead, 2003: 5). Canada's pursuit of inno-vation strategies has also been stalled by high returns on lucrative resource industries such as oil and gas development, which have reduced the inclination of the federal government as well as many companies to invest in research and development that might otherwise advance knowledge-based economic capacity (OECD, 2012c: 48ff.). At the same time, the global reach of technologies and markets has made it possible for enterprises and employment to transcend location, which has had mixed implica-tions for workers. The most highly qualified workers, who possess specialized skills for which there is considerable demand, may be able to pursue rewarding work in any number of locations, but employment prospects are also affected by outsourc-ing of jobs to locales in other nations and reliance in many industries on immigrant and temporary labour sources. Knowledge-sector jobs with the best working condi-tions tend to be clustered in major metropolitan centres and regions with a highly developed infrastructure, including proximity and ready access to core services, trans-portation and communications links, and universities and major research facilities. While considerable investment, along with media and policy attention, is concentrat-ed on innovation and high-level employment options, many of the most innovative firms associated with the new economy have relatively few employees; others rely on large numbers of relatively low-skilled, low-waged production and service workers (Brown and Lauder, 2006; Strathdee, 2005).

Some commentators, therefore, have argued that the structure of work is best characterized as a segmented or dual, rather than a unified, labour market (Piore, 1979; Clairmont and Apostle, 1997). This kind of analysis seeks to explain how mem-bers of subordinate social groups, notably visible minorities as well as female work-ers, are concentrated in lower-paying, more insecure jobs in contrast to white men, who tend to be concentrated in the better jobs. A primary labour market, in which relatively highly qualified and unionized workers are able to demand better wages and working conditions from larger employers, is distinguished from a secondary market in which smaller, more competitive businesses seeking cheaper labour costs require a more unstable labour force. Segmented or dual labour market models are useful in demonstrating that not all workers are competing for the same jobs, and also offer some insight into how educational qualifications can be used to differentiate distinct pools of workers. The practice of streaming in Canadian schools, for instance, operates to select students for particular positions within segmented labour markets (Curtis et al., 1992).

Despite the insights they offer, segmented labour market theories do not provide a complete explanation of inequalities within labour markets. Labour markets are both more diverse and less static than depicted by this approach. The face of work has been altered in many ways by changes in the organization of work, new technologies, demographic shifts, and labour market dynamics. The demise of jobs in traditional labour markets such as manufacturing, combined with the growth of small business and increasing employment in non-traditional occupations, has also blurred the boundaries between primary and secondary segments of the labour force. Immigrant selection criteria increasingly have emphasized skills, qualifications, and other human capital attributes even though many immigrants continue to face specific social or race-based barriers (Li, 2003: 122–3).

Significant continuity and changes in gender segmentation also are evident. Fewer than 20 per cent of women aged 25 and over participated in the paid labour force in 1946 and only about one-third did in the late 1960s, but by 2006 nearly two-thirds (62 per cent) of women were in the labour force. Men's participation rates have declined somewhat over the same time period but still remain relatively high, at about 90 per cent in 1946, 85 per cent in the late 1960s, and just under three-quarters (73.8 per cent) in 2006 (Bernier, 1996: A48–9; Statistics Canada, 2007c).

Table 7.5 presents two ways of looking at overall employment distribution, comparing permanent versus temporary work by major industrial categories, and full-time versus part-time status by occupational categories. The data show that women are represented in substantial numbers and proportions in a wide range of occupational groups. Women's participation in many higher-paying fields, such as managerial, administrative, and professional occupations, has increased in conjunction with more open access to advanced levels of education. However, the data also show that women are most highly concentrated in only a few areas. They are highly concentrated in areas like health care and education, as well as trades sectors and industries related to business and finance, but their work in these fields, as well as in food and accommodation services, tends to be in clerical, sales, and service positions characterized by low wages and benefits, poor working conditions, and relatively little autonomy. Women are slightly more likely than men to be employed in positions classified as temporary, but about one-quarter (26.8 per cent) of women compared to 12.2 per cent of men are in occupations classified as part-time.

While some of these differences can be accounted for in terms of personal preference and differences in qualifications, experience, and other characteristics, the patterns depicted in Table 7.5 provide a glimpse of a more general tendency for precarious and non-standard forms of employment to grow relative to more traditional full-time permanent employment (Vosko, 2007). Trends revealed in the most recent available census data suggest that, other than nursing and teaching for women, managerial positions in the sales and services sectors for men, and information systems analysis, very few of either the largest occupational categories or those that have demonstrated the highest growth since 2001 require specialized credentials beyond high school or specific occupational training (Table 7.6). Comparisons among persons who work full-time on a full-year basis show that women earn on average only two-thirds of the wages earned by men, with the lowest ratios of women's to men's earnings tending to be in sales, services, and other occupations in which there are high concentrations of female workers.

The segmentation of the labour force along gender lines is even more pronounced when part-time and temporary workers are taken into consideration, given that much of this labour is performed by women working for relatively low wages and benefits. Vosko (2003: 27) observes that, despite significant shifts in the nature of work that have created some advances for female workers, women remain highly vulnerable because "the erosion of minimum standards legislation, the deterioration of collective bargaining, unemployment insurance reforms, and cutbacks in the federal public service are fuelling new patterns of gendered labour market inequality." Armstrong and Armstrong (2010: 66) emphasize that even as educational and employment opportunities improve, women continue to be segregated in jobs that parallel the kinds of personal service and domestic labour they carry out in the household. Educational participation has created new social and employment opportunities for women, but traditional gender roles are also reproduced through demands and responsibilities that occur through the intersection of household, schooling, and workplace (Dillabough et al., 2008). Moreover, especially for women and those in the most precarious labour market situations, the amount of labour and related tensions involved in finding jobs, getting to work, caring or arranging care for children and other household members, managing household and leisure activities, and attending to other dimensions of work–family arrangements, is substantial and can pose further vulnerabilities (Corman and Luxton, 2007).

As the evidence and trends outlined in the preceding paragraphs suggest, labour markets are highly complex and changing entities. The possibility that a person will find relatively secure employment with limited education or can follow an educational track that leads to clearly definable, rewarding career opportunities is becoming increasingly remote for labour force entrants. The highly mixed signals that arise from these circumstances contribute to heightened uncertainty and stress for individuals considering or reassessing their employment prospects. The most optimistic assessments suggest that we have moved well beyond a situation described by Osberg et al. (1995: 182–3) in the 1990s as one dominated by problems of "increasing unemployment, the polarization of incomes, rising poverty, and greater dependence on transfer payments—all have their special complexities, but there is a root problem, a lack of jobs." Young workers, recent immigrants, older workers in declining industries, and others who are especially vulnerable to economic shifts must rely on part-time work, periodic retraining, or jobs that do not match their qualifications in order to break into the labour market (Beaujot and Kerr, 2007; Cranford and Vosko, 2006). However, labour market instability and uncertainty are not isolated to these groups. Since the late 1980s, periods of economic restructuring and recession made it increasingly difficult for graduates of trades and vocational programs, who might be expected to have work directly linked to their training, to find and keep such jobs (Bowlby, 1996: 38; Myles and Fawcett, 1990: 16). Subsequent labour market developments have been marked by notable increases in reliance on shifting and temporary types of work as employers seek to maximize flexibility and competitive positioning.

Table 7.5 Employment, by Gender, Industry, and Occupation, Canada, 2011

	Female 000s	(%)	Male 000s	(%)	Total
Industry: Permanent					
Agriculture	30	35.3	55	64.7	85
Other primary industries	48	18.8	208	81.3	256
Utilities	30	24.0	95	76.0	125
Construction	96	13.3	624	86.7	720
Manufacturing	442	28.5	1,110	71.5	1,552
Total goods-producing	646	23.6	2,091	76.4	2,737
Trade	1,071	49.7	1,085	50.3	2,156
Transportation and warehousing	168	26.7	463	73.4	631
Finance, insurance, real estate, and leasing	510	61.6	318	38.4	828
Professional, scientific, and technical services	355	45.8	421	54.3	776
Business, building and other support services	182	45.0	223	55.2	404
Educational services	571	66.2	292	33.8	863
Health care and social assistance	1,350	84.1	255	15.9	1,605
Information, culture, and recreation	237	45.7	274	52.8	512
Accommodation and food services	497	59.9	333	40.1	830
Other services	243	52.8	217	47.2	460
Public administration	424	50.8	410	49.2	834
Total services-producing	5,609	56.7	4,290	43.3	9,899
Total permanent all industries	6,255	49.5	6,381	50.5	12,637
Industry: Temporary					
Agriculture	13	39.4	21	63.6	33
Other primary industries	7	15.9	37	84.1	44
Utilities	5	35.7	10	71.4	14
Construction	15	8.6	159	90.9	175
Manufacturing	41	33.6	81	66.4	122
Total goods-producing	81	20.9	307	79.1	388
Trade	132	54.1	112	45.9	244
Transportation and warehousing	18	26.1	52	75.4	69
Finance, insurance, real estate, and leasing	33	57.9	24	42.1	57
Professional, scientific, and technical services	34	46.6	39	53.4	73
Business, building and other support services	41	37.3	69	62.7	110
Educational services	192	65.5	101	34.5	293
Health care and social assistance	199	84.7	37	15.7	235
Information, culture, and recreation	69	46.0	80	53.3	150
Accommodation and food services	104	59.1	71	40.3	176
Other services	38	57.8	28	42.4	66
Public administration	73	53.2	64	46.7	137

	Female 000s	(%)	Male 000s	(%)	Total
Total services-producing	934	58.0	677	42.0	1,611
Total temporary all industries	1,015	50.8	984	49.2	1,999
Occupation: Full-time					
Management	498	36.2	878	63.8	1,376
Business, finance, and administrative	1,760	67.6	843	32.4	2,603
Natural and applied sciences	260	21.5	949	78.5	1,209
Health	695	78.4	191	21.5	887
Social science, education, government service, and religion	865	67.6	414	32.4	1,279
Art, culture, recreation, and sport	196	50.6	192	49.6	387
Sales and service	1,318	50.2	1,305	49.8	2,623
Trades, transport and equipment operators	128	5.3	2,276	94.7	2,404
Primary industry	71	15.7	382	84.3	453
Processing, manufacturing, and utilities	224	28.9	551	71.0	776
Total full-time	6,016	43.0	7,980	57.0	13,995
Occupation: Part-time					
Management	49	48.5	51	50.5	101
Business, finance, and administrative	413	79.4	107	20.6	520
Natural and applied sciences	19	29.7	45	70.3	64
Health	249	90.2	27	9.8	276
Social science, education, government service, and religion	236	75.2	78	24.8	314
Art, culture, recreation, and sport	117	62.2	71	37.8	188
Sales and service	1,037	67.0	511	33.0	1,548
Trades, transport and equipment operators	36	19.7	147	80.3	183
Primary industry	29	37.7	48	62.3	77
Processing, manufacturing and utilities	19	47.5	21	52.5	40
Total part-time	2,206	66.6	1,106	33.4	3,311

Note: Numbers are rounded.
Source: Statistics Canada CANSIM Tables 2820010 and 2820080.

One of the major contradictions evident in these trends is the coexistence of large numbers of workers who are undereducated and underqualified for available jobs along with a substantial pool of labour market participants who are overqualified and underemployed. Statistics Canada data concerning employment experiences of graduates of post-secondary programs reveal, in general, that those with the highest levels of formal education tend to show the strongest match between job skills and education, with a modestly higher degree of fit for women than for men (Finnie, 2001: 14; Yuen, 2010). Livingstone (2004), through his own research and in summaries of other findings, demonstrates the simultaneous existence of two large groups of

Table 7.6 Ten Most Prevalent Occupations for Men and Women, and Fastest-Growing Occupational Categories, Canada, 2006

Top 10 Occupations, by Employment Numbers	Skill Level*	Total Employment 2006	% of Total Employment	Change 2001–6 (%)
Men				
Retail salespersons and sales clerks	C	285,800	3.2	28.6
Truck drivers	C	276,200	3.1	17.4
Retail trade managers	O	192,200	2.2	–4.0
Janitors, caretakers, and building superintendents	D	154,100	1.7	13.9
Farmers and farm managers	B/C	147,800	1.7	–12.5
Material handlers	C	147,000	1.7	10.4
Automotive service technicians, truck and bus mechanics, and mechanical repairers	B	143,000	1.6	16.6
Carpenters	B	142,400	1.6	30.0
Construction trades helpers and labourers	D	133,600	1.5	55.2
Sales, marketing, and advertising managers	O	102,600	1.2	11.0
Total, top 10 male occupation		1,724,700	19.4	14.5
Total, all occupations (men)		8,884,805	100.0	6.9
Women				
Retail salespersons and sales clerks	C	400,000	5.0	20.7
Cashiers	D	255,500	3.2	16.1
Registered nurses	A	249,400	3.1	15.7
General office clerks	C	244,200	3.1	10.4
Secretaries (except legal and medical)	B	237,300	3.0	–6.5
Elementary school and kindergarten teachers	A	214,600	2.7	10.2
Food counter attendants, kitchen helpers and related occupations	D	194,800	2.4	13.5
Early childhood educators and assistants	B	157,700	2.0	25.2
Food and beverage servers	D	152,000	1.9	–1.9
Light-duty cleaners	D	147,400	1.8	19.8
Total, top 10 female occupations		2,252,900	28.2	12.0
Total, all occupations (women)		7,976,375	100.0	9.8
Occupations with largest increases, 2001–6, by total number of employees				
Retail salespersons and sales clerks	C	685,800	4.1	23.9
Construction trades helpers and labourers	D	143,900	0.9	57.1
Truck drivers	C	286,100	1.7	18.2
Cashiers	D	299,200	1.8	16.9

Top 10 Occupations, by Employment Numbers	Skill Level*	Total Employment 2006	% of Total Employment	Change 2001–6 (%)
Nurse aides, orderlies, and patient service associates	C	169,700	1.0	28.0
Registered nurses	A	265,900	1.6	16.2
Customer service, information, and related clerks	C	191,600	1.1	23.4
Administrative clerks	C	101,700	0.6	53.9
Information systems analysts and consultants	A/B	138,400	0.8	34.2
Carpenters	B	145,000	0.9	30.3
Total men and women, all occupations		16,861,180	100.0	

* Skill levels and occupational categories are based on National Occupational Classification. Skill level refers to credentials or levels of education and training typically required as qualifications for a job.

Skill Level:
O = Management
A = Occupations usually require university education.
B = Occupations usually require college education or apprenticeship training.
C = Occupations usually require secondary school and/or occupation-specific training.
D = On-the-job training is usually provided for occupations.

Source: Statistics Canada (2008b: 13–14).

workers—those whose formal educational credentials exceed their job requirements and those who feel they do not have sufficient skills or training to carry out all their job tasks. More specifically, he shows that **underemployment** and subemployment are subdivided among distinct categories of labour force participants, depending on such factors as the levels of qualifications workers have, the credentials required for entry into certain occupations, the knowledge and skills employed on the job and those that workers have but cannot use in their work, and workers' perceptions about the relationships among these factors. Between one and three out of five workers in North America—and more in working-class positions—are likely to be underemployed according to various dimensions based on the reality or perception that they have recognized skills and credentials they are not able to employ in their jobs, at the same time as these workers are engaging in more formal and informal training on and off the job (Livingstone, 2004: 94–5; Livingstone and Scholtz, 2007: 153–4). More detailed analysis of the skills and capacities associated with various types of education and changing job requirements reveal a much more complex set of phenomena and dynamics than commonly understood (Desjardins and Rubenson, 2011).

In summary, it is difficult to make comprehensive judgments about the degree of match or fit between education and jobs because of the highly complex and changing nature of work and labour markets. Jobs and labour markets, and the manner in which they intersect with education and training, are undergoing massive transformations, but there are highly divergent ways of understanding the dimensions and implications of those changes. The escalation of a long-term shift

Box 7.5 Youth Employment Trends

Young Canadians are experiencing an increasingly more complex and uncertain set of options and circumstances as they navigate their way between schooling and work. Analyzing data for youth aged 22–4 in 2004 drawn from the Youth in Transition Survey, Hango and de Broucker (2007: 11–13) summarize a number of key dimensions of these transitions:

Important background factors associated with education-to-labour-market pathways

- Females are less likely to follow the pathway of dropping out of high school and are more likely to go on to some type of post-secondary program prior to entering the labour force. They are also less likely to delay the start of a post-secondary program than are males.
- In terms of ethnic background, the most salient finding is that Aboriginal youth are more likely than non-Aboriginal youth to leave the educational system with a much lower level of attainment.
- The presence of a long-term limiting condition is a hindrance to further education; these individuals are much less likely to follow pathways leading to the completion of a post-secondary degree or diploma.
- Youth who attended high school in Quebec were more likely than youth from Ontario to drop out of high school; yet if they did graduate from high school and attend a post-secondary program, they were more likely than their counterparts from Ontario to go directly following high school.
- A greater number of siblings led to a greater risk of not finishing high school prior to entering the labour market, as does not living in an intact family (two-parent, non-step family) during high school. As well, the typical universally positive relationship between educational attainment levels across generations was found: youth with parents who had a high level of education were more likely to go to a post-secondary program prior to entering the labour market.

Linking intervening factors to educational pathways

- Marks matter. A very strong relationship was found between grade-point average and dropping out of high school: youth with very low marks in high school were much more likely than those with mid to high marks to drop out and not return. For youth who had attended post-secondary programs, very high marks predicted that the teen would go directly to a post-secondary program after high school rather than delaying.
- Working some hours in high school can be beneficial, while working a great number of hours (over 20) can be detrimental, leading to a greater risk of dropping out of high school. Working over 20 hours a week in high school was also associated with teens delaying their attendance at a post-secondary institution following high school.

- Individuals who had a child or who entered a conjugal union during their teenage years are disproportionately represented among those who dropped out of high school, as well as among those who dropped out but later returned (second-chancers); they were less represented among the paths leading to post-secondary attendance.
- Parental expectations regarding their child's education are generally high, and higher expectations are associated with higher educational attainment.

Linking educational paths to labour market outcomes

- Almost 80 per cent of youth who were not in school in December 2003 were employed. The likelihood of employment is highest for individuals who had delayed post-secondary attendance after high school, but then either graduated from college or university, and for college graduates who had not delayed their post-secondary attendance after high school graduation. . . .
- The odds of employment also increased as the number of months spent out of full-time school increased, for males, for individuals who had no children, and for those who had worked more hours in high school.
- . . . On average, post-secondary graduates (regardless of whether they delayed post-secondary attendance following high school graduation) earned more than the median. High school dropouts (whether or not they returned to school) and those who entered but did not complete a post-secondary program earned less. However, some university graduates were earning less than high school dropouts, though this is at least partly attributable to the university grads having had less opportunity for work experience. . . .
- In addition to the effects of school pathway, several additional interesting results were found for other indicators. For example, women have lower earnings than men, earning almost 28 per cent less than their working male counterparts. Meanwhile, working a greater number of hours in high school had a positive effect on earnings: working on average 20 hours per week increased earnings by about 20 per cent, as compared to not working at all. However, it adversely affected educational attainment. . . .
- The most common occupations were in sales and service, while the least common were in management or business-related. Young adults with post-secondary degrees or diplomas were more represented among management and business-related jobs, as well as professional, scientific, education and government jobs. Meanwhile, young adults with a high school diploma or less were more represented among the goods-producing and primary sectors and those who entered but did not complete a post-secondary program were more represented among the lowest-paying sales and service occupations, likely leading to their low earnings observed earlier.

from jobs related to physical resources and material goods production towards work concentrated in services and knowledge sectors is accompanied by changes in the kinds of competencies and relationships people need to prepare for and conduct their working lives.

The present educational situation in post-secondary institutions can be explained by a combination of factors, including intense competition for many jobs, powerful ideological and rhetorical linkages between social advancement and educational advancement (sometimes supported by general empirical evidence), and anxiety induced by labour market change and uncertainty. These social pressures have fuelled an escalation in levels of educational attainment, and these educational levels exceed what is required across much of the current job market. Even those individuals in a position to make long-term plans for their career futures are subject to the possibility that credential requirements may change or that certain jobs may be substantially reorganized or could disappear altogether before their formal education is complete. The discourse of lifelong learning, acknowledging ongoing transformations in the nature of work and periodic transitions among diverse employment circumstances and learning sites, has replaced conventional notions of a pathway that leads from schooling into a clearly defined career. In general terms, individuals with the highest levels of formal education clearly are in the best position to benefit in terms of finding stable, well-paying, meaningful work. However, even among highly educated workers there is a strong possibility of no available work relevant to their training, while pressures mount for continuous retraining and upgrading. By contrast, those with limited amounts of formal education are more likely to have difficulty finding and keeping work, but when they do, in many cases even they may be overqualified for their jobs. For youth faced with the prospect of seeking work, regardless of their levels of educational attainment, the pressing question of what kinds of job options they should pursue is becoming increasingly uncertain.

Conclusion

This chapter has addressed the relationship between schooling and work. While the goal of preparing youth for entry into the labour force has long been a central concern of educators, just as it has been a recurrent matter for public debate, the chapter has emphasized that there has never been a strict correspondence between formal education and work training. Labour market preparation has been only one of several objectives of education systems. This, combined with the varied needs of employers, the changing nature of most occupations, and the complexity of transition processes between schooling and work, limits the extent to which formal education can respond to labour market demands.

While considerable attention in policy discussions and the media has focused recently on the apparent failure of formal education to produce the kind of workforce required in a competitive global economy, much of that emphasis has offered a relatively uncritical analysis of the kinds of job choices and school–work connections that labour market entrants are confronted with. Clearly, many improvements are needed in the ways that schools approach labour market preparation. It is not sufficient, however, to lay blame with schools or individuals for the mismatch between workers and jobs. A combination of factors that links individual life circumstances and choices with structural characteristics of education and work opportunities contributes to the kinds of life courses that people follow. This chapter has focused mostly on general trends, but the evidence has pointed to the highly uneven and unequal structures of opportunity and reward associated with access to education, labour market options, and socio-economic outcomes. Chapter 8 examines these phenomena in more detail.

Annotated Further Readings

Anisef, Paul, Paul Axelrod, Etta Baichman-Anisef, Carl James, and Anton Turrittin. 2000. *Opportunity and Uncertainty: Life Course Experiences of the Class of '73*. Toronto: University of Toronto Press. This book offers one of the few systematic long-term studies of the educational, occupational, and life pathways followed by students as they complete their schooling and move through adolescence into adulthood.

Bills, David B. 2004. *The Sociology of Education and Work*. Malden, Mass.: Blackwell. Drawing on data on and examples of the changing relations between education and work in the United States, the author provides a clear introduction to major issues associated with the sociological analysis of these relationships focused around competing perspectives that highlight, respectively, meritocracy and credentialism.

Brown, Phillip, Andy Green, and Hugh Lauder. 2001. *High Skills: Globalization, Competitiveness, and Skill Formation*. Oxford: Oxford University Press. The authors critically assess conventional views of the importance of highly skilled knowledge work in the global economy. They demonstrate, through case studies drawn from the United States, the United Kingdom, Japan, Germany, South Korea, and Singapore, that the most optimistic accounts overstate the extent to which highly skilled work pervades developed economies, and outline alternative models of high skills that accompany diverse political economies and policy strategies.

Livingstone, D.W. 2004. *The Education–Jobs Gap: Underemployment or Economic Democracy*. Aurora, ON: Garamond Press. Offering a comprehensive analysis of the relationship between education and work in contemporary economic contexts, this book demonstrates how the broad range of educational experiences and capacities is not given sufficient recognition and scope in many jobs and labour market situations.

Lowe, Graham. 2000. *The Quality of Work: A People-Centred Agenda*. Toronto: Oxford University Press, 2000. The author examines contemporary trends and attitudes regarding the changing nature of work, building from critique towards a framework for the creation of meaningful work opportunities that address people's concerns for greater personal development and fulfillment.

Sawchuk, Peter, and Alison Taylor, eds. 2010. *Challenging Transitions in Learning and Work: Reflections on Policy and Practice*. Rotterdam: Sense Publishers. Several case studies and critical inquiries provide diverse insights into the changing relationships between learning and work, with a Canadian focus.

Shalla, Vivian, and Wallace Clement, eds. 2007. *Work in Tumultuous Times: Critical Perspectives*. Montreal and Kingston: McGill-Queen's University Press. Several authors examine how Canadian society is being restructured by significant social and economic transformations, leading to extensive instability and uncertainty in working and domestic relationships. Contributors highlight how class, gender, and racial inequalities intersect with differences in how people experience and manage them.

Key Terms

Capitalist imperative Pressures to reproduce hierarchy and inequality through schooling and other institutions in order to ensure profitable production and other needs associated with capitalist economies.

Democratic imperative Pressures to ensure that schools and other agencies are governed by priorities for widespread participation, expanded socio-economic opportunities, and social justice for all groups.

Deskilling A process in which workers lose control and autonomy over their work, either through the centralization of decision-making in management and new technologies, or the fragmentation of jobs into more simplified and directed tasks.

Employability The possession of skills and attributes considered essential for individuals to remain part of the labour market and adapt to changing economic conditions.

Global talent pool The portion of the population worldwide with post-secondary credentials, including university degrees and college diplomas normally requiring at least two years of full-time study at the post-secondary level.

Habitus Relatively stable systems of dispositions, habits, or tastes that constitute the basis for how we understand the world.

Knowledge workers Workers, generally with high levels of skills and qualifications, who are engaged in the production, manipulation, and dissemination of knowledge, often involving extensive use of information and communication technologies.

Lifelong learning The notion that learning extends on a continuum from early childhood through adulthood, occurring in a variety of institutional and informal settings rather than being confined to formal learning within selected programs, institutions, and age cohorts.

New economy The shift in emphasis from industrial production within specific industries, firms, and nations to economic activities driven by information and high-level technologies, global competition and international networks, and knowledge-based advancement.

Post-industrial society A form of social and economic organization based on rapid developments related to knowledge, information, advanced technology, and service-sector work. It is made possible by, but does not eradicate the need for, sophisticated advances in the production of raw materials and manufactured goods.

Technological functionalism A perspective that emphasizes industrial and technological development as the basis for educational expansion and emerging knowledge requirements.

Transitions The pathways that people follow from family life, into and out of education, and into various jobs or other social situations throughout their life course.

Underemployment A situation in which a person has educational credentials, skills, or other capacities that are not required for or used in her/his jobs.

Vocational and technical education Education and training programs that lead to certificates or other credentials oriented to specific occupational requirements.

Study Questions

1. Critically discuss the argument that education is failing in its primary purpose to provide the skills and training that individuals require for competitive performance in the new economy.

2. Outline and explain the impact that changing job structures and labour market requirements have had on educational practices over the past century.

3. Many employers and educators are highlighting the importance of a range of fundamental skills rather than specific knowledge for employability in a rapidly changing labour market, as exemplified by the Conference Board of Canada's Employability Skills 2000+ profile, at: www.conferenceboard.ca/topics/education/learning-tools/employability-skills.aspx. Examining this profile, indicate what you consider your level of competency to be with respect to each of the designated categories and skills. Which of these have you gained through various stages of your formal education (and at what levels or types of programs) and which have you achieved on your own or in non-school settings? What conclusions might this assessment provide about the nature and relevance of formal schooling for contemporary work opportunities?

4. Discuss the extent to which Canada has become a post-industrial society. How have the transformations from industrial to post-industrial types of societies affected education and employment prospects for men and women in different circumstances, including those entering the job market and those with extensive work experience.

5. Critics from various perspectives have suggested there is a strong mismatch between education and jobs. Critically compare and contrast the main competing orientations to this mismatch, indicating the extent to which each is supported by available evidence.

6. Outline and explain the degree of correlation between levels of education and levels of employment, income, and labour market success.

7. Debate exists over the question of whether work is becoming more highly skilled or workers are increasingly deskilled. Compare and contrast these positions with reference to research findings and recent trends related to work in Canada.

Chapter 8

Educational Opportunity and Social Reproduction

Learning Objectives

In this chapter, you will:

- be introduced to the concept of opportunity and the major dimensions in which opportunities are understood in relation to education systems;
- gain an understanding of the ways in which education can advance as well as limit opportunities for different individuals and social groups;
- explore variations in educational participation and achievement based on major social characteristics, including gender, race, class, region, and ability status.

Introduction

One of the primary themes in the sociological analysis of education is the assessment of contributions made by formal education both to social equality and to socio-economic opportunity. This interest runs parallel to high social expectations about the value of schooling as a vehicle for social mobility. There is widespread faith in the ability of education to elevate living conditions and advance individual opportunities for all participants. International comparisons of social and economic development among nations, for instance, regard the general levels of education attained by a population as one of the most common indicators of the advancement of a society (UNESCO, 2007) in the same way that learners, their parents, and prospective employers tend to regard schooling as a key determinant of an individual's future success.

While there is little question, in general terms, about the importance of the connection between education and socio-economic opportunity, the degree to which education has been able to contribute effectively to greater social equality has been subject to repeated challenge from different ends of the political spectrum. Compulsory education, along with social welfare, income and tax transfer programs, and other state policies devoted to minimize the impact of poverty and reduce social inequality in Canada, the United States, and other highly developed democratic societies, has not eliminated pronounced gaps that separate the advantaged from the disadvantaged segments of the population. Empirical evidence demonstrates that education on a global scale has had an uneven or ambiguous impact on development, although there continues to be high public confidence in education's ability to drive economic, political, and cultural development (Chabbott and Ramirez, 2006). UNESCO (2007: 2), monitoring educational conditions around the globe, warned in 2007 that, "Despite overall enrolment increases, subnational disparities in school participation persist between regions, provinces or states and between urban and rural areas. Children from poor, indigenous, and disabled populations are also at a systematic disadvantage, as are those living in slums." Four years later, the prognosis remains grim, with UNESCO (2011b: 24–5) observing that, "If current trends continue there could be more children out of school in 2015 than there are today. . . . Deep disparities in opportunities for education linked to wealth, gender, ethnicity, language and wider markers for disadvantage are acting as a brake on progress towards the Education for All goals." The persistence of educational inequality has been accompanied by recurrent debates over the causes of general social inequality and related demands for reforms in education and other social programs.

This chapter focuses on central debates and issues related to the relationship between formal education and social inequality. It addresses questions such as the following:

- What is meant by social inequality and educational opportunity, and how are they related?

- Who benefits from education and what kinds of return do individuals and groups receive from their formal schooling?

- How much does formal education contribute to the reproduction or the eradication of social inequality?

- What are the limitations on education being able to fulfill its promise of better social futures for individuals and social groups?

- What are the prospects that social and educational reform can overcome these limitations?

The Nature and Causes of Social Inequality in Canada

Canadians often pride themselves on the observation that their country ranks ahead of most other nations on indicators related to standard of living, quality of life, and relative equity among groups. Extreme gaps between the haves and have-nots are not nearly as visible as they are in most parts of the world, whether in developing or developed regions. Nonetheless, social inequality in Canada is prevalent along several dimensions. These include disparities in the possession of or access to income and wealth, political power, and ideological power (see, e.g., Clement and Vosko, 2003).

Regardless of which measure is considered, Canadian society is highly stratified according to inequalities of gender, race and ethnicity, class, region, age, and many other social factors (Grabb and Guppy, 2009; McMullen, 2010). Women, who earn on average about two-thirds of the average incomes of men, often continue to be concentrated in subordinate roles in both the household and workplace (Armstrong and Armstrong, 2010: 66; Vosko, 2007). People of Aboriginal ancestry and members of groups considered visible minorities, including many recent immigrants, frequently are marginalized and limited in their ability to gain access to important economic and political positions. While wealth is concentrated among a small core of individuals and firms, large disparities between the privileged and underprivileged are growing. Rice (2002: 117) observes that the new economy, in addition to perpetuating earlier divisions between "good jobs and bad jobs," is also blocking social mobility, with the consequence "that Canada will continue to develop two economies, one for the haves and one for the have-nots. Opportunities will flow to those who have the advantage of educated or well-off parents, while those with poor parents will have limited opportunities." In the decade since that observation was made, accelerating increases in income gaps between the poorest and wealthiest segments of the Canadian population have drawn attention from many other observers (see, e.g., Conference Board of Canada, 2011). Within the former category, households headed by young adults, lone parents, Aboriginal people, and many seniors (especially among women in each of these groups) are much more likely than other households to be living in poverty, often for extended durations (Campaign 2000, 2011).

The chances of finding secure employment, decent wages, and access to adequate living conditions and social support also vary according to where people live. Regional inequalities are acknowledged in government policies that distinguish between the "have-not" provinces—notably in Atlantic Canada—that receive equalization payments from the federal government and the "have" provinces (most typically Ontario, Alberta, and British Columbia). There are also significant inequalities within regions, frequently though not exclusively on a rural/urban and north/south basis. Historically, for instance, the sovereignist movement in Quebec originated out of contradictions, most evident in terms of disparities between anglophones and francophones, both within the province and between Quebec and the rest of Canada (Denis, 1995).

Educational Opportunity and Social Inequality

Formal education is highly implicated in considerations of social inequality because of its importance as a state-managed mechanism to transmit values and regulate credentials and access to highly valued social and economic positions. Educational opportunity is widely accepted as a key mechanism for expanding the distribution of social and economic positions and rewards. Nonetheless, differing claims are made about the meaning and nature of educational opportunity. Lessard (1995: 178–9), citing Lévesque (1979), outlines three distinct meanings of the concept of educational opportunity—equality of access, equality of treatment, and equality of results, each of which corresponds to different political philosophies.

The first meaning, equality of access, refers to the notion that all individuals should be guaranteed little more than the opportunity to attend schools or other formal educational institutions. This view is associated with a conservative or a laissez-faire approach that emphasizes individual responsibility. The state's role is limited to assurances that schools and other vital public services are available to all citizens and that the rules governing these services are fairly applied. Beyond that, people should be expected to look out for their own welfare and be held accountable for their own success or failure. This ideological position, especially when it is combined with concern about government debt, has driven recent reforms to downsize the welfare state through funding and program cuts in education as well as in related areas such as social welfare, health care, and unemployment insurance.

The second concept, equality of treatment, corresponds to a liberal philosophical orientation that stresses that the state must take a more proactive role with respect to education and other social services. Consistent with cultural explanations of inequality, this view argues that persons from varying social backgrounds have distinct needs, interests, and characteristics that have to be taken into account in the planning, delivery, and evaluation of educational programs and services. It is not sufficient simply to "bring people to the classroom door"; instead, the opportunities presented can only be taken advantage of when there are assurances that they are meaningful and relevant to the needs of learners and other clients.

The third approach to educational opportunity, which emphasizes **equality of results**, emerges from a critical or social democratic philosophy grounded in a structural explanation of inequality. In contrast to the first two orientations, this position demands an even greater sense of social responsibility on the part of both the state and the more privileged groups within society. People tend to be poor, unemployed, or **socially disadvantaged** not through any fault of their own but rather because the social system produces poverty, unemployment, and structural inequality as conditions of its ongoing existence. Individuals should not be blamed, for instance, for being born into poor families or for living in communities in which factories close down or fisheries are jeopardized. Therefore, a proactive approach is required to ensure that all members of a population have access to a wide range of educational and social services and programs to guarantee them at least minimum standards of living and opportunities for success.

Individual and Structural Explanations of Social Inequalities

The diverse conceptions of educational opportunity draw attention to competing explanations for the persistence of inequalities both within and outside of schooling. Different theories and public policy perspectives related to social inequality are not only linked with particular assumptions about how the world is organized; they also carry distinct implications regarding prospects for social change. If we assume, for instance, that inequality is a necessary feature of human societies or that it is the product of innate individual characteristics, we may be inclined to believe that little can be done to alter existing social arrangements. By contrast, if we view inequality as the product of social factors, we are more likely to support social policies or government actions such as proposals for affirmative action or tax benefits for the poor. In fact, while various and wide-ranging theories attempt to explain inequality, the most common variants in these debates are positions that, on the one hand, emphasize individual or cultural factors and, on the other hand, stress social structural factors (Bolaria, 2000).

Individual explanations of inequality regard each person as responsible for his or her own success or failure. Disadvantage and poverty are viewed as consequences of low ambition, inadequate skills or abilities, or some other faulty personal characteristics, while those who succeed are considered more capable or talented, exercise personal drive and good judgment, and demonstrate good work habits. These capacities are seen to reside in either the biological or personality structures of individuals.

Social Darwinism, which was popular in the late nineteenth century, for example, promoted the view that individuals were sorted according to their abilities or "fitness" to succeed. The notion of "survival of the fittest" was introduced by sociologist Herbert Spencer (not Charles Darwin, as is often supposed) to indicate how social progress required a naturally competitive selection process to enable the strongest (i.e., those who could contribute the most to socially desirable outcomes) to succeed while the poor and weak should be left to fend for themselves (Ritzer, 2011: 33).

Although this view is highly controversial and has lost favour among most social analysts, it continues to appear in various guises, particularly from the political right. Neo-liberal perspectives, which prioritize individual rights over collective interests, and advanced genetic research, which seeks to map the biological foundations of life forms, emerge as threats to more sociological understandings of human relations (Fuller, 2006). In recent decades, widespread attention has been given to the view that intelligence is distributed and inherited unequally among the population, thereby accounting for higher rates of educational and socio-economic failure among **visible minority** populations such as blacks in the United States (Jensen, 1973; Herrnstein, 1973; Rushton and Bogaert, 1987). Herrnstein and Murray (1994) reignited controversy in the 1990s by arguing in *The Bell Curve* that because of a "cognitive partitioning," through which the population comes to be subdivided into distinct intellectual categories, often on racial lines, it is not possible for everyone to benefit from education. They contend that only select groups should have access to higher education, while those with low IQs should not be expected to graduate from high school.

These views are among the most extreme examples of the individualist orientations to social inequality. They have been widely criticized on several accounts, including their failure to question faulty assumptions about how social characteristics like race, gender, and intelligence are defined and measured, problems with their methodologies and use of data, and their lack of attention to such structural factors as social policy and legislation that restrict opportunities for particular groups (see, e.g., Fraser, 1995). Fischer et al. (1996: 18), observing the impact of social policies and other factors that perpetuate social inequality, state emphatically, "It is not that low intelligence leads to inferior status; it is that inferior status leads to low intelligence test scores." Nonetheless, this approach shares much in common with the widely held liberal assessment that social rewards are allocated on the basis of merit through competition among individuals. The relative success people have in attaining particular social or economic positions is therefore seen to be determined by ability, effort, and personal achievement. This analysis presupposes that social structures and institutions such as education are relatively open, accessible, and fair to all persons.

A variant of the individualist position is found in cultural theories of inequality, which argue that some cultures are more oriented than others to traits that are rewarded in advanced societies. According to this view, persons from modern cultures are better situated than those with a traditional value orientation to identify with goals and adopt characteristics that lead to social and economic success. Traditionalism, "cultures of poverty," and lack of an achievement orientation are presented from this viewpoint as impediments to progress, thereby contributing to the subordination of the culture as a whole as well as to the limitation of opportunities for individuals within those cultures (Hurst, 1992: 229–30). Murray (2012: 209), for instance, characterizes an emerging threat to American social stability constituted by a "new lower class" involving mostly "people who have never quite gotten their acts together and are the despair" of their family and community members. While these views hold little credence among academic researchers, they have gained resilience because of their popularity among critics of the welfare state and others who subscribe to powerful individualist ideologies.

Structural orientations to social inequality do not share the assumptions made by individual and cultural theories. A structural approach does not "blame" individuals or their cultures for possessing deficits or failing to live up to the standards and expectations by which success is determined. Instead, inequality is regarded as socially produced and reproduced on at least two levels. First, structured inequalities permeate social systems and institutional processes. Second, social groups do not share equal access to opportunities, positions, and rewards that accompany those systems and processes. Success and failure, in these regards, are determined by factors other than individual characteristics and efforts. Persons who are talented, capable, intelligent, hardworking, and possess other attributes associated with success in Western societies are distributed widely across various social groups, just as those who do not possess those attributes have diverse social origins. The social system is organized in such a way as to define and produce failure in particular ways, which in turn creates advantages or disadvantages for some groups relative to others. In other words, what counts,

Box 8.1 Climate Change, Environmental Degradation, Poverty, and Gender: Barriers to Basic Education in Developing Nations

Schooling in many nations is constrained by significant barriers to participation, programming, and advancement, revealing the combined impact of schooling and the environments in which schools operate. A report from the United Nations Development Programme (UNDP, 2011: 45ff.) highlights how the requirements to attend to basic daily needs are intensified by climate change and other threats to the environment, making it difficult, especially for girls, to attend school in many developing nations. The report points out the exceptional burden for the world's most disadvantaged people, who are most exposed to both environmental degradation and the social, physical, and economic risks posed by unsafe environments. Several examples cited in the report are presented below.

- People in working-class and minority neighbourhoods, even in developed nations, are most likely to suffer adverse impacts on their health, education, and property values because of the concentration of toxic waste facilities in these areas—to such an extent that "it is clear that environmentally harmful practices accentuate racial and social inequalities" (ibid., 45).
- Desertification, falling water tables, and limited access to other basic resources leave schools in many regions without electricity and clean water. For instance, "[m]ost schools in Madagascar have no running water for adequate hygiene and sanitation, so pupils fall sick regularly, missing classes and underperforming" (ibid., 47).
- Children in much of sub-Saharan Africa, rural India, Pakistan, and many other nations are required to spend time collecting firewood, water, and other resources, contributing to "a high opportunity cost in foregone schooling," especially for girls (UNDP, 2011: 58), but boys are also affected, such as in rural Ethiopia, where "the probability of schooling as the main activity, especially for boys, falls as the time to reach a water source rises" (ibid., 54).
- Natural disasters and conflict related to climate change often induce migration and destruction of livelihoods, increasing the likelihood that "families without assets or other income opportunities, such as wage labour, may pull children out of school," and in some cases "schooling infrastructure may be affected, and teachers may be injured or killed" (ibid., 60).

at least as much as any individual characteristics and dispositions, are the conditions that make it possible to nurture and develop attributes deemed socially desirable in ways that are validated or recognized by institutions and agents that influence access to educational and economic opportunities and other factors associated with success.

In Canada, numerous discriminatory policies at the federal, provincial, and municipal levels have restricted opportunities or prohibited access to services on the basis of race, gender, and other social characteristics. Historically, for instance, there have been policies to prohibit women and people of Asian ancestry from attending universities or registering in specific programs and to limit the length of time that registered Indians could attend public schools. Similarly, lack of access to material resources has restricted the ability of members of socially disadvantaged groups to achieve success in important political, economic, and social spheres of activity.

Competing individual and structural explanations of inequality extend beyond academic analysis into social policy considerations. Various policy alternatives are organized around issues such as what role the state should play in regulating people's lives, providing human services, promoting personal incentive, and recognizing individual or collective rights. Over the past century, intense contestation over these questions frequently has accompanied the rise of—and subsequent efforts to reshape or dismantle—the welfare state.

The Politics of Educational Opportunity

The politics of education in Canada, often parallel to the development of the welfare state, make evident the extent to which alternative understandings of social inequality and educational opportunities play a role in educational practice and decision-making. The history of Canadian education reveals periodic tensions and struggles over the extent to which educational opportunity should be guaranteed and extended by the state. The introduction of mass public schooling in the nineteenth century was itself supported by arguments that all children, regardless of class or social background, should have access to common educational experiences. State-supported schooling ensured that children would be able to attend school even if their parents could not afford to pay tuition costs. Compulsory attendance legislation from the late nineteenth and early twentieth centuries, and later enforcement of truancy regulations to ensure that children were actually in the classroom, expanded the state's role beyond simple assurances that all children had access to schooling. Opposition to these initiatives was countered by arguments that schooling was necessary for the public good and that its domain superseded the interests of any particular individuals or groups. Until recently, the status of education—as one of a limited number of universal social programs available on an open, affordable, and accessible basis to all eligible Canadian residents—has been relatively unchallenged (Rice and Prince, 2000: 169).

The justification of schooling as a resource for the common good has been the basis of repeated attempts (not all of which have been successful) to introduce, modify, or delete particular curricula, programs, and services because they were targeted at other than the general clientele of the public school system. Previous chapters have revealed how, over the years, courses in areas such as physical education, family life, citizenship education, multicultural studies, Aboriginal studies, computer and technological education, and anti-racism education have been added to curricula. Schools have come to take on diverse new roles, including counselling, public health, and other social services. At the same time, education systems remain vulnerable to lobbying to remove curricula, programs, personnel, or materials deemed too costly, unnecessary, or offensive to certain groups.

Debates over the ability of formal schooling to provide conditions for **equality of opportunity** must take into consideration the ideological nature of claims about the "common good." Such claims typically are made on the basis of interests expressed in accordance with the requirements or demands of particular social constituencies, posed in such a way as to represent the general interest. In the most general terms, for instance, there is likely to be widespread agreement with the idea that schools should teach literacy and mathematical and social skills, among other things. However, the kinds of curricula, teaching approaches, learning materials, and modes of evaluation used in the teaching of these areas, and how these are combined with other aspects of the schooling process, involve choices to be made from a range of alternatives. In this way, what is taught, how it is transmitted, and what is conveyed to the learner are rarely universally representative but, instead, are reflections of inequalities and power arrangements that operate both within the education system and through the wider society.

The issue of educational equality also raises questions about the extent to which all students should be subjected to identical educational experiences. The argument that it is sufficient for schools to present a common curriculum to all students places the onus on students, regardless of their social backgrounds, to compete with one another on the basis of universal standards. School programs that integrate or mainstream children from families that do not speak the language of instruction or who are physically or mentally disabled, for instance, are founded on notions that equate equality with "sameness" of treatment. An alternative position recognizes that different groups have distinct needs to which education must respond. Curricula and teaching methods that fail to take social differences into account are disadvantageous to minority students. "Anti-racism education" is based on the view that educators must incorporate into educational processes both acceptance and understanding of racial diversity and pedagogical strategies to combat systemic oppression (Dei, 1996). Similarly, feminist pedagogy emphasizes that gender disparities are reinforced when educators fail to recognize how male and female students have different social experiences that translate into different learning styles.

Inequalities: Alternative Perspectives and Experiences

Current debates over social and educational inequality are shaped by conflicting demands from various interests and perspectives. Governments in several nations, including Canada and its provinces and territories, have been increasingly responsive to neo-liberal and individualist arguments that the state should not, and cannot afford to, offer too broad a range of programs and services in public enterprises like education when these are targeted to the needs of what have come to be defined as "special interests." Affirmative action, education equity, inclusive curricula, multicultural education, English as a second language (ESL), sexuality, and arts and music programs are some of the areas singled out by such critics as "frills" or private issues that are costly, socially divisive, and counterproductive to educational needs in a highly competitive economic environment. Members of minority groups and other people most affected by lack of access to meaningful social and economic opportunity, by contrast, have become increasingly more vocal about their rights and entitlements. These concerns are frequently raised as a consequence of experiences of continuing discrimination and obstacles to the fulfillment of equity objectives. Cutbacks in programs and state services designed to enhance educational and economic opportunities have placed the least privileged segments of the population in an even more vulnerable position when they cannot gain access to the programs and resources required for competitive success.

Differing interpretations of the meaning of educational opportunity and inequality are also associated with differences in how educational opportunity is assessed or measured. The remainder of this chapter will focus on the most common determinants of inequality, addressing such factors as educational attainment, participation rates of different social groups, and relationships among education and income, labour force participation, and other relevant measures.

Before these indicators are examined, however, it is important to emphasize that educational success or failure cannot be understood only in quantitative terms. Acknowledgement must be given to the human and social dimensions that contribute to differing educational experiences and outcomes. Education is not an abstract process but a composite of lived practices with real consequences for people's lives and futures. As emphasized throughout this book, schooling is characterized by a complex array of day-to-day occurrences in educational settings that intersect with external demands and structures. Success and failure take on differing interpretations just as they are produced through the interaction between personal experiences and social structural forces. For instance, we tend to place the greatest social and economic value on the attainment of a university degree, yet the completion of a high school diploma may be a major accomplishment for a person who has returned to school much later in life after being forced in youth to work to support a family following an interruption such as the death of a parent or an unplanned teen pregnancy. Similarly, a mid-range grade may be viewed as a failure by a student whose parents expect nothing less than performance that will lead to admission to an elite university, but the same grade may be a triumph for a student designated by school officials as "at risk" or who is experiencing life difficulties or struggling to maintain an interest in school.

The Assembly of First Nations (1988: 72) points out that notions of educational quality from which measures of success and failure are derived are culturally laden, and emphasizes that educational success from a First Nations perspective should be based on the following goals: "(1) education should prepare children to gain the necessary skills for successful living and to contribute to community and (2) education should reinforce the student's cultural identity." The Canadian Council on Learning (2007b) has reiterated the need to understand educational opportunity and performance by situating educational practices and student experience in an overall social context; they are not merely objects to be measured in quantitative terms (see Box 5.3). Regardless of how opportunity and performance are defined or interpreted, they have important consequences for people's lives and well-being.

Dimensions of Educational Inequality

The following sections examine the most prevalent indicators associated with educational inequality, taking into account that schooling and its outcomes cannot fully be understood in isolation from the social practices that constitute or contribute to school life. The discussion highlights questions about who is enrolled in educational programs, what the characteristics are of students who enrol in and graduate from particular programs, and what the benefits of formal education are for people from particular social backgrounds.

The question of who goes to school can be answered simply, at least in general terms. Almost every Canadian, with the exception of the very youngest and most elderly, is engaged in some educational activity on a regular basis. Nearly one-fifth of the total population is enrolled in full-time formal educational programs. Nearly all children (about 19 out of 20) aged 6 to 16 attend school on a full-time basis, and over 90 per cent of youth or young adults now graduate from high school. Among young adults in the 20–4 age group about 40 per cent were enrolled in full-time educational programs and many more were engaged in part-time studies in 2010–11. In addition, about half of the adult population participate in organized forms of adult learning and at least four out of five Canadians regularly engage in informal learning activities, citing new skills and knowledge they develop in community or personal activities in any given year (Statistics Canada and CMEC, 2011b; Rubenson et al., 2007: 14; Livingstone and Scholtz, 2007).

The composition of school-age populations has undergone significant transformation. Immigration has contributed significantly to the linguistic, racial, and cultural mix in Canadian schools, especially in the largest metropolitan centres. The latest available census data reveal that in 2006, about one in five school-age children in Vancouver and one in seven in Toronto were born outside Canada, with recent immigrants (those arriving between 2001 and 2006) representing up to half of the non-Canadian-born cohort. Immigrants arrive from diverse places and backgrounds; about 60 per cent of recent arrivals were born in Asia and the Middle East, and over half of recent school-age immigrants in Vancouver and Toronto speak languages other than English or French at home (Statistics Canada, 2007a). Aboriginal people are also becoming more concentrated among school-age populations, especially in the Prairie provinces and northern regions. Aboriginal people represent about 3.8 per cent of the Canadian population, but the proportion rises to 6.3 per cent among children aged 14 and under, including one-third of children in Manitoba and over one-quarter in Saskatchewan (Statistics Canada, 2008a).

In addition to racial, cultural, and linguistic diversity, schooling incorporates large proportions of students who encounter various social, economic, and physical challenges. One in ten Canadian children, and nearly one in five of those ages 5 to 14 living with a lone parent, lives in a low-income household (Statistics Canada and CMEC, 2011b: Table A.3.1.2). An estimated 4 per cent of Canadian children of ages 5–14 have physical disabilities or chronic conditions that limit their daily activities, while at least one in four children under the age of 11 exhibits one or more learning or behavioural problems (Kohen et al., 2007; Willms, 2002: 54). Whereas children with special needs were previously segregated into special classrooms or excluded from schools, about 60 per cent of students who receive special education for learning disabilities, emotional and behavioural problems, speech impairment, intellectual or physical disabilities, or other problems are now integrated into regular classrooms for most of their instruction and school-related activities (Bohatyretz and Lipps, 1999: 9; Kohen et al., 2007). Parallel trends in the growth of student diversity are exhibited, in many cases, within post-secondary and adult training institutions.

Educators and educational institutions face a significant challenge to balance student diversity, through strategies that promote integration and inclusion, with external demands for differentiated social and economic outcomes. Major discrepancies in educational participation, performance, and outcomes persist, and educational inequality is especially associated with such factors as gender, race and ethnicity, Aboriginal status, social class, and region.

Gender

Gender-based inequalities are less evident within enrolment patterns than in terms of what happens within educational processes. Because almost all children attend school, there are no significant gender differentiations in enrolments at the elementary and secondary levels. Long-standing gender inequities in post-secondary enrolments have shifted over the past two decades. Overall, proportionately more men than women were enrolled in post-secondary programs until the mid-1980s, after which time the number of women has exceeded the number of men. For example, the ratio of female to male full-time undergraduate university students was 0.8 to 1 in the mid-1970s, but this ratio has steadily risen to current levels approaching 1.4 to 1. Women's participation rates are even higher when part-time students are taken into account. While women's participation rates have remained somewhat lower in graduate studies, women now constitute about 55 per cent of all students in master's programs and just under half (47 per cent) of students in doctoral programs (Statistics Canada and CMEC, 2007: 273–4; CAUT, 2012: 42–4). Some critics, such as Hoff Summers (2000), view these kinds of trends as evidence that schools, influenced by feminism, have contributed to ideologies and practices that produce disadvantage for males. The evidence, however, points to a much more complex picture.

Processes of Gender Segmentation and Reproduction

The literature on educational processes reveals how **gender segmentation** can be reproduced both directly and indirectly within educational programs, even though schools have adopted numerous proactive measures to maintain a posture of gender neutrality. Differentiation according to gender—along with class and race—occurs both through streaming and in the different signals and messages transmitted within the educational experience, as well as in the social and material resources children and youth are equipped with by their family environments (Gaskell, 1992; Andres and Adamuti-Trache, 2008). These signals, operating in conjunction with such other factors as preconceptions held by parents and peers, gender-specific role models, distorted media representations, inadequate curricular materials, teacher biases, insufficient school support, and classroom practices that reinforce stereotypical or segmented gender expectations, influence the production of distinct educational paths or careers for male and female students (Bernhard and Nyhof-Young, 1994; Eyre, 1991). Female students also perceive signals from teachers, in the form of comments or attitudes, to channel them into gender-segregated occupational tracks (Crysdale et al., 1999: 33). In senior grades and post-secondary studies, female teachers are frequently absent or clustered in selected fields, contributing to a lack of role models in the classroom and a potentially limited capacity for consideration of issues of critical importance to female learners. Sometimes, even efforts meant to alleviate gender inequity can have the opposite impact. Kenway and Willis (1998: 208–9) point to a "gender/generation gap" through which some teachers maintain outdated notions of gender that do not take into account significant changes in students' lives and identities.

Children and youth, through their varied interactions with parents, peers, teachers, and other people during schooling and related experiences, are likely to develop a relatively systematic understanding of what the dominant norms and expectations are concerning gender and sexuality (Arnot, 2009). Nonetheless, the messages that students receive about gender and gender roles within schools and through popular media and other relations outside of school can often offset or contradict one another (Moss and Attar, 1999: 143). Despite the availability of an array of educational, career, and personal options that exceeds opportunities open to previous generations, adolescent girls are also under considerable pressure to present themselves in a manner that is at once assertive and modest, assessed against physical and behavioural standards that may be incompatible with one another and difficult to achieve. As Coulter (2012: 8) observes, the pressure that even young girls encounter to be both "bright and beautiful" creates artificial expectations that are even more difficult to fulfill "when teachers deny the actual intelligence of girls and attribute academic success only to uninspired, plodding, hard work, or characterize as 'pushy' those girls with ambition and drive." Adolescent girls are considerably more likely than their male counterparts to hold negative views about themselves and to express lack of confidence about their appearance and capabilities, which often are manifested in serious eating disorders and other problems associated with low self-esteem (Bibby, 2001: 40; Canadian Women's Foundation, 2005: 18–20).

Paradoxically, while many of the tensions and insecurities are directed inwardly for many girls and young women, media and public scrutiny point in another direction, towards phenomena like aggression, bullying, and violence expressed in terms of the problem of "mean girls." Such concerns, though typically overstating the actual occurrence of problem behaviours, draw attention to the complex relationships that adolescent girls and boys must negotiate within contemporary circumstances that pose numerous challenges and uncertainties for them. They cannot be understood without reference to other contextual issues and phenomena, such as the persistence of high instances of sexual assault and violent crimes committed by males against girls and women (Johnson and Dawson, 2011). Concerns about female aggression are sometimes also motivated by a backlash against feminism and other supposed threats to a social order governed by norms that privilege patriarchal, masculinist, and heterosexual standards. These fears also contribute to new ways of labelling and stigmatizing girls' identities and behaviours in relation to those of boys (Landry, 2008).

However, while these may divert attention away from issues that are far more pressing for youth, they also highlight both the risks that youth often face and the shifting expectations about gender, sexuality and sexual orientation, identity, marginality, and overall social positioning that make it difficult for youth to find their way in a changing world. Discourses associated with the relative success or failure of girls and boys, for instance, reinforce a binary view of sex difference. Whether drawing from traditional gender stereotypes or creating new ones, the focus on boys and girls as discrete categories of youth fails to take into account the full range of variances, problems, and capacities encompassed within childhood. At the same time, such categorization ignores how these stereotypes and the standards employed to justify them come about (Martino, 2011; Coulter, 2012).

One way in which the diverse pathways associated with gender can be understood is to examine the areas or programs of study pursued by post-secondary students. Women's increased overall educational participation has been characterized by growing proportions of women in nearly every field of study. Nonetheless, as illustrated in Figure 8.1, the gender-based distribution of university students remains highly uneven. In tandem with women's overall rising post-secondary participation rates, approximate

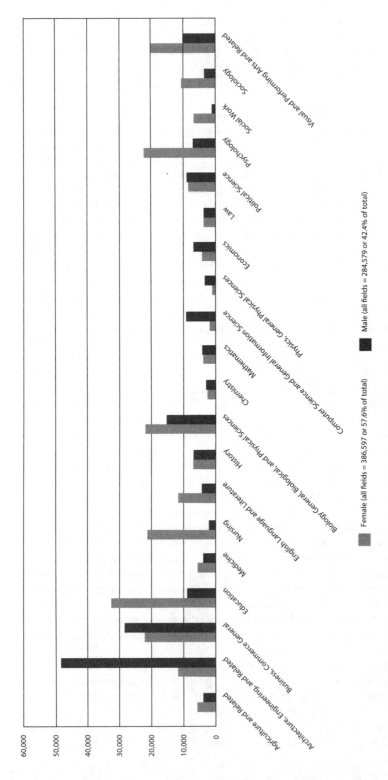

Figure 8.1 Full-Time Equivalent Enrolment in Selected University Undergraduate Programs by Fields of Study and Gender, 2008–9

Source: Data from CAUT (2011: 27–35).

gender parity has been reached or reversed in such traditionally male-dominated fields as agriculture, law, medicine, biological sciences, history, political science, and many business-related fields. Women also have had an increased presence, in both numerical and proportional terms, in economics, mathematics, chemistry, and, to a lesser extent, engineering. The main focus of women's increased university participation remains, however, in fields already dominated by women, notably education, nursing, arts and cultural fields, English (along with other languages not included in the figure), sociology, social work, and psychology. Similar trends pertain for community college enrolment as well, where women are highly concentrated in clerical, human services, or support-related career programs while men dominate in fields related to physical sciences, engineering and applied sciences, and information technologies.

These trends carry through to graduation, which provides a more precise indicator of specified fields of study. Consistent with enrolment trends, substantially more women than men receive undergraduate university degrees in all but a few major disciplinary areas—architecture, engineering and related technologies, mathematics, and computer and information sciences—in which cases men constituted three-quarters or more of degree recipients in 2009–10 (CAUT, 2012: 46). Only limited evidence suggests that the emergence of the new economy or knowledge society discussed in the previous chapter, with its emphasis on innovation, changing business opportunities, and information technology, is contributing to some convergence in fields of study. While degrees and diplomas in fields associated with business, management, and commerce demonstrate some of the highest growth among areas of post-secondary studies for both men and women, growth rates tend to be much higher for men than for women in the main fields related to innovation, such as computers, information technologies, and engineering (Figure 8.2). As a result, too great an emphasis on innovative fields of study, at least as currently posed, may widen rather than narrow gender divides.

The differential educational experiences of males and females contribute to the **social reproduction** of important inequalities beyond the classroom. Figures 8.3 and 8.4 offer two perspectives on intersections among gender inequalities, education, and income. Consistent with patterns observed in the previous chapter, Figure 8.4 demonstrates that average earnings increase for each subsequent level of educational attainment for both men and women. Nonetheless, both figures reveal the persistence of a gender-based wage gap, with women's earnings lower than those of men at every level. The gender gap in earnings generally decreases as education increases, with women periodically having the advantage at the doctoral level. However, relatively few women possess doctoral degrees, in part as a consequence of gender-biased channelling in earlier years of education. As the number of persons with higher levels of credentials has increased over the past two decades, the overall impact on earnings has been different for men and women. Men have generally increased their earnings with each subsequent level of education, while the returns to education for women are less pronounced. Analyzing trends in census data between 1985 and 2000, for instance, Boothby and Drewes (2006: 11) contrast women's earnings relative to those for men, observing that, for women, "Trades certification appears to have had little to no impact on earnings over high-school completers . . . the earnings benefits of continuing on to a college diploma have increased for women, but by a smaller margin than is the case for men . . . [and] earnings for university-educated women have increased very little in relation to high-school completers." As policy and investment decisions come to highlight high-tech and knowledge-sector work, there are dangers that patterns in

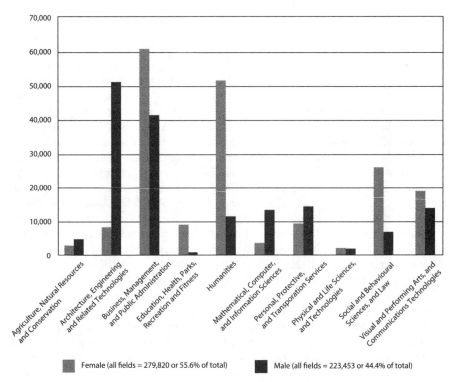

Female (all fields = 279,820 or 55.6% of total)   Male (all fields = 223,453 or 44.4% of total)

Figure 8.2 Full-Time Equivalent Community College Enrolment
by Major Disciplines and Gender, 2008–9

Source: Data from CAUT (2011: 26).

labour market supply and selectivity (such as women's increased overall post-secondary participation concentration in areas like education, health, and general fields of study, in comparison with men's over-representation in engineering, technology, and related fields), combined with more diffuse forms of labour market discrimination, will perpetuate or widen the observed gender gaps (Frenette and Coulombe, 2007: 22, 24). These trends point to the importance of understanding the intersection of family, labour market, and educational factors.

Processes that contribute to gender segregation in education also operate in a similar manner, and reinforce one another, in the spheres of work and family life. Domestic responsibilities, orientations to marriage and family, and personal experiences, among other factors, affect educational attainment and employment and career prospects (Hamilton, 2005). The actual or projected interruption of an education program or career due to pregnancy or family considerations, for instance, normally affects women's lives and opportunities more than it does those of men. As many women have experienced benefits through access to education, both personally and in terms of their ability to acquire better-paying, more secure jobs, there has been some broadening of social opportunities and sharing of tasks in the household and other spheres of life. Nonetheless, especially in working-class families, women continue to bear the highest degree of responsibility for domestic work, caring, and maintenance

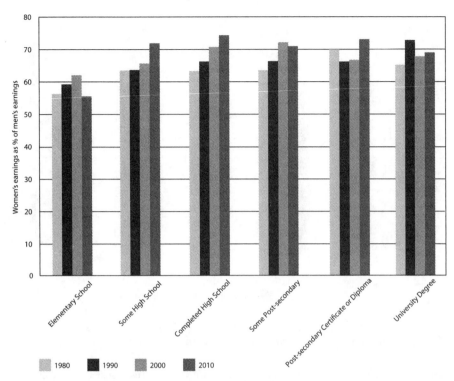

Figure 8.3 Female-to-Male Earnings by Highest Level of Education Completed, Selected Years, 1980–2010

Source: Compiled from data in Statistics Canada, CANSIM Table 2020104.

of activities within communities and non-profit sectors (Neysmith et al., 2012; Pupo and Duffy, 2007). Women in both managerial and professional occupations and in lower-paying and less secure jobs—especially those jobs that entail caring responsibilities—experience substantially higher degrees of work overload and work–life stress than men (Duxbury and Higgins, 2003: 12–13). The enrolment and graduation trends outlined earlier suggest that education will continue to be an important avenue for women to gain entry into non-traditional positions and occupations and will contribute to greater gender parity in terms of labour force participation, wages, and other benefits. In Canada, women's wages have risen more than men's since the late 1980s, in part reflecting the gains in education and occupational choice exercised by younger cohorts of women (Drolet, 2011).

Nonetheless, potential advances in these areas are limited by internal labour market dynamics and persistent gender discrimination, as well as by more general economic restructuring of the kind discussed in Chapter 7, which creates pressure to downsize the labour force, change skill requirements for workers, and minimize labour costs. Overall, among full-time, full-year workers, median earnings for women are about three-quarters of those for men (Cool, 2010: 2). Even when formal education has worked to the initial advantage of women who obtain relatively high-status jobs, women continue to be disadvantaged compared to men over the course of their

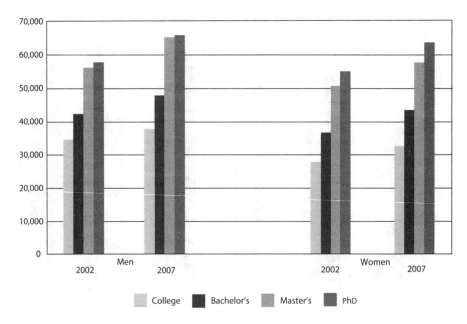

Figure 8.4 Median Earnings ($) of 2000 and 2005 Post-Secondary
Graduates Working Full-Time Two Years after Graduation
(1995 constant dollars)

Note: Excludes graduates who pursued further education in the two years after their graduation.

Source: Compiled from data in Allen and Vaillancourt (2004: 31) and Bayard and Greenlee (2009: 59).

entire careers (Canadian Labour Congress, 2008: 6–7; Frenette and Coulombe, 2007). Despite improvements in women's educational attainment and benefits, evidence demonstrates that gender inequalities still exist with respect to the kinds of educational credentials people receive and in the connections between education and subsequent life circumstances.

Racial and Ethnic Minorities

Increasing racial diversity is one of the major characteristics of contemporary Canadian society. The rising number of people from different social backgrounds is accompanied by growing heterogeneity and complexity in relationships within and among social groups in relation to different social, economic, cultural, and individual circumstances and experiences. Canada's history of education for minority populations is mixed, although schooling has frequently played a strong role in marginalizing and suppressing the interests of large segments of the Aboriginal population as well as black populations and other visible minority groups in some regions. In general terms, evidence suggests that increased educational opportunities, especially since World War II, have been beneficial for racial and ethnic minorities. Nonetheless, several important, and sometimes shifting, differences exist in the educational experiences and achievements among various racial and ethnic groups. In his landmark study of social stratification in Canada, Porter (1965) stressed that barriers to equitable educational participation have contributed to the inability of minority

Box 8.2 Differences in the Relationship between Education and Earnings

In the United States, as in Canada, differences in fields of study and in the economic returns from education are strongly associated with social factors such as gender and race. Analysis conducted through the Center on Education and the Workforce at Georgetown University reveals several striking patterns in who is most likely to have bachelor's degrees in specific fields and the earnings associated with degrees for different majors (Carnevale et al., 2011). The authors observe that

> different majors have different economic value. While going to college is undoubtedly a wise decision, what you take while you're there matters a lot, too. On average . . . Bachelor's degree holders earn 84 per cent more than those with a high school diploma. However, returns to majors run a wide gamut. At the extreme, the highest earning major earns 314 per cent more at the median than the lowest-earning major at the median. (Ibid., 6)

The majors with the highest median earnings are in engineering fields like petroleum and mechanical engineering, in which over 90 per cent of graduates are male; women constitute more than 10 per cent of graduates in only one of the top 10 highest-paying fields—mathematics and computer sciences, in which one-third of majors are female. By contrast, the fields with the lowest median earnings, such as early childhood education, counselling psychology, and social work, are highly feminized (ibid., 17, 93, 170–1). The findings also reveal strong patterns of racial segmentation, with some variations. Graduates of Asian heritage are highly concentrated in some of the highest-paying fields such as computer engineering and other scientific and technological majors, in contrast to African-American graduates, who tend to be most heavily represented in lower-paying fields related to counselling, social work, and health-care services, while Hispanic and other racial minority graduates are dispersed across a wide range of disciplines (ibid., 15–17).

Finally, the study shows that earnings are unevenly distributed within many particular majors or fields. Within engineering, for example, where the median earnings for all full-time, full-year workers with a terminal bachelor's degree were $75,000, male median earnings were $79,000 while those for women were $62,000; median earnings for white workers were $80,000 compared to $72,000 for Asians, $60,000 for African-Americans, $56,000 for Hispanics, and $57,000 for those in other racial or ethnic groups. In education-related majors, which in contrast to engineering are female-dominated, median earnings were $42,000, representing $48,000 for men and $40,000 for women, while the gap across racial groups was smaller, with median incomes ranging between $36,000 for those in the "other" racial and ethnic category to $42,000 for white and African-American graduates (ibid., 34–8).

ethnic groups to attain proportional representation in positions of power and privilege, thereby undermining the claim that our social system is fully **meritocratic** and democratic. Today, although Porter's argument has been challenged and reassessed by many researchers, some of those inequalities remain in place or have been subsumed by new forms of inequality. While Canada's schools include numerous exemplary cases of progressive multicultural and multiracial relationships, serious problems—racial profiling, race-based violence and harassment, and differential educational treatment

Box 8.3 Anti-Racism Education

Anti-racism education builds from an acknowledgement of the diffuse impact of race and racial inequalities, working towards understandings and practices that transcend race-based power relations and other forms of inequality. This process includes not only sensitization to personal identities, stereotypes, and discriminatory actions, but also recognition of the need to address long-lasting legacies of historical and structural injustices. In recent years, often motivated by serious racist incidents, many school boards, provincial education ministries, and other education bodies have introduced anti-racism guidelines along with programs and resources to sensitize educators, students, parents, and others about racism and other forms of discrimination and support the mobilization of anti-racist education and practice.

The Canadian Race Relations Foundation began in 1999 to organize a major national campaign, called "See people who they really are: Unite against racism," that incorporated written and video documentation to assist educators, students, and members of the general public in their efforts to understand and take action to counter racism in Canada (see www.uniteagainstracism.ca). The latest developments in this strategy include the airing of a series of public service announcements in several languages, along with the development of a study guide to enhance awareness of racism and discriminatory practices and their impact (including attention directed to the experiences of slavery and Aboriginal peoples in Canada). This guide also teaches about human rights and outlines strategies to combat racism.

Similarly, school boards and other education authorities have implemented guidelines and procedures typified by the examples below. The Toronto District School Board (2012: 5) guidelines, policies, and procedures concerning anti-racism and ethnocultural equity outline several areas of commitment, some of which include

- ensuring that the principles and practices of anti-racism and ethnocultural equity permeate the curriculum in all subject areas;
- examining and challenging racist and exclusive curriculum in order to ensure inclusivity;
- developing a process to determine whether discriminatory biases related to Aboriginal, racial, ethnocultural, and faith communities are present in existing learning materials, programs, or practices . . . ;
- providing adequate resources and training: to assist all staff in becoming agents of change; to use curriculum effectively in order to promote critical thinking; and to challenge racism and discrimination; . . .

and pathways for particular minority groups—reveal the pervasive impact of both overt racism and more covert forms of discrimination in many aspects of Canadian life.

In terms of overall or average educational achievement, persons of Aboriginal ancestry (discussed more fully in the next section) have significantly lower overall rates of educational attainment and are much less likely to attend and complete post-secondary studies than other Canadians. Among other people within the adult population and in the labour force, those of Jewish and Chinese origin have the highest

- supporting student leadership programs in anti-racism education and equity;
- ensuring that the contributions to Canadian and world history and historiography from Aboriginal, racial, ethnocultural, and faith communities are included accurately in all aspects of the curriculum;
- ensuring that curriculum materials and learning resources are allocated to challenge hate groups and hate propaganda against Aboriginal, racial, ethnocultural, and faith communities, and/or any other social identity.

Similar guidelines and policies have been introduced in other jurisdictions, though the degree of detail and procedures to safeguard implementation or respond to violations vary substantially. In Calgary, for example, which has been the site of recent marches by white supremacist groups, the Calgary Board of Education policy is expressed in an administrative regulation on anti-racism and equity outlining broad principles, some of which include statements of belief:

- THAT a quality environment is characterized by opportunities for all students to engage in relevant curriculum, to be the recipients of just and fair assessment, to have access to full range of services and resources, regardless of the learner's ethno cultural, racial or linguistic background;
- THAT a quality learning environment is free from racism, inequity and discrimination;
- THAT identified instances of racism, inequity and discrimination provide learners and teachers with quality learning opportunities to candidly explore issues, identify systemic barriers, as well as assertively challenge and then responsibly act to alleviate injustices;
- THAT learning materials with racial, cultural and religious biases in content, language or illustration shall evoke critical analyses by teachers and students;
- THAT all students bring linguistic, cultural, educational and personal experiences to school which form their foundations for learning, and consequently, that teachers' practices must reflect respect for an appreciation of diverse cultural experiences, knowledge, languages, preferred ways of learning and backgrounds. (Calgary Board of Education, 2012:1–2)

While these policies and guidelines are useful in fostering dialogue, promoting tolerance, and creating a foundation for safe, inclusive schools, critics are concerned that many such initiatives are not implemented fully or adequately, and do not go far enough in addressing the roots of white privilege and other forms of inequality.

average years of schooling and are most likely to have a university degree. Particularly among the foreign-born, those from Southern European origins tend to have the lowest levels of formal education (Abada et al., 2009: 13–15). These patterns endured throughout much of the twentieth century, but visible minorities—especially Asian men—as well as Southern and Eastern European groups, have experienced considerable gains in their average educational attainment over the last four decades (ibid.; Guppy and Davies, 1998: 23; Finnie et al., 2005: 19–20).

To a certain extent, the modified reproduction of racial and ethnic inequality can be explained by immigration policies and practices that have placed increasing emphasis since the late 1960s on the selective recruitment of highly qualified labour. Until the post–World War II period, the nation's labour market needs were met predominantly by Canadian-born workers augmented periodically by immigrant labour, mostly from Europe or other industrially developed English- or French-speaking nations, to fill low-wage or semi-skilled positions in agriculture and manufacturing sectors. By the late 1960s, the gradual emergence of what is referred to in the previous chapter as the post-industrial or service economy created conditions in which Canada had to look to additional sources to secure qualified workers, especially in many occupations that required professional credentials or specialized skills and training. The aging of the post-war baby-boom generation and their impending retirement, combined with relatively low domestic birth rates, have fuelled further demands for immigrants to sustain the workforce and population base through the twenty-first century. Beginning in 1967, immigration policy and selection criteria were amended to apply a point system recognizing factors like age, credentials, language proficiency, and demand for job skills rather than country and race of origin. These transitions have had significant consequences for the relations between education and minority populations. In particular, recent immigrants represent considerable social and cultural diversity: they are now predominantly from visible minority populations originating in nations throughout Asia and other non-Western regions; they are increasingly well-educated but not always fluent in English or French; and they tend to place a high value on the education of their children.

The impact of these policy changes is evident in comparisons of educational attainments by immigrants and Canadian-born populations. In the years immediately following implementation of the points system (during the 1970s and 1980s), slightly more than half (52 per cent) of immigrants aged 25–64 who arrived in Canada had high school or less (compared to between 55 and 75 per cent of the general population in these age cohorts over the same period). Recent immigrants in general are even more highly educated than the Canadian population. In 2011, the proportion of Canadian-born labour force participants aged 25–54 who had a university degree (25 per cent) was marginally less than those who had no more than high school credentials (28 per cent), whereas among landed immigrants within these age cohorts who had immigrated during the previous 10 years, over half (about 55 per cent) had a university degree and fewer than one out of five had high school or less (calculated from Statistics Canada, CANSIM Table 282-0106).

Intersecting Forms of Diversity

The relationship among race and ethnicity, immigration, and education and the economic benefits associated with education are considerably more complex than these general trends reveal, indicating substantial variations according to class, gender, race, and other significant characteristics. Various immigrant and visible minority groups are clustered at both professional, high-skill, and (especially among visible minority women) lower-status occupational positions (Pendakur, 2000: 151–6; Guppy and Davies, 1998: 122–3). Immigrants, in part due to the credentials and capacities that they bring with them, perform relatively well overall on many economic criteria. Intensified global demand for knowledge-sector workers with specialized skills and advanced credentials elevates the importance of immigration for securing workers to fill positions in many professional occupations and scientific and technical fields. Nonetheless, as the previous chapter has revealed, these sectors constitute relatively limited proportions of the total labour force. Immigrant and migrant labour has been an important source to fill positions in manufacturing and construction industries, as well as in food, accommodation, and other service areas frequently characterized by low wages, poor working conditions, and limited job security. Recent immigrants, in particular, have encountered particular difficulties, relative to persons born in Canada and even compared to previous cohorts of immigrants, in finding secure employment, especially in fields for which they are qualified (Community Foundations of Canada, 2010: 2–3). Such problems typically diminish over time as immigrants settle into the host society, improve their English or French language competency, and gain Canadian contacts and work experience, but this process of labour market integration has slowed down or even ceased for some cohorts of recent immigrants.

Many immigrants, especially women and visible minorities, encounter selective barriers that have long-term implications for career options, occupational mobility, and life prospects. Recent data, including from the 2006 census, reveal that the earnings gap between immigrants and Canadian-born workers has increased, even among the highly educated. In 1980, immigrant men and women who had arrived in the five previous years earned on average 85 per cent of what Canadian-born earners received; by 2005, however, the earnings ratio had widened, with recent immigrants making only 63 per cent and 56 per cent of Canadian-born counterparts for men and women, respectively (Statistics Canada, 2008c: 21). Some of the gap tends to narrow over time, and considerable variations occur both between immigrants and non-immigrants and among different immigrant groups, but, overall, immigrants receive lower returns on education and labour market experiences than do persons born in Canada (Ostrovsky, 2008; Reitz, 2007; Zietsma, 2011).

Several proactive measures have been adopted to counter discriminatory practices, policies, and attitudes and to remove barriers that restrict full participation by racial minorities in all spheres of social life. However, overt discrimination, structural barriers, and complex practices such as limited or non-recognition for foreign credentials and work experience continue to have a differential impact on segments of visible minority and immigrant populations. Some immigrant groups—such as those of Chinese, South Asian, Filipino, West Asian, and Arab origins—are more likely than other Canadians to hold a university degree, while others, including black and Latin American men, are less likely to have a degree, and higher than average proportions of women from Southeast Asia and South Asia have less than high school. In contrast to the small pool of highly qualified immigrants who find ready work in their fields, sizable proportions of the immigrant population (especially among women) begin in a relatively strong employment position yet have almost no career mobility (Creese et al., 1991: 72–3; Li, 2003: 122–3).

Similarly, although education characteristically has an impact on alleviating poverty within the general population, that relationship often does not hold for immigrants, especially those in visible minority groups (Kazemipur and Halli, 2001: 234; National Council of Welfare, 2012). Tran (2004: 11), summarizing trends since the mid-1980s, observes, "Foreign-born visible minority men, especially recent immigrants, saw their labour market outcomes deteriorate faster than Canadian-born non-visible minority men," while among women, "employment rates increased for all except foreign-born visible minorities although foreign-born visible minority women were more highly educated than most other women." In addition, immigrant children and their families, depending on their circumstances and previous experiences, have varying capacities to negotiate the demands associated with new school and community environments. In addition to the process of transition itself, immigrants often are confronted with unfamiliar school rules and procedures, cultural and linguistic barriers, uncertain access to support and resources, economic vulnerability, and sometimes trauma and victimization during or prior to leaving their home countries (Ngo and Schleifer, 2004: 30).

Two prevalent themes emerge in the literature on race, ethnicity, and Canadian schooling. (1) Race—and, to a certain extent, ethnicity—does have an impact on people's educational experiences and social opportunities. (2) Ethnicity and race cannot be understood in isolation from social class, gender, and other important social characteristics. The increasing number and diversity of immigrants, and especially the high concentrations of immigrant populations in larger metropolitan areas, have elevated the profile of race relations and multicultural issues in Canada. These changes have been accompanied by new challenges and opportunities, but they have also raised awareness and frustration over long-standing problems. Recent initiatives to establish Africentric schools in Nova Scotia and Ontario (see Box 5.4), for example, have drawn criticism based on claims that minority rights and segregation are undermining public school values, on the one hand, while highlighting for proponents the historical failure of mainstream education systems to provide adequate cultural validation and educational integration for black students. Similarly, the profusion of media depictions of threats posed by a proliferation of youth gangs, organized in many cases around visible minority or Aboriginal membership, illustrates both the public fears generated over racial diversity and the attraction for some minority group members of alternative lifestyles that promise an escape from the hostility and marginalization they encounter in schools and other social settings.

Several researchers have emphasized the changing and complex nature of race and ethnic relations in Canada, documenting how family, work, schooling, and other institutional environments interact to produce continual modifications and tensions among ethnic identity, ethnic group cohesion, and diverse cultural adaptations (Fleras and Elliott, 2003). Educational policies to promote greater access to post-secondary education have had a significant impact, but have not erased several enduring gaps. In Quebec, for instance, anglophones are more likely to attend and complete university than francophones, reflecting differences in education systems within the province as well as socio-economic and other related factors (Diallo et al, 2009: 41–2). McLaren (2007: 226–7), observing children of West Indian origin in a North York school, notes that underprivileged black students engage in forms of resistance in opposition to dominant school and social expectations if they see that they must attempt to deny their "blackness" to succeed. James (1993), examining the school-to-work transition process for black youth in Toronto, stresses that, while respondents he interviewed tended to assume individual responsibility for their own success or failure, their lives and self-concepts were continually affected by racist stereotypes and structures prevalent both within and beyond schooling. Visible minority and Aboriginal students, though receptive to the substantial opportunities for equity and participation afforded by schooling, remain keenly aware of the many manifestations that they and other students encounter of racism and discrimination (Bibby, 2001: 42–3; James, 2003: 131–64; Schissel and Wotherspoon, 2003: 82–3).

Much as with gender and class, with which they interact, racial and ethnic factors enter into the complex web of social arrangements in such a way as to produce differential experiences and career and educational futures for students of distinct social origins. Research in the United States reveals, for instance, that even in school contexts deemed to be high performing, racially integrated, and situated in relatively affluent areas, schooling culture and social organization can segregate and disadvantage black students relative to their white peers. For black students, both academically and with respect to extracurricular activities,

> their presence in college preparatory courses (known to expand students' knowledge bases in significantly different ways than regular comprehensive high school courses) and their involvement in cultural activities such as band, orchestra, theatre, and Model United Nations, was much lower than that of their Black peers in majority-Black schools. In brief, we found that Black (and Latino) students in the majority-White schools had little to no engagement in specific educational classes or activities that could potentially broaden their cultural horizons. (Carter, 2011: 28)

Jackson (1987: 181) refers to these kinds of school practices, which intersect with the various choices and actions undertaken by students and teachers, as "differentiating practices" that emerge

> as practical organizational solutions to the conflicts and contradictions which both school life and the labour market pose for ethnic minority students. Both the student and the educator may feel justified with their choice of practical solutions, particularly if the student experiences success in his/her courses in the short run. However, this is to disregard the "hidden injury" of long-term educational disadvantage.

The federal government's policy of multiculturalism, in effect since the early 1970s, stands as an important institutional response to the reality of and problems associated with racial and ethnic diversity in Canada. Multiculturalism provides a good example of how state policy has shifted over time in conjunction with differing social realities and conceptions of equality. McAndrew (1995: 165) points out that multiculturalism signifies the state's response to the "pluralist dilemma in education" whereby divergent social interests express "conflicting visions of the role that school plays in either reproducing or transforming ethnic/religious/racial inequalities."

Multiculturalism is intended to foster tolerance and understanding of the broad mosaic of cultural groups within Canadian society. At the same time, it represents the state's interest in perpetuating a common national purpose. In the area of education, in particular, as Fleras and Elliott (1992: 183–5) emphasize, multiculturalism signifies a pronounced change, in jurisdictions outside Quebec, from a preoccupation with integration and assimilation in compliance with English-speaking, white standards of conformity to official recognition of pluralism and diversity, encompassing among its objectives the desire "(a) to diminish the ethnic 'problem'; (b) to eliminate discrimination and promote intergroup harmony; (c) to foster genuine equality and justice for ethnic minorities; and (d) to improve intercultural sharing, understanding, and communication."

In education, multiculturalism has been implemented in various ways across Canada, including such measures as heritage language instruction, the development of curricula to represent diverse cultural traditions, cross-cultural training for educational workers and administrators, and the provision of specific services or opportunities for minority students. The uniqueness of multicultural educational policy and initiatives in each province or region reflects both the fact that education is a provincial responsibility and the reality whereby each jurisdiction has its own distinctive cultural composition and political climate (McAndrew, 1995: 170–4). In general terms, multicultural policy has changed in emphasis since the mid-1980s from an initial concern with cultural understanding and tolerance of racial or ethnic differences towards a more active orientation on race relations, equity issues, and institutional change (Fleras and Elliott, 1992: 68–9). Canadian schools in general have clearly become more sensitive to issues involving cultural diversity and minority learners, although it is difficult to determine how much of this, rather than being the result of the impact of multicultural policies and practices, is due to the reality that many communities are much more racially heterogeneous than they were two or three decades ago.

With respect to anti-racism education, writers such as Alladin (1996) and Henry and Tator (2009: 200ff.) note that, despite several prominent policy statements and initiatives concerned with the eradication of racial bias and discrimination through education, racism continues to be a problem both within schools and in the communities in which they operate. Even programs like ESL, for instance, which are intended to provide training directed to the special needs of students who lack language or social skills essential for success in mainstream classrooms, can marginalize and stigmatize minority children. Rockhill and Tomic (1995: 222) observe that "[t]he segregation of children into special classes for ESL instruction further marks their difference from the other students. When this is coupled with being seen as having a problem, a deficiency or lack, feelings of deviance and shame are reinforced." Multicultural and related programs, in these regards, act in a contradictory way, fostering tolerance of diversity and generating opportunities for minority groups, yet at the same time representing state efforts to manage race and ethnic relations as ongoing problems without providing assurances of full equality for all groups (Kirova, 2008; Wotherspoon, 1995b).

Aboriginal People

Aboriginal people have had a long and often devastating relationship with schooling in Canada. Residential schooling and subsequent encounters with provincial and territorial education systems have contributed to a legacy in which both personal and community experiences of failure, marginalization, and disillusionment are widespread. The Assembly of First Nations (2005: 2), expressing a sentiment echoed by many communities and observers, has declared, with reference to both reserve-based and provincial school systems, that "[t]he current state of First Nations education is unacceptable." Nonetheless, as signified in the title of a recent book, education is also envisioned as "the new buffalo" that will serve as the foundation for cultural survival and empowerment among First Nations and other Aboriginal people (Stonechild, 2006). Aboriginal people represent a relatively small proportion of the total Canadian population, but the Aboriginal population is young, expanding more rapidly than the general population, and highly concentrated in specific regions, including the Prairies and northern territories (Canadian Council on Learning, 2007b: 4).

Before the significance of these factors is discussed in more depth, two general observations are important. First, despite substantial improvements through many promising recent initiatives, Aboriginal people fare considerably less well than other Canadians with respect to educational attainment. Prospects for educational success, in turn, are highly associated with family income or lack of income, housing, crime and victimization in the community, health status, and employment. Second, the Aboriginal population is highly differentiated, representing diverse cultural, legal, social, and economic groupings, identities, and positions (Wotherspoon, 2003).

Problems related to these factors have been most evident for First Nations students living on reserves. Over the course of the decade prior to 2003–4, for instance, the proportion of registered Indians aged 6–16 living on-reserve who were enrolled in full-time schooling declined from 87 per cent to 80 per cent, compared to over 95 per cent of persons of comparable ages in the general population (Indian and Northern Affairs Canada, 2005: 45, 46). Six years later, only one-third (33.3 per cent) of students living on-reserve in their senior year of high school graduated, declining from 35.6 per cent in 2008–9 (Aboriginal Affairs and Northern Development Canada, 2011: 42).

Disparities in educational participation rates are even more pronounced at the post-secondary level. Although the numbers of Aboriginal students and graduates have increased in recent decades, these have been matched or exceeded by overall post-secondary growth. Aboriginal people represent about 5 per cent of the 18–24-year-old age cohort, for example, but only about 3 per cent of all university undergraduate students in Canada; the proportions of the Aboriginal population with university degrees grew by a factor of nearly four times between 1981 and 2006, but the gap in university attainment rates between Aboriginal people and the non-Aboriginal population widened over the same time period (AUCC, 2011: 19). Findings from the longitudinal Youth in Transition Survey, which has tracked the education, work, and life experiences of two large cohorts of young people from across Canada, also reveal that Aboriginal participants are less likely than non-Aboriginal participants to have completed post-secondary programs, with an especially large gap for those with university degrees (Shaenks and Gluszynski, 2009: 30). In 2011, among those aged 25–64, just over half of the off-reserve Aboriginal population (51 per cent of those living in the provinces, with proportions higher among the territorial population), compared with fewer than two out of five in the general population (37 per cent), had high school equivalency or less, while only 11 per cent of the off-reserve Aboriginal population as opposed to 27 per cent of the general population had a university degree (Statistics Canada and Council of Ministers of Education Canada, 2012b: Table D.6.3). Figure 8.5 provides a more detailed look at the distribution of educational credentials across population groups for the population aged 15 and over. The data reveal important differences in educational patterns both within Aboriginal populations and among Aboriginal people, visible minorities, and the population as a whole, suggesting that we must be cautious not to overgeneralize the circumstances that pertain for any social group. Educational attainment is lowest among the Inuit and among registered Indians living on-reserve (close to three-quarters have not yet completed credentials

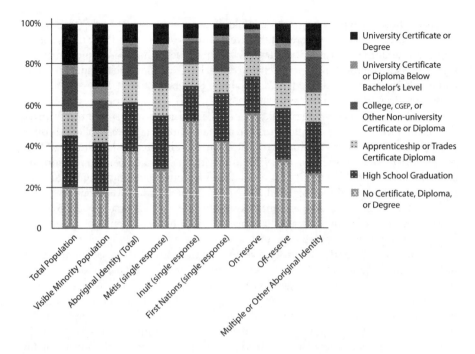

**Figure 8.5 Education by Highest Certificate, Degree, or Diploma,
Ages 15 and Over, Aboriginal Identity Categories,
Visible Minorities, and Total Canadian Population, 2011**

Source: Compiled from data in Statistics Canada, National Household Survey publications 99-012-X2011038, 99-012-X2011044, and 99-012-X2011046.

beyond high school and only about 3 per cent have a university degree), while slightly less than two-thirds of those with Aboriginal identity living off-reserve have Grade 12 or less and just under 10 per cent of Métis and off-reserve Aborginal people have university degrees.

Several factors have contributed to the under-representation and underachievement of Aboriginal peoples in Canadian schooling. As noted earlier, schooling was an important instrument in the early colonization of indigenous peoples by Europeans and in subsequent efforts by the Canadian state to assimilate or acculturate indigenous populations within a dominant framework, often marked by racism and hostility towards Aboriginal peoples and their cultures. As was the case for other visible minorities until well after World War II, First Nations have rarely been given opportunities to represent themselves and their interests in educational decision-making and curricular materials because of the dominant educational orientation towards Anglo-conformity.

In addition, for most Canadians education is a provincial responsibility, whereas education for persons defined by the Indian Act as registered Indians is under federal jurisdiction. One consequence of this divergence has been separate and distinct institutional structures for Aboriginal children, including boarding and residential schools, whose legacy of destruction and pain continues to resonate throughout Aboriginal communities (Schissel and Wotherspoon, 2003; Miller, 1996). This constitutional framework has contributed periodically to jurisdictional disputes that have restricted educational funding and services for First Nations people and produced considerable variations in the nature and quality of educational services provided to different segments of the Aboriginal population. The Assembly of First Nations (2011a: 1) estimates that funding caps imposed by the federal government have meant that First Nations schools have fallen well behind comparable levels of funding for provincial school systems, with an annual average funding shortfall of over 4 per cent between 1996 and 2010. The growing funding gap has meant, as noted in *Maclean's* magazine, that "for the majority of reserve students in Canada, funding equality remains a distant dream" (Sniderman, 2012: 20). Paquette and Fallon (2010: xiii) observe that inadequate funding is only one symptom of a more fundamental problem, that is, a First Nations educational structure that lacks proper governance, oversight, integration, and curricular guidelines is likely to proceed in only "one of two directions: towards assumption by First Nations people of authentic responsibility for the education of their young or towards oblivion as a discredited option in the annals of the history of public education in Canada."

These factors have contributed to the variations in educational attainment among on- and off-reserve registered Indians, non-status Indians, Métis, and Inuit, as shown in Figure 8.5. Compounding these legal and historical circumstances, Aboriginal students have experienced discrimination, lack of culturally sensitive curricula and learning materials, an absence of teachers trained to work with Aboriginal learners and communities, and other problems that have restricted their educational opportunities and success (Satzewich and Wotherspoon, 2000: 126–38). Over two-fifths (42.5 per cent) of First Nations post-secondary students who participated in a national survey in 2011 strongly disagreed with the statement that "First Nations languages, cultures, histories and knowledge are adequately reflected" in their educational institutions, compared to only one-quarter (23 per cent) who strongly agreed (Assembly of First Nations, 2011c: 4).

Recent struggles on the part of Aboriginal peoples to gain input into and control over crucial aspects of their education illustrate the contradictory nature of the relationship between education and socio-economic opportunity. Persistent barriers to educational access and experiences of educational failure have contributed to higher than average rates of unemployment, poverty, and other types of social and economic marginalization among Native peoples. At the same time, education has been regarded by First Nations as a sphere of strategic importance in their quest for self-determination and improved socio-economic conditions. The position paper, "Indian Control of Indian Education," presented by the National Indian Brotherhood (now the Assembly of First Nations) in 1972 and adopted a year later as policy by the federal government, outlined the principles of local control and parental responsibility that would serve as the foundation for subsequent self-government initiatives in the area of education. More recently, the Assembly of First Nations (2010) has reasserted the 1972 vision statement and principles, augmenting the policy framework with a series of explicit objectives to achieve effective First Nations control of lifelong education. Since First Nations began to take control of educational services in the early 1970s, the number of band-operated schools increased steadily to current levels of 518, enrolling three out of five eligible on-reserve First Nations students attending kindergarten, elementary, and secondary school (Standing Senate Committee on Aboriginal Affairs, 2011: 9). The shift to band control has been accompanied by the development of new curricula and teaching/learning aids with First Nations content, cross-cultural training programs, teacher-training programs designed to increase the number of teachers of Aboriginal ancestry, school–community liaisons, and diverse initiatives designed to improve the chances of success for Aboriginal students in both band-controlled and provincial schools. The degree to which educational success occurs in basic education has longer-term implications. Finnie et al. (2005: 22), assessing the relative impact of family background characteristics on post-secondary enrolment, observe that the "negative effect of native ethnicity is played out early on, during the high school years . . . or before, rather than at the point of entry into post-secondary schooling."

The Mixed Significance of Changes in Aboriginal Education

The impact of these developments has been mixed (Assembly of First Nations, 1988; Castellano et al., 2000; Kirkness and Bowman, 1992; Schissel and Wotherspoon, 2003). Growing sensitivity to the need for educational improvement among Aboriginal communities, combined with appropriate programming, services, and personnel, has contributed to increasing educational participation and attainment rates among Aboriginal populations at almost all levels. As part of its jurisdictional obligation to First Nations, the federal government transfers to bands funding for eligible post-secondary students. This support is a crucial factor enabling many First Nations students to pursue advanced education, typically numbering in recent years about 20,000 students and producing about 3,500–3,600 graduates on an annual basis (Assembly of First Nations, 2011b: 18). While these numbers represent dramatic increases since the program was first introduced (just over 800 First Nations students were funded to attend post-secondary programs in 1969–70 and about 8,600 were enrolled by the mid-1980s), the number of funded students has declined since the mid-1990s, when as many as 27,000 students and 4,000 graduates a year were supported by federal funding (ibid., 18; Standing Committee on Aboriginal Affairs and Northern Development, 2007). Because of funding limits and other changes to the program, bands have few options but to pass these limits on to students in one of two ways: "reduce the amount of funding available for each student, or reduce the total number of students receiving financial aid" (AUCC, 2011: 20). Although the actual number of Aboriginal students and graduates is higher than these figures indicate, since many First Nations students and other Aboriginal groups do not qualify for or receive federal funding, the trends nonetheless point to the more general difficulties many Aboriginal students are confronted with in being able to continue into and finance post-secondary programs. The Assembly of First Nations suggests that, apart from the small number of students who are funded annually, at least two to three times that number are prevented from pursuing post-secondary studies because of lack of funding in a context of rising education-related costs (Assembly of First Nations, 2011b: 17; Standing Committee on Public Accounts, 2005: 10).

Despite these barriers, significant numbers of Aboriginal people return to school later in life to upgrade basic education or to achieve higher credentials. More than half of university and college students of Aboriginal ancestry, compared to just over one-third of the general post-secondary student body, are age 22 and over (Canadian Millennium Scholarship Foundation, 2005: 5). Nearly half (48 per cent) of First Nations students who complete post-secondary programs are over 30 years old at the time of graduation (Assembly of First Nations, 2011b: 19). Census data reveal that for those aged 20–4, the non-Aboriginal population has close to double the participation rate of the Aboriginal population (40.5 per cent to 24.1 per cent, respectively), but Aboriginal people have higher participation rates, by factors of two to four times for each age cohort from 30 to 64 (Statistics Canada, 2003: 47). Despite the persistence of numerous obstacles and resistance to change, some elementary and secondary schools have made significant progress to accommodate Aboriginal learners and communities, with demonstrated improvements in student attendance, academic achievement, student motivation and work habits, staff awareness, and the incorporation of positive role models.

Several jurisdictions have begun to incorporate a comprehensive, integrated approach into their educational planning and delivery, recognizing that the most severe problems faced by learners cannot be resolved through schooling alone. The Royal Commission on Aboriginal Peoples, in placing education at the core of its far-reaching aim to achieve full participation in the economy and self-sufficiency of Aboriginal people, has stimulated several innovative educational developments (Castellano et al., 2000), along with numerous parallel initiatives. In Saskatchewan, for instance, the Minister of Education is advised by a First Nations and Métis Education Provincial Advisory Committee, with representation by key education and Aboriginal stakeholders and agencies. The Committee's expressed vision poses

> education as a lifelong process that begins when an individual is born and con-
> tinues through all stages of life. The school, then, is just one part of an individual's
> education and must recognize the role of Elders, family and the community in
> teaching and learning. We also see acceptance of the concept of lifelong learning
> as essential to progress in Aboriginal education, and to the growth of awareness
> among all those involved in education. Our recommendations related to lifelong
> learning are aimed at achieving respect for diverse perspectives on learning, and
> recognition of education as a multifaceted process that occurs continuously, in
> and beyond school. (Saskatchewan Ministry of Education, 2012)

Similar initiatives and principles have been adopted in other jurisdictions. Manitoba, for example, has an Aboriginal Education Directorate with a mandate to provide leadership and co-ordination in areas of Aboriginal education and training both within the education ministry and in partnership with First Nations communities and organizations throughout the province. Nova Scotia's education department has a Mi'kmaq Liaison Office, and other provincial and territorial education ministries have introduced a wide range of programs to support and monitor Aboriginal educational improvement. Insofar as there is an impetus within First Nations, federal, and provincial governance to foster such an integrated approach to social and educational development, it is possible that more meaningful opportunities can be provided to large segments of the Aboriginal population.

Nonetheless, several problems remain. The gradual path towards progress in meeting many of the needs of First Nations students and communities remains hindered by lack of resolution of the kinds of critical problems that Kirkness and Bowman (1992: 52–3) reported on several years ago, including poor attendance and motivation, high dropout rates, poverty and racism, tensions between schools and families, high mobility, and language difficulties. Many of these concerns, along with frustration over the slow pace of efforts by Aboriginal Elders, parents, and other community members to gain effective input into and control over their education, have been repeatedly expressed to various educational and policy-making bodies, but they have met with little productive response (Royal Commission on Aboriginal Peoples, 1996a, 1996b). Aboriginal students generally express highly positive assessments of schools and teachers, and stress the importance of education for life success, but they also encounter racism, institutional barriers, and cultural divisions that can significantly impede their educational progress (Assembly of First Nations, 2005; Silver and Mallett, 2002: 29–30; Schissel and Wotherspoon, 2003: 82–92). At the post-secondary level, Aboriginal students are most likely to suggest that financial barriers and poor grades are deterrents to higher education, but high proportions also attribute a lack of welcoming environment as a barrier to continuing their studies (CMSA, 2005: 4). Among the core challenges confronting educators and Aboriginal communities

Box 8.4 The Educational Attainment of Aboriginal People

The *Report* of the Royal Commission on Aboriginal Peoples (1996b: 433–4, 440, 476–7) remains highly relevant for its insights into crucial historical and contemporary issues. The Idle No More movement that gained national prominence beginning in late 2012 adopted a vision that draws attention to core relationships outlined in the *Report* and to the lack of meaningful action on many of those issues in the intervening 16 years. These include the following concise summary of the factors that have contributed to the restriction of opportunities for educational success and limited integration into the labour force among Aboriginal youth:

In Aboriginal societies, as in many societies, children are regarded as a precious gift. Control over the education of their children has been a pressing priority of Aboriginal peoples for decades. This is not surprising. The destiny of a people is intricately bound to the way its children are educated. Education is the transmission of cultural DNA from one generation to the next. It shapes the language and pathways of thinking, the contours of character and values, the social skills and creative potential of the individual. It determines the productive skills of a people.

Aboriginal peoples are diverse in their histories, environments and cultures, but their deep commitment to education cuts across all boundaries. In our public hearings, Aboriginal parents, elders, youth and leaders came forward to tell us of the vital importance of education in achieving their vision of a prosperous future. Education is seen as the vehicle for both enhancing the life of the individual and reaching collective goals.

For more than 25 years, Aboriginal peoples have been articulating their goals for Aboriginal education. They want education to prepare them to participate fully in the economic life of their communities and in Canadian society. But this is only part of their vision. Presenters told us that education must develop children and youth as Aboriginal citizens, linguistically and culturally competent to assume the responsibilities of their nations. Youth that emerge from school must be grounded in a strong, positive Aboriginal identity. Consistent with Aboriginal traditions, education must develop the whole child, intellectually, spiritually, emotionally and physically.

Current education policies fail to realize these goals. The majority of Aboriginal youth do not complete high school. They leave the school system are the following, as summarized in the context of a forum organized through the Council of Ministers of Education Canada (2011):

- Aboriginal students, both male and female, perform at lower levels than other students—and this gap is not closing fast enough.
- Transience levels are very high for Aboriginal students, as individuals and families move frequently on- and off-reserve.
- The number of well-trained Aboriginal teachers remains low.
- Existing curricula and teaching methods do not sufficiently reflect Aboriginal needs and values.

without the requisite skills for employment, and without the language and cultural knowledge of their people. Rather than nurturing the individual, the schooling experience typically erodes identity and self-worth. Those who continue in Canada's formal education systems told us of regular encounters with racism, racism expressed not only in interpersonal exchanges but also through the denial of Aboriginal values, perspectives and cultures in the curriculum and the life of the institution.

The human costs of this failure are immense. It saps the creative potential of individuals, communities, and nations. Yet, despite the painful experiences Aboriginal people carry with them from formal education systems, they still see education as the hope for the future, and they are determined to see education fulfil its promise. . . .

By the time they enter high school, many Aboriginal youth have spent eight years or more in an education system from which they and their parents feel alienated. In public schools, the absence of support for Aboriginal identities is overwhelming: no Aboriginal high school teachers; only a limited curriculum dealing with contemporary Aboriginal languages, cultures, history, and political issues; an emphasis on intellectual cognitive achievement at the expense of spiritual, social, and physical development; and the marginalization of youth in decision-making about their education.

At the high school level, most parents are even less involved in their children's education than at elementary school levels. Their exclusion from decision-making is intensified where there are no local high schools, where teachers and administrators are non-Aboriginal, and where Aboriginal parents are in a minority. Issues of culturally appropriate curriculum, language education, parental involvement, and funding for curriculum development and culture programs are all present in the education of youth, as in the education of the child. Additional challenges encountered in the education of youth are the need for youth empowerment; the need for local high schools; the opportunity to return to high school; and the transition from high school to economic activity and careers.

Source: *Report of the Royal Commission on Aboriginal Peoples, Vol. 3, Gathering Strength*, 1996. Pages 433–4, 440, 476–7. Reproduced with the permission of the Minister of Public Works and Government Services, 2008, and courtesy of the Privy Council Office.

Aboriginal people have had some success in converting educational credentials, particularly in professional fields, administration, and business and commerce, into labour market and economic advances. Especially for many Aboriginal people living off-reserve, high levels of credentials tend to offer relatively high returns on employment and income prospects (Luffman and Sussman, 2007; Sharpe et al., 2009). However, the Aboriginal population, both overall and with respect to those with higher credentials, remains highly segmented, often concentrated within specific areas. Aboriginal people pursuing post-secondary studies remain relatively under-represented in the most prestigious or highly skilled fields, mostly concentrated instead in such areas as human services, trades and construction, and technologies for men and commercial and human services and clerical programs for women (Assembly of First Nations, 2011b: 19; Luffman and Sussman, 2007). Hull (2000: 108) observes that educational pathways and returns are highly mediated by class, gender, Aboriginal status, and region for Aboriginal people:

> It is clear that, by and large, registered Indian women continue to have weaker labour market participation and success than registered Indian men and that there continue to be high concentrations of men and women in particular occupations. It also appears that within urban areas registered Indians experience greater extremes of occupational success on the one hand, and government dependency on the other. These extremes are closely related to educational attainment.

In many cases, however, educational improvements have not been sufficient to overcome deeper problems like absence of sufficient jobs and discrimination. In addition to limited employment opportunities in many communities in which Aboriginal people are concentrated, or lack of available jobs to match education or work experience, many Aboriginal people indicate that "being Aboriginal" can produce difficulties in their search for jobs (Statistics Canada, 1993). Subsequent surveys of residents of urban communities across Canada reveal that, regardless of the city, "Almost all urban Aboriginal peoples agree that others behave in an unfair or negative way towards Aboriginal people. Majorities say they have been teased or insulted because of their Aboriginal background" (Environics Institute, 2010: 78). Indian and Northern Affairs Canada (2004) acknowledges that systemic factors such as human resources practices that are not culturally sensitive, as well as attitudinal factors such as stereotyping, discrimination, and racism, compound the barriers that restrict equitable employment options for Aboriginal people. Aboriginal people with the highest educational credentials tend to receive significant returns for their education, but considerable evidence points to the reality that Aboriginal people in general are more likely than other Canadians to experience a diminished relationship between education and social and economic opportunities (Canadian Race Relations Foundation, 2000: 24–6).

Social Class

Despite a long tradition of analysis of the relationship between social class and other dimensions of social inequality, until recently a surprisingly small body of systematic data has been available to document those relations with respect to Canadian education. This problem, in large part, is a consequence of differences in the definition and measurement of class inequality. The most common conceptions of **class**, derived from structural functionalist analysis, emphasize social stratification, relying on such indicators as income, occupation, parental education, and other variables that can be empirically measured and compared (McMullin, 2010: 7–9; Forcese, 1997: 22–8). These kinds of indicators can be readily identified, but require considerable resources and massive databases, such as census sources, if they are to be analyzed in a comprehensive way.

Alternative conceptions, including those derived from Marxist analysis or others following the critical analysis of contemporary European researchers such as Pierre Bourdieu, emphasize class as a relational concept that requires much more intensive scrutiny of what people do and how they do it in relation to other people, productive property, and labour processes (McMullin, 2010; Nakhaie, 1996; Veltmeyer, 1986). This kind of analysis has become increasingly prevalent in studying educational inequality. It is most effective where detailed information makes it possible to understand how class relations, educational backgrounds, and other significant social factors intersect with one another. Regardless of how class is defined and operationalized, however, the interaction between social class and educational inequality is a persistent, and potentially growing, phenomenon.

The strong two-way association between social background and education exists because social privilege increases the chances of gaining higher educational credentials, which in turn increase the likelihood of subsequent socio-economic success. As we have already observed with respect to gender, race, and ethnic inequality, nearly all groups have experienced some benefits from the expansion of Canada's education system in the latter part of the twentieth century. Porter et al. (1982: 313), in an analysis of students' educational plans and paths in Ontario, concluded that the education system is somewhat meritocratic in that, regardless of social background, students tend to have high aspirations and access to educational opportunities, and that factors like mental ability and self-concept do count. About two-thirds of all Canadians have more education than their parents, while only 7 per cent have less formal education than their parents; in 1993, "just over half the population had attended a post-secondary institution, compared with a little over 10 per cent of their parents . . . while 70 per cent of the parents had not graduated from high school, only 30 per cent of their children had failed to do so" (Fournier et al., 1995: 24, 26). While a strong association continues between parental education and prospects for university graduation, the combined impact of increased post-secondary participation across the population and the growing numbers of university-educated parents suggests that intergenerational educational mobility remains strong in Canada (Turcotte, 2011a).

However, these opportunities are not distributed equally. The rapid expansion of post-secondary education in the late 1960s and early 1970s produced some relative gains in educational opportunities for women and some ethnic minorities, but overall patterns of class inequality have remained relatively stable (Anisef and Okihiro, 1982: 131). Class plays a strong role in influencing students' aspirations, usually indirectly through its impact on the programs students entered into, their parents' expectations, and the self-concepts of the learners (Porter et al., 1982: 313). Clark (1960), in an influential article written at the time that education systems began to expand dramatically, draws attention to the "cooling out" function played by junior colleges, making it possible for students to gain post-secondary credentials even when their aspirations to achieve higher-status university degrees are not able to be fulfilled. Subsequent researchers have focused on which students are and are not likely to succeed educationally. Forcese (1997: 133), for example, argues that educational institutions tend to serve as "gatekeepers to 'success'" rather than as facilitators for upward social mobility because they restrict the numbers of students from lower-class backgrounds who benefit from formal education:

> Education was to have been the means of overcoming the inheritance of social class. However, as presently constituted, the educational system favours the already privileged, and screens out the already disadvantaged. Rather than defeating stratification, formal education is a cause of persisting and increasingly rigid stratification.

More recent research confirms the tendency for educational inequality to be reproduced across generations. Class-related factors, including parental income, wealth, occupation, and education, recur prominently in both Canadian and comparative studies that examine indicators associated with education. Ornstein (2007: 150), examining historical relationships between education and class in the United States, cautions that globalization is likely to restrict opportunities for class mobility that were limited in the first place: "Only if inequalities of income and wealth are kept within a limited range can education be used as an equalizer. . . . Because . . . measures [to address these issues] are not being implemented, we are witnessing a rise of a new aristocratic class, based on wealth and power." Expressed in less dramatic terms, Guppy and Davies (1998: 123) conclude from a comprehensive overview of education trends in Canada that, in comparison with gender and ethnicity, "class background seems to be the far more enduring source of educational inequality" once general educational improvements are taken into account. Family income affects not only educational directions, but also the ability graduates have to secure jobs and higher incomes (Grayson, 1997).

The likelihood that a young Canadian will engage in post-secondary studies, especially at a university level, increases with each successive level of parental education and household income (Knighton and Mirza, 2002; Turcotte, 2011a). Even though more Canadians, regardless of background, are participating in higher education, relatively enduring patterns of inequality persist. Although family income has relatively little impact on the likelihood of participation in community colleges, persons from high-income families are more than twice as likely to attend university than those from low-income families (Berger, 2009a: 48–9). Siedule (1992: 19), comparing the impact of such socio-economic factors as family income, family structure, province of residence, and ethnic background, demonstrates that the difference between favourable and unfavourable conditions can make a difference of up to five years in the amount of education a person attains. Over a decade later, Finnie et al. (2005: 22) observe that the likelihood of university attendance increases by as much as 5 per cent for each additional year of parental education, with an overall result that, when other factors are held constant, "the relative university attendance rates for those whose parents have a high school diploma and those with at least some university education are 29 versus 53 per cent in the case of men, and 37 versus 65 per cent for women."

Class background intersects with other crucial factors to influence prospects for educational success, as demonstrated in the analysis by Curtis et al. (1992: 10) of the Ontario 25–34-year-old population:

> More than a third of the people whose fathers were industrial workers, or were self-employed, dropped out of high school. Nearly half of those whose fathers were unskilled workers dropped out. Those people from single-mother and poor

visible-minority households probably fared even worse. On the other hand, less than 10 per cent of the people whose fathers were company managers or professionals dropped out of high school. . . . Employers' and professional-class kids are much more likely to go to university than are working-class kids—somewhere between two-and-a-half to four times as likely.

These findings indicate some educational mobility—people from diverse backgrounds are represented at all levels—but they also reveal that the chances for educational opportunity are greater for those who are already relatively well situated. The data in Figures 8.6 and 8.7 demonstrate that the likelihood of post-secondary attendance increases in conjunction with parental income and education levels. Family background has an impact on the level of post-secondary studies as well as overall participation rates. Whereas community college programs draw students from all socio-economic backgrounds, university enrolment patterns are more strongly associated with family income (shown in Figure 8.6) and parental education. The strong association between parental education and university participation is especially pronounced, revealing that the prospect of attending university is at least twice as likely for persons with a parent or guardian with a university degree than for those whose parents have trade or college-level credentials, and three times more than for those from households where parents or guardians do not have any credentials beyond high school.

The mechanisms by which class inequalities are reproduced are highly complex, consistent with the analysis offered by such writers as Bernstein, Bourdieu, Gramsci, Apple, and others discussed in previous chapters. Researchers have begun to analyze in greater empirical detail the mechanisms that contribute to selectivity and inequality in educational pathways. Canadian evidence points to the strong impact that parental education and family income have—along with other factors such as Aboriginal status,

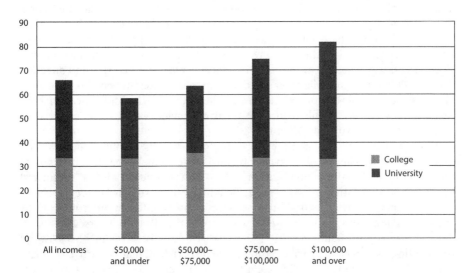

Figure 8.6 Post-Secondary Participation Rates (%) by Family Income (Youth Aged 21 in 2006), Canada

Source: Compiled from data in Finnie et al. (2012: 25).

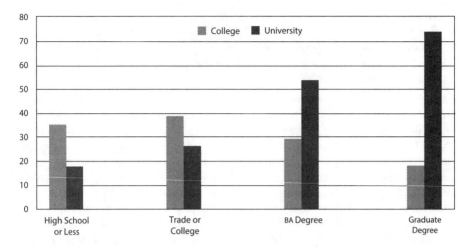

Figure 8.7 Post-Secondary Participation Rates (%) by Parent/Guardian's Education (Youth Aged 21 in 2006), Canada

Source: Compiled from data in Finnie et al. (2012: 25).

disability status, and rural versus urban residence—on prospects for post-secondary studies; these data reveal, at the same time, that some differences can be mitigated while others become stronger, depending on how these factors overlap or intersect with one another (Finnie et al., 2011: 29–30). Individual predispositions and experiences combine with signals from peers, family members, and educators in such a way as to lead into certain pathways or trajectories, as opposed to others, regarding such matters as how long to stay in school, what subjects to study, what careers to seek, and how much effort to apply to particular courses (Andres Bellamy, 1993). Class-related elements enter into the degree of influence that parents can have on their children's education, for instance, through the extent to which family members can provide time and money to support educational studies, and involvement in networks where interaction with other parents, teachers, and employers provides advantageous feedback and direction (Lareau, 2000: 116–19). While often posed in terms of distinctions between high status and less socially valued attributes or forms of cultural capital, class differences can both be transmitted and potentially reduced by regular behaviours such as parental reading with children (de Graaf et al., 2000: 107–8).

Previous chapters have cited literature that points to the strong association between parental income and other markers of advantage on the selection of high school courses required for admission to university and post-secondary studies (Krahn and Taylor, 2007). Many other considerations, including individual self-confidence, ability to read and perform well in test situations, selective use of information from teachers and career counsellors, and job interview skills, are also likely to be associated with class (Grayson, 1997; Tanner et al., 1995: 52–4). Differentials in family background offer varying capacities to provide resources and experiences that, in turn, contribute to substantial variations in reading ability, school grades, school quality, and subjective orientations that influence subsequent educational and career options (Bourque and Doray, 2009). Frenette (2007: 23) highlights the importance of understanding the interplay among these factors:

differences in academic performance across the income distribution may themselves be the result of differences in family income. Families with more financial resources may spend more money on books for children, take their children to museums, spend more on daycare in the early years, locate in neighbourhoods with better schools, etc. These actions may result in higher performance on standardized and scholastic tests, and thus, in a higher probability of attending university in the future.

The Program of International Student Assessment, based on reading, science, and mathematics skills tests administered to youth in more than 30 nations in selected years, demonstrates that socio-economic differences tend to be less pronounced in Canada than in most other OECD nations, and that a variety of factors, including parental interest in their children's education, reading at home, and numerous aspects of school climate, influenced student outcomes. Nonetheless, the survey also demonstrates that **socio-economic status** (SES), whether determined by parental background or school composition, continues to be one of the strongest determinants of student performance in all Canadian provinces and participating nations (Bussière et al., 2007: 41–2; Bussière et al., 2009).

Public concern about access to higher education has increased with the prominence accorded to the notion of a knowledge or information society. Across social groups, educational attainment is perceived to be a fundamental tool for social and economic participation and an avenue for advancement. Educational success remains tied to a belief in individualism and competitiveness, which may serve an ideological purpose that acts in the interests of those who benefit most from existing social arrangements. However, there is also pragmatic acceptance that education, whether directly or indirectly, is critical for successfully navigating contemporary social life. Research on youth who have left school before high school graduation, for example, shows that

International Contrast Case Study

Educational Inequalities and Disadvantage in Rich Nations

Results from comparative tests of educational achievement indicate the varied roles that schools play, in conjunction with social, demographic, economic, and policy factors, in the reproduction of educational inequalities. In considering the essential determinants of participation in advanced societies, the UNICEF Innocenti Research Centre highlights the need to understand that children's well-being involves much more than simply fiscal resources, presenting data that address the fundamental question of "how far behind are the least advantaged children being allowed to fall?" (UNICEF, 2010: 5). With respect to education, comparisons of inequalities based on reading, math, and science scores make it possible

to inform two commonly contested issues. First, they undermine the argument that steady progress towards equality of opportunity in education means that differences in educational outcomes are now mostly a reflection of the distribution of natural abilities.

continued

As [the data] show, different OECD countries have very different patterns of bottom-end inequality in educational outcomes; and it is reasonable to assume that this is the result not of differences in the distribution of natural abilities but of differences in policies which, over time, limit the extent to which less able students fall behind. [The comparison], for example, shows that lower-achieving students in Finland, Ireland and Canada are far less likely to fall a long way behind their peers than are students in Austria, France or Belgium.

The pattern of bottom-end inequality in educational outcomes therefore reflects more than the lottery of birth and circumstance. It may reflect differences in national efforts to reduce socio-economic disadvantage. Or it may reflect efforts to weaken the link between socio-economic disadvantage and school achievement (children whose mothers did not complete secondary school, for example, are at substantially greater risk of having low reading literacy scores, but that risk is two or three times greater in some countries than in others).[1] It is likely, also, that different degrees of inequality reflect different degrees of policy concern, over time, for those at risk of falling behind.

Second, international comparisons of inequality in educational outcomes also inform the issue of whether a trade-off must be made between investing in low-achieving students and maximizing the potential of those in the higher reaches of the ability range. [The analysis] suggests an answer to this question by showing that there is no relationship between greater inequality and better performance at the median. In fact the most unequal countries tend towards slightly lower scores at the 50th percentile. The two countries with the lowest bottom-end inequality in reading literacy, Finland and South Korea, are also the two countries with the highest median levels of educational achievement. A child born in either of these countries therefore has both a lower chance of falling a long way behind his or her peers and a higher chance of scoring above the average reading literacy mark for the OECD as a whole. (UNICEF, 2010: 11–12)

Note

1. UNICEF (2002).

Discussion Questions

1. To what extent do differences in educational achievement reflect individual characteristics (such as natural ability, talent, motivation, and hard work) as opposed to social and policy factors? Discuss your response.

2. Why is it important to pay attention to the gaps between the most and least advantaged in highly developed nations? What are the consequences of not doing so? Discuss with reference to Canada and at least one other nation.

those who do not continue tend to blame themselves, at least in part, for their actions, while the majority of dropouts now return later in life to complete their basic credentials and proceed to post-secondary studies (Tanner et al., 1995; Hango and de Broucker, 2007: 23). Nonetheless, numerous barriers that restrict access to higher education are increasingly recognized by the Canadian public. Findings from national and Ontario surveys, for instance, reveal that between two-thirds to three-quarters of respondents consider students from low-income families to have below-average opportunities to attend post-secondary programs; qualified Aboriginal students and students with disabilities are also perceived by at least one-third to one-half or more of respondents to have limited opportunities (Hart, 2012: 22; Canadian Council on Learning, 2006a: 33–4).

Continued belief in the legitimacy of schooling to facilitate individual access to jobs and other social rewards is based, in part, on the kinds of evidence outlined above. Many people do benefit from converting their educational achievements into social mobility and success. Hunter and Leiper (1993), for instance, suggest that factors like human capital theory and "market signalling," in which employers rely on educational credentials as an indication of future employee productivity, interact to produce a strong relationship between formal education and earnings. Even when the evidence is contradictory and individuals are aware of significant barriers to social mobility, the stakes are sufficiently high to ensure that most of us play by the rules—i.e., while not all of us can achieve educational success, and educational success does not in itself guarantee a good job, the consequences of not having an education are severe enough to motivate people to get as much education as they can. A persistent and growing gap in average family wealth exists between families whose major income recipient is a university graduate and those families whose primary income earner is not a university graduate (Morissette et al., 2002: 18; Berger and Parkin, 2009: 9–10).

Poverty is one of the more widely recognized costs of low educational achievement. There is a strong two-way relationship in that poverty rates are highest among those with the lowest levels of education, and educational problems are often most severe among those living in poverty. Persons living in poverty are most highly concentrated among those with the least education—nearly one in six persons with high school or less spent at least one year between 2005 and 2010 living below the after-tax low-income cut-off line, compared to about one in sixteen persons with a university degree (including those whose incomes were low while they were studying), and 3 per cent of those with less than high school, compared to 0.6 per cent of those with a university degree, were poor for the entire six-year period (Statistics Canada, CANSIM Table 282-0807).

Being poor also increases the risk of further educational difficulties. The likelihood that a student will drop out before completing high school (a trend that also holds for those who do not return for additional education) is substantially higher than average among those in lower socio-economic groups and those whose parents had little formal education (Gilbert and Frank, 1998: 15–17; Zeman, 2007). These trends reflect, in part, class-based differences both in dispositions towards education transmitted from parents to children and in the cultural and economic resources that students are able to draw upon in the classroom (Andres Bellamy, 1993). Andres and Adamuti-Trache (2008: 140), in their analysis of the pathways followed by people in British Columbia over the course of the 15-year period following high school graduation, observe that "those from advantaged family backgrounds fare best in every way" considered in

Box 8.5 The Impact of Poverty on Education

Amid general economic prosperity, poverty prevails within many segments of the Canadian population. Poverty influences educational experiences and outcomes, and it is associated with educational attainment. Low income is linked with many factors that have a detrimental impact on educational success, including nutritional and health problems and living conditions that may not be conducive to full educational participation. Campaign 2000 (2011: 1, 6–7, 12), a national network of groups dedicated to education and action to end child poverty, reports on major dimensions, causes, and consequences of child poverty:

As Campaign 2000 issues its twentieth monitoring report on child and family poverty, we are struck by the lack of progress over two decades. The economy has more than doubled in size, yet the incomes of families in the lowest decile have virtually stagnated. The gap between rich and poor families has continued to widen, leaving average-income families also struggling to keep up. With considerable evidence from academic, community-based and government research and from extensive testimony from people with lived experience of poverty, we probably know more about how to eradicate poverty in Canada than we did twenty years ago. Yet, structural barriers hinder significant progress on eradicating poverty.

At the same time, the younger generation—children of the baby boomers—are struggling more than their parents. They carry a heavy debt burden if they have pursued post-secondary education and often put off establishing long-term relationships and family formation. Many young people are unemployed or underemployed. . . .

[C]urrently, just finding employment is not a guaranteed way out of poverty. Most recent figures show that about 1 in 3 low-income children has at least one parent who is working full-time but is still in poverty. These parents are not finding jobs with sufficient pay, reasonable amounts of hours of work, and decent benefits that would allow them to move above the poverty line. Better public policies that work with pro-active employers are needed to enable families to achieve economic independence.

The gap in the amounts of time and money that families have is increasing more rapidly that the income gap alone according to new research that examines family income and time use over three decades. The incomes of families at the top of the scale are increasing without significant increases in hours of paid work by parents, while families in the middle range must work more hours to keep the same level of earnings. In other words, families in the lower and middle income ranges are working more hours but not earning significantly more wages while increased work yields greater income for families at the top.[1] . . .

Some Children and Families Are at Greater Risk

- **Lone mothers are still at higher risk for poverty.** While some progress has been achieved, female-led lone parent families are at greater risk of poverty. More than half (52.1 per cent) of female lone mothers with children under six live in poverty.[2] Lone mothers face the challenge of being the sole provider while also having to find adequate child care and secure housing, both of which are often unaffordable. Many also struggle to balance education or training, community service and/or paid work with family responsibilities.

- **Children of immigrants, of Aboriginal identity,[3] in racialized families and those with a disability are clearly at a higher risk for poverty.** This is often the result of persistent social and economic inequality which threatens social cohesion.
- **Having a child with a disability affects parents' employment status.** Almost 2 in 5 (38.4 per cent) reported working less hours in order to care for a child with a disability; about 1 in 4 parents had not accepted employment. More than 6 in 10 mothers compromised on their work schedule in contrast to 1 in 10 fathers.[4] . . .

Cost—A Barrier to Post-Secondary Education

The cost of post-secondary education is disproportionately high for racialized Canadians who earn on average 81.4 cents to every $1 earned by their non-racialized counterparts[5] and end up spending a higher proportion of their income on university fees.[6] Racialized Canadians are consequently more likely to be in debt and in low-paid jobs after graduating from a post-secondary institution.

Changes to the Post-Secondary Student Support Program (PSSSP) that provides federal funding to Aboriginal students pursuing post-secondary studies has, since 2001, led to over an estimated 20,000 post-secondary candidates in Aboriginal communities being denied money to pursue higher education.[7] For the young and rapidly growing Aboriginal population,[8] post-secondary opportunities are essential to ensure that young people have access to the job market and to achieving their potential.

Since the early 1990s, a series of government funding cuts for colleges and universities along with the deregulation of university fees has led post-secondary institutions to disproportionately rely on tuition fees to meet their costs. The cuts have not only affected the personal finances of students and their families, but have also limited the accessibility of post-secondary education to low- to middle-income families as many avoid accumulating such high levels of debt.[9]

Notes

1. Burton, P., Phipps, S., 2011. "Families, Time, and Well-Being in Canada," *Canadian Public Policy* 37, 3.
2. Statistics Canada. 2006 Census of Population. Catalogue no. 97-563-X, 97-563-XCB2006028, and The Vanier Institute of the Family. 2010. *Families Count: Profiling Canada's Families IV*. Ottawa, 4 Oct.
3. Aboriginal identity refers to those persons who report identifying with at least one Aboriginal group: North American Indian, Métis or Inuit, and/or those who reported being a Treaty Indian or a Registered

continued

Indian, as defined by the Indian Act of Canada, and/or those who reported they were members of an Indian band or First Nation. Information retrieved from Statistics Canada.

4. Statistics Canada. *Participation and Activity Limitation Survey*, 2006.

5. Canadian Federation of Students. 2010. *The Racialised Impact of Tuition Fees: Assessing the Social Cost of Post-Secondary Education*, and Block, S., and G. Galabuzi. 2011. *Canada's Colour Coded Labour Market: The Gap for Racialized Workers*. Wellesley Institute and the Canadian Centre for Policy Alternatives.

6. Canadian Federation of Students, *The Racialised Impact of Tuition Fees*.

7. Canadian Federation of Students. 2010. *Public Education for the Public Good: A National Vision for Canada's Post-Secondary Education System*, p. 17.

8. Ibid., p. 16.

9. Ibid., p. 14.

Source: Campaign 2000. 2011. At: www.campaign2000.ca.

their research. Social origins, and especially the resources available within families to support educational pursuits, also account for much of the variation observed in relation to other indicators, including gender, immigration status, and race and ethnicity (Boyd, 2009; Coulter, 2012).

There is growing awareness of the impact that poverty and associated risk factors have both during early childhood and throughout the life course. Low income and poverty are associated with nutritional deficiencies, ill health, emotional and behavioural disorders, and social disruptions that produce frequent absences from school, attention deficits, engagement in risky behaviours, and other factors that adversely affect school performance (Lee, 2004; Statistics Canada and CMEC, 2007: 15). These problems accumulate over time, so that health risks are greatest among adults who have the lowest levels of educational attainment (Raphael, 2011; Roberge et al., 1995: 17). Particularly for older students, economic pressures sometimes force youth to combine schooling and work. Although some students who combine schooling with moderate hours of work may have increased chances for academic success in high school or post-secondary studies, those who are forced to work longer hours, thereby reducing the time available to attend class, complete assignments, or meet other school-related demands are more likely to encounter educational difficulties (Bushnik, 2003; Motte and Schwartz, 2009).

Schools themselves, as well as the circumstances of those living in poverty, can also contribute to lower educational achievement among the poor. Olson (1995: 205) contends that children from working-class and poorer families are penalized in part because schooling, teaching, and the curriculum are organized and oriented in such a way as to be irrelevant to the needs and interests of those children. Curtis et al. (1992: 66) argue that, in addition to strong class differences (along with racial, ethnic, and gender ones) in the distribution of students into higher and lower educational streams, resources are diverted from programs in vocational and general education, where the less privileged are likely to be found, into special programs like French immersion, classes for "gifted" students, and private schools that typically serve students from more privileged backgrounds. Educational outcomes are highly affected by the complex mix of educational practices, the culture of school organizations, the extent and use of school resources, students' socio-economic backgrounds, and the mix of students within specific schools and classrooms (Frempong and Willms, 2002).

Recent trends suggest that class and educational inequalities are likely to compound one another further. With about one in ten Canadian children living in poverty (Campaign 2000, 2011: 2), youth from disadvantaged backgrounds, as well as those with disabilities, are less likely than other youth to complete high school and more likely to experience difficulties in labour market participation (Hango and de Broucker, 2007: 26). Despite consistent evidence, there has been an absence of comprehensive policy to address problems for low-income households, whose family members endure heavier responsibilities for financing their own education and securing social support as educational costs rise and government services and financial support erode.

This problem has implications for students at all levels of schooling, given the importance of financial and cultural capital for educational success, but it may be most visible among those who proceed to post-secondary studies. The issue of access to higher education has gained prominence in the face of concerns by student organizations, educators, and other groups about the impact of increasing tuition fees and changes to financial assistance and student loan programs that place greater burdens on individuals or family support networks. Some evidence suggests that after 1989–90, when tuition fees first began to rise significantly, the gap in university participation rates widened initially, as students from families with the lowest socio-economic status were increasingly disadvantaged relative to those from higher SES family backgrounds (Bouchard and Zhao, 2000: 28). Although this gap levelled off beginning in 1999, it began to rise again after 2005 (Berger, 2009a: 48), revealing an ongoing association between post-secondary participation and both household income and parents' education.

Tuition fees are increasing in an environment in which there are high degrees of uncertainty and fluctuation in employment opportunities for young people. Moreover, changes to sources of financial assistance, such as the Canada Student Loan Program, have altered the nature and amounts of funding available to students. Tuition increases do not in themselves account for reduced accessibility to university since students have generally tended to be drawn from relatively privileged backgrounds, and other barriers, such as lack of services for non-traditional groups and those most in need of assistance, do restrict access (Levin, 1990: 52–6). In addition to financial concerns, several factors, such as school grades, cultural resources, and motivation, pose barriers to post-secondary studies, but Berger, Motte, and Parkin (2007: 54) emphasize that low-income youth are most likely to experience problems in all of these regards and therefore are most apt to defer or steer away from post-secondary studies. The impact of tuition increases has also been mitigated somewhat by special assistance or tuition support programs for students from low-income families and designated groups, but these programs tend to have restricted terms of reference and capacity to support only a small proportion of eligible students.

Further differentiation or selectivity in access to post-secondary studies occurs as some students combine school and work, others rely on family sources or borrowed funds to cover their educational costs, and still others opt to enter the labour market directly. Income inequality is evident in the tendency for students to look increasingly to support from parents or other friends and family members to finance at least part of their studies. Close to three-quarters of post-secondary students report that they rely on some form of financial assistance from parents (ibid., 84). The funds that students must raise on their own or receive in support from parents or other family members varies across provinces and income levels, but tend to be higher in Canada, especially in Quebec and for those in upper-income groups, than in the United States (Belley et al., 2011: 25). Students are also burdened with increasingly higher debt loads through borrowing from private sources and government student loan programs. Nearly half of graduates receiving college certificates or diplomas since the early 1990s and close to 60 per cent of those receiving university degrees owed debt from student loan programs at the time of graduation (Dubois, 2006: 5; Berger, 2009b: 189). The average indebtedness for undergraduate university students at the time of graduation continues to increase steadily, approaching $27,000 in 2009 after more than doubling (in constant dollars) over the previous two decades (ibid., 189–90). With rising costs associated with education in a context of uncertainty about job prospects, students are increasingly concerned about the capacity to pay back their debt after they complete their studies (Canadian Alliance of Student Associations, 2010: 35–6).

These trends make it more difficult for students from less privileged backgrounds to attend the post-secondary programs of their choice, or worse, they may restrict access altogether (Berger, 2009a: 45ff.; Ouellette, 2006). In cases in which tuition fees have been unregulated and escalated most dramatically, particularly in some professional degree programs such as medicine, law, and dentistry, over-representation of students from upper-income groups has increased relative to those from middle- and lower-income groups (Frenette, 2005b; Ouellette, 2006). Evidence also indicates that accumulated debt and other fiscal barriers are affecting students' ability to enter or complete college programs that have typically offered greater post-secondary options for students from diverse social and economic backgrounds (Berger et al., 2007: 130–1).

Given these concerns, attention to issues of access to post-secondary studies is being extended to questions about student retention and completion. For various reasons, many post-secondary students interrupt their studies periodically, sometimes for substantial lengths of time and in other cases without returning to complete their programs. Determining factors include inadequate financial resources, isolation and lack of support networks, personal and family commitments, work opportunities, and limited commitment to or interest in their studies. Available data suggest that between one-fifth and one-quarter of students who enter post-secondary programs in Canada leave prior to completion. While students do not complete their post-secondary studies for a variety of reasons, a striking correspondence exists between the factors associated with post-secondary attendance and those related to post-secondary completion (Lambert et al., 2004; Ma and Frempong, 2008). These factors often interact strongly with one another, as illustrated by the case of First Nations students who are alienated by educational institutions that do not take into account personal, cultural, and economic factors (Monture-Angus, 1995: 81–4; Paquette and Fallon, 2010). In short, class inequalities continue to shape and are reinforced by the education system.

Students with Disabilities

People with disabilities have been one of the least well-served groups in the long-term quest for equitable educational and social participation. Misunderstanding, discrimination, and exclusion from school, work, and other core spheres of social life are common experiences among persons with disabilities.

Changes in the way that students with a disability are treated by education systems have broadly corresponded with public attitudes towards and treatment of the disabled in society, with gradual movement towards accommodation for different types of disability accompanying greater understanding of the complexity of disability and disability issues. For much of Canada's history, persons with physical, behavioural, or cognitive disabilities have tended to be stigmatized, marginalized, or left as dependants subject to the predilections of family or private caregivers. Throughout much of the twentieth century, disability issues came to be framed increasingly through a medical model in which disabilities were regarded as pathologies or forms of impairment that required management and treatment by health-care professionals and other experts (Titchkosky, 2003). Medical approaches to disability continue to prevail, often for legitimate reasons, but sometimes with highly contested or disturbing consequences, as in the extensive prescription of mood-altering drugs to children and youth diagnosed with behavioural or learning disabilities (Maté, 1999). Crystallized around the successful quest to include disability rights in the 1982 Canadian Charter of Rights and Freedoms, persons with disability and their advocates have focused on the rights of the disabled, including provision for equity, autonomy, and participation in all spheres of social life.

In education, extensive debate has focused on the extent to which students should be included or integrated into regular programs and classes as opposed to having specially designated programs. This focus has recently shifted to acknowledge the need for educational institutions to provide more extensive services and programs to ensure that students with disabilities have viable options to participate fully in education at all levels where they are eligible. In the process, educational participation and attainment levels among persons with disabilities have improved, but remain below national averages. For Canadians ages 16–64, persons with disabilities are about 1.5 to 2 times more likely to have less than high school, and about half as likely to have a university degree, than those without a disability, but much of this gap disappears for those in the 15–24 cohort (Canadian Council on Learning, 2007a). About 6 per cent of students who graduated from Canadian universities in 2006 reported having a disability, which is more than twice the level reported in 1995 but below age-adjusted rates of disability in the population as a whole (CAUT, 2007: 21; Statistics Canada, 2007d). The proportions of respondents in national surveys of Canadian university undergraduate students self-identifying as disabled rose from below 3 per cent in 1998–9 to 9 per cent in 2010–11; among the latter, over half of the reported disabilities were related to learning or mental health (CAUT, 2012: 40; Prairie Research Associates, 2011: 8–9). A substantial gap remains in university participation rates between students identified as having a disability and those not so identified, though students with disabilities are only slightly less likely than those who do not have a disability to pursue post-secondary studies at the college level (Finnie et al., 2011: 16). The importance of educational equity is underscored by observations discussed throughout this chapter and elsewhere in the book of the strong associations between educational prospects and economic and social well-being.

Close to 175,000 school-age children were reported in 2006 to have some form of disability, representing 4.6 per cent of all children aged 5–14 years in Canada, compared to 4.0 per cent in 2001 (Statistics Canada, 2007d: 23–5). These include various forms of disability, such as difficulties with hearing, sight, speech, and mobility, although learning disabilities and chronic health conditions account for the majority of cases. There is considerable variation across provinces and disability categories in the levels of success and the kinds of services and programs available for students with disabilities. All but about 4 per cent of school-age children in Canada attend schools, with about 60 per cent of elementary school-age children with mild or moderate disabilities in Canada integrated in regular school classes, ranging from about half of those in Quebec and British Columbia to close to three-quarters of those in Prince Edward Island and New Brunswick (Canadian Council on Learning, 2007a; Kohen et al., 2007). Children and youth with more severe disabilities or limited physical or cognitive activity are more likely to be placed in special programs or educated in other ways.

These trends highlight the continuing need to improve educational services for students with disabilities as well as the complex arrangements that these improvements can sometimes entail. Without special funding agreements or collaboration with other agencies, for instance, it can be prohibitively expensive for many school districts to provide costly equipment, tutors, or aides required to meet the needs of relatively small numbers of students. Educational institutions, often driven by legal rulings and human rights challenges, have begun recently to implement more comprehensive policies and services guided by principles of **reasonable accommodation**, which seek to ensure that, except in cases that would cause undue hardship to the organization, appropriate physical arrangements, supports, and practices are in place to ensure that each individual with a disability will be able to participate fully in educational programs and activities.

Innovations in technologies, new software programs, and alternative means of educational delivery increase educational options and limit the impact of barriers to educational participation for many students, but these are often costly or not widely available. Such initiatives can contribute to environments more conducive to educational participation by students with disabilities. Nonetheless, Frazee (2003: 13) cautions that, without full appreciation for what these measures mean in the context of real learning situations, they can also perpetuate disadvantage "by imposing conditions upon inclusion, once again holding out the offer of equal participation as contingent upon their capacity to emulate valued social norms." Accessible buildings and appropriate services and supports are important preconditions to address needs of students with disabilities, but these represent only part of a broader social environment. Research conducted for the Canadian Council on Learning (2009b: 4) reveals that, in addition to issues related to physical accessibility, persons with disabilities also encounter barriers related to financial issues (such as high-cost programs and administrative demands) and attitudes among instructors and others that often inhibit their adult learning experiences. Titchkosky (2011: 7) stresses that issues related to access extend well beyond physical and material needs to encompass "access to a general feeling of legitimate participation, meaningfulness, and belonging." Many students with disabilities continue to encounter both attitudinal and physical barriers in and out of educational settings that restrict their prospects to function fully on a day-to-day basis or compel them to lower their educational aspirations. Even the analysis of disability in relation to education occurs through concepts or discourses that situate disability outside of or apart from regular educational practices and possibilities. Moore et al. (2008), drawing upon a critical pedagogy framework, stress the necessity to combat these issues by employing a rights-based orientation in which the voices of youth and adults living with disabilities have a central place.

Regional Inequality

Canadians receive unequal amounts of and returns from education on the basis of where they live. These differences reflect disparities between urban and rural settings, provincial and regional diversity, and inequalities within a single geographical site such as a city or metropolitan area.

Educational indicators are generally more favourable for persons living in cities in comparison with those who reside in rural areas. Rural residents have less formal education, on average, than urban residents do. There is a declining, but persistent, gap in educational attainment between rural and urban populations. Data from the 2006 census reveal that, among persons aged 25–64, just over one-quarter (26 per cent) of urban residents, compared to 11 per cent of those in rural communities, had university degrees (Statistics Canada, 2008d: 25). Conversely, one-fifth of the urban population and over one-third of persons living in predominantly rural regions had less than high school (Rothwell and Turcotte, 2006: 6). Some of these differences can be accounted for by the fact that educational institutions, especially at the post-secondary level, are concentrated in urban areas, as are jobs and services associated with higher levels of education, as well as recent immigrants, who are typically more highly educated than the Canadian-born population.

Rural/urban disparities, however, also appear among the school-age population. Dropout rates, overall, are higher among rural than urban residents, and rural students who drop out of school tend to leave earlier. Despite declining dropout rates across Canada (in 1990–1, nearly 17 per cent of 20- to 24-year-olds were not in school and did not have a high school diploma, compared to 8.5 per cent by 2009–10), the dropout rate in smaller towns and sparsely populated areas, at over 15 per cent, remains above national levels from the 1990s (Gilmore, 2010). Rural residents typically have lower university participation rates than those from urban areas but slightly higher rates of participation in community colleges and CEGEPs. Analysis of a national cohort of youth born in 1984 reveals that by 2006 (at ages 21–2), 45 per cent of those from urban communities compared to 32 per cent of those from rural communities had attended university, whereas college participation rates were 32 per cent for urban youth and 35 per cent for their rural counterparts (Finnie et al., 2011: 15).

Patterns of educational inequality are evident in comparisons across provinces and territories, as the data in Tables 8.1 and 8.2 illustrate. Levels of educational attainment fall below national averages in regions that tend to be poorer. In most of the Atlantic provinces, Quebec, Manitoba, Saskatchewan, and the Northwest Territories, between 16 and 21 per cent of the populations (and 46 per cent in Nunavut) have not completed high school, and in nearly all of them the proportion of the population with post-secondary (college or university) credentials is below the national average of 52 per cent. The converse is true for provinces that have traditionally been considered the "have" provinces and that are the primary destination of highly qualified recent immigrants, such as Ontario and British Columbia (as well as the one exception, the Yukon Territory), which meet or exceed the national average levels of educational attainment. Comparative studies of reading skills and adult literacy reveal broadly similar

Table 8.1 Educational Attainment, by Province and Territory, 2011 (% of Population Aged 25–64)

	Less Than High School	Graduated from High School	Apprenticeship or Trades Certificate or Diploma	Post-Secondary Certificate or Diploma (college or university)	University Degree
Canada*	11	26	12	25	27
Newfoundland and Labrador	18	21	23	21	17
Prince Edward Island	16	24	10	28	22
Nova Scotia	13	24	14	24	25
New Brunswick	16	27	10	27	19
Quebec	14	20	18	23	25
Ontario	9	26	6	28	30
Manitoba	13	31	10	23	23
Saskatchewan	13	31	18	17	21
Alberta	11	28	15	22	24
British Columbia	8	30	13	22	28
Yukon Territory	12	21	11	30	26
Northwest Territories	21	20	10	27	22
Nunavut	46	14	9	18	13

* Canadian total for provinces only.
Source: Compiled from Statistics Canada and CMEC (2012: Table D.6.3).

trends, with lower scores more prevalent among rural populations in Newfoundland and Labrador, New Brunswick, Quebec, and Nunavut (Statistics Canada and CMEC, 2007: 104–6; Knighton et al., 2010: 17).

Some levelling out occurs, however, when current levels of educational participation are considered, reflecting the increasingly high overall proportions of young people engaged in basic and continuing education. The data in Table 8.2 reveal relatively little variation across provinces in levels of educational participation among youth. In nearly all cases, with the exception of Nunavut and the Northwest Territories, between 77 and 87 per cent of the 15–19 age cohort were in school in 2010–11, while rates of university participation among 20- to 24-year-olds were below the national average of

Table 8.2 Dimensions of Educational Participation, by Province and Territory

	Education Participation Rate (% of 15–19 age cohort enrolled in secondary or post-secondary studies), 2010–11	College Participation Rate (% of 20–4 age cohort) 2010–11	University Participation Rate (% of 20–4 age cohort) 2010–11	High School Dropout Rate, 2007–10 (average)**	Unemployment Rate (% of labour force 15–24 age cohort), 2011	Percentage of the School-Age Population (ages 5–19) of Low Income, 2009
Canada*	82	11	27	8.9	14.2	9
Newfoundland and Labrador	83	15	21	7.4	20.8	7
Prince Edward Island	81	10	27	8.9	15.2	6
Nova Scotia	82	7	27	8.6	16.7	8
New Brunswick	82	9	23	8.1	17.5	8
Quebec	81	12	27	11.7	13.4	8
Ontario	87	14	29	7.8	15.8	9
Manitoba	79	7	24	11.4	11.6	9
Saskatchewan	78	6	23	9.4	10.4	10
Alberta	77	8	22	10.4	10.7	8
British Columbia	79	10	28	6.2	14.0	12
Yukon	69	10	n.a.	15.5	n.a.	n.a.
Northwest Territories	76	8	8	30.1	n.a.	n.a.
Nunavut	65	8	14	50.0	n.a.	n.a.

* Provinces only.
** Percentage of 20-to 24-year-olds without a high school diploma and not in school.

Sources: Compiled from Statistics Canada and CMEC (2011a: Tables C.2.1, E.1.2.1, A.3.1.2.); Gilmore (2011); Statistics Canada, CANSIM Table 2820002.

27 per cent in Newfoundland and Labrador, New Brunswick, the Prairie provinces, and the Territories. Labour market prospects for youth have some impact on these rates, particularly in western Canada where there tend to be higher dropout rates, slightly lower university participation rates, and lower youth unemployment rates.

There are also regional differences in people's attitudes towards schooling and educational performance. Ironically, persons living in regions with the lowest levels of education tend to have more positive views of schooling than those with higher levels. Various public opinion surveys reveal that people in the Prairie provinces and Atlantic Canada tend to have more favourable attitudes about schools and improved quality of education than those from provinces with the highest urban concentrations of population (Williams and Millinoff, 1990: 37–8; Canadian Education Association, 2007: 7, 10). Such poll results reflect, at times, public reaction to unpopular educational reforms in specific provinces, such as Ontario in the late 1990s. They also reveal strong convictions that education is important to the future of rural communities and to options for individuals from those communities. Rural communities face a perpetual challenge to address the reality that many of their youth look to education as a channel for educational, economic, and social opportunities that exist in cities or other regions (Knight, 1993: 306–7; Wotherspoon, 1998: 138). Corbett (2009: 8) highlights the challenges and contradictions associated with the development of strategies to provide a solid educational foundation for rural youth, enticing them to live in rural areas, and equipping them with experiences and life choices conducive to living with the demands of a cosmopolitan world.

Observed differences in educational attainment and attitudes towards schooling reflect several important dimensions of Canadian social reality. To a large extent, education systems in Canada have emerged and developed amid debates over the degree to which competing economic and social considerations should drive educational planning and programs. On the one hand, imperatives such as economies of scale, efficiency, and cost considerations have led to consolidation of schools and school districts and centralization of programs and resources. Regions with stronger economic bases are in a better position than poorer regions to provide both the resources to finance a strong educational system and employment opportunities for people with educational credentials. Similarly, smaller provinces and rural or isolated areas with limited populations are less likely to be able to offer a complete range of educational programs and services than are city schools or larger school districts. On the other hand, educational institutions are under pressure to be responsive to local concerns and to provide meaningful services. Schools with low enrolments may not be cost-efficient, but they may be able to offer several advantages to students and community members—greater opportunities for teacher–student interaction, sensitivity to parental concerns, higher morale, and benefits for students with educational difficulties or from disadvantaged backgrounds—that tend not to be found in larger school settings (Leithwood and Jantzi, 2007). In rural areas and smaller communities, especially, schools are essential for more than their educational offerings, serving as focal points for sports and recreation, social organizations, and cultural events that contribute to an enhanced quality of life within the community. Nonetheless, such schools often remain at risk through an absence of adequate resources and stability (Bolaria et al., 1995: 433–5).

The structure of educational finance in Canada has been shaped by efforts to compensate for some of the most severe consequences of regional inequalities. Until the end of the twentieth century, funding for elementary and secondary education in nearly all provinces (except New Brunswick and Prince Edward Island) came predominantly from tax revenue generated at the school board or district level, augmented by grants from provincial governments to equalize school spending between poorer and wealthier districts. Federal–provincial arrangements generally have operated on a similar principle, with equalization payments and special funding programs for post-secondary education based on the transfer of funds from the federal government to ensure that the "have-not" provinces are able to provide comparable services to those available in the "have" provinces (Dibski, 1995: 69–70). Such programs have sought to ensure that a basic range and level of educational services, along with health care and other social services, are available to residents in all provinces and regions.

Ongoing changes to cost-sharing formulas and funding arrangements, however, have tended to shift the burden of funding downward while centralizing fiscal constraints, thereby heightening fears that inequalities among districts will increase (Barlow and Robertson, 1994: 12; Sattler, 2012). The federal government provides provinces and territories with educational support through the Canada Social Transfer and other "investment" programs that transfer funding to assist in such areas as early childhood development, childhood learning, job training, and post-secondary education. Nonetheless, these kinds of arrangements remain unstable and inadequate for several reasons, including the shifting terrain of federal–provincial relations, rising costs and demand for education of various kinds, federal initiatives to contain social spending and co-ordinate programs, and the pre-eminence that health care (in addition to policy areas like security) has gained over education and other social programs on the policy agenda. The pace of parallel measures taken periodically by provincial governments to restrain education spending, centralize control over many educational decision-making matters, eliminate or place limits on local school district discretionary spending and taxation powers, and reduce the numbers of school boards has recently slowed but has not entirely been reversed (Young et al., 2007: 41–7, 148ff.; Lessard and Brassard, 2009). While these developments likely will produce some long-overdue innovations in educational organization and programming—especially as attention is paid to the importance of strategic educational investment and promotion of a knowledge economy—they also increase the likelihood that programs and services for selected groups, such as people with special educational needs or residents in smaller communities, will be reduced or cut out altogether.

Conclusion

This chapter has examined several dimensions and consequences of educational inequality in Canada. The expansion of the education system and broadening of conceptions of educational opportunity over the past century have resulted in substantial gains in educational attainment among nearly all segments of the population. This expansion has been especially important for women, as well as for members of many visible minority and Aboriginal populations, providing access to educational programs and subsequent social and economic positions reliant on advanced educational credentials, which traditionally have not been open to them. Considerable evidence indicates that not only does education contribute to social mobility but it also limits the extent to which social inequalities may be reproduced from one generation to the next. There is a real basis to claims that educational gains can lead to increased social and economic opportunities and that individuals can benefit from education regardless of their social background.

However, substantial obstacles continue to stand in the way of full equality of access to and benefit from education for many segments of the population. Gender equity has been achieved in participation rates at most levels of formal education, but gender segregation remains in areas of study concentration and in the ability to translate educational credentials into subsequent educational and career advancement. Similarly, visible minorities and people with physical disabilities have demonstrated considerable gains in levels of educational participation and attainment, but their ability to translate those advances into socio-economic success also depends on such factors as personal experiences of discrimination and their structural location in Canadian society. With a few notable exceptions, persons of Aboriginal ancestry, in particular, remain a considerable distance away from education and employment equity with the population as a whole. Issues related to sexism, racism, poverty, disability, regional disparities, and other factors often compound one another, contributing to distinctly different probabilities that people from diverse social backgrounds will achieve educational and social success.

In summary, then, there is a contradictory relationship between formal education and social and economic opportunity. Education is a vital ingredient in most recipes for success, sometimes as a contributing factor but more often as part of an overall package associated with relative privilege or disadvantage. Several policy and organizational changes, such as improved educational access for minorities, education equity initiatives, multiculturalism, teacher training for greater sensitivity to the educational needs of distinct categories of learners, and inclusive curricula, have enhanced opportunities for people who have been typically disadvantaged. However, schooling, both actively, in terms of how it responds to and rewards people on a differential basis, and tacitly, in terms of the gaps, silences, and failures to confront socio-economic disparities on a systematic basis, also contributes to the ongoing reproduction of social inequality.

To be sure, there will be new opportunities for some individuals as jobs are created that reward intelligence, initiative, and technical proficiency as opposed to socio-economic background. Nonetheless, recent policy and program changes in the direction of funding cutbacks, restrictions on or deletion of support services for students, greater individual responsibility for educational costs and options, and realignment of educational priorities in conjunction with wider fiscal planning are likely to minimize the chances that those from less privileged social backgrounds will receive equitable access to and benefits from formal education. Significant challenges, debates, and reforms surrounding contemporary education are the focus of the next chapter.

....

Annotated Further Readings

Castellano, Marlene Brant, Lynne Davis, and Louise Lahache, eds. 2000. *Aboriginal Education: Fulfilling the Promise*. Vancouver: University of British Columbia Press. The authors highlight several promising developments, as well as crucial challenges, that characterize education for Canada's Aboriginal people in the wake of the 1996 report of the Royal Commission on Aboriginal Peoples.

Fennell, Shailaja, and Madeleine Arnot, eds. 2008. *Gender Education and Equality in a Global Context: Conceptual Frameworks and Policy Perspectives*. London: Routledge. Contributors from several nations examine the meaning and nature of gender and equality as social and economic relations shift in a global context. Research and theoretical discussions are framed around diverse educational forms, challenges, and possibilities.

Grabb, Edward, and Neil Guppy, eds. 2009. *Social Inequality in Canada: Patterns, Problems, and Policies*, 5th edn. Toronto: Pearson Education. This collection incorporates theoretical and analytical chapters that explore major dimensions and consequences of social inequality in Canada. Both historical and contemporary issues are addressed, covering such themes as gender, age, socio-economic and regional inequality, and education.

Henry, Frances, and Carol Tator. 2009. *The Colour of Democracy: Racism in Canadian Society*, 4th edn. Toronto: Thomson Nelson. The authors emphasize how racism continues to be a factor in Canadian society even within legal and formal frameworks that restrict discrimination against racial and ethnic groups and other minorities. Attention is given to structural racism and how it operates in various social locations, including extensive discussion of racism and education.

Levine-Rasky, Cynthia, ed. 2009. *Canadian Perspectives on the Sociology of Education*. Toronto: Oxford University Press. Covering both theoretical and empirical contributions to the analysis of relationships between school and society, this volume includes chapters that explore several dimensions of educational inequality in Canada, including race, gender and identity, socio-economic inequality, streaming, rural schooling, and the impact of educational reform.

McMullin, Julie. 2010. *Understanding Social Inequality: Intersections of Class, Age, Gender, Ethnicity, and Race in Canada*, 2nd edn. Toronto: Oxford University Press. The book presents several case studies that explore social inequality in Canada, beginning with a framework that demonstrates how major dimensions of social inequality intersect with one another.

Willms, J. Douglas, ed. 2002. *Vulnerable Children: Findings from Canada's National Longitudinal Survey of Children and Youth*. Edmonton: University of Alberta Press and Human Resources Development Canada. This book covers crucial causes, consequences, and dimensions of negative life experiences associated with vulnerability, including racial and ethnic discrimination, parenting concerns, family violence, poverty, and learning and behavioural disorders.

Key Terms

Class A social grouping based on social and economic relations, defined in terms of people's position with respect to ownership and control of assets that contribute to the production of new goods and services.

Equality of opportunity The view that all persons should have the same chance to succeed or fail on their own merits, regardless of their social background.

Equality of results The notion that intervention by the state or other agencies is necessary to guarantee that all persons will achieve at least minimum agreed-upon standards of living and access to other essential resources and opportunities.

Gender segmentation The concentration of males and females within distinct and separate jobs, education programs, and other social sites, often associated with differential status and benefits.

Meritocratic The principle that persons are selected for social positions based on merit or achievement in accordance with universal standards and criteria.

Reasonable accommodation The requirement that an institution or service provider will make arrangements or provisions to remove barriers that discriminate against an individual or group protected under human rights legislation. Based on the recognition that equal treatment can sometimes be discriminatory towards particular individuals or groups, such as persons with disability or cultural minorities, this approach also acknowledges that accommodation cannot be extended to the point of causing undue hardship on the service provider.

Social Darwinism A view that societies change through internal evolutionary processes; commonly employed to justify existing social inequalities that reflect "survival of the fittest."

Socially disadvantaged Those who are unable to attain important social and economic resources as a result of barriers or inadequate opportunities relative to standards that prevail among a nation or social group as a whole.

Social reproduction The process by which social structures and systems of inequality are maintained over time.

Socio-economic status (SES) A measure of the relative social and economic position of a person or group, determined by such factors as income, wealth, occupation, education level, family background, and prestige accorded an occupation.

Visible minority A term used in Canada to refer to non-Caucasian persons of specified racial or ethnic origins other than Aboriginal.

Study Questions

1. To what extent is educational achievement the outcome of individual effort as opposed to social factors? Explain your answer.

2. Discuss the extent to which education contributes to or restricts opportunities for social and economic success among diverse racial and ethnic groups in Canada.

3. Explain why, despite efforts to ensure that schooling is inclusive and responsive to all students, strong educational inequalities persist among social groups. Provide specific examples to illustrate how processes of inclusion and exclusion may affect particular students in different ways.

4. Which groups have benefited the most from educational expansion over the past five decades? Explain your response.

5. Examine the policies and procedures for a school board or government in your region (many of these are accessible through websites or other publicly available formats). Does the jurisdiction you have selected have explicit anti-racism or anti-discrimination guidelines and policies? If not, explore or consider why these have not been adopted; if so, explore the extent to which these have been implemented and effective in reducing racism and discrimination within that particular setting.

6. Discuss the importance of university education in the context of a knowledge society. To what extent is university open to and able to provide equitable opportunities for students from diverse social backgrounds? To what extent should people look to universities as opposed to other forms of education in order to improve these prospects?

Chapter 9

Contemporary Educational Challenges and Reforms

Learning Objectives

In this chapter, you will:

- gain an understanding of the major challenges and controversies surrounding education systems in the twenty-first century, including educational reform, technological change, social diversity, and globalization and social change;

- explore questions central to understanding how sociological analysis may be able to address emerging educational systems and issues.

Introduction

Previous chapters have emphasized the need to understand education as a dynamic and often contradictory endeavour. While education systems have been remarkably resilient over time (to the point that some critics consider them obsolete), formal educational institutions and their participants are continually challenged to rethink and reshape themselves to keep pace with important social, economic, and political transformations. Posed another way, the uneven pace at which transformations occur across three levels (the context, content, and structure of schooling) has fuelled periodic tensions and uncertainty over the role and relevance of education in a changing world. The social and economic contexts in which education systems operate are being rapidly transformed by shifts in technologies, knowledge forms, social relationships, and personal identities and life courses. The content of schooling is also changing, although typically in a more gradual manner. Educational participants are becoming increasingly more diverse, bringing with them desires and capacities to modify programs, curricula, knowledge, and resources for appropriate educational practices. Educators are challenged with finding ways to capture the attention of students whose lives are infused with the immediacy, attractions, and distractions of digital technologies. Finally, while the institutional structure and organization of educational services are also being transformed, these changes have tended to be much less dramatic than changes in socio-economic contexts and educational processes. These relationships have contributed to a proliferation of alternative educational venues and forms at the same time that existing institutional arrangements are being reconfigured, challenged, or defended by various groups.

The first two chapters identified sociology as a discipline concerned with an understanding of relations between individuals and societies, and formal education as a social institution that contributes to the development of individual capacities and social competencies. The contemporary social world is markedly different from that of Durkheim and other early social scientists who began to introduce the sociological analysis of education. Early school systems and the research that examined them were oriented to knowledge and skills deemed relevant to life in particular national or regional contexts in which confident assumptions were typically asserted about shared value orientations, projected horizons for careers or households, and rational planning for the future. Sociology and other social sciences were heralded as instruments for determining optimal educational arrangements and curricula at least as much as they were devoted to critical understanding of emerging educational developments. Yet, within any types of social and educational transformations, fundamental questions arise concerning what kinds of educational arrangements and supports must be in place to ensure that children and youth are able to develop the skills, capacities, and understandings required to negotiate the demands of those changing worlds.

One of the defining characteristics of life in advanced capitalist societies has been the dramatic reconfiguration of individual experiences, institutional arrangements, and social relationships to the extent that notions of individuality, society, and social organization are undergoing fundamental reassessment. We are influenced by, and able to interact with, persons, organizations, and processes that extend far beyond the sites in which we conduct most of our face-to-face daily encounters. We have access to levels and forms of knowledge, technological devices and applications, consumer products, and lifestyle choices well beyond what could likely be imagined by sociologists and educators in the late nineteenth and early twentieth centuries. However, just as early sociologists struggled with the mixed promises and dangers inherent to the development of industrial capitalism and liberal democracies, so do contemporary sociologists wrestle with the direction and consequences of current social and economic trajectories.

These tensions, which are expressed in varied and sometimes conflicting ways, are captured in notions of a "risk society" in which the products and consequences of human intervention in nature and society have created serious threats—climate change, environmental devastation, nuclear and chemical weapons, technological dependency, public health epidemics, and large-scale violent conflict—that may exceed our capacity to control them (Beck, 1992; Giddens, 1990). In such a context, not only does the individual bear an increasing degree of responsibility to engage in strategies and actions to compensate for the insecurity and uncertainty of life, but the institutions and mechanisms designed to foster social protection and rational planning or certainty carry potential dangers of their own (Baumann, 1989, 2006). Previous chapters have pointed to various ways in which these dynamics are being experienced and played out in and around education, including heightened involvement in education and training initiatives in response to volatile labour markets, intensification of work and stresses that accompany overload and uncertainty across various spheres of life, changing life course patterns, **marketization**—i.e., the extension of market relations in education—and aggressive patterns of commodification and consumption. Education is expected to equip people to identify and confront the major challenges of the day at the same time that it supplies qualified personnel and knowledge to those social and economic systems that contribute to many of those problems.

This chapter draws together major themes and issues highlighted throughout the book by exploring key issues and challenges that continue to drive educational reform in Canada and other nations. At the heart of contemporary debates over education are concerns about how best to accommodate the demands and uncertainties associated with a globalizing world. The transformations that accompany what is often characterized as a knowledge society convey promises of advanced levels of prosperity and enhanced conditions of life, but they also carry with them high levels of risk and uncertainty in personal and collective circumstances and deep inequalities in resources, capacities, and opportunities. Beginning with a brief discussion of the dynamics associated with educational change, the chapter explores how these relationships intersect with three contemporary educational issues: calls for increased **accountability** and rational planning in education; the impact of new technologies on education; and the implications of social diversity and globalization for education.

Understanding Conflicting Visions of Educational Reform

Education systems have benefited in some ways from the re-emergence of discourses that place human capital development and knowledge at the centre of strategies to build a highly skilled labour force. Educational expansion is a key component in the quest to adapt to a knowledge-based economy governed by advanced technologies, accelerated information-processing capacities, innovation, and flexibility. This approach has coincided with de-emphasis on fiscal restraint and renewed government spending on social and economic programs. However, two subsequent developments have placed limits on government investment in education in Canada and many other nations. First, the 11 September 2001 terrorist attacks in the United States and Western military engagement in the Middle East diverted the focus of much state policy and resources throughout most of North America and Europe to issues related to security and the military. Second, the global financial crisis that began in 2008 and the ensuing economic uncertainty have prompted policies of fiscal restraint that many governments, including those at both federal and provincial levels in Canada, have employed to justify reduced spending and restructuring in education and other social policy areas. Attempts also have been made to reshape education systems to capture new resources and ameliorate criticism from public, government, and corporate interests.

Previous chapters have revealed that, despite being held in generally high regard, education systems have not been immune to a general crisis of confidence in government and public institutions and have attracted criticism along the way. Critics continue to level serious charges against existing education systems—our education system has not maintained competitiveness with educational outputs in the most advanced nations; students are not learning essential skills and performing as well as they must to succeed in the global economy; schools are too costly to maintain in their present form; too much attention is placed on frivolous programs to the neglect of the basics; greater discipline and respect for traditional values are needed in the schools; education systems and personnel need to be more open and accountable to the public; schools need to be more responsive to market forces; taxpayers (or "consumers") who are paying for education require a wider array of educational choices. The catalogue of criticisms is long.

Defenders of public education assert that the critics are creating a distorted portrayal and offering misguided proposals for educational reform that may be even more damaging than the alleged problems. By way of rebuttal, critics respond that many of the people who speak out on behalf of education systems are teachers, bureaucrats, and others whose self-interest lies in preserving the educational status quo. Governments have followed suit by implementing a variety of reforms to constrain and reallocate educational costs, expand public and parental choice, and address issues of accountability, openness, and public participation.

Overriding the aforementioned specific concerns, a new hegemony has arisen to suggest that existing education systems must undergo more fundamental changes to meet the demands of new social and economic realities. This vision advances beyond an earlier notion of back-to-basics education by placing a reformed general education system into a broader continuum of ongoing training, innovation, and skill development (United Nations Development Programme, 2001: 84–5). The OECD (2002: 21) poses the dilemma as a significant area of concern for contemporary societies:

> A democratic society, genuinely committed to the encouragement of lifelong learning for all its people, is faced with a great challenge in the system of education it inherits from the antecedent meritocratic society. Can a system designed to sort and reward the most able be reformed in such a way as to help everyone fulfil their (very diverse) potential? Or, if reform is impossible, is a kind of educational revolution on the agenda for learning?

More recent reports have posed the mandate to cultivate education and skills more bluntly. "Without adequate investment in skills," claims another report produced through the OECD (2012a: 10), "people languish on the margins of society, technological progress does not translate into economic growth, and countries can no longer compete in an increasingly knowledge-based global society."

Global linkages with education are not new—the modern world was shaped by interactions across nations, including processes of colonization and conflict as well as trade and cultural enrichment. Indeed, being considered an educated person often traditionally included the capacity to understand and traverse diverse national contexts. However, educators and students now encounter relatively few areas of life that have been untouched by more recent transformations occurring on a global scale. Global dynamics, in conjunction with rapid technological developments and the shift towards a service-based economy, have come to signify many of the defining characteristics of the contemporary world.

Globalization is readily understood as a general pattern—defined by Giddens (1990: 64), for instance, as "the intensification of worldwide social relations which link distant localities in such a way that local happenings are shaped by events occurring many miles away and vice versa"—but diverse and conflicting interpretations compete regarding the specific nature, dimensions, and implications of global phenomena. Much of the emphasis on globalization emerged through economic and political discourses that have intensified since the 1970s in relation to market liberalization and expanded commodification, accompanied by reductions in the state's capacity to regulate business and trade and provide services not central to economic development. However, globalization also refers to a wide range of other political, economic, social, cultural, and associational trends, many of which have been unfolding over long periods of time. Numerous interrelated processes are associated with globalization: increased fluidity across various types of borders (such as national boundaries and categories of identity); greater awareness of events and connections that involve others regardless of locale; compression of time and space; the internationalization of labour markets and divisions of labour; accelerating expansion of new social networks and information flows; the growth of transnational organizations and alliances; diminishing influence or autonomy of nation-states; and greater individualization.

Whether focused on particular dimensions or on interactions among global is-sues, assessments and discourses concerning globalization are often sharply divided. The transformations occurring in conjunction with globalization are portrayed in various ways as progressive and necessary or as dangerous and threatening, signi-fied in part through distinctions between "globalization from above" (in relation to measures advanced by economic and political elites) and "globalization from below" (with reference to alternatives promoted through popular movements that mobilize broad public support). Struggles related to globalization have been popularized in the mass media, typically framed through graphic, militaristic images of battalions of police in riot gear beating or facing off against young protestors hurtling projectiles or smashing windows and cars as plumes of smoke and gas rise over them. Such scenes, over the past decade and a half, have been common at major political and economic summits. Recent examples also include events associated with the Occupy movement protests in cities across North America and other parts of the world in late 2011 and with the marches that occurred in conjunction with a strike by Quebec students and their supporters a few months later in opposition to government measures to increase post-secondary tuition and later to restrict public demonstrations.

These popular actions and government responses symbolize the polarizing dynam-ics that emerge as part of globalization, but they do not reveal the more nuanced (and sometimes even more socially regressive and destructive) aspects of global develop-ments. Burbules and Torres (2000: 13) caution that globalization cannot adequately be understood simply as a phenomenon that is inherently either "good" or "bad"; rather, it must be assessed through a series of tensions and choices that transcend dichotomies, including those

> between the global and the local; between economic and cultural dimensions of globalization; between globalization viewed as a trend toward homogenization around Western (or, even more narrowly, around American) norms and culture, and globalization viewed as an era of increased contact between diverse cultures, leading to an increase in hybridization and novelty; and between the material and rhetorical effects of globalization.

Conflicting orientations to these and related issues have significant implications for schooling. The vehemence with which contending views about educational reform are expressed signifies the importance of education to both public and personal life. As Chapter 3 has emphasized, many of these debates are not new—the history of public education is riddled with an ongoing litany of critiques, defences, and counter-critiques about education systems and their efficacy. Whatever positions are advocated, widespread concern clearly exists over the necessity to maintain an accessible, equitable system of quality education in the face of significant social and economic changes.

Education debates tend to be characterized by diverse strands that emerge around fundamental contradictions. Alternative understandings of globalization and its im-pact tend to reflect and intensify ongoing tensions between what Carnoy and Levin (1985) term capitalist and democratic imperatives in education, as discussed in Chapter 7. Apple (2000: 17–18), following Gintis (1980), argues that these tensions are indicative of underlying contention over **property rights**, where individual rights and liberties are governed by market relations, contracts, and the possession of pri-vate property, and **person rights**, in which people's rights and freedoms are granted on the basis of citizenship and moral claims. Support for initiatives such as market-based education reforms, reduction of state funding for education, and an emphasis on standardized curricula exemplify some of the ways in which capitalist imperatives and property rights have begun to influence educational decision-making. On the other hand, movements to broaden public access to education, to foster **inclusive schooling** that represents and serves the full range of diversity within communities, and to develop curricula and programs oriented to social justice issues are indicative of approaches to educational reform guided by democratic considerations and human rights. Framing these issues more broadly, Spring (2007) contrasts a dominant "industrial-consumer paradigm" of education—governed by economic productivity and an ethos of consumption—with an alternative paradigm in which emphasis is on quality-of-life issues oriented to promote longevity and subjective well-being.

The ideological struggles that occur over core social rights and priorities have many consequences for schooling. As cases and examples cited in previous chapters have demonstrated, there tends to be greater acceptance in Canada of the essential role played by governments in funding and operating education systems, at least at the elementary and secondary school levels, in contrast to the United States and many other nations where important dimensions of public school teaching, curricula, and finance have been undermined or threatened. At the same time, even in Canada individuals and family members are being called upon to spend increasing amounts of money to fund or support educational activities while private and commercial alternatives are advancing as part of new educational markets. As school systems position themselves to accommodate social changes and competing educational interests, the school year becomes increasingly more crowded with new curricular demands that have to compete for attention and space with existing educational objectives and practices. In the process, many teachers are reporting that, at a time when they are expected to be creative and innovative, they are held back as it becomes increasingly more difficult to keep pace with what is expected of them (Canadian Education Association and Canadian Teachers' Federation, 2012: 13). These challenges and paradoxes are likely to intensify: while the development of knowledge-based societies and new information technologies are fuelled by knowledge, education, and innovation, they also contribute to conditions in which the forms of knowledge, and how these are produced, recognized, and regulated, are likely to diversify and become the focus of ongoing challenges.

Rational Planning and Educational Accountability

Debate over how to measure and interpret educational quality and outcomes has accompanied strongly divergent views about how to reform the education system to improve its performance. One set of issues in which competing educational interests and ideologies have become highly visible is debate over accountability and choice, and related emphasis on market-driven alternatives such as **charter schools**, educational voucher systems, and parental choice models. Some proponents of reform have argued that educational competition and accountability can be increased by implementing merit pay for teachers, basing their salaries or providing incentive bonuses in accordance with student performance or test results. Others see reform as a matter of continuous monitoring and critical reflection by educators, sometimes as a professional responsibility and in other cases in collaboration with other groups, including administrators and community members.

Wilkinson (1994: 17) summarizes the three main factors normally involved in such debates—concern over the declining quality of education in Canada in the face of increasing international competitiveness; concern over the kinds of values transmitted through schooling; and frustration over the lack of responsiveness to change within the educational bureaucracy. Ungerleider (2003: 221–2) points to the need for decisive leadership at all levels to guide public schooling, informed by a solid foundation of knowledge and understanding of the complexities of schooling.

Some of these arguments have been outlined in previous chapters. The issues of concern illustrate how various groups—such as business and neo-liberal interests calling for competitiveness in education and religious organizations seeking the promotion of faith-based values in schooling—come to be aligned within the New Right. By contrast, many other segments of the population, including education and teachers' organizations, organized labour, coalitions to promote social justice, and people who subscribe to more inclusive notions of social equality, have expressed considerable opposition to proposals for market-driven educational reforms.

Fundamental to these debates are competing conceptions about what the goals and purposes of education are and whose interests schooling should serve. Advocates of varying positions agree that public education requires some reform to meet the needs of diverse groups of learners in a rapidly changing social and economic context. Many critics, however, argue that extensive changes reaching beyond the current system are necessary to compensate for a lack of quality, imagination, choice, and effective outcomes in public education.

Proponents of property rights and market-based educational choice make their case by highlighting relationships between educational and economic indicators to demonstrate the deficiencies of the present system. Demands for drastic educational reform were bolstered in the early 1990s by data suggesting that Canada was receiving poor returns on its education investments, as signified by its relatively poor or "mediocre" ranking on labour market activity, economic performance, and student rankings in comparative scores on standardized mathematics, science, and literacy tests (Economic Council of Canada, 1992: 40; Schweitzer, 1995: 47). Although this critique has been tempered somewhat by findings that Canadian students, both in general and within most provinces, have fared relatively better than those in most other comparable nations including the United States, declines in the relative performance of some Canadian students have bolstered concerns from various perspectives that the education system is not fully meeting contemporary needs (Canadian Council on Learning, 2011: 4, 12; Knighton et al., 2010: 39).

In part, the emphasis on test scores and other indicators of educational performance reveals a desire by educators, policy-makers, and parents for systematic feedback on education activities. In terms of assessment of and reporting on individual student performance, for instance, school jurisdictions across the country have sought compromises between those parents and teachers who want test scores that produce a numerical or letter grade purporting to show exactly where one student stands in relation to others and those who feel that anecdotal reporting and commentary about educational processes provide a truer reflection of a student's ability and progress (Lewington, 1995: A1).

Assessing Educational Performance

In education, following innovations in the health-care domain, there has been growing emphasis on the application of **evidence-based decision-making**. The principle of drawing upon a solid foundation of research-based findings to guide educational practice has widespread support among educators, policy-makers, and other groups, although there is less agreement as to how best to implement such a process (Levin and Seward, 2003). Just as parents wish to know how well their children are doing in comparison with others, educators and other interested groups want information about how well different education systems and their outputs measure up against one another. Teachers now spend considerable amounts of their time engaging in critical reflection and planning based on various forms of assessment and indicators from test scores and other types of feedback. On a broader scale, the Canadian Council on Learning was initiated in 2004 as an independent organization, funded by the federal government, as a mechanism to promote lifelong learning, facilitate and exchange research on different dimensions of learning, and foster the application of research in educational decision-making. Among its varied activities, the council has focused attention on developing strategies to address serious data gaps, particularly with respect to post-secondary education, that have made it difficult to draw meaningful comparisons and implement effective changes (Canadian Council on Learning, 2007d: 8). These data gaps are likely to grow further with the dissolution of the Council following the withdrawal of federal funding support in 2010. The elimination of the mandatory long-form census for 2011 will only add to these gaps in information. In the absence of reliable alternatives, Canada will have little national capacity to maintain an adequate base of comprehensive data required for adequate monitoring and analysis of educational performance and change. In one of its final reports, the Canadian Council of Learning (2011: 38) flags the key issues:

> how will Canadians be provided with the authoritative, independent and detailed information on the state of learning in this country that is such a necessary driver of future educational progress? Who will carry forward the national educational agenda that will be a crucial determinant of the future opportunities and prosperity of Canadians and their communities in CCL's absence?

On a narrower plane, educators and education bodies—driven by political pressures and by genuine desire for a knowledge base that may contribute to improved educational performance—have shed much of their initial reluctance to engage in comparative testing of students. Nonetheless, the results from various comparative databases remain highly volatile, especially when they are used to promote the agendas of particular bodies, such as the Fraser Institute, which has published school-by-school "report cards" on educational performance in Alberta, British Columbia, Ontario, and Quebec in its pursuit of market-driven education reform. De Broucker and Sweetman (2002: 8), noting the potential that comparative educational indicators have to be employed in narrow ways by specific groups, stress that "It is all too common to focus on problems, and they certainly exist, but problems are in fact 'news' (and often covered by the news media), whereas the 'un-newsworthy' is mostly good compared to that experienced by other countries."

Since the 1990s, Canada (through various federal government departments, provincial governments, and the Council of Ministers of Education Canada) has participated in recurrent cycles of initiatives like the Trends in International Mathematics and Science Study, the Progress in International Reading Literacy Study, the Program for International Student Assessment, and the Pan-Canadian Assessment Program. These programs, which variously employ standardized tests to compare mathematics, reading, writing, literacy, and science skills at particular age or grade levels across jurisdictions, signify a growing desire for data to provide a comparative baseline for guiding educational assessment and decision-making. Parallel to these developments are movements towards a national curriculum and core curricula in several provinces that provide specified areas of study and learning materials for all learners at particular stages of their studies. Government inquiries conducted over the past two decades, including commissions on learning and education undertaken in Alberta, Ontario, and Newfoundland and Labrador, have acknowledged that issues surrounding problems of assessment, evaluation, and reporting are highly complex. At the same time, consistent with the prevailing trends, their recommendations pointed to the implementation of more systematic procedures for testing and assessing students and education system performance to reduce these issues to quantifiable outcomes.

Debates over testing in Canada, however, have been somewhat muted in comparison to the United States. Legislation in the US, notably the federal No Child Left Behind Act, has generated extensive controversy and skewed educational pathways for many students by linking funding allocation to student outcomes (Irons and Harris, 2007; Meier and Wood, 2004). More generally, in both the US and Canada, numerous critics have pointed out that standardized tests, curricula, and performance indicators do not reflect the true nature and quality of education and tend to discount socioeconomic background and other factors that can influence outcomes. For standardized tests that compare student performance in different provinces and countries to be valid and fair, there must be some assurance that students in each jurisdiction have had an opportunity to cover the material or acquire the skills being tested. Consequently, testing tends to be restricted to a narrow range of all material that is likely to be covered in a subject area. It remains highly debatable as to how accurately test scores reflect student ability either within a given subject area or in more general terms. This selectivity often means that oral and visual skills and other competencies possessed by many otherwise low-performing minority students or marginalized youth are ignored in educational assessments (Kearns, 2011). Low scores based on culturally biased or narrow standardized tests, in turn, sometimes result in inappropriate assessment and program placement that may undermine prospects for education success by Aboriginal youth and other minority students (Peltier, 2010: 127). Testing and evaluation, particularly when they are oriented to empirical or "objective" measures, generally focus on relatively discrete bits of information rather than on critical thinking and wider, more complex activities usually regarded as essential within educational practices. Given that the school day consists of both formal curricular expectations and social and other dimensions of the "hidden" curriculum, there is no necessary correlation between the number of school days and the amount or quality of education in a given school jurisdiction.

Test data must be carefully presented and interpreted to be meaningful. Media and political commentary often ignores the fact that most international and interprovincial comparisons of test results draw on different populations or subgroups of students. Some jurisdictions with lower "average" test scores often include a wider range of students than other jurisdictions that draw from more selective student bodies that would be expected to produce higher score results (Gilliss, 1995: 121–3). Some rethinking of comparative test results has accompanied findings that demonstrate the impact of specific factors—notably socio-economic inequality—on overall performance. In particular, especially within Canada, jurisdictions with the most favourable outcomes tend to be those in which the participants from the lowest socio-economic

Box 9.1 Social and Economic Imperatives and School Ratings

Interest in issues of school choice and accountability has paralleled the desires by many parents to ensure that their children receive a solid educational foundation that ensures they will be competitive for further education and employment opportunities in an information society. One of the best-known and most controversial mechanisms devoted to fostering school choice and to providing parents with information about school performance is a report card on schools in several provinces, including Alberta, British Columbia, Ontario, and Quebec, issued periodically by the Fraser Institute. The report cards rank schools at particular levels in each province according to a composite index composed of provincial test score results and patterns from particular grades in such areas as reading, writing, and numeracy. Proponents of the reporting initiative point to the benefits it offers to educators and parents in providing useful information that can drive educational improvement over time, though this is typically expressed in language framed around notions of educational consumers and marketplaces, as Peter Cowley (2007: 6), one of the authors of the report cards, reveals:

> It was in the context of this rather dismal educational landscape [of government policies that discouraged expansion of private schooling] that The Fraser Institute initiated the school performance measurement project. Its main product—report cards on individual school performance—would, to the extent possible, establish one of the conditions necessary for a free market in education; namely, the availability to consumers, in this case parents, of reliable information on the comparative value of services provided by competing suppliers, in this case schools.
>
> These annual audits of school performance would assist parents in two ways.
>
> First, they would enable parents to make more informed decisions when choosing a school for their children. Second, they would enable parents to advocate more effectively for improvement at their children's schools. These two purposes would be served by bringing together in the report cards a variety of objective data on student results at individual schools in such a way as to make comparisons among schools easy. The results would then be published in an understandable format and made available to the widest possible audience.

categories do well and that show the least difference among learners from the top and bottom socio-economic categories (Willms, 1997: 20; Bussière et al., 2001: 32–3; Bussière et al., 2007: 41; OECD, 2010b).

Testing and assessment procedures can often generate a unique logic apart from the outcomes they are overtly intended to measure. Ball (2004) refers to many recent processes employed by governments and education administrators to report on school activities as "performativity," which can serve a dual function of reporting and impression management. The use of performance indicators and other standards to measure educational effectiveness provides decision-makers with a wide range of information that may be used to gauge and compare different individuals, institutions,

Critics, by contrast, point to serious bias and deficiencies in the aims and methodology employed in the report cards, ignoring social dimensions in favour of economic imperatives. A British Columbia teacher (Waber, 2006: 6–7) identifies several specific internal flaws and wider omissions in the reporting procedures—including ranking schools on a provincial level rather than by the characteristics the report seeks to highlight, confusing **educational governance** (especially public versus private) with other factors that influence performance, ignoring class size, ignoring budgetary factors, and obscuring demographic factors related to students' social backgrounds—and condemns the reports more broadly:

> The focus of the *Report Card* is exceedingly narrow. To identify schools that effectively meet the expectations of the larger community, parents should have access not only to their academic results but also to objective information regarding their success in nurturing non-academic, behavioral, attitudinal and social skills. But even the formula that [report authors] Cowley and Easton use to calculate academic ratings is questionable. Their weighting of the scores for reading, writing, numeracy, gender differences, and meeting expectations exaggerates the differences between schools and school systems.
>
> The shortcomings of the *Report Card* are glaring. It glosses over, or fails to consider, some of the influences that others have found responsible for large differences in academic achievement. Until its authors take into account the numbers of students who require ESL and special needs instruction in each school, the effect of selective admission, the vagaries of the gender gap and the differences in per-pupil cost, a ranking that includes both public and independent schools lacks validity.

Other critics, such as Gutstein (2010: 49–50), stress that, rather than focusing on methodological details, it is crucial to recognize the more fundamental agenda that drives the published rankings and related measures, which is to promote market alternatives to public schools. Similarly, Raptis (2012) observes that in addition to "penalizing" many schools composed predominantly of low-income students, the rankings, along with media reports in which they are disseminated, constitute a more dangerous discourse employed in the interest of powerful political forces.

or units. In the process, it creates a significant amount of new work in gathering information, meeting to discuss reporting and decision-making procedures, reporting, and debriefing, which, in turn, can take time away from teaching and learning processes. At the same time, akin to dangers that teachers may respond to standardized testing by "teaching to the text" in order to generate the best results rather than focusing on other activities, the staff and schools being assessed learn to be proficient in how they highlight the best results and minimize limitations, presenting themselves in the most favourable way possible. The impetus for much evidence-based practice in education is viewed by some critics as an attack on teacher professionalism driven by technical agendas in which knowledge is reduced to limited bits of factual information devoid of a clear understanding of social contexts and human relationships (Clegg, 2005: 417–18). Lessard (2004: 34, 48) uses the case of educational reforms in Quebec to illustrate the tensions and contradictions carried by a "logic of indicators" driven by mechanical applications of enterprise culture, in contrast with efforts to pursue effective pedagogical innovations grounded in classroom practice.

As has been noted throughout this book, schooling and learning are about much more than simply acquiring and repeating information. Many critics ignore the more indeterminate human and social dimensions of education as they seek to generate standardized achievement test scores and quantitative measures of educational accountability for specific ends. Evidence from New Zealand, Australia, the United Kingdom, and several American states, where educational measurement and accountability have been key elements of market-based school reforms, indicates that these measures have been employed more fully to control education, discipline teachers, and appease parents than to contribute to more effective teaching and learning (Smyth et al., 2000). Discourses of accountability and measurement are often silent on the cultural and political dimensions to learning. Persons from distinct social backgrounds have varying degrees of access to information deemed as valuable or valid from the dominant cultural perspective. In many educational settings, not high test scores but the extent to which all students can gain access to meaningful social opportunities and experiences is the mark of student and school success. Bacon (1995: 87), expressing the concerns of many Canadian teachers, emphasizes that:

> Outcomes are not just things that are measurable. For example, appreciation of cultural diversity, adaptability to change, values clarification, a sense of personal worth and responsibility, and character development are all important outcomes but are difficult to measure. Nor are these things the sole responsibility of the school. These responsibilities are shared with parents and others in society.

One former business executive, commenting on his reversal of an earlier assessment that schools should be governed more like businesses, stresses that he has since "learned that a school is not a business. Schools are unable to control the quality of their raw material, they are dependent upon the vagaries of politics for a reliable revenue stream, and they are constantly mauled by a howling horde of disparate, competing customer groups that would send the best CEO screaming into the night" (Vollmer, 2003: 42). Posed another way, the determination of educational quality is a highly contested process that involves several levels of human judgment

> the common denominator among all attempts to judge educational quality is the imposition of human judgement with all of its complex and conflicted assumptions, values, biases, cultural predispositions, and so forth. In this respect, the narrowest of quality evaluation schemes founded purely on standardized tests is no more objectively valid than the most uncomplicated of holistic quality judgements. All parties to the educational process do the same thing in this matter, they impose—or attempt to impose—their ideas about the knowledge, beliefs, values, and attitudes the schools ought to foster. (Paquette, 1989: 23)

Education and New Technologies

The revolutionizing possibilities and imperatives associated with the "information age" are integral to contemporary educational reform processes. The rapid pace of innovation in new information and communications technologies (ICTs) has been accompanied by greater levels of adoption of computer and digital technologies at work and school, and in the home and daily life. Computers and handheld devices, advanced data-processing systems, technology transfer programs, and electronic information networks, notably the Internet and World Wide Web, have affected our expectations about education in the same way that they have altered many general patterns of living and working. Educational institutions encounter rising expectations about their ability both to incorporate information technologies and social media into their own activities and to train persons who have the capacity to master and develop new technologies in innovative ways. The wider social transformations associated with life in a digital world have also contributed to questions about whether traditional educational models and institutions have become obsolete. Like most educational issues, these are complex matters that often reveal contradictory dimensions to how people view these developments and what their implications are for education systems.

Technological innovations have been eagerly embraced by some segments of education communities and resisted or regarded with disdain by others. It is important to distinguish, in these varied responses, between the use and impact of technologies as they relate to individual learners and educators, and those associated with education systems or processes as a whole. Individuals may use computers, social media, or network systems, for instance, to conduct research and write term papers, to organize attendance records or grade reports, to introduce graphic presentations or simulations to classes, or to exchange information with people in other educational settings. These applications may be used as resources to facilitate administrative, teaching, or learning practices for individuals without substantially altering teaching or learning processes. Technological innovations may also be applied in a slightly more engaged manner involving changes that apply to individuals and to education systems, such as the teaching of courses in computers or data-processing or the introduction of distance education courses by television, teleconferencing, or computers. Such applications, however, still are combined with more traditional educational practices. Canadian provincial and territorial curricula typically include guidelines to integrate media with core curricular areas and opportunities to study media education and engage with various media in the school context. However, with the rapidly changing digital environment, schools and educators often struggle to keep pace with emerging developments and the immediate as well as longer-term implications conveyed through these transformations.

Technological change has the potential to alter education in fundamental ways. In the extreme, information and communications technologies suggest an imperative for new paradigms based on drastic alterations to our whole way of thinking, learning, interacting, and living. Selwyn (2012: 4) identifies three principal ways in which educational institutions may be transformed by digital technologies—"virtual schooling," or digital delivery of educational services; digitally driven "reschooling," whereby schools are reconfigured internally through the use of new technologies; and digitally driven "deschooling," where existing school structures and processes are no longer required. Information technologies are commonly posed as inescapable realities that set the pace and standard for work and socio-economic survival in the emergent global scheme of things. Schooling, if it is to be relevant, must ensure that students gain competencies related to some of the technical aspects associated with

Box 9.2 Internet Skills among Canadian Youth

Educators and education systems are struggling to keep pace with a world in which Internet use is a taken-for-granted phenomenon in the lives of children and youth. A survey of over 5,000 Canadian students in Grades 4 to 11 reveals the growing confidence that boys and girls alike have with some computer-related skills (ERIN Research, 2005: 57, 59):

Kids rated their own skill level in ten common areas of their lives. Most of the skills, listed in [the following table], relate to the world of schools and friends—only two are specifically computer-based (skill using the Internet and skill playing computer games). The rating scale runs from 0 to 100 with 50 as the midpoint. If people rate their skills accurately, the average rating would be 50. If most people thought that they were better than average, then the mean rating would be higher than 50.

In fact most of the ratings exceed 50, meaning that students as a group tend to be rather confident in their abilities. "Using the Internet" is, by a slight margin, the top-ranked skill. Both girls and boys feel confident in their Internet abilities.

It is no surprise that heavy Internet use is associated with skill using the Net and skill playing computer games. But what about shopping or making friends or making people laugh? One hypothesis is that kids who are good shoppers recognize that the Internet is one tool of the trade and they spend time online to advance their interest in shopping. Likewise, the Net is a medium for making new friends (e.g., via MSN), and it is a huge source of humorous material (several of the top-ranked "favourite sites" deal primarily in jokes).

Kids who are interested in making new friends will use the Net as one channel of social interaction and will therefore increase the time they spend online. On the other hand, those who are interested in math, science, reading, and the arts may find less to advance their interests on the Net and spend less time online. What the hypothesis states is that shopping, making friends and

new technologies, which means that the infrastructure must be sufficiently equipped with these technologies—and be able to adapt and innovate within ongoing processes of change. Spurred by varying forms of government support and corporate funding, several initiatives have emerged in recent years to promote the introduction and use of new technologies and information-based learning systems at virtually all levels of education and training.

Educators and curriculum planning bodies are also paying increased attention to significant moral, cultural, and social issues that accompany new digital media and their application. The balance between regulation to prevent abuse or inadequate content conveyed through networked devices and innovative learning opportunities is often a delicate one that can be upset by uncertainty, as well as by over-reacting or failing to respond in various ways to unanticipated new conditions. In recognition of the complex array of intersecting social and technical being funny are skills that, for today's youth, are embedded in electronic communications. The Internet is an extension of everyday social life and an integral part of these skill sets.

Table 9.1 Girls' and Boys' Self-Ratings of 10 Skills

(Skill rating: 0 = not as good; 50 = about the same; 100 = better)

Skill	Girls	Boys	Total
Using the Internet*	62	68	65
Making friends	66	62	64
Telling jokes, making people laugh	60	65	63
Reading*	66	58	62
Playing computer games*	50	71	61
Sports*	51	64	58
Math and science*	52	57	54
Visual arts*	55	47	51
Shopping*	62	33	47
Playing a musical instrument or singing	51	42	47

* Statistically significant gender difference accounting for 1 per cent or more of the variance.

Source: © Media Awareness Network, *Young Canadians in a Wired World*, Ottawa, Canada, 2008, at: www.media-awareness.ca, quoted with permission.

dimensions emerging with the proliferation of ICTs and digital information, educational jurisdictions in Canada and other nations have begun to integrate into school curricula both media literacy (i.e., the capacity to engage critically with digital and other mass media) and **digital literacy** (which encompasses the various skills necessary to operate as producers and consumers of knowledge in a digital world). Importantly, digital literacy includes both technical knowledge and the capacity to understand, synthesize, and critically engage with information produced through various media (van Hamel, 2011: 11–12). As with many other curricular changes, the extent to which schooling can foster effective critical literacies related to media will depend on adequate support and commitment throughout education systems. Among other critical factors, this support must include assurances that formal objectives will not be subordinated by competing demands that enter into educational practice.

Digital Transformations within Education

Educational innovations now in place or underway include the delivery of entire educational programs by computer-based curricular modules and other forms of e-learning, the transformation of classrooms into fully "wired" learning centres, and electronic networks that provide for "virtual" campuses or schools. There is growing official support to integrate new technologies more comprehensively into education. In the mid-1990s, Ontario's Royal Commission on Learning (1994: 26–7) stressed that "it is crucial that every classroom in every school be part of the information highway," driven by the conviction "that information technology is one of the engines needed to drive the necessary transformation of the education system." By the end of the decade, initiatives like SchoolNet, organized through Industry Canada in conjunction with provincial and territorial governments, were promoted as vehicles that would link all public schools and libraries through the Internet with the aim to prepare learners for the knowledge-based society. Some of these initiatives have not been as successful as initially anticipated, but they have been supplanted by an immense range of alternatives at local, national, and international levels. The most common types of developments have included

- purchase and action plans to incorporate computers and other electronic devices, programs, software, and communication networks into the ongoing activities of educational institutions;
- the establishment of computer-assisted learning and computer-based training programs, especially for students with special needs and other targeted groups;
- the introduction of hands-on learning technologies in classrooms and technology support programs for educators;
- use of information networks for distance learning and modular learning programs;
- electronic linkages among new institutional networks of participants and partners in education and other fields.

The introduction of new technologies and information networks has widespread appeal because of the advantages they offer to both educators and learners. Routine tasks can sometimes be integrated into computer programs in an efficient, cost-effective manner that benefits and enhances the interest of the learner, teacher, or administrator. Information and materials previously beyond the reach of many educational institutions, particularly in remote areas or those with limited supporting resources, are now often readily available to all participants who have access to computer facilities or advanced communications technology. Information and service networks; learning packages in CD- or DVD-ROM form; multi-media kits; distance education programs; and online, wireless, or satellite transmission of information enable educators, students, and even parents to access an unprecedented range of resources. The digitization of library resources, journals and books, and other materials provides unprecedented access to important learning and research resources. Students who acquire computer and programming skills and gain facility with information transmission and retrieval processes have access to competitive job markets driven by technological change. Moreover, computer-literate students and school personnel contribute to the pool of highly qualified people required to advance further technological progress. Information technology and the networks it fosters also promote co-operation and innovation among educational institutions and between education and other sectors of the economy.

Challenges to the Digital Revolution

It is important to examine critically the extent to which education can and should be modified by technological change. Tran (1995: 50–1) poses a number of fundamental questions that continue to be relevant as educators contend with how best to integrate ICTs into the classroom. These include the following:

- What is the goal of education and how do computer systems contribute to this goal?
- What are the best approaches to teaching students, training teachers, and evaluating programs?
- How is computer technology related to various subject areas?
- How far can new technology be incorporated without damaging major learning objectives?

Some proponents of the expansion of computer technology in the classroom have portrayed teachers and other school personnel as uninformed or rigid detractors who resist changes that have already been embraced by students and employers (Lewington and Orpwood, 1993: 100).

However, computers and new information systems often have been introduced into schools without a thorough assessment of how they will be incorporated into daily school routines, how they affect teachers' work, and what kinds of training and support resources are available. Even when school systems and personnel are firmly committed to the expansion of new technologies, for instance, deficiencies in areas such as in-service training, technical support, and access to hardware and software will undermine the potential contributions these technologies can make to educational practices. Cuban (2001: 177–8) observes that, even as computer use has become ubiquitous in North American schools, there have been no clear advances in educational outcomes related to academic achievement and efficiency, no clearly defined agreement on what constitutes computer literacy, and no technological revolution in teaching and learning in most classrooms. Interviews with a panel of teachers reveal five major concerns among educators about how digital technologies are employed in Canadian schools: schools tend to emphasize training students to use technologies rather than enhancing learning through the use of technologies; teaching related to new technologies is too often mechanistic and teacher-driven rather than undertaken as a shared responsibility that facilitates students' learning; many teachers, especially those concerned about classroom management early in their careers, limit use of technologies and their applications for fear they will disrupt attention to other learning objectives; teacher training tends to emphasize technological use rather than ways to enhance learning through technologies and new media; and school regulations and media filters limit options for teachers to incorporate network-related tools within effective learning situations (Steeves, 2012b: 4).

From the perspective of learners, new technologies constitute additional forms of cultural and fiscal capital that differentially affect opportunities for success or failure. Increasing numbers of people have access to computers, "smart" devices, and Internet connections at home, school, workplaces, and public wireless access points. New technologies tend to be adopted more widely over time once their utility is established and basic start-up costs drop. At the same time, differential means and opportunities possessed by families, communities, and institutions to keep abreast of up-to-date, compatible forms of information technology and support contribute to the persistence of gaps in technological access and use. Network-linked technologies have become an indispensable means of communication and information for growing segments of the population, offering numerous advantages and pleasures but also increasing risks such as cyberbullying, information theft, and vulnerability posed by dissemination of highly personal details through sexting or other initially private messages. Craft (2011: 8–9) contrasts two dominant discourses associated with childhood and youth in the context of these technological developments. One discourse poses the digital revolution as "endangering," with youth seen to be vulnerable and at risk in an uncertain world; the other sees new communications technologies as "enabling," with youth empowered by innovation, creativity, and technological sophistication. While proponents of various ideological and political positions may emphasize one or the other of these orientations, evidence suggests that the realities depicted through these representations tend to be intermingled in the experiences of young people. Many Canadian youth, for example, tend to express confidence in their ability to manage the risks conveyed through digital technologies, but they also acknowledge the networked society to be one in which private space has disappeared with the expansion of surveillance by parents, teachers, and online businesses (Steeves, 2012a: 16, 37). Selwyn (2012: 15), assessing the changing relationship between educational technologies and school structures, observes the need for a balanced approach to establish "exactly how the relationships between formality and informality within schools may be adjusted and altered in ways that can shift the frames of in-school technology use without undermining basic institutional structures and interests."

Digital Divides and Social Inequalities

The explosion of computer technology over the past two decades has fostered considerable interest in a phenomenon widely described as the **digital divide** with reference to the inequitable nature of information technology access, use, and returns. The digital divide separates people with ready access to computer technology and Internet connections from those without such access. Sciadis (2002: 4–5) emphasizes several variants of digital divides, based on two main sets of factors. One set of issues concerns the unequal distribution of access to information and communications technologies across significant sociological and demographic categories, including age, gender, class, and geography. Data from 2006 reveal that about 94 per cent of 15-year-olds in Canada, compared to an average of 80 per cent of those the same age in all OECD nations, reported frequent use of computers at home (Statistics Canada and CMEC, 2012: Table C.5.5). Some evidence suggests that the widespread penetration of computer technologies throughout much of the world has closed some of these gaps, but access to and use of ICTs in developing nations and poorer regions remain well below comparable levels in highly developed and affluent nations (Dutta et al., 2012). Sciadis (2002: 18) observes that, while more people in all categories are employing computer technologies with increasing frequency, the divide between the top and bottom income groups has persisted or even widened (ibid., 5).

In Canada, programs sponsored by government and industry groups to supply home computers to students in households with limited resources attest to the distance that remains to be covered before the nation is fully networked (see, e.g.,

Sky's the Limit Youth Organization, 2010). Internationally, initiatives such as the One Laptop Per Child program have been undertaken to close the divide by providing low-cost computers to youth in some of the world's poorest regions, but there are serious limitations to these types of interventions. Success in some areas has been offset by widening gaps in computer use in Peru and other nations due to inadequate computer skills among teachers and administrators, limited technical support, software issues, lack of Internet access, hidden support costs, and other financial and cultural barriers (Bajak, 2012; Shrestha, 2007).

A second area of concern is related to differences in access and capabilities with respect to specific technologies, including analogue and digital devices. One dimension of uneven skill levels associated with ICTs is a generational divide in application, capabilities, and attitudes related to new technologies. A cross-Canada survey (Ipsos Reid, 2007: 2), comparing responses of persons aged 55 and over with those between ages 18 and 55, for instance, reveals that

> Behaviourally, older Canadians lag behind the younger groups in each of 20 common online activities Canadians have ever participated in. The gap is largest for listening to Internet radio (34 per cent), downloading free MP3 files (32 per cent), visiting blogs (23 per cent), conducting online banking (21 per cent), researching courses and schools (21 per cent), comparison shopping (20 per cent), searching for real estate (18 per cent), researching trips (17 per cent), using the Internet at work for personal reasons (17 per cent), and purchasing online (14 per cent). These divides are evident in surveys of Canadian school-age youth.
>
> These trends are significant to relationships at work, school, and other social spheres as children and youth become increasingly immersed in and adept with a wide range of technologies and applications beyond capacities held by their parents, teachers and supervisors. Educational institutions, including universities that have often been at the cutting edge of new technologies, are scrambling to expand technologies and programs that incorporate ICTs as ever-emerging technologies emerge. Consequently, by the time the "established" order begins to incorporate or respond to favourite networking sites and devices, youth who are the most "connected" have already moved on to new ones.

Source: The Canadian Inter@ctive Reid Report, © Ipsos Reid.

By 2012, Internet access had become nearly universal (95 per cent) among Canadians younger than 55 years of age, compared to access rates of just over two-thirds (68 per cent) for those ages 55 and over, while corresponding rates of mobile phone access were nearly three times higher for the under 55 age cohort (47 per cent) than for those ages 55 and over (16 per cent) (Ipsos Reid, 2012: 2). With successive generations moving through the life course since the widespread introduction of the Internet and wireless technologies, plus the widening reach of digital technologies across the globe, there is some convergence, though age differences are likely to continue, reflecting changing demands and interests associated with particular life stages.

These issues have significant implications for schooling. Educational activity, in general, tends to facilitate the use of digital technologies both directly and indirectly. Data from Statistics Canada reveal that students, especially in younger age cohorts, are more engaged than non-students in Internet use for both educational and other purposes (McKeown and Underhill, 2007). By contrast, despite the promise that computers may hold for expanding education and training possibilities, students'

International Case Study

Variations in Access to Computers and Software

The capacity to participate actively in contemporary education, work, and social settings is becoming increasingly dependent on computers and related information technologies. As the world becomes more fully wired and integrated, students continue to experience substantial variations in the extent to which they have access to technologies and technological support at home and

Table 9.2 Percentage of 15-Year-Old Students in Schools Whose Principals Reported Shortage or Inadequacy of Computer Hardware or Software, by Province and Selected Countries, 2009

	% with Computer Shortage or Inadequacy	% with Software Shortage or Inadequacy
Province		
Newfoundland and Labrador	28	27
Prince Edward Island	8	15
Nova Scotia	22	13
New Brunswick	37	24
Quebec	28	21
Ontario	39	22
Manitoba	29	22
Saskatchewan	16	11
Alberta	23	13
British Columbia	22	21
Selected OECD/G8 Countries		
Canada	31	20
Australia	29	21
Denmark	26	14
Finland	42	41
Germany	29	28
Italy	29	39
Ireland	51	39
Japan	14	22
South Korea	8	19
New Zealand	43	24
Norway	37	38
Russian Federation	63	57
Sweden	52	35
Switzerland	17	16
United Kingdom	32	20
United States	26	15

Source: Data from Statistics Canada and CMEC (2012b: Table C.5.6).

school. The data in Table 9.2 illustrate some of these discrepancies, revealing that in a number of Canadian jurisdictions as well as in other highly developed nations one-quarter or more of all schools are reported to lack adequate computer or software resources. These figures also suggest an upward spiral in the adoption of information technologies. As computer use becomes more widely accepted as a basic part of education in a given context, expectations about having access to the latest technologies and digital services are likely to rise.

Regardless of the situation in most highly developed nations, students in many developing parts of the world have even fewer opportunities to use computers at school and in other settings. In developed nations, including even those like Sweden or Finland in which relatively high rates of computer and software shortages or inadequacies are reported, one computer is available for about every five to ten or fewer students; in contrast, in developing nations this ratio is frequently many times higher, most notably in cases like Guatemala (with a ratio of about 100 students per computer), Morocco (174:1), Dominican Republic (179:1), and Ghana, where there is only one computer, on average, per 586 learners (International Telecommunication Union, 2010: 35–6). These relationships are even more skewed when the actual uses of computers are taken into account, as the figures include computers that are used strictly or partially for administrative use as well as those that are part of pedagogical practice.

Access to computers or mobile technology in schools is only one dimension of wider inequalities evident in the nature and quality of educational services related to ICTs and other factors that can be delivered in different parts of the world. Broadband Internet access is available to nearly all schools (though there are exceptions, such as in remote rural regions) in much of the developed world, but rates of broadband connectivity are about 50 per cent in middle-income and developing countries in the Americas, and are lower than 10 per cent in some parts of Africa; some of the latter, in turn, notably Ethiopia, Senegal, and Ghana, face the more fundamental challenge of having no electricity in a majority of schools (International Telecommunication Union, 2010: 38–40). However, some developing regions and nations are highly connected, with new technologies integrated into schooling and providing educational opportunities to students in areas that previously lacked adequate schooling options. In the course of these changes, understood in relation to other major issues that confront educators and schools in many developing nations, there are serious concerns that educational inequalities are likely to increase both within nations and globally.

Discussion Questions

1. What major factors are likely to account for variations in access to adequate computing facilities and software in Canada and other developed nations? Provide a sociological explanation for this issue.

2. To what extent is it important and even possible for all students in Canada and other nations to have equal access to current information technologies? Why do you consider this to be the case?

use of computers for personal enjoyment, gaming, and communications has tended to match or prevail over word processing and other activities related to schoolwork (Corbett and Willms, 2002: 14). Results from international surveys reveal that computers are available in school on a regular basis for increasing proportions of the student population, though important variations exist in computer use—boys are more likely than girls (52 per cent and 41 per cent, respectively) to report frequent use of computers at school, while the rates of those who report frequent computer use at school range from 28 per cent in Quebec to 65 per cent or more in Saskatchewan and Manitoba (Statistics Canada and CMEC, 2012b: Tables C.5.3, C.5.5).

Educational applications of technology can also be undermined by the inability of educators to appreciate the potential held by digital technologies because of their own lack of understanding and facility with ongoing changes. Clifford (2005: 15) portrays graphically the gap between "cyberkids" and technologically illiterate educators:

> Many young people spend a lot of time online and gaming, yet educators have very little understanding of the intellectual skills they actually use there. Cyberkids multi-task, plugged into ipods, MSN and their cell phones all at once. They send text messages and video clips wherever, whenever. Writing, they'd rather hunker down crosslegged in a busy hallway than sit quietly, straight-backed, with feet flat on the floor in the ergonomically approved positions most of us were taught in Grade 10 typing classes. They pull their laptops out of back-packs and connect to the wireless network in their favorite coffee shop. Talking about it as old fogies, we chuckle together about the generation gap and how we know that we just don't get it. If there are young people nearby, they generally keep their mouths shut. "How do you listen to those headphones and actually concentrate on what you are supposed to be doing?" we ask them, like anthropologists trying to win our way into the exotic rituals of a jungle tribe.

Gender-related differences extend to how computers are used and the kinds of computer-related training undertaken in schooling. Males remain much more actively involved than females in computer studies and computer use at all levels of education, particularly in fields that involve computer programming and advanced applications, as opposed to data entry, word processing, or clerical uses (Collis, 1991; Dryburgh, 2002). In many educational settings, women's positions are undermined by tendencies to privilege technical knowledge over social skills and by masculinist cultural assumptions and social practices associated with information technologies (Butterwick et al., 2007: 286; Rose and Jenson, 2007: 66–7). Among Canadian teens, half or more of all males, compared to just over one-third of females, identify their computer and the Internet as a source of enjoyment, with males substantially more likely to identify video and computer gaming as a major source of enjoyment. Females, on the other hand, are slightly more likely than males to designate e-mail communications as a source of enjoyment (Bibby, 2001: 24). Differences in computer use and applications tend to be associated, in turn, with gender-differentiated labour market and employment patterns (Taylor, 2005).

Much of the discussion over the implementation of new technologies in education concerns the specific advantages or disadvantages of technology while ignoring wider political and pedagogical considerations. Among the most ardent promoters of computer and advanced technological innovations in education are business interests, corporations, specialists, or government personnel whose profits or career advancement are linked with prospects for widespread adoption of their products or services in educational settings, or parents who seek competitive advantage for their children (Mangan, 1994). Education poses a highly lucrative market for business and commercial interests both directly and indirectly, through sales of information and communications technology and related products to educational institutions, broader influence over educational decision-making, and cultivation of product identification and marketing to students and their families.

The rhetoric associated with new technologies sometimes helps to foster a misleading sense of urgency in which it appears imperative for us to master technology or else become doomed to failure. As funding and program priorities shift towards computer technology, other programs and services may be cut or undermined. Some critics point out that it is easy to become mesmerized by graphics, simulations, and other technical capabilities, as well as by imagery related to technological revolutions and information highways, to such an extent that fundamental moral and human dimensions of education are forgotten (Beattie, 1996: 104–5). In its most extreme forms, technology can decontextualize education, reduce knowledge to isolated bits or fragments of information, and undermine the kinds of face-to-face contact and social interaction that are vital to many learning processes (Nelsen, 1997). Computerized education, paralleling changes to workplace environments in which technologies replace human activities for purposes of control, efficiency, and cost-saving, can often restrict rather than enhance people's capacity to develop and apply higher-level skills related to thinking and complex reasoning, communication, and problem-solving (Levy and Murnane, 2007). Moreover, the potentially empowering aspects of some new technologies are likely to remain limited as long as digital and information systems are embedded within power relations in which the capacity to monitor, regulate, predict, and modify human behaviour corresponds with opportunities to increase private profit or advance interests of the most powerful groups (Monahan, 2005). More explicitly, the triumph of technology within education, insofar as it has occurred, is viewed by many critics as a further extension of agendas to advance the free-market, liberal capitalist, neo-conservative agenda.

Computers and other new technologies, as with many other factors associated with teaching and learning, play a contradictory role in educational relationships. Information technology can stimulate interest, increase access to resources and programs, enhance innovation and flexibility, facilitate connections among educational participants, and ensure that education is attuned to emergent global trends. It can also work to the disadvantage of educators and learners who do not have access to or are unable to master technological developments. It may democratize access to information, but it can also contribute to centralized control, increased monitoring of individual activity, and limits to freedom. It can open up new employment and creative possibilities, but it can also contribute to the reproduction of existing social inequalities and the emergence of new dimensions by which more privileged groups come to distance themselves from the underprivileged. Underlying all of these concerns is the recognition that schooling, by nature, tends to be highly nuanced and complex. As an institution constituted by social as well as technical relationships and formal and informal practices, schooling cannot be understood in isolation from the broader contexts within which both social change and technological innovation operate.

Education and Social Diversity

As educational institutions struggle to remain relevant and viable, they must contend with the ongoing challenge of how best to define their mandates and serve the students and communities they intend to reach. One of the most prominent characteristics of contemporary educational institutions is the tremendous range of diversity among students and other participants. This phenomenon reflects the changing composition of populations, the recognition that more people are attending and staying in school for longer periods of time, the integration of previously excluded groups into educational settings, and more fluid boundaries between different forms of schooling and other social and educational sites. In all of these regards, internal and external transformations are challenging and reconfiguring the educational landscape, marked by shifting conceptions of what knowledge and education represent in a globalizing context.

In addition to the array of choices created by new institutional arrangements and programs, increased attention is being paid to various kinds of lifelong learning and informal learning that occur in community and work settings and other sites beyond formal educational institutions. As trends discussed throughout the book demonstrate, more people are undertaking a growing variety of informal and alternative educational activities even as they participate in formal education for longer periods of time. These developments suggest that most conventional educational institutions will be able to maintain large student numbers, but they also pose challenges for institutions to adapt and modify their activities to accommodate new types of learners and demands while taking into consideration innovations and activities from alternative or competing educational services and channels.

Corresponding with the focus on alternative sites and models of educational delivery is a broadening of our understandings about what constitutes knowledge. As well as growing emphasis on the kinds of scientific and technical knowledge that contribute to innovations that are central to the growth of knowledge-based or information societies, greater recognition is accorded indigenous knowledge and other knowledge systems that are not rooted in Western historical traditions (Battiste and Henderson, 2009). The increasing presence of immigrants from varied national contexts makes it likely that engagement with and interaction among diverse knowledge systems and traditions will increase in many parts of Canada. The capacity to share and learn from knowledge of different types can provide social participants with useful opportunities to foster innovation and cultural enrichment, but it is also important to pay attention to tensions and problems these interactions may generate. Efforts to include particular knowledge systems within educational programming may produce resistance or struggles with proponents of more traditional or competing curricular priorities, while risking the possibility that the knowledge is presented in a fragmented, partial, or inaccurate way. New hierarchies of knowledge are also emerging, especially as resources and status are more likely to be accorded to scientific and technical knowledge while other types of knowledge tend to be less fully integrated into programming or receive only nominal recognition.

As knowledge is accepted as a fundamental driver of social and economic transformation, schools and other educational institutions have some prospects to benefit from enhanced social importance and resources. However, these changes also mean increased scrutiny to ensure that schooling is delivering the kinds of outcomes regarded as essential by employers, governments, and other stakeholders. All of these developments have exerted increasing new pressures on public schooling and traditional modes of educational delivery to remain open, accessible, and meaningful to a diverse range of learners and their communities. Diversity can be one of the major strengths of democratic public institutions, but it also poses practical challenges in how it is best accommodated.

The educational world has become more complex as educational constituencies have broadened. Education is beginning earlier in life, with expanded preschool and early childhood initiatives, and is continuing well beyond high school and post-secondary levels for most people. Demographic changes, immigration, increasing Aboriginal populations, changes in families and workplaces, modifications to the life course, and broader concerns about personal, community, and social security are altering the nature of student bodies and the attitudes and expectations they carry with them. Educational institutions and participants are positioning themselves to respond to admonitions that the stakes of getting an education—and getting the proper kinds of education—are growing.

Various educational programs and services have also emerged in response to the needs of diverse constituencies. These include

- adult education, university degree programs for mature students, and integration programs for persons who return to school later in life;
- ESL, heritage language, cultural education, and anti-racism education programs;
- programs for Aboriginal students and educational institutions and initiatives under First Nations control;
- educational programs and services for the visually or hearing-impaired, or for persons with other physical or mental disabilities;
- alternative schools or classes for intellectually gifted, emotionally impaired, or learning-disabled students;
- expansion of distance education, web-based courses, and other options for students who cannot attend classes in person as a result of geography, time, work, mobility, or other restrictions;
- increased acknowledgement and recognition of alternative forms of knowledge, including indigenous knowledge and knowledge acquired on the job or in other social settings, and assessment and recognition mechanisms for prior learning;
- co-operative education and other learning programs that combine formal schooling with vocational training or community or work experience;
- scholarship or mentoring programs to encourage female students to complete studies in fields like natural sciences and computers and to promote male literacy and reading skills;
- internationalization of education, exchange programs, and co-operative arrangements between educational institutions in different nations;
- global citizenship and comparative education programs.

Many of these changes are positive insofar as they expand educational opportunities and provide options for education and training appropriate to people's circumstances and needs. Expanded educational services may provide particular benefits for segments of the population that typically have been excluded from all but the most basic levels of education. It is crucial, at the same time, to analyze and not take for granted issues like sponsorship, control, funding, accessibility, and delivery of programs and services in order to gain a full understanding of the nature and implications of educational change and innovation.

Box 9.3 Roots of Empathy

Educational reform is often accused of being susceptible to emerging fads, jargon, and innovations that have little sustained impact on educational outcomes. With all of the distractions concerning educational innovation in complex societies, it is important not to lose sight of the centrality of human interactions within educational practice. Several schools in Canada and other nations provide opportunities for students to integrate learning with community service and caring relationships with others across the age spectrum.

Many schools are establishing programs that enable students to interact with seniors in care homes, residences, schools, and community settings, providing unique opportunities for learning, social engagement, and understanding of such issues as aging, disability, mental illness, and death. In British Columbia, for example, the provincial Retired Teachers' Association (BCRTA) established an award to recognize programs in the province's public schools that fostered student–senior interaction. Five such programs were honoured in 2012, including a program in Williams Lake where part of the curriculum is delivered in a seniors' residence near the elementary school, enabling time to work and engage with seniors; a kindergarten program in Invermere that includes weekly classes in an assisted and independent living centre to enable students and seniors to read, work, and play together; a music program in Fruitvale in which a senior musician provides harmonica training for Grade 3 students; a program in Surrey that enables kindergarten students to work on art and music projects with "Grandfriends" at an extended-care facility; and a Humanitarian Club in a Langley High School that engages members in several activities, including weekly visits with residents in a local retirement centre (BCRTA, 2012).

The highly successful program called Roots of Empathy, founded by Canadian educator and parent/child advocate Mary Gordon in 1996, offers another prominent example of how paying attention to fundamental social relationships can make a difference in even some of the most challenging circumstances. The program, which is endorsed by provincial education ministries and school boards across the country, pairs elementary school students with parents and infants from within the community, enabling participants to develop close interpersonal connections while learning about human development, positive parenting skills, and activities linked to core curricular areas. The program has expanded, through an evidence-based approach building on strong integration with

This is especially true of fiscally or politically motivated reforms, or those that treat education in an abstract way as an industry or business. Economically, it often makes sense to close community or neighbourhood schools with low enrolments, to increase class sizes or tuition fees, or to prioritize education programs that contribute to high student achievement and employment. However, sometimes less tangible social, pedagogical, and ethical dimensions are also crucial to educational practice and decision-making. Educators, administrators, and policy-makers need to be aware of the questions and limitations that surround the appropriateness and applicability of such indicators.

both the communities in which it operates and key dimensions of the schools' curricula, to several other national and educational settings. Guided by principles of participatory democracy and inclusion, the initiative provides students with opportunities to observe and reflect on human development and interactions by teaming with infants and parents in their neighbourhoods. Roots of Empathy (2012) summarizes the program's main features:

Emotional Literacy

At the heart of the program are a neighbourhood infant and parent who visit the classroom every three weeks over the school year. A trained Roots of Empathy Instructor coaches students to observe the baby's development and to label the baby's feelings. In this experiential learning, the baby is the "Teacher" and a lever, which the instructor uses to help children identify and reflect on their own feelings and the feelings of others. This "emotional literacy" taught in the program lays the foundation for more safe and caring classrooms, where children are the "Changers." They are more competent in understanding their own feelings and the feelings of others (empathy) and are therefore less likely to physically, psychologically and emotionally hurt each other through bullying and other cruelties. In the Roots of Empathy program children learn how to challenge cruelty and injustice. Messages of social inclusion and activities that are consensus-building contribute to a culture of caring that changes the tone of the classroom. The Instructor also visits before and after each family visit to prepare and reinforce teachings using a specialized lesson plan for each visit. Research results from national and international evaluations of Roots of Empathy indicate significant reductions in aggression and increases in pro-social behaviour.

Empathy

The cognitive aspect of empathy is perspective-taking and the affective aspect is emotion. Roots of Empathy educates both the mind and the heart.

Empathy is a key ingredient to responsible citizenship and responsive parenting. Information on infant safety and development helps children to be more aware of issues of infant vulnerability such as Sudden Infant Death Syndrome (SIDS), Shaken Baby Syndrome, Fetal Alcohol Spectrum Disorder (FASD) and second-hand smoke. Observations of a loving parent–child relationship give children a model of responsible parenting.

Risk and Empowerment: Education in the Global Context

Accelerated globalization and new information and communication technologies have fostered a sometimes confusing and uncertain array of educational realities and choices for educational participants and those trying to shape or make sense of education. Life options, for many students and their families, are becoming even more precarious. As they make their way through education systems and other learning sites, the numerous possibilities that learners are likely to encounter for applying and extending their learning may be offset by their capacity to finance their schooling or pay off student debt, their uneven prospects to attain meaningful work, and the numerous other complications that arise in a changing world.

Children in the initial stages of their educational pathways have unprecedented opportunities to interact with peers from across the globe, gain exposure to vast bodies of knowledge and information, and develop skills and capacities for ongoing creativity and social enhancement. In this shifting social landscape, questions about how to organize and deliver educational activities, while ensuring that all children and youth have viable prospects to pursue these learning options, remain crucial. Nonetheless, in a context of what seems to be a relatively straightforward matter for communities and governments to devote greater resources and attention to educational matters, substantial barriers limit the likelihood that the desired objectives can be achieved.

On a global scale, the factors preventing children from attending or completing school include extreme poverty, economic and social vulnerability, slavery and sexual exploitation, conflict and war, refugee status, environmental disasters, nutrition and health problems, and other forms of dislocation (Brock, 2011). The worst of these problems are typically encountered in some developing parts of the world, but even in regions where children and youth face limited exposure to these concerns, there are significant connections and implications.

A key feature of globalization is the growing capacity for decisions made by governments, corporations, and citizens in specific parts of the world to become interconnected with those in other regions. In North American school jurisdictions, education for global citizenship, involving complex understandings about globalization, knowledge about events, conditions, and practices in other parts of the world, and skills essential for life in a globally connected world, has not yet extended beyond limited or somewhat superficial levels (Myers, 2010). Cases in which public attention, through the immediacy offered by information technologies and communication networks, can convert tragedies and triumphs that occur in distant locales into major world events may offer numerous learning possibilities in a highly connected world that also produces significant distractions and deviations from important priorities. Global connections are also being enhanced in other ways as immigration levels from diverse source countries increase and geographic mobility and travel options expand within Canada and internationally.

Canadian educational institutions and classrooms reach and often bring together students with a variety of social backgrounds and learning needs. Those whose social and economic conditions are relatively stable and secure, regardless of racial, ethnic, and family origins, coexist with others from households in which refugee status, residential schooling, or other experiences have involved serious trauma, deprivation, or injury. The dynamics within specific regional or national contexts are important in assessing how to address policies and practices that intensify global climate change, human trafficking, or ethnic conflict, for example, but the roots and solutions to these issues also transcend boundaries. It is important that Canadian learners and citizens know about issues like poverty, inequality, and discrimination in their own communities, just as they also need to know about such issues as how Canadian corporations may be implicated in environmentally destructive and socially oppressive practices or how the relatively affluent and privileged life chances many of them enjoy are possible because of limited industrial regulation or low labour costs in other parts of the world. With rising individualism and ideological, political, fiscal, and social barriers that make collective organization difficult, it is increasingly more important to find ways to ensure that learners have means to share knowledge that is critical for strong citizenship at both local and global levels. These types of learning include opportunities to understand ongoing struggles such as those associated with civil rights, feminism, anti-racism, labour, and other social movements that would enable citizens to develop tools to explore the roots, limitations, and possibilities associated with mobilizing effective social change.

However, there are serious challenges and resistance to the kinds of critical engagement necessary to foster effective global citizenship education. The focus on skills, employability, and core curricula limits the space available for critical reflection within already crowded curricula in many educational programs. Market-focused economic imperatives and policies and practices oriented to advance the interests of powerful corporations or political groups further undermine broader chances for democratic engagement while exacerbating many of the problems that such engagement seeks to address. Reactions to high-profile incidences of violence and mass shootings in several educational institutions in North America and Europe, combined with broader concerns about terrorist threats, have heightened a climate of fear that has reinforced discourses and policies focusing on themes of social control and public security. The calls by some American politicians and lobbyists to arm teachers, in the wake of the horrific killings at a Newtown, Connecticut, elementary school in December 2012, are representative of such a discourse of fear and social control.

Many politicians and decision-makers in Canada, the United States, and other jurisdictions, under the guise of ensuring public order or serving national interests, have introduced measures to intensify surveillance, suspend or restrict rights in particular situations, and increase penalties or incarceration for certain types of offenders and offences (Saltman and Gabbard, 2011). These actions typically affect some minority populations more severely than others, but they also provide the state or other centrally authorized groups with the discretion to draw upon or apply them more generally in other situations (Monahan and Torres, 2011). These trends have several consequences for schooling, including the potential for heightened attention to matters of discipline and control while limiting other viable educational choices, especially for those deemed to be in higher-risk populations, and diversion of public resources from education to control-related activities.

The trends discussed throughout this chapter demonstrate that education reform and decision-making are much more complex than commonly assumed. A vast literature, spanning several fields, has emerged to explain or move beyond questions about why schooling appears impervious to so many reform initiatives (Rowan and Miskel, 1999; Sarason, 1996; Fullan, 2007). There are few absolute or readily agreed-upon answers to questions about such issues as the optimal class size for teaching and learning at different levels, the impact of mainstreaming of special-needs students within regular classrooms on different groups of students, the extent to which decisions over school closures should consider community interests as well as cost factors, the amount of formal recognition that should be given to different education credentials, and the relative merit of training workers as opposed to educating citizens. These specific issues point towards more fundamental questions that have been at the heart of educational controversies for several generations. Liberal educational values dedicated to broadly based knowledge, critical reflection, and citizen engagement may seem out of step in a world driven by technological and commercial imperatives. Education,

Box 9.4 Core Educational Challenges in the Twenty-First Century

Education systems are undergoing substantial modification as they come to be aligned in accordance with fundamental social, economic, and cultural transformations. Education is positioned as a central driver of social and economic change, but it is also being realigned to adjust to various external pressures. A growing body of literature offers numerous descriptions, analyses, and prescriptions for emerging educational directions, many of which have been discussed in this chapter and other places throughout the book. Many of the core trends and pressures facing education are summarized succinctly by Peters and Besley (2006: 172):

Main Trends and Pressures Facing Education

1. *Globalization and increasing competition*
   - Increased globalization (as world economic integration).
   - Increased levels of national and international competition.
   - Increased power and importance of global and multinational corporations.
   - Increased importance of research to global multinationals.
   - Importance of regional and international trade and investment agreements.
   - The growing economic and political importance of the Asian economies, including China.

2. *Public-sector changes*
   - Declining socio-political priority of education as an entirely state-funded activity.
   - Corporatization and privatization of the public sector.
   - Greater interpenetration of public and private enterprises.
   - Growth of managerialism (New Public Management) and new contractualism.

though, involves much more than technical knowledge and specific skills. Education also plays a vital role in democratic societies by enriching human life and empowering citizens, enhancing their capacity to contribute to their societies in meaningful ways. These debates and issues are not new. Schooling, from its inception, has been understood as an institution that can serve many purposes. However, it is likely that debates over these kinds of issues will intensify as the role of education in a globally changing society comes under further public scrutiny.

Conclusion

This book has emphasized that an essential starting point for an understanding of educational issues lies in the observation that education and schooling are complex, multi-dimensional, and contradictory endeavours. Each chapter has pointed to instances in which educational structures and practices intersect with and resemble other social institutions, as well as to instances in which education contains unique

- Localization and autonomy: decentralization, devolution, and delegation of authority to local communities and government agencies.
- Demands for increased efficiency and accountability.

3. *Increasing importance of knowledge*
   - Increasing economic, social, and cultural importance of knowledge.
   - Commodification and mercantilization of knowledge.
   - Increasing role and importance of telecommunications and information technologies.
   - New political, legal, and ethical problems of "information economy" (e.g., intellectual property, copyright, plagiarism).

4. *Employment*
   - Changing nature of advanced economies to knowledge-based industries.
   - Changing structure of the labour market (e.g., casualization, feminization of the workforce).
   - Demand for highly skilled, technically competent workforce, with an emphasis on generic and transferable "core" skills.

5. *Education policy*
   - Increasing multicultural and international nature of societies and education institutions.
   - Increased demand from a highly diversified, "massified" student population.
   - Need for lifelong learning and "second-chance" education.
   - The vocationalization of education through partnerships with business and the promotion of entrepreneurial culture.
   - Erosion of state education by non-traditional providers.
   - Individualization and customization of programs for learners.

Source: Michael A. Peters and A.C. Tina Besley. 2006. *Building Knowledge Cultures: Education and Development in the Age of Knowledge Capitalism.* Lanham, MD: Rowman & Littlefield.

and sometimes conflicting dimensions. These observations can be confusing and sometimes frustrating to students, participants, and researchers, but they also contribute to possibilities to generate essential understandings and changes. Education is a social activity concerned with the development and transformation of human beings. As education is converted into various informal and institutional forms, it reflects and modifies the social world of which it is a part. Consequently, education has personal and social importance, as well as wider economic and political significance.

These issues, in turn, point to important questions linked to social policy formulation and research in education. Some of these, as we have seen, have been addressed by research and analysis, but because all of them involve conflicting choices and interpretations, they require much more intensive scrutiny. A sampling of these questions is listed below:

- What is really meant by quality education? Who should be responsible for determining and assessing educational quality?

- Who should pay for education? To what extent, and at what levels, should the state cover education costs as opposed to leaving responsibility with individuals, families, employers, or other agencies?

- To what extent should learners be segregated from, or integrated with, other learners according to ability and special needs?

- To what extent should specific groups or communities, defined by such factors as religion, cultural values, political beliefs, or economic interests, be able to establish and control their own educational institutions? If such schools are established, who should pay for them and what kinds of guidelines, if any, should be in place to ensure their consistency with federal or provincial standards?

- How should we define and measure educational success?

- To what extent should educational priorities and programs be determined by labour markets and a focus on jobs?

- How do education systems need to change in order to provide effective knowledge and sustainable actions related to environmental issues and planetary concerns?

- How much should public education be focused on local concerns as opposed to global issues?

- How much autonomy should educators and education specialists, as opposed to parents and community members, have to plan and deliver educational services?

- How can parents and communities best become involved in education to ensure educational success among children and youth?

- How much priority should governments and communities place on education relative to other important areas like health care, social and community security, and economic development?

While sociological analysis, in conjunction with other forms of inquiry, can help provide a foundation and tools from which to assess these issues, it cannot provide absolute answers. This book began with an overview of key debates central to sociological inquiry that must be taken into consideration when addressing questions such as the ones posed here. Our analysis should be guided by a recognition that social structures and institutions, which give shape to our experiences and provide definition for social issues, also are constructed and can be changed through human activity.

Sociology enables us to gain insights about our lives by examining the relationships between individuals and social forces. In sociological research and analysis, as with all other dimensions of human social life, we must make decisions about what to study, how to examine it, and what to do about our findings. The answers we come up with emerge only from the choices made by people as they interact with one another and their social circumstances. Education, in this sense, is a critical process in our ability to broaden our basis of social understanding, increase our ability to make meaningful life decisions, and transform our world in ways that can be beneficial to all of us.

This chapter has highlighted emergent debates and issues associated with contemporary demands for educational reform. There is a broad range of positions about what education should be about and how it should be organized. These tend to be focused on divergent views that stress, on the one hand, an understanding of education as a commodity that can be marketed like other goods and services and, on the other hand, an emphasis on the personal, transformative characteristics of education for social justice. The centrality of the diverse forms of education to human life suggests that education will continue to be contested, leaving open questions about how to ensure that all people are able to develop and use their capacities in meaningful ways.

Annotated Further Readings

Cuban, Larry. 2000. *Oversold and Underused: Computers in the Classroom*. Cambridge, MA.: Harvard University Press. The author investigates the claims made by proponents and critics of computers in education systems, providing strong evidence about the limits and prospects associated with the integration of new technologies within existing classroom settings.

de Broucker, Patrice, and Arthur Sweetman, eds. 2002. *Towards Evidence-Based Policy for Canadian Education*. Montreal and Kingston: McGill-Queen's University Press. Contributors from diverse academic and policy perspectives highlight relevant issues, advances, and concerns related to educational measurement and research oriented to the improvement of educational practices and outcomes.

Jenson, Jennifer, Chloë Brushwood Rose, and Brian Lewis, with Richard Smith, Stan Shapson, Penny Milton, and Robert Kennedy. 2007. *Policy Unplugged: Dis/Connections between Technology Policy and Practices in Canadian Schools*. Montreal and Kingston: McGill-Queen's University Press. Researchers and educators offer an overview and assess the impact of federal and provincial policies, programs, and funding practices for technology in K–12 schools. The authors highlight in particular the existence and consequences of a gap between high-level policies and specific practices.

Monahan, Torin, and Rodolfo D. Torres, eds. 2010. *Schools Under Surveillance: Cultures of Control in Public Education*. New Brunswick, NJ: Rutgers University Press. This collection draws together recent research and analysis of various forms of surveillance within public education, focusing on issues related to testing and accountability as well as more direct forms of monitoring and control, and exploring their implications for class, race, gender, and other forms of social inequality.

Portelli, John P., and R. Patrick Solomon, eds. 2001. *The Erosion of Democracy in Education: From Critique to Possibilities*. Calgary: Detselig. This collection draws on examples from different Canadian contexts to highlight serious concerns arising from recent educational reforms and to work towards an alternative, progressive vision for education.

Robertson, Heather-jane. 1998. *No More Teachers, No More Books: The Commercialization of Canada's Schools*. Toronto: McClelland & Stewart. The author offers a pointed critique of the ways in which powerful lobby groups and business interests are attacking and reshaping schools in order to expand opportunities for commercialization and ensure stronger alignment with market forces.

Suárez-Orozca, Marcelo M., ed. 2007. *Learning in the Global Era: International Perspectives on Globalization and Education*. Berkeley and Los Angeles: University of California Press. Scholars representing different academic disciplines analyze the impact of global shifts in technology, cultural diversity, and social relationships on education and learners, drawing on experiences and research from several regional and national settings.

Subedi, Binaya, ed. 2010. *Critical Global Perspectives: Rethinking Knowledge about Global Societies.* Charlotte, NC: Information Age Publishing. Posing questions about what it means to know and teach about the world in a global context, authors from diverse nations and disciplines explore issues related to curriculum, gender, culture, race and ethnicity, and teacher education.

Ungerleider, Charles. 2003. *Failing Our Kids: How We Are Ruining Our Public Schools.* Toronto: McClelland & Stewart. The author, drawing on extensive experience as an educational researcher, administrator, and policy-maker, examines conflicting challenges that are posing dangers for public schools. He makes a highly informed case for the development of strong schools that can contribute effectively to economic development and informed citizenship.

Key Terms

Accountability The expectation that public education, like other state-provided services, has clearly defined objectives that members of the public can identify and assess as to how well and how cost-effectively they are being met.

Charter schools Schools based on a contract or charter that outlines specific arrangements and performance commitments, made between school representatives and school boards or government bodies.

Digital divide The gap between individuals, groups, and regions based on differential access to and use of computers and information communications technologies.

Digital literacy The skills and capacities required for people to become effective and critical producers as well as consumers of media-related information in contemporary societies.

Educational governance The laws, procedures, regulations, and institutional arrangements that outline how education systems are organized and operated within a specific jurisdiction.

Evidence-based decision-making The systematic assessment and application of comprehensive research-based knowledge to inform decision-making and practice in education, health care, and other realms.

Inclusive schooling A concept that emphasizes schools as agencies that actively incorporate and respond to diverse student needs, regardless of social, physical, or cultural characteristics.

Marketization A process in which social relationships are transformed by defining people as consumers and social services such as education are considered as profit-making endeavours or commodities that are produced, bought, and sold in a market environment.

Person rights The basis for a vision of democracy in which all people are assured specific social entitlements and opportunities for meaningful participation in social, political, and economic life by virtue of their residence or citizenship within a jurisdiction.

Property rights The notion that social, economic, and political participation is based on market relations, private property, and contractual arrangements.

Study Questions

1. Considerable recent controversy has been generated over the issue of whether there should be an overarching public system of education or a variety of educational alternatives that allow parents optimal choice for their children's schooling. Discuss whether the provision of education should be a public or private matter, critically assessing the strengths and limitations of the main positions within this debate.

2. Critically discuss the extent to which educational practices have been affected by, and should be modified to adapt to, current developments in information and communications technologies.

3. Discuss the role of formal educational institutions in a context that places increasing emphasis on lifelong learning. To what extent should the role and mandate of school be broadened, relative to alternatives that place greater emphasis on learning at home, on the job, and in other sites?

4. Discuss the extent to which parents and other community members should be involved in decision-making within local schools. Should schools respond primarily to local interests or address broader concerns?

5. Discuss the extent to which, and the ways in which, educational reform is necessary in order to fulfill contemporary social and economic expectations.

6. By exploring mass media or websites, identify an issue or situation in which particular individuals or groups are advocating for a specific type of educational reform. Describe the arguments in favour of reform and opposing or alternative views, if any. Analyze this issue critically—explore such questions as what interests are represented by those taking different stances in the debate; what the consequences or implications might be for educational participants and other specific groups in the community and elsewhere if these changes are made or resisted; and what factors might account for or explain these developments.

Websites

www.afn.ca/index.php/en/policy-areas/education
The Assembly of First Nations website includes policies, position papers, research, and resources related to education and other matters of importance to First Nations across Canada.

www.2asanet.org/soe
This site, maintained by the Sociology of Education section of the American Sociology Association, is directed primarily to professionals and researchers engaged in the field. It contains a summary description of the sociology of education and emerging issues, as well as many useful links to other databases and relevant sites.

www.caut.ca
The Canadian Association of University Teachers, which represents academic staff at Canadian universities, reports on its website major developments, issues, and analyses relevant to post-secondary education.

www.policyalternatives.ca
The Canadian Centre for Policy Alternatives is an independent organization that conducts research and fosters public dialogue on a variety of issues related to social and economic justice. Its activities include widespread coverage of issues related to education in Canada, including publication of the quarterly journal *Our Schools/Our Selves*.

www.ccl-cca.ca/ccl
The Canadian Council on Learning was established in 2004 to foster and exchange knowledge about all aspects of learning relevant to Canada. The organization was dissolved in 2012, but its website remains open in order to share research findings, reports, and statements on Canadian education and learning through the life course, focused through five thematic areas—Aboriginal learning, adult learning, early childhood learning, health and learning, and work and learning.

www.cfs-fcee.ca/html/english/home/index.php
The Canadian Federation of Students provides a student voice and perspective on post-secondary issues, policies, student debt, and emerging matters of concern to its membership (drawn from university and college students in institutions across Canada) and others interested in educational matters. The cfs site includes position papers, research and analysis, and links to other major education information sites.

www.cdnsba.org
The Canadian School Boards Association represents school boards and school board associations across Canada. The association's website includes information and links on issues of educational policy and governance, research, and other important developments related to elementary and secondary education.

www.cmec.ca
The home page for the Council of Ministers of Education Canada provides access to major databases and reports and studies conducted through that organization, as well as links to each of the provincial and territorial ministries of education and other important Canadian and international education bodies.

www.crr.ca
The Canadian Race Relations Foundation, a non-profit, arm's length organization established by an Act of Parliament in 1996, is dedicated to the elimination of racism in Canada. Its website includes resources focusing on awareness of racism and other forms of discrimination, anti-racism initiatives and training, research reports, and links to relevant organizational websites across Canada and internationally.

www.educationworld.com
Education World provides a comprehensive range of information and links of interest to educators and others in education-related fields. It covers lesson plans and reviews of emerging issues in education, with strong emphasis on technological developments and integration of technology within educational settings.

www.eric.ed.gov
ERIC, the Educational Resources Information Center, contains a comprehensive database of information (mostly abstracts of journal articles and reports) on various aspects and fields related to education, including sociology of education. It is a valuable reference tool and starting point for research into both contemporary and historical educational issues.

www.hrsdc.gc.ca/eng/home.shtml
Human Resources and Skills Development Canada provides information on jobs, education and training initiatives, children and youth, Aboriginal people, persons with disabilities, and other factors relevant to workplace and community participation. The website includes extensive research and reports in addition to basic information about government programs and employment in Canada.

www.iportal.usask.ca/index.php?sid=230692801&t=index
The Indigenous Studies Portal (iPortal) was established at the University of Saskatchewan Library to provide a common starting point for resources for Indigenous studies. It includes electronic resources of various types, such as books, articles, archival documents, theses, and photographs, covering education, Indigenous knowledge, history, decolonization, and many other thematic areas.

www.oecd.org
The website of the Organisation for Economic Co-operation and Development provides useful and up-to-date information for international comparisons and developments. It includes report summaries, statistics, and links to major documents on education and related thematic areas that highlight significant trends and issues for 30 member countries and several dozen other nations.

www.safeschoolscoalition.org/index.html
The Safe Schools Coalition is an international partnership, with both public and private affiliates, to support gay, lesbian, bisexual, and transgender youth. It is dedicated to ensuring that schools are safe places for all children, teachers, and parents, regardless of gender identity or sexual orientation. This website has several resources useful for educators, students, and researchers, including detailed publications, reports, and position statements related to its mandate, information on gay–straight alliances, and links to websites in the US, Canada, and other nations.

www.sociosite.net/topics/education.php
The Social Science Information System, housed at the Faculty of Social Sciences at the University of Amsterdam, offers links to sites of interest to sociologists and other social scientists, with sections on numerous thematic areas including the Sociology of Education.

www.wallnetwork.ca
The site for the Work and Lifelong Learning national research network includes information and links relevant to an understanding of how work and learning are changing in a global economy. Definitions, discussion papers, and research findings document the nature and extent of learning in various forms and contexts, including informal learning and other forms of learning that occur outside of formal educational institutions.

www.statcan.gc.ca/start-debut-eng.html; www.statcan.gc.ca/start-debut-fra.html
Statistics Canada provides comprehensive data and information on education and numerous related areas on its website and through links with other sites. Census data, diverse databases and reports on both current and historical dimensions of Canadian social and economic life, and learning resources for students and educators are available.

www.tcrecord.org
The website for *Teachers' College Record* offers an online journal, discussion groups, and other items of interest to educators, educational researchers, and students. Free registration is required for access to numerous items relevant to many significant dimensions of teaching and learning.

www.unesco.org/new/en/unesco
The United Nations Educational, Scientific and Cultural Organization seeks to foster dialogue, mutual respect, and improved living conditions for people on a global scale. Its website includes useful resources and information relevant to education as well as related social and cultural issues, including reports and programs on education in specific nations and on a comparative level.

References

Abada, Teresa, Feng Hou, and Bali Ram. 2009. "Ethnic Differences in Educational Attainment among the Children of Canadian Immigrants," *Canadian Journal of Sociology* 34, 1: 1–30.

Aboriginal Affairs and Northern Development Canada. 2011. *2010–2011 Department Performance Report: Aboriginal Affairs and Northern Development Canada and Canadian Polar Commission.* Ottawa: Treasury Board of Canada Secretariat.

Acker, Sandra. 1999. *The Realities of Teachers' Work: Never a Dull Moment.* London: Cassell.

Addams, Jane. 1999 [1910]. *Twenty Years at Hull House: with autobiographical notes,* ed. and intro. Victoria Bissel Brown. Boston: Bedford St Martin's.

Albas, Daniel, and Cheryl Albas. 1993. "Disclaimer Mannerisms of Students: How To Avoid Being Labelled as Cheaters," *Canadian Review of Sociology and Anthropology* 31, 4: 422–45.

Alladin, Ibrahim. 1996. *Racism in Canadian Schools.* Toronto: Harcourt Brace.

Allen, May, and Chantal Vaillancourt. 2004. *Class of 2000: Profile of Postsecondary Graduates and Student Debt.* Ottawa: Minister of Industry, Statistics Canada Catalogue no. 81-595-MIE2004016.

Altenbaugh, Richard J. 1995. "The Irony of Gender," in Mark B. Ginsburg, ed., *The Politics of Teachers' Work and Lives.* New York: Garland Publishing, 73–90.

Althusser, Louis. 1971. "Ideology and Ideological State Apparatuses," in Althusser, ed., *Lenin and Philosophy and Other Essays.* New York: Monthly Review Press, 172–86.

Anderson, James G. 1968. *Bureaucracy in Education.* Baltimore: Johns Hopkins University Press.

Andres, Lesley, and E. Dianne Looker. 2001. "Rurality and Capital: Educational Expectations and Attainment of Rural, Urban/Rural and Metropolitan Youth," *Canadian Journal of Higher Education* 31, 2: 1–45.

Andres, Lesley, and Maria Adamuti-Trache. 2008. "Life-Course Transitions, Social Class, and Gender: A 15-Year Perspective of the Lived Lives of Canadian Young Adults," *Journal of Youth Studies* 11, 2: 115–45.

Andres Bellamy, Lesley. 1993. "Life Trajectories, Action, and Negotiating the Transition from High School," in Anisef and Axelrod (1993: 137–57).

———. 1994. "Capital, Habitus, Field, and Practice: An Introduction to the Work of Pierre Bourdieu," in Erwin and MacLennan (1994: 120–36).

Angus Reid Group. 1999. "Canadians' Assessment and Views of the Education System," press release, Toronto, 22 June.

Anisef, Paul, and Paul Axelrod, eds. 1993. *Transitions: Schooling and Employment in Canada.* Toronto: Thompson Educational Publishing.

———, ———, Etta Baichman-Anisef, Carl James, and Anton Turritin. 2000. *Opportunity and Uncertainty: Life Course Experiences of the Class of '73.* Toronto: University of Toronto Press.

——— and Norman Okihiro. 1982. *Losers and Winners: The Pursuit of Equality and Social Justice in Higher Education.* Toronto: Butterworths.

Apple, Michael W. 1986. *Teachers and Texts: A Political Economy of Class and Gender Relations in Education.* New York: Routledge & Kegan Paul.

———. 1995. *Education and Power,* 2nd edn. New York: Routledge.

———. 2000. *Official Knowledge: Democratic Education in a Conservative Age.* New York: Routledge.

———. 2004. *Ideology and Curriculum,* 3rd edn. New York: RoutledgeFalmer.

———. 2006. "Rhetoric and Reality in Critical Educational Studies in the United States," *British Journal of Sociology of Education* 27, 5: 679–87.

———, Wayne Au, and Luis Armando Gandin, eds. 2009. *The Routledge International Handbook of Critical Education.* New York: Routledge.

———, Stephen J. Ball, and Luis Armando Gandin, eds. 2010. *The Routledge International Handbook of the Sociology of Education.* Abingdon, UK: Routledge.

Arbus, Judith. 1990. "Grateful To Be Working: Women Teachers during the Great Depression," in Frieda Forman, Mary O'Brien, Jane Haddad, Dianne Hallman, and Philinda Masters, eds, *Feminism and Education: A Canadian Perspective.* Toronto: Centre for Women's Studies in Education, 169–90.

Armstrong, Pat, and Hugh Armstrong. 2010. *The Double Ghetto: Canadian Women and Their Segregated Work,* 3rd edn. Toronto: Oxford University Press.

Arnot, Madeleine. 2009. *Educating the Gendered Citizen: Sociological Engagements with National and Global Agendas.* London: Routledge.

——— and Jo-Anne Dillabough. 1999. "Feminist Politics and Democratic Values in Education," *Curriculum Inquiry* 29, 2: 159–89.

—— and Mairtin Mac An Ghaill, eds. 2006. *The RoutledgeFalmer Reader in Gender and Education*. London: Routledge.

—— and Kathleen Weiler, eds. 1993. *Feminism and Social Justice in Education: International Perspectives*. London: Falmer.

Aronowitz, Stanley, and Henry A. Giroux. 1993. *Education Still under Siege*, 2nd edn. Toronto: OISE Press.

Ashton, David, and Graham Lowe. 1991. "School-to-Work Transitions in Britain and Canada: A Comparative Perspective," in Ashton and Lowe, eds, *Making Their Way: Education, Training and the Labour Market in Canada and Britain*. Toronto: University of Toronto Press, 1–14.

Ashton, David N., and Johnny Sung. 1997. "Education, Skill Formation, and Economic Development: The Singaporean Approach," in Halsey et al. (1997: 207–18).

Assembly of First Nations. 1988. *Tradition and Education: Towards a Vision of Our Future, National Review of First Nations Education*, vol. 1. Ottawa: Assembly of First Nations.

——. 2005. *First Nations Education Action Plan*. Ottawa: Assembly of First Nations, 31 May.

——. 2010. *First Nations Control of First Nations Education: It's Our Vision, It's Our Time*. Ottawa: Assembly of First Nations, July.

——. 2011a. *Fact Sheet: First Nations Education Funding*. Ottawa: Assembly of First Nations, National Panel Briefing Binder Resource Documents, Mar.

——. 2011b. *National Chief's Virtual Summit on Post-Secondary Education*. Ottawa: Assembly of First Nations,

——. 2011c. *Virtual Summit, AFN Survey of First Nation Post-Secondary Students 2011*. Ottawa: Assembly of First Nations.

Association of Universities and Colleges of Canada (AUCC). 2011. *Trends in Higher Education*, vol. 1, Enrolment. Ottawa: AUCC.

Aurini, Janice, and Scott Davies. 2005. "Choice without Markets: Homeschooling in the Context of Private Education," *British Journal of Sociology of Education* 26, 4: 461–74.

Axelrod, Paul. 1997. *The Promise of Schooling: Education in Canada, 1800–1914*. Toronto: University of Toronto Press.

——. 2002. *Values in Conflict: The University, the Marketplace and the Trials of Liberal Education*. Montreal and Kingston: McGill-Queen's University Press.

Bacon, Allan. 1995. "The Teachers' Perspective on Accountability," *Canadian Journal of Education* 20, 1: 85–91.

Baez, Javier Eduardo, and Indhira Vanessa Santos. 2007. *Children's Vulnerability to Weather Shocks: A Natural Disaster as a Natural Experiment*. New York: Social Science Research Network.

Bajak, Frank. 2012. "More to Learning than Laptops: Peru's Plan to Equip All Students with Their Own Computers Gets Mixed Grades," Saskatoon *Sunday Phoenix*, 8 July, B6.

Baker, David P. 2011. "The Future of the Schooled Society: The Transforming Culture of Education in Postindustrial Society," in Maureen T. Hallinan, ed., *Frontiers in Sociology of Education*. Dordrecht: Springer, 11–33.

Baldwin, John R., and Desmond Beckstead. 2003. *Knowledge Workers in Canada's Economy, 1971–2001*. Ottawa: Minister of Industry, Analytical Paper, Statistics Canada Catalogue no. 11-624-MIE No. 004 (Oct.).

Ball, Stephen J. 1981. "The Sociology of Education in Developing Countries," *British Journal of Sociology of Education* 2, 3: 301-13.

——. 2004. "Performativities and Fabrications in the Education Economy: Towards the Performative Society," in Ball, ed., *The RoutledgeFalmer Reader in Sociology of Education*. New York: RoutledgeFalmer, 143–55.

——. 2008. "Some Sociologies of Education: A History of Problems and Places, and Segments and Gazes," *Sociological Review* 56, 4: 650–69.

Ballantine, Jeanne H., and Joan Z. Spade, eds. 2012. *Schools and Society: A Sociological Approach to Education*, 4th edn. Thousand Oaks, CA.: Sage.

Banks, Olive. 1976. *The Sociology of Education*, 3rd ed. London: B.T. Batsford.

Barlow, Maude, and Heather-jane Robertson. 1994. *Class Warfare: The Assault on Canada's Schools*. Toronto: Key Porter Books.

Bascia, Nina. 2009. "Teachers as Professionals: Salaries, Benefits and Unions," in Lawrence J. Saha and A. Gary Dworkin, eds, *International Handbook of Research on Teachers and Teaching*. New York: Springer, 481–9.

——. 2010. *Reducing Class Size: What Do We Know?* Toronto: Canadian Education Association.

Battiste, Marie. 2000. "Introduction: Unfolding the Lessons of Colonization," in Battiste, ed., *Reclaiming Indigenous Voice and Vision*. Vancouver: University of British Columbia Press, xvi–xxx.

———— and James (Sa'ke'j) Youngblood Henderson. 2009. "Naturalizing Indigenous Knowledge in Eurocentric Education," *Canadian Journal of Native Education* 32, 1: 5–18, 129–30.

Bauer, Gabrielle. 2001. "Why Boys Must Be Boys: Is Your Son's School Giving Him What He Needs To Succeed?" *Canadian Living* (Nov.).

Bauman, Zygmunt. 1989. *Modernity and the Holocaust*. Ithaca, NY: Cornell University Press.

————. 2006. *Liquid Fear*. Cambridge: Polity Press.

Bayard, Justin, and Edith Greenlee. 2009. *Graduating in Canada: Profile, Labour Market Outcomes and Student Debt of the Class of 2005*. Ottawa: Minister of Industry, Statistics Canada Catalogue no. 81-595-M No. 074.

Beattie, Catherine. 1996. "The Computer in Schools: Visions, Illusions, and Mistakes," in Geoffrey Milburn, ed., *"Ring Some Alarm Bells in Ontario": Reactions to the Report of the Royal Commission on Learning*. London, ON.: Althouse Press, 95–107.

Beaujot, Roderic, and Don Kerr. 2007. *Emerging Youth Transition Patterns in Canada: Opportunities and Risks: Discussion Paper*. Ottawa: Government of Canada Policy Research Initiative.

Beck, Ulrich. 1992. *Risk Society: Towards a New Modernity*. London: Sage.

Becker, Howard S. 1952. "Social Class Variations in the Teacher–Pupil Relationship," *Journal of Educational Sociology* 25: 451–65.

————. 1953. "The Teacher in the Authority System of the Public School," *Journal of Educational Sociology* 26: 128–41.

————. 1996. "School Is a Lousy Place To Learn Anything In," in Robert G. Burgess, ed., *Howard Becker on Education*. Buckingham, UK: Open University Press, 99–112. Originally published in *American Behavioral Scientist* (1972): 85–105.

————, Blanche Geer, Everett C. Hughes, and Anselm L. Strauss. 1961. *Boys in White: Student Culture in Medical School*. Chicago: University of Chicago Press.

Bell, Daniel. 1973. *The Coming of Post-Industrial Society*. New York: Basic Books.

Bellas, Marcia L. 1999. "Emotional Labour in Academia: The Case of Professors," *Annals, American Academy of Political and Social Science* 561: 96–110.

Belley, Philippe, Marc Frenette, and Lance Lochner. 2011. *Post-Secondary Attendance by Parental Income in the U.S. and Canada: What Role for Financial Aid Policy?* Cambridge, Mass.: National Bureau of Economic Research, Working Paper no. 17218, July.

Berger, Joseph. 2009a. "Participation in Post-Secondary Education: Recent Trends," in Berger et al. (2009: 26–62).

————. 2009b. "Student Debt in Canada," in Berger et al. (2009: 182–205).

————, Anne Motte, and Andrew Parkin. 2007, 2009. *The Price of Knowledge: Access and Student Finance in Canada*, 3rd edn, 4th edn. Montreal: Canada Millennium Scholarship Foundation.

———— and Andrew Parkin. 2009. "The Value of a Degree: Education, Employment and Earnings in Canada," in Berger et al. (2009: 6–23).

Bernard, Jessie. 1964. *Academic Women*. University Park, PA: Pennsylvania State University Press.

Bernhard, Judith K., and Joyce Nyhof-Young. 1994. "Towards Increased Participation of Women in Science and Technology: Social Theory and Interventions for Girls in Ontario Elementary Schools," in Erwin and MacLennan (1994: 397–416).

Bernier, Rachel. 1996. "The Labour Force Survey: 50 Years Old in 1996," in Statistics Canada, *Labour Force Annual Averages 1995*. Ottawa: Minister of Industry, Science and Technology, A33–50.

Bernier, Suzanne. 1995. "Youth Combining School and Work," *Education Quarterly Review* 2, 4: 10–23.

Bernstein, Basil. 1977. "Class and Pedagogies: Visible and Invisible," in Jerome Karabel and A.H. Halsey, eds, *Power and Ideology in Education*. New York: Oxford University Press, 511–34.

Berthelot, Jocelyn. 2006. *Une école pour le monde, une école pour tout le monde. L'éducation québécoise dans le contexte de la mondialisation*. Montréal: VLB Éditeur.

Bibby, Reginald W. 2001. *Canada's Teens: Today, Yesterday, and Tomorrow*. Toronto: Stoddart.

Bills, David B. 2004. *The Sociology of Education and Work*. Malden, MA: Blackwell.

Birchard, Karen. 2002. "European Report Compares Student Conditions in Eight Countries," *University Affairs* (Dec.): 24.

Black Learners Advisory Committee. 1994. *BLAC Report on Education. Redressing Inequity—Empowering Black Learners*. Halifax: Black Learners Advisory Committee.

Blackmore, Jill. 1999. *Troubling Women: Feminism, Leadership and Educational Change*. Buckingham, UK: Open University Press.

Blaise, Mindy, and Affrica Taylor. 2012. "Using Queer Theory to Rethink Gender Equity in Early Childhood Education," *Young Children* 67, 1: 88–97.

Blau, Peter M., and Otis Dudley Duncan. 1967. *The American Occupational Structure*. New York: John Wiley and Sons.

Blouin, Patric. 2006. "A Profile of Elementary and Secondary School Principals in Canada: First Results from the 2004–2005 Survey of Principals," *Education Matters* 3, 2. Statistics Canada Catalogue no. 81-004-XIE.

Bohatyretz, Sandra, and Garth Lipps. 1999. "Diversity in the Classroom: Characteristics of Elementary Students Receiving Special Education," *Education Quarterly Review* 6, 2: 7–19.

Bolaria, B. Singh. 2000. "An Introduction to Social Issues and Contradictions: Sociological Perspectives," in Bolaria, ed., *Social Issues and Contradictions in Canadian Society*, 3rd edn. Toronto: Harcourt Brace & Company, 1–19.

———, Harley D. Dickinson, and Terry Wotherspoon. 1995. "Rural Issues and Problems," in Bolaria, ed., *Social Issues and Contradictions in Canadian Society*, 2nd edn. Toronto: Harcourt Brace & Company, 419–43.

Boothby, Daniel, and Torben Drewes. 2006. "Postsecondary Education in Canada: Returns to University, College and Trades Education," *Canadian Public Policy* 32, 1: 1–22.

Bouchard, Brigitte, and John Zhao. 2000. "University Education: Recent Trends in Participation, Accessibility and Returns," *Education Quarterly Review* 6, 4: 24–32.

Bourdieu, Pierre. 1977. "Cultural Reproduction and Social Reproduction," in Jerome Karabel and A.H. Halsey, eds, *Power and Ideology in Education*. New York: Oxford University Press, 487–511.

———. 1984 [1979]. *Distinction: A Social Critique of the Judgement of Taste*. Cambridge, MA: Harvard University Press.

——— and Jean-Claude Passeron. 1979. *The Inheritors: French Students and Their Relations to Culture*. Chicago: University of Chicago Press.

Bourgon, Lyndsie. 2008. "MAs Are Becoming the New BA," *The Sheaf* (University of Saskatchewan), 3 Jan., A4.

Bourque, Claude Julie, et Pierre Doray. 2009. "Les représentations sociales du travail dans des parcours de retour aux études aux niveaux collégial et universitaire," *Revue Interventions Économiques* 40, 1: 1–16.

Bowlby, Geoff. 1996. "Relationship between Postsecondary Graduates' Education and Employment," *Education Quarterly Review* 3, 2: 35–44.

Bowles, Samuel, and Herbert Gintis. 1976. *Schooling in Capitalist America: Educational Reform and the Contradictions of Economic Life*. New York: Basic Books.

Boyd, Monica. 2009. "Social Origins and the Educational and Occupational Aspirations of the 1.5 and Second Generations," *Canadian Review of Sociology* 46, 4: 339–69.

Bracey, Gerald W. 2006. "The High-Skills Hoax," *Phi Delta Kappan* 88, 1: 93–4.

Bradley, John. 2011. "False Accusations: A Growing Fear in the Classroom," *Education Canada* 51, 1: 4–9.

Braithwaite, Max. 1979. *Why Shoot the Teacher?* Toronto: McClelland & Stewart.

Braverman, Harry. 1974. *Labor and Monopoly Capital: The Degradation of Work in the Twentieth Century*. New York: Monthly Review Press.

Braverman, Samantha. 2011. "Most Americans Opposed to Banning Any Books," *Harris Poll* 47 (12 Apr.). At: harrisinteractive.com/NewsRoom/HarrisPolls/tabid/447/mid/1508/articleId/754/ctl/ReadCustom Default/Default.aspx.

British Columbia. 1875. *Annual Report of the Public Schools, 1875*. Victoria: Province of British Columbia.

———. 1904. *Annual Report of the Public Schools, 1904*. Victoria: Province of British Columbia.

———. 1988. *A Legacy for Learners: The Report of the Royal Commission on Education*. Victoria: Province of British Columbia.

British Columbia Retired Teachers' Association (BCRTA). 2012. "2012 BCRTA Golden Star Award Winners." Vancouver: BCRTA announcement, July. At: www.bcrta.ca/committees/2012%20BCRTA%20 Golden%20Star%20Award%20Winners.pdf.

British Columbia School Trustees' Association. 1980. "Rules Required for Teachers in Revelstoke Area, 1915," *BCSTA Reports*, 17 Oct.

Brock, Colin. 2011. *Education as a Global Concern*. New York: Continuum.

Brockington, Riley. 2011. *Summary Public School Indicators for Canada, the Provinces and Territories, 2009/2010*. Ottawa: Statistics Canada, Catalogue no. 81-595M, No. 95.

Brookes, Anne-Louise. 1992. *Feminist Pedagogy: An Autobiographical Approach*. Halifax: Fernwood.

Broster, Ruth, and Ken Brien. 2010. "Cyber-Bullying of Educators by Students: Evolving Legal and Policy Developments," *Education Law Journal* 20, 1: 35–61.

Brown, Phillip. 2003. "The Opportunity Trap: Education and Employment in a Global Economy," *European Educational Research Journal* 2, 1: 142–80.

———— and Hugh Lauder. 2006. "Globalisation, Knowledge and the Myth of the Magnet Economy," *Globalisation, Societies and Education* 4, 1: 25–57.

————, Andy Green, and Hugh Lauder. 2001. *High Skills: Globalization, Competitiveness, and Skill Formation*. Oxford: Oxford University Press.

Bruce, Christopher J., and Arthur M. Schwartz. 1997. "Education: Meeting the Challenge," in Bruce, R.D. Kneebone, and K.J. McKenzie, eds, *A Government Reinvented: A Study of Alberta's Deficit Elimination Program*. Toronto: Oxford University Press, 383–416.

Burbules, Nicholas C., and Carlos Alberto Torres. 2000. "Globalization and Education: An Introduction," in Burbules and Torres, eds, *Globalization and Education: Critical Perspectives*. New York: Routledge, 1–26.

Burman, Erica. 2005. "Childhood, Neo-liberalism and the Feminization of Education," *Gender and Education* 17, 4: 351–67.

Bushnik, Tracey. 2003. *Learning, Earning and Leaving: The Relationship between Working While in High School and Dropping Out*. Ottawa: Minister of Industry, Education, Skills and Learning, Research Paper, Catalogue no. 81-595-MIE, No. 004.

Bussière, Patrick, Fernando Cartwright, Robert Crocker, Xin Ma, Jillian Oderkirk, and Yanhong Zhang. 2001. *Measuring Up: The Performance of Canada's Youth in Reading, Mathematics and Science*. Ottawa: Minister of Industry Canada.

————, Tamara Knighton, and Dianne Pennock. 2007. *Measuring Up: Canadian Results of the OECD PISA Study. The Performance of Canada's Youth in Science, Reading and Mathematics. 2006 First Results for Canadians Aged 15*. Ottawa: Minister of Industry, Statistics Canada Catalogue no. 81-590-XIE2007001.

————, Roland Hébert, and Tamara Knighton. 2009. "Educational Outcomes at Age 21 Associated with Reading Ability at Age 15," *Education Matters: Insights on Education, Learning, and Training in Canada* 6, 2 (17 June). Statistics Canada Catalogue no. 81-004-X.

Butler, Judith. 1990. *Gender Trouble: Feminism and the Subversion of Identity*. London: Routledge.

Butterwick, Shauna, Kaela Jubas, and Hong Zhu. 2007. "Gender Matters in IT and Skills Hierarchies and Women's On the Job Learning," in Lesley Farnell and Tara Fenwick, eds, *Educating the Global Workforce: Knowledge, Knowledge Work and Knowledge Workers*. Abingdon, UK: Routledge, 278–88.

Calgary Board of Education. 2012. "Administrative Regulations: Part 4 Staff. AR4027.3. Anti-Racism and Equity," Calgary Board of Education. At: www.cbe.ab.ca/policies/adminregs.asp.

Campaign 2000. 2007. *It Takes a Nation to Raise a Generation: Time for a National Poverty Reduction Strategy, 2007 Report Card on Child and Family Poverty*. Toronto: Campaign 2000, 26 Nov. At: www.campaign2000.ca/reportcards.html.

————. 2011. *Revisiting Family Security in Insecure Times: 2011 Report Card on Child and Family Poverty in Canada*. Toronto: Campaign 2000. At: www.campaign2000.ca/reportcards.html.

Canadian Alliance of Student Associations. 2010. *Canadian Student Survey. Next Steps: Upper-Year Canadian PSE Students' Future Plans and Debt*. Ottawa: Canadian Alliance of Student Associations.

Canadian Association of University Teachers (CAUT). 2007. *CAUT Almanac of Post-Secondary Education in Canada, 2007*. Ottawa: CAUT.

————. 2011. *CAUT Almanac of Post-Secondary Education in Canada, 2011–2012*. Ottawa: CAUT.

————. 2012. *CAUT Almanac of Post-Secondary Education in Canada, 2012–2013*. Ottawa: CAUT.

Canadian Chamber of Commerce. 2012. *Top 10 Barriers to Competitiveness*. Ottawa: Canadian Chamber of Commerce, May.

Canadian Council on Learning. 2006a. *Canadian Attitudes on Post-Secondary Education*. Ottawa: Canadian Council on Learning.

————. 2006b. "School Enrolment Trends in Canada," *Lessons in Learning* (26 Sept.). Ottawa: Canadian Council on Learning.

————. 2007a. "Canada Slow To Overcome Limits for Disabled Learners," *Lessons in Learning* (26 Feb.). Ottawa: Canadian Council on Learning.

————. 2007b. *Redefining How Success Is Measured in First Nations, Inuit and Métis Learning*. Ottawa: Canadian Council on Learning.

————. 2007c. *Report on Learning in Canada 2007, Post-Secondary Education in Canada—Strategies for Success*. Ottawa: Canadian Council on Learning.

———. 2007d. *The State of Learning in Canada: No Time for Complacency, Report on Learning in Canada 2007.* Ottawa: Canadian Council on Learning.

———. 2007e. *2007 Survey of Canadian Attitudes toward Learning: Results for Elementary and Secondary School Learning.* Ottawa: Canadian Council on Learning.

———. 2009a. *2008 Survey of Canadian Attitudes toward Learning: Results for Learning throughout the Lifespan.* Ottawa: Canadian Council on Learning.

———. 2009b. *Strategies for Overcoming Barriers to Training and Education for Canadians with Disabilities.* Ottawa: Canadian Council on Learning.

———. 2011. *What Is the Future of Learning in Canada?* Ottawa: Canadian Council on Learning, Oct.

Canadian Council on Social Development. 2003. "Census Analysis: Census Shows Growing Polarization of Income in Canada." At: www.ccsd.ca/pr/2003/censusincome.htm.

Canadian Education Association. 2007. *Public Education in Canada: Facts, Trends and Attitudes 2007.* Toronto: Canadian Education Association.

——— . 2012. *Public Survey Results.* Results from the 2012 CEA Attitudes towards Public Education Survey, 28 Aug. Toronto: Canadian Education Association.

——— and Canadian Teachers' Federation. 2012. *Teaching the Way We Aspire to Teach: Now and in the Future. Teachers' Vision for Teaching and Learning in Canada's Public Schools.* Toronto and Ottawa: Canadian Education Association and Canadian Teachers' Federation.

Canadian Federation of Humanities and Social Sciences. 2012. "Post-Secondary Pyramid—Equity Audit 2010." Ottawa: Canadian Federation of Humanities and Social Sciences. At: fedcan.ca/content/en/333/ivory-towers.html.

Canadian Institute of Public Opinion. 1976. "One-in-Three Believe Education Has Slipped," *Gallup Report,* 27 Mar.

Canadian Labour Congress. 2008. *Women in the Workforce: Still a Long Way from Equality.* Ottawa: Canadian Labour Congress (Mar.).

Canadian Millennium Scholarship Foundation (CMSF). 2005. *Changing Course: Improving Aboriginal Access to Post-Secondary Education in Canada.* Montreal: CMSF, Research Notes #2. At: www.millenniumscholarships.ca/images/Publications/mrn-changing-course-en.pdf.

Canadian Race Relations Foundation (CRRF). 2000. *Racism in Our Schools: What To Know about It; How To Fight It.* Ottawa: Canadian Race Relations Foundation.

——— and Association for Canadian Studies (CRRF/ACS). 2011. *A Four Country Survey of Opinion on Racism and Prejudice in 2010: Canada, the United States, Germany and Spain.* Ottawa: Canadian Race Relations Foundation and Association for Canadian Studies, Jan.

Canadian Teachers' Federation. 1993. *Progress Revisited: The Quality of (Work) Life of Women Teachers.* Ottawa: Canadian Teachers' Federation.

———. 1997. *Behind the Charter School Myths.* Ottawa: Canadian Teachers' Federation.

———. 2005. "Canadian Teachers Face Longer Hours of Work and More Challenging Working Conditions Compared to Four Years Ago: National Survey," news release, 15 July. At: www.ctf-fce.ca/archive/docs/en/PRESS/2005/pr05-14.htm.

———. 2006. "Beyond the Bake Sale: Exposing the Many Faces of Commercialization in Canada's Schools," news release, 15 May. At: www.ctf-fce.ca/archive/docs/en/PRESS/2006/pr06-12.htm.

———. 2012. *Teaching in Canada.* Ottawa: Canadian Teachers' Federation. At: www.ctf-fce.ca/MembersLink/Default.aspx?cats=MO.

Canadian Women's Foundation. 2005. *Girls in Canada 2005.* Toronto: Canadian Women's Foundation, Sept.

Cappon, Paul. 2007. "Evaluating Post-Secondary Education," Canadian Council on Learning, 20 Sept. At: www.ccl-cca.ca/CCL/Newsroom/Articles/20070920EvaluatingPost-SecondaryEducation.html.

Carnevale, Anthony P., Jeff Strohl, and Michelle Melton. 2011. *What's It Worth? The Economic Value of College Majors.* Washington: Georgetown University Center on Education and the Workforce.

Carnoy, Martin. 1974. *Education as Cultural Imperialism.* New York: D. McKay Co.

——— and Henry M. Levin. 1985. *Schooling and Work in the Democratic State.* Stanford, CA: Stanford University Press.

Carr-Saunders, A.M. 1966. "Professionalism in Historical Perspective," in H.M. Vollmer and D.L. Mills, eds, *Professionalization.* Englewood Cliffs, NJ: Prentice-Hall, 2–9.

Carter, Prudence. 2011. "Putting the Horse before the Cart: The Culture of Schooling," *Education Canada* 51, 1: 26–9.

Castellano, Marlene Brant, Lynne Davis, and Louise Lahache, eds. 2000. *Aboriginal Education: Fulfilling the Promise.* Vancouver: University of British Columbia Press.

Central Advisory Council for Education (The Plowden Report). 1967. *Children and Their Primary Schools*, 2 vols. London: Her Majesty's Stationery Office.

Chabbott, Colette, and Francisco O. Ramirez. 2006. "Development and Education," in Hallinan (2006: 163–87).

Chafe, J.W. 1969. *Chalk, Sweat, and Cheers: A History of the Manitoba Teachers' Society*. Winnipeg: Manitoba Teachers' Society.

Chalmers, John W. 1968. *Teachers of the Foothills Province: The Story of the Alberta Teachers' Association*. Toronto: University of Toronto Press.

Charland, Jean-Pierre. 2000. *L'entreprise éducative au Québec, 1840–1900*. Québec: Les presses de l'Université Laval.

Chomsky, Noam. 2011. "The Function of Schools: Subtler and Cruder Methods of Control," in Saltman and Gabbard (2011: 26–35).

Chrisjohn, Roland, and Tanya Wasacase. 2009. "Half-Truths and Whole Lies: Rhetoric in the 'Apology' and the Truth and Reconciliation Commission," in Gregory Younging, Jonathan Dewar, and Mike DeGagne, eds, *Response, Responsibility, and Renewal: Canada's Truth and Reconciliation Journey*. Ottawa: Aboriginal Healing Foundation, 219–29.

Chubb, John E., and Terry M. Moe. 1990. *Politics, Markets, and America's Schools*. Washington: Brookings Institution.

Cicourel, Aaron V., and John J. Kitsuse. 1963. *The Educational Decision-Makers*. Indianapolis: Bobbs-Merrill.

Clairmont, Don, and Richard Apostle. 1997. "Work: A Segmentation Perspective," in Axel Van den Berg and Joseph Smucker, eds, *The Sociology of Labour Markets: Efficiency, Equity, Security*. Scarborough, ON: Prentice-Hall Allyn and Bacon, 388–404.

Clark, Burton R. 1960. "The 'Cooling-Out' Function in Higher Education," *American Journal of Sociology* 65, 6: 569–76.

———. 1962. *Educating the Expert Society*. San Francisco: Chandler.

Clark, Warren. 1991. *The Class of '86: A Compendium of Findings of the 1988 National Graduates Survey of 1986 Graduates with Comparisons to the 1984 National Graduates Survey*. Ottawa: Employment and Immigration Canada.

———. 2000. "100 Years of Education," *Canadian Social Trends* 59 (Winter): 3–7.

Clegg, Sue. 2005. "Evidence-based Practice in Educational Research: A Critical Realist Critique of Systematic Review," *British Journal of Sociology in Education* 26, 3: 415–28.

Clement, Wallace. 1974. *The Canadian Corporate Elite: An Analysis of Economic Power*. Toronto: McClelland & Stewart.

——— and Leah F. Vosko, eds. 2003. *Changing Canada: Political Economy as Transformation*. Montreal and Kingston: McGill-Queen's University Press.

——— and Glenn Williams. 1989. *The New Canadian Political Economy*. Montreal and Kingston: McGill-Queen's University Press.

Clifford, Pat. 2005. "Cyberkids," *Education Canada* 45, 2: 14–16.

———. 2008. "End Notes: An Edutainment Version of 'No Child Left Behind'," *Education Canada* 48, 4: 76.

Cobb, William H. 2000. *Radical Education in the Rural South: Commonwealth College*. Detroit: Wayne State University Press.

Cohen, Stanley. 1972. *Folk Devils and Moral Panics*. London: MacGibbon and Kee.

Coleman, James S. 1968. "The Concept of Equality of Educational Opportunity," *Harvard Educational Review* 38, 1: 7–22.

——— et al. 1966. *Equality of Educational Opportunity*. Washington: US Government Printing Office.

Collard, John, and Cecilia Reynolds, eds. 2005. *Leadership, Gender and Culture in Education: Male and Female Perspectives*. New York: Open University Press.

Collins, Patricia Hill. 2006. "Going Public: Doing the Sociology That Had No Name," in Dan Clawson, Robert Zussman, Joya Misra, Naomi Gerstel, Randall Stokes, Douglas L. Anderton, and Michael Burawoy, eds, *Public Sociology: Fifteen Eminent Sociologists Debate Politics and the Profession in the Twenty-First Century*. Berkeley: University of California Press, 101–13.

Collins, Randall. 1971. "Functional and Conflict Theories of Educational Stratification," *American Sociological Review* 36, 6: 1002–19.

———. 2006. "Comparative and Historical Patterns of Education," in Hallinan (2006: 213–39).

Collis, Betty. 1991. "Adolescent Females and Computers: Real and Perceived Barriers," in Gaskell and McLaren (1991: 147–61).

Community Foundations of Canada. 2010. *Canada's Vital Signs 2010*. Ottawa: Community Foundations of Canada. At: www.vitalsignscanada.ca/nr-2010-research-findings-e.html.

Conference Board of Canada. 2011. "Income Gap between the Rich and Poor Increasing Faster in Canada Than in the United States," news release 12–33, Ottawa, 13 Sept. At: www.conference board.ca/hcp/default.aspx.

Connell, R.W. 2000. *The Men and the Boys*. Berkeley: University of California Press.

———, D.J. Ashenden, S. Kessler, and G.W. Dowsett. 1982. *Making the Difference: Schools, Families and Social Division*. Sydney: George Allen & Unwin.

Contenta, Sandro. 1993. *Rituals of Failure: What Schools Really Teach*. Toronto: Between the Lines.

Cool, Julie. 2010. *Wage Gap between Women and Men*. Ottawa: Library of Parliament, Background Paper No. 2010-30-E, 29 July.

Corbett, Bradley A., and J. Douglas Willms. 2002. "Information and Communication Technology: Access and Use," *Education Quarterly Review* 8, 4: 8–15.

Corbett, Michael. 2009. "Rural Schooling in Mobile Modernity: Returning to the Places I've Been," *Journal of Research in Rural Education* 24, 7: 1–13.

Corman, June, and Meg Luxton. 2007. "Social Reproduction and the Changing Dynamics of Unpaid Household and Caregiving Work," in Shalla and Clement (2007: 262–88).

Corporation des Enseignants du Québec (CEQ). 1974. "Our Schools Serve the Ruling Class," in George Martell, ed., *The Politics of the Canadian Public School*. Toronto: James Lorimer, 172–85.

Corrigan, Philip, Bruce Curtis, and Robert Lanning. 1987. "The Political Space of Schooling," in Wotherspoon (1987: 21–43).

Côté, James E., and Anton Allahar. 2006. *Critical Youth Studies: A Canadian Focus*. Toronto: Pearson Prentice-Hall.

Cottingham, Mollie E. 1958. "The Canadian Conference on Education," *The B.C. Teacher* 37, 8: 398–9, 407–8.

Coulter, Rebecca Priegert. 1993. "Schooling, Work and Life: Reflections of the Young in the 1940s," in Coulter and Ivor F. Goodson, eds, *Rethinking Vocationalism: Whose Work/Life Is It?* Toronto: Our Schools/Our Selves, 69–86.

———. 2012. "What About the Girls?" *Education Canada* 52, 3: 6–9.

Council of Ministers of Education Canada (CMEC). 2001. *The Development of Education in Canada*. Toronto: Council of Ministers of Education Canada.

———. 2010. *Strengthening Aboriginal Success: Moving Toward Learn Canada 2020*. Toronto: Council of Ministers of Education Canada, CMEC Summit on Aboriginal Education Summary Report.

———. 2011. "Overview: CMEC Educators' Forum on Aboriginal Education." Ottawa: Council of Ministers of Education Canada. At: www.cmec.ca/Programs/aboriginaled/forum-2011/Pages/default.aspx.

Cowley, Peter. 2007. "Bringing Education into the Market Place: Part I—The Report Cards on Schools," *Fraser Forum* (Sept.): 6–9.

Craft, Anna. 2011. *Creativity and Education Futures: Learning in a Digital Age*. Stoke-on-Trent, UK: Trentham Books.

Craig, Wendy M., and Yossi Harel. 2004. "Bullying, Physical Fighting and Victimization," in Candace Currie, Chris Roberts, Antony Morgan, Rebecca Smith, Wolfgang Settertobulte, Oddrun Samdal, and Vivian Barnekow Rasmussen, eds, *Young People's Health in Context: Health Behaviour in School-aged Children (HBSC) Study: International Report from the 2001/2002 Survey*. Geneva: World Health Organization, 133–44.

Cranford, Cynthia J., and Leah H. Vosko. 2006. "Conceptualizing Precarious Employment: Mapping Wage Work across Social Location and Occupational Context," in Vosko, ed., *Precarious Employment: Understanding Labour Market Insecurity in Canada*. Montreal and Kingston: McGill-Queen's University Press, 43–66.

Crawley, Mike. 1995. *Schoolyard Bullies: Messing with British Columbia's Education System*. Victoria: Orca Book Publishers.

Creese, Gillian, Neil Guppy, and Martin Meissner. 1991. *Ups and Downs on the Ladder of Success: Social Mobility in Canada*. Ottawa: Minister of Industry, Science and Technology, Statistics Canada Catalogue no. 11-612.

Cremin, Lawrence A. 1988. *American Education: The Metropolitan Experience, 1876–1980*. New York: Harper & Row.

Crompton, Susan. 2002. "I Still Feel Overqualified for My Job," *Canadian Social Trends* 67 (Winter): 23–6.

Crosby, Andrew. 2010. "The International Student Experience in Canadian Post-Secondary Education: Democratic Racism, Anti-Racism Education, and Internationalization at Home," *Our Schools/Our Selves* 19, 13: 399–413.

Crysdale, Stewart, Alan J.C. King, and Nancy Mandell. 1999, *On Their Own? Making the Transition from School to Work in the Information Age*. Montreal and Kingston: McGill-Queen's University Press.

—— and Harry MacKay. 1994. *Youth's Passage through School to Work: A Comparative Longitudinal Study*. Toronto: Thompson Educational Publishing.

Cuban, Larry. 2001. *Oversold and Underused: Computers in the Classroom*. Cambridge, MA: Harvard University Press.

Cummins, Jim, and Marcel Danesi. 1990. *Heritage Languages: The Development and Denial of Canada's Linguistic Resources*. Toronto: Our Schools/Our Selves Education Foundation.

Currie, Candace, Saoirse Nic Gabhainn, Emmanuelle Godeau, Chris Roberts, Rebecca Smith, Dorothy Currie, Will Picket, Matthias Richter, Antony Morgan, and Vivian Barnekow, eds. 2008. *Inequalities in Young People's Health. HBSC International Report from the 2005/2006 Survey*. Edinburgh: HBSC International Coordinating Centre and World Health Organization.

Currie, Jan, and Janice Newson, eds. 1998. *Universities and Globalization: Critical Perspectives*. Thousand Oaks, CA: Sage.

Curtis, Bruce. 1988. *Building the Educational State: Canada West, 1836–1871*. Barcombe, Lewes: Falmer.

——, D.W. Livingstone, and Harry Smaller. 1992. *Stacking the Deck: The Streaming of Working-Class Kids in Ontario Schools*. Toronto: Our Schools/Our Selves Education Foundation.

Danylewycz, Marta, Beth Light, and Alison Prentice. 1991. "The Evolution of the Sexual Division of Labor in Teaching: Nineteenth Century Ontario and Quebec Case Study," in Gaskell and McLaren (1991: 33–60).

—— and Alison Prentice. 1986. "Teachers' Work: Changing Patterns and Perceptions in the Emerging School Systems of Nineteenth and Early Twentieth Century Central Canada," *Labour/Le Travail* 17: 59–80.

Darder, Antonia, Marta P. Baltodano, and Rodolfo D. Torres. 2009."Critical Pedagogy: An Introduction", in Darder, Baltodano and Torres, eds, *The Critical Pedagogy Reader*, 2nd edn. New York: Routledge, 1–20.

Davey, Ian E. 1978. "The Rhythm of Work and the Rhythm of School," in McDonald and Chaiton (1978: 221–53).

Davies, Scott. 1995. "Leaps of Faith: Shifting Currents in Critical Sociology of Education," *American Journal of Sociology* 100, 6: 1448–78.

—— and Janice D. Aurini. 2008. "School Choice as Concerted Cultivation: The Case of Canada," in Martin Forsey, Scott Davies, and Geoffrey Walford, eds, *The Globalisation of School Choice?* Oxford: Symposium Books, 55–71.

—— and Neil Guppy. 2010. *The Schooled Society: An Introduction to the Sociology of Education*, 2nd edn. Toronto: Oxford University Press.

——, Linda Quirke, and Janice Aurini. 2006. "Institutional Theory Goes to the Market: The Challenge of Rapid Growth in Private K–12 Education," in Heinz Meyer and Brian Rowan, eds, *The New Institutionalization and the Study of Education*. Albany, NY: SUNY Press, 103–22.

—— and David Zarifa. 2009. "New Institutional Theory and the Weberian Tradition," in Levine-Rasky (2009: 3–16).

Deafening Silence. 2010. "Overeducating the Economy: Taxi Drivers vs. Calutron Girls," Deafening Silence weblog, 1 Mar. At: www.defsi.typepad.com/deafening_silence/2010/03/overeducating-the-economy-taxi-drivers-vs-calutron-girls.html.

de Broucker, Patrice, and Arthur Sweetman. 2002. "Introduction," in de Broucker and Sweetman, eds, *Towards Evidence-Based Policy for Canadian Education*. Kingston, ON: John Deutsch Institute for the Study of Economic Policy/Statistics Canada, 1–14.

de Graaf, Nan Dirk, Paul M. de Graaf, and Gerbert Kraaykamp. 2000. "Parental Cultural Capital and Educational Attainment in the Netherlands: A Refinement of the Cultural Capital Perspective," *Sociology of Education* 73, 2: 92–111.

Dehli, Kari. 1993. "Subject to the New Global Economy: Power and Positioning in Ontario Labour Market Policy Formation," in Rebecca Priegert Coulter and Ivor F. Goodson, eds, *Rethinking Vocationalism: Whose Work/Life Is It?* Toronto: Our Schools/Our Selves Education Foundation, 113–41.

Dei, George J. Sefa. 1996. *Anti-Racism Education: Theory and Practice*. Halifax: Fernwood.

——. 2006. "Black-Focused Schools: A Call for Re-visioning," *Education Canada* 46, 3: 27–31.

—— and Agnes Calliste, eds. 2000. *Power, Knowledge and Anti-Racism Education: A Critical Reader*. Halifax: Fernwood.

————, Irma Marcia James, Leeno Luke Karumanchery, Sonia James-Wilson, and Jasmin Zine. 2000. *Removing the Margins: The Challenges and Possibilities of Inclusive Schooling*. Toronto: Canadian Scholars' Press.

————, Leeno Luke Karumanchery, and Nisha Karumanchery-Luik. 2004. *Playing the Race Card: Exposing White Power and Privilege*. New York: Peter Lang.

de Janvry, Alain, Elisabeth Sadoulet, Pantelis Solomon, and Renos Vakis. 2006. *Uninsured Risk and Asset Protection: Can Conditional Transfer Programs Serve as Safety Nets?* Social Protection Discussion Paper No. 0604. Washington: World Bank.

de León, Pedro Garcia, Corinne Heckmann, and Gara Rojas González. 2012. "What Will the Global Talent Pool Look Like in 2020?" *OECD Education Today*, 31 May. At: www.oecdeducationtoday .blogspot.fr/2012/05/what-will-global-talent-pool-look-like.html.

Denis, Wilfrid B. 1995. "The Meech Lake Shuffle: French and English Language Rights in Canada," in B. Singh Bolaria, ed., *Social Issues and Contradictions in Canadian Society*, 2nd edn. Toronto: Harcourt Brace & Company, 161–92.

Dennison, John D. 1981. "The Community College in Canada: An Educational Innovation," in J. Donald Wilson, ed., *Canadian Education in the 1980's*. Calgary: Detselig, 213–30.

Desjardins, Eric, and Kjell Rubenson. 2011. *An Analysis of Skill Mismatch Using Direct Measures of Skills*. Paris: OECD Education Working Papers 63 (Oct.). At: www.oecd-ilibrary.org/education/ an-analysis-of-skill-mismatch-using-direct-measures-of-skills_5kg3nh9h52g5-en.

Dewey, John. 1966. *Democracy and Education*. New York: Free Press.

Diallo, Bayero, Claude Trottier, and Pierre Doray. 2009. *What Do We Know about the Pathways and Transitions of Canadian Students in Post-Secondary Education?* Note I: Transitions Project. Montreal: Canada Millennium Scholarship Foundation, Dec.

Dibski, Dennis. 1995. "Financing Education," in Ghosh and Ray (1995: 66–80).

Dillabough, Jo-Anne. 2004. "Class, Culture, and the 'Predicaments of Masculine Domination': Encountering Pierre Bourdieu," *British Journal of Sociology of Education* 25, 4: 489–506.

————, Julie McLeod, and Martin Mills. 2008. "In Search of Allies and Others: 'Troubling' Gender and Education," *Discourse: Studies in the Cultural Politics of Education* 29, 3: 301–10.

Dolby, Nadine, and Greg Dimitriadis, eds. 2004. *Learning to Labor in New Times*. New York: Routledge.

Dominion Bureau of Statistics. 1924. *The Canada Year Book 1922–23*. Ottawa: King's Printer.

————. 1963. *Survey of Higher Education 1954–1961*. Ottawa: Queen's Printer.

Dorn, Charles M. 2003. "Sociology and the End of Arts Education," *Arts Education Policy Review* 104, 5: 3–13.

Downie, Bryan M. 1978. *Collective Bargaining and Conflict Resolution in Education: The Evolution of Public Policy in Ontario*. Kingston, ON: Queen's University Industrial Relations Centre, Research and Current Issues Series No. 36.

Dreeben, Robert. 1968. *On What Is Learned in School*. Reading, MA: Addison-Wesley.

Drolet, Marie. 2005. *Participation in Post-Secondary Education in Canada: Has the Role of Parental Income and Education Changed over the 1990s?* Ottawa: Minister of Industry. Statistics Canada Analytical Studies Branch Working Paper Series No. 243, Catalogue no. 11F0019MIE.

————. 2011. "Why Has the Gender Wage Gap Narrowed?" *Perspectives on Labour and Income* 23, 1: 3–13. Statistics Canada Catalogue no. 75-001-XWE.

Drucker, Peter F. 1993. *Post-Capitalist Society*. New York: HarperCollins.

Dryburgh, Heather. 2002. "Learning Computer Skills," *Education Quarterly* Review 8, 2: 8–18.

Dubois, Julie. 2006. *Trends in Student Borrowing and Pathways: Evidences from the 1990, 1995 and 2000 Classes. Final Report*. Ottawa: Human Resources and Skills Development Canada.

Dunleavy, Jodene, and Penny Milton. 2008. "Student Engagement for Effective Teaching and Deep Learning," *Education Canada* 48, 5: 5–9.

Durkheim, Émile. 1933 [1893]. *The Division of Labor in Society*. New York: Free Press.

————. 1956 [1922]. *Education and Society*. Glencoe, IL: Free Press.

Dutta, Soumitra, Beñat Bilbao-Osorio, and Thierry Geiger. 2012. "The Networked Readiness Index 2012: Benchmarking ICT Progress and Impacts for the Next Decade," in Dutta and Bilbao-Osorio, eds, *The Global Information Technology Report 2012: Living in a Hyperconnected World*. Geneva: World Economic Forum and INSEAD, 3–34.

Duxbury, Linda, and Chris Higgins. 2003. *Work–Life Conflict in Canada in the New Millennium: A Status Report. Final Report*, Oct. Ottawa: Health Canada.

Easton, Stephen T. 1988. *Education in Canada: An Analysis of Elementary, Secondary and Vocational Schooling*. Vancouver: Fraser Institute.

Economic Council of Canada. 1991. *Employment in the Service Economy*. Ottawa: Minister of Supply and Services Canada.

———. 1992. *A Lot to Learn: Education and Training in Canada. A Statement by the Economic Council of Canada*. Ottawa: Minister of Supply and Services Canada.

Edmonton Public Schools and Faculty of Education, University of Alberta. 2000. *Small Class Size Project: Final Report*. Edmonton: Edmonton Public Schools and University of Alberta.

Education International. 2009. *Education International Report to the Expert Committee on the Application of the 1966 ILO/UNESCO Recommendation on the Status of Teachers and 1997 UNESCO Recommendation on the Status of Higher Education Teaching Personnel*. Brussels: Education International, Sept.

Eid, Paul, Johanne Magliore, and Michèle Turenne. 2011. *Racialized Profiling and Systemic Discrimination of Racialized Youth: Report of the Consultation on Racial Profiling and Its Consequences*. Quebec: Commission des droits de la personne et des droits de la jeunesse.

Ellsworth, Elizabeth. 1992. "Why Doesn't This Feel Empowering? Working through the Repressive Myths of Critical Pedagogy," in Carmen Luke and Jennifer Gore, eds, *Feminisms and Critical Pedagogy*. New York: Routledge, 90–119.

Environics Institute. 2010. *Urban Aboriginal Peoples Study: Main Report*. Toronto: Environics Institute.

ERIN Research Inc. 2005. *Young Canadians in a Wired World. Phase II Student Survey*. Ottawa: Media Awareness Network.

Erwin, Lorna, and David MacLennan, eds. 1994. *Sociology of Education in Canada: Critical Perspectives on Theory, Research & Practice*. Toronto: Copp Clark Longman.

Eyre, Linda. 1991. "Gender Relations in the Classroom: A Fresh Look at Coeducation," in Gaskell and McLaren (1991: 193–219).

Fahmy-Eid, Nadia. 2003. "The History of Women's Education: Assessment and New Perspectives for the Future," *Historical Studies in Education/Revue d'histoire de l'éducation* 15, 1: 18–36.

Fennell, Shailaja, and Madeleine Arnot, eds. 2008. *Gender Education and Equality in a Global Context: Conceptual Frameworks and Policy Perspectives*. London: Routledge.

Ferrao, Vincent. 2010. "Paid Work," in *Women in Canada: A Gender-Based Statistical Report*. Ottawa: Statistics Canada Catalogue no. 89-503X, Dec.

Fine, Sean. 2001. "Schools Told to Fix Boys' Low Grades," *Globe and Mail*, 27 Aug., A1, A7.

Finnie, Ross. 2001. "Graduates' Earnings and the Job Skills–Education Match," *Education Quarterly Review* 7, 2: 7–21.

———, Eric Lascelles, and Arthur Sweetman. 2005. *Who Goes? The Direct and Indirect Effects of Family Background on Access to Post-Secondary Education*. Ottawa: Minister of Industry, Statistics Canada Analytical Studies Research Paper Series No. 237, Catalogue no. 11F1109MIE.

———, Stephen Childs, and Andrew Wismer. 2011. *Access to Post-Secondary Education among Under-Represented and Minority Groups: Measuring the Gaps, Assessing the Causes*. Ottawa: Education Policy Research Initiative, Working Paper no. 2011-01, Jan.

———, Richard E. Mueller, and Andrew Wismer. 2012. *Access and Barriers to Post-Secondary Education: Evidence from the YITS*. Ottawa: Education Policy Research Initiative, Working Paper no. 2012-01, Feb.

Fischer, Claude S., Michael Hout, Martin Sanchez Jankowski, Samuel R. Lucas, Ann Swindler, and Kim Voss. 1996. *Inequality by Design: Cracking the Bell Curve Myth*. Princeton, NJ: Princeton University Press.

Fiske, Edward B., and Helen F. Ladd. 2000. *When Schools Compete: A Cautionary Tale*. Washington: Brookings Institution Press.

Fleming, Thomas. 1986. "'Our Boys in the Field': School Inspectors, Superintendents and the Changing Character of School Leadership in British Columbia," in Nancy M. Sheehan, J. Donald Wilson, and David C. Jones, eds, *Schools in the West: Essays in Canadian Educational History*. Calgary: Detselig, 285–303.

Fleras, Augie, and Jean Leonard Elliott. 1992. *Multiculturalism in Canada: The Challenge of Diversity*. Scarborough, ON: Nelson Canada.

——— and ———. 2003. *Unequal Relations: An Introduction to Race and Ethnic Dynamics in Canada*, 4th edn. Toronto: Prentice-Hall.

Floud, Jean, A.H. Halsey, and F.M. Martin. 1956. *Social Class and Educational Opportunity*. London: Heinemann.

Forcese, Dennis. 1997. *The Canadian Class Structure*, 4th edn. Toronto: McGraw-Hill Ryerson.

Foucault, Michel. 1977. *Discipline and Punish: The Birth of the Prison*. New York: Pantheon Books.

———. 1980. *Power/Knowledge: Selected Interviews and Other Writings, 1972–1977*. New York: Pantheon Books.

Fournier, Elaine, George Butlin, and Philip Giles. 1995. "Intergenerational Change in the Education of Canadians," *Education Quarterly Review* 2, 2: 22–33.

Fraser, Steven, ed. 1995. *The Bell Curve Wars: Race, Intelligence, and the Future of America*. New York: Basic Books.

Frank, Blye, Michael Kehler, Trudy Lovell, and Kevin Davis. 2003. "A Tangle of Trouble: Boys, Masculinity and Schooling—Future Directions," *Educational Review* 55, 2: 119–33.

Frazee, Catherine. 2003. *Thumbs Up! Inclusion, Rights and Equality as Experienced by Youth with Disabilities*. Toronto: Laidlaw Foundation, Working Paper Series, Perspectives on Social Inclusion.

Freedman, Joe. 1995. *The Charter School Idea: Breaking Educational Gridlock*. Red Deer, Alta: Society for Advancing Educational Research.

Freire, Paulo. 1970. *Pedagogy of the Oppressed*. New York: Herder and Herder.

———. 1985. *The Politics of Education: Culture, Power and Liberation*. South Hadley, MA: Bergin and Garvey.

Frempong, George, and J. Douglas Willms. 2002. "Can School Quality Compensate for Socioeconomic Disadvantage?" in Willms, ed., *Vulnerable Children: Findings from Canada's National Longitudinal Survey of Children and Youth*. Edmonton: University of Alberta Press and Human Resources Development Canada, 277–303.

Frenette, Marc. 2005. *The Impact of Tuition Fees on University Access: Evidence from a Large-Scale Price Deregulation in Professional Programs*. Ottawa: Statistics Canada Analytical Studies Branch Research Paper Series Number 263, Catalogue no. 11F0019MIE.

———. 2007. *Why Are Youth from Lower-Income Families Less Likely To Attend University? Evidence from Academic Abilities, Parental Influences, and Financial Constraints*. Ottawa: Statistics Canada Analytical Studies Branch Research Paper Series Number 295, Catalogue no. 11F0019MIE.

——— and Simon Coulombe. 2007. *Has Higher Education among Young Women Substantially Reduced the Gender Gap in Employment and Earnings?* Ottawa: Minister of Industry, Statistics Canada Analytical Studies Branch Research Paper Series Number 301, Catalogue no. 11F0019MIE.

Frideres, James S. 2011. *First Nations in the Twenty-First Century*. Toronto: Oxford University Press.

Froese-Germain, Bernie. 2011. "The Voice of Canadian Teachers on Teachers and Learning," *Teacher Voice*, 8 Nov. At: www.ctf-fce.ca/priorities/default.aspx?ArtID=1929&lang=EN&year=2011&index_id=65551.

Fullan, Michael. 2007. *The New Meaning of Educational Change*, 4th edn. New York: Teachers College Press.

Fuller, Bruce. 2000. "Introduction: Growing Charter Schools, Decentering the State," in Fuller, ed., *Inside Charter Schools: The Paradox of Radical Decentralization*. Cambridge, MA: Harvard University Press, 1–11.

Fuller, Steve. 2006. *The New Sociological Imagination*. London: Sage.

Gaffield, Chad. 1982. "Schooling, the Economy, and Rural Society in Nineteenth-Century Ontario," in Joy Parr, ed., *Childhood and Family in Canadian History*. Toronto: McClelland & Stewart, 69–92.

Galarneau, Diane, Howard Krebs, René Morissette, and Xuelin Zhang. 2001. *The Quest for Workers: A New Portrait of Job Vacancies in Canada*. Ottawa: Minister of Industry, Evolving Workplace Series, Statistics Canada Catalogue no. 71-584-MPE No. 2.

Gallen, Verna, Bruce Karlenzig, and Isobel Tamney. 1995. "Teacher Workload and Work Life in Saskatchewan," *Education Quarterly Review* 2, 4: 49–58.

Gaskell, Jane. 1992. *Gender Matters from School to Work*. Toronto: OISE Press.

——— and Arlene McLaren. 1991. "Women as Mothers, Women as Teachers," in Gaskell and McLaren (1991: 19–32).

——— and ———, eds. 1991. *Women and Education*, 2nd edn. Calgary: Detselig.

———, ———, and Myra Novogrodsky. 1989. *Claiming an Education: Feminism and Canadian Schools*. Toronto: Our Schools/Our Selves.

Gerth, H.H., and C. Wright Mills. 1946. *From Max Weber: Essays in Sociology*. New York: Oxford University Press.

Ghosh, Ratna, and Douglas Ray, eds. 1995. *Social Change and Education in Canada*, 3rd edn. Toronto: Harcourt Brace.

Giddens, Anthony. 1987. *Sociology: A Brief but Critical Introduction*, 2nd edn. San Diego: Harcourt Brace Jovanovich.

————. 1990. *The Consequences of Modernity*. Stanford, CA: Stanford University Press.

Gidney, R.D., and W.P.J. Millar. 2012. *How Schools Worked: Public Education in English Canada, 1900–1940*. Montreal and Kingston: McGill-Queen's University Press.

Gilbert, Sid, and Jeff Frank. 1998. "Educational Pathways," in Human Resources Development Canada and Statistics Canada, *High School May Not Be Enough: An Analysis of Results from the School Leavers Follow-up Survey, 1995*. Ottawa: Minister of Public Works and Government Services Canada, Catalogue no. 81-585-XBE, 9–20.

Gilliss, Geraldine. 1995. "The Grade Is Made If One Looks at the Data Carefully," in Thomas T. Schweitzer, Robert K. Crocker, and Gilliss, *The State of Education in Canada*. Montreal: Institute for Research on Public Policy, 119–26.

Gilmore, Jason. 2011. "Trends in Dropout Rates and the Labour Market Outcomes of Young Dropouts," *Education Matters: Insights on Education, Learning and Training in Canada* 7, 4. Ottawa: Statistics Canada Catalogue no. 81-004-X.

Gintis, Herbert. 1980. "Communication and Politics," Socialist Review 10 (Mar.–June): 189–232.

———— and Samuel Bowles. 1980. "Contradiction and Reproduction in Educational Theory," in Len Barton, Roland Meighan, and Stephen Walker, eds, *Schooling, Ideology and the Curriculum*. Barcombe, Lewes: Falmer, 51–65.

Giroux, Henry A. 1983. *Theory and Resistance in Education*. South Hadley, MA: Bergin and Garvey.

————. 1988. *Teachers as Intellectuals*. Westport, CT: Bergin and Garvey.

———— and Peter McLaren, eds. 1989. *Critical Pedagogy, the State, and Cultural Struggle*. Albany: State University of New York Press.

Goffman, Erving. 1961. *Asylums*. Garden City, NY: Doubleday.

Gonick, Cy. 2010. "Radical Winnipeg," *Canadian Dimension* 44, 1: 17–21.

Gorbutt, David. 1972. "The New Sociology of Education," *Education for Teaching* 89 (Autumn): 3–11.

Gordon, Edward. 2009. "The Global Talent Crisis," *The Futurist* 43, 5: 34–9.

Gore, Jennifer M. 1993. *The Struggle for Pedagogies: Critical and Feminist Discourses as Regimes of Truth*. New York: Routledge.

Government of Canada. 2001. *Achieving Excellence: Investing in People, Knowledge and Opportunity*. Ottawa: Industry Canada, Catalogue no. C2-596/2001. Reprinted by permission of Public Works and Government Services Canada.

————. 2002. *Knowledge Matters: Skills and Learning for Canadians: Canada's Innovation Strategy*. Ottawa: Minister of Industry.

Government of Saskatchewan. 2003. *School Plus: Well-Being and Educational Success for All Children and Youth*. Regina: Saskatchewan Learning.

Grabb, Edward, and Neil Guppy, eds. 2009. *Social Inequality in Canada: Patterns, Problems and Policies*, 5th edn. Toronto: Pearson Education Canada.

Gracey, Harry L. 1977. "Learning the Student Role: Kindergarten as Academic Boot Camp," in Dennis H. Wrong and Gracey, eds, *Readings in Introductory Sociology*, 3rd edn. New York: Macmillan, 215–26.

Gramsci, Antonio. 1971. "The Intellectuals," in Quintin Hoare and Geoffrey Nowell Smith, eds and trans, *Selections from the Prison Notebooks of Antonio Gramsci*. London: Lawrence and Wishart, 13–23.

Grayson, J. Paul. 1997. *Who Gets Jobs? Initial Labour Market Experiences of York Graduates*. Toronto: Institute for Social Research, York University.

Grieshaber-Otto, Jim, and Matt Sanger. 2002. *Perilous Lessons: The Impact of the WTO Services Agreement (GATS) on Canada's Public Education System*. Ottawa: Canadian Centre for Policy Alternatives.

Grubel, Herbert. 2012. "Stopping Teachers' Strikes Permanently." Vancouver: Fraser Institute commentary, 14 Mar. At: www.fraserinstitute.org/research-news/news/display.aspx?id=18100.

Guppy, Neil, and Scott Davies. 1998. *Education in Canada: Recent Trends and Future Challenges*. Ottawa: Statistics Canada.

———— and ————. 1999. "Understanding Canadians' Declining Confidence in Public Education," *Canadian Journal of Education* 24, 3: 265–80.

————, Robert Crocker, Scott Davies, Claire LaPointe, and Larry Sackney. 2005. *Parent and Teacher Views on Education: A Policy-maker's Guide*. Kelowna, BC: Society for the Advancement of Excellence in Education.

Guss, Lois. 1993. "Residential School Survivor," in Linda Jaine, ed., *Residential Schools: The Stolen Years*. Saskatoon: University Extension Press, University of Saskatchewan, 91–4. Reprinted by permission of University Extension Press.

Gutstein, Donald. 2010. "War on Public Education Rages: Right-wing 'Think Tanks' on the Attack," *Our Schools/Our Selves* 20, 1: 47–54.

Hale, Jon N. 2007. "Early Pedagogical Influences on the Mississippi Freedom Schools: Myles Horton and Critical Education in the Deep South," *American Educational History Journal* 34, 2: 315–29.

Hall, Christine. 2004. "Theorizing Changes in Teachers' Work," *Canadian Journal of Educational Administration and Policy* 32, 1. At: www.umanitoba.ca/publications/cjeap/articles/noma/theorising. change.html.

Hall, E.M., and L.A. Dennis. 1968. *Living and Learning: The Report of the Provincial Committee on Aims and Objectives of Education in the Schools of Ontario* (Hall-Dennis Report). Toronto: Ontario Department of Education.

Hallinan, Maureen T., ed. 2006. *Handbook of the Sociology of Education*. New York: Kluwer Academic/ Plenum Publishers.

Halsey, A.H., Hugh Lauder, Phillip Brown, and Amy Stewart Wells. 1997. *Education: Culture, Economy, Society*. New York: Oxford University Press.

Hamilton, Roberta. 2005. *Gendering the Vertical Mosaic: Feminist Perspectives on Canadian Society*, 2nd edn. Toronto: Pearson Prentice-Hall.

Hammer, Kate. 2012. "Africentric School Principal Leaving Job," *Globe and Mail*, 19 June.

Hango, Darcy. 2010. *Labour Market Experiences of Youth after Leaving School: Exploring the Effect of Educational Pathways over Time*. Ottawa: Minister of Industry, Statistics Canada Catalogue no. 81-595-M No. 087.

———— and Patrice de Broucker. 2007. *Education-to-Labour Market Pathways of Canadian Youth: Findings from the Youth in Transition Survey*. Ottawa: Minister of Industry, Statistics Canada Catalogue no. 81-515-MIE – No. 054. At: www.statcan.gc.ca/pub/81-595-m/81-595-m2007054-eng.pdf.

Hare, Jan, and Michelle Pidgeon. 2011. "The Way of the Warrior: Indigenous Youth Navigating the Challenges of Schooling," *Canadian Journal of Education* 34, 2: 93–111.

Hargreaves, Andy. 2003. *Teaching in the Knowledge Society: Education in the Age of Insecurity*. New York: Teachers College Press.

Hargreaves, David H. 1967. *Social Relations in a Secondary School*. London: Routledge & Kegan Paul.

Harrison, Trevor W., and Jerrold L. Kachur, eds. 1999. *Contested Classrooms: Education, Globalization and Democracy in Alberta*. Edmonton: University of Alberta Press.

Hart, Doug. 2012. *Public Attitudes towards Education in Ontario 2012: The 18th OISE Survey*. Toronto: Ontario Institute for Studies in Education of the University of Toronto.

Heisz, Andrew. 2007. *Income Inequality and Redistribution in Canada: 1976–2004*. Ottawa: Minister of Industry, Statistics Canada Analytical Studies Branch Research Paper Series No. 298 (May).

————, A. Jackson, and G. Picot. 2002. *Winners and Losers in the Labour Market of the 1990s*. Ottawa: Statistics Canada Analytical Studies Branch Research Paper Series No. 184 (Feb.).

Henchey, Norman. 1977. "Pressures for Professional Autonomy and Public Controls," in Hugh A. Stevenson and J. Donald Wilson, eds, *Precepts, Policy and Process: Perspectives on Contemporary Canadian Education*. London, ON: Alexander, Blake Associates.

Henry, Frances, and Carol Tator. 2009. *The Colour of Democracy: Racism in Canadian Society*, 4th edn. Toronto: Thomson Nelson.

Hepburn, Claudia Rebanks. 1999. "The Case for School Choice: Models from the United States, New Zealand, Denmark, and Sweden." Vancouver: Fraser Institute Critical Issues Bulletin (Sept.).

Herrnstein, Richard J. 1973. *IQ in the Meritocracy*. Boston: Little Brown.

———— and Charles Murray. 1994. *The Bell Curve: Intelligence and Class Structure in American Life*. New York: Free Press.

Hochschild, Arlie Russell. 1983. *The Managed Heart: Commercialization of Human Feeling*. Berkeley: University of California Press.

Hoff Sommers, Christina. 2000. *The War against Boys: How Misguided Feminism Is Harming Our Young Men*. New York: Simon and Schuster.

Holt, John. 1964. *How Children Fail*. New York: Pitman.

hooks, bell. 2000. *Feminist Theory: From Margin to Center*, 2nd edn. Cambridge, MA: South End Press.

Horton, Myles, and Paulo Freire. 1990. *We Make the Road by Walking: Conversations on Education and Social Change*. Philadelphia: Temple University Press.

Houston, Susan E. 1982. "The 'Waifs and Strays' of a Late Victorian City: Juvenile Delinquents in Toronto," in Joy Parr, ed., *Childhood and Family in Canadian History*. Toronto: McClelland & Stewart, 129–42.

————— and Alison Prentice. 1988. *Schooling and Scholars in Nineteenth-Century Ontario*. Toronto: University of Toronto Press.

Hughes, Karen D., and Graham S. Lowe. 2000. "Surveying the 'Post-Industrial' Landscape: Information Technologies and Labour Market Polarization in Canada," *Canadian Review of Sociology and Anthropology* 37, 1: 28–53.

Hull, Jeremy. 2000. *Aboriginal Post-Secondary Education and Labour Market Outcomes: Canada, 1996*. Ottawa: Indian and Northern Affairs Canada Research and Analysis Directorate.

Human Resources Development Canada. 1996. "Labour Market Polarization . . . What's Going On?" *Applied Research Bulletin* 2, 2: 5–7.

Hunter, Alfred J., and Jean McKenzie Leiper. 1993. "On Formal Education, Skills and Earnings: The Role of Educational Certificates in Earnings Determination," *Canadian Journal of Sociology* 18, 1: 21–42.

Hurst, Charles E. 1992. *Social Inequality: Forms, Causes, and Consequences*. Boston: Allyn and Bacon.

Illich, Ivan. 1970. *Deschooling Society*. New York: Harper and Row.

Industry Canada. 1992. *A Lot to Learn: Education and Training in Canada*. Ottawa: Industry Canada.

Indian and Northern Affairs Canada. 2004. "Backgrounder: Aboriginal Workforce Participation Initiative," news release, 18 Nov. At: www.ainc-inac.gc.ca/nr/prs/s-d2004/02525abk_e.html.

—————. 2005. *Basic Departmental Data 2004*. Ottawa: Minister of Public Works and Government Services Canada.

International Labour Organization. 2011. "Joint Message from UNESCO, UNDP, UNICEF, ILO and Education International on the occasion of World Teachers' Day," news release, 5 Oct. At: www.ilo.org/global/industries-and-sectors/education/WCMS_164605/lang--en/index.htm.

International Telecommunication Union. 2010. *Monitoring the WSIS Targets, A Mid-term Review. World Telecommunication/ICT Development Report 2010*. Geneva: International Telecommunication Union.

Ipsos Reid. 2003. "A Good Understanding of the Basics (91%) Tops 7 Goals as to What Parents Say Their Children Need for a Successful Education—But Only Half (51%) Are Satisfied with Their Child's Progress towards This Goal," press release, Toronto, 23 Feb.

—————. 2007. "'Digital Divide' Remains Wide—Only Six-in-Ten Canadians Aged 55+ Have Access to the Internet," news release. Vancouver: Ipsos Reid, 15 Feb.

—————. 2012. *The Ipsos Canadian Inter@ctive Reid Report: 2012 Fact Guide*. Vancouver: Ipsos Reid.

Irons, E. Jane, and Sandra Harris. 2007. *The Challenges of No Child Left Behind: Understanding the Issues of Excellence, Accountability, and Choice*. Lanham, Md: Rowman & Littlefield.

Isenbarger, Lynn, and Michalinos Zembylas. 2006. "The Emotional Labour of Caring in Teaching," *Teaching and Teacher Education* 22, 1: 120–34.

Jackson, Nancy S. 1987. "Ethnicity and Vocational Choice," in Young (1987: 165–82).

—————. 1993. "Rethinking Vocational Learning," in Rebecca Priegert Coulter and Ivor F. Goodson, eds, *Rethinking Vocationalism: Whose Work/Life Is It?* Toronto: Our Schools/Our Selves Education Foundation, 166–80.

—————. 1994. "Rethinking Vocational Learning: The Case of Clerical Skills," in Erwin and MacLennan (1994: 341–51).

Jackson, Philip W. 1968. *Life in Classrooms*. New York: Holt, Rinehart and Winston.

Jaenen, Cornelius J. 1986. "Education for Francization: The Case of New France in the Seventeenth Century," in Jean Barman, Yvonne Hébert, and Don McCaskill, eds, *Indian Education in Canada*, vol. 1: The Legacy. Vancouver: University of British Columbia Press, 45–63.

James, Carl E. 1993. "Getting There and Staying There: Blacks' Employment Experience," in Anisef and Axelrod (1993: 3–20).

—————. 2003. *Seeing Ourselves: Exploring Race, Ethnicity and Culture*, 3rd edn. Toronto: Thompson Educational Publishing.

Jencks, Christopher, et al. 1972. *Inequality: A Reassessment of the Effect of Family and Schooling in America*. New York: Basic Books.

Jenks, Chris. 1998. "Introduction," in Jenks, ed., *Core Sociological Dichotomies*. London: Sage, 1–7.

Jensen, Arthur. 1973. *Educability and Group Difference*. New York: Harper and Row.

Johnson, F. Henry. 1968. *A Brief History of Canadian Education*. Toronto: McGraw-Hill.

Johnson, Holly, and Myrna Dawson. 2011. *Violence against Women in Canada: Research and Policy Perspectives*. Toronto: Oxford University Press.

Johnson, Norma. 2011. "Feedback: The Weight of Credentials," *Canadian Nurse* (Oct.). At: www.canadian-nurse.com/index.php?option=com_content&view=article&catid=8%3Afeedback&id=547%3Athe-weight-of-credentials&Itemid=35&lang=en.

Johnson, Susan Moore. 2005. "The Prospects for Teaching as a Profession," in Larry V. Hedges and Barbara Schneider, eds, *The Social Organization of Schooling*. New York: Russell Sage Foundation, 72–90.

Jones, Kerry Reimer, and Anthony Nnajiofor Ezeife. 2011. "School Size as a Factor in the Academic Achievement of Elementary School Students," *Psychology* 2, 8: 859–68.

Kailin, Julie. 2002. *Antiracist Education: From Theory to Practice*. Lanham, Md: Rowman & Littlefield.

Kanagarajah, Sri. 2006. *Business Dynamics in Canada 2003*. Ottawa: Minister of Industry, Statistics Canada Catalogue no. 61-534-XIE2006 (Mar.).

Kanpol, Barry. 1992. *Towards a Theory and Practice of Teacher Cultural Politics: Continuing the Postmodern Debate*. Norwood, NJ: Ablex Publishing.

Karabel, Jerome, and A.H. Halsey. 1977. "Educational Research: A Review and an Interpretation," in Karabel and Halsey, eds, *Power and Ideology in Education*. New York: Oxford University Press, 1–85.

Katz, Joseph. 1969. *Society, Schools and Progress in Canada*. Toronto: Pergamon Press.

Kazemipur, Abdolmohammad, and Shiva S. Halli. 2001. "The Changing Colour of Poverty in Canada," *Canadian Review of Sociology and Anthropology* 38, 2: 217–38.

Kearns, Laura-Lee. 2011. "High-Stakes Standardized Testing and Marginalized Youth: An Examination of Those Who Fail," *Canadian Journal of Education* 34, 2: 112–30.

Kehler, Michael. 2010. "Boys, Books and Homophobia: Exploring the Practices and Policies of Masculinities in School," *McGill Journal of Education* 45, 3: 351–70.

Kelly, Jennifer. 1998. *Under the Gaze: Learning to Be Black in White Society*. Halifax: Fernwood.

Kenway, Jane, and D. Langmead. 1998. "Governmentality, the 'Now' University and the Future of Knowledge Work," *Australian Universities' Review*, 41, 2: 28–31.

——— and Helen Modra. 1992. "Feminist Pedagogy and Emancipatory Possibilities," in Luke and Gore (1992: 138–66).

——— and Sue Willis. 1998. *Answering Back: Girls, Boys and Feminism in Schools*. London: Routledge.

Kerckhoff, Alan C. 2006. "Transition from School to Work in Comparative Perspective," in Maureen T. Hallinan, ed., *Handbook of the Sociology of Education*. New York: Springer, 453–74..

Kincheloe, Joe L. 2007. "Critical Pedagogy in the Twenty-First Century: Evolution for Survival," in Peter McLaren and Kincheloe, eds, *Critical Pedagogy: Where Are We Now?* New York: Peter Lang, 9–42.

King, Alan J.C., William F. Boyce, and Matthew A. King. 1999. *Trends in the Health of Canadian Youth*. Ottawa: Health Canada.

——— and Marjorie J. Peart. 1992. *Teachers in Canada: Their Work and Quality of Life*. Ottawa: Canadian Teachers' Federation.

Kirkness, Verna, and Sheena Selkirk Bowman. 1992. *First Nations and Schools: Triumphs and Struggles*. Toronto: Canadian Education Association.

Kirova, Anna. 2008. "Critical and Emerging Discourses in Multicultural Education Literature: A Review," *Canadian Ethnic Studies* 40, 1: 101–24.

Klein, Naomi. 2009. *No Logo*, 10th Anniversary Edition. Toronto: Vintage Canada.

Knight, Doug. 1993. "Understanding Change in Education in Rural and Remote Regions of Canada," in Earle Newton and Knight, eds, *Understanding Change in Education: Rural and Remote Regions of Canada*. Calgary: Detselig, 299–310.

Knighton, Tamara, Pierre Brochu, and Tomasz Gluszynski. 2010. *Measuring Up: Canadian Results of the OECD PISA Study. The Performance of Canada's Youth in Reading, Mathematics and Science, 2009 First Results for Canadians Aged 15*. Ottawa: Minister of Industry, Statistics Canada Catalogue no. 81-590-XIE.

——— and Sheba Mirza. 2002. "Postsecondary Participation: The Effects of Parents' Education and Household Income," *Education Quarterly Review* 8, 3: 25–32.

Kohen, Dafna, Sharanjit Uppal, Anne Guevremont, and Fernando Cartwright. 2007. "Children with Disabilities and the Educational System: A Provincial Perspective," *Education Matters* 4, 1. At: www.statcan.gc.ca/pub/81-004-x/2007001/9631-eng.htm.

Kozol, Jonathan. 1967. *Death at an Early Age: The Destruction of the Hearts and Minds of Negro Children in Boston Public Schools*. New York: Houghton Mifflin.

Krahn, Harvey, and Alison Taylor. 2007. "'Streaming' in the 10th Grade in Four Canadian Provinces in 2000," *Education Matters* 4, 2. At: www.statcan.gc.ca/pub/81-004-x/2007002/9994-eng.htm.

Labaree, David F. 2010. *Someone Has to Fail: The Zero-Sum Game of Public Schooling*. Cambridge, MA: Harvard University Press.

Lacey, Colin. 1970. *Hightown Grammar: The School as a Social System*. Manchester: Manchester University Press.

Ladson-Billings, Gloria, and William F. Tate IV. 1995. "Toward a Critical Race Theory of Education," *Teachers College Record* 97, 1: 47–68.

Lambert, Mylène, Klarka Zeman, Mary Allan, and Patrick Bussière. 2004. *Who Pursues Postsecondary Education, Who Leaves and Why? Results from the Youth in Transition Survey.* Ottawa: Culture, Tourism and the Centre for Education Statistics Research Paper no. 026, Statistics Canada Catalogue no. 81-595-MIE2004026.

Lambert, Susan. 2011. "Strike Will Have Little Impact on Kids," *Vancouver Sun*, 1 Sept., A15. Reprinted with permission from the BC Teachers' Federation, Vancouver, Canada.

Landry, Nicole E.R. 2008. *The Mean Girl Motive: Negotiating Power and Femininity.* Black Point, NS: Fernwood Publishing.

Lareau, Annette. 2000. *Home Advantage: Social Class and Parental Intervention in Elementary Education*, updated edn. Lanham, Md: Rowman & Littlefield.

———— and Erin McNamara Horvat. 1999. "Moments of Social Inclusion and Exclusion: Race, Class, and Cultural Capital in Family-School Relationships," *Sociology of Education* 72, 1: 37–53.

———— and Elliott B. Weininger. 2003. "Cultural Capital in Educational Research: A Critical Assessment," *Theory and Society* 32, 5–6: 567–606.

Lauder, Hugh, Phillip Brown, Jo-Anne Dillabough, and A.H. Halsey. 2006. "The Prospects for Education: Individualization, Globalization, and Social Change," in Lauder et al., eds, *Education, Globalization & Social Change.* Oxford: Oxford University Press, 1–70.

Lauen, Douglas Lee, and Karolyn Tyson. 2009. "Perspectives from the Disciplines: Sociological Contributions to Education Policy Research and Debates," in Gary Sykes, Barbara Schneider, and David N. Plank, eds, *Handbook of Education Policy Research.* New York: Routledge, 71–82.

Lauwerys, Joseph. 1973. *The Purposes of Education: Results of a CEA Survey.* Toronto: Canadian Education Association.

Lawr, Douglas, and Robert Gidney, eds. 1973. *Educating Canadians: A Documentary History of Public Education.* Toronto: Van Nostrand Reinhold.

Lawson, Robert F., and Roger R. Woock. 1987. "Policy and Policy Actors in Canadian Education," in Ratna Ghosh and Douglas Ray, eds, *Social Change and Education in Canada.* Toronto: Harcourt Brace Jovanovich, 133–42.

Lawton, Stephen B. 1995. *Busting Bureaucracy to Reclaim Our Schools.* Montreal: Institute for Research on Public Policy.

Leacy, F.H. 1983. *Historical Statistics of Canada*, 2nd edn. Ottawa: Statistics Canada.

LeBlanc, Jules. 1974. "Becoming Political: The Growth of the Quebec Teachers' Union," in Martell (1974: 151–64).

Lee, Mark. 2004. "Socio-Economic Inequalities," in William Boyce, ed., *Young People in Canada: Their Health and Well-Being.* Ottawa: Health Canada, 9–15.

Lehmann, Wolfgang. 2007. "'I Just Didn't Feel Like I Fit In': The Role of Habitus in University Drop-out Decisions," *Canadian Journal of Higher Education* 37, 2: 89–110.

Leithwood, Kenneth, and Doris Jantzi. 2009. "A Review of Empirical Evidence about School Size Effects: A Policy Perspective," *Review of Educational Research* 79, 1: 464–90.

Lessard, Claude. 1995. "Equality and Inequality in Canadian Education," in Ghosh and Ray (1995: 178–95).

————. 2004. "L'Obligation de Résultats en Éducation: De Quoi s'agit-il? Le contexte Québecoise d'une Demande Sociale, un rhétorique du changement et une extension de la recherché," in Lessard et Philippe Meirieu, eds, *L'Obligation de Résultats en Éducation.* Saint-Nicolas, QC: Les Presses de l'Université Laval, 23–49.

———— with André Brassard. 2009. "Educational Governance in Canada: 1990–2003," in Levine-Rasky (2009: 255–74).

Lévesque, M. 1979. *L'égalité des chances en éducation, considérations théoriques et approches empiriques.* Québec: Conseil Supérieur de l'Education.

Levin, Benjamin. 1990. "Tuition Fees and University Accessibility," *Canadian Public Policy* 16, 1: 51–9.

————. 2005. *Governing Education.* Toronto: University of Toronto Press.

————. 2009. "20 Minutes to Change a Life?" *Education Canada* 49, 3: 16–17.

———— and Shirley Seward. 2003. *Consultations on the Government of Canada's Proposal to Establish a Canadian Learning Institute*, Summary Report. Ottawa: Human Resources and Development Canada Strategic Policy, Canadian Learning Institute Project (Feb.).

Levine-Rasky, Cynthia, ed. 2009. *Canadian Perspectives on the Sociology of Education.* Toronto: Oxford University Press.

Levinson, David L., and Alan R. Sadovnik. 2002. "Education and Sociology: An Introduction," in Levinson, Peter W. Cookson Jr, and Sadovnik, eds, *Education and Sociology: An Encyclopedia*. New York: RoutledgeFalmer, 1–16.

Levy, Frank, and Richard J. Murnane. 2007. "How Computerized Work and Globalization Shape Human Skill Demands," in Marcelo M. Suárez-Orozca, ed., *Learning in the Global Era: International Perspectives on Globalization and Education*. Berkeley: University of California Press, 158–74.

Lewington, Jennifer. 1995. "Report Cards Get a New Twist," *Globe and Mail*, 13 Nov., A1.

———— and Graham Orpwood. 1993. *Overdue Assignment: Taking Responsibility for Canada's Schools*. Toronto: John Wiley & Sons.

Leydesdorff, Loet, and Henry Etkowitz. 1997. "A Triple Helix of University–Industry–Government Relations," in Etkowitz and Leydesdorff, eds, *Universities and the Global Knowledge Economy: A Triple Helix of University–Industry–Government Relations*. London: Pinter, 155–62.

Li, Chris, Ginette Gervais, and Aurélie Duval. 2006. *The Dynamics of Overqualification: Canada's Underemployed University Graduates*. Ottawa: Minister of Industry, Analytical Paper, Statistics Canada Catalogue no. 11-621-MIE2006039.

Li, Peter S. 1996. *The Making of Post-War Canada*. Toronto: Oxford University Press.

Lin, Jane. 2006. "The Teaching Profession: Trends from 1999 to 2005," *Education Matters* 3, 4 (Dec.), Statistics Canada Catalogue no. 81-004-XIE. At: www.statcan.gc.ca/pub/81-004-x/4153365-eng.htm.

Livingstone, D.W. 1983. *Class, Ideologies and Educational Futures*. London: Routledge.

————. 1985. *Social Crisis and Schooling*. Toronto: Garamond Press.

————. 1987. "Crisis, Classes and Educational Reform in Advanced Capitalism," in Wotherspoon (1987: 57–67).

————. 1994. "Searching for Missing Links: Neo-Marxist Theories of Education," in Erwin and MacLennan (1994: 55–82).

————. 2004. *The Education–Jobs Gap: Underemployment or Economic Democracy*. Toronto: Garamond Press.

———— and Antonie Scholtz. 2007. "Contradictions of Labour Processes and Workers' Use of Skills in Advanced Capitalist Economies," in Shalla and Clement (2007: 131–62).

Lockhart, Alexander. 1979. "Educational Opportunities and Economic Opportunities—the 'New' Liberal Equality Syndrome," in John A. Fry, ed., *Economy, Class and Social Reality: Issues in Contemporary Canadian Society*. Toronto: Butterworths, 224–37.

————. 1991. *School Teaching in Canada*. Toronto: University of Toronto Press.

Longo, Nicholas V. 2007. *Why Community Matters: Connecting Education with Civic Life*. Albany, NY: State University of New York Press.

Looker, E, Dianne. 2010. "Can I Get There from Here? Canadian Rural–Urban Participation Rates in Post-Secondary Education," in Ross Finnie, Marc Frenette, Richard E. Muller, and Arthur Sweetman, eds, *Pursuing Higher Education in Canada: Economic, Social and Policy Dimensions*. Montreal and Kingston: McGill-Queen's University Press, 269–92.

Lortie, Dan C. 1975. *Schoolteacher: A Sociological Study*. Chicago: University of Chicago Press.

Love, James. 1978. "The Professionalization of Teachers in Mid-Nineteenth Century Upper Canada," in McDonald and Chaiton (1978: 109–28).

Lowe, Graham S. 2000. *The Quality of Work: A People-Centred Agenda*. Toronto: Oxford University Press.

————. 2002. "Leveraging the Skills of Knowledge Workers," *Isuma: Canadian Journal of Policy Research* 3, 1: 79–86.

————. 2007. *21st Century Job Quality: Achieving What Canadians Want*. Ottawa: Canadian Policy Research Networks Research Report W37 Work and Learning.

Luffman, Jacqueline, and Deborah Sussman. 2007. "The Aboriginal Labour Force in Western Canada," *Perspectives on Labour and Income* 8, 1: 13–27. Ottawa: Statistics Canada Catalogue no. 75-001-XIE.

Luhmann, Niklas, and Karl-Eberhard Schorr. 2000. *Problems of Reflection in the System of Education*, trans. Rebecca A. Neuwirth. Münster: Waxmann.

Luke, Carmen, and Jennifer Gore, eds. 1992. *Feminisms and Critical Pedagogy*. New York: Routledge.

Lynch, Kathleen. 1989. *The Hidden Curriculum: Reproduction in Education, an Appraisal*. London: Falmer.

Ma, Xin, and George Frempong. 2008. *Non-Completion of Postsecondary Education and Profile of Postsecondary Dropouts*. Ottawa: Human Resources Development Canada, Learning Policy Directorate Strategic Policy and Research, Learning Research Series Report SP-837-05-08E, May.

McAndrew, Marie. 1995. "Ethnicity, Multiculturalism, and Multicultural Education in Canada," in Ghosh and Ray (1995: 165–77).

MacBeath, John. 2012. *Future of the Teaching Profession*. Brussels and Cambridge: Education International Research Institute and University of Cambridge.

Macdonald, Doune. 1999. "Teacher Attrition: A Review of Literature," *Teaching and Teacher Education* 15, 8: 835–48.

McDonald, Neil, and Alf Chaiton, eds. 1978. *Egerton Ryerson and His Times: Essays on the History of Education*. Toronto: Macmillan.

McKeown, Larry, and Cathy Underhill. 2007. "Learning Online: Factors Associated with Use of the Internet for Educational Purposes," *Education Matters* 4, 4 (30 Oct.). At: www5.statcan.gc.ca/bsolc/olc-cel/olc-cel?lang=eng&catno=81-004-X200700410375.

McLaren, Arlene, and Jim Gaskell. 1995. "Now You See It, Now You Don't: Gender as an Issue in School Science," in Jane Gaskell and John Willinsky, eds, *Gender Informs Curriculum: From Enrichment to Transformation*. New York: Teachers College Press, 136–56.

McLaren, Peter. 2007. *Life in Schools: An Introduction to Critical Pedagogy in the Foundations of Education*, 5th edn. New York: Addison-Wesley Longman.

McLeod, Keith. 1993. "Bilingualism, Multilingualism and Multiculturalism: A Retrospective of Western Canada Since the 1870s," in Marcel Danesi, McLeod and Sonia Morris, eds, *Heritage Languages and Education: The Canadian Experience*. Oakville, ON: Mosaic Press, 33–52.

McMullin, Julie. 2010. *Understanding Social Inequality: Intersections of Class, Age, Gender, Ethnicity, and Race in Canada*, 2nd edn. Toronto: Oxford University Press.

McNeil, Linda M. 1986. *Contradictions of Control: School Structure and School Knowledge*. New York: Routledge & Kegan Paul.

McRobbie, Angela. 1978. "Working Class Girls and the Culture of Femininity," in Women's Studies Group, Centre for Contemporary Cultural Studies, *Women Take Issue*. Birmingham: University of Birmingham, Centre for Contemporary Cultural Studies, 96–108.

———. 2009. *The Aftermath of Feminism: Gender, Culture and Social Change*. Los Angeles: Sage.

Mandell, Nancy, and Stewart Crysdale. 1993. "Gender Tracks: Male-Female Perceptions of Home–School–Work Transitions," in Anisef and Axelrod (1993: 19–41).

Mangan, J. Marshall. 1994. "The Politics of Educational Computing in Ontario," in Erwin and MacLennan (1994: 263–77).

Mann, Jean. 1980. "G.M. Weir and H.B. King: Progressive Education or Education for the Progressive State," in J. Donald Wilson and David C. Jones, eds, *Schooling and Society in 20th Century British Columbia*. Calgary: Detselig, 91–118.

Mannheim, Karl. 1936. *Ideology and Utopia: An Introduction to the Sociology of Knowledge*. New York: Harcourt, Brace and World.

Manzer, Ronald. 1994. *Public Schools and Political Ideas: Canadian Educational Policy in Historical Perspective*. Toronto: University of Toronto Press.

Martel, Denis, Jocelyn Gagnon, Joanne Pelletier-Murphy, and Johanne Grenier. 1999. "Pygmalion en éducation physique: un mythe bien réel," *Canadian Journal of Education* 24, 1: 42–56.

Martell, George, ed. 1974. *The Politics of the Canadian Public School*. Toronto: James Lorimer.

Martin, Wilfred. 1976. *The Negotiated Order of the School*. Toronto: Macmillan.

———. 1982. *Teachers' Pets and Class Victims*. St John's: Publications Committee, Faculty of Education, Memorial University of Newfoundland.

——— and Allan J. Macdonell. 1982. *Canadian Education: A Sociological Analysis*, 2nd edn. Scarborough, ON: Prentice-Hall.

Martineau, Harriett. 1837. *Society in America*, 3 vols. London: Saunders and Otley.

Martino, Wayne. 2011. "Failing Boys! Beyond Crisis, Moral Panic and Limiting Stereotypes," *Education Canada* 51, 4: 16–20.

Marx, Karl. 1963 [1869]. *The Eighteenth Brumaire of Louis Bonaparte*. New York: International Publishers.

———. 1977 [1862–3]. *Capital: A Critique of Political Economy*, vol. 1. New York: Vintage Books.

——— and Friedrich Engels. 1965 [1848]. *Manifesto of the Communist Party*. Peking: Foreign Languages Press.

Maté, Gabor. 1999. *Scattered Minds: A New Look at the Origins and Healing of Attention Deficit Disorder*. Toronto: Alfred A. Knopf.

Meier, Debra, and George Wood, eds. 2004. *Many Children Left Behind: How the No Child Left Behind Act Is Damaging Our Children and Our Schools*. Boston: Beacon Press.

Meyer, Heinz-Deiter, and Brian Rowan. 2006. "Institutional Analysis and the Study of Education," in Meyer and Rowan, eds, *The New Institutionalism in Education*. Albany, NY: State University of New York Press, 1–13.

Meyer, John W. 1977. "The Effects of Education as an Institution," 83, 1: 55–77.

Miller, James R. 1996. *Shingwauk's Vision: A History of Native Residential Schools.* Toronto: University of Toronto Press.

Mills, C. Wright. 1951. *White Collar: The American Middle Classes.* New York: Oxford University Press.

———. 1956. *The Power Elite.* New York: Oxford University Press.

Molnar, Alex. 2005. *School Commercialism: From Democratic Ideal to Market Commodity.* New York: Routledge.

Mombourquette, Angela. 2011. "For Gay Teachers, Coming Out Is a Lot Harder Than It Sounds," Halifax *Chronicle Herald*, 14 Nov.

Monahan, Torin. 2005. *Globalization, Technological Change, and Public Education.* New York: Routledge.

——— and Rodolfo D. Torres, eds. 2010. *Schools under Surveillance: Cultures of Control in Public Education.* New Brunswick, NJ: Rutgers University Press.

Monture-Angus, Patricia. 1995. *Thunder in My Soul: A Mohawk Woman Speaks.* Halifax: Fernwood.

Moore, Shannon A., Richard C. Mitchell and Luke Melchior. 2008. "Rights-Based Critical Disability Studies," in Moore and Mitchell, eds, *Power, Pedagogy and Praxis: Social Justice in the Globalized Classroom.* Rotterdam: Sense Publishers, 233–45.

Morissette, René, Xuelin Zhang, and Marie Drolet. 2002. "Are Families Getting Richer?" *Canadian Social Trends* 66 (Autumn): 15–19.

Mortensen, Thomas. 2012. "State Funding: A Race to the Bottom," *The Presidency* 15, 1: 26–9.

Moscovitch, Allan, and Glenn Drover. 1987. "Social Expenditures and the Welfare State: The Canadian Experience in Historical Perspective," in Moscovitch and Jim Albert, eds, *The "Benevolent" State: The Growth of Welfare in Canada.* Toronto: Garamond Press, 13–43.

Moss, Gemma, and Dena Attar. 1999. "Boys and Literacy: Gendering the Reading Curriculum," in Jon Prosser, ed., *School Culture.* Thousand Oaks, Calif.: Sage, 133–44.

Motte, Anne, and Saul Schwartz. 2009. *Are Student Employment and Academic Success Linked?* Montreal: Canadian Millennium Scholarship Foundation, Millennium Research Note #9.

Muir, J. Douglas. 1968. *Collective Bargaining by Canadian Public School Teachers.* Task Force on Labour Relations Study No. 11. Ottawa: Information Canada.

Murphy, Raymond. 1994. "A Weberian Approach to Credentials: Credentials as a Code of Exclusionary Closure," in Erwin and MacLennan (1994: 102–19).

Murray, Charles. 2012. *Coming Apart: The State of White America, 1960–2010.* New York: Crown Forum.

Myers, Douglas. 1973. "Introduction," in Myers, ed., *The Failure of Educational Reform in Canada.* Toronto: McClelland & Stewart, 11–13.

Myers, John P. 2010. "The Curriculum of Globalization: Considerations for International and Global Education in the 21st Century," in Binaya Subedi, ed., *Critical Global Perspectives: Rethinking Knowledge about Global Societies.* Charlotte, NC: Information Age Publishing, 103–20.

Myles, John, and Gail Fawcett. 1990. *Job Skills and the Service Economy.* Ottawa: Economic Council of Canada, Working Paper No. 4.

Nakhaie, M. Reza. 1996. "The Reproduction of Class Relations by Gender in Canada," *Canadian Journal of Sociology* 21, 4: 523–58.

National Center for Science Education (NCSE). 2012. "Opposition to Oklahoma's Antiscience Bill," 28 Mar. At: www.ncse.com/news/2012/03/opposition-to-oklahomas-antiscience-bill-007279.

National Council of Welfare. 2007. "Persistence of Poverty by Highest Level of Education, 1999–2004," *Poverty Statistics 2004.* Ottawa: National Council of Welfare. At: www.ncwcnbes.net/documents/researchpublications/ResearchProjects/PovertyProfile/2004/Persistence-EducationENG.pdf.

———. 2012. *A Snapshot of Racialized Poverty in Canada. Poverty Profile: Special Edition.* Ottawa: National Council of Welfare.

Nayak, Anoop. 2003. *Race, Place and Globalization: Youth Cultures in a Changing World.* New York: Berg Publishers.

Naylor, Charlie. 2002. "Teacher Workload and Stress: An International Perspective on Human Costs and Systemic Failure," *Our Schools/Our Selves* 11, 3: 125–50.

——— and Anne C. Schaefer. 2002. "Teacher Workload and Stress: A British Columbia Perspective," *Education Quarterly Review* 8, 3: 33–6.

Neatby, Hilda. 1953. *So Little for the Mind.* Toronto: Clarke, Irwin.

Nelsen, Randle W. 1997. "Reading, Writing and Relationships among the Electronic Zealots: Distance Education and the Traditional University," in Nelsen, ed., *Inside Canadian Universities: Another Day at the Plant.* Kingston, ON: Cedarcreek Publications, 184–210.

————. 2007. *Fun and Games and Higher Education: The Lonely Crowd Revisited.* Toronto: Between the Lines.

———— and David Nock, eds. 1978. *Reading, Writing, and Riches: Education and the Socio-Economic Order in North America.* Kitchener, ON: Between the Lines.

Neysmith, Sheila M., Marge Reitsma-Street, Stephanie Baker Collins, and Elaine Porter. 2012. *Beyond Caring Labour to Provisional Work.* Toronto: University of Toronto Press.

Ng, Roxanna. 1991. "Teaching against the Grain: Contradictions for Minority Teachers," in Gaskell and McLaren (1991: 99–115).

Ngo, Hieu Van, and Barbara Schleifer. 2004. "Immigrant Children and Youth in Focus," *Canadian Issues* (Spring): 29–33. At: canada.metropolis.net/pdfs/Van_ngo_e.pdf.

Nikiforuk, Andrew. 1993. *School's Out: The Catastrophe in Public Education and What We Can Do About It.* Toronto: Macfarlane Walter & Ross.

Nolan, Kathleen, and Jean Anyon. 2004. "Learning To Do Time: Willis's Model of Cultural Reproduction in an Era of Postindustrialism, Globalization, and Mass Incarceration," in Nadine Dolby and Greg Dimitriadis, eds, *Learning to Labor in New Times.* New York: Routledge, 133–50.

Nugent, Becky, and Diana Calhoun Bell. 2006. *Toward Deprivatized Pedagogy.* Cresskill, NJ: Hampton Press.

Oderkirk, Jillian. 1996. "Computer Literacy—A Growing Requirement," *Education Quarterly* Review 3, 3: 9–29.

Ogbu, John. 1994. "Racial Stratification and Education in the United States: Why Inequality Persists," *Teachers College Record* 96: 264–98.

Ogle, Jennifer Paff, and Molly Eckman. 2002. "Dress-Related Responses to the Columbine Shootings: Other-Imposed and Self-Designed," *Family and Consumer Sciences Research Journal* 31, 2: 155–94.

O'Haire, Noreen. 2005. *CTF Survey on Gender and Leadership.* Ottawa: Canadian Teachers' Federation. At: www.ctf-fce.ca/e/programs/pd/gender_issues/SurveyOnGenderIdentity_PDP_ Fall2004_4-4_EN.pdf.

Oliff, Phil, and Michael Leachman. 2011. *New School Year Brings Steep Cuts in State Funding for Schools.* Washington: Center on Budget and Policy Priorities, Oct. At: www.cbpp.org/files/9-1-11sfp.pdf.

Olson, Paul. 1995. "Poverty and Education in Canada," in Ghosh and Ray (1995: 196–208).

Ontario Human Rights Commission. 2003. *The Ontario Safe Schools Act: School Discipline and Discrimination.* Consultation Paper prepared by Ken Bhattacharjee, 8 July. Toronto: Ontario Human Rights Commission. At: www.ohrc.on.ca/en/resources/discussion_consultation/Safe SchoolsConsultRepENG.

Organisation for Economic Co-operation and Development (OECD). 2001. *OECD Economic Outlook* 70 (Dec.). Paris: OECD.

————. 2002. *Understanding the Brain: Towards a New Learning Science.* Paris: OECD.

————. 2010a. *Off to a Good Start? Jobs for Youth.* Paris: OECD.

————. 2010b. *PISA 2009 Results: Overcoming Social Background—Equity in Learning Opportunities and Outcomes,* vol. 2. Paris: OECD.

————. 2011. *Education at a Glance 2011: OECD Indicators.* Paris: OECD.

————. 2012a. *Better Skills, Better Jobs, Better Lives: A Strategic Approach to Skills Policies.* Paris: OECD.

————. 2012b. *Education at a Glance 2012: OECD Indicators.* Paris: OECD.

————. 2012c. *OECD Economic Surveys: Canada. June 2012.* Paris: OECD.

Ornstein, Allan. 2007. *Class Counts: Education, Inequality, and the Shrinking Middle Class* Lanham, MD: Rowman & Littlefield.

Ornstein, Michael, Penni Stewart, and Janice Drakich. 1998. "The Status of Women Faculty in Canadian Universities," *Education Quarterly* Review 5, 2: 9–29.

Osberg, Lars. 2006. "Pulling Apart—The Growing Gulfs in Canadian Society," *Policy Options* 27, 4: 8–11.

———— and Andrew Sharpe. 2004. "Has Economic Well-Being Improved in Canada and the United States?" in Edward N. Wolffe, ed., *What Has Happened to the Quality of Life in the Advanced Industrialized Nations?* Cheltenham, UK: Edward Elgar, 123–52.

————, Fred Wien, and Jan Grude. 1995. *Vanishing Jobs: Canada's Changing Workplaces.* Toronto: James Lorimer.

Ostrovsky, Yuri. 2008. *Earnings Inequality and Earnings Instability of Immigrants in Canada.* Ottawa: Statistics Canada, Analytical Studies Branch Research Paper Series no. 309 (9 Apr.), Statistics Canada Catalogue no. 11F0019MWE.

Ouellette, Sylvie. 2006. *How Students Fund Their Postsecondary Education: Findings from the Postsecondary Education Participation Survey.* Ottawa: Culture, Tourism and the Centre for Education Statistics Research Paper No. 042 (Apr.), Statistics Canada Catalogue no. 81-595-MIE2006042.

Ozga, Jennifer, and Martin Lawn. 1981. *Teachers, Professionalism and Class: A Study of Organized Teachers*. London: Falmer.

Pacholik, Barb. 2007. "Size Matters in Schools, Study Says," *Regina Leader-Post*, 5 Sept., A1–2.

Paquette, Jerry. 1989. "The Quality Conundrum: Assessing What We Cannot Agree On," in Stephen B. Lawton and Rouleen Wignall, eds, *Scrimping or Squandering? Financing Canadian Schools*. Toronto: OISE Press, 11–28.

——— and Gérald Fallon. 2010. *First Nations Education Policy in Canada: Progress or Gridlock?* Toronto: University of Toronto Press.

Parelius, Robert James, and Ann Parker Parelius. 1987. *The Sociology of Education*, 2nd edn. Englewood Cliffs, NJ: Prentice-Hall.

Parsey, John M., and John K. Friesen. 1953. "Folk Schools in Canada," *School Review* 61, 3: 141–50.

Parsons, Talcott. 1959. "The School Class as a Social System: Some of Its Functions in American Society," *Harvard Educational Review* 29, 4: 297–318. Reprinted by permission of the publisher.

Paton, J.M. 1962. *The Role of Teachers' Organizations in Canadian Education*. Toronto: W.J. Gage.

Payne, Charles M. 2003. "More Than a Symbol of Freedom: Education for Liberation and Democracy," *Phi Delta Kappan* 85, 1: 22–8.

Peltier, Sharla. 2010. "Facilitating Language and Lifelong Learning for Students with Aboriginal Indian Dialects," *Canadian Journal of Native Education* 32 (Suppl.): 114–42.

Pendakur, Ravi. 2000. *Immigrants and the Labour Force: Policy, Regulation, and Impact*. Montreal and Kingston: McGill-Queen's University Press.

Peters, Michael A., and A.C. Tina Besley. 2006. *Building Knowledge Cultures: Education and Development in the Age of Knowledge Capitalism*. Lanham, MD: Rowman & Littlefield.

Phillips, Charles E. 1957. *The Development of Education in Canada*. Toronto: W.J. Gage.

Pierson, Paul. 2001. "Coping with Permanent Austerity: Welfare State Restructuring in Affluent Democracies," in Pierson, ed, *The New Politics of the Welfare State*. Oxford: Oxford University Press, 410–56.

Piore, Michael J. 1979. *Birds of Passage: Migrant Labour in Industrial Societies*. New York: Cambridge University Press.

Poelzer, Irene. 1990. *Saskatchewan Women Teachers, 1905–1920: Their Contributions*. Saskatoon: Lindenblatt and Hamonic.

Pomerantz, Shauna, and Rebecca Raby. 2011. "'Oh, She's So Smart': Girls' Complex Engagements with Post/Feminist Narratives of Academic Success," *Gender and Education* 23, 5: 549–64.

Popkewitz, Thomas S. 1991. *A Political Sociology of Educational Reform: Power/Knowledge in Teaching, Teacher Education, and Research*. New York: Teachers College Press.

Porfilio, Brad J., and Paul R. Carr. 2010. "The Neo-Liberal Social Order, Youth and Resistance," in Porfilio and Carr, eds, *Youth Culture, Education and Resistance: Subverting the Commercial Ordering of Life*. Rotterdam: Sense Publishing, 1–18.

Portelli, John P., and R. Patrick Solomon, eds. 2001. *The Erosion of Democracy in Education*. Calgary: Detselig.

Porter, John. 1965. *The Vertical Mosaic: An Analysis of Social Class and Power in Canada*. Toronto: University of Toronto Press.

———, Marion Porter, and Bernard R. Blishen. 1982. *Stations and Callings: Making It through the School System*. Toronto: Methuen.

Prairie Research Associates. 2011. *Canadian University Consortium Undergraduate University Student Survey Master Report*. Winnipeg: Prairie Research Associates, for Canadian University Consortium.

Prentice, Alison. 1977. *The School Promoters: Education and Social Class in Mid-Nineteenth Century Upper Canada*. Toronto: McClelland & Stewart.

——— and Susan E. Houston, eds. 1975. *Family, School and Society in Nineteenth Century Canada*. Toronto: Oxford University Press.

——— and Marjorie R. Theobald. 1991. "The Historiography of Women Teachers: A Retrospect," in Prentice and Theobald, eds, *Women Who Taught: Perspectives on the History of Women and Teaching*. Toronto: University of Toronto Press, 3–33.

Press, Harold, Gerald Galway, and Eldred Barnes. 2002. "Teacher Labour Market Conditions in Canada: Balancing Demand and Supply," *School Business Affairs* (Nov.): 28–32.

Priesnitz, Wendy. 2008. *Challenging Assumptions in Education*, 2nd edn. Toronto: Alternate Press.

Pupo, Noreen, and Ann Duffy. 2007. "Blurring the Distinction between Public and Private Spheres: The Commodification of Household Work—Gender, Class, Community, and Global Dimensions," in Shalla and Clement (2007: 289–325).

Raham, Helen. 1996. "Revitalizing Public Education in Canada: The Potential of Choice and Charter Schools," *Fraser Forum* (Aug.), special issue.

Randhawa, B.S. 1991. "Inequities in Educational Opportunities and Life Chances," in Terry Wotherspoon, ed., *Hitting the Books: The Politics of Educational Retrenchment*. Toronto and Saskatoon: Garamond Press and the Social Research Unit, 139–58.

Raphael, Dennis. 2011. *Poverty in Canada: Implications for Health and Quality of Life*, 2nd edn. Toronto: Canadian Scholars' Press.

Raptis, Helen. 2005. "A Tale of Two Women: Edith Lucas, Mary Ashworth, and the Changing Nature of Educational Policy in British Columbia, 1937–1977," *Historical Studies in Education/Revue d'histoire de l'éducation* 17, 2: 293–319.

———. 2012. "Ending the Reign of the Fraser Institute's School Rankings," *Canadian Journal of Education* 35, 1: 187–201.

Ray, Brian D. 2001. "Homeschooling in Canada," *Education Canada* 41, 1: 28–31.

Reardon, Sara. 2011. "Climate Change Sparks Battles in Classroom," *Science* 333 (5 Aug.): 688–9.

Rees, Ruth. 1990. "Gender Distribution in Canada's Schools: It's Still as Bad as You Think," *Our Schools/Our Selves* 2, 3: 20–2.

Regnier, Robert, and Brian D. MacLean. 1987. "Hegemony in Education: The Nuclear Industry in Northern Schools," in Wotherspoon (1987: 165–79).

Reitz, Jeffrey G. 2007. "Immigrant Employment Success in Canada, Part II: Understanding the Decline," *Journal of International Migration and Integration* 8, 1: 37–62.

Repo, Satu. 1974. "BC Teachers Turn Political," in Martell (1974: 200–17).

———. 1998. *Making Schools Matter: Good Teachers at Work*. Toronto: James Lorimer.

Reynolds, Cecilia. 1990. "Too Limiting a Liberation: Discourse and Actuality in the Case of Women Teachers," in Frieda Forman, Mary O'Brien, Jane Haddad, Dianne Hallman, and Philinda Masters, eds, *Feminism and Education: A Canadian Perspective*. Toronto: Centre for Women's Studies in Education, 145–68.

———. 2002. "Introduction: New Questions about Women and School Leadership," in Reynolds, ed., *Women and School Leadership: International Perspectives*. Albany: State University of New York Press, 1–8.

———, Robert White, Carol Brayman, and Shaun Moore. 2008. "Women and Secondary School Principal Rotation/Succession: A Study of the Beliefs of Decision Makers in Four Provinces," *Canadian Journal of Education* 31, 1: 32–54.

Rice, James R. 2002. "Being Poor in the Best of Times," in G. Bruce Doern, ed., *How Ottawa Spends 2002–2003: The Security Aftermath and National Priorities*. Toronto: Oxford University Press, 102–20.

——— and Michael J. Prince. 2000. *Changing Politics of Canadian Social Policy*. Toronto: University of Toronto Press.

Richie, Shawna. 2010. *Innovation in Action: An Examination of Charter Schools in Alberta*. Calgary: Canada West Foundation.

Ringrose, Jessica. 2007. "Successful Girls? Complicating Post-Feminist, Neoliberal Discourses of Educational Achievement and Gender Equality," *Gender and Education* 19, 4: 471–89.

Rist, Ray C. 1970. "Student Social Class and Teacher Expectations: The Self-Fulfilling Prophecy in Ghetto Education," *Harvard Educational Review* 40: 411–50.

Ritzer, George. 2011. *Classical Sociological Theory*, 6th edn. New York: McGraw-Hill.

Rizvi, Fazal, Bob Lingard, and Jennifer Lavia. 2006. "Postcolonialism and Education: Negotiating a Contested Terrain," *Pedagogy, Culture and Society* 14, 3: 249–62.

Robelen, Erik W. 2012. "N.H. Parents Gain Leverage to Challenge Curricula," *Education Week* 31, 17 (18 Jan.): 6.

Roberge, Roger, Jean-Marie Berthelot, and Michael Wolfson. 1995. "Health and Socio-Economic Inequalities," *Canadian Social Trends* 37 (Summer): 15–19.

Roberts, Julian V. 2007. "Public Confidence in Criminal Justice in Canada: A Comparative and Contextual Analysis," *Canadian Journal of Criminology and Criminal Justice* 49, 2: 153–84.

Robertson, Heather-jane. 1998. *No More Teachers, No More Books: The Commercialization of Canada's Schools*. Toronto: McClelland & Stewart.

———. 2007. *Great Expectations: Essays on Schools and Society*. Ottawa: Canadian Centre for Policy Alternatives.

———, David McGrane, and Erika Shaker. 2003. *For Cash and Future Considerations: Ontario Universities and Public–Private Partnerships*. Ottawa: Canadian Centre for Policy Alternatives.

Robertson, Susan. 2000. *A Class Act: Changing Teachers' Work, the State, and Globalisation*. London: Falmer.

Rockhill, Kathleen, and Patricia Tomic. 1995. "Situating ESL between Speech and Silence," in Jane Gaskell and John Willinsky, eds, *Gender In/forms Curriculum: From Enrichment to Transformation.* New York: Teachers College Press, 209–29.

Roots of Empathy. 2012. "Roots of Empathy: What We Do," program summary. Toronto: Roots of Empathy. At: www.rootsofempathy.org/en/what-we-do/about-our-program.html.

Rose, Chloë Brushwood, and Jennifer Jenson. 2007. "Gender Inequality and Professional School Culture: Teachers at Work with Technology," in Jenson, Rose, and Brian Lewis, with Richard Smith, Stan Shapson, Penny Milton, and Robert Kennedy, *Policy Unplugged: Dis/Connections between Technology Policy and Practices in Canadian Schools.* Montreal and Kingston: McGill-Queen's University Press, 48–67.

Rosenthal, Robert, and Lenore Jacobson. 1968. *Pygmalion in the Classroom: Teacher Expectation and Pupils' Intellectual Development.* New York: Holt, Rinehart and Winston.

Rothwell, Neil, and Martin Turcotte. 2006. "The Influence of Education on Civic Engagement: Differences across Canada's Rural–Urban Spectrum," *Rural and Small Town Canada Analysis Bulletin* 7, 1 (July), Statistics Canada Catalogue no. 21-006-XIE. At: www.statcan.ca/english/freepub/21-006-XIE/21-006-XIE2006001.pdf.

Rowan, Brian, and Cecil G. Miskel. 1999. "Institutional Theory and the Study of Educational Organizations," in Joseph Murphy and Karen Seashore Louis, eds, *Handbook of Research on Educational Administration: A Project of the American Educational Research Association,* 2nd edn. San Francisco: Jossey-Bass, 359–83.

Royal Commission on Aboriginal Peoples. 1996a. *Report of the Royal Commission on Aboriginal Peoples, vol. 1, Looking Forward, Looking Back.* Ottawa: Minister of Supply and Services Canada.

———. 1996b. *Report of the Royal Commission on Aboriginal Peoples, vol. 3, Gathering Strength.* Ottawa: Minister of Supply and Services Canada.

Royal Commission on Learning. 1994. *For the Love of Learning,* vol. 4, *Making It Happen.* Toronto: Queen's Printer for Ontario.

Royal Commission on the Relations of Capital and Labour in Canada. 1889. *Report of the Royal Commission on the Relations of Capital and Labour in Canada.* Ottawa: Government of Canada.

Rubenson, Kjell, Richard Desjardins, and Ee-Seul Yoon. 2007. *Adult Learning in Canada: A Comparative Perspective. Results from the Adult Literacy and Life Skills Survey.* Ottawa: Minister of Industry, Statistics Canada Catalogue no. 89-552-XIE no. 17 (Oct.).

Runté, Robert. 1998. "The Impact of Centralized Examinations on Teacher Professionalism," *Canadian Journal of Education* 23, 2: 166–81.

Rushton, Philippe, and Anthony Bogaert. 1987. "Race Differences in Sexual Behavior: Testing an Evolutionary Hypothesis," *Journal of Research on Personality* 21: 529–51.

Ryan, James, Katrina Pollock, and Fab Antonelli. 2009. "Teacher Diversity in Canada: Leaky Pipelines, Bottlenecks, and Glass Ceilings," *Canadian Journal of Education* 32, 3: 591–617.

Saha, Lawrence J. 2008. "Sociology of Education," in Thomas L. Good, ed, *21st Century Education: A Reference Handbook,* vol. 1. Thousand Oaks, CA: 299–307.

Saltman, Kenneth J., and David A. Gabbard, eds. 2011. *Education as Enforcement: The Militarization and Corporatization of Schools,* 2nd edn. New York: Routledge.

Samuelson, Les. 1991. "The Neo-Conservative Sacrifice of Youth: Quality of Youth Employment and Its Consequences," in Terry Wotherspoon, ed., *Hitting the Books: The Politics of Educational Retrenchment.* Toronto and Saskatoon: Garamond Press and the Social Research Unit, 119–38.

Sarason, Seymour B. 1996. *Revisiting "The Culture of the School and the Problem of Change."* New York: Teachers College Press.

Saskatchewan Education. 1996. *Building Communities of Hope: Best Practices for Meeting the Learning Needs of At-Risk and Indian and Métis Students.* Regina: Saskatchewan Education.

Saskatchewan Ministry of Education. 2009. *2009 Saskatchewan Education Indicators Report, Prekindergarten to Grade 12.* Regina: Government of Saskatchewan, Dec.

———, First Nations and Metis Education Provincial Advisory Committee. 2012. "Principles and Guidelines." At: www.education.gov.sk.ca/FNMEPAC.

Saskatchewan Teachers' Federation. 1995. *The Workload and Worklife of Saskatchewan Teachers: Full-Time Teachers 1994–95.* Saskatoon: Saskatchewan Teachers' Federation Research Report No. 1.

Sattler, Peggy. 2012. "Education Governance Reform in Ontario: Neoliberalism in Context," *Canadian Journal of Educational Administration and Policy* 128 (16 Jan.): 1–28.

Satzewich, Vic, and Terry Wotherspoon. 2000. *First Nations: Race, Class, and Gender Relations.* Regina: Canadian Plains Research Centre.

Sawchuk, Peter H., and Alison Taylor. 2010. "Understanding Challenging Transitions in Learning and Work," in Sawchuk and Taylor, eds, *Challenging Transitions in Learning and Work: Reflections on Policy and Practice*. Rotterdam: Sense Publishers, 1–24.

Schecter, Stephen. 1977. "Capitalism, Class, and Educational Reform in Canada," in Leo Panitch, ed., *The Canadian State: Political Economy and Political Power*. Toronto: University of Toronto Press, 373–416.

Schissel, Bernard. 2006. *Still Blaming Children: Youth Conduct and the Politics of Child Hating*. Black Point, NS: Fernwood.

—— and Terry Wotherspoon. 2003. *The Legacy of School for Aboriginal People: Education, Oppression, and Emancipation*. Toronto: Oxford University Press.

Sciadas, George. 2002. *The Digital Divide in Canada*. Ottawa: Statistics Canada Research Paper, 1 Oct., Catalogue no. 56F0009XIE.

Schweitzer, Thomas T. 1995. *The State of Education in Canada*. Montreal: Institute for Research on Public Policy.

Sears, Alan. 2003. *Retooling the Mind Factory: Education in a Lean State*. Aurora, ON: Garamond Press.

Selman, Gordon, Michael Cooke, Mark Selman, and Paul Dempler. 1997. *The Foundations of Adult Education in Canada*, 2nd edn. Toronto: Thompson Educational Publishing.

Selwyn, Neil. 2012. "School 2.0: Rethinking the Future of Schools in the Digital Age," in Athanassios Jimoyiannis, ed., *Research on e-Learning and ICT in Education*. New York: Springer, 3–16.

Sewid-Smith, Daisy. 1991. "In Time Immemorial," in Dorothy Jensen and Cheryl Brooks, eds, *In Celebration of Our Survival: The First Nations of British Columbia*. Vancouver: University of British Columbia Press, 16–32.

Shack, Sybil. 1973. *The Two-Thirds Minority: Women in Canadian Education*. Toronto: Guidance Centre, University of Toronto.

Shaienks, Danielle, and Tomasz Gluszynski. 2007. *Participation in Postsecondary Education: Graduates, Continuers and Drop Outs, Results from YITS Cycle 4*. Ottawa: Culture, Tourism and the Centre for Education Statistics Research Paper no. 059, Statistics Canada Catalogue no. 81-595-MIE2007059.

—— and ——. 2009. *Education and Labour Market Transitions in Young Adulthood*. Ottawa: Culture, Tourism and the Centre for Education Statistics Research Paper no. 075, Statistics Canada Catalogue no. 81-595-M2009075.

Shakeshaft, Charol. 2004. *Educator Sexual Misconduct: A Synthesis of Existing Literature*. Washington: US Department of Education Policy and Program Study Service #2004-09.

Shalla, Vivian, and Wallace Clement, eds. 2007. *Work in Tumultuous Times: Critical Perspectives*. Montreal and Kingston: McGill-Queen's University Press.

Sharpe, Andrew, François Arsenault, Simon Lapointe, and Fraser Cowan. 2009. *The Effect of Increasing Aboriginal Educational Attainment on the Labour Force, Output and the Fiscal Balance*. Ottawa: Centre for the Study of Living Standards, CSLS Research Report 2009-3, May.

Shor, Ira. 1980. *Critical Teaching and Everyday Life*. Boston: South End Press.

Short, Donn. 2011. "Safe Schools: The Threat from Within?" *Education Canada* 51, 3: 4–8.

Shrestha, Alok. 2007. "$100 Computer! Is It Worth What It Seems To Be?" *Panorama*, 18 Nov. At: www.tigweb.org/youth-media/panorama/article.html?ContentID=17063.

Siedule, Tom. 1992. *The Influence of Socioeconomic Background on Education*. Ottawa: Economic Council of Canada, Working Paper No. 34.

Silver, Jim, and Kathy Mallett, with Janice Greene and Freeman Simard. 2002. *Aboriginal Education in Winnipeg Inner-City Schools*. Winnipeg: Canadian Centre for Policy Alternatives and Winnipeg Inner-City Research Alliance.

Simon, Roger. 2001. "Now's the Time: Foreword," in Portelli and Solomon (2001: 11–13).

Sims, Jinny. 2004. "Open Letter to Don Wright, Commissioner, Commission to Review Teacher Collective Bargaining," 27 Sept. Vancouver: British Columbia Teachers' Federation Negotiations. At: bctf.ca/BargainingAndContracts.aspx?id=4920.

Singer, Alan, and Michael Pezone. 2003. "Education for Social Change: From Theory to Practice," *Workplace: A Journal for Academic Labor* 5, 2. At: www.louisville.edu/journal/workplace/issue5p2/singerpezone.html.

Skolrood, Arthur Harold. 1967. "The British Columbia Teachers' Federation: A Study of Its Historical Development, Interests and Activities from 1916 to 1963," Ed.D. thesis, University of Oregon.

Sky's the Limit Youth Organization. 2010. "Building Digital Skills: Increasing Computer Access to Under-Resourced Youth in Canada," submission to Government of Canada, The Digital Economy in Canada Public Consultation. At: www.digitaleconomy.gc.ca/eic/site/028.nsf/eng/00420.html.

Smaller, Harry, Rosemary Clark, Doug Hart, David Livingstone, and Zahra Noormohammed. 2000. "Teacher Learning, Informal and Formal: Results of a Canadian Teachers' Survey," New Approaches to Lifelong Learning Working Paper 14-2000. At: http://hdl.handle.net/1807/2728.

Smith, Andrea. 2009. "Indigenous Peoples and Boarding Schools: A Comparative Study," Report prepared for Secretariat of the United Nations Permanent Forum on Indigenous Issues, eighth session, New York, May. At: www.un.org/esa/socdev/unpfii/documents/E_C_19_2009_crp1.pdf.

———, Barry H. Schneider, and Martin D. Ruck. 2005. "'Thinking About Makin' It': Black Canadian Students' Beliefs Regarding Education and Academic Achievement," *Journal of Youth and Adolescence* 34, 4: 347–59.

Smith, David, Diego S. De León, Janet Krstevski, and Susan M. Cantrell. 2012. *Solving the Skills Paradox: Seven Ways to Close Your Critical Skills Gaps.* Toronto: Accenture Canada.

Smith, Dorothy E. 1987. *The Everyday World as Problematic: A Feminist Sociology.* Boston: Northeastern University Press.

Smith, Matthew, and Peter McLaren. 2010. "Critical Pedagogy: An Overview," *Childhood Education* 86, 5 (Suppl.): 332–4.

Smyth, John. 2001. *Critical Politics of Teachers' Work: An Australian Perspective.* New York: Peter Lang.

———, Alastair Dow, Robert Hattam, Alan Reid, and Geoffrey Shacklock. 2000. *Teachers' Work in a Globalizing Economy.* London: Falmer.

Sniderman, Andrew Stobo. 2012. "Aboriginal Students: An Education Underclass," *Maclean's* 125, 31 (13 Aug.): 20–1.

Spring, Joel. 2007. *A New Paradigm for Global School Systems: Education for a Long and Happy Life.* Mahwah, NJ: Lawrence Erlbaum Associates.

———. 2011. *The American School, a Global Context: From the Puritans to the Obama Administration*, 8th edn. New York: McGraw-Hill.

Srivastava, Sarita. 2007. "'Let's Talk': The Pedagogy and Politics of Anti-Racist Change," in Mark Coté, Richard J.P. Day, and Greig de Peuter, eds, *Utopian Pedagogy: Radical Experiments against Neoliberal Globalization.* Toronto: University of Toronto Press, 294–313.

Standing Committee on Aboriginal Affairs and Northern Development. 2007. *No Higher Priority: Aboriginal Post-Secondary Education in Canada: Report of the Standing Committee on Aboriginal Affairs and Northern Development.* Ottawa: House of Commons.

Standing Committee on Public Accounts. 2005. *Education Program and Post-Secondary Student Support*, Report of the Standing Committee on Public Accounts. Ottawa: House of Commons, June.

Standing Senate Committee on Aboriginal Peoples. 2011. *Reforming First Nations Education: From Crisis to Hope*, Report of the Standing Senate Committee on Aboriginal Peoples. Ottawa: Parliament of Canada, Dec.

Statistics Canada. 1973. *Education in Canada 1973.* Ottawa: Information Canada.

———. 1984. *Education in Canada 1983.* Ottawa: Minister of Supply and Services Canada.

———. 1993. *Schooling, Work and Related Activities, Income, Expenses and Mobility: 1991 Aboriginal Peoples' Survey.* Ottawa: Minister of Industry, Science and Technology, Catalogue no. 89-534.

———. 2001a. *Education in Canada, 2000.* Ottawa: Minister of Industry, Catalogue no. 81-229.

———. 2001b. "Trends in the Use of Private Education," *The Daily*, 4 July.

———. 2003. *Education in Canada: Raising the Standard* (2001 Census, Analysis Series). Ottawa: Statistics Canada Catalogue no. 96-F0030-X1E2001012.

———. 2007a. *Immigration in Canada: A Portrait of the Foreign-born Population, 2006 Census.* Ottawa: Minister of Industry (Mar.), Statistics Canada Catalogue no. 97-557-XIE2006.

———. 2007b. "Labour Force Survey Estimates (LFS), by Educational Attainment, Sex and Age Group, Annually," Table 2820004, CANSIM Multidimensional database. At: dc2.chass.utoronto.ca/cgi-bin/cansimdim/c2_getArrayDim.pl.

———. 2007c. "Labour Force Survey Estimates (LFS), by National Occupational Classification for Statistics (NOC-S) and Sex," CANSIM Multidimensional database. At: dc2.chass.utoronto.ca/cgi-bin/cansim-dim/c2_seriesCart.pl.

———. 2007d. *Participation and Activity Limitation Survey 2006: Analytical Report.* Ottawa: Minister of Industry, Social and Aboriginal Statistics Division Analytical Paper (Dec.), Catalogue no. 89-628-XIE2007002. At: dc2.chass.utoronto.ca.cyber.usask.ca/cgi-bin/cansimdim/c2_getArray Dim.pl.

———. 2007e. "Shopping for Back to School," *Back to School . . . by the Numbers.* Ottawa: Statistics Canada media release, 13 Sept. At: www42.statcan.ca/smr08/smr08_088_e.htm.

————. 2008a. *Aboriginal Identity, Sex, and Age Groups for the Population of Canada*. Ottawa: Statistics Canada, 2006 Census of Canada, Catalogue no. 97-558-xcb2006007 (15 Jan.).

————. 2008b. *Canada's Changing Labour Force, 2006 Census*. Ottawa: Minister of Industry (Mar.), Catalogue no. 97-559-XIE2006001. At: www12.statcan.gc.ca/english/census06/analysis/labour/pdf/97-559-XIE2006001.pdf.

————. 2008c. *Earnings and Income of Canadians over the Past Quarter Century, 2006 Census*. Ottawa: Minister of Industry (May), Catalogue no. 97-563-XIE2006001.

————. 2008d. *Educational Portrait of Canada, 2006 Census*. Ottawa: Minister of Industry (Mar.), Catalogue no. 97-560-XIE2006001.

————. 2008e. "Labour Force Activity, Highest Certificate, Diploma or Degree, Aboriginal Identity, Age Groups and Sex for the Population 15 Years and Over, 2006 Census." Ottawa: Minister of Industry, Catalogue no. 97-559-XCB2006019. At: www12.statcan.ca/english/census06/data/topics/ListProducts.cfm?Temporal=2006&APATH=3&THEME=7.

————. 2011a. *Education Indicators in Canada: Handbook for the Pan-Canadian Education Indicators Program*. Toronto: Canadian Education Statistics Council, Dec., Catalogue No. 81-582-GIE.

————. 2011b. "Employment, Unadjusted for Seasonal Variation, by Type of Employee for Selected Industries Classified Using the North American Industry Classification System (NAICS)," CANSIM Multidimensional database Table 281-0024. At: www5.statcan.gc.ca/cansim/a26?lang=eng&retrLang=eng&id=2810024&paSer=&pattern=&stByVal=1&p1=1&p2=-1&tabMode=dataTable&csid=.

————. 2012. "Labour Force Survey Estimates (LFS), by National Occupational Classification for Statistics (NOC-S) and Sex," CANSIM Multidimensional database. Table 282-0010. At: www5.statcan.gc.ca/cansim/a26?lang=eng&retrLang=eng&id=2820010&tabMode=dataTable&srchLan=-1&p1=-1&p2=9.

————. 2013. *Summary Elementary and Secondary School Indicators for Canada, the Provinces and Territories, 2006/2007 to 2010/2011*. Ottawa: Minister of Industry. Culture, Tourism and the Centre for Education Statistics Research Paper, Catalogue no. 81-595-M – No. 099.

———— and Council of Ministers of Education Canada (CMEC). 2011a. *Education Indicators in Canada: An International Perspective 2011*. Toronto: Canadian Education Statistics Council.

———— and ————. 2011b. *Education Indicators in Canada: Report of the Pan-Canadian Education Indicators Program 2011*. Toronto: Canadian Education Statistics Council, Catalogue no. 81-582-XPE.

———— and ————. 2012a. *Economic Downturn and Educational Attainment*. Toronto: Canadian Education Statistics Council, Catalogue no. 81-559-X, June.

———— and ————. 2012b. *Education Indicators in Canada: Report of the Pan-Canadian Education Indicators Program 2012*. Toronto: Canadian Education Statistics Council, Catalogue no. 81-582-XPE.

———— and Organisation for Economic Co-operation and Development (OECD). 2011. *Literacy for Life: Further Results from the Adult Literacy and Life Skills Survey, Second International ALL Report*. Paris and Ottawa: OECD Publishing and Minister of Industry. Statistics Canada Catalogue no. 89-604-XWE2011001.

St Denis, Verna. 2010. *A Study of Aboriginal Teachers' Professional Knowledge and Experience in Canadian Schools*. Toronto: Canadian Teachers' Federation, Mar.

Stebbins, Robert A. 1971. "The Meaning of Disorderly Behavior: Teacher Definition of a Classroom Situation," *Sociology of Education* 44, 2: 217–36.

————. 1975. *Teachers and Meaning: Definitions of Classroom Situations*. Leiden: E.J. Brill.

Steeves, Valerie. 2012a. *Young Canadians in a Wired World. Phase II: Talking to Youth and Parents about Life Online*. Ottawa: MediaSmarts.

————. 2012b. *Young Canadians in a Wired World. Phase III: Teachers' Perspectives*. Ottawa: MediaSmarts.

Steinberg, Shirley R., and Joe L. Kincheloe, eds. 1997. *Kinderculture: The Corporate Construction of Childhood*. Boulder, CO: Westview Press.

Stelmach, Bonnie. 2004. "Unlocking the Schoolhouse Doors: Institutional Constraints on Parent and Community Involvement in a School Improvement Initiative," *Canadian Journal of Educational Administration and Policy* 31 (18 June). At: www.umanitoba.ca/publications/cjeap/articles/stelmach.html.

Stevenson, David Lee. 2006. "The Fit and Misfit of Sociological Research and Educational Policy," in Hallinan (2006: 547–63).

Stonechild, Blair. 2006. *The New Buffalo: The Struggle for Aboriginal Post-Secondary Education in Canada*. Winnipeg: University of Manitoba Press.

Strategic Counsel. 2007. *A Summary Report to the Association of Universities and Colleges of Canada: Attitudes and Perceptions of Higher Education.* Toronto: Strategic Counsel, Mar.

Strathdee, Rob. 2005. "Globalization, Innovation, and the Declining Significance of Qualifications-Led Social and Economic Change," *Journal of Educational Policy* 20, 4: 437–56.

Stromquist, Nelly P., and Karen Monkman. 2000. "Defining Globalization and Assessing Its Implications on Knowledge and Education," in Stromquist and Monkman, eds, *Globalization and Education: Integration and Contestation across Cultures.* Lanham, Md: Rowman & Littlefield, 3–26.

Suárez-Orozca, Marcelo M., ed. 2007. *Learning in the Global Era: International Perspectives on Globalization and Education.* Berkeley: University of California Press.

Subedi, Binaya, ed. 2010. *Critical Global Perspectives: Rethinking Knowledge about Global Societies.* Charlotte, NC: Information Age Publishing.

Sullivan, Alice. 2002. "Bourdieu and Education: How Useful Is Bourdieu's Theory for Researchers?" *Netherlands Journal of Social Sciences* 38, 2: 144–66.

Sutherland, Neil. 1976. *Children in English-Speaking Canada: Framing the Twentieth-Century Consensus.* Toronto: University of Toronto Press.

Sweet, Robert, and Paul Gallagher. 1999. "Private Training Institutions in Canada: New Directions for a Public Resource," *Journal of Educational Administration and Foundations* 13, 2: 54–77.

——— and Nancy Mandell. 2005. "Exploring Limits to Parental Involvement in Their Children's Homework," in Sweet and Paul Anisef, eds, *Preparing for Post-Secondary Education: New Roles for Governments and Families.* Montreal and Kingston: McGill-Queen's University Press, 273–88.

Tanner, Julian, Harvey Krahn, and Timothy F. Hartnagel. 1995. *Fractured Transitions from School to Work: Revisiting the Dropout Problem.* Toronto: Oxford University Press.

Tardif, Maurice, and Claude Lessard. 1999. *Le Travail Enseignant au Quotidien: Contribution à l'étude du travail dans les métiers et les professions d'interactions humaines.* Saint-Nicolas, QC: Les Presses de l'Université Laval.

——— and ———. 2004. "Introduction," in Maurice Tardif et Claude Lessard, eds, *La profession d'enseignant aujourd'hui: Évolutions, perspectives et enjeux internationaux.* St Nicolas, QC, and Bruxelles: Les Presses de l'Universié Laval et De Boeck, 1–18.

Taylor, Alison. 2001. *The Politics of Educational Reform in Alberta.* Toronto: University of Toronto Press.

———. 2005. "Finding the Future That Fits," *Gender and Education* 17, 2: 165–87.

———. 2007. *Pathways for Youth to the Labour Market: An Overview of High School Initiatives.* Ottawa: Canadian Policy Research Network and Canadian Council on Learning.

Tetley, William. 1982. "Language and Education Rights in Quebec and Canada (A Legislative History and Personal Political Diary)," *Law and Contemporary Problems* 45, 4: 177–219.

Titchkosky, Tanya. 2003. *Disability, Self and Society.* Toronto: University of Toronto Press.

———. 2011. *The Question of Access: Disability, Space, Meaning.* Toronto: University of Toronto Press.

Titley, E. Brian. 1982. "Tradition, Change and Education in French Canada," in Titley and Miller (1982: 45–56).

——— and Peter J. Miller, eds. 1982. *Education in Canada: An Interpretation.* Calgary: Detselig.

Tomkins, George S. 1977. "Canadian Education and the Development of a National Consciousness: Historical and Contemporary Perspectives," in Alf Chaiton and Neil McDonald, eds, *Canadian Schools and Canadian Identity.* Toronto: Gage, 6–28.

———. 1981. "Stability and Change in the Canadian Curriculum," in J. Donald Wilson, ed., *Canadian Education in the 1980's.* Calgary: Detselig, 135–58.

Toronto District School Board. 2012. "Equity Foundation Statement and Commitments to Equity Policy Implementation," Toronto District School Board, Equitable and Inclusive Schools: Students, Parent and Community Guidelines, Policies, and Procedures. At: www.tdsb.on.ca/_site/ViewItem.asp?siteid=15&menuid=682&pageid=546.

Torres, Carlos Alberto, and Theodore R. Mitchell, eds. 1998. *Sociology of Education: Emerging Perspectives.* Albany: State University of New York Press.

Tran, Dien. 1995. "Communication Technology and Education in Canada," in Ghosh and Ray (1995: 45–53).

Tran, Kelly. 2004. "Visible Minorities in the Labour Force: 20 Years of Change," *Canadian Social Trends* 73 (Summer): 7–11.

Trani, Randy K., and Robert K. Irvine. 2010. *Fallacies in Education: Why Schools Are Mired in Mediocrity.* Lanham, Md: Rowman & Littlefield.

Tremblay, Claire. 2012. "Canada's A Grade Teachers," *Teacher Voice*, Feb.

Truth and Reconciliation Commission of Canada. 2012. *They Came for the Children: Canada, Aboriginal Peoples and Residential Schools.* Winnipeg: Truth and Reconciliation Commission of Canada.

Tulchinsky, Gerald. 2008. *Canada's Jews: A People's Journey.* Toronto: University of Toronto Press.

Turcotte, Martin. 2011a. "Intergenerational Education Mobility: University Completion in Relation to Parents' Education Level," *Canadian Social Trends* 92 (Winter): 37–43.

———. 2011b. "Women and Education," in *Women in Canada: A Gender-Based Statistical Report.* Ottawa: Statistics Canada Catalogue no. 89-503X, Dec.

Ungerleider, Charles S. 1994. "Power, Politics, and the Professionalization of Teachers in British Columbia," in Erwin and MacLennan (1994: 370–9).

———. 2003. *Failing Our Kids: How We Are Ruining Our Public Schools.* Toronto: McClelland & Stewart.

United Nations Children's Fund (UNICEF). 2002. *A League Table of Educational Disadvantage in Rich Nations,* Innocenti Report Card No. 4. Florence, Italy: UNICEF, Innocenti Research Centre, Nov.

———. 2010. *The Children Left Behind: A League Table of Inequality in Child Well-Being in the World's Rich Countries,* Innocenti Report Card No. 9. Florence, Italy: UNICEF, Innocenti Research Centre.

United Nations Development Programme. 2001. *Human Development Report 2001: Making New Technologies Work for Human Development.* New York: Oxford University Press.

———. 2011. *Human Development Report 2011. Sustainability and Equity: A Better Future for All.* New York: Palgrave Macmillan.

United Nations Educational, Scientific and Cultural Organization (UNESCO). 2007. *Education for All by 2015: Will We Make It?* EFA Global Monitoring Report 2008. Paris: UNESCO.

———. 2011a. *Global Education Digest 2011: Comparing Education Statistics Across the World.* Montreal: UNESCO Institute for Statistics.

———. 2011b. *The Hidden Crisis: Armed Conflict and Education.* EFA Global Monitoring Report 2011. Paris: UNESCO.

———. 2012. *Report of Homophobic Bullying in Educational Institutions,* prepared for the International Consultation on Homophobic Bullying in Educational Institutions. Paris: UNESCO, Mar.

Usalcas, Jeannine. 2011. "Aboriginal People and the Labour Market: Estimates from the Labour Force Survey, 2008–2010." Ottawa: Minister of Industry, Statistics Canada Labour Statistics Division, Catalogue no. 71-588-X, no. 3.

Vanderstraeten, Rof. 2003. "Explorations in the Systems-Theoretical Study of Education," in Carlos Alberto Torres and Ari Antikainen, eds, *The International Handbook of the Sociology of Education: An International Assessment of New Research and Theory.* Lanham, Md: Rowman & Littlefield, 42–57.

van Hamel, Anton. 2011. *From Consumer to Citizen: Digital Media and Youth Civic Engagement.* Ottawa: Media Awareness Network.

Veltmeyer, Henry. 1986. *The Canadian Class Structure.* Toronto: Garamond Press.

Vinken, Henk. 2007. "New Life Course Dynamics?" *Young* 15, 1: 9–30.

Vollmer, Jamie Robert. 2003. "The Blueberry Story: The Teacher Gives the Businessman a Lesson," *Our Schools/Our Selves* 12, 3: 41–2.

Vosko, Leah F. 2003. "Gender Differentiation and the Standard/Non-Standard Employment Distinction: A Genealogy of Policy Interventions in Canada," in Danielle Juteau, ed., *Social Differentiation: Patterns and Processes.* Toronto: University of Toronto Press, 25–80.

———. 2007. "Gendered Labour Market Insecurities: Manifestations of Precarious Employment in Different Locations," in Shalla and Clement (2007: 52–97).

Waber, Dietmar. 2006. "Examining the Examiners: Reflections on Non-Partisanship, the Fraser Institute and the Report Card on Schools," *Education Canada* 46, 3: 4–8.

Walford, Geoffrey, and W.S.F. Pickering, eds. 1998. *Durkheim and Modern Education.* London: Routledge.

Walkerdine, Valerie. 1998. *Counting Girls Out: Girls and Mathematics,* new edn. London: Falmer.

Waller, Willard. 1965. *The Sociology of Teaching.* New York: John Wiley & Sons.

Warburton, Rennie. 1986. "The Class Relations of Public School Teachers in British Columbia," *Canadian Review of Sociology and Anthropology* 23, 2: 210–29.

Weaver-Hightower, Marcus. 2003. "The 'Boy Turn' in Research on Gender and Education," *Review of Educational Research* 73, 4: 471–98.

Weber, Sandra, and Claudia Mitchell. 1999. "Teacher Identity and Popular Culture," in Jon Prosser, ed., *School Culture*. Thousand Oaks, CA: Sage, 145–60.

Weiler, Kathleen. 1988. *Women Teaching for Change: Gender, Class and Power*. New York: Bergin and Garvey.

Weis, Lois. 1990. *Working Class without Work: High School Students in a De-industrializing Economy*. New York: Routledge.

———, Cameron McCarthy, and Greg Dimitriadis, eds. 2006. *Ideology, Curriculum and the New Sociology of Education: Revisiting the Work of Michael Apple*. New York: Routledge.

White, Patrick. 2008. "Afrocentric: Bad Word, Good Idea," *Globe and Mail*, 18 Jan., L1, L3.

Whitty, Geoff. 1997. "Marketization, the State, and the Re-Formation of the Teaching Profession," in Halsey et al. (1997: 299–310).

Wickstrom, Rod A. 1994. "Educational Change: Can We Make Sense of Reality?" *Education Canada* 34, 4: 4–10.

Wilkinson, Bruce W. 1994. *Educational Choice: Necessary But Not Sufficient*. Montreal: Institute for Research on Public Policy.

Willard, Doug. 2001. "Keeping Canada's Teaching Profession Alive and Well," *Hill Times*, 8 Oct.

Williams, Tom R., and Holly Millinoff. 1990. *Canada's Schools: A Report Card for the 1990s: A CEA Opinion Poll*. Toronto: Canadian Education Association.

Willis, Paul. 1977. *Learning to Labor: How Working Class Kids Get Working Class Jobs*. New York: Columbia University Press.

Willms, J. Douglas. 1997. *Literacy Skills of Canadian Youth*. Ottawa: Minister of Industry, Statistics Canada Catalogue no. 89-552-MIE no. 1.

———. 2002. "The Prevalence of Vulnerability," in Willms, ed., *Vulnerable Children: Findings from Canada's National Longitudinal Survey of Children and Youth*. Edmonton: University of Alberta Press and Human Resources Development Canada, 45–69.

Wilson, J. Donald. 1981. "Religion and Education: The Other Side of Pluralism," in Wilson, ed., *Canadian Education in the 1980's*. Calgary: Detselig, 97–113.

———. 1991. "'I Am Ready To Be of Assistance When I Can': Lottie Bowron and Rural Women Teachers in British Columbia," in Alison Prentice and Marjorie R. Theobald, eds, *Women Who Taught: Perspectives on the History of Women and Teaching*. Toronto: University of Toronto Press, 202–29.

———, Robert M. Stamp, and Louis-Philippe Audet, eds. 1970. *Canadian Education: A History*. Scarborough, ON: Prentice-Hall.

Wolfe, David A. 2002. "Innovation Policy for the Knowledge-Based Economy: From the Red Book to the White Paper," in G. Bruce Doern, ed., *How Ottawa Spends 2002–2003: The Security Aftermath and National Priorities*. Toronto: Oxford University Press, 137–56.

Woods, Peter. 1983. *Sociology and the School: An Interactionist Viewpoint*. Boston: Routledge & Kegan Paul.

Worth, W.H. 1972. *A Future of Choices—A Choice of Futures: A Report of the Commission on Educational Planning* (Worth Report). Edmonton: Queen's Printer.

Wotherspoon, Terry. 1984. "Ideals and Sausage Factories: Schools in Capitalist Society," in John A. Fry, ed., *Contradictions in Canadian Society: Readings in Introductory Sociology*. Toronto: John Wiley & Sons, 207–18.

———, ed. 1987. *The Political Economy of Canadian Schooling*. Toronto: Methuen.

———. 1989. "Immigration and the Production of a Teaching Force: Policy Implications for Education and Labour," *International Migration* 27, 4: 543–62.

———. 1991. "Educational Reorganization and Retrenchment," in Wotherspoon, ed., *Hitting the Books: The Politics of Educational Retrenchment*. Toronto and Saskatoon: Garamond Press and Social Research Unit, 15–58.

———. 1993. "From Subordinate Partners to Dependent Employees: State Regulation of Public School Teachers in Nineteenth Century British Columbia," *Labour/Le Travail* 31 (Spring): 75–110.

———. 1995a. "The Incorporation of Public School Teachers into the Industrial Order: British Columbia in the First Half of the Twentieth Century," *Studies in Political Economy* 46 (Spring): 119–51.

———. 1995b. "Multiculturalism and the Management of Race and Ethnic Relations in Canadian Schooling," in Wotherspoon and Paul Jungbluth, eds, *Multicultural Education in a Changing Global Economy: Canada and the Netherlands*. Munster: Waxmann, 41–60.

———. 1998. "Education, Place, and the Sustainability of Rural Communities in Saskatchewan," *Journal of Research in Rural Education* 14, 3: 131–41.

———. 2003. "Aboriginal People, Public Policy, and Social Differentiation in Canada," in Danielle Juteau, ed., *Social Differentiation: Patterns and Processes*. Toronto: University of Toronto Press, 155–204.

————. 2006. "Teachers' Work in Canadian Aboriginal Communities," *Comparative Education Review* 50, 4: 672–94.

Wyn, Johanna, Sandra Acker, and Elisabeth Richards. 2000. "Making a Difference: Women in Management in Australian and Canadian Faculties of Education," *Gender and Education* 12, 4: 435–47.

Yuen, Jennifer. 2010. "Job–Education Match and Mismatch: Wage Differentials," *Perspectives on Labour and Income* 11, 4 (Apr.): 16–26.

Youdell, Deborah. 2010. "Recognizing the Subjects of Education: Engagements with Judith Butler," in Apple, Ball, and Gandin (2010: 132–42).

Young, Jon, ed. 1987. *Breaking the Mosaic: Ethnic Identities in Canadian Schooling*. Toronto: Garamond Press.

————, Benjamin Levin, and Dawn Wallin. 2007. *Understanding Canadian Schools: An Introduction to Educational Administration*, 4th edn. Scarborough, ON: Nelson.

Young, Leslie. 2012. "Canadians Give Public School System Middling Grades," Global News, 4 Sept. At: www.globalnews.ca/news/282208/poll-canadians-give-public-school-system-middling-grades.

Young, Michael F.D., ed. 1971. *Knowledge and Control: New Directions for the Sociology of Education*. London: Collier-Macmillan.

Younghusband, Lynda. 2006. "Teacher Stress and Working Environments: Implications for Teaching and Learning," *Newfoundland Quarterly* 98, 4: 8–11.

Zeman, Klarka. 2007. "A First Look at Provincial Differences in Educational Pathways from High School to College and University," *Education Matters* 4, 2 (19 June).

Zietsma, Danielle. 2011. "Immigrants Working in Regulated Occupations," *Perspectives on Labour and Income* 11, 2 (Feb.): 13–28.

Index